VB.NET
CORE CLASSES
IN A NUTSHELL

A Desktop Quick Reference

Related titles from O'Reilly

In a Nutshell references

C# in a Nutshell

VB.NET Language in a Nutshell

ADO.NET in a Nutshell

ASP.NET in a Nutshell

.NET Windows Forms in a Nutshell

Also available

C# and VB.NET Conversion Pocket Reference

C# Essentials

COM and .NET Component Services

Learning C#

Learning Visual Basic .NET

Mastering Visual Studio .NET

.NET Framework Essentials

Programming ASP.NET

Programming C#

Programming .NET Web Services

Programming Visual Basic .NET

VB.NET
CORE CLASSES
IN A NUTSHELL

A Desktop Quick Reference

Budi Kurniawan & Ted Neward

O'REILLY®

Beijing • Cambridge • Farnham • Köln • Paris • Sebastopol • Taipei • Tokyo

VB.NET Core Classes in a Nutshell

by Budi Kurniawan and Ted Neward
with Brian Jepson, Matthew MacDonald, Martin Smith, and Steve Spainhour

Published by O'Reilly & Associates, Inc., 1005 Gravenstein Highway North,
Sebastopol, CA 95472.

O'Reilly & Associates books may be purchased for educational, business, or sales
promotional use. Online editions are also available for most titles
(*safari.oreilly.com*). For more information, contact our corporate/institutional sales
department: (800) 998-9938 or *corporate@oreilly.com*.

Editors: Ron Petrusha and Brian Jepson

Production Editors: Catherine Morris and Linley Dolby

Cover Designer: Pam Spremulli

Printing History:

June 2002:   First Edition.

Library of Congress Cataloging-in-Publication Data

Kurniawan, Budi
   VB.NET core classes in a nutshell / Budi Kurniawan.
     p. cm.
   Includes index.
   ISBN 0-596-00257-2
   1. Microsoft Visual BASIC 2. BASIC (Computer program language) I. Title

QA76.73.B3 K875 2002
005.2'768--dc21   2002070420

[M]

Table of Contents

Preface

This book is a desktop reference for the core classes in Microsoft's .NET Framework Class Library (FCL). It is intended as a companion volume to *Visual Basic .NET Language in a Nutshell*, Second Edition, which provides a reference to the Visual Basic language.

Visual Basic .NET Core Classes in a Nutshell is divided into two parts. Part I, which consists of a single chapter, offers a very brief overview of and introduction to the .NET FCL.

Part II is a quick reference to the core classes of the FCL—22 of the most important namespaces of the FCL and their more than 700 types, complete with namespace maps, type descriptions, member signatures using VB .NET syntax, and useful cross references and annotations. Part II is also available on the CD-ROM that accompanies the book (see "What's on the CD").

Who This Book Is For

As a reference guide to the core classes, we think you'll find *Visual Basic .NET Core Classes in a Nutshell* to be an essential book regardless of your level of experience with Visual Basic. Whether you are an experienced Visual Basic developer or a relatively new programmer just beginning to work with Visual Basic and the .NET platform, you'll find that Visual Basic .NET Core Classes in a Nutshell provides an extremely helpful description of each type in the namespaces documented in Part II, along with a useful list of type members that features VB syntax.

How This Book Is Structured

This book consists of two parts: a single-chapter introduction, and a reference guide to 22 of the core namespaces of the .NET Framework Class Library.

The single chapter in Part I, *Introduction*, examines the significance of the .NET Framework Class Library, provides a summary of its contents, discusses the types found in .NET namespaces, and offers some suggestions for exploring the FCL.

Part II consists of 22 chapters, each of which is devoted to one of the 22 namespaces documented in this book. These namespaces provide the core (or system-level) classes defined in the .NET FCL. Excluded are the namespaces whose classes are designed to provide support for application development. The most notable of these excluded namespaces and their child namespaces are System.Data, System.Web, and System.Windows.Forms.

Part II includes chapters that document the following .NET FCL namespaces:

Microsoft.Win32
System
System.Collections
System.Collections.Specialized
System.Diagnostics
System.Globalization
System.IO
System.IO.IsolatedStorage
System.Net
System.Net.Sockets
System.Reflection
System.Reflection.Emit
System.Runtime.InteropServices
System.Runtime.Serialization
System.Runtime.Serialization.Formatters
System.Text
System.Text.RegularExpressions
System.Threading
System.Timers
System.XML
System.XML.XPath
System.Xml.Xsl

Chapter 2 explains how to get the most from this reference.

What's on the CD

The CD that accompanies this book contains *VB.NET Core Classes in a Nutshell for Microsoft Visual Studio .NET*. This software plugs directly into Microsoft Visual Studio .NET and makes the contents of Part II of the book, *.NET Core Classes Quick Reference*, available to you as a fully integrated member of Visual Studio .NET Dynamic Help.

By making *VB.NET Core Classes in a Nutshell* a part of your Visual Studio .NET development environment, you gain the following benefits:

- Continuous access to the contents of the .NET Core Classes Quick Reference as you work in the online Visual Studio .NET development environment

- Ability to browse the contents of the book in the Visual Studio .NET Help Contents window

- Constantly updated Dynamic Help links to relevant Quick Reference entries as you write Microsoft Visual Basic .NET code (these links appear in a separate Dynamic Help window link group named O'Reilly Help)

- Links to Quick Reference topics when you use either the Help Search facility or interactive Index

- Access to the O'Reilly web site, *http://www.oreilly.com*, for additional books and articles on Visual Basic .NET and the .NET Framework

- Cross-links between Quick Reference topics and related information in MSDN documentation.

For last-minute changes and more information on this software, please read the Release Notes on the CD.

To use *VB.NET Core Classes in a Nutshell for Microsoft Visual Studio .NET* you must be running an officially released version of Visual Basic .NET or Visual Studio .NET on your computer or laptop. To install *VB.NET Core Classes in a Nutshell for Microsoft Visual Studio .NET*:

1. Place the CD in the CD player.

2. Double-click on the file named *VBNETCoreClassesinaNutshell.msi*

3. Follow the instructions contained in the install program windows. Be sure to read and to accept the terms of the software license before proceeding.

To uninstall *VB.NET Core Classes in a Nutshell for Microsoft Visual Studio .NET*, repeat the above procedure, but click on the Remove button when the program prompts you to select an install option.

Making *VB.NET Core Classes in a Nutshell Quick Reference* available as a Visual Studio .NET plug-in is an experiment for both O'Reilly & Associates and Microsoft. We want very much to hear your comments and ideas.

Please send your comments to:

bookquestions@oreilly.com

If you discover errors in content or encounter any problems in using this product, please report them to:

bookquestions@oreilly.com

For updates and more information, visit:

http://examples.oreilly.com/vbnetcore

Conventions Used in This Book

The following typographical conventions are used in this book.

Italic is used for:

- Directory pathnames and filenames

- Domain names and URLs

- New terms where they are first defined

`Constant width` is used for:

- Code examples and output

- Names and keywords in C# programs, including method or field names, variable names, and class names

- XML and HTML element tags

- Registry keys

`Constant width italic` is used for:

- Replaceable parameter names or user-provided elements in syntax

---

 This icon designates a note, which is an important aside to the nearby text.

How to Contact Us

We have tested and verified the information in this book to the best of our ability, but you may find that features have changed (or even that we have made mistakes!). Please let us know about any errors you find, as well as your suggestions for future editions, by writing to:

O'Reilly & Associates, Inc.
1005 Gravenstein Highway North
Sebastopol, CA 95472
(800) 998-9938 (in the U.S. or Canada)
(707) 829-0515 (international/local)
(707) 829-0104 (fax)

To ask technical questions or comment on the book, send email to:

bookquestions@oreilly.com

We have a web site for the book, where we'll list examples, errata, and any plans for future editions. You can access this page at:

http://www.oreilly.com/catalog/vbdotnetcorenut

For more information about this book and others, see the O'Reilly web sites:

http://www.oreilly.com
http://dotnet.oreilly.com

How the Reference Was Generated

Part II was generated using .NET's reflection API. Using reflection, we drilled down into selected classes, structures, enumerations, delegates, and interfaces from the Framework Class Library, and extracted detailed information on each type and its members. Next, we structured this information as DocBook XML, which we used to generate the printed pages. We also used in-house tools to generate the online Microsoft Help 2.0 version that accompanies this book.

Acknowledgments

This book would not be possible without the contribution and support of many individuals, including family, friends, and the hardworking folks at O'Reilly & Associates, Inc.

Brian Jepson and Lenny Muellner of O'Reilly developed the programs responsible for generating Part II and Appendix E. Brian also developed the namespace maps that are found in the overviews that begin each chapter of the Reference with input from Ted Neward and Peter Drayton. Ted Neward, Matthew MacDonald, Martin Smith, Steve Spainhour, and Brian Jepson wrote the more than 700 namespace and type descriptions that make the API reference so valuable.

Brad Merrill of Microsoft wrote the sections on regular expressions and provided content for Appendix A.

Brad Abrams and members of his .NET Framework team contributed to the design of the API reference and provided technical review that immeasurably improved its quality. Daniel Creeron provided an outstanding technical review of the book.

VB.NET Core Classes in a Nutshell for Visual Studio .NET was made possible by the work of many individuals. Mike Sierra of O'Reilly converted the API Reference to Microsoft Help 2.0 format and did the work necessary to integrate its content with the Visual Studio .NET dynamic help system. He was assisted by Lenny Muellner and Erik Ray. Greg Dickerson and Chris Valdez of the O'Reilly Tech Support group tested each version of the software. Kipper York and Shane McRoberts of the Microsoft Help team provided invaluable technical assistance at crucial moments, and Eric Promislow and Vladimir Baikalov of ActiveState built the install package that plugs our Help collection into Visual Studio .NET. Frank Gocinski of the Visual Studio .NET Integration Program was instrumental in helping us become full partners in the program. A special tip of the hat to Rob Howard of Microsoft who supported our original vision and helped us make the right connections to get this project off the ground.

PART I

Introduction

This introduction consists of a single chapter that examines the significance of the .NET Framework Class Library (FCL) and the ways it differs from the .Win32 API and from COM automation. It also provides an overview of the functionality contained in the FCL.

CHAPTER 1

Introduction

The .NET Framework is Microsoft's new computing platform that simplifies the design, development, and deployment of computer applications. Developed particularly to facilitate the creation of Internet applications and distributed Internet applications, the .NET Framework features the .NET Framework Class Library (FCL), a systematic class framework to be used for the development of system tools and utilities as well as application software. This chapter assesses the significance of the .NET FCL and discusses accessing it from Visual Basic code.

Before the .NET FCL

Although programmers using languages like C++ have been using frameworks for system and application development from the very inception of their language (the Microsoft Foundation Class Library, or MFC, for instance, is a framework for developers of Windows applications using C++), comprehensive frameworks or class libraries are comparatively rare in Visual Basic programming. For the most part, programmers of previous versions of Visual Basic depended on two major sources to extend the Visual Basic language: the Win32 API, and ActiveX servers exposed through COM automation.

The Win32 API

The Win32 API is a procedural library that allows the developer to create programs that run under Windows and take advantage of core Windows operating system services. The Win32 API has been enhanced on a regular basis since it was introduced to support Windows NT 3.0, and it now consists of several thousand functions and constants located in a number of dynamic link libraries (DLLs). Because it is a loose collection of functions, there are'nt necessarily any consistent conventions in naming functions or in designating function parameters. The function-based style of programming using the Win32 API has a number of limitations:

Lack of consistency across the entire Win32 API

Although a collection of Win32 API functions may be interdependent, at the same time each function tends to be a more or less independent entity that is called in isolation from other functions in your program. This tends to make the Win32 API as a whole difficult for all programmers to learn and master.

Focus on C programmers

The Win32 API originally was developed as a set of functions that would be called primarily from C code. Although the Win32 API can be called from Visual Basic code, writing code that relies heavily on calls to external DLLs has always been something of an adventure in Visual Basic. Much of the challenge centers on the fact that the type systems used by C and Visual Basic are not completely compatible, so that Visual Basic data types have to be converted to data types expected by C language routines.

To get some sense of the difference in style between the function-based, procedural programming that characterizes the Win32 API and the object-oriented programming that characterizes the .NET Framework, Examples 1-1 and 1-2 contain the source code for a console mode routine that launches the application responsible for handling the data file whose name the user enters in a text box. Example 1-1 is written in Visual Basic 6.0 (although it could have run under any version from VB 4 through VB 6) and relies extensively on Win32 API calls, and particularly on calls to the registry API. Example 1-2 is written for Visual Basic .NET and relies on the .NET Framework Class Library, and particularly on its Registry and RegistryKey classes.

Example 1–1. Launching an application using the Win32 API

```
Option Explicit

Private Declare Function RegCloseKey Lib "advapi32.dll" ( _
        ByVal hKey As Long) As Long
Private Declare Function RegOpenKey Lib "advapi32.dll" _
        Alias "RegOpenKeyA" ( _
        ByVal hKey As Long, ByVal lpSubKey As String, _
        phkResult As Long) As Long
Public Declare Function RegQueryValue Lib "advapi32.dll" _
        Alias "RegQueryValueA" ( _
        ByVal hKey As Long, ByVal lpSubKey As String, _
        ByVal lpValue As String, lpcbValue As Long) As Long
Private Declare Function RegQueryValueEx Lib "advapi32.dll" _
        Alias "RegQueryValueExA" ( _
        ByVal hKey As Long, ByVal lpValueName As String, _
        ByVal lpReserved As Long, lpType As Long, _
        lpData As Any, lpcbData As Long) As Long
Public Declare Function WinExec Lib "kernel32" ( _
        ByVal lpCmdLine As String, ByVal nCmdShow As Long) _
        As Long

Public Const MAX_PATH = 260

Private Const HKEY_CLASSES_ROOT = &H80000000

Private Const ERROR_SUCCESS = 0&

Public Const REG_DWORD = 4
```

Example 1-1. Launching an application using the Win32 API (continued)

```
Public Const REG_SZ = 1

Public Const SW_SHOWNORMAL = 1

Private Sub Main()
    Dim strFile As String, strExten As String
    Dim strProgID As String, strExe As String
    Dim lPos As Long
    Dim hKey As Long, lStrLen As Long

    strFile = InputBox("Enter Name of File to Open: ", _
                        "Open File", "")
    If strFile = "" Then Exit Sub

    ' Get file extension
    lPos = InStrRev(1, strFile, ".")
    If lPos = 0 Then
        MsgBox "Filename must include an extension."
        Exit Sub
    Else
        strExten = Mid(strFile, lPos)
    End If

    ' Get programmatic identifier
    If RegOpenKey(HKEY_CLASSES_ROOT, strExten, hKey) <> _
                    ERROR_SUCCESS Then
        MsgBox "File extension not found."
        Exit Sub
    End If
    lStrLen = 0
    Call RegQueryValue(hKey, "", "", lStrLen)
    strProgID = Space(lStrLen)
    Call RegQueryValue(hKey, "", strProgID, lStrLen)
    RegCloseKey hKey

    ' Get associated application
    strProgID = Left(strProgID, lStrLen - 1) & _
                "\shell\open\command"
    If RegOpenKey(HKEY_CLASSES_ROOT, strProgID, hKey) <> _
                    ERROR_SUCCESS Then
        MsgBox "Open command key not found..."
        Exit Sub
    End If

    lStrLen = 0
    Call RegQueryValue(hKey, "", "", lStrLen)
    strExe = Space(lStrLen)
    Call RegQueryValue(hKey, "", strExe, lStrLen)
    RegCloseKey hKey

    ' Launch application and pass its filename as a parameter
    lPos = InStr(1, strExe, " %1")
    If lPos > 0 Then _
        strExe = Left(strExe, lPos)
    strExe = strExe & " " & strFile
```

```
      Call WinExec(strExe, SW_SHOWNORMAL)
End Sub
```

Example 1-1 is a relatively long program, largely because of the intricacies of working with the Win32 API. We need, of course, to declare all registry-related functions with their parameters, as well as all constants that we intend to use. In addition, each registry access requires that we do the following:

1. Open the relevant registry key.

2. Determine the length of the string we want to retrieve.

3. Set the string buffer to the appropriate length.

4. Retrieve the registry value.

5. Adjust the string containing the registry value by removing its terminating null character.

6. Close the open registry key.

In contrast, the VB.NET program in Example 1-2 is considerably shorter and simpler. In contrast to the numerous `Declare` and `Const` statements in Example 1-1, the program only needs to use the `Imports` statement to indicate which namespaces it will access. Registry access is also significantly simpler. The program relies on two classes: the shared Registry class, which provides access to HKEY_CLASSES_ROOT (HKCR), one of the top-level registry keys; and the RegistryKey class, which represents a registry key. As a result, once the program obtains a reference to HKEY_CLASSES_ROOT, registry access consists of the following steps:

1. Open the appropriate subkey by calling the top-level key's open method, passing it the path to the subkey to be opened.

2. Retrieve the newly opened key's default value.

3. Close the open registry key.

Example 1-2. Launching an application using the .NET FCL

```
Option Strict On

Imports System
Imports Microsoft.Win32
Imports Microsoft.VisualBasic

Public Module modMain
    Public Sub Main()
        Dim strExten, strProgID, strExe As String
        Dim oProgID, oOpenCmd As RegistryKey

        Dim strFile As String = InputBox("Enter Name of File to Open: ", _
                                         "Open File", "")
        If strFile = "" Then Exit Sub

        ' Get file extension
        Dim iPos As Integer = InStrRev(strFile, ".")
        Try
            strExten = Mid(strFile, iPos)
```

Example 1-2. Launching an application using the .NET FCL (continued)

```
      Catch
         MsgBox("Filename must include an extension.")
         Exit Sub
      End Try

      ' Get Programmatic Identifier
      Dim oHKCR As RegistryKey = Registry.ClassesRoot
      Try
         oProgID = oHKCR.OpenSubkey(strExten)
         strProgID = CStr(oProgID.GetValue(Nothing))
         oProgID.Close()
      Catch
         MsgBox("File extension not found.")
         Exit Sub
      End Try

      ' Get associated application
      Try
         oOpenCmd = oHKCR.OpenSubkey(strProgID & _
                     "\shell\open\command")
         strExe = CStr(oOpenCmd.GetValue(Nothing))
         oOpenCmd.Close()
      Catch
         MsgBox("Open command key not found...")
         Exit Sub
      End Try

      ' Launch application and pass its filename as a parameter
      iPos = InStr(1, strExe, " %1")
      If iPos > 0 Then _
         strExe = Left(strExe, iPos)
      strExe = strExe & " " & strFile

      Call Shell(strExe, AppWinStyle.NormalFocus)
   End Sub
End Module
```

COM Automation

In place of the function-based programming using the Win32 API, COM automation represented a clear step forward. COM was a more or less object-oriented technology that held out the promise of language independence; as long as a language understood the Component Object Model, it should be able to access and take advantage of COM components.

Example 1-3 shows a VB 6 program written using COM automation that, like the programs in Examples 1-1 and 1-2, launches the application responsible for handling the data file whose name the user enters in a text box. Like the VB.NET program in Example 1-2, it is a short and fairly simple program that relies on the WScript object available from the Windows Script Host object model.

Example 1-3. Launching an application using COM automation

```
Option Explicit

Private Sub Main()
```

Example 1–3. Launching an application using COM automation (continued)

```
On Error Resume Next

Dim lPos As Long
Dim strFile As String, strExten As String
Dim strProgID As String, strExe As String

strFile = InputBox("Enter Name of File to Open: ", _
                   "Open File", "")
If strFile = "" Then Exit Sub

' Get file extension
lPos = InStrRev(strFile, ".")
If lPos = 0 Then
    MsgBox "Filename must include an extension."
    Exit Sub
Else
    strExten = Mid(strFile, lPos)
End If

' Initialize WSH Shell object
Dim oShell As WshShell
Set oShell = New WshShell

' Get programmatic identifier
strProgID = oShell.RegRead("HKCR\" & strExten & "\")
If Err.Number <> 0 Then
    MsgBox "File extension not found."
    Exit Sub
End If

' Get associated application
strProgID = "HKCR\" & strProgID & "\shell\open\command\"
strExe = oShell.RegRead(strProgID)
If Err.Number <> 0 Then
    MsgBox "Open command key not found..."
    Exit Sub
End If

' Launch application and pass it filename as a parameter
lPos = InStr(1, strExe, " %1")
If lPos > 0 Then _
    strExe = Left(strExe, lPos)
strExe = strExe & " " & strFile

oShell.Run strExe, 5, True
End Sub
```

Despite its substantial popularity, COM suffered from a number of limitations:

- COM itself offered a model for binary code reuse; it did not offer a model for source code reuse. An implication of this is that, although COM offered interfaced-based inheritance (a feature that predominantly advanced programmers were interested in), it did not support code-based inheritance.

- Although COM offered the promise of a language-independent architecture, reality often fell far short of the promise. The root of the problem was the fact that seamless interoperability with COM presupposed that each language was able to create and manipulate common automation-compatible data types. This, however, was not the case. As a result, although COM made some real advances in the area of language independence, it also had some real weaknesses.

- COM was extremely complex, and for the most part only C++ programmers were able to work with COM directly. For VB programmers, the Visual Basic environment masked much of the complexity of COM. The inevitable result was that Visual Basic failed to give the developer full control over COM when it was needed, and many Visual Basic programmers often lacked sufficient familiarity with COM to take advantage even of those features that they were able to control.

In addition, COM did not offer an integrated class library comparable to the .NET FCL. Instead, the developers of each application or operating system service were free to implement whatever object model made sense to extend their application. As a result, there are major gaps in the functionality made available through COM automation, and there is not a good deal of consistency across object models.

The .NET platform and the .NET Framework Class Library were developed in an effort to address these weaknesses of COM.

The .NET Framework Class Library

The .NET Framework includes the .NET Framework Class Library (FCL), a vast collection of thousands of *types* (that is, of classes, interfaces, structures, delegates, and enumerations) that aim at encapsulating the functionality of core system and application services in order to make application programming easier and faster. There are classes that you can use to manipulate the file system, access databases, serialize objects, and launch and synchronize multiple threads of execution, to name just a few.

To make working with these classes easy, classes with similar functionality are grouped together in namespaces. Therefore, there is a namespace containing types for drawing, a number of namespaces for .NET remoting, etc. In fact, the "intrinsic" functions of the Visual Basic language (such as *InStr*, *Len*, and *UBound*) are implemented as class methods in the Microsoft.VisualBasic namespace. In total, the .NET FCL places more than 80 namespaces at your disposal.

The .NET FCL includes classes with the following functionality:

Data type definition
Some members of the System namespace, such as the Object, String, Int32, and Single classes, form the data types used by Visual Basic .NET (as well as by other .NET languages that rely on the .NET Common Type System).

Exceptions
When an exception is generated, the CLR provides exception information to the Exception class (in the System namespace) or to one of the derived classes found throughout the .NET FCL.

Events and event handlers

The signature of event handlers is represented by the EventHandler delegate (in the System namespace) or one of its derived delegates. The event information passed to an event handler is represented by the EventArgs class (in the System namespace) or one of its derived classes.

Attributes

Attributes allow custom items of information about a program element to be stored with an assembly's metadata. Since this information becomes a permanent part of the program element's description, it is always available and can be used to modify the design time, compile time, or runtime behavior of a program element. Attributes are classes derived from the Attribute class (in the System namespace) or one of its derived classes found throughout the .NET FCL.

Collections and data structures

The .NET FCL features a number of general-purpose and more specialized collection classes. The general-purpose classes include the Array class (in the System namespace) and the ArrayList and CollectionBase classes (in the System.Collection namespace). Specialized classes include the Stack class, a last-in, first-out structure, the Queue class, a first-in, first-out structure, in the System.Collection namespace, and the ListDictionary class, a linked list dictionary class, in the System.Collection.Specialized namespace.

Control creation

The .NET FCL provides full support for custom Windows and web controls that integrate with design-time environments like Visual Studio through a number of classes, including the Container class in the System.ComponentModel namespace or the CollectionEditor class in the System.ComponentModel.Design namespace.

Configuration settings

Using the .NET FCL, you have easy access to application configuration information from configuration files using classes such as AppSettingsReader and DictionarySectionHandler in the System.Configuration namespace. You can also access registry data using the Registry, RegistryHive, and RegistryKey classes in the Microsoft.Win32 namespace. Finally, you can access ActiveDirectory information using the members of the System.DirectoryServices namespace.

Debugging, profiling, and diagnostics

The .NET FCL makes a large number of debugging, diagnostic, and informational classes available that can help in locating and fixing bugs, as well as in improving overall performance. These include the Debug, Debugger, EventLog, and PerformanceCounter classes in the System.Diagnostics namespace.

Drawing

The FCL provides a full set of graphics objects, such as the Color structure, the Brush class, the Font class, and the Graphics class in the System.Drawing namespace.

Input/output

The FCL allows you to read the standard input, standard output, and standard error streams, as well as to access the file system, through classes like File, FileInfo, StreamReader, and StreamWriter in the System.IO namespace.

Availability of metadata

Through the Type class in the System namespace and classes like Assembly, Module, EventInfo, MethodInfo, and ParameterInfo in the System.Reflection namespace, the .NET FCL provides support for reading metadata (the data that describes particular program elements) at any time.

Remote calls

Through classes such as ObjRef, RemotingConfiguration, and RemotingServices in the System.Runtime.Remoting namespace, the .NET FCL adds support for remoting (calls that cross process or machine boundaries).

String handling and manipulation

Interestingly, in the .NET Framework, strings are immutable. This means that simple operations such as string concatenation involve an enormous performance penalty. The StringBuilder class in the System.Text namespace makes it possible to perform string concatenation efficiently. The RegEx and Match classes in System.Text.RegularExpressions make it possible to perform regular expression searches on strings.

Control of threading

In previous versions of Visual Basic, threading was a factor that enormously impacted VB applications but over which the VB developer had no control. With classes like Thread, Mutex, and Monitor in the System.Threading namespace, the .NET FCL for the first time places threading under the direct control of the VB.NET developer.

Data access

The .NET FCL features a brand new data access technology, ADO.NET. It is represented by classes like the DataSet class in the System.Data namespace, the OleDbConnection, OleDbCommand, and OleDbDataReader classes in the System.Data.OleDb namespace, and the SqlConnection, SqlCommand, and SqlDataReader classes in the System.Data.SqlClient namespace.

Windows desktop applications

The forms and controls that made Visual Basic the premier Rapid Application Development package for Windows have their equivalent in the .NET FCL. These classes, such as the Form class, the Button class, and the TextBox class, are found in the System.Windows.Forms namespace.

Web application development

In addition to Windows controls, the .NET FCL features two sets of controls for web application development. HTML server controls execute on the server but otherwise correspond more or less directly to standard client-side HTML controls. They are found in the System.Web.UI.HTMLControls namespace. Web controls (also known as ASP controls) are server controls that abstract the functionality of controls in a web application. They are found in the System.Web.UI.WebControls namespace.

Web services

A web service is simply a function call over the Internet. The .NET FCL supports the development of web services through the types in the System.Web.Services namespace.

As you can see, the functionality offered by the .NET FCL is extensive—and in this overview of the .NET FCL, we've only emphasized the highlights.

Working with the .NET FCL

Despite its vast size, the .NET FCL is a manageable collection of classes and their methods. This is because, unlike more traditional development tools such as the Win32 API, the .NET FCL is a collection of types (classes, interfaces, delegates, events, structures, modules, and enumerations) and their members organized into namespaces. A *namespace* is simply a logical grouping of classes that can in turn contain other namespaces, so that a collection of namespaces forms an inverse hierarchical tree. Organization of types into namespaces helps to prevent collisions in the event that types are identically named.

Although the .NET system of namespaces does not have a single root, we can consider the System namespace at the top of the .NET FCL hierarchy. It includes a wide variety of basic system classes, including data types, exception types, and types defining the most important attributes.

Defining Accessible Namespaces

The types in a namespace, in turn, reside in an assembly, which is simply a logical unit of deployment. An assembly provides the Microsoft Intermediate Language (MSIL) code for its contents, which is packaged in a Windows portable executable (PE) file. An assembly also specifies security permissions for itself, maintains a list of the types that it defines and their scopes, and specifies rules for resolving references to external types.

The assemblies in which namespaces of the .NET FCL reside are Windows dynamic link libraries (.DLLs). Typically, a single assembly contains multiple namespaces. In addition, however, a single namespace can reside in multiple assemblies. The System namespace, for example, resides in both *mscorlib.dll* and *system.dll*.

 You can use ILDASM, the Intermediate Language disassembler included with the .NET Framework SDK, to see which namespaces and types are available in a particular assembly or DLL.

Namespaces are made available to Visual Studio or to the Visual Basic compiler by identifying the assembly in which the namespace resides. When using Visual Studio as the development environment for your Visual Basic projects, this is done by using the References dialog, as follows:

---

1. Select Project → Add Reference from the main menu, or right-click on References in the Solution Explorer window and select Add Reference from the popup menu.

2. When the Add Reference dialog appears, make sure the .NET tab is selected, as shown in Figure 1-1. (The tab should be selected by default.)

3. Select one or more DLL whose types you'd like to reference, then click the Select button. The assemblies you've added should appear in the Selected Components data grid. (See Figure 1-2.) Repeat this step if necessary until each assembly whose types you wish to access is displayed in the Selected Components data grid in the lower portion of the dialog.

4. Click the OK button to close the dialog.

Component Name	Version	Path
mscorlib	1.0.3300.0	C:\WINDOWS\Microsoft.NET...
msdatasrc	7.0.3300.0	C:\Program Files\Microsoft.NE...
msddslmp	7.0.3300.0	C:\Program Files\Microsoft.NE...
msddsp	7.0.3300.0	C:\Program Files\Microsoft.NE...
office	7.0.3300.0	C:\WINDOWS\Microsoft.NET...
RegCode	1.0.3300.0	C:\WINDOWS\Microsoft.NET...
stdole	7.0.3300.0	C:\Program Files\Microsoft.NE...
System.Configuration.Install.dll	1.0.3300.0	C:\WINDOWS\Microsoft.NET...
System.Data.dll	1.0.3300.0	C:\WINDOWS\Microsoft.NET...
System.Design.dll	1.0.3300.0	C:\WINDOWS\Microsoft.NET...
System.DirectoryServices.dll	1.0.3300.0	C:\WINDOWS\Microsoft.NET...
System.dll	1.0.3300.0	C:\WINDOWS\Microsoft.NET...

Figure 1-1. The .NET tab of the Add Reference dialog

The Add Reference dialog does not list the assemblies whose references have already been added to a Visual Studio .NET project. You can see which assemblies are currently referenced by a project by expanding the References tree in the Solution Explorer window.

When compiling using the VB.NET command-line compiler, assemblies are made available to the compiler by using the /r: (or /reference:) compiler switch.

Figure 1–2. *Selecting assemblies whose namespaces and types will be referenced*

Commas are used to separate DLLs if multiple DLLs are referenced. For example, the following command might compile a standard Windows desktop application:

```
vbc MyWinApp.vb /t:winexe /r:system.dll,system.windows.forms.dll
```

You may have noticed that you don't need to specify the path to .NET DLLs in order to access them. This is because they are registered in the Global Assembly Cache (or GAC), a location in which the Common Language Runtime expects to find its shared libraries.

References to some namespaces are added to every project created in the Visual Studio environment. The following are the project types supported by Visual Studio .NET, along with the .NET DLLs each project type automatically references:

ASP.NET web applications
  System.dll

  System.Data.dll

  System.Drawing.dll

  System.Web.dll

System.XML.dll

ASP.NET web services
System.dll

System.Data.dll

System.Web.dll

System.Web.Services.dll

System.XML.dll

Class libraries
System.dll

System.Data.dll

System.XML.dll

Console applications
System.dll

System.Data.dll

System.XML.dll

Web control libraries
System.dll

System.Data.dll

System.Drawing.dll

System.Management.dll

System.Web.dll

System.XML.dll

Windows applications
System.dll

System.Data.dll

System.Drawing.dll

System.Windows.Forms.dll

System.XML.dll

Windows control libraries
System.dll

System.Data.dll

System.Drawing.dll

System.Windows.Forms.dll

System.XML.dll

Windows services
   System.dll

   System.Data.dll

   System.ServiceProcess.dll

   System.XML.dll

All Visual Studio .NET projects written using Visual Basic also transparently reference two .NET DLLs: *mscorlib.dll* (which contains portions of the System namespace, as well as namespaces such as System.Collections, System.IO, System.Reflection, and System.Threading), and *Microsoft.VisualBasic.dll* (which defines the functions, procedures, constants, and attributes of the Visual Basic .NET language). The Visual Basic command-line compiler also references these two DLLs automatically, although it doesn't automatically reference any additional .NET assemblies.

Accessing Types in Namespaces

Once you've added a reference to an assembly, you can access any of the types in its namespaces by providing a fully qualified reference to the type. For instance, the code in Example 1-4 instantiates objects of the HashTable and DictionaryEntry classes, and also calls a method of the Console class.

Example 1–4. Using fully qualified namespace names

```
Option Strict On

Public Module modMain
   Public Sub Main
      ' Define hashtable
      Dim States As New System.Collections.HashTable()
      ' Add items
      States.Add("NY", "New York")
      States.Add("CA", "California")
      States.Add("MI", "Michigan")
      States.Add("VT", "Vermont")
      States.Add("WA", "Washington")

      ' Define and fill DictionaryEntry object
      Dim dict(States.Count - 1) As _
              System.Collections.DictionaryEntry
      Dim item As System.Collections.DictionaryEntry
      States.CopyTo(dict, 0)

      ' Iterate dictionary
      For Each Item in dict
        System.Console.WriteLine( _
           Microsoft.VisualBasic.Strings.UCase(CStr(item.Key)) _
           & ": " & CStr(item.Value))
      Next
   End Sub
End Module
```

In each case, the source code includes the fully qualified name of the type it instantiates or accesses; the Console class is a type in the System namespace, while the HashTable and DictionaryEntry classes are both types in the System.Collections namespace. Note that even the namespace of the supposedly "intrinsic" Visual Basic *UCase* function must be specified or a compiler error ("Name 'UCase' is not declared.") results if you attempt to compile the program using the Visual Basic command-line compiler. The *UCase* function, as you can see from the code in Example 1-4, is a member of the Strings class in the Microsoft.VisualBasic namespace.

Importing Namespaces

Needless to say, fully qualifying the name of each .NET type quickly becomes rather tiresome, particularly for types that are nested deep within a hierarchical namespace. You can, however, use the Imports directive to import a particular namespace, thereby allowing the compiler to resolve the reference to a particular type and eliminating the need for you to provide a fully qualified path to the type. For example, the code fragment shown in Example 1-4, when rewritten to use the Imports directive, appears as shown in Example 1-5 (new and modified lines of code appear in boldface).

Example 1-5. Importing namespaces with the Imports directive

```
Option Strict On

Imports System
Imports System.Collections
Public Module modMain

Public Sub Main
    ' Define hashtable
    Dim States As New HashTable()
    ' Add items
    States.Add("NY", "New York")
    States.Add("CA", "California")
    States.Add("MI", "Michigan")
    States.Add("VT", "Vermont")
    States.Add("WA", "Washington")

    ' Define and fill DictionaryEntry object
    Dim dict(States.Count - 1) As DictionaryEntry
    Dim item As DictionaryEntry
    States.CopyTo(dict, 0)

    ' Iterate dictionary
    For Each Item in dict
        Console.WriteLine(CStr(item.Key) & ": " & _
                          CStr(item.Value))
    Next
End Sub

End Module
```

Note that while no namespaces are automatically imported by the command line compiler, Visual Studio automatically imports a number of namespaces, again depending on the project type. The project types and the namespaces that they automatically import are as follows:

ASP.NET web applications
Microsoft.VisualBasic

System

System.Collections

System.Configuration

System.Data

System.Drawing

System.Web

System.Web.UI

System.Web.UI.HTMLControls

System.Web.UI.WebControls

ASP.NET web services
Microsoft.VisualBasic

System

System.Collections

System.Data

System.Diagnostics

Class libraries
Microsoft.VisualBasic

System

System.Collections

System.Data

System.Diagnostics

Console applications
Microsoft.VisualBasic

System

System.Collections

System.Data

System.Diagnostics

Web control libraries
Microsoft.VisualBasic

System

System.Collections

System.Data

System.Diagnostics

System.Management

Windows applications
Microsoft.VisualBasic

System

System.Collections

System.Data

System.Diagnostics

System.Drawing

System.Windows.Forms

Windows control libraries
Microsoft.VisualBasic

System

System.Collections

System.Data

System.Diagnostics

System.Drawing

System.Windows.Forms

Windows services
Microsoft.VisualBasic

System

System.Collections

System.Data

System.Diagnostics

In addition, the *AssemblyInfo.vb* file automatically imports two additional namespaces, System.Reflection and System.Runtime.InteropServices, into every project.

You can have Visual Studio automatically import a particular namespace, which makes it available to all of the source code files in a project, as follows:

1. Select Project → Properties from the main menu, or right-click on the project name in the Solution Explorer window and select Properties from the popup menu to open the properties dialog.

2. Select Common Properties → Imports in the treeview control on the right to display the Imports property page.

3. Enter the fully qualified name of the namespace you'd like to import in the Namespace dialog and click the Add Import button. Repeat this step for each namespace you'd like to automatically import in the project.

4. Click OK to close the property page.

While the use of the Imports directive can save a substantial amount of typing, it does mean that the compiler is left to identify the namespace containing a particular type. This means that, if identically named types are found in the imported namespaces, Visual Basic will not be able to determine which type you wish to instantiate. For example, consider the code in Example 1-6, which defines two custom namespaces, each with a class named Person.

Example 1-6. Classes with the same name

```
Option Strict On

Namespace Extensions.Classes

    Public Class Person
        Dim sName As String

        Public Sub New(Name As String)
            sName = Name
        End Sub

        Public Property Name() As String
            Get
                Return sName
            End Get
            Set
                sName = Value
            End Set
        End Property
    End Class
End Namespace

Namespace Extensions.Demographics
    Public Enum Gender As Short
        Male = 2
        Female = 1
    End Enum

    Public Class Person
        Dim shAge As Short
        Dim chGender As Gender

        Public Property Age() As Short
            Get
                Return shAge
            End Get
            Set
                shAge = Value
            End Set
        End Property

        Public Property Gender() As Gender
            Get
                Return chGender
```

Example 1–6. Classes with the same name (continued)

```
        End Get
        Set
            chGender = Value
        End Set
    End Property
  End Class
End Namespace
```

This code can be compiled into a dynamic link library. We can then attempt to access the Person class using code like that in Example 1-7.

Example 1–7. A type collision

```
Option Strict On

Imports Extensions.Classes
Imports Extensions.Demographics
Imports System

Module modMain
    Public Sub Main()
        Dim oPerson As New Person("John Doe")
        Console.WriteLine(oPerson.Name)

        Dim oPerson2 As New Person
        oPerson2.Age = 32
        oPerson2.Gender = Gender.Female
        Console.WriteLine(oPerson2.Gender.ToString)
    End Sub
End Module
```

However, when we attempt to compile this code, the VB.NET command-line compiler raises two instances of the following compiler error:

> error BC30561: 'Person' is ambiguous, imported from the namespaces or types 'Extensions.Demographics, Extensions.Classes'.

To resolve this problem of type collisions, two solutions are available. The first is to use the fully qualified namespace name to indicate the namespace containing the type we want to instantiate, just as if we hadn't used the Imports statement. The second is to assign an alias to a namespace and to use that alias to identify the namespace containing the type we want to instantiate. To do this, we also use the Imports directive, which then has the following syntax:

```
Imports aliasname = namespace
```

where aliasname is the alias by which the namespace will be referenced in code, and namespace is the fully qualified namespace name.

We can then modify our code example from Example 1-7 to take advantage of aliasing. The result is shown in Example 1-8 (again, modified lines are shown in boldface).

Example 1–8. Using aliasing to prevent type naming conflicts

```
Option Strict On

Imports cl = Extensions.Classes
Imports Extensions.Demographics
Imports System

Module modMain
    Public Sub Main()
        Dim oPerson As New cl.Person("John Doe")
        Console.WriteLine(oPerson.Name)

        Dim oPerson2 As New Person
        oPerson2.Age = 32
        oPerson2.Gender = Gender.Female
        Console.WriteLine(oPerson2.Gender.ToString)
    End Sub
End Module
```

Note that we have aliased a single namespace, which has magically resolved the ambiguous reference to both namespaces. The use of an alias, however, means that all further references to types in the Extensions.Classes namespace must use the alias in order to resolve the reference to the type, or we must use the fully qualified name of the type.

The Types of a .NET Namespace

Once you've made a namespace accessible to your code, you can access any of the types it contains. In this section, we'll survey the types that a .NET namespace can contain.

Classes

In VB.NET, classes are reference types; that is, when you create an instance of a class in code, you work with a pointer (or reference) to the object rather than with the object itself. This is similar to previous versions of Visual Basic.

When a .NET class is instantiated, its constructor (or its New subroutine) executes. Each .NET class can have one or more constructors (that is, constructors can be overloaded), and the constructor can either be parameterless or parameterized. Visual Basic .NET provides three ways to initialize a variable and invoke its constructor. These are illustrated in the following three sets of statements, each of which instantiates a System.IO.FileInfo object:

```
' Single statement
Dim oFile As New FileInfo("c:\documents\notes.txt")

' Single Statement with separate call to constructor
Dim oFile As FileInfo = New FileInfo("c:\documents\notes.txt")

' Separate declaration and initialization
Dim oFile As FileInfo
oFile = New FileInfo("c:\documents\notes.txt")
```

Once we create an instance of a class, we can invoke its properties and methods. In addition, we can handle its events (assuming that it exposes events) if we instantiate the object using the WithEvents keyword. For example:

```
Dim WithEvents cn As New SqlConnection()
```

Visual Basic .NET, unlike previous versions of Visual Basic, supports both instance and shared members. *Instance members* exist for each instance of a class; in previous versions of Visual Basic, all members of a class were instance members. *Shared members* are members that are not associated with a specific instance of a class or a structure, but rather are common to all instances of a class. Accessing a shared member of a class does not require that the class be instantiated; it can be accessed using the class name only. In addition, if the shared member is a property, it has a single value for all instances of the class.

In Example 1-8, we accessed the shared WriteLine method of the Console class, as follows:

```
Console.WriteLine(oPerson.Name)
```

Note that, to do this, we didn't have to instantiate an instance of the Console class; we simply called the Console class directly. A peculiarity of Visual Basic is that you can invoke shared members using either the class name or the name of an instance variable. The following code fragment, which does create an instance of the Console class, also works:

```
Dim con As Console
con.WriteLine(oPerson2.Gender.ToString)
```

Structures

Structures are very similar to classes, except that they are value types rather than reference types. Most of the primitive data types (Boolean, Byte, Char, Int16, Int32, etc.) defined in the FCL are implemented as structures. Because structures don't support parameterless constructors, you don't use the New keyword to instantiate them.

You work with structures just as you work with .NET classes, except that the New keyword is not used in declaring a structure:

```
' Declaration and initialization
Dim num1 As Int16 = 10

' Separate declaration and initialization
Dim num2 As Int16
num2 = 10
```

Enumerations

An enumeration is a related set of constants. You don't have to instantiate enumerations to take advantage of their members. When working with enumerations in

.NET, however, you must specify the name of the enumeration in order to access one of its constants. For example:

```
Dim dy As String = WeekdayName(1, False, FirstDayOfWeek.Sunday)
```

Interfaces

Interfaces are virtual base classes; that is, they consist of members (methods, properties, and events) that have no implementation. Instead, derived classes must provide the implementation. For example, the following code fragment uses interface inheritance to define a new class:

```
Class CustomCompare
    Implements System.IComparable

    Public Function CompareTo(obj As Object) As Integer _
                    Implements System.IComparable.CompareTo
        ' Implementation of IComparable.ICompareTo
    End Function
End Class
```

Delegates

A delegate is a reference type that represents a strongly typed function pointer. All delegates are explicitly or implicitly derived from the System.Delegate class, which includes a number of members that provide information about the delegate, create object instances, or invoke the delegate. Delegates can be used in event procedures, for asynchronous callbacks, and wherever the address of a function is expected. The following example uses a delegate to define the thread procedure to be passed to the ThreadPool class's QueueUserWorkItem method:

```
Option Strict On

    Imports Microsoft.VisualBasic
    Imports System
    Imports System.Threading
    Imports System.Windows.Forms

Public Class ThreadedForm : Inherits Form

    Protected WithEvents btnStart As Button
    Protected lblOutput As Label

    Public Shared Sub Main()
        Dim thrdForm As New ThreadedForm()
        Application.Run(thrdForm)
    End Sub

    Public Sub New()

        Me.Height = 200
        Me.Width = 400

        btnStart = New Button()
        btnStart.Text = "&Start"
        btnStart.Top = 50
```

```
           btnStart.Left = 100
           btnStart.Width = 75
           btnStart.Height = 50
           Me.Controls.Add(btnStart)

           lblOutput = New Label()
           lblOutput.Top = 125
           lblOutput.Left = 100
           lblOutput.Width = 200
           lblOutput.Height = 75
           Me.Controls.Add(lblOutput)
           Me.Text = "Asynchronous Callback Example"
       End Sub

       Protected Sub btnStart_Click(sender As Object, _
                                 e As EventArgs) _
                   Handles btnStart.Click
           btnStart.Enabled = False
           Dim thrdProc As WaitCallback = AddressOf ThreadProcedure
           ThreadPool.QueueUserWorkItem(thrdProc, 1000000)
       End Sub

       Protected Sub ThreadProcedure(o As Object)
           Dim i As Integer
           If TypeOf o Is Integer Then
              i = DirectCast(o, Integer)
           Else
              Exit Sub
           End If
           Dim lCtr As Long
           For lCtr = 0 to 10000000
              If lCtr Mod 1000000 = 0 Then
                 lblOutput.Text = lblOutput.Text & "X"
              End If
           Next
       End Sub

   End Class
```

Approaching the .NET FCL

It may seem that, given both the newness and the enormity of the .NET platform,
a substantial learning curve is required to "learn" the .NET FCL. In fact, this isn't
the case; you can begin to take advantage of the class library immediately by
selecting those classes, structures, and enumerations and their members that are of
immediate interest to you and ignoring the rest. You can then gradually expand
your familiarity with the .NET FCL as needed.

This incremental approach to learning the .NET FCL is possible because Visual
Basic was written to run under the .NET platform, and much of the Visual Basic
language (or at least the functions and procedures not implemented directly by the
Visual Basic compiler) actually wrap functionality found in the .NET FCL.

The clearest example of this is to be found in the data types supported by Visual
Basic. While Visual Basic's data types appear to be intrinsic, in fact they are
defined by the .NET FCL; Visual Basic merely provides wrappers for each of the
.NET data types for which it offers native support. This, in fact, is one of the major

strengths of the .NET Framework: it features the Common Type System (CTS), which allows components and applications written in one .NET-compliant language to more or less seamlessly interoperate with components written in other .NET-compliant languages. Table 1-1 shows the "intrinsic" Visual Basic data types and their corresponding .NET FCL data types.

Table 1-1. VB.NET data types and their corresponding .NET FCL data types

VB.NET data type	.NET FCL data type
Boolean	System.Boolean
Byte	System.Byte
Char	System.Char
Date	System.DateTime
Decimal	System.Decimal
Double	System.Double
Integer	System.Int32
Long	System.Int64
Object	System.Object
Short	System.Int16
Single	System.Single
String	System.String

That the standard VB data types are merely wrappers for CTS data types is indicated by the Visual Basic *SystemTypeName* function, which returns the name of a CTS data type that corresponds to a particular "intrinsic" VB data type. For example, the code fragment:

```
Dim i as Integer = 12345
Dim s As String = "New World"

Console.WriteLine(SystemTypeName(TypeName(i)))
Console.WriteLine(SystemTypeName(TypeName(s)))
```

shows that the VB Integer corresponds to the .NET System.Int32 data type, while the VB String data type corresponds to the .NET System.String data type. In other words, we could also declare and initialize our two variables as follows:

```
Dim i as System.Int32 = 12345
Dim s As System.String = "New World"
```

The fact that VB data types are really CTS data types means that we can access the fields, properties, and methods of CTS datatypes from VB variables. Consider, for example, the following code fragment:

```
Dim d As Double
Dim b As Byte
Dim s As String = InputBox("Enter a number (0-255): ")

If IsNumeric(s) Then
    d = CDbl(s)
    If b.MaxValue >= d And b.MinValue <= d Then
```

```
      b = CByte(s)
   End If
   Console.WriteLine(TypeName(b) & " value: " & b)
End If
```

The code simply checks whether the numeric equivalent of a string entered by the user is within the range of the VB Byte data type by retrieving the values of the System.Byte data type's MinValue and MaxValue fields.

 Because they don't exist in the Framework Class Library, two intrinsic data types found in previous versions of VB have been removed from the language. The first is the Currency data type. In its place, use the Decimal data type, which in the .NET platform is a standard data type. (In previous versions of VB, the Decimal was a subtype of the Variant data type, and variables could be cast as decimals only by calling the *CDec* conversion function.) The second is the Variant data type, which has been replaced by the Object data type as VB's "universal" data type.

Moreover, the reverse is also true: given a CTS data type, we can pass it as a parameter to methods that work on Visual Basic data types. For example:

```
Option Strict On
Imports Microsoft.VisualBasic
Imports System

Public Module modMain

Public Sub Main
   Dim iNum As Int32 = 1234
   Dim sNum As System.String = CStr(iNum)

   Console.WriteLine(Mid(sNum,3,2))
End Sub

End Module
```

This code includes two instances of calls to VB.NET methods using CTS data types. The first is the call to the *CStr* conversion function, which is passed a variable of type Int32. The second is the call to the *Mid* string manipulation function, which is passed a variable of type System.String.

This means that, when working with Visual Basic data types, you can continue to call intrinsic Visual Basic functions, and call the members of .NET data types when they provide important functionality not available directly from Visual Basic. The following sections detail some of those functions.

Array Class

Just as Visual Basic scalar data types are in fact CTS scalar data types, so Visual Basic arrays are actually members of the .NET System.Array class. Some of its members that are not readily available in Visual Basic .NET are shown in the following table:

Name	Member type	Description
BinarySearch	Shared method	Searches a one-dimensional array for a particular value
Clear	Shared method	Sets a range of array elements to zero, False, or a null reference, depending on the members' data type
Copy	Shared method	Copies a portion of one array to another and performs any necessary type conversions
CopyTo	Method	Copies all the elements of a one-dimensional array to another one-dimensional array starting at a particular index position
IndexOf	Shared method	Returns the index of the first occurrence of a particular value in an array
IsFixedSize	Property	Returns a Boolean indicating whether an Array object has a fixed size
IsReadOnly	Property	Returns a Boolean indicating whether the elements in Array object are read-only
LastIndexOf	Shared method	Returns the index of the last occurrence of a particular value in an array
Rank	Property	Returns an Integer indicating the number of dimensions of the array
Reverse	Shared method	Reverses the elements in all or part of a one-dimensional array
Sort	Shared method	Sorts a one-dimensional array

Boolean Structure

The following table lists the members of the System.Boolean structure that are not readily available in the Visual Basic .NET language:

Name	Member type	Description
FalseString	Shared field	Returns the string representation of the Boolean value False. This is a read-only constant value.
Parse	Shared method	Converts a string (whose value must be either Boolean.TrueString or Boolean.FalseString) to its Boolean equivalent.
TrueString	Shared field	Returns the string representation of the Boolean value True. This is a read-only constant value.

Byte Structure

The Visual Basic .NET Byte data type is synonymous with the .NET System.Byte data type. The following table lists some of the members of the Byte class that are not readily available in Visual Basic:

Name	Member type	Description
MaxValue	Shared field	A constant representing the largest possible value of an instance of the Byte class
MinValue	Shared field	A constant representing the smallest possible value of an instance of the Byte class
Parse	Shared method	Converts the numeric representation of a string to its Byte equivalent

Char Structure

Char, a new data type in VB.NET, corresponds to the System.Char data type. Some of the members of the latter that offer functionality not available in VB.NET are shown in the following table:

Name	Member type	Description
GetUnicodeCategory	Shared method	Returns a member of the UnicodeCategory enumeration (in the System.Globalization namespace) indicating the character type of a Char object.
IsControl	Shared method	Returns a Boolean indicating whether a particular Unicode character is a control character.
IsDigit	Shared method	Returns a Boolean indicating whether a particular Unicode character is a decimal digit. (The decimal and thousands separators are not considered digits.)
IsLetter	Shared method	Returns a Boolean indicating whether a particular Unicode character is a letter of the alphabet.
IsLetterOrDigit	Shared method	Returns a Boolean indicating whether a particular Unicode character is a digit or a letter of the alphabet.
IsLower	Shared method	Returns a Boolean indicating whether a particular Unicode character is a lowercase letter. The method returns True only for letters of the alphabet; that is, Char.IsLetter must also return True.
IsNumber	Shared method	Returns a Boolean indicating whether a particular Unicode character is a decimal or hexadecimal digit.
IsPunctuation	Shared method	Returns a Boolean indicating whether a particular Unicode character is a punctuation mark.

Name	Member type	Description
IsSeparator	Shared method	Returns a Boolean indicating whether a particular Unicode character is a separator character (e.g., a space). The method does not return True if the character is a numeric separator.
IsSymbol	Shared method	Returns a Boolean indicating whether a particular Unicode character is a symbol.
IsUpper	Shared method	Returns a Boolean indicating whether a particular Unicode character is an uppercase letter. The method returns True only for letters of the alphabet; that is, Char.IsLetter must also return True.
IsWhiteSpace	Shared method	Returns a Boolean indicating whether a particular Unicode character is white space.
MaxValue	Shared field	A constant containing the largest possible value of Char object.
MinValue	Shared field	A constant containing the smallest possible value of a Char object.
Parse	Shared method	Converts a particular character in a string to a Char object.

DateTime Structure

The Visual Basic Date data type corresponds to the .NET Framework's DateTime structure. The following table lists the DateTime members whose functionality is not available in the date/time functions supported by the VB.NET language:

Name	Member type	Description
AddMilliseconds	Method	Adds a designated number of milliseconds to the DateTime instance
AddTicks	Method	Adds a designated number of ticks to the DateTime instance
CompareTo	Method	Compares the current DateTime instance to an object and returns an indication of their relative values
DaysInMonth	Shared method	Returns the number of days in a designated month and year
FromOADate	Shared method	Converts an OLE Automation Date value to a DateTime instance
GetDateTimeFormats	Method	Returns a String array containing all the string representations supported by the standard DateTime format specifiers
IsLeapYear	Shared method	Returns a Boolean indicating whether a particular year is a leap year
MaxValue	Shared field	A constant containing the largest possible value of a DateTime instance
Millisecond	Property	Retrieves the milliseconds component of a DateTime instance

Name	Member type	Description
MinValue	Shared field	A constant containing the smallest possible value of a DateTime instance
Now	Shared property	Returns the current local date and time
Parse	Shared method	Converts a string representation of a date/time to a DateTime instance
ParseExact	Shared method	Converts a string representation of a date/time in a specified format to its DateTime equivalent
Ticks	Property	Returns a Long containing the number of ticks that represent the date and time value of this instance
TimeOfDay	Property	Returns the current time of day
Today	Shared property	Returns the current date
ToFileTime	Method	Converts the DateTime instance to the format of the local system's file time
ToLocalTime	Method	Converts the current coordinated universal time (UTC) to local time
ToLongDateString	Method	Converts a DateTime instance to its long date string representation
ToLongTimeString	Method	Converts a DateTime instance to its long time string representation
ToOADate	Method	Converts the value of this instance to a Double representing the OLE Automation date
ToShortDateString	Method	Converts a DateTime instance to its short date string representation
ToShortTimeString	Method	Converts a DateTime instance to its short time string representation
ToUniversalTime	Method	Converts the value of the DateTime instance to coordinated universal time (UTC)
UtcNow	Shared property	Returns a DateTime instance that represents the current local date and time expressed as the coordinated universal time (UTC)

Decimal Structure

The VB.NET Decimal data type corresponds directly to the System.Decimal structure. The CTS Decimal structure includes the following members whose functionality is not readily available in VB.NET:

Name	Member type	Description
FromOACurrency	Shared method	Converts a Long containing an OLE Automation Currency value (e.g., a VB6 or VBScript Currency value) to a Decimal value
GetBits	Shared method	Converts a particular Decimal value to its binary representation and returns that value as an Integer

Name	Member type	Description
MaxValue	Shared field	A constant containing the largest possible value of a Decimal object
MinValue	Shared field	A constant containing the smallest possible value of a Decimal object
ToOACurrency	Shared method	Converts a Decimal value to an OLE Automation Currency value (e.g., a VB6 or VBScript Currency value), which it returns as a Long

Double Structure

The VB.NET Double data type corresponds to the .NET Framework's System.Double data type. The following table lists the members of the latter that offer functionality not found in the Visual Basic .NET language:

Name	Member type	Description
Epsilon	Shared field	A constant containing the smallest positive Double value greater than zero
MaxValue	Shared field	A constant containing the largest possible value of a Double object
MinValue	Shared field	A constant containing the smallest possible value of a Double object
NaN	Shared field	A constant containing the representation of a value that is not a number (NaN)
NegativeInfinity	Shared field	A constant containing a number that represents negative infinity
PositiveInfinity	Shared field	A constant containing a number that represents positive infinity
IsInfinity	Shared method	Returns a Boolean indicating whether the value of a Double object represents positive or negative infinity
InNaN	Shared method	Returns a Boolean indicating whether a Double object contains a value that is not a number (NaN)
IsNegativeInfinity	Shared method	Returns a Boolean indicating whether the value of a Double object represents negative infinity
IsPositiveInfinity	Shared method	Returns a Boolean indicating whether the value of a Double object represents positive infinity
Parse	Shared method	Converts the string representation of a number to its Double equivalent

Int16 Structure

The VB.NET Short data type corresponds directly to the System.Int16 structure. The members of the latter structure that offer unique functionality are shown in the following table:

Name	Member type	Description
MaxValue	Shared field	A constant containing the largest possible value of an Int16 object
MinValue	Shared field	A constant containing the smallest possible value of an Int16 object
Parse	Shared method	Converts the string representation of a number to its Int16 equivalent

Int32 Structure

The VB.NET Integer data type corresponds directly to the System.Int32 structure. The members of the Int32 structure that offer unique functionality are shown in the following table:

Name	Member type	Description
MaxValue	Shared field	A constant containing the largest possible value of an Int32 object
MinValue	Shared field	A constant containing the smallest possible value of an Int32 object
Parse	Shared method	Converts the string representation of a number to its Int32 equivalent

Int64 Structure

The VB.NET Long data type corresponds directly to the System.Int64 structure. The members of the Int64 structure that offer unique functionality are shown in the following table:

Name	Member type	Description
MaxValue	Shared field	A constant containing the largest possible value of an Int64 object
MinValue	Shared field	A constant containing the smallest possible value of an Int64 object
Parse	Shared method	Converts the string representation of a number to its Int64 equivalent

Object Class

The VB.NET Object data type corresponds to the System.Object class. System.Object, however, offers no functionality that is not available through the standard Visual Basic language.

Single Structure

The VB.NET Single data type corresponds to the .NET Framework's System.Single data type. The following table lists the members of the latter that offer functionality not found in the Visual Basic .NET language:

Name	Member type	Description
Epsilon	Shared field	A constant containing the smallest positive Single value greater than zero
MaxValue	Shared field	A constant containing the largest possible value of a Single object
MinValue	Shared field	A constant containing the smallest possible value of a Single object
NaN	Shared field	A constant containing the representation of a value that is not a number (NaN)
NegativeInfinity	Shared field	A constant containing a number that represents negative infinity
PositiveInfinity	Shared field	A constant containing a number that represents positive infinity
IsInfinity	Shared method	Returns a Boolean indicating whether the value of a Single object represents positive or negative infinity
InNaN	Shared method	Returns a Boolean indicating whether a Single object contains a value that is not a number (NaN)
IsNegativeInfinity	Shared method	Returns a Boolean indicating whether the value of a Single object represents negative infinity
IsPositiveInfinity	Shared method	Returns a Boolean indicating whether the value of a Single object represents positive infinity
Parse	Shared method	Converts the string representation of a number to its Single equivalent

String Class

The VB.NET String data type is equivalent to the System.String class. The members of the String class that offer functionality not incorporated in the VB.NET language are shown in the following table:

Name	Member type	Description
Chars	Property	Returns a Char instance representing the character at a particular position in a string
Clone	Method	Returns an additional reference to a particular String instance
CompareOrdinal	Shared method	Compares two strings without considering locale settings

Name	Member type	Description
CopyTo	Method	Copies a designated number of characters starting at a particular position in a string to a character array
Empty	Shared field	A constant representing an empty string
EndsWith	Method	Returns a Boolean indicating whether the String instance ends with the substring passed to the method as an argument
Format	Shared method	Replaces each format specification in a string with its corresponding value
IndexOf	Method	Returns the position of the first occurrence of a character or a substring within the string instance
IndexOfAny	Method	Returns the index of the first occurrence in this String instance of any element in a character array
Insert	Method	Inserts a substring at a designated position of a String instance
LastIndexOf	Method	Returns the position of the last occurrence of a designated character or substring within the string instance
LastIndexOfAny	Method	Returns the position of the last occurrence in this String instance of any of a set of characters in a character array
PadLeft	Method	Right aligns the characters in a String instance by padding them with a space or another designated character
PadRight	Method	Left aligns the characters in a String instance by padding them with a space or another designated character
Remove	Method	Deletes a specified number of characters from a String instance beginning at a designated position
StartsWith	Method	Returns a Boolean indicating whether the String instance begins with a designated substring or character
ToCharArray	Method	Copies the characters in the String instance to a Unicode character array

Non-CTS Data Types

Note, however, that because they are not part of the Common Language Specification (the specification that defines the core functionality that a .NET platform must implement), VB does not wrap the following CTS data types:

System.SByte
Description: Signed byte

Value Range: -128 to 127

System.UInt16
Description: Unsigned 16-bit integer

Value Range: 0 to 65,535

System.UInt32
Description: Unsigned 32-bit integer

Value Range: 0 to 4,294,967,295

System.UInt64
Description: Unsigned 64-bit integer

Value Range: 0 to 18,446,744,073,709,551,615

PART II

.NET Core Classes
Quick Reference

CHAPTER 2

Reference

The quick-reference section that follows packs a lot of information into a small space. This introductory section explains how to get the most out of that information. It describes how the quick reference is organized and how to read the individual quick reference entries.

Finding a Quick-Reference Entry

The quick reference is organized into chapters, one per namespace. Each chapter begins with an overview of the namespace and includes a hierarchy diagram for the types (classes, interfaces, enumerations, delegates, and structs) in the namespace. Following the overview are quick-reference entries for all of the types in the namespace.

Figure 2-1 is a sample diagram showing the notation used in this book. This notation is similar to that used in *Java in a Nutshell* (O'Reilly) but borrows some features from UML.

Classes marked as MustInherit are shown as a slanted rectangle, and classes marked as NonInheritable are shown as an octagonal rectangle. Inheritance is shown as a solid line from the subtype, ending with a hollow triangle that points to the base class. There are two notations that indicate interface implementation. The lollipop notation is used most of the time, since it is easier to read. In some cases, especially where many types implement a given interface, the shaded box notation with the dashed line is used.

Important relationships between types (associations) are shown with a dashed line ending with an arrow. The figures don't show every possible association. Some types have strong containing relationships with one another. For example, a System.Net.WebException object instance includes a System.Net.WebResponse object instance that represents the HTTP response containing the error details (HTTP status code and error message). To show this relationship, a filled diamond is attached to the containing type with a solid line that points to the contained type.

Entries are organized alphabetically by type *and* namespace, so that related types are grouped near each other. Thus, in order to look up a quick reference entry for a particular type, you must also know the name of the namespace that contains that type. Usually, the namespace is obvious from the context, and you should have no trouble looking up the quick-reference entry you want. Use the tabs on the outside edge of the book and the dictionary-style headers on the upper outside corner of each page to help you find the namespace and type you are looking for.

Occasionally, you may need to look up a type for which you do not already know the namespace. In this case, refer to Appendix A. This index allows you to look up a type by its name and find out what namespace it is part of.

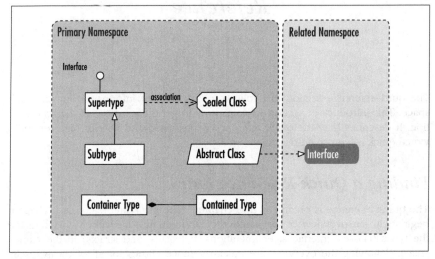

Figure 2–1. Class hierarchy notation

Reading a Quick-Reference Entry

Each quick-reference entry contains quite a bit of information. The sections that follow describe the structure of a quick-reference entry, explaining what information is available, where it is found, and what it means. While reading the descriptions that follow, you will find it helpful to flip through the reference section itself to find examples of the features being described.

Type Name, Namespace, Assembly, Type Category, and Flags

Each quick-reference entry begins with a four-part title that specifies the name, namespace (followed by the assembly in parentheses), and type category of the type, and may also specify various additional flags that describe the type. The type name appears in bold at the upper left of the title. The namespace and assembly appear, in smaller print, in the lower left, below the type name.

The upper-right portion of the title indicates the type category of the type (class, delegate, enum, interface, or struct). The "class" category may include modifiers such as `NonInheritable` or `MustInherit`.

In the lower-right corner of the title, you may find a list of flags that describe the type. The possible flags and their meanings are as follows:

ECMA
> The type is part of the ECMA CLI specification.

Serializable
> The type, or a base class, implements System.Runtime.Serialization.ISerializable or has been flagged with the System.Serializable attribute.

Marshal by reference
> This class, or a superclass, derives from System.MarshalByRefObject.

Context bound
> This class, or a superclass, derives from System.ContextBoundObject.

Disposable
> The type implements the System.IDisposable interface.

Flag
> The enumeration is marked with the System.FlagsAttribute attribute.

Description

The title of each quick-reference entry is followed by a short description of the most important features of the type. This description may be anywhere from a couple of sentences to several paragraphs long.

Synopsis

The most important part of every quick-reference entry is the synopsis, which follows the title and description. The synopsis for a type looks a lot like its source code, except that the member bodies are omitted and some additional annotations are added. If you know VB.NET syntax, you know how to read the type synopsis.

The first line of the synopsis contains information about the type itself. It begins with a list of type modifiers, such as `MustInherit` and `NonInheritable`. These modifiers are followed by the `Class`, `Delegate`, `Enum`, `Interface`, or `Struct` keyword and then by the name of the type. The type name may be followed by a colon (:) and a base class or interfaces that the type implements.

The type definition line is followed by a list of the members that the type defines. This list includes only those members that are explicitly declared in the type, are overridden from a base class, or are implementations of an interface member. Members that are simply inherited from a base class are not shown; you will need to look up the base class definition to find those members.

Once again, if you understand basic VB.NET syntax, you should have no trouble making sense of these lines. The listing for each member includes the modifiers, type, and name of the member. For methods, the synopsis also includes the type and name of each method parameter. The member names are in boldface, so it is easy to scan the list of members looking for the one you want. The names of method parameters are in italics to indicate that they are not to be used literally. The member listings are printed on alternating gray and white backgrounds to keep them visually separate.

Member availability and flags

Each member listing is a single line that defines the syntax for that member. These listings use VB.NET syntax, so their meaning is immediately clear to any VB.NET programmer. There is some auxiliary information associated with each member synopsis, however, that requires explanation.

The area to the right of the member synopsis is used to display a variety of flags that provide additional information about the member. Some of these flags indicate additional specification details that do not appear in the member syntax itself.

The following flags may be displayed to the right of a member synopsis:

Overrides
>   Indicates that a method overrides a method in one of its base classes. The flag is followed by the name of the base class that the method overrides.

Implements
>   Indicates that a method implements a method in an interface. The flag is followed by the name of the interface that is implemented.

=
>   For enumeration fields and constant fields, this flag is followed by the constant value of the field. Only constants of primitive and String types and constants with the value `Nothing` are displayed. Some constant values are specification details, while others are implementation details. Some constants are platform dependent, such as System.BitConverter.IsLittleEndian. Platform-dependent values shown in this book conform to the System.PlatformID.Win32NT platform (32-bit Windows NT, 2000, or XP). The reason that symbolic constants are defined, however, is so you can write code that does not rely directly upon the constant value. Use this flag to help you understand the type, but do not rely upon the constant values in your own programs.

Functional grouping of members

Within a type synopsis, the members are not listed in strict alphabetical order. Instead, they are broken down into functional groups and listed alphabetically within each group. Constructors, events, fields, methods, and properties are all listed separately. Instance methods are kept separate from shared (class) methods. Public members are listed separately from protected members. Grouping members by category breaks a type down into smaller, more comprehensible segments, making the type easier to understand. This grouping also makes it easier for you to find a desired member.

Functional groups are separated from each other in a type synopsis with VB.NET comments, such as:

```
Public Constructors
```

or:

```
' Protected Instance Properties
```

or:

```
' Events
```

The various functional categories are as follows (in the order in which they appear in a type synopsis):

Constructors
> Displays the constructors for the type. Public constructors and protected constructors are displayed separately in subgroupings. If a type defines no constructor at all, the VB.NET compiler adds a default parameterless constructor that is displayed here. If a type defines only private constructors, it cannot be instantiated, so no constructor appears. Constructors are listed first because the first thing you do with most types is instantiate them by calling a constructor.

Fields
> Displays all of the fields defined by the type, including constants. Public and protected fields are displayed in separate subgroups. Fields are listed here, near the top of the synopsis, because constant values are often used throughout the type as legal values for method parameters and return values.

Properties
> Lists all the properties of the type, breaking them down into subgroups for public and protected shared properties and public and protected instance properties. After the property name, its accessors (get or set) are shown.

Shared Methods
> Lists the shared methods (class methods) of the type, broken down into subgroups for public shared methods and protected shared methods.

Public Instance Methods
> Contains all the public instance methods.

Protected Instance Methods
> Contains all the protected instance methods.

Class Hierarchy

For any type that has a non-trivial inheritance hierarchy, the synopsis is followed by a "Hierarchy" section. This section lists all of the base classes of the type, as well as any interfaces implemented by those base classes. It will also list any interfaces implemented by an interface. In the hierarchy listing, arrows indicate base class to derived class relationships, while the interfaces implemented by a type follow the type name in parentheses. For example, the following hierarchy indicates that System.IO.Stream implements IDisposable and extends MarshalByRefObject, which itself extends Object:

```
System.Object | System.MarshalByRefObject | System.IO.Stream(System.IDisposable)
```

If a type has subtypes, the "Hierarchy" section is followed by a "Subtypes" section that lists those subtypes. If an interface has implementations, the "Hierarchy" section is followed by an "Implementations" section that lists those implementations. While the "Hierarchy" section shows ancestors of the type, the "Subtypes" or "Implementations" section shows descendants.

Cross References

The hierarchy section of a quick-reference entry is followed by a number of optional cross reference sections that indicate other related types and methods that may be of interest. These sections are the following:

Passed To
> This section lists all of the members (from other types) that are passed an object of this type as an argument, including properties whose values can be set to this type. This is useful when you have an object of a given type and want to know where it can be used.

Returned By
> This section lists all of the members that return an object of this type, including properties whose values can take on this type. This is useful when you know that you want to work with an object of this type, but don't know how to obtain one.

Valid On
> For attributes, this lists the attribute targets that the attribute can be applied to.

Associated Events
> For delegates, this lists the events it can handle.

A Note About Type Names

Throughout the quick reference, you'll notice that types are sometimes referred to by type name alone and at other times referred to by type name and namespace. If namespaces were always used, the type synopses would become long and hard to read. On the other hand, if namespaces were never used, it would sometimes be difficult to know what type was being referred to. The rules for including or omitting the namespace name are complex, but they can be summarized approximately as follows:

- If the type name alone is ambiguous, the namespace name is always used.

- If the type is part of the System namespace or is a very commonly used type like System.Collection.ICollection, the namespace is omitted.

- If the type being referred to is part of the current namespace (and has a quick-reference entry in the current chapter), the namespace is omitted. The namespace is also omitted if the type being referred to is part of a namespace that contains the current namespace.

CHAPTER 3

Microsoft.Win32

The Microsoft.Win32 namespace includes types you can use to interact with the Microsoft Windows platform. These types concentrate on two aspects of Windows-specific programming: receiving operating system events and manipulating the registry. Essentially, the classes, delegates, and enumerations in this namespace provide a type-safe object wrapper around a few select functions in the Windows API.

Use the Registry class to access the root level registry keys, which are provided as RegistryKey objects. These have built-in methods for retrieving and modifying key values. The SystemEvents class allows you to respond to system events such as timers, preference changes, and shutdown operations. All other types in this namespace are used to support the SystemEvents class, by providing delegates for each event and custom System.EventArgs objects that provide additional information to the corresponding event handlers. Figure 3-1 shows the inheritance diagram for this namespace.

PowerModeChangedEventArgs   Class

Microsoft.Win32 (system.dll)

This class creates a custom System.EventArgs object for the PowerModeChangedEventHandler delegate. It provides additional information to your event handler, identifying the new power mode that the system has entered.

```
Public Class PowerModeChangedEventArgs : Inherits EventArgs
' Public Constructors
   Public Sub New(ByVal mode As PowerModes)
' Public Instance Properties
   Public ReadOnly Property Mode As PowerModes
End Class
```

Hierarchy: System.Object→ System.EventArgs→ PowerModeChangedEventArgs

Passed To: PowerModeChangedEventHandler.{BeginInvoke(), Invoke()}

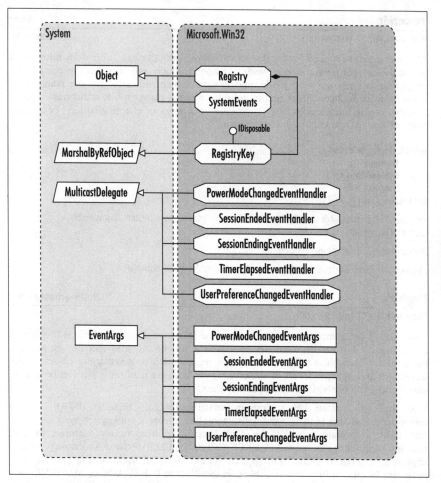

Figure 3–1. The Microsoft.Win32 namespace

PowerModeChangedEventHandler

Delegate

Microsoft.Win32 (system.dll)

serializable

This delegate defines the signature that an event handler must use to receive the System-Events.PowerModeChanged event. This event is raised when the computer enters or exits suspend mode, and when the power consumption level changes. A computer requires Advanced Power Management (APM) or Advanced Configuration and Power Interface (ACPI) support in order to use these operating system features. APM/ACPI is usually supported on (but not restricted to) portable computers and devices.

```
Public Delegate Sub PowerModeChangedEventHandler(ByVal sender As Object, _
    ByVal e As PowerModeChangedEventArgs)
```

Associated Events: SystemEvents.PowerModeChanged()

PowerModes

Enum

Microsoft.Win32 (system.dll) *serializable*

This enumeration is used for the PowerModeChangedEventArgs class. It provides information about the current power modes, such as Suspend, which indicates that the computer is preparing to enter suspend mode, and Resume, which indicates that the computer is about to leave it. StatusChange simply indicates that the power mode status has changed, possibly due to automatic power-down settings, a weak or charging battery, or a transition between AC power and battery power.

```
Public Enum PowerModes
    Resume = 1
    StatusChange = 2
    Suspend = 3
End Enum
```

Hierarchy: System.Object→ System.ValueType→ System.Enum(System.IComparable, System.IFormattable, System.IConvertible)→ PowerModes

Returned By: PowerModeChangedEventArgs.Mode

Passed To: PowerModeChangedEventArgs.PowerModeChangedEventArgs()

Registry

NotInheritable Class

Microsoft.Win32 (mscorlib.dll)

This class is the starting point when using the Windows registry, which is the central repository used by most Windows applications for storing user-specific settings and preferences. Each shared field of this class represents a root RegistryKey object, which has values and multiple levels of subkeys. These keys are read-only, but can be manipulated using the methods of the RegistryKey class.

Most applications store their settings in CurrentUser (HKEY_CURRENT_USER). The recommended standard is to use the Software subkey, create a subkey for your organization, and then create a subkey for each specific application (for example, Internet Explorer preferences are stored in HKEY_CURRENT_USER\Software\Microsoft\Internet Explorer). Analogous global settings that should affect all users on the current computer can be placed in a similar subkey in LocalMachine (HKEY_LOCAL_MACHINE). For example, setup programs often use this key to store information about installed applications. The full collection of user settings for all the users of the current computer can be retrieved from the Users key, as can the default settings for new users, which are contained in the .DEFAULT subkey of users. CurrentUser is actually a mapped subkey of Users, much as CurrentConfig is a subkey of LocalMachine.

The ClassesRoot key contains information used for Windows 3.1–compatible DDE and OLE support. Information for file viewers, Windows Explorer extensions, and file associations is also stored in this key. You can use the PerformanceData key to retrieve performance-related information. This data is not actually stored in the registry. Instead, it is automatically collected from the appropriate system object managers when this key is accessed. Lastly, the DynData key is used to support Virtual Device Drivers (VxDs) and allow them to provide real-time data to remote Win32 applications. It is used only in Windows 95, 98, and ME systems.

Much more information about the system registry is available from Microsoft's Windows platform documentation.

```
Public NotInheritable Class Registry
' Public Shared Fields
```

Public Shared ReadOnly **ClassesRoot** As RegistryKey	=*HKEY_CLASSES_ROOT [0x80000000]*
Public Shared ReadOnly **CurrentConfig** As RegistryKey	=*HKEY_CURRENT_CONFIG [0x80000005]*
Public Shared ReadOnly **CurrentUser** As RegistryKey	=*HKEY_CURRENT_USER [0x80000001]*
Public Shared ReadOnly **DynData** As RegistryKey	=*HKEY_DYN_DATA [0x80000006]*
Public Shared ReadOnly **LocalMachine** As RegistryKey	=*HKEY_LOCAL_MACHINE [0x80000002]*
Public Shared ReadOnly **PerformanceData** As RegistryKey	=*HKEY_PERFORMANCE_DATA [0x80000004]*
Public Shared ReadOnly **Users** As RegistryKey	=*HKEY_USERS [0x80000003]*

End Class

RegistryHive

Microsoft.Win32 (mscorlib.dll)

Enum

serializable

This enumeration provides values for the RegistryKey.OpenRemoteBaseKey() method. These values identify a registry key, just like the fields in the Registry class.

```
Public Enum RegistryHive
    ClassesRoot = &H080000000
    CurrentUser = &H080000001
    LocalMachine = &H080000002
    Users = &H080000003
    PerformanceData = &H080000004
    CurrentConfig = &H080000005
    DynData = &H080000006
End Enum
```

Hierarchy: System.Object→ System.ValueType→ System.Enum(System.IComparable, System.IFormattable, System.IConvertible)→ RegistryHive

Passed To: RegistryKey.OpenRemoteBaseKey()

RegistryKey

Microsoft.Win32 (mscorlib.dll)

NotInheritable Class

marshal by reference, disposable

The RegistryKey class contains the core functionality for reading and writing to the Windows registry. Each RegistryKey object represents an individual key in the registry. You can use the properties of this class to find out how many values this key contains (ValueCount), how many subkeys (SubKeyCount) there are, and the fully qualified key name (Name).

To open a subkey for modification, use the overloaded version of the OpenSubKey() method—which allows you to specify the writable parameter—and set it to true. You can open subkeys that are several levels deep by separating keys with a backslash (\). You can also use methods such as CreateSubKey() and DeleteSubKey(). In the registry, keys are logical groupings, and values are the entries used to store the actual data. You can use the GetValue(), SetValue(), and DeleteValue() methods to manipulate a named value in the current key.

Changes to the registry are propagated across the system automatically and are flushed to disk automatically by the system. You should never need to use methods such as Flush(), unless you require absolute certainty that a registry change has been written to disk. The OpenRemoteBaseKey() method opens the registry on a remote computer, provided both machines are running the remote registry service and have remote administration enabled.

```
Public NotInheritable Class RegistryKey : Inherits MarshalByRefObject: Implements IDisposable
    ' Public Instance Properties
    Public ReadOnly Property Name As String
```

Public ReadOnly Property **SubKeyCount** As Integer
Public ReadOnly Property **ValueCount** As Integer
' *Public Shared Methods*
Public Shared Function **OpenRemoteBaseKey**(ByVal hKey As RegistryHive, ByVal machineName As String) _
  As RegistryKey
' *Public Instance Methods*
Public Sub **Close**()
Public Function **CreateSubKey**(ByVal subkey As String) As RegistryKey
Public Sub **DeleteSubKey**(ByVal subkey As String)
Public Sub **DeleteSubKey**(ByVal subkey As String, ByVal throwOnMissingSubKey As Boolean)
Public Sub **DeleteSubKeyTree**(ByVal subkey As String)
Public Sub **DeleteValue**(ByVal name As String)
Public Sub **DeleteValue**(ByVal name As String, ByVal throwOnMissingValue As Boolean)
Public Sub **Flush**()
Public Function **GetSubKeyNames**() As String()
Public Function **GetValue**(ByVal name As String) As Object
Public Function **GetValue**(ByVal name As String, ByVal defaultValue As Object) As Object
Public Function **GetValueNames**() As String()
Public Function **OpenSubKey**(ByVal name As String) As RegistryKey
Public Function **OpenSubKey**(ByVal name As String, ByVal writable As Boolean) As RegistryKey
Public Sub **SetValue**(ByVal name As String, ByVal value As Object)
Overrides Public Function **ToString**() As String
' *Protected Instance Methods*
Overrides Protected Sub **Finalize**()
End Class

Hierarchy: System.Object→ System.MarshalByRefObject→ RegistryKey(System.IDisposable)

SessionEndedEventArgs
Class

Microsoft.Win32 (system.dll)

This class is a custom System.EventArgs object for the SystemEvents.SessionEnded delegate. It provides additional information to your event handler about why the current session has ended.

Public Class **SessionEndedEventArgs** : Inherits EventArgs
' *Public Constructors*
Public Sub **New**(ByVal reason As SessionEndReasons)
' *Public Instance Properties*
Public ReadOnly Property **Reason** As SessionEndReasons
End Class

Hierarchy: System.Object→ System.EventArgs→ SessionEndedEventArgs

Passed To: SessionEndedEventHandler.{BeginInvoke(), Invoke()}

SessionEndedEventHandler
Delegate

Microsoft.Win32 (system.dll)
serializable

This delegate defines the signature that an event handler must use to receive the System-Events.SessionEnded event. This event is raised just before the system finishes its logoff or shutdown procedure.

Public Delegate Sub **SessionEndedEventHandler**(ByVal sender As Object, ByVal e As SessionEndedEventArgs)

Associated Events: SystemEvents.SessionEnded()

SessionEndingEventArgs   Class

Microsoft.Win32 (system.dll)

This class is a custom System.EventArgs object for the SystemEvents.SessionEnding delegate. It provides additional information to your event handler about why the session is ending, and allows you to request that the session continue, by setting the Cancel property to true. Note that this is only a request, and you may not always be able to successfully cancel a shutdown operation.

Public Class **SessionEndingEventArgs** : Inherits EventArgs
' *Public Constructors*
  Public Sub **New**(ByVal reason As SessionEndReasons)
' *Public Instance Properties*
  Public Property **Cancel** As Boolean
  Public ReadOnly Property **Reason** As SessionEndReasons
End Class

Hierarchy: System.Object→ System.EventArgs→ SessionEndingEventArgs

Passed To: SessionEndingEventHandler.{BeginInvoke(), Invoke()}

SessionEndingEventHandler   Delegate

Microsoft.Win32 (system.dll)   *serializable*

This delegate defines the signature that an event handler must use to receive the System-Events.SessionEnding event. This event is raised when the user has chosen to log off or shutdown the system. It occurs before the SystemEvents.SessionEnded event. SessionEnding-EventArgs provides a Cancel property, which you can set in the event handler to cancel the pending shutdown.

Public Delegate Sub **SessionEndingEventHandler**(ByVal sender As Object, ByVal e As SessionEndingEventArgs)

Associated Events: SystemEvents.SessionEnding()

SessionEndReasons   Enum

Microsoft.Win32 (system.dll)   *serializable*

This enumeration specifies information for the Reason property of the SessionEndingEvent-Args and SessionEndedEventArgs event arguments. It specifies whether the user who started the current application is logging off (Logoff) (in which case the system may continue to run) or whether the operating system is shutting down (SystemShutdown).

Public Enum **SessionEndReasons**
    Logoff = 1
    SystemShutdown = 2
End Enum

Hierarchy: System.Object→ System.ValueType→ System.Enum(System.IComparable, System.IFormattable, System.IConvertible)→ SessionEndReasons

Returned By: SessionEndedEventArgs.Reason, SessionEndingEventArgs.Reason

Passed To: SessionEndedEventArgs.SessionEndedEventArgs(), SessionEndingEventArgs.SessionEndingEventArgs()

SystemEvents

NotInheritable Class

Microsoft.Win32 (system.dll)

This class provides global events for select Windows operating system events. You can write event handlers to receive these. Some of the events include notifications that occur when user settings are changed (DisplaySettingsChanged, TimeChanged, and UserPreferenceChanged) or when the system state changes (LowMemory, PowerModeChangedSessionEnded, and SessionEnding). You can also receive notifications about new fonts (InstalledFontsChanged) and palette switching in 256-color mode (PaletteChanged).

System event handlers are executed on a different thread than the rest of your program. For this reason, code in the event handler must be thread-safe. If your event handler needs access to other objects from your program, you can use the shared method InvokeOnEventsThread() to instantiate these objects on the system event listener thread. This way, they are easily accessible to the event handler code.

Do not perform time-consuming tasks in a system event handler, as it may cause problems with other applications that are also trying to handle the event.

```
Public NotInheritable Class SystemEvents
' Public Shared Methods
   Public Shared Function CreateTimer(ByVal interval As Integer) As IntPtr
   Public Shared Sub InvokeOnEventsThread(ByVal method As Delegate)
   Public Shared Sub KillTimer(ByVal timerId As IntPtr)
' Events
   Public Event DisplaySettingsChanged As EventHandler
   Public Event EventsThreadShutdown As EventHandler
   Public Event InstalledFontsChanged As EventHandler
   Public Event LowMemory As EventHandler
   Public Event PaletteChanged As EventHandler
   Public Event PowerModeChanged As PowerModeChangedEventHandler
   Public Event SessionEnded As SessionEndedEventHandler
   Public Event SessionEnding As SessionEndingEventHandler
   Public Event TimeChanged As EventHandler
   Public Event TimerElapsed As TimerElapsedEventHandler
   Public Event UserPreferenceChanged As UserPreferenceChangedEventHandler
   Public Event UserPreferenceChanging As UserPreferenceChangingEventHandler
End Class
```

TimerElapsedEventArgs

Class

Microsoft.Win32 (system.dll)

This class is a custom System.EventArgs object used for the SystemEvents.TimerElapsed delegate. It provides additional information to your event handler, identifying the ID of the timer that has changed.

```
Public Class TimerElapsedEventArgs : Inherits EventArgs
' Public Constructors
   Public Sub New(ByVal timerId As IntPtr)
' Public Instance Properties
   Public ReadOnly Property TimerId As IntPtr
End Class
```

Hierarchy: System.Object→ System.EventArgs→ TimerElapsedEventArgs

Passed To: TimerElapsedEventHandler.{BeginInvoke(), Invoke()}

TimerElapsedEventHandler   Delegate

Microsoft.Win32 (system.dll)   *serializable*

This delegate defines the signature an event handler must use to receive the System-Events.TimerElapsed event. This event is raised whenever a windows timer interval expires.

Public Delegate Sub **TimerElapsedEventHandler**(ByVal sender As Object, ByVal e As TimerElapsedEventArgs)

Associated Events: SystemEvents.TimerElapsed()

UserPreferenceCategory   Enum

Microsoft.Win32 (system.dll)   *serializable*

This enumeration is used for the UserPreferenceChangedEventArgs class. It provides information identifying the type of preference that was changed.

Public Enum **UserPreferenceCategory**
    Accessibility = 1
    Color = 2
    Desktop = 3
    General = 4
    Icon = 5
    Keyboard = 6
    Menu = 7
    Mouse = 8
    Policy = 9
    Power = 10
    Screensaver = 11
    Window = 12
    Locale = 13
End Enum

Hierarchy: System.Object→ System.ValueType→ System.Enum(System.IComparable, System.IFormattable, System.IConvertible)→ UserPreferenceCategory

Returned By: UserPreferenceChangedEventArgs.Category, UserPreferenceChangingEventArgs.Category

Passed To: UserPreferenceChangedEventArgs.UserPreferenceChangedEventArgs(), UserPreferenceChangingEventArgs.UserPreferenceChangingEventArgs()

UserPreferenceChangedEventArgs   Class

Microsoft.Win32 (system.dll)

This class is a custom System.EventArgs object used for the UserPreferenceChangedEventHandler delegate. It provides additional information to your event handler, identifying the type of preference that was changed.

Public Class **UserPreferenceChangedEventArgs** : Inherits EventArgs
' *Public Constructors*
    Public Sub **New**(ByVal category As UserPreferenceCategory)
' *Public Instance Properties*
    Public ReadOnly Property **Category** As UserPreferenceCategory
End Class

Hierarchy: System.Object→ System.EventArgs→ UserPreferenceChangedEventArgs

Passed To: UserPreferenceChangedEventHandler.{BeginInvoke(), Invoke()}

UserPreferenceChangedEventHandler
Delegate

Microsoft.Win32 (system.dll)
serializable

This delegate defines the signature an event handler must use to receive the System-Events.UserPreferenceChanged event. This event is raised when a user applies configuration changes, usually through one of the setting modules in the Control Panel. Note that not all changes raise this event, so it is best to first test it to make sure it accomplishes everything you need before you rely on it.

```
Public Delegate Sub UserPreferenceChangedEventHandler(ByVal sender As Object, _
    ByVal e As UserPreferenceChangedEventArgs)
```

Associated Events: SystemEvents.UserPreferenceChanged()

UserPreferenceChangingEventArgs
Class

Microsoft.Win32 (system.dll)

This class represents the event arguments sent to a UserPreferenceChangingEventHandler. Category specifies the UserPreferenceCategory of user preferences that is changing.

```
Public Class UserPreferenceChangingEventArgs : Inherits EventArgs
' Public Constructors
    Public Sub New(ByVal category As UserPreferenceCategory)
' Public Instance Properties
    Public ReadOnly Property Category As UserPreferenceCategory
End Class
```

Hierarchy: System.Object→ System.EventArgs→ UserPreferenceChangingEventArgs

Passed To: UserPreferenceChangingEventHandler.{BeginInvoke(), Invoke()}

UserPreferenceChangingEventHandler
Delegate

Microsoft.Win32 (system.dll)
serializable

This delegate receives the SystemEvents.UserPreferenceChanging event, which is similar to SystemEvents.UserPreferenceChanged, except it is raised as the event is changing, not after it has changed.

```
Public Delegate Sub UserPreferenceChangingEventHandler(ByVal sender As Object, _
    ByVal e As UserPreferenceChangingEventArgs)
```

Associated Events: SystemEvents.UserPreferenceChanging()

CHAPTER 4

System

In many respects, the System namespace serves as the core namespace for the .NET libraries, in much the same way java.lang does for Java programmers or stdlib.h does for C/C++ programmers. For example, the ECMA-compliant primitive-type value types are defined in the System namespace, along with complementary composite types and base types. These are used in the synthesis of type generation, which is done by the compiler on the .NET programmer's behalf (for an example of this on-the-fly type synthesis, see Array). Figure 4-1 shows many of the types in this namespace.

System serves as the home for key base-type definitions, including Object, the root of every type in the .NET hierarchy. Every type in the system ultimately extends this class, making it the "root of all evil" in .NET. In addition, this namespace contains ValueType, the base type for all value types in .NET (such as the primitive types listed later in this chapter, shown in Figure 4-5), and Type, which in turn represents compile-time type information about other types defined within the .NET environment (the type metadata).

ECMA-compliant primitive-type value types include the fundamental types used for all .NET applications, which are basic value types such as Int32, Single, Double, Decimal, Char, Byte, and Boolean. All of the primitive types are aliased in VB.NET with keywords such as Integer, Double, and Boolean. See the description of each type for more details. In addition to these fundamental types, there are composite types such as DateTime and TimeSpan, used to handle date- and time-based calculations without having to drop down to integer math, and Uri, used to represent references to a Universal Resource Identifier, which is the more generic form of the ubiquitous HTTP URL identifier used on the Web.

In addition to these primitive and composite types, several interfaces defined here are intended as support interfaces. For example, the interfaces IConvertible, IComparable, and ICloneable let types support the same basic operations (conversion, comparison, and cloning, respectively) that the primitive types offer.

Along with the base types described earlier, System contains base types that programmers do not directly reference, such as the following:

System.Array

> The base type for any array-type declaration, allowing .NET developers to refer to any type (or rank) array without having to specify exact type.

System.Delegate and System.MulticastDelegate

> Base types for delegate types (see Figure 4-2) created using the **Delegate** keyword in VB.NET.

System.Attribute

> The base type required for any type that wishes to be used as an attribute on other types, or methods, fields, etc. (see Figure 4-2).

Because delegates are often used in conjunction with events and event handlers, System also contains the definitions for EventHandler, the universal delegate type, and EventArgs, the base type representing data sent as part of an event-handler call.

System also serves as the heart of the exception-handling hierarchy in .NET, defining the base type Exception, which is the base type for all exceptions. The exception hierarchy is then bifurcated into two realms: *system exceptions*, which are exceptions generated by or relating to the runtime itself, and *application exceptions*, which are exceptions relating to the target business domain and typically are used on a per-application basis. SystemException serves as the base type for the former, and ApplicationException is the base type for the latter. Figure 4-3 and Figure 4-4 show the exceptions in the System namespace.

System also contains two definitions of some importance to the .NET programmer: the IDisposable interface, used to help programmers define cleanup and resource-release semantics for their types, and the GC class, which gives the .NET programmer access to the CLR garbage collector.

The System namespace also contains a few interoperability types. Guid represents the OSF UUID type that was made famous by COM. The attributes STAThreadAttribute and MTAThreadAttribute indicate to the runtime which sort of COM apartment-threading model the .NET component should use (but only when COM interoperability comes into play).

Finally, System defines the fundamental types such as Console and Environment. These give the .NET programmer access to the standard-in/standard-out streams (i.e., the command-shell console) and the environment variables of a given process, respectively. Most .NET applications will use ASP.NET or Windows Forms to present a graphical user interface. However, applications such as compilation tools, XML filters, and batch jobs use console I/O and environment variables extensively.

Activator
NotInheritable Class

System (mscorlib.dll)

This class is used to *activate* objects; that is, it either creates an object or obtains a handle to an existing object. This class is generally used in a variety of specialized conditions. For example, Activator can create an object within another AppDomain and hold a handle to that object. This effectively gives a multidomain container application (such as ASP.NET) the ability to reach into another AppDomain to perform tasks within that domain (such as closing down the AppDomain in the event of a user request to shut down the application server).

Activator's methods come in two distinct flavors: CreateInstance() and CreateInstanceFrom(). These create new objects when given particular criteria (such as the type to create and

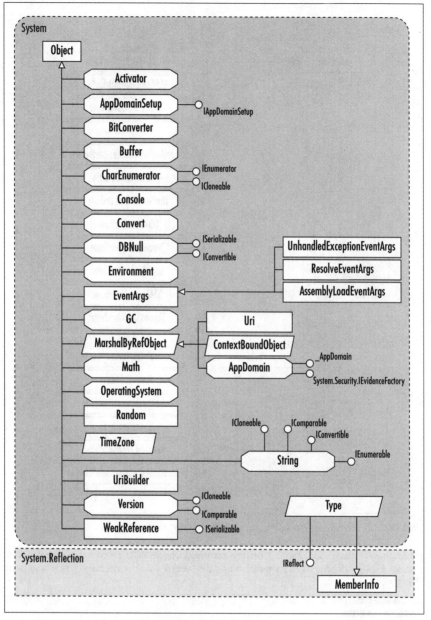

Figure 4–1. The System namespace

the assembly from which to create it). The GetObject() method uses published System.Runtime.Remoting.RemotingConfiguration data to locate another object and obtain a handle to it (usually in preparation for some remote-object method invocations).

All of the methods in Activator return a System.Runtime.Remoting.ObjectHandle, not the actual object itself; this object is actually a proxy to the created/remote object. As such,

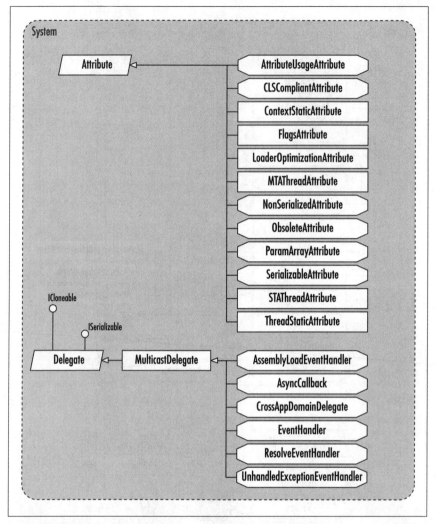

Figure 4–2. Attributes and delegates in the System namespace

programmers must call Unwrap() on the returned ObjectHandle to use the object. (Note that an explicit downcast is required, since the return value is declared to be a generic Object.)

```
Public NotInheritable Class Activator
' Public Shared Methods
   Public Shared Function CreateComInstanceFrom(ByVal assemblyName As String, ByVal typeName As String) _
      As ObjectHandle
   Public Shared Function CreateInstance(ByVal type As Type) As Object
   Public Shared Function CreateInstance(ByVal type As Type, ByVal bindingAttr As System.Reflection.BindingFlags, _
      ByVal binder As System.Reflection.Binder, ByVal args As Object(), _
      ByVal culture As System.Globalization.CultureInfo) As Object
   Public Shared Function CreateInstance(ByVal type As Type, ByVal bindingAttr As System.Reflection.BindingFlags, _
      ByVal binder As System.Reflection.Binder, ByVal args As Object(), _
      ByVal culture As System.Globalization.CultureInfo, ByVal activationAttributes As Object()) As Object
```

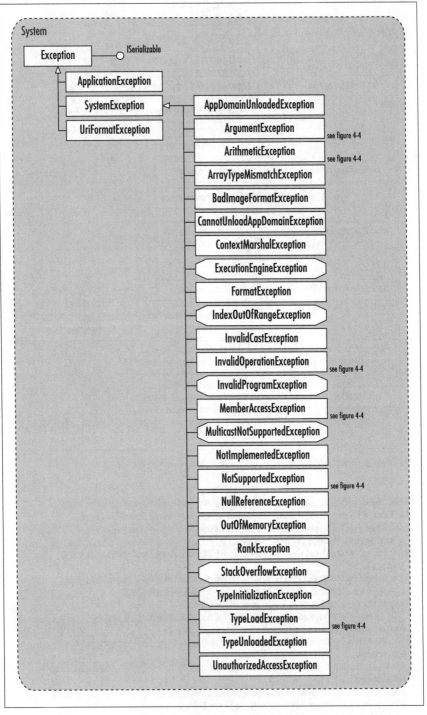

Figure 4–3. Exceptions in the System namespace

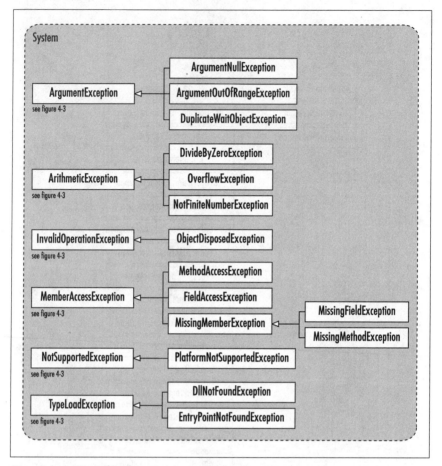

Figure 4-4. Specialized exceptions in the System namespace

```
Public Shared Function CreateInstance(ByVal type As Type, ByVal nonPublic As Boolean) As Object
Public Shared Function CreateInstance(ByVal type As Type, ByVal args As Object()) As Object
Public Shared Function CreateInstance(ByVal type As Type, ByVal args As Object(), _
   ByVal activationAttributes As Object()) As Object
Public Shared Function CreateInstance(ByVal assemblyName As String, ByVal typeName As String) _
   As ObjectHandle
Public Shared Function CreateInstance(ByVal assemblyName As String, ByVal typeName As String, _
   ByVal ignoreCase As Boolean, ByVal bindingAttr As System.Reflection.BindingFlags,
   ByVal binder As System.Reflection.Binder, ByVal args As Object(),                 _
   ByVal culture As System.Globalization.CultureInfo, ByVal activationAttributes As Object(),  _
   ByVal securityInfo As System.Security.Policy.Evidence) As ObjectHandle
Public Shared Function CreateInstance(ByVal assemblyName As String, ByVal typeName As String, _
   ByVal activationAttributes As Object()) As ObjectHandle
Public Shared Function CreateInstanceFrom(ByVal assemblyFile As String, ByVal typeName As String) _
   As ObjectHandle
Public Shared Function CreateInstanceFrom(ByVal assemblyFile As String, ByVal typeName As String, _
   ByVal ignoreCase As Boolean, ByVal bindingAttr As System.Reflection.BindingFlags,
   ByVal binder As System.Reflection.Binder, ByVal args As Object(),                 _
                                                                                    _
```

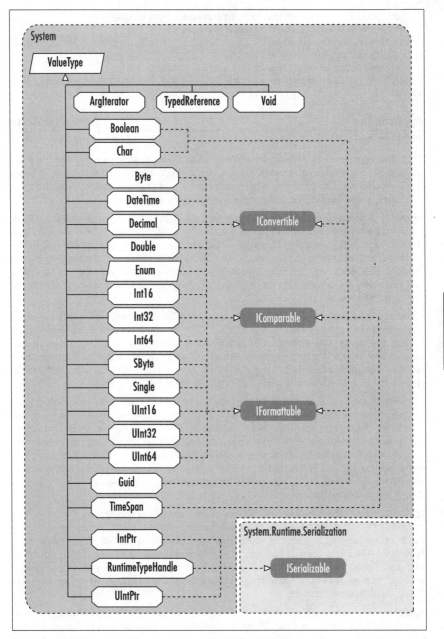

Figure 4-5. Value types in the System namespace

ByVal culture As System.Globalization.CultureInfo, ByVal activationAttributes As Object(),
ByVal securityInfo As System.Security.Policy.Evidence) As ObjectHandle
Public Shared Function **CreateInstanceFrom**(ByVal assemblyFile As String, ByVal typeName As String, _
ByVal activationAttributes As Object()) As ObjectHandle
Public Shared Function **GetObject**(ByVal type As Type, ByVal url As String) As Object
Public Shared Function **GetObject**(ByVal type As Type, ByVal url As String, ByVal state As Object) As Object
End Class

AppDomain

NotInheritable Class

System (mscorlib.dll)

ECMA, marshal by reference

This class represents an abstract separation within the executing process, which mimics the separation between processes running on a single machine. As a result, a single .NET process can host multiple other processes that offer the isolation found between processes, while keeping the low overhead of a single process.

Every .NET process created has at least one AppDomain, even when running a simple command shell–driven application, such as *Hello, world*, created by the shim code at the start of a .NET executable file. Applications that act as containers, however, can create multiple AppDomains, loading assemblies into each AppDomain independently of one another. This is, in fact, precisely how ASP.NET keeps multiple web applications separate from one another, so that an exception thrown from within one won't tear down the entire IIS process.

Creating a new AppDomain involves using the shared CreateDomain() method. This method is overloaded four ways, but the most common use is simply to pass in a friendly name for the AppDomain. When finished with a given AppDomain, use the Unload() method to close down the AppDomain and all objects stored within it. Should a .NET programmer wish to obtain a reference to the AppDomain she is currently executing within, the shared property CurrentDomain returns the current AppDomain.

Each AppDomain contains an entirely separate list of loaded assemblies accessible via the GetAssemblies() method, which returns the list of assemblies loaded for this particular AppDomain. AppDomains can also create instances of types within the given AppDomain, using the CreateInstance() family of methods. An AppDomain can also load and execute the entry point of an assembly using the ExecuteAssembly() method, or it can load an assembly directly using one of the Load() methods. AppDomains even support the ability to create dynamic (that is, transient or temporary) assemblies through the DefineDynamicAssembly() method.

AppDomains also offer a number of .NET events for interested consumers, notifying .NET programmers when an assembly has been loaded (AssemblyLoad), when an exception has been thrown out of a thread within that assembly (UnhandledException), or when the AppDomain—or the process containing it—is being unloaded and torn down (DomainUnload and ProcessExit). .NET programmers can use these events to perform necessary actions, such as loading an assembly from an alternative location when an assembly fails to load (AssemblyResolve).

AppDomain also contains a number of properties, which act in a role similar to environment variables within a process. These AppDomain properties are, like environment variables, simple name-value mapping pairs, retrievable in one of two ways: via the GetData() method or via a set of predefined properties on the AppDomain class (such as BaseDirectory).

Public NotInheritable Class **AppDomain** : Inherits MarshalByRefObject : Implements _AppDomain, _
System.Security.IEvidenceFactory
' *Public Shared Properties*
Public Shared ReadOnly Property **CurrentDomain** As AppDomain

' *Public Instance Properties*
Public ReadOnly Property **BaseDirectory** As String Implements _AppDomain.BaseDirectory
Public ReadOnly Property **DynamicDirectory** As String Implements _AppDomain.DynamicDirectory
Public ReadOnly Property **Evidence** As Evidence Implements IEvidenceFactory.Evidence
Public ReadOnly Property **FriendlyName** As String Implements _AppDomain.FriendlyName
Public ReadOnly Property **RelativeSearchPath** As String Implements _AppDomain.RelativeSearchPath
Public ReadOnly Property **SetupInformation** As AppDomainSetup
Public ReadOnly Property **ShadowCopyFiles** As Boolean Implements _AppDomain.ShadowCopyFiles
' *Public Shared Methods*
Public Shared Function **CreateDomain**(ByVal friendlyName As String) As AppDomain
Public Shared Function **CreateDomain**(ByVal friendlyName As String, _
  ByVal securityInfo As System.Security.Policy.Evidence) As AppDomain
Public Shared Function **CreateDomain**(ByVal friendlyName As String, _
  ByVal securityInfo As System.Security.Policy.Evidence, ByVal info As AppDomainSetup) As AppDomain
Public Shared Function **CreateDomain**(ByVal friendlyName As String, _
  ByVal securityInfo As System.Security.Policy.Evidence, ByVal appBasePath As String, _
  ByVal appRelativeSearchPath As String, ByVal shadowCopyFiles As Boolean) As AppDomain
Public Shared Function **GetCurrentThreadId**() As Integer
Public Shared Sub **Unload**(ByVal domain As AppDomain)
' *Public Instance Methods*
Public Sub **AppendPrivatePath**(ByVal path As String) Implements _AppDomain.AppendPrivatePath
Public Sub **ClearPrivatePath**() Implements _AppDomain.ClearPrivatePath
Public Sub **ClearShadowCopyPath**() Implements _AppDomain.ClearShadowCopyPath
Public Function **CreateComInstanceFrom**(ByVal assemblyName As String, ByVal typeName As String) _
  As ObjectHandle
Public Function **CreateInstance**(ByVal assemblyName As String, ByVal typeName As String) As ObjectHandle _
  Implements _AppDomain.CreateInstance
Public Function **CreateInstance**(ByVal assemblyName As String, ByVal typeName As String, _
  ByVal ignoreCase As Boolean, ByVal bindingAttr As System.Reflection.BindingFlags, _
  ByVal binder As System.Reflection.Binder, ByVal args As Object(), _
  ByVal culture As System.Globalization.CultureInfo, ByVal activationAttributes As Object(), _
  ByVal securityAttributes As System.Security.Policy.Evidence) As ObjectHandle _
  Implements _AppDomain.CreateInstance
Public Function **CreateInstance**(ByVal assemblyName As String, ByVal typeName As String, _
  ByVal activationAttributes As Object()) As ObjectHandle Implements _AppDomain.CreateInstance
Public Function **CreateInstanceAndUnwrap**(ByVal assemblyName As String, ByVal typeName As String) _
  As Object
Public Function **CreateInstanceAndUnwrap**(ByVal assemblyName As String, ByVal typeName As String, _
  ByVal ignoreCase As Boolean, ByVal bindingAttr As System.Reflection.BindingFlags, _
  ByVal binder As System.Reflection.Binder, ByVal args As Object(), _
  ByVal culture As System.Globalization.CultureInfo, ByVal activationAttributes As Object(), _
  ByVal securityAttributes As System.Security.Policy.Evidence) As Object
Public Function **CreateInstanceAndUnwrap**(ByVal assemblyName As String, ByVal typeName As String, _
  ByVal activationAttributes As Object()) As Object
Public Function **CreateInstanceFrom**(ByVal assemblyFile As String, ByVal typeName As String) As ObjectHandle _
  Implements _AppDomain.CreateInstanceFrom
Public Function **CreateInstanceFrom**(ByVal assemblyFile As String, ByVal typeName As String, _
  ByVal ignoreCase As Boolean, ByVal bindingAttr As System.Reflection.BindingFlags, _
  ByVal binder As System.Reflection.Binder, ByVal args As Object(), _
  ByVal culture As System.Globalization.CultureInfo, ByVal activationAttributes As Object(), _
  ByVal securityAttributes As System.Security.Policy.Evidence) As ObjectHandle _
  Implements _AppDomain.CreateInstanceFrom
Public Function **CreateInstanceFrom**(ByVal assemblyFile As String, ByVal typeName As String, _
  ByVal activationAttributes As Object()) As ObjectHandle Implements _AppDomain.CreateInstanceFrom
Public Function **CreateInstanceFromAndUnwrap**(ByVal assemblyName As String, ByVal typeName As String) _
  As Object

System

Public Function **CreateInstanceFromAndUnwrap**(ByVal assemblyName As String, ByVal typeName As String, _
  ByVal ignoreCase As Boolean, ByVal bindingAttr As System.Reflection.BindingFlags, _
  ByVal binder As System.Reflection.Binder, ByVal args As Object(), _
  · ByVal culture As System.Globalization.CultureInfo, ByVal activationAttributes As Object(), _
  ByVal securityAttributes As System.Security.Policy.Evidence) As Object

Public Function **CreateInstanceFromAndUnwrap**(ByVal assemblyName As String, ByVal typeName As String, _
  ByVal activationAttributes As Object()) As Object

Public Function **DefineDynamicAssembly**(ByVal name As System.Reflection.AssemblyName, _
  ByVal access As System.Reflection.Emit.AssemblyBuilderAccess) As AssemblyBuilder _
  Implements _AppDomain.DefineDynamicAssembly

Public Function **DefineDynamicAssembly**(ByVal name As System.Reflection.AssemblyName, _
  ByVal access As System.Reflection.Emit.AssemblyBuilderAccess, _
  ByVal evidence As System.Security.Policy.Evidence) As AssemblyBuilder _
  Implements _AppDomain.DefineDynamicAssembly

Public Function **DefineDynamicAssembly**(ByVal name As System.Reflection.AssemblyName, _
  ByVal access As System.Reflection.Emit.AssemblyBuilderAccess, _
  ByVal evidence As System.Security.Policy.Evidence, ByVal requiredPermissions As System.Security.PermissionSet, _
  ByVal optionalPermissions As System.Security.PermissionSet, _
  ByVal refusedPermissions As System.Security.PermissionSet) As AssemblyBuilder _
  Implements _AppDomain.DefineDynamicAssembly

Public Function **DefineDynamicAssembly**(ByVal name As System.Reflection.AssemblyName, _
  ByVal access As System.Reflection.Emit.AssemblyBuilderAccess, _
  ByVal requiredPermissions As System.Security.PermissionSet, _
  ByVal optionalPermissions As System.Security.PermissionSet, _
  ByVal refusedPermissions As System.Security.PermissionSet) As AssemblyBuilder _
  Implements _AppDomain.DefineDynamicAssembly

Public Function **DefineDynamicAssembly**(ByVal name As System.Reflection.AssemblyName, _
  ByVal access As System.Reflection.Emit.AssemblyBuilderAccess, ByVal dir As String) As AssemblyBuilder _
  Implements _AppDomain.DefineDynamicAssembly

Public Function **DefineDynamicAssembly**(ByVal name As System.Reflection.AssemblyName, _
  ByVal access As System.Reflection.Emit.AssemblyBuilderAccess, ByVal dir As String, _
  ByVal evidence As System.Security.Policy.Evidence) As AssemblyBuilder _
  Implements _AppDomain.DefineDynamicAssembly

Public Function **DefineDynamicAssembly**(ByVal name As System.Reflection.AssemblyName, _
  ByVal access As System.Reflection.Emit.AssemblyBuilderAccess, ByVal dir As String, _
  ByVal evidence As System.Security.Policy.Evidence, ByVal requiredPermissions As System.Security.PermissionSet), _
  ByVal optionalPermissions As System.Security.PermissionSet, _
  ByVal refusedPermissions As System.Security.PermissionSet) As AssemblyBuilder _
  Implements _AppDomain.DefineDynamicAssembly

Public Function **DefineDynamicAssembly**(ByVal name As System.Reflection.AssemblyName, _
  ByVal access As System.Reflection.Emit.AssemblyBuilderAccess, ByVal dir As String, _
  ByVal evidence As System.Security.Policy.Evidence, ByVal requiredPermissions As System.Security.PermissionSet, _
  ByVal optionalPermissions As System.Security.PermissionSet, _
  ByVal refusedPermissions As System.Security.PermissionSet, ByVal isSynchronized As Boolean) As AssemblyBuilder _
  Implements _AppDomain.DefineDynamicAssembly

Public Function **DefineDynamicAssembly**(ByVal name As System.Reflection.AssemblyName, _
  ByVal access As System.Reflection.Emit.AssemblyBuilderAccess, ByVal dir As String, _
  ByVal requiredPermissions As System.Security.PermissionSet, _
  ByVal optionalPermissions As System.Security.PermissionSet, _
  ByVal refusedPermissions As System.Security.PermissionSet) As AssemblyBuilder _
  Implements _AppDomain.DefineDynamicAssembly

Public Sub **DoCallBack**(ByVal callBackDelegate As CrossAppDomainDelegate) _
  Implements _AppDomain.DoCallBack

Public Function **ExecuteAssembly**(ByVal assemblyFile As String) As Integer _
  Implements _AppDomain.ExecuteAssembly

Public Function **ExecuteAssembly**(ByVal assemblyFile As String, _
  ByVal assemblySecurity As System.Security.Policy.Evidence) As Integer _
  Implements _AppDomain.ExecuteAssembly

Public Function **ExecuteAssembly**(ByVal assemblyFile As String, _
  ByVal assemblySecurity As System.Security.Policy.Evidence, ByVal args As String()) As Integer _
  Implements _AppDomain.ExecuteAssembly

Public Function **GetAssemblies**() As Assembly() Implements _AppDomain.GetAssemblies

Public Function **GetData**(ByVal name As String) As Object Implements _AppDomain.GetData

Public Function **GetType**() As Type

Overrides Public Function **InitializeLifetimeService**() As Object

Public Function **IsFinalizingForUnload**() As Boolean

Public Function **Load**(ByVal assemblyRef As System.Reflection.AssemblyName) As Assembly _
  Implements _AppDomain.Load

Public Function **Load**(ByVal assemblyRef As System.Reflection.AssemblyName, _
  ByVal assemblySecurity As System.Security.Policy.Evidence) As Assembly Implements _AppDomain.Load

Public Function **Load**(ByVal rawAssembly As Byte()) As Assembly Implements _AppDomain.Load

Public Function **Load**(ByVal rawAssembly As Byte(), ByVal rawSymbolStore As Byte()) As Assembly _
  Implements _AppDomain.Load

Public Function **Load**(ByVal rawAssembly As Byte(), ByVal rawSymbolStore As Byte(), _
  ByVal securityEvidence As System.Security.Policy.Evidence) As Assembly Implements _AppDomain.Load

Public Function **Load**(ByVal assemblyString As String) As Assembly Implements _AppDomain.Load

Public Function **Load**(ByVal assemblyString As String, ByVal assemblySecurity As System.Security.Policy.Evidence) _
  As Assembly Implements _AppDomain.Load

Public Sub **SetAppDomainPolicy**(ByVal domainPolicy As System.Security.Policy.PolicyLevel) _
  Implements _AppDomain.SetAppDomainPolicy

Public Sub **SetCachePath**(ByVal path As String) Implements _AppDomain.SetCachePath

Public Sub **SetData**(ByVal name As String, ByVal data As Object) Implements _AppDomain.SetData

Public Sub **SetDynamicBase**(ByVal path As String)

Public Sub **SetPrincipalPolicy**(ByVal policy As System.Security.Principal.PrincipalPolicy) _
  Implements _AppDomain.SetPrincipalPolicy

Public Sub **SetShadowCopyFiles**()

Public Sub **SetShadowCopyPath**(ByVal path As String) Implements _AppDomain.SetShadowCopyPath

Public Sub **SetThreadPrincipal**(ByVal principal As System.Security.Principal.IPrincipal) _
  Implements _AppDomain.SetThreadPrincipal

Overrides Public Function **ToString**() As String

' Events

Public Event **AssemblyLoad** As AssemblyLoadEventHandler Implements _AppDomain.AssemblyLoad

Public Event **AssemblyResolve** As ResolveEventHandler Implements _AppDomain.AssemblyResolve

Public Event **DomainUnload** As EventHandler Implements _AppDomain.DomainUnload

Public Event **ProcessExit** As EventHandler Implements _AppDomain.ProcessExit

Public Event **ResourceResolve** As ResolveEventHandler Implements _AppDomain.ResourceResolve

Public Event **TypeResolve** As ResolveEventHandler Implements _AppDomain.TypeResolve

Public Event **UnhandledException** As UnhandledExceptionEventHandler _
  Implements _AppDomain.UnhandledException

End Class

Hierarchy: Object→ MarshalByRefObject→ AppDomain(_AppDomain,
System.Security.IEvidenceFactory)

Returned By: System.Threading.Thread.GetDomain()

AppDomainSetup
NotInheritable Class

System (mscorlib.dll)
serializable

This class allows you to configure some settings for an application domain before creating an AppDomain object. Create an instance of this class, set its properties, and pass it to the appropriate AppDomain factory method.

```
Public NotInheritable Class AppDomainSetup : Implements IAppDomainSetup
' Public Constructors
   Public Sub New()
' Public Instance Properties
   Public Property ApplicationBase As String Implements IAppDomainSetup.ApplicationBase
   Public Property ApplicationName As String Implements IAppDomainSetup.ApplicationName
   Public Property CachePath As String Implements IAppDomainSetup.CachePath
   Public Property ConfigurationFile As String Implements IAppDomainSetup.ConfigurationFile
   Public Property DisallowPublisherPolicy As Boolean
   Public Property DynamicBase As String Implements IAppDomainSetup.DynamicBase
   Public Property LicenseFile As String Implements IAppDomainSetup.LicenseFile
   Public Property LoaderOptimization As LoaderOptimization
   Public Property PrivateBinPath As String Implements IAppDomainSetup.PrivateBinPath
   Public Property PrivateBinPathProbe As String Implements IAppDomainSetup.PrivateBinPathProbe
   Public Property ShadowCopyDirectories As String Implements IAppDomainSetup.ShadowCopyDirectories
   Public Property ShadowCopyFiles As String Implements IAppDomainSetup.ShadowCopyFiles
End Class
```

Returned By: AppDomain.SetupInformation

Passed To: AppDomain.CreateDomain()

AppDomainUnloadedException
Class

System (mscorlib.dll)
serializable

This exception signals an attempt to access an AppDomain that has been unloaded by AppDomain.Unload().

```
Public Class AppDomainUnloadedException : Inherits SystemException
' Public Constructors
   Public Sub New()
   Public Sub New(ByVal message As String)
   Public Sub New(ByVal message As String, ByVal innerException As Exception)
' Protected Constructors
   Protected Sub New(ByVal info As System.Runtime.Serialization.SerializationInfo, _
      ByVal context As System.Runtime.Serialization.StreamingContext)
End Class
```

Hierarchy: Object→ Exception(System.Runtime.Serialization.ISerializable)→ SystemException→ AppDomainUnloadedException

ApplicationException
Class

System (mscorlib.dll)
ECMA, serializable

Derive from this class to create your own application-specific exceptions when a system-supplied exception is inappropriate. For example, if an application's methods receive an invalid argument, it makes sense to throw an ArgumentException. However, if an internal calculation results in a value that violates your business rules, you might choose to throw an application exception. Application exceptions should be treated as nonfatal.

```
Public Class ApplicationException : Inherits Exception
' Public Constructors
   Public Sub New()
   Public Sub New(ByVal message As String)
   Public Sub New(ByVal message As String, ByVal innerException As Exception)
' Protected Constructors
   Protected Sub New(ByVal info As System.Runtime.Serialization.SerializationInfo, _
      ByVal context As System.Runtime.Serialization.StreamingContext)
End Class
```

Hierarchy: Object→ Exception(System.Runtime.Serialization.ISerializable)→ ApplicationException

Subclasses: System.Reflection.{ InvalidFilterCriteriaException, TargetException, TargetInvocationException, TargetParameterCountException}

ArgIterator   Structure
System (mscorlib.dll)

The .NET runtime uses this class to handle methods that take a variable number of parameters (i.e., methods with a parameter marked as ParamArray). The use of this class is completely hidden by language features. Unless you are writing a language compiler that needs to implement this feature, you do not need to use this class.

```
Public Structure ArgIterator
' Public Constructors
   Public Sub New(ByVal arglist As RuntimeArgumentHandle)
' Public Instance Methods
   Public Sub End()
   Overrides Public Function Equals(ByVal o As Object) As Boolean
   Overrides Public Function GetHashCode() As Integer
   Public Function GetNextArg() As TypedReference
   Public Function GetNextArg(ByVal rth As RuntimeTypeHandle) As TypedReference
   Public Function GetNextArgType() As RuntimeTypeHandle
   Public Function GetRemainingCount() As Integer
End Structure
```

Hierarchy: Object→ ValueType→ ArgIterator

ArgumentException   Class
System (mscorlib.dll)   *ECMA, serializable*

This exception indicates that illegal data was passed to a method or constructor call. Note that *illegal* data is entirely contextual—the data may be a legitimate .NET value, but inappropriate for the use in question. Although .NET languages are type-safe in that you can't pass a string as a parameter when an integer is expected, there is nothing to keep you from passing a null or invalid value, such as sending (2001, 13, 32) to Date-Time's constructor. However, there is no 32nd day of the 13th month of the year 2001, and if you try to initialize such a date, you'll get an exception.

The ArgumentException class (or one of its subclasses, ArgumentNullException or ArgumentOut-OfRangeException) indicates that a method argument violated such a constraint. If you need to implement this exception in your own code, consider using one of its subclasses instead, since they represent common argument exceptions.

```
Public Class ArgumentException : Inherits SystemException
' Public Constructors
   Public Sub New()
```

Public Sub **New**(ByVal message As String)
Public Sub **New**(ByVal message As String, ByVal innerException As Exception)
Public Sub **New**(ByVal message As String, ByVal paramName As String)
Public Sub **New**(ByVal message As String, ByVal paramName As String, ByVal innerException As Exception)
' Protected Constructors
   Protected Sub **New**(ByVal info As System.Runtime.Serialization.SerializationInfo, _
   ByVal context As System.Runtime.Serialization.StreamingContext)
' Public Instance Properties
   Overrides Public ReadOnly Property **Message** As String
   Overridable Public ReadOnly Property **ParamName** As String
' Public Instance Methods
   Overrides Public Sub **GetObjectData**(ByVal info As System.Runtime.Serialization.SerializationInfo, _
   ByVal context As System.Runtime.Serialization.StreamingContext)
End Class

Hierarchy: Object→ Exception(System.Runtime.Serialization.ISerializable)→ SystemException→
ArgumentException

Subclasses: ArgumentNullException, ArgumentOutOfRangeException, DuplicateWaitObjectException

ArgumentNullException   Class

System (mscorlib.dll)   *ECMA, serializable*

This exception is a subclass of ArgumentException and indicates that a null parameter
value was received by a method that does not accept nulls.

Public Class **ArgumentNullException** : Inherits ArgumentException
' Public Constructors
   Public Sub **New**()
   Public Sub **New**(ByVal paramName As String)
   Public Sub **New**(ByVal paramName As String, ByVal message As String)
' Protected Constructors
   Protected Sub **New**(ByVal info As System.Runtime.Serialization.SerializationInfo, _
   ByVal context As System.Runtime.Serialization.StreamingContext)
End Class

Hierarchy: Object→ Exception(System.Runtime.Serialization.ISerializable)→ SystemException→
ArgumentException→ ArgumentNullException

ArgumentOutOfRangeException   Class

System (mscorlib.dll)   *ECMA, serializable*

This exception is a subclass of ArgumentException and indicates that a method received an
out-of-range parameter value.

Public Class **ArgumentOutOfRangeException** : Inherits ArgumentException
' Public Constructors
   Public Sub **New**()
   Public Sub **New**(ByVal paramName As String)
   Public Sub **New**(ByVal paramName As String, ByVal actualValue As Object, ByVal message As String)
   Public Sub **New**(ByVal paramName As String, ByVal message As String)
' Protected Constructors
   Protected Sub **New**(ByVal info As System.Runtime.Serialization.SerializationInfo, _
   ByVal context As System.Runtime.Serialization.StreamingContext)
' Public Instance Properties
   Overridable Public ReadOnly Property **ActualValue** As Object
   Overrides Public ReadOnly Property **Message** As String

' *Public Instance Methods*
    Overrides Public Sub **GetObjectData**(ByVal info As System.Runtime.Serialization.SerializationInfo, _
        ByVal context As System.Runtime.Serialization.StreamingContext)
End Class

Hierarchy: Object→ Exception(System.Runtime.Serialization.ISerializable)→ SystemException→
ArgumentException→ ArgumentOutOfRangeException

ArithmeticException   Class
System (mscorlib.dll)   *ECMA, serializable*

This is the base class for all math-related exceptions. You can throw this class from
your own code, but use a subclass (if one exists) that specifically addresses the type of
error you have encountered.

Public Class **ArithmeticException** : Inherits SystemException
' *Public Constructors*
    Public Sub **New**()
    Public Sub **New**(ByVal message As String)
    Public Sub **New**(ByVal message As String, ByVal innerException As Exception)
' *Protected Constructors*
    Protected Sub **New**(ByVal info As System.Runtime.Serialization.SerializationInfo, _
        ByVal context As System.Runtime.Serialization.StreamingContext)
End Class

Hierarchy: Object→ Exception(System.Runtime.Serialization.ISerializable)→ SystemException→
ArithmeticException

Subclasses: DivideByZeroException, NotFiniteNumberException, OverflowException

Array   MustInherit Class
System (mscorlib.dll)   *ECMA, serializable*

Unlike other environments (such as C++), .NET has arrays of first-class type, in that all
array types are derivatives of the base type Array. All methods are available on any array
type, regardless of its declaration. In fact, the CLR is required to synthesize a *pseudotype*
that matches the declaration. Thus, when you declare a variable of type String(), the CLR
creates an anonymous type, deriving from Array specifically for storing Strings in a one-
dimensional array.

The Array class has a number of useful array-related methods, such as checking for
bounds violations (attempting to access an element of the array that isn't in the array's
declared size) and retrieval of array length. In addition, because Array also implements
the ICloneable, System.Collections.IList, System.Collections.ICollection, and System.Collections.IEnu-
merable interfaces, arrays can be used anywhere these interface types are expected.

Arrays are reference types. This means that the statement ArrayB = ArrayA results in two
objects that reference the same array. Use ArrayB = ArrayA.Clone() to create a duplicate
copy of an array. This will be a shallow copy with identical references to subobjects. To
create a deep copy in which each array has its own copy of subobjects, you must loop
through the array and assign values manually.

The Array class also contains useful shared methods. These include IndexOf(), which
returns the offset of the first matching occurrence of an object in an array. For one-
dimensional arrays, you can also use Reverse() to reverse a subset of rows, and Sort() to
sort a subset of rows (provided the objects in the array implement the IComparable interface). If the objects in the array do not implement that interface, you can implement
System.Collections.IComparer in a custom class and pass an instance of it to Sort().

The shared Copy() method works like the C function memmove: it copies a portion of an array to a different position in the current array (or to a different array). When copying between multidimensional arrays, the array is treated like a long one-dimensional array in which each element occupies a separate row. (For example, if an array has three columns, copying five elements from the beginning of the array copies all three elements in the first row and the first two elements from the second row.) The source and destination ranges can overlap without causing a problem.

Note that you can create both multidimensional arrays and ragged arrays (arrays of arrays). Arrays are fixed in size and zero-based by default, although you can use the CreateInstance() method to create an array with a different lower bound. This is not recommended, as the array won't be CLS (Common Language Specification)–compliant. Lastly, if you need a dynamically resizable array, consider the collection System.Collections.ArrayList, which provides Add() and Remove() methods.

```
Public MustInherit Class Array : Implements ICloneable, IList, ICollection , IEnumerable
' Public Instance Properties
   Overridable Public ReadOnly Property IsFixedSize As Boolean Implements IList.IsFixedSize
   Overridable Public ReadOnly Property IsReadOnly As Boolean Implements IList.IsReadOnly
   Overridable Public ReadOnly Property IsSynchronized As Boolean Implements ICollection.IsSynchronized
   Public ReadOnly Property Length As Integer
   Public ReadOnly Property Rank As Integer
   Overridable Public ReadOnly Property SyncRoot As Object Implements ICollection.SyncRoot
' Public Shared Methods
   Public Shared Function BinarySearch(ByVal array As Array, ByVal index As Integer, ByVal length As Integer, _
      ByVal value As Object)  As Integer
   Public Shared Function BinarySearch(ByVal array As Array, ByVal index As Integer, ByVal length As Integer, _
      ByVal value As Object, ByVal comparer As System.Collections.IComparer) As Integer
   Public Shared Function BinarySearch(ByVal array As Array, ByVal value As Object) As Integer
   Public Shared Function BinarySearch(ByVal array As Array, ByVal value As Object, _
      ByVal comparer As System.Collections.IComparer) As Integer
   Public Shared Sub Clear(ByVal array As Array, ByVal index As Integer, ByVal length As Integer)
   Public Shared Sub Copy(ByVal sourceArray As Array, ByVal destinationArray As Array, ByVal length As Integer)
   Public Shared Sub Copy(ByVal sourceArray As Array, ByVal sourceIndex As Integer, ByVal destinationArray As Array, _
      ByVal destinationIndex As Integer, ByVal length As Integer)
   Public Shared Function CreateInstance(ByVal elementType As Type, ByVal length As Integer) As Array
   Public Shared Function CreateInstance(ByVal elementType As Type, ByVal lengths As Integer()) As Array
   Public Shared Function CreateInstance(ByVal elementType As Type, ByVal lengths As Integer(), _
      ByVal lowerBounds As Integer()) As Array
   Public Shared Function CreateInstance(ByVal elementType As Type, ByVal length1 As Integer, _
      ByVal length2 As Integer) As Array
   Public Shared Function CreateInstance(ByVal elementType As Type, ByVal length1 As Integer, _
      ByVal length2 As Integer, ByVal length3 As Integer)  As Array
   Public Shared Function IndexOf(ByVal array As Array, ByVal value As Object) As Integer
   Public Shared Function IndexOf(ByVal array As Array, ByVal value As Object, ByVal startIndex As Integer) As Integer
   Public Shared Function IndexOf(ByVal array As Array, ByVal value As Object, ByVal startIndex As Integer, _
      ByVal count As Integer)  As Integer
   Public Shared Function LastIndexOf(ByVal array As Array, ByVal value As Object) As Integer
   Public Shared Function LastIndexOf(ByVal array As Array, ByVal value As Object, ByVal startIndex As Integer) _
      As Integer
   Public Shared Function LastIndexOf(ByVal array As Array, ByVal value As Object, ByVal startIndex As Integer, _
      ByVal count As Integer)  As Integer
   Public Shared Sub Reverse(ByVal array As Array)
   Public Shared Sub Reverse(ByVal array As Array, ByVal index As Integer, ByVal length As Integer)
   Public Shared Sub Sort(ByVal array As Array)
   Public Shared Sub Sort(ByVal keys As Array, ByVal items As Array)
   Public Shared Sub Sort(ByVal keys As Array, ByVal items As Array, _
      ByVal comparer As System.Collections.IComparer)
```

Public Shared Sub **Sort**(ByVal keys As Array, ByVal items As Array, ByVal index As Integer, ByVal length As Integer)
Public Shared Sub **Sort**(ByVal keys As Array, ByVal items As Array, ByVal index As Integer, ByVal length As Integer, _
   ByVal comparer As System.Collections.IComparer)
Public Shared Sub **Sort**(ByVal array As Array, ByVal comparer As System.Collections.IComparer)
Public Shared Sub **Sort**(ByVal array As Array, ByVal index As Integer, ByVal length As Integer)
Public Shared Sub **Sort**(ByVal array As Array, ByVal index As Integer, ByVal length As Integer, _
   ByVal comparer As System.Collections.IComparer)
' Public Instance Methods
Overridable Public Function **Clone**() As Object Implements ICloneable.Clone
Overridable Public Sub **CopyTo**(ByVal array As Array, ByVal index As Integer) Implements ICollection.CopyTo
Overridable Public Function **GetEnumerator**() As IEnumerator Implements IEnumerable.GetEnumerator
Public Function **GetLength**(ByVal dimension As Integer) As Integer
Public Function **GetLowerBound**(ByVal dimension As Integer) As Integer
Public Function **GetUpperBound**(ByVal dimension As Integer) As Integer
Public Function **GetValue**(ByVal index As Integer) As Object
Public Function **GetValue**(ByVal indices As Integer()) As Object
Public Function **GetValue**(ByVal index1 As Integer, ByVal index2 As Integer) As Object
Public Function **GetValue**(ByVal index1 As Integer, ByVal index2 As Integer, ByVal index3 As Integer) As Object
Public Sub **Initialize**()
Public Sub **SetValue**(ByVal value As Object, ByVal index As Integer)
Public Sub **SetValue**(ByVal value As Object, ByVal indices As Integer())
Public Sub **SetValue**(ByVal value As Object, ByVal index1 As Integer, ByVal index2 As Integer)
Public Sub **SetValue**(ByVal value As Object, ByVal index1 As Integer, ByVal index2 As Integer, _
   ByVal index3 As Integer)
End Class

Returned By: System.Collections.ArrayList.ToArray(), Enum.GetValues()

Passed To: Multiple types

ArrayTypeMismatchException   Class

System (mscorlib.dll)   *ECMA, serializable*

This exception is thrown when you store an element in an array that has a different type than the array's declared type. For example, trying to store a String object into an array declared to hold Int32 instances causes this exception to be thrown.

Public Class **ArrayTypeMismatchException** : Inherits SystemException
' Public Constructors
Public Sub **New**()
Public Sub **New**(ByVal message As String)
Public Sub **New**(ByVal message As String, ByVal innerException As Exception)
' Protected Constructors
Protected Sub **New**(ByVal info As System.Runtime.Serialization.SerializationInfo, _
   ByVal context As System.Runtime.Serialization.StreamingContext)
End Class

Hierarchy: Object→ Exception(System.Runtime.Serialization.ISerializable)→ SystemException→
ArrayTypeMismatchException

AssemblyLoadEventArgs   Class

System (mscorlib.dll)   *ECMA*

This class is used by the .NET Framework to pass information to the AppDomain.AssemblyLoad event. This information consists of a System.Reflection.Assembly object that represents the newly loaded assembly.

```
Public Class AssemblyLoadEventArgs : Inherits EventArgs
' Public Constructors
     Public Sub New(ByVal loadedAssembly As System.Reflection.Assembly)
' Public Instance Properties
     Public ReadOnly Property LoadedAssembly As Assembly
End Class
```

Hierarchy: Object→ EventArgs→ AssemblyLoadEventArgs

Passed To: AssemblyLoadEventHandler.{BeginInvoke(), Invoke()}

AssemblyLoadEventHandler   Delegate

System (mscorlib.dll)   *ECMA, serializable*

This delegate represents the event-handler method for the AppDomain.AssemblyLoad event.

```
Public Delegate Sub AssemblyLoadEventHandler(ByVal sender As Object, ByVal args As AssemblyLoadEventArgs)
```

Associated Events: AppDomain.AssemblyLoad()

AsyncCallback   Delegate

System (mscorlib.dll)   *ECMA, serializable*

This delegate type is used as part of asynchronous operations on delegates in general. Delegates can be executed in an asynchronous fashion, using a random thread out of the system-managed thread pool. Frequently, however, programmers desire notification of the asynchronously executing delegate's completion, and the AsyncCallback is used to achieve that.

Using an AsyncCallback is fairly straightforward. At the asynchronous delegate's invocation, pass in an instance of this delegate (referring to a void-returning IAsyncResult-accepting method) as part of the BeginInvoke() call. When the asynchronously executing delegate has finished execution, the method on the other end of the AsyncCallback is invoked, with an IAsyncResult object as the sole parameter. (This IAsyncResult object contains the output parameters from the delegate's call: the return value, along with any out or ref parameters declared as part of the method's signature.)

```
Public Delegate Sub AsyncCallback(ByVal ar As IAsyncResult)
```

Passed To: Multiple types

Attribute   MustInherit Class

System (mscorlib.dll)   *ECMA, serializable*

This is the base class for all custom attributes. Attributes are the .NET programmer's means of inserting additional metadata into a type's definition. For example, the .NET Serialization mechanism uses an attribute to indicate which fields in a type should not be serialized (see the System.Reflection.FieldAttributes.NotSerialized enumeration value). .NET programmers are free to create their own attributes (called *custom attributes*, although from a certain perspective all attributes are inherently custom) by creating a new type that claims Attribute as its base class type.

By themselves, attributes offer no modification to a type's behavioral semantics; that is, attributes don't modify the type's methods or execution in any way. In fact, attribute instances aren't even created until they are retrieved out of the type's metadata via the Reflection APIs. The entire purpose of an attribute is to act as a marker inside the type's metadata for consumption by some other API, library, or facility. For example, the Serialization APIs in the .NET Framework Class Library use the Serializable attribute to indicate which types are serializable. However, by themselves, the attributes carry no code to perform the actual act of serialization. This must be done by passing the instance of the type into instances of the Serialization classes, in which the attribute is retrieved, examined, and "appropriate" action is taken.

Attributes can be attached to any metadata component in the .NET system. This means fields, methods, properties, events, types (classes and value types), assemblies, modules, and more can all be the target of attribute declarations. (An attribute indicates which types it is restricted to by using the AttributeTargets enumeration.)

The base Attribute class provides helper functions for testing custom attributes, including the IsDefined() method, which examines a code element and indicates whether its metadata is decorated with a specified type of attribute. To use this method, you must provide the element using the appropriate reflection type (e.g., System.Reflection.Assembly or System.Reflection.ParameterInfo). You can also use the GetCustomAttribute() method to get a reference to an attribute of a specified type, or the GetCustomAttributes() to get an array that contains all matching attributes. When applied to a class or class member, these methods consider all ancestors. To disable this default behavior, use one of the overloaded methods that allows you to supply the inherit parameter, and set it to false.

Custom attributes should override the TypeId property so that it supplies a user-defined identifier that uniquely describes the instance of this attribute on the type. This is entirely because more than one instance of an attribute can be associated with any particular metadata-token (field, type, parameter, and so on) instance.

```
Public MustInherit Class Attribute
' Protected Constructors
  Protected Sub New()
' Public Instance Properties
  Overridable Public ReadOnly Property TypeId As Object
' Public Shared Methods
  Public Shared Function GetCustomAttribute(ByVal element As System.Reflection.Assembly, _
    ByVal attributeType As Type) As Attribute
  Public Shared Function GetCustomAttribute(ByVal element As System.Reflection.Assembly, _
    ByVal attributeType As Type, ByVal inherit As Boolean) As Attribute
  Public Shared Function GetCustomAttribute(ByVal element As System.Reflection.MemberInfo, _
    ByVal attributeType As Type) As Attribute
  Public Shared Function GetCustomAttribute(ByVal element As System.Reflection.MemberInfo, _
    ByVal attributeType As Type, ByVal inherit As Boolean) As Attribute
  Public Shared Function GetCustomAttribute(ByVal element As System.Reflection.Module, _
    ByVal attributeType As Type) As Attribute
  Public Shared Function GetCustomAttribute(ByVal element As System.Reflection.Module, _
    ByVal attributeType As Type, ByVal inherit As Boolean) As Attribute
  Public Shared Function GetCustomAttribute(ByVal element As System.Reflection.ParameterInfo, _
    ByVal attributeType As Type) As Attribute
  Public Shared Function GetCustomAttribute(ByVal element As System.Reflection.ParameterInfo, _
    ByVal attributeType As Type, ByVal inherit As Boolean) As Attribute
  Public Shared Function GetCustomAttributes(ByVal element As System.Reflection.Assembly) As Attribute()
  Public Shared Function GetCustomAttributes(ByVal element As System.Reflection.Assembly, _
    ByVal inherit As Boolean) As Attribute()
  Public Shared Function GetCustomAttributes(ByVal element As System.Reflection.Assembly, _
    ByVal attributeType As Type) As Attribute()
  Public Shared Function GetCustomAttributes(ByVal element As System.Reflection.Assembly, _
    ByVal attributeType As Type, ByVal inherit As Boolean) As Attribute()
  Public Shared Function GetCustomAttributes(ByVal element As System.Reflection.MemberInfo) As Attribute()
  Public Shared Function GetCustomAttributes(ByVal element As System.Reflection.MemberInfo, _
    ByVal inherit As Boolean) As Attribute()
  Public Shared Function GetCustomAttributes(ByVal element As System.Reflection.MemberInfo, _
    ByVal type As Type) As Attribute()
```

System

Public Shared Function **GetCustomAttributes**(ByVal element As System.Reflection.MemberInfo, _
ByVal type As Type, ByVal inherit As Boolean) As Attribute()

Public Shared Function **GetCustomAttributes**(ByVal element As System.Reflection.Module) As Attribute()

Public Shared Function **GetCustomAttributes**(ByVal element As System.Reflection.Module, _
ByVal inherit As Boolean) As Attribute()

Public Shared Function **GetCustomAttributes**(ByVal element As System.Reflection.Module, _
ByVal attributeType As Type) As Attribute()

Public Shared Function **GetCustomAttributes**(ByVal element As System.Reflection.Module, _
ByVal attributeType As Type, ByVal inherit As Boolean) As Attribute()

Public Shared Function **GetCustomAttributes**(ByVal element As System.Reflection.ParameterInfo) As Attribute()

Public Shared Function **GetCustomAttributes**(ByVal element As System.Reflection.ParameterInfo, _
ByVal inherit As Boolean) As Attribute()

Public Shared Function **GetCustomAttributes**(ByVal element As System.Reflection.ParameterInfo, _
ByVal attributeType As Type) As Attribute()

Public Shared Function **GetCustomAttributes**(ByVal element As System.Reflection.ParameterInfo, _
ByVal attributeType As Type, ByVal inherit As Boolean) As Attribute()

Public Shared Function **IsDefined**(ByVal element As System.Reflection.Assembly, ByVal attributeType As Type) _
As Boolean

Public Shared Function **IsDefined**(ByVal element As System.Reflection.Assembly, ByVal attributeType As Type, _
ByVal inherit As Boolean) As Boolean

Public Shared Function **IsDefined**(ByVal element As System.Reflection.MemberInfo, ByVal attributeType As Type) _
As Boolean

Public Shared Function **IsDefined**(ByVal element As System.Reflection.MemberInfo, ByVal attributeType As Type, _
ByVal inherit As Boolean) As Boolean

Public Shared Function **IsDefined**(ByVal element As System.Reflection.Module, ByVal attributeType As Type) _
As Boolean

Public Shared Function **IsDefined**(ByVal element As System.Reflection.Module, ByVal attributeType As Type, _
ByVal inherit As Boolean) As Boolean

Public Shared Function **IsDefined**(ByVal element As System.Reflection.ParameterInfo, ByVal attributeType As Type) _
As Boolean

Public Shared Function **IsDefined**(ByVal element As System.Reflection.ParameterInfo, ByVal attributeType As Type, _
ByVal inherit As Boolean) As Boolean

' *Public Instance Methods*

Overrides Public Function **Equals**(ByVal obj As Object) As Boolean

Overrides Public Function **GetHashCode**() As Integer

Overridable Public Function **IsDefaultAttribute**() As Boolean

Overridable Public Function **Match**(ByVal obj As Object) As Boolean

End Class

Subclasses: Multiple types

Valid On: All

AttributeTargets   Enum

System (mscorlib.dll)   *ECMA, serializable, flag*

This enumeration is used to set the AttributeUsageAttribute.ValidOn property when creating a custom attribute. It allows you to specify the code elements for which a custom attribute can be used. You can use a bitwise combination of these values to specify multiple elements.

Using this attribute is the only means by which a custom attribute can declare a restriction of its usage against various metadata types. For example, when using the System.Reflection.AssemblyKeyFileAttribute attribute, which simply tells the compiler which public/private keyfile to use to sign the assembly, it makes no sense to apply to any other metadata type besides the assembly. Therefore, the AssemblyKeyFileAttribute attribute has an AttributeUsageAttribute (see the AttributeUsageAttribute entry) declared on it with the value Assembly. As a result, any attempt to use the AssemblyKeyFileAttribute attribute on anything other than an assembly results in a compilation error.

```
Public Enum AttributeTargets
    Assembly = &H000000001
    Module = &H000000002
    Class = &H000000004
    Struct = &H000000008
    Enum = &H000000010
    Constructor = &H000000020
    Method = &H000000040
    Property = &H000000080
    Field = &H000000100
    Event = &H000000200
    Interface = &H000000400
    Parameter = &H000000800
    Delegate = &H000001000
    ReturnValue = &H000002000
    All = &H000003FFF
End Enum
```

Hierarchy: Object→ ValueType→ Enum(IComparable, IFormattable, IConvertible)→ AttributeTargets

Returned By: AttributeUsageAttribute.ValidOn

Passed To: AttributeUsageAttribute.AttributeUsageAttribute()

AttributeUsageAttribute

NotInheritable Class

System (mscorlib.dll)

ECMA, serializable

This attribute is used when developing a custom attribute class. It allows you to specify how your custom attribute must be used. The ValidOn property uses a bitwise combination of values from AttributeTargets to specify the code elements that can use your custom attribute. It's read-only and must be initialized using the constructor, as in (AttributeUsage(AttributeTargets.Field | AttributeTargets.Property)).

The AllowMultiple property specifies whether the attribute can be used more than once for the same element. The Inherited attribute specifies whether your custom attribute will be applied to derived classes and overridden members. These are indicated using the usual *named parameter* syntax supported by attributes, as in (AttributeUsage(Inherited = true, AllowMultiple = true))

```
Public NotInheritable Class AttributeUsageAttribute : Inherits Attribute
' Public Constructors
    Public Sub New(ByVal validOn As AttributeTargets)
' Public Instance Properties
    Public Property AllowMultiple As Boolean
    Public Property Inherited As Boolean
    Public ReadOnly Property ValidOn As AttributeTargets
End Class
```

Hierarchy: Object→ Attribute→ AttributeUsageAttribute

Valid On: Class

BadImageFormatException

System (mscorlib.dll)

Class

ECMA, serializable

This exception occurs when .NET tries to load a DLL or executable that is either corrupt or invalid for the platform on which you are running.

Public Class **BadImageFormatException** : Inherits SystemException
' *Public Constructors*
  Public Sub **New**()
  Public Sub **New**(ByVal message As String)
  Public Sub **New**(ByVal message As String, ByVal inner As Exception)
  Public Sub **New**(ByVal message As String, ByVal fileName As String)
  Public Sub **New**(ByVal message As String, ByVal fileName As String, ByVal inner As Exception)
' *Protected Constructors*
  Protected Sub **New**(ByVal info As System.Runtime.Serialization.SerializationInfo, _
    ByVal context As System.Runtime.Serialization.StreamingContext)
' *Public Instance Properties*
  Public ReadOnly Property **FileName** As String
  Public ReadOnly Property **FusionLog** As String
  Overrides Public ReadOnly Property **Message** As String
' *Public Instance Methods*
  Overrides Public Sub **GetObjectData**(ByVal info As System.Runtime.Serialization.SerializationInfo, _
    ByVal context As System.Runtime.Serialization.StreamingContext)
  Overrides Public Function **ToString**() As String
End Class

Hierarchy: Object→ Exception(System.Runtime.Serialization.ISerializable)→ SystemException→ BadImageFormatException

BitConverter

System (mscorlib.dll)

NotInheritable Class

This class provides shared methods that can be used to convert portions of a byte array to simple value types. It also contains the overloaded **GetBytes**() method, which converts simple data types to byte arrays. These functions can be useful for creating custom reader and writer classes. For example, a typical writer class might take specific data, convert it to a byte array, then pass the byte array to some type of stream object.

Public NotInheritable Class **BitConverter**
' *Public Shared Fields*
  Public Shared ReadOnly **IsLittleEndian** As Boolean   *=True*
' *Public Shared Methods*
  Public Shared Function **DoubleToInt64Bits**(ByVal value As Double) As Long
  Public Shared Function **GetBytes**(ByVal value As Boolean) As Byte()
  Public Shared Function **GetBytes**(ByVal value As Char) As Byte()
  Public Shared Function **GetBytes**(ByVal value As Double) As Byte()
  Public Shared Function **GetBytes**(ByVal value As Short) As Byte()
  Public Shared Function **GetBytes**(ByVal value As Integer) As Byte()
  Public Shared Function **GetBytes**(ByVal value As Long) As Byte()
  Public Shared Function **GetBytes**(ByVal value As Single) As Byte()
  Public Shared Function **GetBytes**(ByVal value As UInt16) As Byte()
  Public Shared Function **GetBytes**(ByVal value As UInt32) As Byte()
  Public Shared Function **GetBytes**(ByVal value As UInt64) As Byte()
  Public Shared Function **Int64BitsToDouble**(ByVal value As Long) As Double
  Public Shared Function **ToBoolean**(ByVal value As Byte(), ByVal startIndex As Integer) As Boolean
  Public Shared Function **ToChar**(ByVal value As Byte(), ByVal startIndex As Integer) As Char
  Public Shared Function **ToDouble**(ByVal value As Byte(), ByVal startIndex As Integer) As Double

Public Shared Function **ToInt16**(ByVal value As Byte(), ByVal startIndex As Integer) As Short
Public Shared Function **ToInt32**(ByVal value As Byte(), ByVal startIndex As Integer) As Integer
Public Shared Function **ToInt64**(ByVal value As Byte(), ByVal startIndex As Integer) As Long
Public Shared Function **ToSingle**(ByVal value As Byte(), ByVal startIndex As Integer) As Single
Public Shared Function **ToString**(ByVal value As Byte()) As String
Public Shared Function **ToString**(ByVal value As Byte(), ByVal startIndex As Integer) As String
Public Shared Function **ToString**(ByVal value As Byte(), ByVal startIndex As Integer, ByVal length As Integer) _
    As String
Public Shared Function **ToUInt16**(ByVal value As Byte(), ByVal startIndex As Integer) As UInt16
Public Shared Function **ToUInt32**(ByVal value As Byte(), ByVal startIndex As Integer) As UInt32
Public Shared Function **ToUInt64**(ByVal value As Byte(), ByVal startIndex As Integer) As UInt64
End Class

Boolean   Structure

System (mscorlib.dll)   *ECMA, serializable*

This is a simple value type that contains either true or false. When converting to or from
a string or comparing with a string, the TrueString and FalseString fields are used (these
return True and False). This type is available in VB.NET through the Boolean alias.

Public Structure **Boolean** : Implements IComparable, IConvertible
' *Public Shared Fields*
    Public Shared ReadOnly **FalseString** As String   *=False*
    Public Shared ReadOnly **TrueString** As String   *=True*
' *Public Shared Methods*
    Public Shared Function **Parse**(ByVal value As String) As Boolean
' *Public Instance Methods*
    Public Function **CompareTo**(ByVal obj As Object) As Integer Implements IComparable.CompareTo
    Overrides Public Function **Equals**(ByVal obj As Object) As Boolean
    Overrides Public Function **GetHashCode**() As Integer
    Public Function **GetTypeCode**() As TypeCode Implements IConvertible.GetTypeCode
    Overrides Public Function **ToString**() As String
    Public Function **ToString**(ByVal provider As IFormatProvider) As String Implements IConvertible.ToString
End Structure

Hierarchy: Object→ ValueType→ Boolean(IComparable, IConvertible)

Returned By: Multiple types

Passed To: Multiple types

Buffer   NotInheritable Class

System (mscorlib.dll)

The Buffer class provides shared methods used to manipulate a region of unmanaged
memory as though it were an array of Bytes. Byte arrays are traditionally used in unmanaged code to represent blocks of contiguous memory. This class includes the Byte-
Length() method, which indicates the total number of bytes in an array, and the GetByte()
and SetByte() methods, which allow you to retrieve or set a specific Byte object in an
array by specifying a zero-based index. Additionally, the BlockCopy() method can be
used to move contiguous groups of bytes from one position in a buffer to another.

Note that BlockCopy ignores types when conducting its byte-shuffling operations. If you
use BlockCopy to insert an otherwise incompatible type into the buffer, the copy goes
through, but unpredictable results will arise later when you try to work with the buffer
as its original type. For example, if you use the BlockCopy method to insert an Int32 into
an array of String objects, the copy goes through, but the next time the array is

accessed, there is no longer a String reference. It is an Int32, and what the CLR will do at that point is undocumented.

```
Public NotInheritable Class Buffer
' Public Shared Methods
   Public Shared Sub BlockCopy(ByVal src As Array, ByVal srcOffset As Integer, ByVal dst As Array, _
      ByVal dstOffset As Integer, ByVal count As Integer)
   Public Shared Function ByteLength(ByVal array As Array) As Integer
   Public Shared Function GetByte(ByVal array As Array, ByVal index As Integer) As Byte
   Public Shared Sub SetByte(ByVal array As Array, ByVal index As Integer, ByVal value As Byte)
End Class
```

Byte   Structure

System (mscorlib.dll)   *ECMA, serializable*

This simple value type represents an unsigned 8-bit integer that can vary in value from 0 to 255. The Parse() method converts a number in a string (such as 122) into a Byte object. This type is available in VB.NET through the Byte alias.

```
Public Structure Byte : Implements IComparable, IFormattable, IConvertible
' Public Shared Fields
   Public const MaxValue As Byte                                           =255
   Public const MinValue As Byte                                             =0
' Public Shared Methods
   Public Shared Function Parse(ByVal s As String) As Byte
   Public Shared Function Parse(ByVal s As String, ByVal provider As IFormatProvider) As Byte
   Public Shared Function Parse(ByVal s As String, ByVal style As System.Globalization.NumberStyles) As Byte
   Public Shared Function Parse(ByVal s As String, ByVal style As System.Globalization.NumberStyles, _
      ByVal provider As IFormatProvider) As Byte
' Public Instance Methods
   Public Function CompareTo(ByVal value As Object) As Integer Implements  IComparable.CompareTo
   Overrides Public Function Equals(ByVal obj As Object) As Boolean
   Overrides Public Function GetHashCode() As Integer
   Public Function GetTypeCode() As TypeCode Implements  IConvertible.GetTypeCode
   Overrides Public Function ToString() As String
   Public Function ToString(ByVal provider As IFormatProvider) As String Implements  IConvertible.ToString
   Public Function ToString(ByVal format As String) As String
   Public Function ToString(ByVal format As String, ByVal provider As IFormatProvider) As String _
      Implements  IFormattable.ToString
End Structure
```

Hierarchy: Object→ ValueType→ Byte(IComparable, IFormattable, IConvertible)

Returned By: Multiple types

Passed To: Multiple types

CannotUnloadAppDomainException   Class

System (mscorlib.dll)   *ECMA, serializable*

This exception signals that an attempt to invoke AppDomain.Unload() failed. This indicates that you either tried to unload the default application domain (AppDomain.CurrentDomain), the domain has a thread that cannot be stopped, or the domain has already been unloaded.

```
Public Class CannotUnloadAppDomainException : Inherits SystemException
' Public Constructors
   Public Sub New()
   Public Sub New(ByVal message As String)
```

```
Public Sub New(ByVal message As String, ByVal innerException As Exception)
' Protected Constructors
   Protected Sub New(ByVal info As System.Runtime.Serialization.SerializationInfo, _
      ByVal context As System.Runtime.Serialization.StreamingContext)
End Class
```

Hierarchy: Object→ Exception(System.Runtime.Serialization.ISerializable)→ SystemException→
CannotUnloadAppDomainException

Char   Structure

System (mscorlib.dll)   *ECMA, serializable*

This simple value type represents a 16-bit Unicode character (from hexadecimal 0x0000
to 0xFFFF). You can convert a character to upper- or lowercase and get its numeric representation using the methods of a Char object. You can also test if it is a number, letter,
or symbol by using the methods prefixed with Is. For exact information, use the GetUni-
codeCategory() method to get an enumerated value from System.Globalization.UnicodeCate-
gory. This classifies the character into one of about thirty categories.

This type is aliased as Char in VB.NET. If you need an array of chars, use the String class.

```
Public Structure Char : Implements IComparable, IConvertible
' Public Shared Fields
   Public const MaxValue As Char                                    = [amp ] H0000FFFF
   Public const MinValue As Char                                    = [amp ] H00000000
' Public Shared Methods
   Public Shared Function GetNumericValue(ByVal c As Char) As Double
   Public Shared Function GetNumericValue(ByVal s As String, ByVal index As Integer) As Double
   Public Shared Function GetUnicodeCategory(ByVal c As Char) As UnicodeCategory
   Public Shared Function GetUnicodeCategory(ByVal s As String, ByVal index As Integer) As UnicodeCategory
   Public Shared Function IsControl(ByVal c As Char) As Boolean
   Public Shared Function IsControl(ByVal s As String, ByVal index As Integer) As Boolean
   Public Shared Function IsDigit(ByVal c As Char) As Boolean
   Public Shared Function IsDigit(ByVal s As String, ByVal index As Integer) As Boolean
   Public Shared Function IsLetter(ByVal c As Char) As Boolean
   Public Shared Function IsLetter(ByVal s As String, ByVal index As Integer) As Boolean
   Public Shared Function IsLetterOrDigit(ByVal c As Char) As Boolean
   Public Shared Function IsLetterOrDigit(ByVal s As String, ByVal index As Integer) As Boolean
   Public Shared Function IsLower(ByVal c As Char) As Boolean
   Public Shared Function IsLower(ByVal s As String, ByVal index As Integer) As Boolean
   Public Shared Function IsNumber(ByVal c As Char) As Boolean
   Public Shared Function IsNumber(ByVal s As String, ByVal index As Integer) As Boolean
   Public Shared Function IsPunctuation(ByVal c As Char) As Boolean
   Public Shared Function IsPunctuation(ByVal s As String, ByVal index As Integer) As Boolean
   Public Shared Function IsSeparator(ByVal c As Char) As Boolean
   Public Shared Function IsSeparator(ByVal s As String, ByVal index As Integer) As Boolean
   Public Shared Function IsSurrogate(ByVal c As Char) As Boolean
   Public Shared Function IsSurrogate(ByVal s As String, ByVal index As Integer) As Boolean
   Public Shared Function IsSymbol(ByVal c As Char) As Boolean
   Public Shared Function IsSymbol(ByVal s As String, ByVal index As Integer) As Boolean
   Public Shared Function IsUpper(ByVal c As Char) As Boolean
   Public Shared Function IsUpper(ByVal s As String, ByVal index As Integer) As Boolean
   Public Shared Function IsWhiteSpace(ByVal c As Char) As Boolean
   Public Shared Function IsWhiteSpace(ByVal s As String, ByVal index As Integer) As Boolean
   Public Shared Function Parse(ByVal s As String) As Char
   Public Shared Function ToLower(ByVal c As Char) As Char
```

Public Shared Function **ToLower**(ByVal c As Char, ByVal culture As System.Globalization.CultureInfo) As Char
Public Shared Function **ToString**(ByVal c As Char) As String
Public Shared Function **ToUpper**(ByVal c As Char) As Char
Public Shared Function **ToUpper**(ByVal c As Char, ByVal culture As System.Globalization.CultureInfo) As Char
' *Public Instance Methods*
Public Function **CompareTo**(ByVal value As Object) As Integer Implements IComparable.CompareTo
Overrides Public Function **Equals**(ByVal obj As Object) As Boolean
Overrides Public Function **GetHashCode**() As Integer
Public Function **GetTypeCode**() As TypeCode Implements IConvertible.GetTypeCode
Overrides Public Function **ToString**() As String
Public Function **ToString**(ByVal provider As IFormatProvider) As String Implements IConvertible.ToString
End Structure

Hierarchy: Object→ ValueType→ Char(IComparable, IConvertible)

Returned By: Multiple types

Passed To: Multiple types

CharEnumerator

NotInheritable Class

System (mscorlib.dll)

ECMA, serializable

This class allows you to access and iterate through individual chars in an array. You can manually retrieve a CharEnumerator from a String object using the String.GetEnumerator() method and then using the MoveNext() method to step through the string. However, VB.NET provides built-in support with the convenient For Each construct, which uses a CharEnumerator transparently.

By convention, a CharEnumerator starts just before the first character. When using a CharEnumerator manually, you need to call the MoveNext() method before you can access the first character.

Public NotInheritable Class **CharEnumerator** : Implements IEnumerator, ICloneable
' *Public Instance Properties*
Public ReadOnly Property **Current** As Char
' *Public Instance Methods*
Public Function **Clone**() As Object Implements ICloneable.Clone
Public Function **MoveNext**() As Boolean Implements IEnumerator.MoveNext
Public Sub **Reset**() Implements IEnumerator.Reset
End Class

Returned By: String.GetEnumerator()

CLSCompliantAttribute

NotInheritable Class

System (mscorlib.dll)

ECMA, serializable

This attribute indicates that a program element is compliant with the CLS. If you use non–CLS compliant classes (such as UInt32) in a class marked as compliant, the compiler generates a compliance warning.

By default, types without this attribute are not CLS-compliant unless they are contained in a CLS-compliant type or assembly. You can specifically mark non–CLS compliant members inside a CLS-compliant type using <CLSCompliant(False)>.

Public NotInheritable Class **CLSCompliantAttribute** : Inherits Attribute
' *Public Constructors*
Public Sub **New**(ByVal isCompliant As Boolean)
' *Public Instance Properties*

Public ReadOnly Property **IsCompliant** As Boolean
End Class

Hierarchy: Object→ Attribute→ CLSCompliantAttribute

Valid On: All

Console
NotInheritable Class

System (mscorlib.dll)
ECMA

The Console class provides shared methods that allow you to create console, or command-line, applications. If you attempt to use these methods in a Windows Forms
application, they are ignored. For a console application, data is transmitted through
three streams. Input is received from the *standard input stream*, output is written
through the *standard output stream*, and error data is written to the *standard error output stream*. These streams are provided through the In property, which is a Sys-
tem.IO.TextReader object, and through the Out and Error properties, which are
System.IO.TextWriter objects. You can use the methods of these objects directly, or you can
use the methods provided by the Console class. For example, you can use the Write()
method to write any basic data type to the console window (or use WriteLine() to write
data with a trailing hard return). You can also use the ReadLine() method to cause the
console window to wait for input. When the user presses the Enter key, this method
returns with a string containing the input characters (except the final hard return).

You can use the SetIn(), SetOut(), and SetError() methods to bind the console to different
stream objects, such as System.IO.FileStream. To reset the streams to their default objects,
use the methods prefixed with OpenStandard. . ..

Public NotInheritable Class **Console**
  ' Public Shared Properties
    Public Shared ReadOnly Property **Error** As TextWriter
    Public Shared ReadOnly Property **In** As TextReader
    Public Shared ReadOnly Property **Out** As TextWriter
  ' Public Shared Methods
    Public Shared Function **OpenStandardError**() As Stream
    Public Shared Function **OpenStandardError**(ByVal bufferSize As Integer) As Stream
    Public Shared Function **OpenStandardInput**() As Stream
    Public Shared Function **OpenStandardInput**(ByVal bufferSize As Integer) As Stream
    Public Shared Function **OpenStandardOutput**() As Stream
    Public Shared Function **OpenStandardOutput**(ByVal bufferSize As Integer) As Stream
    Public Shared Function **Read**() As Integer
    Public Shared Function **ReadLine**() As String
    Public Shared Sub **SetError**(ByVal newError As System.IO.TextWriter)
    Public Shared Sub **SetIn**(ByVal newIn As System.IO.TextReader)
    Public Shared Sub **SetOut**(ByVal newOut As System.IO.TextWriter)
    Public Shared Sub **Write**(ByVal value As Boolean)
    Public Shared Sub **Write**(ByVal value As Char)
    Public Shared Sub **Write**(ByVal buffer As Char())
    Public Shared Sub **Write**(ByVal buffer As Char(), ByVal index As Integer, ByVal count As Integer)
    Public Shared Sub **Write**(ByVal value As Decimal)
    Public Shared Sub **Write**(ByVal value As Double)
    Public Shared Sub **Write**(ByVal value As Integer)
    Public Shared Sub **Write**(ByVal value As Long)
    Public Shared Sub **Write**(ByVal value As Object)
    Public Shared Sub **Write**(ByVal value As Single)
    Public Shared Sub **Write**(ByVal value As String)

System

Public Shared Sub **Write**(ByVal format As String, ByVal arg0 As Object)
Public Shared Sub **Write**(ByVal format As String, ParamArray arg As Object())
Public Shared Sub **Write**(ByVal format As String, ByVal arg0 As Object, ByVal arg1 As Object)
Public Shared Sub **Write**(ByVal format As String, ByVal arg0 As Object, ByVal arg1 As Object, ByVal arg2 As Object)
Public Shared Sub **Write**(ByVal format As String, ByVal arg0 As Object, ByVal arg1 As Object, ByVal arg2 As Object, _
   ByVal arg3 As Object)
Public Shared Sub **Write**(ByVal value As UInt32)
Public Shared Sub **Write**(ByVal value As UInt64)
Public Shared Sub **WriteLine**()
Public Shared Sub **WriteLine**(ByVal value As Boolean)
Public Shared Sub **WriteLine**(ByVal value As Char)
Public Shared Sub **WriteLine**(ByVal buffer As Char())
Public Shared Sub **WriteLine**(ByVal buffer As Char(), ByVal index As Integer, ByVal count As Integer)
Public Shared Sub **WriteLine**(ByVal value As Decimal)
Public Shared Sub **WriteLine**(ByVal value As Double)
Public Shared Sub **WriteLine**(ByVal value As Integer)
Public Shared Sub **WriteLine**(ByVal value As Long)
Public Shared Sub **WriteLine**(ByVal value As Object)
Public Shared Sub **WriteLine**(ByVal value As Single)
Public Shared Sub **WriteLine**(ByVal value As String)
Public Shared Sub **WriteLine**(ByVal format As String, ByVal arg0 As Object)
Public Shared Sub **WriteLine**(ByVal format As String, ParamArray arg As Object())
Public Shared Sub **WriteLine**(ByVal format As String, ByVal arg0 As Object, ByVal arg1 As Object)
Public Shared Sub **WriteLine**(ByVal format As String, ByVal arg0 As Object, ByVal arg1 As Object, _
   ByVal arg2 As Object)
Public Shared Sub **WriteLine**(ByVal format As String, ByVal arg0 As Object, ByVal arg1 As Object, _
   ByVal arg2 As Object, ByVal arg3 As Object)
Public Shared Sub **WriteLine**(ByVal value As UInt32)
Public Shared Sub **WriteLine**(ByVal value As UInt64)
End Class

ContextBoundObject
MustInherit Class

System (mscorlib.dll)
serializable, marshal by reference, context bound

An object inheriting from ContextBoundObject shares characteristics with an object inheriting from MarshalByRefObject. The difference is that a context further subdivides a domain. While instances of MarshalByRefObject are passed to other domains by reference and must interact through proxy objects, instances of ContextBoundObject are passed by reference to other contexts, even in the same domain. Unlike domains, contexts can provide a rich environment with other services such as synchronization, transactions, just-in-time activation, and security.

For more information, consult the System.Runtime.Remoting.Contexts namespace.

Public MustInherit Class **ContextBoundObject** : Inherits MarshalByRefObject
' Protected Constructors
   Protected Sub **New**()
End Class

Hierarchy: Object→ MarshalByRefObject→ ContextBoundObject

ContextMarshalException
Class

System (mscorlib.dll)
serializable

This exception is thrown when a marshaler fails to move an object across a context boundary. This is usually the case if a nonserializable object is passed as a parameter to a cross-context call, such as an instance of the CrossAppDomainDelegate.

```
Public Class ContextMarshalException : Inherits SystemException
' Public Constructors
   Public Sub New()
   Public Sub New(ByVal message As String)
   Public Sub New(ByVal message As String, ByVal inner As Exception)
' Protected Constructors
   Protected Sub New(ByVal info As System.Runtime.Serialization.SerializationInfo, _
     ByVal context As System.Runtime.Serialization.StreamingContext)
End Class
```

Hierarchy: Object→ Exception(System.Runtime.Serialization.ISerializable)→ SystemException→ ContextMarshalException

ContextStaticAttribute
Class

System (mscorlib.dll)
serializable

This attribute designates that a shared field should not be shared between contexts. Each context accesses a separate copy of this field and is able to set and retrieve values without accidentally overwriting data set by another context. Just as thread-local storage is used to store data in a per-thread fashion, this is used to store shared data in a per-context fashion.

```
Public Class ContextStaticAttribute : Inherits Attribute
' Public Constructors
   Public Sub New()
End Class
```

Hierarchy: Object→ Attribute→ ContextStaticAttribute

Valid On: Field

Convert
NotInheritable Class

System (mscorlib.dll)
ECMA

This class provides shared helper methods that convert base data types to other base data types. You can also convert objects to base data types, provided they implement the IConvertible interface and cast objects to different types with the ChangeType() method.

CLR languages typically allow widening conversions (e.g., Int16 to Int32) through direct assignment. Narrowing conversions require the Convert class or explicit casting. The Convert class does not generate an exception when you lose numeric precision, but it does throw an overflow exception if the source value is too large for the destination data type.

Note that implicit and explicit conversions can return different results than the Convert class. Namely, they truncate significant digits in a narrowing conversion (for example, changing 32.6 to the integer 32), while the Convert class rounds the number automatically (converting 32.6 to 33). The Convert class uses banker's rounding, meaning that the fraction 1/2 is rounded down for even numbers (so 4.5 becomes 4) and rounded up for odd numbers (so 5.5 becomes 6). This helps combat rounding bias.

The ToString() methods are functionally equivalent to the Object.ToString() method of the corresponding base data types. The conversions from strings to numeric or date data are functionally equivalent to the Parse() method of the appropriate data type (e.g., Int32.Parse()). For string conversions, you can also supply an IFormatProvider object to specify culture-specific formatting information used to interpret or encode a string.

For Boolean conversions, any nonzero number becomes true, except for strings, which are compared against the Boolean.TrueString and Boolean.FalseString fields. When converted to a number, a Boolean false becomes a 0, and a Boolean true becomes a 1.

Some conversion methods are provided only for symmetry and always throw an Invalid-CastException. These include any conversion between date and any data type other than string.

```
Public NotInheritable Class Convert
' Public Shared Fields
   Public Shared ReadOnly DBNull As Object
' Public Shared Methods
   Public Shared Function ChangeType(ByVal value As Object, ByVal conversionType As Type) As Object
   Public Shared Function ChangeType(ByVal value As Object, ByVal typeCode As TypeCode) As Object
   Public Shared Function ChangeType(ByVal value As Object, ByVal typeCode As TypeCode, _
      ByVal provider As IFormatProvider) As Object
   Public Shared Function ChangeType(ByVal value As Object, ByVal conversionType As Type, _
      ByVal provider As IFormatProvider) As Object
   Public Shared Function FromBase64CharArray(ByVal inArray As Char(), ByVal offset As Integer, _
      ByVal length As Integer) As Byte()
   Public Shared Function FromBase64String(ByVal s As String) As Byte()
   Public Shared Function GetTypeCode(ByVal value As Object) As TypeCode
   Public Shared Function IsDBNull(ByVal value As Object) As Boolean
   Public Shared Function ToBase64CharArray(ByVal inArray As Byte(), ByVal offsetIn As Integer, _
      ByVal length As Integer, ByVal outArray As Char(), ByVal offsetOut As Integer) As Integer
   Public Shared Function ToBase64String(ByVal inArray As Byte()) As String
   Public Shared Function ToBase64String(ByVal inArray As Byte(), ByVal offset As Integer, ByVal length As Integer) _
      As String
   Public Shared Function ToBoolean(ByVal value As Boolean) As Boolean
   Public Shared Function ToBoolean(ByVal value As Byte) As Boolean
   Public Shared Function ToBoolean(ByVal value As Char) As Boolean
   Public Shared Function ToBoolean(ByVal value As Date) As Boolean
   Public Shared Function ToBoolean(ByVal value As Decimal) As Boolean
   Public Shared Function ToBoolean(ByVal value As Double) As Boolean
   Public Shared Function ToBoolean(ByVal value As Short) As Boolean
   Public Shared Function ToBoolean(ByVal value As Integer) As Boolean
   Public Shared Function ToBoolean(ByVal value As Long) As Boolean
   Public Shared Function ToBoolean(ByVal value As Object) As Boolean
   Public Shared Function ToBoolean(ByVal value As Object, ByVal provider As IFormatProvider) As Boolean
   Public Shared Function ToBoolean(ByVal value As SByte) As Boolean
   Public Shared Function ToBoolean(ByVal value As Single) As Boolean
   Public Shared Function ToBoolean(ByVal value As String) As Boolean
   Public Shared Function ToBoolean(ByVal value As String, ByVal provider As IFormatProvider) As Boolean
   Public Shared Function ToBoolean(ByVal value As UInt16) As Boolean
   Public Shared Function ToBoolean(ByVal value As UInt32) As Boolean
   Public Shared Function ToBoolean(ByVal value As UInt64) As Boolean
   Public Shared Function ToByte(ByVal value As Boolean) As Byte
   Public Shared Function ToByte(ByVal value As Byte) As Byte
   Public Shared Function ToByte(ByVal value As Char) As Byte
   Public Shared Function ToByte(ByVal value As Date) As Byte
   Public Shared Function ToByte(ByVal value As Decimal) As Byte
   Public Shared Function ToByte(ByVal value As Double) As Byte
   Public Shared Function ToByte(ByVal value As Short) As Byte
```

```
Public Shared Function ToByte(ByVal value As Integer) As Byte
Public Shared Function ToByte(ByVal value As Long) As Byte
Public Shared Function ToByte(ByVal value As Object) As Byte
Public Shared Function ToByte(ByVal value As Object, ByVal provider As IFormatProvider) As Byte
Public Shared Function ToByte(ByVal value As SByte) As Byte
Public Shared Function ToByte(ByVal value As Single) As Byte
Public Shared Function ToByte(ByVal value As String) As Byte
Public Shared Function ToByte(ByVal value As String, ByVal provider As IFormatProvider) As Byte
Public Shared Function ToByte(ByVal value As String, ByVal fromBase As Integer) As Byte
Public Shared Function ToByte(ByVal value As UInt16) As Byte
Public Shared Function ToByte(ByVal value As UInt32) As Byte
Public Shared Function ToByte(ByVal value As UInt64) As Byte
Public Shared Function ToChar(ByVal value As Boolean) As Char
Public Shared Function ToChar(ByVal value As Byte) As Char
Public Shared Function ToChar(ByVal value As Char) As Char
Public Shared Function ToChar(ByVal value As Date) As Char
Public Shared Function ToChar(ByVal value As Decimal) As Char
Public Shared Function ToChar(ByVal value As Double) As Char
Public Shared Function ToChar(ByVal value As Short) As Char
Public Shared Function ToChar(ByVal value As Integer) As Char
Public Shared Function ToChar(ByVal value As Long) As Char
Public Shared Function ToChar(ByVal value As Object) As Char
Public Shared Function ToChar(ByVal value As Object, ByVal provider As IFormatProvider) As Char
Public Shared Function ToChar(ByVal value As SByte) As Char
Public Shared Function ToChar(ByVal value As Single) As Char
Public Shared Function ToChar(ByVal value As String) As Char
Public Shared Function ToChar(ByVal value As String, ByVal provider As IFormatProvider) As Char
Public Shared Function ToChar(ByVal value As UInt16) As Char
Public Shared Function ToChar(ByVal value As UInt32) As Char
Public Shared Function ToChar(ByVal value As UInt64) As Char
Public Shared Function ToDateTime(ByVal value As Boolean) As Date
Public Shared Function ToDateTime(ByVal value As Byte) As Date
Public Shared Function ToDateTime(ByVal value As Char) As Date
Public Shared Function ToDateTime(ByVal value As Date) As Date
Public Shared Function ToDateTime(ByVal value As Decimal) As Date
Public Shared Function ToDateTime(ByVal value As Double) As Date
Public Shared Function ToDateTime(ByVal value As Short) As Date
Public Shared Function ToDateTime(ByVal value As Integer) As Date
Public Shared Function ToDateTime(ByVal value As Long) As Date
Public Shared Function ToDateTime(ByVal value As Object) As Date
Public Shared Function ToDateTime(ByVal value As Object, ByVal provider As IFormatProvider) As Date
Public Shared Function ToDateTime(ByVal value As SByte) As Date
Public Shared Function ToDateTime(ByVal value As Single) As Date
Public Shared Function ToDateTime(ByVal value As String) As Date
Public Shared Function ToDateTime(ByVal value As String, ByVal provider As IFormatProvider) As Date
Public Shared Function ToDateTime(ByVal value As UInt16) As Date
Public Shared Function ToDateTime(ByVal value As UInt32) As Date
Public Shared Function ToDateTime(ByVal value As UInt64) As Date
Public Shared Function ToDecimal(ByVal value As Boolean) As Decimal
Public Shared Function ToDecimal(ByVal value As Byte) As Decimal
Public Shared Function ToDecimal(ByVal value As Char) As Decimal
Public Shared Function ToDecimal(ByVal value As Date) As Decimal
Public Shared Function ToDecimal(ByVal value As Decimal) As Decimal
Public Shared Function ToDecimal(ByVal value As Double) As Decimal
Public Shared Function ToDecimal(ByVal value As Short) As Decimal
```

System

Public Shared Function **ToDecimal**(ByVal value As Integer) As Decimal
Public Shared Function **ToDecimal**(ByVal value As Long) As Decimal
Public Shared Function **ToDecimal**(ByVal value As Object) As Decimal
Public Shared Function **ToDecimal**(ByVal value As Object, ByVal provider As IFormatProvider) As Decimal
Public Shared Function **ToDecimal**(ByVal value As SByte) As Decimal
Public Shared Function **ToDecimal**(ByVal value As Single) As Decimal
Public Shared Function **ToDecimal**(ByVal value As String) As Decimal
Public Shared Function **ToDecimal**(ByVal value As String, ByVal provider As IFormatProvider) As Decimal
Public Shared Function **ToDecimal**(ByVal value As UInt16) As Decimal
Public Shared Function **ToDecimal**(ByVal value As UInt32) As Decimal
Public Shared Function **ToDecimal**(ByVal value As UInt64) As Decimal
Public Shared Function **ToDouble**(ByVal value As Boolean) As Double
Public Shared Function **ToDouble**(ByVal value As Byte) As Double
Public Shared Function **ToDouble**(ByVal value As Char) As Double
Public Shared Function **ToDouble**(ByVal value As Date) As Double
Public Shared Function **ToDouble**(ByVal value As Decimal) As Double
Public Shared Function **ToDouble**(ByVal value As Double) As Double
Public Shared Function **ToDouble**(ByVal value As Short) As Double
Public Shared Function **ToDouble**(ByVal value As Integer) As Double
Public Shared Function **ToDouble**(ByVal value As Long) As Double
Public Shared Function **ToDouble**(ByVal value As Object) As Double
Public Shared Function **ToDouble**(ByVal value As Object, ByVal provider As IFormatProvider) As Double
Public Shared Function **ToDouble**(ByVal value As SByte) As Double
Public Shared Function **ToDouble**(ByVal value As Single) As Double
Public Shared Function **ToDouble**(ByVal value As String) As Double
Public Shared Function **ToDouble**(ByVal value As String, ByVal provider As IFormatProvider) As Double
Public Shared Function **ToDouble**(ByVal value As UInt16) As Double
Public Shared Function **ToDouble**(ByVal value As UInt32) As Double
Public Shared Function **ToDouble**(ByVal value As UInt64) As Double
Public Shared Function **ToInt16**(ByVal value As Boolean) As Short
Public Shared Function **ToInt16**(ByVal value As Byte) As Short
Public Shared Function **ToInt16**(ByVal value As Char) As Short
Public Shared Function **ToInt16**(ByVal value As Date) As Short
Public Shared Function **ToInt16**(ByVal value As Decimal) As Short
Public Shared Function **ToInt16**(ByVal value As Double) As Short
Public Shared Function **ToInt16**(ByVal value As Short) As Short
Public Shared Function **ToInt16**(ByVal value As Integer) As Short
Public Shared Function **ToInt16**(ByVal value As Long) As Short
Public Shared Function **ToInt16**(ByVal value As Object) As Short
Public Shared Function **ToInt16**(ByVal value As Object, ByVal provider As IFormatProvider) As Short
Public Shared Function **ToInt16**(ByVal value As SByte) As Short
Public Shared Function **ToInt16**(ByVal value As Single) As Short
Public Shared Function **ToInt16**(ByVal value As String) As Short
Public Shared Function **ToInt16**(ByVal value As String, ByVal provider As IFormatProvider) As Short
Public Shared Function **ToInt16**(ByVal value As String, ByVal fromBase As Integer) As Short
Public Shared Function **ToInt16**(ByVal value As UInt16) As Short
Public Shared Function **ToInt16**(ByVal value As UInt32) As Short
Public Shared Function **ToInt16**(ByVal value As UInt64) As Short
Public Shared Function **ToInt32**(ByVal value As Boolean) As Integer
Public Shared Function **ToInt32**(ByVal value As Byte) As Integer
Public Shared Function **ToInt32**(ByVal value As Char) As Integer
Public Shared Function **ToInt32**(ByVal value As Date) As Integer
Public Shared Function **ToInt32**(ByVal value As Decimal) As Integer
Public Shared Function **ToInt32**(ByVal value As Double) As Integer
Public Shared Function **ToInt32**(ByVal value As Short) As Integer

Public Shared Function **ToInt32**(ByVal value As Integer) As Integer
Public Shared Function **ToInt32**(ByVal value As Long) As Integer
Public Shared Function **ToInt32**(ByVal value As Object) As Integer
Public Shared Function **ToInt32**(ByVal value As Object, ByVal provider As IFormatProvider) As Integer
Public Shared Function **ToInt32**(ByVal value As SByte) As Integer
Public Shared Function **ToInt32**(ByVal value As Single) As Integer
Public Shared Function **ToInt32**(ByVal value As String) As Integer
Public Shared Function **ToInt32**(ByVal value As String, ByVal provider As IFormatProvider) As Integer
Public Shared Function **ToInt32**(ByVal value As String, ByVal fromBase As Integer) As Integer
Public Shared Function **ToInt32**(ByVal value As UInt16) As Integer
Public Shared Function **ToInt32**(ByVal value As UInt32) As Integer
Public Shared Function **ToInt32**(ByVal value As UInt64) As Integer
Public Shared Function **ToInt64**(ByVal value As Boolean) As Long
Public Shared Function **ToInt64**(ByVal value As Byte) As Long
Public Shared Function **ToInt64**(ByVal value As Char) As Long
Public Shared Function **ToInt64**(ByVal value As Date) As Long
Public Shared Function **ToInt64**(ByVal value As Decimal) As Long
Public Shared Function **ToInt64**(ByVal value As Double) As Long
Public Shared Function **ToInt64**(ByVal value As Short) As Long
Public Shared Function **ToInt64**(ByVal value As Integer) As Long
Public Shared Function **ToInt64**(ByVal value As Long) As Long
Public Shared Function **ToInt64**(ByVal value As Object) As Long
Public Shared Function **ToInt64**(ByVal value As Object, ByVal provider As IFormatProvider) As Long
Public Shared Function **ToInt64**(ByVal value As SByte) As Long
Public Shared Function **ToInt64**(ByVal value As Single) As Long
Public Shared Function **ToInt64**(ByVal value As String) As Long
Public Shared Function **ToInt64**(ByVal value As String, ByVal provider As IFormatProvider) As Long
Public Shared Function **ToInt64**(ByVal value As String, ByVal fromBase As Integer) As Long
Public Shared Function **ToInt64**(ByVal value As UInt16) As Long
Public Shared Function **ToInt64**(ByVal value As UInt32) As Long
Public Shared Function **ToInt64**(ByVal value As UInt64) As Long
Public Shared Function **ToSByte**(ByVal value As Boolean) As SByte
Public Shared Function **ToSByte**(ByVal value As Byte) As SByte
Public Shared Function **ToSByte**(ByVal value As Char) As SByte
Public Shared Function **ToSByte**(ByVal value As Date) As SByte
Public Shared Function **ToSByte**(ByVal value As Decimal) As SByte
Public Shared Function **ToSByte**(ByVal value As Double) As SByte
Public Shared Function **ToSByte**(ByVal value As Short) As SByte
Public Shared Function **ToSByte**(ByVal value As Integer) As SByte
Public Shared Function **ToSByte**(ByVal value As Long) As SByte
Public Shared Function **ToSByte**(ByVal value As Object) As SByte
Public Shared Function **ToSByte**(ByVal value As Object, ByVal provider As IFormatProvider) As SByte
Public Shared Function **ToSByte**(ByVal value As SByte) As SByte
Public Shared Function **ToSByte**(ByVal value As Single) As SByte
Public Shared Function **ToSByte**(ByVal value As String) As SByte
Public Shared Function **ToSByte**(ByVal value As String, ByVal provider As IFormatProvider) As SByte
Public Shared Function **ToSByte**(ByVal value As String, ByVal fromBase As Integer) As SByte
Public Shared Function **ToSByte**(ByVal value As UInt16) As SByte
Public Shared Function **ToSByte**(ByVal value As UInt32) As SByte
Public Shared Function **ToSByte**(ByVal value As UInt64) As SByte
Public Shared Function **ToSingle**(ByVal value As Boolean) As Single
Public Shared Function **ToSingle**(ByVal value As Byte) As Single
Public Shared Function **ToSingle**(ByVal value As Char) As Single
Public Shared Function **ToSingle**(ByVal value As Date) As Single
Public Shared Function **ToSingle**(ByVal value As Decimal) As Single

System

Public Shared Function **ToSingle**(ByVal value As Double) As Single
Public Shared Function **ToSingle**(ByVal value As Short) As Single
Public Shared Function **ToSingle**(ByVal value As Integer) As Single
Public Shared Function **ToSingle**(ByVal value As Long) As Single
Public Shared Function **ToSingle**(ByVal value As Object) As Single
Public Shared Function **ToSingle**(ByVal value As Object, ByVal provider As IFormatProvider) As Single
Public Shared Function **ToSingle**(ByVal value As SByte) As Single
Public Shared Function **ToSingle**(ByVal value As Single) As Single
Public Shared Function **ToSingle**(ByVal value As String) As Single
Public Shared Function **ToSingle**(ByVal value As String, ByVal provider As IFormatProvider) As Single
Public Shared Function **ToSingle**(ByVal value As UInt16) As Single
Public Shared Function **ToSingle**(ByVal value As UInt32) As Single
Public Shared Function **ToSingle**(ByVal value As UInt64) As Single
Public Shared Function **ToString**(ByVal value As Boolean) As String
Public Shared Function **ToString**(ByVal value As Boolean, ByVal provider As IFormatProvider) As String
Public Shared Function **ToString**(ByVal value As Byte) As String
Public Shared Function **ToString**(ByVal value As Byte, ByVal provider As IFormatProvider) As String
Public Shared Function **ToString**(ByVal value As Byte, ByVal toBase As Integer) As String
Public Shared Function **ToString**(ByVal value As Char) As String
Public Shared Function **ToString**(ByVal value As Char, ByVal provider As IFormatProvider) As String
Public Shared Function **ToString**(ByVal value As Date) As String
Public Shared Function **ToString**(ByVal value As Date, ByVal provider As IFormatProvider) As String
Public Shared Function **ToString**(ByVal value As Decimal) As String
Public Shared Function **ToString**(ByVal value As Decimal, ByVal provider As IFormatProvider) As String
Public Shared Function **ToString**(ByVal value As Double) As String
Public Shared Function **ToString**(ByVal value As Double, ByVal provider As IFormatProvider) As String
Public Shared Function **ToString**(ByVal value As Short) As String
Public Shared Function **ToString**(ByVal value As Short, ByVal provider As IFormatProvider) As String
Public Shared Function **ToString**(ByVal value As Short, ByVal toBase As Integer) As String
Public Shared Function **ToString**(ByVal value As Integer) As String
Public Shared Function **ToString**(ByVal value As Integer, ByVal provider As IFormatProvider) As String
Public Shared Function **ToString**(ByVal value As Integer, ByVal toBase As Integer) As String
Public Shared Function **ToString**(ByVal value As Long) As String
Public Shared Function **ToString**(ByVal value As Long, ByVal provider As IFormatProvider) As String
Public Shared Function **ToString**(ByVal value As Long, ByVal toBase As Integer) As String
Public Shared Function **ToString**(ByVal value As Object) As String
Public Shared Function **ToString**(ByVal value As Object, ByVal provider As IFormatProvider) As String
Public Shared Function **ToString**(ByVal value As SByte) As String
Public Shared Function **ToString**(ByVal value As SByte, ByVal provider As IFormatProvider) As String
Public Shared Function **ToString**(ByVal value As Single) As String
Public Shared Function **ToString**(ByVal value As Single, ByVal provider As IFormatProvider) As String
Public Shared Function **ToString**(ByVal value As String) As String
Public Shared Function **ToString**(ByVal value As String, ByVal provider As IFormatProvider) As String
Public Shared Function **ToString**(ByVal value As UInt16) As String
Public Shared Function **ToString**(ByVal value As UInt16, ByVal provider As IFormatProvider) As String
Public Shared Function **ToString**(ByVal value As UInt32) As String
Public Shared Function **ToString**(ByVal value As UInt32, ByVal provider As IFormatProvider) As String
Public Shared Function **ToString**(ByVal value As UInt64) As String
Public Shared Function **ToString**(ByVal value As UInt64, ByVal provider As IFormatProvider) As String
Public Shared Function **ToUInt16**(ByVal value As Boolean) As UInt16
Public Shared Function **ToUInt16**(ByVal value As Byte) As UInt16
Public Shared Function **ToUInt16**(ByVal value As Char) As UInt16
Public Shared Function **ToUInt16**(ByVal value As Date) As UInt16
Public Shared Function **ToUInt16**(ByVal value As Decimal) As UInt16
Public Shared Function **ToUInt16**(ByVal value As Double) As UInt16

Public Shared Function **ToUInt16**(ByVal value As Short) As UInt16
Public Shared Function **ToUInt16**(ByVal value As Integer) As UInt16
Public Shared Function **ToUInt16**(ByVal value As Long) As UInt16
Public Shared Function **ToUInt16**(ByVal value As Object) As UInt16
Public Shared Function **ToUInt16**(ByVal value As Object, ByVal provider As IFormatProvider) As UInt16
Public Shared Function **ToUInt16**(ByVal value As SByte) As UInt16
Public Shared Function **ToUInt16**(ByVal value As Single) As UInt16
Public Shared Function **ToUInt16**(ByVal value As String) As UInt16
Public Shared Function **ToUInt16**(ByVal value As String, ByVal provider As IFormatProvider) As UInt16
Public Shared Function **ToUInt16**(ByVal value As String, ByVal fromBase As Integer) As UInt16
Public Shared Function **ToUInt16**(ByVal value As UInt16) As UInt16
Public Shared Function **ToUInt16**(ByVal value As UInt32) As UInt16
Public Shared Function **ToUInt16**(ByVal value As UInt64) As UInt16
Public Shared Function **ToUInt32**(ByVal value As Boolean) As UInt32
Public Shared Function **ToUInt32**(ByVal value As Byte) As UInt32
Public Shared Function **ToUInt32**(ByVal value As Char) As UInt32
Public Shared Function **ToUInt32**(ByVal value As Date) As UInt32
Public Shared Function **ToUInt32**(ByVal value As Decimal) As UInt32
Public Shared Function **ToUInt32**(ByVal value As Double) As UInt32
Public Shared Function **ToUInt32**(ByVal value As Short) As UInt32
Public Shared Function **ToUInt32**(ByVal value As Integer) As UInt32
Public Shared Function **ToUInt32**(ByVal value As Long) As UInt32
Public Shared Function **ToUInt32**(ByVal value As Object) As UInt32
Public Shared Function **ToUInt32**(ByVal value As Object, ByVal provider As IFormatProvider) As UInt32
Public Shared Function **ToUInt32**(ByVal value As SByte) As UInt32
Public Shared Function **ToUInt32**(ByVal value As Single) As UInt32
Public Shared Function **ToUInt32**(ByVal value As String) As UInt32
Public Shared Function **ToUInt32**(ByVal value As String, ByVal provider As IFormatProvider) As UInt32
Public Shared Function **ToUInt32**(ByVal value As String, ByVal fromBase As Integer) As UInt32
Public Shared Function **ToUInt32**(ByVal value As UInt16) As UInt32
Public Shared Function **ToUInt32**(ByVal value As UInt32) As UInt32
Public Shared Function **ToUInt32**(ByVal value As UInt64) As UInt32
Public Shared Function **ToUInt64**(ByVal value As Boolean) As UInt64
Public Shared Function **ToUInt64**(ByVal value As Byte) As UInt64
Public Shared Function **ToUInt64**(ByVal value As Char) As UInt64
Public Shared Function **ToUInt64**(ByVal value As Date) As UInt64
Public Shared Function **ToUInt64**(ByVal value As Decimal) As UInt64
Public Shared Function **ToUInt64**(ByVal value As Double) As UInt64
Public Shared Function **ToUInt64**(ByVal value As Short) As UInt64
Public Shared Function **ToUInt64**(ByVal value As Integer) As UInt64
Public Shared Function **ToUInt64**(ByVal value As Long) As UInt64
Public Shared Function **ToUInt64**(ByVal value As Object) As UInt64
Public Shared Function **ToUInt64**(ByVal value As Object, ByVal provider As IFormatProvider) As UInt64
Public Shared Function **ToUInt64**(ByVal value As SByte) As UInt64
Public Shared Function **ToUInt64**(ByVal value As Single) As UInt64
Public Shared Function **ToUInt64**(ByVal value As String) As UInt64
Public Shared Function **ToUInt64**(ByVal value As String, ByVal provider As IFormatProvider) As UInt64
Public Shared Function **ToUInt64**(ByVal value As String, ByVal fromBase As Integer) As UInt64
Public Shared Function **ToUInt64**(ByVal value As UInt16) As UInt64
Public Shared Function **ToUInt64**(ByVal value As UInt32) As UInt64
Public Shared Function **ToUInt64**(ByVal value As UInt64) As UInt64
End Class

CrossAppDomainDelegate   Delegate

System (mscorlib.dll)   *serializable*

This delegate invokes a method in a different application domain using the AppDomain.DoCallBack() method. You can then invoke a delegate instance within another AppDomain, which provides you with the ability to check on an AppDomain's status or information.

Public Delegate Sub **CrossAppDomainDelegate**()

Passed To: AppDomain.DoCallBack()

DateTime   Structure

System (mscorlib.dll)   *ECMA, serializable*

This simple value type represents a moment in time from 12:00:00 A.M., 1/1/0001 C.E. (Common Era), to 11:59:59 P.M., 12/31/9999 C.E., which is measured to the nearest *tick*, or 100-nanosecond interval. You can use this type in greater-than/less-than comparisons, sorting, and in calculations using other DateTime or TimeSpan instances. You can also use convenient Add. . . methods, such as AddSeconds(), with a positive or negative value.

To extract part of a date, use properties such as Day and Minute. All properties except Ticks represent a single component of a compound date, not the whole date. You can convert a string into a DateTime using the shared Parse() or ParseExact() methods, which require that the date match the pattern specified by a supplied format string.

The DateTime class also provides valuable shared functions that can determine the number of days in a month (DaysInMonth()), evaluate whether a year is a leap year (IsLeapYear()), and retrieve the date stamp from a file (FromFileTime()). You can also get the current date from the shared property Today (or UtcNow for the coordinated universal time).

Public Structure **DateTime** : Implements IComparable, IFormattable, IConvertible
' Public Constructors
  Public Sub **New**(ByVal year As Integer, ByVal month As Integer, ByVal day As Integer)
  Public Sub **New**(ByVal year As Integer, ByVal month As Integer, ByVal day As Integer, _
    ByVal calendar As System.Globalization.Calendar)
  Public Sub **New**(ByVal year As Integer, ByVal month As Integer, ByVal day As Integer, ByVal hour As Integer, _
    ByVal minute As Integer, ByVal second As Integer)
  Public Sub **New**(ByVal year As Integer, ByVal month As Integer, ByVal day As Integer, ByVal hour As Integer, _
    ByVal minute As Integer), ByVal second As Integer, ByVal calendar As System.Globalization.Calendar)
  Public Sub **New**(ByVal year As Integer, ByVal month As Integer, ByVal day As Integer, ByVal hour As Integer, _
    ByVal minute As Integer), ByVal second As Integer, ByVal millisecond As Integer)
  Public Sub **New**(ByVal year As Integer, ByVal month As Integer, ByVal day As Integer, ByVal hour As Integer, _
    ByVal minute As Integer, ByVal second As Integer, ByVal millisecond As Integer,
    ByVal calendar As System.Globalization.Calendar)   −
  Public Sub **New**(ByVal ticks As Long)
' Public Shared Fields
  Public Shared ReadOnly **MaxValue** As Date   *=12/31/9999 11:59:59 PM*
  Public Shared ReadOnly **MinValue** As Date   *=1/1/0001 12:00:00 AM*
' Public Shared Properties
  Public Shared ReadOnly Property **Now** As Date
  Public Shared ReadOnly Property **Today** As Date
  Public Shared ReadOnly Property **UtcNow** As Date
' Public Instance Properties
  Public ReadOnly Property **Date** As Date
  Public ReadOnly Property **Day** As Integer

Public ReadOnly Property **DayOfWeek** As DayOfWeek
Public ReadOnly Property **DayOfYear** As Integer
Public ReadOnly Property **Hour** As Integer
Public ReadOnly Property **Millisecond** As Integer
Public ReadOnly Property **Minute** As Integer
Public ReadOnly Property **Month** As Integer
Public ReadOnly Property **Second** As Integer
Public ReadOnly Property **Ticks** As Long
Public ReadOnly Property **TimeOfDay** As TimeSpan
Public ReadOnly Property **Year** As Integer
' *Public Shared Methods*
Public Shared Function **Compare**(ByVal t1 As Date, ByVal t2 As Date) As Integer
Public Shared Function **DaysInMonth**(ByVal year As Integer, ByVal month As Integer) As Integer
Public Shared Function **Equals**(ByVal t1 As Date, ByVal t2 As Date) As Boolean
Public Shared Function **FromFileTime**(ByVal fileTime As Long) As Date
Public Shared Function **FromOADate**(ByVal d As Double) As Date
Public Shared Function **IsLeapYear**(ByVal year As Integer) As Boolean
Public Shared Function **Parse**(ByVal s As String) As Date
Public Shared Function **Parse**(ByVal s As String, ByVal provider As IFormatProvider) As Date
Public Shared Function **Parse**(ByVal s As String, ByVal provider As IFormatProvider, _
ByVal styles As System.Globalization.DateTimeStyles) As Date
Public Shared Function **ParseExact**(ByVal s As String, ByVal formats As String(), ByVal provider As IFormatProvider _
, ByVal style As System.Globalization.DateTimeStyles) As Date
Public Shared Function **ParseExact**(ByVal s As String, ByVal format As String, ByVal provider As IFormatProvider) _
As Date
Public Shared Function **ParseExact**(ByVal s As String, ByVal format As String, ByVal provider As IFormatProvider, _
ByVal style As System.Globalization.DateTimeStyles) As Date
Public Shared Date operator Sub -(ByVal d As Date, ByVal t As TimeSpan)
Public Shared TimeSpan operator Sub -(ByVal d1 As Date, ByVal d2 As Date)
Public Shared Date operator Sub +(ByVal d As Date, ByVal t As TimeSpan)
Public Shared Boolean operator Sub !=(ByVal d1 As Date, ByVal d2 As Date)
Public Shared Boolean operator Sub <(ByVal t1 As Date, ByVal t2 As Date)
Public Shared Boolean operator Sub <=(ByVal t1 As Date, ByVal t2 As Date)
Public Shared Boolean operator Sub ==(ByVal d1 As Date, ByVal d2 As Date)
Public Shared Boolean operator Sub >(ByVal t1 As Date, ByVal t2 As Date)
Public Shared Boolean operator Sub >=(ByVal t1 As Date, ByVal t2 As Date)
' *Public Instance Methods*
Public Function **Add**(ByVal value As TimeSpan) As Date
Public Function **AddDays**(ByVal value As Double) As Date
Public Function **AddHours**(ByVal value As Double) As Date
Public Function **AddMilliseconds**(ByVal value As Double) As Date
Public Function **AddMinutes**(ByVal value As Double) As Date
Public Function **AddMonths**(ByVal months As Integer) As Date
Public Function **AddSeconds**(ByVal value As Double) As Date
Public Function **AddTicks**(ByVal value As Long) As Date
Public Function **AddYears**(ByVal value As Integer) As Date
Public Function **CompareTo**(ByVal value As Object) As Integer Implements IComparable.CompareTo
Overrides Public Function **Equals**(ByVal value As Object) As Boolean
Public Function **GetDateTimeFormats**() As String()
Public Function **GetDateTimeFormats**(ByVal format As Char) As String()
Public Function **GetDateTimeFormats**(ByVal format As Char, ByVal provider As IFormatProvider) As String()
Public Function **GetDateTimeFormats**(ByVal provider As IFormatProvider) As String()
Overrides Public Function **GetHashCode**() As Integer
Public Function **GetTypeCode**() As TypeCode Implements IConvertible.GetTypeCode
Public Function **Subtract**(ByVal value As TimeSpan) As Date

Public Function **Subtract**(ByVal value As Date) As TimeSpan
Public Function **ToFileTime**() As Long
Public Function **ToLocalTime**() As Date
Public Function **ToLongDateString**() As String
Public Function **ToLongTimeString**() As String
Public Function **ToOADate**() As Double
Public Function **ToShortDateString**() As String
Public Function **ToShortTimeString**() As String
Overrides Public Function **ToString**() As String
Public Function **ToString**(ByVal provider As IFormatProvider) As String Implements IConvertible.ToString
Public Function **ToString**(ByVal format As String) As String
Public Function **ToString**(ByVal format As String, ByVal provider As IFormatProvider) As String _
Implements IFormattable.ToString
Public Function **ToUniversalTime**() As Date
End Structure

Hierarchy: Object→ ValueType→ DateTime(IComparable, IFormattable, IConvertible)

Returned By: Multiple types

Passed To: Multiple types

DayOfWeek
Enum

System (mscorlib.dll)
serializable

This enumeration is used by the DateTime.DayOfWeek property.

Public Enum **DayOfWeek**
    Sunday = 0
    Monday = 1
    Tuesday = 2
    Wednesday = 3
    Thursday = 4
    Friday = 5
    Saturday = 6
End Enum

Hierarchy: Object→ ValueType→ Enum(IComparable, IFormattable, IConvertible)→ DayOfWeek

Returned By: DateTime.DayOfWeek, System.Globalization.Calendar.GetDayOfWeek(),
System.Globalization.DateTimeFormatInfo.FirstDayOfWeek

Passed To: System.Globalization.Calendar.GetWeekOfYear(),
System.Globalization.DateTimeFormatInfo.{FirstDayOfWeek, GetAbbreviatedDayName(), GetDayName()}

DBNull
NotInheritable Class

System (mscorlib.dll)
serializable

DBNull indicates the absence of information, typically in a database application in which
a field does not contain any data. The types in the System.Data.SqlTypes namespace have
built-in support for DBNull.

Note that Value is not the same as the Nothing keyword in VB.NET. The Nothing keyword
can be used to release an object by clearing the reference. System.DBNull.Value, on the
other hand, is a reference to a special value (a member of the singleton class DBNull)
that is used to indicate missing information.

This class has some other uses, namely in COM Interop, in which it represents a
VT_EMPTY variant (as opposed to a VT_NULL variant, which is a null reference).

Public NotInheritable Class **DBNull** : Implements System.Runtime.Serialization.ISerializable, IConvertible
' *Public Shared Fields*
  Public Shared ReadOnly **Value** As DBNull
' *Public Instance Methods*
  Public Sub **GetObjectData**(ByVal info As System.Runtime.Serialization.SerializationInfo,
    ByVal context As System.Runtime.Serialization.StreamingContext) Implements ISerializable.GetObjectData
  Public Function **GetTypeCode**() As TypeCode Implements IConvertible.GetTypeCode
  Overrides Public Function **ToString**() As String
  Public Function **ToString**(ByVal provider As IFormatProvider) As String Implements IConvertible.ToString
End Class

Decimal

Structure

System (mscorlib.dll)

ECMA, serializable

This simple value type is commonly used for financial calculations, which can preserve a significant number of fractional digits with no round-off error. Decimals are stored as 12-byte signed integers scaled by a variable power of 10. This means that a decimal data type can effectively hold 28 significant digits without losing any information. With a scale of 0 (no decimal places), the largest possible value is approximately 7.92×10^{28}. This type is available in VB.NET through the Decimal alias.

Public Structure **Decimal** : Implements IFormattable, IComparable , IConvertible
' *Public Constructors*
  Public Sub **New**(ByVal value As Double)
  Public Sub **New**(ByVal value As Integer)
  Public Sub **New**(ByVal bits As Integer())
  Public Sub **New**(ByVal lo As Integer, ByVal mid As Integer, ByVal hi As Integer, ByVal isNegative As Boolean, _
    ByVal scale As Byte)
  Public Sub **New**(ByVal value As Long)
  Public Sub **New**(ByVal value As Single)
  Public Sub **New**(ByVal value As UInt32)
  Public Sub **New**(ByVal value As UInt64)
' *Public Shared Fields*
  Public Shared ReadOnly **MaxValue** As Decimal   =7922816251426433759354395033 5
  Public Shared ReadOnly **MinusOne** As Decimal   =-1
  Public Shared ReadOnly **MinValue** As Decimal   =-79228162514264337593543950335
  Public Shared ReadOnly **One** As Decimal   =1
  Public Shared ReadOnly **Zero** As Decimal   =0
' *Public Shared Methods*
  Public Shared Function **Add**(ByVal d1 As Decimal, ByVal d2 As Decimal) As Decimal
  Public Shared Function **Compare**(ByVal d1 As Decimal, ByVal d2 As Decimal) As Integer
  Public Shared Function **Divide**(ByVal d1 As Decimal, ByVal d2 As Decimal) As Decimal
  Public Shared Function **Equals**(ByVal d1 As Decimal, ByVal d2 As Decimal) As Boolean
  Public Shared Function **Floor**(ByVal d As Decimal) As Decimal
  Public Shared Function **FromOACurrency**(ByVal cy As Long) As Decimal
  Public Shared Function **GetBits**(ByVal d As Decimal) As Integer()
  Public Shared Function **Multiply**(ByVal d1 As Decimal, ByVal d2 As Decimal) As Decimal
  Public Shared Function **Negate**(ByVal d As Decimal) As Decimal
  Public Shared Function **Parse**(ByVal s As String) As Decimal
  Public Shared Function **Parse**(ByVal s As String, ByVal provider As IFormatProvider) As Decimal
  Public Shared Function **Parse**(ByVal s As String, ByVal style As System.Globalization.NumberStyles) As Decimal
  Public Shared Function **Parse**(ByVal s As String, ByVal style As System.Globalization.NumberStyles, _
    ByVal provider As IFormatProvider) As Decimal
  Public Shared Function **Remainder**(ByVal d1 As Decimal, ByVal d2 As Decimal) As Decimal
  Public Shared Function **Round**(ByVal d As Decimal, ByVal decimals As Integer) As Decimal

System

Public Shared Function **Subtract**(ByVal d1 As Decimal, ByVal d2 As Decimal) As Decimal

Public Shared Function **ToByte**(ByVal value As Decimal) As Byte

Public Shared Function **ToDouble**(ByVal d As Decimal) As Double

Public Shared Function **ToInt16**(ByVal value As Decimal) As Short

Public Shared Function **ToInt32**(ByVal d As Decimal) As Integer

Public Shared Function **ToInt64**(ByVal d As Decimal) As Long

Public Shared Function **ToOACurrency**(ByVal value As Decimal) As Long

Public Shared Function **ToSByte**(ByVal value As Decimal) As SByte

Public Shared Function **ToSingle**(ByVal d As Decimal) As Single

Public Shared Function **ToUInt16**(ByVal value As Decimal) As UInt16

Public Shared Function **ToUInt32**(ByVal d As Decimal) As UInt32

Public Shared Function **ToUInt64**(ByVal d As Decimal) As UInt64

Public Shared Function **Truncate**(ByVal d As Decimal) As Decimal

Public Shared Decimal operator Sub %(ByVal d1 As Decimal, ByVal d2 As Decimal)

Public Shared Decimal operator Sub *(ByVal d1 As Decimal, ByVal d2 As Decimal)

Public Shared Decimal operator Sub /(ByVal d1 As Decimal, ByVal d2 As Decimal)

Public Shared Decimal operator Sub --(ByVal d As Decimal)

Public Shared Decimal operator Sub -(ByVal d As Decimal)

Public Shared Decimal operator Sub -(ByVal d1 As Decimal, ByVal d2 As Decimal)

Public Shared Decimal operator Sub +(ByVal d As Decimal)

Public Shared Decimal operator Sub +(ByVal d1 As Decimal, ByVal d2 As Decimal)

Public Shared Decimal operator Sub ++(ByVal d As Decimal)

Public Shared Boolean operator Sub !=(ByVal d1 As Decimal, ByVal d2 As Decimal)

Public Shared Boolean operator Sub <(ByVal d1 As Decimal, ByVal d2 As Decimal)

Public Shared Boolean operator Sub <=(ByVal d1 As Decimal, ByVal d2 As Decimal)

Public Shared Boolean operator Sub ==(ByVal d1 As Decimal, ByVal d2 As Decimal)

Public Shared Boolean operator Sub >(ByVal d1 As Decimal, ByVal d2 As Decimal)

Public Shared Boolean operator Sub >=(ByVal d1 As Decimal, ByVal d2 As Decimal)

Public Shared explicit operator Sub **Byte**(ByVal value As Decimal)

Public Shared explicit operator Sub **Char**(ByVal value As Decimal)

Public Shared explicit operator Sub **Decimal**(ByVal value As Double)

Public Shared explicit operator Sub **Decimal**(ByVal value As Single)

Public Shared explicit operator Sub **Double**(ByVal value As Decimal)

Public Shared explicit operator Sub **Short**(ByVal value As Decimal)

Public Shared explicit operator Sub **Integer**(ByVal value As Decimal)

Public Shared explicit operator Sub **Long**(ByVal value As Decimal)

Public Shared explicit operator Sub **SByte**(ByVal value As Decimal)

Public Shared explicit operator Sub **Single**(ByVal value As Decimal)

Public Shared explicit operator Sub **UInt16**(ByVal value As Decimal)

Public Shared explicit operator Sub **UInt32**(ByVal value As Decimal)

Public Shared explicit operator Sub **UInt64**(ByVal value As Decimal)

Public Shared implicit operator Sub **Decimal**(ByVal value As Byte)

Public Shared implicit operator Sub **Decimal**(ByVal value As Char)

Public Shared implicit operator Sub **Decimal**(ByVal value As Short)

Public Shared implicit operator Sub **Decimal**(ByVal value As Integer)

Public Shared implicit operator Sub **Decimal**(ByVal value As Long)

Public Shared implicit operator Sub **Decimal**(ByVal value As SByte)

Public Shared implicit operator Sub **Decimal**(ByVal value As UInt16)

Public Shared implicit operator Sub **Decimal**(ByVal value As UInt32)

Public Shared implicit operator Sub **Decimal**(ByVal value As UInt64)

' *Public Instance Methods*

Public Function **CompareTo**(ByVal value As Object) As Integer Implements IComparable.CompareTo

Overrides Public Function **Equals**(ByVal value As Object) As Boolean

Overrides Public Function **GetHashCode**() As Integer

Public Function **GetTypeCode**() As TypeCode Implements IConvertible.GetTypeCode

Overrides Public Function **ToString**() As String
Public Function **ToString**(ByVal provider As IFormatProvider) As String Implements IConvertible.ToString
Public Function **ToString**(ByVal format As String) As String
Public Function **ToString**(ByVal format As String, ByVal provider As IFormatProvider) As String _
    Implements IFormattable.ToString
End Structure

Hierarchy: Object→ ValueType→ Decimal(IFormattable, IComparable, IConvertible)

Returned By: Convert.ToDecimal(), IConvertible.ToDecimal(), System.IO.BinaryReader.ReadDecimal(),
System.Runtime.InteropServices.CurrencyWrapper.WrappedObject,
System.Runtime.Serialization.FormatterConverter.ToDecimal(),
System.Runtime.Serialization.IFormatterConverter.ToDecimal(),
System.Runtime.Serialization.SerializationInfo.GetDecimal(), System.Xml.XmlConvert.ToDecimal()

Passed To: Multiple types

Delegate

MustInherit Class

System (mscorlib.dll)

ECMA, serializable

A delegate is used to provide a decoupling of caller from callee; that is, a delegate points to a given method (instance or shared) in a class, and callers can call through the delegate without having to know the target of the call. In many respects, the delegate is conceptually similar to the C/C++ *function pointer*, with a number of important advantages. A delegate is strongly typed, meaning that only methods that match the delegate's declared signature are acceptable when constructing the delegate instance, and the compiler enforces the delegate's declared signature when called. A delegate can distinguish between a shared and an instance method. This avoids the C++ application associated with pointers to member functions, which require a literal pointer to the object upon which to invoke the method.

Delegates are usually constructed by the language compiler, varying in syntax from language to language. In VB.NET, the construct Public Delegate Sub CallBackDelegate(param1 as Integer, param2 as String) declares a new type that derives from the Delegate type (its immediate superclass is actually MulticastDelegate). This new CallbackDelegate type is also declared with a constructor (to take the method to call when the delegate is invoked) and an Invoke method (to do the actual call), along with asynchronous versions of Invoke (the BeginInvoke and EndInvoke methods).

In many cases, you will want to use delegates as an *invocation chain*, where a single call to the delegate should result in a series of calls against a collection of delegate targets. (This is most easily seen in .NET's publish-subscribe event-handling idiom—VB.NET's Event keyword.) To achieve this, Delegate contains shared methods allowing delegates to combine into a single delegate instance that calls into multiple delegate targets. The Combine() method takes two existing delegate instances (with identical signatures) and returns a single delegate instance that calls both targets when invoked. (There is another form of Combine() that takes an array of delegates instead of just a pair.) Remove() does the opposite of Combine(), removing a delegate from the multicast call chain. (See the MulticastDelegate entry for more information on multicast delegates.)

Delegates can also be invoked using the DynamicInvoke() method, without knowing the actual concretely generated Delegate subtype. This method expects an array of object references, whose type should match those of the expected parameters to the delegate. If any of the parameters to DynamicInvoke() do not match those expected by the target method, an exception is thrown. Delegates can also be constructed in the same generic fashion using one of the overloaded forms of CreateDelegate().

Delegates can be invoked either synchronously or asynchronously. To invoke a delegate synchronously (that is, block until the call(s) return), simply use the delegate as if it is a method. The call to a delegate is executed completely before execution resumes in the calling method. Should you wish the call to the delegate to occur in parallel with the calling method, use the BeginInvoke method to start execution and the EndInvoke method to wait for the asynchronous delegate call's completion (if it hasn't finished by the time the EndInvoke call is made). If any of the delegate's parameters are declared as ref or out parameters, these parameters will be available on the parameter list to EndInvoke.

```
Public MustInherit Class Delegate : Implements ICloneable, System.Runtime.Serialization.ISerializable
' Protected Constructors
   Protected Sub New(ByVal target As Object, ByVal method As String)
   Protected Sub New(ByVal target As Type, ByVal method As String)
' Public Instance Properties
   Public ReadOnly Property Method As MethodInfo
   Public ReadOnly Property Target As Object
' Public Shared Methods
   Public Shared Function Combine(ByVal delegates As Delegate()) As Delegate
   Public Shared Function Combine(ByVal a As Delegate, ByVal b As Delegate) As Delegate
   Public Shared Function CreateDelegate(ByVal type As Type, ByVal method As System.Reflection.MethodInfo) _
      As Delegate
   Public Shared Function CreateDelegate(ByVal type As Type, ByVal target As Object, ByVal method As String) _
      As Delegate
   Public Shared Function CreateDelegate(ByVal type As Type, ByVal target As Object, ByVal method As String, _
      ByVal ignoreCase As Boolean)  As Delegate
   Public Shared Function CreateDelegate(ByVal type As Type, ByVal target As Type, ByVal method As String) _
      As Delegate
   Public Shared Function Remove(ByVal source As Delegate, ByVal value As Delegate) As Delegate
   Public Shared Boolean operator Sub !=(ByVal d1 As Delegate, ByVal d2 As Delegate)
   Public Shared Boolean operator Sub ==(ByVal d1 As Delegate, ByVal d2 As Delegate)
' Public Instance Methods
   Overridable Public Function Clone() As Object Implements ICloneable.Clone
   Public Function DynamicInvoke(ByVal args As Object()) As Object
   Overrides Public Function Equals(ByVal obj As Object) As Boolean
   Overrides Public Function GetHashCode() As Integer
   Overridable Public Function GetInvocationList() As Delegate()
   Overridable Public Sub GetObjectData(ByVal info As System.Runtime.Serialization.SerializationInfo, _
      ByVal context As System.Runtime.Serialization.StreamingContext)  Implements  ISerializable.GetObjectData
' Protected Instance Methods
   Overridable Protected Function CombineImpl(ByVal d As Delegate) As Delegate
   Overridable Protected Function DynamicInvokeImpl(ByVal args As Object()) As Object
   Overridable Protected Function GetMethodImpl() As MethodInfo
   Overridable Protected Function RemoveImpl(ByVal d As Delegate) As Delegate
End Class
```

Subclasses: MulticastDelegate

Returned By: MulticastDelegate.{CombineImpl(), GetInvocationList(), RemoveImpl()}

Passed To: Microsoft.Win32.SystemEvents.InvokeOnEventsThread(),
MulticastDelegate.{CombineImpl(), RemoveImpl()}, System.Reflection.EventInfo.{AddEventHandler(),
RemoveEventHandler()}, System.Runtime.InteropServices.Expando.IExpando.AddMethod()

DivideByZeroException
Class

System (mscorlib.dll)
ECMA, serializable

This exception is thrown when a math operation attempts to divide by zero.

Public Class **DivideByZeroException** : Inherits ArithmeticException
 ' Public Constructors
  Public Sub **New**()
  Public Sub **New**(ByVal message As String)
  Public Sub **New**(ByVal message As String, ByVal innerException As Exception)
 ' Protected Constructors
  Protected Sub **New**(ByVal info As System.Runtime.Serialization.SerializationInfo, _
    ByVal context As System.Runtime.Serialization.StreamingContext)
End Class

Hierarchy: Object→ Exception(System.Runtime.Serialization.ISerializable)→ SystemException→ ArithmeticException→ DivideByZeroException

DllNotFoundException
Class

System (mscorlib.dll)
serializable

This exception indicates that the file specified in a DLL import could not be found (see System.Runtime.InteropServices.DllImportAttribute). This exception is thrown only when you attempt to link against a method declared using the P/Invoke features of .NET. Any managed DLL (such as those produced by C# or Visual Basic .NET) that cannot be found instead generates TypeLoadExceptions when you attempt to resolve types out of an assembly that cannot be found.

Public Class **DllNotFoundException** : Inherits TypeLoadException
 ' Public Constructors
  Public Sub **New**()
  Public Sub **New**(ByVal message As String)
  Public Sub **New**(ByVal message As String, ByVal inner As Exception)
 ' Protected Constructors
  Protected Sub **New**(ByVal info As System.Runtime.Serialization.SerializationInfo, _
    ByVal context As System.Runtime.Serialization.StreamingContext)
End Class

Hierarchy: Object→ Exception(System.Runtime.Serialization.ISerializable)→ SystemException→ TypeLoadException→ DllNotFoundException

Double
Structure

System (mscorlib.dll)
ECMA, serializable

This represents a 64-bit double-precision floating number as a value type. The value of a double can range, approximately from -1.8×10^{308} to 1.8×10^{308} and can be set to one of the following fields: PositiveInfinity, NegativeInfinity, and NaN (not a number). This type is aliased as Double in VB.NET.

Public Structure **Double** : Implements IComparable, IFormattable, IConvertible
 ' Public Shared Fields

Public const **Epsilon** As Double	*=4.94065645841247E-324*
Public const **MaxValue** As Double	*=1.79769313486232E+308*
Public const **MinValue** As Double	*=-1.79769313486232E+308*
Public const **NaN** As Double	*=NaN*
Public const **NegativeInfinity** As Double	*=-Infinity*
Public const **PositiveInfinity** As Double	*=Infinity*

 ' Public Shared Methods

Public Shared Function **IsInfinity**(ByVal d As Double) As Boolean
Public Shared Function **IsNaN**(ByVal d As Double) As Boolean
Public Shared Function **IsNegativeInfinity**(ByVal d As Double) As Boolean
Public Shared Function **IsPositiveInfinity**(ByVal d As Double) As Boolean
Public Shared Function **Parse**(ByVal s As String) As Double
Public Shared Function **Parse**(ByVal s As String, ByVal provider As IFormatProvider) As Double
Public Shared Function **Parse**(ByVal s As String, ByVal style As System.Globalization.NumberStyles) As Double
Public Shared Function **Parse**(ByVal s As String, ByVal style As System.Globalization.NumberStyles, _
 ByVal provider As IFormatProvider) As Double
Public Shared Function **TryParse**(ByVal s As String, ByVal style As System.Globalization.NumberStyles, _
 ByVal provider As IFormatProvider, ByRef result As Double) As Boolean
' Public Instance Methods
Public Function **CompareTo**(ByVal value As Object) As Integer Implements IComparable.CompareTo
Overrides Public Function **Equals**(ByVal obj As Object) As Boolean
Overrides Public Function **GetHashCode**() As Integer
Public Function **GetTypeCode**() As TypeCode Implements IConvertible.GetTypeCode
Overrides Public Function **ToString**() As String
Public Function **ToString**(ByVal provider As IFormatProvider) As String Implements IConvertible.ToString
Public Function **ToString**(ByVal format As String) As String
Public Function **ToString**(ByVal format As String, ByVal provider As IFormatProvider) As String _
 Implements IFormattable.ToString
End Structure

Hierarchy: Object→ ValueType→ Double(IComparable, IFormattable, IConvertible)

Returned By: Multiple types

Passed To: Multiple types

DuplicateWaitObjectException   Class
System (mscorlib.dll)   *ECMA, serializable*

This exception is thrown when an object shows up more than once in the array passed
to System.Threading.WaitHandle.WaitAll() or System.Threading.WaitHandle.WaitAny().

Public Class **DuplicateWaitObjectException** : Inherits ArgumentException
' Public Constructors
Public Sub **New**()
Public Sub **New**(ByVal parameterName As String)
Public Sub **New**(ByVal parameterName As String, ByVal message As String)
' Protected Constructors
Protected Sub **New**(ByVal info As System.Runtime.Serialization.SerializationInfo, _
 ByVal context As System.Runtime.Serialization.StreamingContext)
End Class

Hierarchy: Object→ Exception(System.Runtime.Serialization.ISerializable)→ SystemException→
ArgumentException→ DuplicateWaitObjectException

EntryPointNotFoundException   Class
System (mscorlib.dll)   *ECMA, serializable*

This exception indicates that an entry point could not be found when .NET loaded an
assembly flagged for execution; that is, an AppDomain was instructed to execute an
assembly, but no method in that assembly was marked with the .entrypoint metadata
flag.

Public Class **EntryPointNotFoundException** : Inherits TypeLoadException
' Public Constructors

```
   Public Sub New()
   Public Sub New(ByVal message As String)
   Public Sub New(ByVal message As String, ByVal inner As Exception)
' Protected Constructors
   Protected Sub New(ByVal info As System.Runtime.Serialization.SerializationInfo, _
      ByVal context As System.Runtime.Serialization.StreamingContext)
End Class
```

Hierarchy: Object→ Exception(System.Runtime.Serialization.ISerializable)→ SystemException→ TypeLoadException→ EntryPointNotFoundException

Enum   MustInherit Class

System (mscorlib.dll)   *ECMA, serializable*

This is the base class for all enumerations. In VB.NET, you can use the Enum keyword to create an enumeration type consisting of named constants and their values. By default, the underlying type used for enumeration elements is Int32, but you can use any integer data type.

```
Public MustInherit Class Enum : Inherits ValueType : Implements IComparable , IFormattable, IConvertible
' Protected Constructors
   Protected Sub New()
' Public Shared Methods
   Public Shared Function Format(ByVal enumType As Type, ByVal value As Object, ByVal format As String) As String
   Public Shared Function GetName(ByVal enumType As Type, ByVal value As Object) As String
   Public Shared Function GetNames(ByVal enumType As Type) As String()
   Public Shared Function GetUnderlyingType(ByVal enumType As Type) As Type
   Public Shared Function GetValues(ByVal enumType As Type) As Array
   Public Shared Function IsDefined(ByVal enumType As Type, ByVal value As Object) As Boolean
   Public Shared Function Parse(ByVal enumType As Type, ByVal value As String) As Object
   Public Shared Function Parse(ByVal enumType As Type, ByVal value As String, ByVal ignoreCase As Boolean) _
      As Object
   Public Shared Function ToObject(ByVal enumType As Type, ByVal value As Byte) As Object
   Public Shared Function ToObject(ByVal enumType As Type, ByVal value As Short) As Object
   Public Shared Function ToObject(ByVal enumType As Type, ByVal value As Integer) As Object
   Public Shared Function ToObject(ByVal enumType As Type, ByVal value As Long) As Object
   Public Shared Function ToObject(ByVal enumType As Type, ByVal value As Object) As Object
   Public Shared Function ToObject(ByVal enumType As Type, ByVal value As SByte) As Object
   Public Shared Function ToObject(ByVal enumType As Type, ByVal value As UInt16) As Object
   Public Shared Function ToObject(ByVal enumType As Type, ByVal value As UInt32) As Object
   Public Shared Function ToObject(ByVal enumType As Type, ByVal value As UInt64) As Object
' Public Instance Methods
   Public Function CompareTo(ByVal target As Object) As Integer Implements IComparable.CompareTo
   Overrides Public Function Equals(ByVal obj As Object) As Boolean
   Overrides Public Function GetHashCode() As Integer
   Public Function GetTypeCode() As TypeCode Implements IConvertible.GetTypeCode
   Overrides Public Function ToString() As String
   Public Function ToString(ByVal provider As IFormatProvider) As String Implements IConvertible.ToString
   Public Function ToString(ByVal format As String) As String
   Public Function ToString(ByVal format As String, ByVal provider As IFormatProvider) As String _
      Implements IFormattable.ToString
End Class
```

Hierarchy: Object→ ValueType→ Enum(IComparable, IFormattable, IConvertible)

Subclasses: Multiple types

Environment

System (mscorlib.dll)   *ECMA*

This class represents an application's operating environment, which includes details about the operating system, the current user, and other environment variables. This information is provided through shared properties and some helper methods.

You can retrieve command-line arguments as a string from CommandLine or as an array of strings using GetCommandLineArgs(). Use the GetLogicalDrives() method to get an array of strings containing drive names (for example, C:\), and use the GetFolderPath() method to get the physical location of a special system folder. You can also retrieve environment variables by key name using the GetEnvironmentVariable() method and automatically replace environment variables in a string with the ExpandEnvironmentVariables() method, as long as they are delimited with the percent sign (%). For example, on a system with the environment variable MAC_ADDR set to 123456789012, the string MAC_ADDR=%MAC_ADDR% would be converted to MAC_ADDR=123456789012.

```
Public NotInheritable Class Environment
' Public Shared Properties
   Public Shared ReadOnly Property CommandLine As String
   Public Shared Property CurrentDirectory As String
   Public Shared Property ExitCode As Integer
   Public Shared ReadOnly Property MachineName As String
   Public Shared ReadOnly Property NewLine As String
   Public Shared ReadOnly Property OSVersion As OperatingSystem
   Public Shared ReadOnly Property StackTrace As String
   Public Shared ReadOnly Property SystemDirectory As String
   Public Shared ReadOnly Property TickCount As Integer
   Public Shared ReadOnly Property UserDomainName As String
   Public Shared ReadOnly Property UserInteractive As Boolean
   Public Shared ReadOnly Property UserName As String
   Public Shared ReadOnly Property Version As Version
   Public Shared ReadOnly Property WorkingSet As Long
' Public Instance Properties
   Public ReadOnly Property HasShutdownStarted As Boolean
' Public Shared Methods
   Public Shared Sub Exit(ByVal exitCode As Integer)
   Public Shared Function ExpandEnvironmentVariables(ByVal name As String) As String
   Public Shared Function GetCommandLineArgs() As String()
   Public Shared Function GetEnvironmentVariable(ByVal variable As String) As String
   Public Shared Function GetEnvironmentVariables() As IDictionary
   Public Shared Function GetFolderPath(ByVal folder As SpecialFolder) As String
   Public Shared Function GetLogicalDrives() As String()
End Class
```

Environment.SpecialFolder

Enum

System (mscorlib.dll)   *serializable*

This enumeration is used by the Environment.GetFolderPath() method to allow you to retrieve the physical path of commonly used system (or "special") folders, including everything from the Internet cache to the Start menu.

```
Public Enum Environment.SpecialFolder
      Programs = 2
      Personal = 5
      Favorites = 6
```

```
    Startup = 7
    Recent = 8
    SendTo = 9
    StartMenu = 11
    DesktopDirectory = 16
    Templates = 21
    ApplicationData = 26
    LocalApplicationData = 28
    InternetCache = 32
    Cookies = 33
    History = 34
    CommonApplicationData = 35
    System = 37
    ProgramFiles = 38
    CommonProgramFiles = 43
End Enum
```

Hierarchy: Object→ ValueType→ Enum(IComparable, IFormattable, IConvertible)→ SpecialFolder

EventArgs   Class

System (mscorlib.dll)   *ECMA, serializable*

See the EventHandler entry for details regarding the EventArgs/EventHandler idiom for delegates in .NET. If .NET developers wish to follow this idiom, they should create new subtypes of EventArgs for each new collection of data to be sent to interested parties; otherwise, they should pass Empty, indicating that no event data is to be passed as part of this event notification.

```
Public Class EventArgs
' Public Constructors
   Public Sub New()
' Public Shared Fields
   Public Shared ReadOnly Empty As EventArgs                        =System.EventArgs
End Class
```

Subclasses: Multiple types

Passed To: EventHandler.{BeginInvoke(), Invoke()}

EventHandler   Delegate

System (mscorlib.dll)   *ECMA, serializable*

Shortly after Beta 1 of .NET was released, Microsoft .NET developers realized that prolific use of delegates could easily lead to type-bloat; since each declared delegate created a new type in the system, a large number of delegates would lead to a huge number of types to load, verify, and initialize. In Beta 2, Microsoft introduced an idiom that, it's hoped, will keep type-bloat down to reasonable levels in .NET.

Microsoft defines two types, EventHandler (a delegate type) and EventArgs, a glorified C construct. EventHandler is declared to expect two parameters: an object reference indicating the sender of the event, and an event data parameter (the EventArgs or some derived-type instance).

This delegate represents the base type for .NET event handlers. (In Beta 2 and later, all .NET Framework Class Library types with declared events use this same idiom, so as to remain consistent.) Its arguments include a sender parameter, which refers to the object that issued the event, and an e parameter, which contains additional event data. Events that do not require additional information use the EventHandler delegate directly.

Events that need to send additional information derive their own custom delegate from this type. Custom event delegates look similar, except that they replace the EventArgs parameter with a custom object derived from EventArgs. This object contains additional properties or methods that are specific to the event.

Public Delegate Sub **EventHandler**(ByVal sender As Object, ByVal e As EventArgs)

Associated Events: Multiple types

Exception   Class

System (mscorlib.dll)   *ECMA, serializable*

This is the base class for all .NET exceptions. .NET Framework exceptions are generally derived from SystemException, and user-defined exceptions are generally derived from ApplicationException.

In some cases, one exception may throw another; this is often the case when using layered architectures. For example, a persistence layer may throw a persistence-related exception (DatabaseNotFoundException), whose semantics are undefined at a higher level (such as the UI layer). In this case, a middle layer may throw a new exception-derived type (such as PersistenceException), but doesn't wish to lose the original source of the exception—instead, it wraps the original exception by setting it to be the InnerException. In this way, a layer can communicate a lower-level exception to higher layers without losing information or violating encapsulation.

The StackTrace property is a string containing the stacktrace. This permits determination of the call sequence leading up to the line that threw the exception. HelpLink contains a link to a help file with information about the exception. Message contains a text message that describes the exception.

Public Class **Exception** : Implements System.Runtime.Serialization.ISerializable
' *Public Constructors*
  Public Sub **New**()
  Public Sub **New**(ByVal message As String)
  Public Sub **New**(ByVal message As String, ByVal innerException As Exception)
' *Protected Constructors*
  Protected Sub **New**(ByVal info As System.Runtime.Serialization.SerializationInfo, _
    ByVal context As System.Runtime.Serialization.StreamingContext)
' *Public Instance Properties*
  Overridable Public Property **HelpLink** As String
  Public ReadOnly Property **InnerException** As Exception
  Overridable Public ReadOnly Property **Message** As String
  Overridable Public Property **Source** As String
  Overridable Public ReadOnly Property **StackTrace** As String
  Public ReadOnly Property **TargetSite** As MethodBase
' *Protected Instance Properties*
  Protected Property **HResult** As Integer
' *Public Instance Methods*
  Overridable Public Function **GetBaseException**() As Exception
  Overridable Public Sub **GetObjectData**(ByVal info As System.Runtime.Serialization.SerializationInfo, _
    ByVal context As System.Runtime.Serialization.StreamingContext) Implements ISerializable.GetObjectData
  Overrides Public Function **ToString**() As String
End Class

Subclasses: ApplicationException, SystemException,
System.IO.IsolatedStorage.IsolatedStorageException

Returned By: System.IO.ErrorEventArgs.GetException(),
System.Reflection.ReflectionTypeLoadException.LoaderExceptions,
System.Threading.ThreadExceptionEventArgs.Exception

Passed To: Multiple types

ExecutionEngineException

NotInheritable Class

System (mscorlib.dll)

ECMA, serializable

This exception indicates that an error has occurred deep within the innards of the .NET CLR.

```
Public NotInheritable Class ExecutionEngineException : Inherits SystemException
' Public Constructors
  Public Sub New()
  Public Sub New(ByVal message As String)
  Public Sub New(ByVal message As String, ByVal innerException As Exception)
End Class
```

Hierarchy: Object→ Exception(System.Runtime.Serialization.ISerializable)→ SystemException→ ExecutionEngineException

FieldAccessException

Class

System (mscorlib.dll)

ECMA, serializable

This exception is thrown when you try to access a protected or private field that you would not normally have access to. Most compilers will not let you compile code that does this directly. However, late-bound code can sneak by the compiler and throw this exception at runtime. For example, if you lack sufficient privileges to modify a field using System.Reflection.FieldInfo.SetValue(), this exception is thrown.

```
Public Class FieldAccessException : Inherits MemberAccessException
' Public Constructors
  Public Sub New()
  Public Sub New(ByVal message As String)
  Public Sub New(ByVal message As String, ByVal inner As Exception)
' Protected Constructors
  Protected Sub New(ByVal info As System.Runtime.Serialization.SerializationInfo, _
    ByVal context As System.Runtime.Serialization.StreamingContext)
End Class
```

Hierarchy: Object→ Exception(System.Runtime.Serialization.ISerializable)→ SystemException→ MemberAccessException→ FieldAccessException

FlagsAttribute

Class

System (mscorlib.dll)

ECMA, serializable

This attribute indicates that an enumeration should be treated as a set of on/off flags (i.e., a bit field). Unlike enumerated constants, bit fields can be combined with a bitwise OR operation.

```
Public Class FlagsAttribute : Inherits Attribute
' Public Constructors
  Public Sub New()
End Class
```

Hierarchy: Object→ Attribute→ FlagsAttribute

Valid On: Enum

FormatException
Class

System (mscorlib.dll)
ECMA, serializable

This exception signals that an error occurred during the handling of a format string. Format strings are used by methods such as Console.WriteLine() to replace a format specification with one or more parameters. This exception may be triggered by supplying too few arguments to replace all the format strings (for example, supplying only two arguments to Console.WriteLine() when your format string is "{0} {1} {2}").

Public Class **FormatException** : Inherits SystemException
' Public Constructors
  Public Sub **New**()
  Public Sub **New**(ByVal message As String)
  Public Sub **New**(ByVal message As String, ByVal innerException As Exception)
' Protected Constructors
  Protected Sub **New**(ByVal info As System.Runtime.Serialization.SerializationInfo, _
    ByVal context As System.Runtime.Serialization.StreamingContext)
End Class

Hierarchy: Object→ Exception(System.Runtime.Serialization.ISerializable)→ SystemException→ FormatException

Subclasses: UriFormatException, System.Net.CookieException, System.Reflection.CustomAttributeFormatException

GC
NotInheritable Class

System (mscorlib.dll)
ECMA

This class allows you to control garbage collection programmatically. Garbage collection is the .NET service that periodically scans for unreferenced objects and reclaims the memory they occupy.

The garbage-collection service distinguishes between older and more recently allocated memory using *generations*. The most recently allocated memory is considered generation zero, and the oldest memory is in generation MaxGeneration. Because new allocations are likely to be freed before long-standing memory allocations, the garbage collector improves its performance by concentrating on lower generations of memory. You can find out the generation of an object using the GetGeneration() method. You can also get the number of memory bytes that are currently allocated using the GetTotalMemory() method. A forceFullCollection parameter indicates whether this method should wait a short interval before returning to collect and finalize some objects.

To force a *full sweep* garbage collection, use the Collect() method. You can improve performance by specifying the maximum generation that will be examined. Generally, it is best to let .NET perform garbage collection automatically when the system is idle.

Some developers have lamented a noticeable lack of *deterministic finalization* within a garbage-collected system; that is, because the object's lifetime is under the control of the garbage collector, there is no guarantee that an object is destroyed as soon as it becomes unreferenced. One approach used to try to compensate for this phenomenon is to call GC repeatedly in an effort to force the object's cleanup. This is both time-consuming and wasteful of the garbage collector's efforts, since a collection may involve not only recollection, but readjustment of object locations in memory. If a programmer requires more explicit control over when an object is cleaned up, the class can be declared as implementing the IDisposable interface (which consists of a single method, Dispose()). Use of IDisposable is recommended over the use of Finalize() methods. This is due to a variety of reasons too numerous to explore here.

The KeepAlive() method is used to preserve the life of an object that is not strongly referenced. This is sometimes required when interacting with methods in unmanaged code (such as Win32 APIs or COM). The KeepAlive() method works in an unusual manner: it makes an object ineligible for garbage collection from the start of the current routine to the point where the KeepAlive() method is called. This unusual system prevents problems that could otherwise be created by compiler optimizations.

```
Public NotInheritable Class GC
' Public Shared Properties
   Public Shared ReadOnly Property MaxGeneration As Integer
' Public Shared Methods
   Public Shared Sub Collect()
   Public Shared Sub Collect(ByVal generation As Integer)
   Public Shared Function GetGeneration(ByVal obj As Object) As Integer
   Public Shared Function GetGeneration(ByVal wo As WeakReference) As Integer
   Public Shared Function GetTotalMemory(ByVal forceFullCollection As Boolean) As Long
   Public Shared Sub KeepAlive(ByVal obj As Object)
   Public Shared Sub ReRegisterForFinalize(ByVal obj As Object)
   Public Shared Sub SuppressFinalize(ByVal obj As Object)
   Public Shared Sub WaitForPendingFinalizers()
End Class
```

Guid   Structure
System (mscorlib.dll)   *serializable*

This value type represents a Globally Unique Identifier (GUID). A GUID is a 128-bit integer (16 bytes) that can be used across all computers and networks and will be statistically unique (for all practical purposes, the number cannot be duplicated coincidentally). GUIDs are used to identify COM (but not .NET) objects uniquely for registration purposes.

```
Public Structure Guid : Implements IFormattable, IComparable
' Public Constructors
   Public Sub New(ByVal b As Byte())
   Public Sub New(ByVal a As Integer, ByVal b As Short, ByVal c As Short, ByVal d As Byte())
   Public Sub New(ByVal g As String)
' Public Shared Fields
   Public Shared ReadOnly Empty As Guid                  =00000000-0000-0000-0000-000000000000
' Public Shared Methods
   Public Shared Function NewGuid() As Guid
   Public Shared Boolean operator Sub !=(ByVal a As Guid, ByVal b As Guid)
   Public Shared Boolean operator Sub ==(ByVal a As Guid, ByVal b As Guid)
' Public Instance Methods
   Public Function CompareTo(ByVal value As Object) As Integer Implements IComparable.CompareTo
   Overrides Public Function Equals(ByVal o As Object) As Boolean
   Overrides Public Function GetHashCode() As Integer
   Public Function ToByteArray() As Byte()
   Overrides Public Function ToString() As String
   Public Function ToString(ByVal format As String) As String
   Public Function ToString(ByVal format As String, ByVal provider As IFormatProvider) As String _
      Implements IFormattable.ToString
End Structure
```

Hierarchy: Object→ ValueType→ Guid(IFormattable, IComparable)

Returned By: System.Reflection.Emit.UnmanagedMarshal.IIDGuid, System.Runtime.InteropServices.IRegistrationServices.GetManagedCategoryGuid(), System.Runtime.InteropServices.Marshal.{GenerateGuidForType(), GetTypeLibGuid(), GetTypeLibGuidForAssembly()},

System.Runtime.InteropServices.RegistrationServices.GetManagedCategoryGuid(), Type.GUID,
System.Xml.XmlConvert.ToGuid()

Passed To: System.Reflection.Emit.ModuleBuilder.DefineDocument(),
System.Runtime.InteropServices.IRegistrationServices.RegisterTypeForComClients(),
System.Runtime.InteropServices.Marshal.QueryInterface(),
System.Runtime.InteropServices.RegistrationServices.RegisterTypeForComClients(),
Type.GetTypeFromCLSID(), System.Xml.XmlConvert.ToString()

IAsyncResult

Interface

System (mscorlib.dll)

ECMA

This interface is used in asynchronous programming to act as a placeholder for the result of the async call. It is most commonly used when an instance of a delegate type is fired using the BeginInvoke method. (This idiom is used extensively throughout the .NET Framework Class Library.)

Asynchronous method calls can be harvested in a number of ways. A programmer can poll the call by checking the IsCompleted property of the IAsyncResult object to see if the call has completed yet. This, while perhaps the simplest approach, is also likely the most wasteful, as the caller needs to be in some sort of spin loop, repeatedly checking the property until a true is received.

A variant of the polling spin loop is to use the AsyncWaitHandle property of IAsyncResult. This is a standard Win32 handle that can be used in some of the synchronization primitives provided in the System.Threading namespace. Specifically, this property is a System.Threading.WaitHandle instance, meaning that the programmer can call any of the Wait methods: WaitOne(), WaitAny(), or WaitAll(). The net effect is the same—put the calling thread to sleep until the async call completes.

Although not formally part of the IAsyncResult interface, a corresponding EndInvoke method is supported by delegates. The EndInvoke method blocks the calling thread until the async call completes. Alternatively, at the point of the async delegate call, a programmer can specify a callback delegate to call when the async call completes. This callback, a delegate instance of type AsyncCallback, is passed this IAsyncResult instance as part of the call. An optional generic argument can also be passed in as part of the async call, and this generic argument is available on the IAsyncResult through the AsyncState property.

Public Interface **IAsyncResult**
' Public Instance Properties
   Public ReadOnly Property **AsyncState** As Object
   Public ReadOnly Property **AsyncWaitHandle** As WaitHandle
   Public ReadOnly Property **CompletedSynchronously** As Boolean
   Public ReadOnly Property **IsCompleted** As Boolean
End Interface

Returned By: Multiple types

Passed To: Multiple types

ICloneable

Interface

System (mscorlib.dll)

ECMA

ICloneable is a marker interface, indicating that an object can be cloned (that is, have a completely identical copy created). It consists of a single method, Clone(), which is called by clients wishing to create a complete copy of the ICloneable-implementing class.

When speaking of cloning, the terms *deep copy cloning* and *shallow copy cloning* indicate how deeply into the object graph a clone operation will carry itself. A deep copy not only clones the object called, but in turn seeks to clone any objects to which it holds reference. This sort of operation must be handled by the programmer, usually by calling Clone() in turn on each object this object references. A shallow copy is a complete bitwise copy of this object; any objects referenced by this object are also referenced by the cloned object.

The simplest way to implement a shallow clone is to use the Object.MemberwiseClone() method to copy this object's fields directly and then return. A deep clone also calls MemberwiseClone(), but then also asks each object reference held within this object to Clone() itself.

```
Public Interface ICloneable
' Public Instance Methods
    Public Function Clone() As Object
End Interface
```

Implemented By: Multiple types

IComparable   Interface
System (mscorlib.dll)   *ECMA*

This interface is implemented by classes that can be ordered in a list. Classes such as String and Int32 implement this interface. You can also implement it in your own classes to create a type-specific method that allows your objects to be sorted in arrays. This interface does not allow classes to be compared with the greater-than and less-than operators. This interface simply provides a well-known protocol for doing comparisons of objects.

To implement IComparable, override the CompareTo() method. This method accepts another instance of your IComparable object and returns an integer that indicates the result of the comparison. (Zero means equal, less than zero indicates that the supplied object is less than the current instance, and greater than zero indicates that the object is greater than the current instance.) Note that the actual value of the integer is irrelevant other than its positive, negative, or zero status (similar to the way strcmp works in C). Also note that because CompareTo() accepts an argument of IComparable type, care must be taken to ensure that it is a legitimate comparison—for example, myInt.CompareTo(myString) throws an ArgumentException.

```
Public Interface IComparable
' Public Instance Methods
    Public Function CompareTo(ByVal obj As Object) As Integer
End Interface
```

Implemented By: Multiple types

IConvertible   Interface
System (mscorlib.dll)

The IConvertible interface allows conversion of an object to basic data types and allows the conversion methods in the Convert class to use that object. When implementing the IConvertible interface, create your own type-specific methods for each of the supplied conversion methods.

Note that IConvertible allows one-way conversion from a custom type to other data types, but does not allow a conversion from a basic data type to a custom type.

```
Public Interface IConvertible
' Public Instance Methods
    Public Function GetTypeCode() As TypeCode
```

Public Function **ToBoolean**(ByVal provider As IFormatProvider) As Boolean
Public Function **ToByte**(ByVal provider As IFormatProvider) As Byte
Public Function **ToChar**(ByVal provider As IFormatProvider) As Char
Public Function **ToDateTime**(ByVal provider As IFormatProvider) As Date
Public Function **ToDecimal**(ByVal provider As IFormatProvider) As Decimal
Public Function **ToDouble**(ByVal provider As IFormatProvider) As Double
Public Function **ToInt16**(ByVal provider As IFormatProvider) As Short
Public Function **ToInt32**(ByVal provider As IFormatProvider) As Integer
Public Function **ToInt64**(ByVal provider As IFormatProvider) As Long
Public Function **ToSByte**(ByVal provider As IFormatProvider) As SByte
Public Function **ToSingle**(ByVal provider As IFormatProvider) As Single
Public Function **ToString**(ByVal provider As IFormatProvider) As String
Public Function **ToType**(ByVal conversionType As Type, ByVal provider As IFormatProvider) As Object
Public Function **ToUInt16**(ByVal provider As IFormatProvider) As UInt16
Public Function **ToUInt32**(ByVal provider As IFormatProvider) As UInt32
Public Function **ToUInt64**(ByVal provider As IFormatProvider) As UInt64
End Interface

Implemented By: Multiple types

ICustomFormatter   Interface

System (mscorlib.dll)

This interface provides a custom formatter, which returns string information for supplied objects based on custom criteria. The ICustomFormatter interface contains a single Format() method. This method accepts a format string and an IFormatProvider object and uses this criteria to determine which string to return for the specified object.

Public Interface **ICustomFormatter**
' *Public Instance Methods*
   Public Function **Format**(ByVal format As String, ByVal arg As Object, ByVal formatProvider As IFormatProvider) _
      As String
End Interface

IDisposable   Interface

System (mscorlib.dll)   *ECMA*

This interface provides a last-ditch cleanup hook with well-known timing semantics (similar in concept to a C++ destructor). This is called *deterministic finalization*.

As part of normal garbage-collection operation, the CLR looks for (and calls if available) the object's Finalize method right before it removes an object from heap memory. Unfortunately, because the CLR may not garbage-collect the object as soon as it becomes available for collection, objects may hold onto resources for longer than necessary. The IDisposable interface is intended to work with language constructs to let you ensure that key resources are released in a time-efficient manner.

Any object whose type implements the IDisposable interface must have a corresponding Dispose() method defined for it.

If a type provides a Finalize method, then it should also inherit this interface and provide a corresponding Dispose() method. In addition, once the Dispose() method is called, part of its implementation should be to call the GC.SuppressFinalize() method to prevent the garbage collector from finalizing this object again when garbage collection occurs.

Public Interface **IDisposable**
' *Public Instance Methods*
  Public Sub **Dispose**()
End Interface

Implemented By: Multiple types

IFormatProvider   Interface
System (mscorlib.dll)   *ECMA*

This interface provides a way to retrieve an object that controls formatting through the
GetFormat() method. For example, the System.Globalization.CultureInfo class can return a Sys-
tem.Globalization.NumberFormatInfo object, a System.Globalization.DateTimeFormatInfo object, or a
null reference, depending on the supplied formatType parameter.

Public Interface **IFormatProvider**
' *Public Instance Methods*
  Public Function **GetFormat**(ByVal formatType As Type) As Object
End Interface

Implemented By: System.Globalization.{ CultureInfo, DateTimeFormatInfo, NumberFormatInfo}

Returned By: System.IO.TextWriter.FormatProvider

Passed To: Multiple types

IFormattable   Interface
System (mscorlib.dll)   *ECMA*

This interface is implemented in your objects to provide a custom ToString() method that
accepts a format string and an IFormatProvider instance. You can then use this information
to determine how the return string should be rendered. All numeric value types in the
System namespace implement this interface.

Public Interface **IFormattable**
' *Public Instance Methods*
  Public Function **ToString**(ByVal format As String, ByVal formatProvider As IFormatProvider) As String
End Interface

Implemented By: Multiple types

IndexOutOfRangeException   NotInheritable Class
System (mscorlib.dll)   *ECMA, serializable*

This exception signals an attempt to access an index beyond the bounds of a collection
or array.

Public NotInheritable Class **IndexOutOfRangeException** : Inherits SystemException
' *Public Constructors*
  Public Sub **New**()
  Public Sub **New**(ByVal message As String)
  Public Sub **New**(ByVal message As String, ByVal innerException As Exception)
End Class

Hierarchy: Object→ Exception(System.Runtime.Serialization.ISerializable)→ SystemException→
IndexOutOfRangeException

Int16
Structure

System (mscorlib.dll)
ECMA, serializable

This is the value type for 16-bit integers (which can range from –32768 to 32767). This is also available in VB.NET through the Short alias.

Public Structure **Int16** : Implements IComparable, IFormattable, IConvertible
' *Public Shared Fields*
   Public const **MaxValue** As Short =32767
   Public const **MinValue** As Short =-32768
' *Public Shared Methods*
   Public Shared Function **Parse**(ByVal s As String) As Short
   Public Shared Function **Parse**(ByVal s As String, ByVal provider As IFormatProvider) As Short
   Public Shared Function **Parse**(ByVal s As String, ByVal style As System.Globalization.NumberStyles) As Short
   Public Shared Function **Parse**(ByVal s As String, ByVal style As System.Globalization.NumberStyles, _
     ByVal provider As IFormatProvider) As Short
' *Public Instance Methods*
   Public Function **CompareTo**(ByVal value As Object) As Integer Implements IComparable.CompareTo
   Overrides Public Function **Equals**(ByVal obj As Object) As Boolean
   Overrides Public Function **GetHashCode**() As Integer
   Public Function **GetTypeCode**() As TypeCode Implements IConvertible.GetTypeCode
   Overrides Public Function **ToString**() As String
   Public Function **ToString**(ByVal provider As IFormatProvider) As String Implements IConvertible.ToString
   Public Function **ToString**(ByVal format As String) As String
   Public Function **ToString**(ByVal format As String, ByVal provider As IFormatProvider) As String _
     Implements IFormattable.ToString
End Structure

Hierarchy: Object→ ValueType→ Int16(IComparable, IFormattable, IConvertible)

Returned By: Multiple types

Passed To: Multiple types

Int32
Structure

System (mscorlib.dll)
ECMA, serializable

This is the value type for 32-bit integers (which can range from –2,147,483,648 to 2,147,483,647). This is also available in VB.NET through the Integer alias.

Public Structure **Int32** : Implements IComparable, IFormattable, IConvertible
' *Public Shared Fields*
   Public const **MaxValue** As Integer =2147483647
   Public const **MinValue** As Integer =-2147483648
' *Public Shared Methods*
   Public Shared Function **Parse**(ByVal s As String) As Integer
   Public Shared Function **Parse**(ByVal s As String, ByVal provider As IFormatProvider) As Integer
   Public Shared Function **Parse**(ByVal s As String, ByVal style As System.Globalization.NumberStyles) As Integer
   Public Shared Function **Parse**(ByVal s As String, ByVal style As System.Globalization.NumberStyles, _
     ByVal provider As IFormatProvider) As Integer
' *Public Instance Methods*
   Public Function **CompareTo**(ByVal value As Object) As Integer Implements IComparable.CompareTo
   Overrides Public Function **Equals**(ByVal obj As Object) As Boolean
   Overrides Public Function **GetHashCode**() As Integer
   Public Function **GetTypeCode**() As TypeCode Implements IConvertible.GetTypeCode
   Overrides Public Function **ToString**() As String
   Public Function **ToString**(ByVal provider As IFormatProvider) As String Implements IConvertible.ToString
   Public Function **ToString**(ByVal format As String) As String

```
Public Function ToString(ByVal format As String, ByVal provider As IFormatProvider) As String _
   Implements IFormattable.ToString
End Structure
```

Hierarchy: Object→ ValueType→ Int32(IComparable, IFormattable, IConvertible)

Returned By: Multiple types

Passed To: Multiple types

Int64   Structure

System (mscorlib.dll)   *ECMA, serializable*

This is the value type for 64-bit integers (which can range, approximately, from -9.22×10^{18} to 9.22×10^{18}). This is also available in VB.NET through the Long alias.

```
Public Structure Int64 : Implements IComparable, IFormattable, IConvertible
' Public Shared Fields
   Public const MaxValue As Long                                    =9223372036854775807
   Public const MinValue As Long                                    =-9223372036854775808
' Public Shared Methods
   Public Shared Function Parse(ByVal s As String) As Long
   Public Shared Function Parse(ByVal s As String, ByVal provider As IFormatProvider) As Long
   Public Shared Function Parse(ByVal s As String, ByVal style As System.Globalization.NumberStyles) As Long
   Public Shared Function Parse(ByVal s As String, ByVal style As System.Globalization.NumberStyles, _
      ByVal provider As IFormatProvider) As Long
' Public Instance Methods
   Public Function CompareTo(ByVal value As Object) As Integer Implements IComparable.CompareTo
   Overrides Public Function Equals(ByVal obj As Object) As Boolean
   Overrides Public Function GetHashCode() As Integer
   Public Function GetTypeCode() As TypeCode Implements IConvertible.GetTypeCode
   Overrides Public Function ToString() As String
   Public Function ToString(ByVal provider As IFormatProvider) As String Implements IConvertible.ToString
   Public Function ToString(ByVal format As String) As String
   Public Function ToString(ByVal format As String, ByVal provider As IFormatProvider) As String _
      Implements IFormattable.ToString
End Structure
```

Hierarchy: Object→ ValueType→ Int64(IComparable, IFormattable, IConvertible)

Returned By: Multiple types

Passed To: Multiple types

IntPtr   Structure

System (mscorlib.dll)   *ECMA, serializable*

This is the value type used to store unmanaged pointers or handles (e.g., IntPtr objects are used in the System.IO.FileStream class to hold file handles).

Using this type allows your pointers to be platform-independent, as IntPtr is automatically mapped to a 32-bit integer on 32-bit operating systems and to a 64-bit integer on 64-bit operating systems. The IntPtr type is CLS-compliant and should be used in preference of the UIntPtr.

```
Public Structure IntPtr : Implements System.Runtime.Serialization.ISerializable
' Public Constructors
   Public Sub New(ByVal value As Integer)
   Public Sub New(ByVal value As Long)
```

' *Public Shared Fields*
   Public Shared ReadOnly **Zero** As IntPtr   *=0*
' *Public Shared Properties*
   Public Shared ReadOnly Property **Size** As Integer
' *Public Shared Methods*
   Public Shared Boolean operator Sub **!=**(ByVal value1 As IntPtr, ByVal value2 As IntPtr)
   Public Shared Boolean operator Sub **==**(ByVal value1 As IntPtr, ByVal value2 As IntPtr)
   Public Shared explicit operator Sub **Integer**(ByVal value As IntPtr)
   Public Shared explicit operator Sub **Long**(ByVal value As IntPtr)
   Public Shared explicit operator Sub **IntPtr**(ByVal value As Integer)
   Public Shared explicit operator Sub **IntPtr**(ByVal value As Long)
' *Public Instance Methods*
   Overrides Public Function **Equals**(ByVal obj As Object) As Boolean
   Overrides Public Function **GetHashCode**() As Integer
   Public Function **ToInt32**() As Integer
   Public Function **ToInt64**() As Long
   Overrides Public Function **ToString**() As String
End Structure

Hierarchy: Object→ ValueType→ IntPtr(System.Runtime.Serialization.ISerializable)

Returned By: Multiple types

Passed To: Multiple types

InvalidCastException   Class

System (mscorlib.dll)   *ECMA, serializable*

This exception signals a failure during a cast or explicit conversion.

Public Class **InvalidCastException** : Inherits SystemException
' *Public Constructors*
   Public Sub **New**()
   Public Sub **New**(ByVal message As String)
   Public Sub **New**(ByVal message As String, ByVal innerException As Exception)
' *Protected Constructors*
   Protected Sub **New**(ByVal info As System.Runtime.Serialization.SerializationInfo, _
     ByVal context As System.Runtime.Serialization.StreamingContext)
End Class

Hierarchy: Object→ Exception(System.Runtime.Serialization.ISerializable)→ SystemException→ InvalidCastException

InvalidOperationException   Class

System (mscorlib.dll)   *ECMA, serializable*

This exception indicates that a user attempted to use a method when the object was not in an appropriate state. For example, this exception is thrown if you attempt to write data with a System.Xml.XmlTextWriter that is already closed.

Public Class **InvalidOperationException** : Inherits SystemException
' *Public Constructors*
   Public Sub **New**()
   Public Sub **New**(ByVal message As String)
   Public Sub **New**(ByVal message As String, ByVal innerException As Exception)

' *Protected Constructors*
```
Protected Sub New(ByVal info As System.Runtime.Serialization.SerializationInfo, _
    ByVal context As System.Runtime.Serialization.StreamingContext)
End Class
```

Hierarchy: Object→ Exception(System.Runtime.Serialization.ISerializable)→ SystemException→ InvalidOperationException

Subclasses: ObjectDisposedException, System.Net.{ ProtocolViolationException, WebException}

InvalidProgramException
NotInheritable Class

System (mscorlib.dll)
ECMA, serializable

This exception indicates that the .NET execution engine found some invalid code or metadata in a program. This can be caused by a compiler bug that generates malformed MSIL (Microsoft Intermediate Language) instructions.

```
Public NotInheritable Class InvalidProgramException : Inherits SystemException
' Public Constructors
    Public Sub New()
    Public Sub New(ByVal message As String)
    Public Sub New(ByVal message As String, ByVal inner As Exception)
End Class
```

Hierarchy: Object→ Exception(System.Runtime.Serialization.ISerializable)→ SystemException→ InvalidProgramException

IServiceProvider
Interface

System (mscorlib.dll)

This interface defines a mechanism for retrieving a service object. A class implementing this interface provides a service object to other objects through its GetService() method.

```
Public Interface IServiceProvider
' Public Instance Methods
    Public Function GetService(ByVal serviceType As Type) As Object
End Interface
```

LoaderOptimization
Enum

System (mscorlib.dll)
serializable

This enumeration is used for the LoaderOptimizationAttribute constructor. It specifies whether your application will use more than one AppDomain. Use the MultiDomain value if your application contains many domains that use the same code, and use MultiDomainHost if your application hosts multiple domains with unique code—in which case resources are shared for globally available assemblies only. NotSpecified reverts to SingleDomain, unless the default domain or host specifies otherwise.

```
Public Enum LoaderOptimization
    NotSpecified = 0
    SingleDomain = 1
    MultiDomain = 2
    MultiDomainHost = 3
End Enum
```

Hierarchy: Object→ ValueType→ Enum(IComparable, IFormattable, IConvertible)→ LoaderOptimization

Returned By: AppDomainSetup.LoaderOptimization, LoaderOptimizationAttribute.Value

Passed To: AppDomainSetup.LoaderOptimization,
LoaderOptimizationAttribute.LoaderOptimizationAttribute()

LoaderOptimizationAttribute   NotInheritable Class
System (mscorlib.dll)

This attribute can be used only on your application's Main method. It sets the type of default optimization used to share internal resources across application domains. It is most relevant when you use the AppDomain class to create more than one domain from your application. By default, if you do not use this attribute, the .NET Framework makes optimizations with the assumption that your application has only a single domain.

```
Public NotInheritable Class LoaderOptimizationAttribute : Inherits Attribute
' Public Constructors
   Public Sub New(ByVal value As Byte)
   Public Sub New(ByVal value As LoaderOptimization)
' Public Instance Properties
   Public ReadOnly Property Value As LoaderOptimization
End Class
```

Hierarchy: Object→ Attribute→ LoaderOptimizationAttribute

Valid On: Method

LocalDataStoreSlot   NotInheritable Class
System (mscorlib.dll)

The CLR allocates a multislot local data store to each process when it starts. These slots are used for thread-specific and context-specific data, and are not shared between threads or contexts. The LocalDataStoreSlot class encapsulates one of these slots. It's used by the GetData() and SetData() methods in the System.Threading.Thread and System.Runtime.Remoting.Contexts.Context classes.

```
Public NotInheritable Class LocalDataStoreSlot
' Protected Instance Methods
   Overrides Protected Sub Finalize()
End Class
```

Returned By: System.Threading.Thread.{AllocateDataSlot(), AllocateNamedDataSlot(), GetNamedDataSlot()}

Passed To: System.Threading.Thread.{GetData(), SetData()}

MarshalByRefObject   MustInherit Class
System (mscorlib.dll)   *ECMA, serializable, marshal by reference*

MarshalByRefObject is the base class for objects that are marshaled by reference across AppDomain boundaries. If you attempt to transmit an object that derives from this class to another domain (e.g., as a parameter in a method call to a remote machine), an object reference is sent. (In actuality, this is an object proxy, which provides the same interface—methods, properties, and so forth.) If the other domain uses this reference (e.g., sets an object property or calls one of its methods), the call is automatically marshaled back to the original domain in which the object was created, and it is invoked there, using the proxy object the .NET Framework creates automatically.

You can inherit from this class to create a remotable object. Values that should be marshaled by reference include unmanaged pointers and file handles, which do not have any meaning in another domain. Objects that are marshaled by reference live until their lifetime lease expires. The MarshalByRefObject class includes methods for getting and setting the ILease object from the System.Runtime.Remoting.Lifetime namespace. More information about remoting can be found in the System.Runtime.Remoting namespace.

```
Public MustInherit Class MarshalByRefObject
' Protected Constructors
   Protected Sub New()
' Public Instance Methods
   Overridable Public Function CreateObjRef(ByVal requestedType As Type) As ObjRef
   Public Function GetLifetimeService() As Object
   Overridable Public Function InitializeLifetimeService() As Object
End Class
```

Subclasses: Multiple types

Math

NotInheritable Class

System (mscorlib.dll)

ECMA

This class provides shared helper functions for many trigonometric, logarithmic, and other mathematical operations, including methods for rounding numbers, getting absolute values, retrieving the largest whole divisor (Floor()), and determining the remainder (IEEERemainder()). The constants *pi* and *e* are provided as fields.

```
Public NotInheritable Class Math
' Public Shared Fields
   Public const E As Double                                      =2.71828182845905
   Public const PI As Double                                     =3.14159265358979
' Public Shared Methods
   Public Shared Function Abs(ByVal value As Decimal) As Decimal
   Public Shared Function Abs(ByVal value As Double) As Double
   Public Shared Function Abs(ByVal value As Short) As Short
   Public Shared Function Abs(ByVal value As Integer) As Integer
   Public Shared Function Abs(ByVal value As Long) As Long
   Public Shared Function Abs(ByVal value As SByte) As SByte
   Public Shared Function Abs(ByVal value As Single) As Single
   Public Shared Function Acos(ByVal d As Double) As Double
   Public Shared Function Asin(ByVal d As Double) As Double
   Public Shared Function Atan(ByVal d As Double) As Double
   Public Shared Function Atan2(ByVal y As Double, ByVal x As Double) As Double
   Public Shared Function Ceiling(ByVal a As Double) As Double
   Public Shared Function Cos(ByVal d As Double) As Double
   Public Shared Function Cosh(ByVal value As Double) As Double
   Public Shared Function Exp(ByVal d As Double) As Double
   Public Shared Function Floor(ByVal d As Double) As Double
   Public Shared Function IEEERemainder(ByVal x As Double, ByVal y As Double) As Double
   Public Shared Function Log(ByVal d As Double) As Double
   Public Shared Function Log(ByVal a As Double, ByVal newBase As Double) As Double
   Public Shared Function Log10(ByVal d As Double) As Double
   Public Shared Function Max(ByVal val1 As Byte, ByVal val2 As Byte) As Byte
   Public Shared Function Max(ByVal val1 As Decimal, ByVal val2 As Decimal) As Decimal
   Public Shared Function Max(ByVal val1 As Double, ByVal val2 As Double) As Double
   Public Shared Function Max(ByVal val1 As Short, ByVal val2 As Short) As Short
   Public Shared Function Max(ByVal val1 As Integer, ByVal val2 As Integer) As Integer
   Public Shared Function Max(ByVal val1 As Long, ByVal val2 As Long) As Long
   Public Shared Function Max(ByVal val1 As SByte, ByVal val2 As SByte) As SByte
   Public Shared Function Max(ByVal val1 As Single, ByVal val2 As Single) As Single
```

System

Public Shared Function **Max**(ByVal val1 As UInt16, ByVal val2 As UInt16) As UInt16
Public Shared Function **Max**(ByVal val1 As UInt32, ByVal val2 As UInt32) As UInt32
Public Shared Function **Max**(ByVal val1 As UInt64, ByVal val2 As UInt64) As UInt64
Public Shared Function **Min**(ByVal val1 As Byte, ByVal val2 As Byte) As Byte
Public Shared Function **Min**(ByVal val1 As Decimal, ByVal val2 As Decimal) As Decimal
Public Shared Function **Min**(ByVal val1 As Double, ByVal val2 As Double) As Double
Public Shared Function **Min**(ByVal val1 As Short, ByVal val2 As Short) As Short
Public Shared Function **Min**(ByVal val1 As Integer, ByVal val2 As Integer) As Integer
Public Shared Function **Min**(ByVal val1 As Long, ByVal val2 As Long) As Long
Public Shared Function **Min**(ByVal val1 As SByte, ByVal val2 As SByte) As SByte
Public Shared Function **Min**(ByVal val1 As Single, ByVal val2 As Single) As Single
Public Shared Function **Min**(ByVal val1 As UInt16, ByVal val2 As UInt16) As UInt16
Public Shared Function **Min**(ByVal val1 As UInt32, ByVal val2 As UInt32) As UInt32
Public Shared Function **Min**(ByVal val1 As UInt64, ByVal val2 As UInt64) As UInt64
Public Shared Function **Pow**(ByVal x As Double, ByVal y As Double) As Double
Public Shared Function **Round**(ByVal d As Decimal) As Decimal
Public Shared Function **Round**(ByVal d As Decimal, ByVal decimals As Integer) As Decimal
Public Shared Function **Round**(ByVal a As Double) As Double
Public Shared Function **Round**(ByVal value As Double, ByVal digits As Integer) As Double
Public Shared Function **Sign**(ByVal value As Decimal) As Integer
Public Shared Function **Sign**(ByVal value As Double) As Integer
Public Shared Function **Sign**(ByVal value As Short) As Integer
Public Shared Function **Sign**(ByVal value As Integer) As Integer
Public Shared Function **Sign**(ByVal value As Long) As Integer
Public Shared Function **Sign**(ByVal value As SByte) As Integer
Public Shared Function **Sign**(ByVal value As Single) As Integer
Public Shared Function **Sin**(ByVal a As Double) As Double
Public Shared Function **Sinh**(ByVal value As Double) As Double
Public Shared Function **Sqrt**(ByVal d As Double) As Double
Public Shared Function **Tan**(ByVal a As Double) As Double
Public Shared Function **Tanh**(ByVal value As Double) As Double
End Class

MemberAccessException

Class

System (mscorlib.dll)

ECMA, serializable

This is the superclass of several exceptions that indicate a failed attempt to access a class member.

Public Class **MemberAccessException** : Inherits SystemException
' *Public Constructors*
  Public Sub **New**()
  Public Sub **New**(ByVal message As String)
  Public Sub **New**(ByVal message As String, ByVal inner As Exception)
' *Protected Constructors*
  Protected Sub **New**(ByVal info As System.Runtime.Serialization.SerializationInfo, _
    ByVal context As System.Runtime.Serialization.StreamingContext)
End Class

Hierarchy: Object→ Exception(System.Runtime.Serialization.ISerializable)→ SystemException→ MemberAccessException

Subclasses: FieldAccessException, MethodAccessException, MissingMemberException

MethodAccessException

Class

System (mscorlib.dll)

ECMA, serializable

This exception indicates a failed attempt to access a method.

```
Public Class MethodAccessException : Inherits MemberAccessException
' Public Constructors
   Public Sub New()
   Public Sub New(ByVal message As String)
   Public Sub New(ByVal message As String, ByVal inner As Exception)
' Protected Constructors
   Protected Sub New(ByVal info As System.Runtime.Serialization.SerializationInfo, _
      ByVal context As System.Runtime.Serialization.StreamingContext)
End Class
```

Hierarchy: Object→ Exception(System.Runtime.Serialization.ISerializable)→ SystemException→ MemberAccessException→ MethodAccessException

MissingFieldException

Class

System (mscorlib.dll)

ECMA, serializable

MissingMemberException indicates an attempt to access a nonexistent field.

```
Public Class MissingFieldException : Inherits MissingMemberException
' Public Constructors
   Public Sub New()
   Public Sub New(ByVal message As String)
   Public Sub New(ByVal message As String, ByVal inner As Exception)
   Public Sub New(ByVal className As String, ByVal fieldName As String)
' Protected Constructors
   Protected Sub New(ByVal info As System.Runtime.Serialization.SerializationInfo, _
      ByVal context As System.Runtime.Serialization.StreamingContext)
' Public Instance Properties
   Overrides Public ReadOnly Property Message As String
End Class
```

Hierarchy: Object→ Exception(System.Runtime.Serialization.ISerializable)→ SystemException→ MemberAccessException→ MissingMemberException→ MissingFieldException

MissingMemberException

Class

System (mscorlib.dll)

ECMA, serializable

This is the superclass of several exceptions that indicate an attempt to access a nonexistent member. Although the compiler detects explicit attempts of this sort, it does not protect against attempts to access nonexistent members using reflection.

```
Public Class MissingMemberException : Inherits MemberAccessException
' Public Constructors
   Public Sub New()
   Public Sub New(ByVal message As String)
   Public Sub New(ByVal message As String, ByVal inner As Exception)
   Public Sub New(ByVal className As String, ByVal memberName As String)
' Protected Constructors
   Protected Sub New(ByVal info As System.Runtime.Serialization.SerializationInfo, _
      ByVal context As System.Runtime.Serialization.StreamingContext)
' Protected Instance Fields
   protected ClassName As String
   protected MemberName As String
```

System

```
    protected Signature As Byte()
' Public Instance Properties
    Overrides Public ReadOnly Property Message As String
' Public Instance Methods
    Overrides Public Sub GetObjectData(ByVal info As System.Runtime.Serialization.SerializationInfo, _
        ByVal context As System.Runtime.Serialization.StreamingContext)
End Class
```

Hierarchy: Object→ Exception(System.Runtime.Serialization.ISerializable)→ SystemException→
MemberAccessException→ MissingMemberException

Subclasses: MissingFieldException, MissingMethodException

MissingMethodException   Class

System (mscorlib.dll)   *ECMA, serializable*

This exception indicates an attempt to access a nonexistent method.

```
Public Class MissingMethodException : Inherits MissingMemberException
' Public Constructors
    Public Sub New()
    Public Sub New(ByVal message As String)
    Public Sub New(ByVal message As String, ByVal inner As Exception)
    Public Sub New(ByVal className As String, ByVal methodName As String)
' Protected Constructors
    Protected Sub New(ByVal info As System.Runtime.Serialization.SerializationInfo, _
        ByVal context As System.Runtime.Serialization.StreamingContext)
' Public Instance Properties
    Overrides Public ReadOnly Property Message As String
End Class
```

Hierarchy: Object→ Exception(System.Runtime.Serialization.ISerializable)→ SystemException→
MemberAccessException→ MissingMemberException→ MissingMethodException

MTAThreadAttribute   NotInheritable Class

System (mscorlib.dll)

This attribute is used entirely for COM interoperability in .NET; it has no effect on a
pure .NET application or system.

This attribute can be used only on the Main method of the application. It sets the
default threading model to MTA (multithreaded apartment). Alternatively, you can use
the STAThreadAttribute attribute for a single-threaded apartment model.

```
Public NotInheritable Class MTAThreadAttribute : Inherits Attribute
' Public Constructors
    Public Sub New()
End Class
```

Hierarchy: Object→ Attribute→ MTAThreadAttribute

Valid On: Method

MulticastDelegate

MustInherit Class

System (mscorlib.dll)

serializable

This is the base class for multicast delegates. Multicast delegates are identical to normal delegates, except that their invocation list can hold more than one method at a time. You can use Delegate.Combine() to add a method to the list and Delegate.Remove() to remove one. When you invoke a multicast delegate, the methods are invoked synchronously one after the other. An error in one method can prevent the delegate from calling the other methods in its list.

Multicast delegates can also be invoked asynchronously, meaning that the entire call chain is invoked serially by a single thread out of the system thread pool. If it is desirable to invoke each delegate in the chain on its own asynchronous thread instead, then use GetInvocationList() to obtain the list of delegates and asynchronously invoke each one.

```
Public MustInherit Class MulticastDelegate : Inherits Delegate
' Protected Constructors
    Protected Sub New(ByVal target As Object, ByVal method As String)
    Protected Sub New(ByVal target As Type, ByVal method As String)
' Public Shared Methods
    Public Shared Boolean operator Sub !=(ByVal d1 As MulticastDelegate, ByVal d2 As MulticastDelegate)
    Public Shared Boolean operator Sub ==(ByVal d1 As MulticastDelegate, ByVal d2 As MulticastDelegate)
' Public Instance Methods
    Overrides NotOverridable Public Function Equals(ByVal obj As Object) As Boolean
    Overrides NotOverridable Public Function GetHashCode() As Integer
    Overrides NotOverridable Public Function GetInvocationList() As Delegate()
    Overrides Public Sub GetObjectData(ByVal info As System.Runtime.Serialization.SerializationInfo, _
        ByVal context As System.Runtime.Serialization.StreamingContext)
' Protected Instance Methods
    Overrides NotOverridable Protected Function CombineImpl(ByVal follow As Delegate) As Delegate
    Overrides NotOverridable Protected Function DynamicInvokeImpl(ByVal args As Object()) As Object
    Overrides NotOverridable Protected Function RemoveImpl(ByVal value As Delegate) As Delegate
End Class
```

Hierarchy: Object→ Delegate(ICloneable, System.Runtime.Serialization.ISerializable)→ MulticastDelegate

Subclasses: Multiple types

MulticastNotSupportedException

NotInheritable Class

System (mscorlib.dll)

serializable

This exception is thrown when two uncombinable delegates are combined; see Delegate and MulticastDelegate for details regarding what constitutes *combinable* delegates.

```
Public NotInheritable Class MulticastNotSupportedException : Inherits SystemException
' Public Constructors
    Public Sub New()
    Public Sub New(ByVal message As String)
    Public Sub New(ByVal message As String, ByVal inner As Exception)
End Class
```

Hierarchy: Object→ Exception(System.Runtime.Serialization.ISerializable)→ SystemException→ MulticastNotSupportedException

NonSerializedAttribute
NotInheritable Class

System (mscorlib.dll)

This attribute lets you mark properties of fields in a class as nonserializable, so that they are ignored during a serialization operation. Typical examples of nonserializable data include pointers, handles, and other data structures that can't be recreated during deserialization.

By default, a class is not eligible for serialization unless it implements System.Runtime.Serialization.ISerializable or is marked with a SerializableAttribute. Once a class is marked as serializable, you must mark all fields or properties that are not to be serialized with a NonSerializedAttribute.

Public NotInheritable Class **NonSerializedAttribute** : Inherits Attribute
' *Public Constructors*
   Public Sub **New**()
End Class

Hierarchy: Object→ Attribute→ NonSerializedAttribute

Valid On: Field

NotFiniteNumberException
Class

System (mscorlib.dll)
ECMA, serializable

This exception is thrown when certain languages encounter floating-point infinity or NaN (not a number) values. These values can be represented in VB with Double.Negative-Infinity, Double.PositiveInfinity, and Double.NaN. (Similar fields are available in Single.)

Public Class **NotFiniteNumberException** : Inherits ArithmeticException
' *Public Constructors*
   Public Sub **New**()
   Public Sub **New**(ByVal offendingNumber As Double)
   Public Sub **New**(ByVal message As String)
   Public Sub **New**(ByVal message As String, ByVal offendingNumber As Double)
   Public Sub **New**(ByVal message As String, ByVal offendingNumber As Double, ByVal innerException As Exception)
' *Protected Constructors*
   Protected Sub **New**(ByVal info As System.Runtime.Serialization.SerializationInfo, _
     ByVal context As System.Runtime.Serialization.StreamingContext)
' *Public Instance Properties*
   Public ReadOnly Property **OffendingNumber** As Double
' *Public Instance Methods*
   Overrides Public Sub **GetObjectData**(ByVal info As System.Runtime.Serialization.SerializationInfo, _
     ByVal context As System.Runtime.Serialization.StreamingContext)
End Class

Hierarchy: Object→ Exception(System.Runtime.Serialization.ISerializable)→ SystemException.→ ArithmeticException→ NotFiniteNumberException

NotImplementedException
Class

System (mscorlib.dll)
serializable

This exception signals an attempt to access an unimplemented method or operation.

Suppose you have a base class with a number of unimplemented methods. You may have reason not to mark them as MustInherit (perhaps you want to let programmers develop subclasses that only implement some of the base class methods). You can throw this exception in those methods, letting users of the subclass know that they are not implemented.

```
Public Class NotImplementedException : Inherits SystemException
' Public Constructors
   Public Sub New()
   Public Sub New(ByVal message As String)
   Public Sub New(ByVal message As String, ByVal inner As Exception)
' Protected Constructors
   Protected Sub New(ByVal info As System.Runtime.Serialization.SerializationInfo, _
      ByVal context As System.Runtime.Serialization.StreamingContext)
End Class
```

Hierarchy: Object→ Exception(System.Runtime.Serialization.ISerializable)→ SystemException→ NotImplementedException

NotSupportedException   Class

System (mscorlib.dll)   *ECMA, serializable*

This exception indicates an attempt to use an unsupported method. For example, if you try to seek on a stream that is based on unidirectional input—for example, a standard input stream from a console utility such as *sort.exe*—this exception could be thrown.

```
Public Class NotSupportedException : Inherits SystemException
' Public Constructors
   Public Sub New()
   Public Sub New(ByVal message As String)
   Public Sub New(ByVal message As String, ByVal innerException As Exception)
' Protected Constructors
   Protected Sub New(ByVal info As System.Runtime.Serialization.SerializationInfo, _
      ByVal context As System.Runtime.Serialization.StreamingContext)
End Class
```

Hierarchy: Object→ Exception(System.Runtime.Serialization.ISerializable)→ SystemException→ NotSupportedException

Subclasses: PlatformNotSupportedException

NullReferenceException   Class

System (mscorlib.dll)   *ECMA, serializable*

This exception is thrown when you try to dereference a null pointer (for example, accessing an instance field on an object reference that currently points to no instance).

```
Public Class NullReferenceException : Inherits SystemException
' Public Constructors
   Public Sub New()
   Public Sub New(ByVal message As String)
   Public Sub New(ByVal message As String, ByVal innerException As Exception)
' Protected Constructors
   Protected Sub New(ByVal info As System.Runtime.Serialization.SerializationInfo, _
      ByVal context As System.Runtime.Serialization.StreamingContext)
End Class
```

Hierarchy: Object→ Exception(System.Runtime.Serialization.ISerializable)→ SystemException→ NullReferenceException

Object   Class

System (mscorlib.dll)   *ECMA, serializable*

This class is the root of all .NET types, including value types and reference types. Some CLR languages such as C# and VB.NET do not require a type to inherit from Object explicitly. If no base type is listed in a class declaration, it is assumed that the type is to inherit from Object. Therefore, all types derive from it implicitly and can use any of its methods.

Use the GetType() method to obtain a description of your object's internal metadata as a Type object. Use the ToString() method to get a String that represents your object. By default, this is the fully qualified type name of your object, but most classes override this method to provide something more useful, such as a string representation of the object's content. For example, System.Drawing.Point.ToString() might return (10,5).

The MemberwiseClone() method returns a new object of the same type that is a member-by-member duplicate. This object is called a shallow copy because any subobjects are not copied. Instead, the references are duplicated, meaning that both the original and cloned type refer to the same subobjects. MemberwiseClone() is protected, so it can be called only from methods of your derived object. Usually, you will implement the ICloneable interface for your objects and call MemberwiseClone() from a customized IClone-able.Clone() method.

Use the Equals() method to test for reference equality. Derived value-type classes override this method to provide value equality (which returns true for identical content, even if it is stored in different objects at different memory addresses). Note that the equality operator (== in C#, = in VB.NET) does not call Equals() unless the equality operator is overloaded for the appropriate type (as it is with String, for example).

The ReferenceEquals() method, while perhaps seeming somewhat similar, compares object identity rather than object equality. That is, while Equals() might return true for two independent objects that contain the same state, ReferenceEquals() checks to see if the two references passed to it point to the same object. These two objects are identical, which is only the case when both references point to the same location in memory. ReferenceEquals() is the only safe way to test references for identity.

The GetHashCode() method returns a hash code so the object can be used as a key in a System.Collections.Hashtable collection. By default, GetHashCode() returns a unique hash code for each object, which is sufficient for reference types but must be overridden by all value types so that equivalent types return identical hash codes.

```
Public Class Object
' Public Constructors
    Public Sub New()
' Public Shared Methods
    Public Shared Function Equals(ByVal objA As Object, ByVal objB As Object) As Boolean
    Public Shared Function ReferenceEquals(ByVal objA As Object, ByVal objB As Object) As Boolean
' Public Instance Methods
    Overridable Public Function Equals(ByVal obj As Object) As Boolean
    Overridable Public Function GetHashCode() As Integer
    Public Function GetType() As Type
    Overridable Public Function ToString() As String
' Protected Instance Methods
    Overrides Protected Sub Finalize()
    Protected Function MemberwiseClone() As Object
End Class
```

Subclasses: Multiple types

Returned By: Multiple types

Passed To: Multiple types

ObjectDisposedException | Class

System (mscorlib.dll) | *ECMA, serializable*

This exception is thrown when certain operations are performed on an object that has been disposed. For example, trying to read from an I/O stream that has been closed by the System.IO.Stream.Close() method should raise this exception.

```
Public Class ObjectDisposedException : Inherits InvalidOperationException
' Public Constructors
   Public Sub New(ByVal objectName As String)
   Public Sub New(ByVal objectName As String, ByVal message As String)
' Protected Constructors
   Protected Sub New(ByVal info As System.Runtime.Serialization.SerializationInfo, _
      ByVal context As System.Runtime.Serialization.StreamingContext)
' Public Instance Properties
   Overrides Public ReadOnly Property Message As String
   Public ReadOnly Property ObjectName As String
' Public Instance Methods
   Overrides Public Sub GetObjectData(ByVal info As System.Runtime.Serialization.SerializationInfo, _
      ByVal context As System.Runtime.Serialization.StreamingContext)
End Class
```

Hierarchy: Object→ Exception(System.Runtime.Serialization.ISerializable)→ SystemException→ InvalidOperationException→ ObjectDisposedException

ObsoleteAttribute | NotInheritable Class

System (mscorlib.dll) | *ECMA, serializable*

This attribute is used to mark program elements that will be removed in future versions or are no longer fully supported. The use of an element with this attribute (e.g., calling a method or setting a property marked with ObsoleteAttribute) causes a compile-time warning. You can set the Message property to supply a string to display to the user, typically specifying a workaround or the program element that should be used as a replacement. You can also use the IsError property to specify that the compiler treats the use of this element as an error. The default is false. These properties are set through the constructor, as in <Obsolete ("OldMethod has been replaced by NewMethod", True)>.

```
Public NotInheritable Class ObsoleteAttribute : Inherits Attribute
' Public Constructors
   Public Sub New()
   Public Sub New(ByVal message As String)
   Public Sub New(ByVal message As String, ByVal error As Boolean)
' Public Instance Properties
   Public ReadOnly Property IsError As Boolean
   Public ReadOnly Property Message As String
End Class
```

Hierarchy: Object→ Attribute→ ObsoleteAttribute

Valid On: Class, Struct, Enum, Constructor, Method, Property, Field, Event, Interface, Delegate

OperatingSystem

NotInheritable Class

System (mscorlib.dll)   *serializable*

This class represents the current operating system by combining an instance of the PlatformID and Version classes. It is returned by the Environment.OSVersion property.

Public NotInheritable Class **OperatingSystem** : Implements ICloneable
' *Public Constructors*
   Public Sub **New**(ByVal platform As PlatformID, ByVal version As Version)
' *Public Instance Properties*
   Public ReadOnly Property **Platform** As PlatformID
   Public ReadOnly Property **Version** As Version
' *Public Instance Methods*
   Public Function **Clone**() As Object Implements ICloneable.Clone
   Overrides Public Function **ToString**() As String
End Class

Returned By: Environment.OSVersion

OutOfMemoryException

Class

System (mscorlib.dll)   *ECMA, serializable*

This exception indicates that the .NET runtime has exhausted all available memory and usually means the CLR is in deep danger of dying altogether.

Public Class **OutOfMemoryException** : Inherits SystemException
' *Public Constructors*
   Public Sub **New**()
   Public Sub **New**(ByVal message As String)
   Public Sub **New**(ByVal message As String, ByVal innerException As Exception)
' *Protected Constructors*
   Protected Sub **New**(ByVal info As System.Runtime.Serialization.SerializationInfo, _
     ByVal context As System.Runtime.Serialization.StreamingContext)
End Class

Hierarchy: Object→ Exception(System.Runtime.Serialization.ISerializable)→ SystemException→
OutOfMemoryException

OverflowException

Class

System (mscorlib.dll)   *ECMA, serializable*

This exception indicates an attempt to store a value that exceeds the limit of the target type. This could be caused by an arithmetic operation, cast, or conversion.

Public Class **OverflowException** : Inherits ArithmeticException
' *Public Constructors*
   Public Sub **New**()
   Public Sub **New**(ByVal message As String)
   Public Sub **New**(ByVal message As String, ByVal innerException As Exception)
' *Protected Constructors*
   Protected Sub **New**(ByVal info As System.Runtime.Serialization.SerializationInfo, _
     ByVal context As System.Runtime.Serialization.StreamingContext)
End Class

Hierarchy: Object→ Exception(System.Runtime.Serialization.ISerializable)→ SystemException→
ArithmeticException→ OverflowException

ParamArrayAttribute

NotInheritable Class

System (mscorlib.dll)

ECMA

This attribute is used on a method to indicate that it can accept a variable number of parameters. The method has an array as its last parameter, and the list of values passed to the method are stored in the array. In VB.NET, use the ParamArray keyword to create methods with a variable number of arguments, rather than using this attribute directly.

```
Public NotInheritable Class ParamArrayAttribute : Inherits Attribute
' Public Constructors
   Public Sub New()
End Class
```

Hierarchy: Object→ Attribute→ ParamArrayAttribute

Valid On: Parameter

PlatformID

Enum

System (mscorlib.dll)

serializable

This enumerated value indicates the type of operating platform that .NET is currently running on and is returned by the OperatingSystem.Platform property. Win32Windows indicates a Windows 9x–based operating system, while Win32NT indicates an operating system based on Windows NT, including Windows 2000, XP, and .NET Server. Win32S is a layer that can run on 16-bit versions of Windows (Windows 3.x) to provide access to some 32-bit applications.

```
Public Enum PlatformID
   Win32S = 0
   Win32Windows = 1
   Win32NT = 2
End Enum
```

Hierarchy: Object→ ValueType→ Enum(IComparable, IFormattable, IConvertible)→ PlatformID

Returned By: OperatingSystem.Platform

Passed To: OperatingSystem.OperatingSystem()

PlatformNotSupportedException

Class

System (mscorlib.dll)

serializable

This exception signals an attempt to access a class or member that is not available on the current platform. For example, many properties from System.Diagnostics.Process are not available on Windows 95, 98, or ME.

```
Public Class PlatformNotSupportedException : Inherits NotSupportedException
' Public Constructors
   Public Sub New()
   Public Sub New(ByVal message As String)
   Public Sub New(ByVal message As String, ByVal inner As Exception)
' Protected Constructors
   Protected Sub New(ByVal info As System.Runtime.Serialization.SerializationInfo, _
      ByVal context As System.Runtime.Serialization.StreamingContext)
End Class
```

Hierarchy: Object→ Exception(System.Runtime.Serialization.ISerializable)→ SystemException→ NotSupportedException→ PlatformNotSupportedException

Random

System (mscorlib.dll)

Class

ECMA, serializable

This class encapsulates a *pseudorandom number* (one chosen from a list of pregenerated numbers, but that is statistically random). After creating an instance of this class, use the Next(), NextDouble(), or NextBytes() methods to return random information. NextDouble() returns a fraction value between 0.0 and 1.0, while Next() returns an integer between 0 and the maximum bound that you specify. NextBytes() fills a supplied array of bytes with random numbers.

When creating a Random object, you supply a seed value to the constructor, which determines the place on the list from where the random number is drawn. If you supply the same seed value to multiple Random instances, you will receive the same random number. Computers are incapable of generating truly random numbers, and Random should not be used for cryptographic algorithms. For a cryptographically strong random number generator, see the System.Security.Cryptography.RandomNumberGenerator in the .NET Framework SDK Documentation.

```
Public Class Random
' Public Constructors
   Public Sub New()
   Public Sub New(ByVal Seed As Integer)
' Public Instance Methods
   Overridable Public Function Next() As Integer
   Overridable Public Function Next(ByVal maxValue As Integer) As Integer
   Overridable Public Function Next(ByVal minValue As Integer, ByVal maxValue As Integer) As Integer
   Overridable Public Sub NextBytes(ByVal buffer As Byte())
   Overridable Public Function NextDouble() As Double
' Protected Instance Methods
   Overridable Protected Function Sample() As Double
End Class
```

RankException

System (mscorlib.dll)

Class

ECMA, serializable

This exception signals an attempt to send an array of the wrong rank to a method. For example, this exception is thrown when you pass a multidimensional array to Array.Sort() or Array.Reverse().

```
Public Class RankException : Inherits SystemException
' Public Constructors
   Public Sub New()
   Public Sub New(ByVal message As String)
   Public Sub New(ByVal message As String, ByVal innerException As Exception)
' Protected Constructors
   Protected Sub New(ByVal info As System.Runtime.Serialization.SerializationInfo, _
       ByVal context As System.Runtime.Serialization.StreamingContext)
End Class
```

Hierarchy: Object→ Exception(System.Runtime.Serialization.ISerializable)→ SystemException→ RankException

ResolveEventArgs Class

System (mscorlib.dll)

This object is provided to methods with the ResolveEventHandler signature, indicating additional information about the reference that could not be resolved in the Name property.

Public Class **ResolveEventArgs** : Inherits EventArgs
' Public Constructors
   Public Sub **New**(ByVal name As String)
' Public Instance Properties
   Public ReadOnly Property **Name** As String
End Class

Hierarchy: Object→ EventArgs→ ResolveEventArgs

Passed To: System.Reflection.ModuleResolveEventHandler.{BeginInvoke(), Invoke()}, ResolveEventHandler.{BeginInvoke(), Invoke()}

ResolveEventHandler Delegate

System (mscorlib.dll) *serializable*

This delegate defines the event handler that can be created to respond to AppDomain.TypeResolve, AppDomain.ResourceResolve, and AppDomain.AssemblyResolve events. These events are raised when the runtime cannot find a type, assembly, or resource. Use this delegate to catch that event, then find and return the assembly that contains the missing type, resource, or assembly.

Public Delegate Function **ResolveEventHandler**(ByVal sender As Object, ByVal args As ResolveEventArgs) _
   As Assembly

Associated Events: AppDomain.{AssemblyResolve(), ResourceResolve(), TypeResolve()}

RuntimeTypeHandle Structure

System (mscorlib.dll) *ECMA, serializable*

This structure is a handle to the internal metadata representation of a type. The Value property provides an IntPtr reference. You can use this class with the Type.GetTypeFromHandle()shared method.

Public Structure **RuntimeTypeHandle** : Implements System.Runtime.Serialization.ISerializable
' Public Instance Properties
   Public ReadOnly Property **Value** As IntPtr
' Public Instance Methods
   Public Sub **GetObjectData**(ByVal info As System.Runtime.Serialization.SerializationInfo, _
     ByVal context As System.Runtime.Serialization.StreamingContext) Implements ISerializable.GetObjectData
End Structure

Hierarchy: Object→ ValueType→ RuntimeTypeHandle(System.Runtime.Serialization.ISerializable)

Returned By: ArgIterator.GetNextArgType(), Type.{GetTypeHandle(), TypeHandle}

Passed To: ArgIterator.GetNextArg(), Type.GetTypeFromHandle()

SByte
Structure
System (mscorlib.dll)   *ECMA, serializable*

This structure represents an 8-bit signed integer (from –128 to 127). It is not CLS-compliant. Use Int16 instead.

```
Public Structure SByte : Implements IComparable, IFormattable, IConvertible
' Public Shared Fields
    Public const MaxValue As SByte                                           =127
    Public const MinValue As SByte                                          =-128
' Public Shared Methods
    Public Shared Function Parse(ByVal s As String) As SByte
    Public Shared Function Parse(ByVal s As String, ByVal provider As IFormatProvider) As SByte
    Public Shared Function Parse(ByVal s As String, ByVal style As System.Globalization.NumberStyles) As SByte
    Public Shared Function Parse(ByVal s As String, ByVal style As System.Globalization.NumberStyles, _
        ByVal provider As IFormatProvider) As SByte
' Public Instance Methods
    Public Function CompareTo(ByVal obj As Object) As Integer Implements  IComparable.CompareTo
    Overrides Public Function Equals(ByVal obj As Object) As Boolean
    Overrides Public Function GetHashCode() As Integer
    Public Function GetTypeCode() As TypeCode Implements  IConvertible.GetTypeCode
    Overrides Public Function ToString() As String
    Public Function ToString(ByVal provider As IFormatProvider) As String Implements  IConvertible.ToString
    Public Function ToString(ByVal format As String) As String
    Public Function ToString(ByVal format As String, ByVal provider As IFormatProvider) As String _
        Implements  IFormattable.ToString
End Structure
```

Hierarchy: Object→ ValueType→ SByte(IComparable, IFormattable, IConvertible)

Returned By: Convert.ToSByte(), Decimal.ToSByte(), IConvertible.ToSByte(), System.IO.BinaryReader.ReadSByte(), Math.{Abs(), Max(), Min()}, System.Runtime.Serialization.FormatterConverter.ToSByte(), System.Runtime.Serialization.IFormatterConverter.ToSByte(), System.Runtime.Serialization.SerializationInfo.GetSByte(), System.Xml.XmlConvert.ToSByte()

Passed To: Multiple types

SerializableAttribute
NotInheritable Class
System (mscorlib.dll)

This attribute is used in the class definition to indicate that a class can be serialized. By default, all fields in the class are serialized except for the fields that are marked with a NonSerializedAttribute.

It is not necessary to use this attribute if a given type implements the System.Runtime.Serialization.ISerializable interface, which indicates that a class provides its own methods for serialization.

```
Public NotInheritable Class SerializableAttribute : Inherits Attribute
' Public Constructors
    Public Sub New()
End Class
```

Hierarchy: Object→ Attribute→ SerializableAttribute

Valid On: Class, Struct, Enum, Delegate

Single

Structure

System (mscorlib.dll)

ECMA, serializable

This represents a 32-bit single-precision floating number as a value type. The value of a single can range approximately from -3.4×10^{38} to 3.4×10^{38}, and can also be set to one of the following fields: PositiveInfinity, NegativeInfinity, and NaN (not a number). In VB.NET, this type is aliased as Single.

Public Structure **Single** : Implements IComparable, IFormattable, IConvertible
' *Public Shared Fields*
   Public const **Epsilon** As Single =*1.401298E-45*
   Public const **MaxValue** As Single =*3.402823E+38*
   Public const **MinValue** As Single =*-3.402823E+38*
   Public const **NaN** As Single =*NaN*
   Public const **NegativeInfinity** As Single =*-Infinity*
   Public const **PositiveInfinity** As Single =*Infinity*
' *Public Shared Methods*
   Public Shared Function **IsInfinity**(ByVal f As Single) As Boolean
   Public Shared Function **IsNaN**(ByVal f As Single) As Boolean
   Public Shared Function **IsNegativeInfinity**(ByVal f As Single) As Boolean
   Public Shared Function **IsPositiveInfinity**(ByVal f As Single) As Boolean
   Public Shared Function **Parse**(ByVal s As String) As Single
   Public Shared Function **Parse**(ByVal s As String, ByVal provider As IFormatProvider) As Single
   Public Shared Function **Parse**(ByVal s As String, ByVal style As System.Globalization.NumberStyles) As Single
   Public Shared Function **Parse**(ByVal s As String, ByVal style As System.Globalization.NumberStyles, _
     ByVal provider As IFormatProvider) As Single
' *Public Instance Methods*
   Public Function **CompareTo**(ByVal value As Object) As Integer Implements IComparable.CompareTo
   Overrides Public Function **Equals**(ByVal obj As Object) As Boolean
   Overrides Public Function **GetHashCode**() As Integer
   Public Function **GetTypeCode**() As TypeCode Implements IConvertible.GetTypeCode
   Overrides Public Function **ToString**() As String
   Public Function **ToString**(ByVal provider As IFormatProvider) As String Implements IConvertible.ToString
   Public Function **ToString**(ByVal format As String) As String
   Public Function **ToString**(ByVal format As String, ByVal provider As IFormatProvider) As String _
     Implements IFormattable.ToString
End Structure

Hierarchy: Object→ ValueType→ Single(IComparable, IFormattable, IConvertible)

Returned By: BitConverter.ToSingle(), Convert.ToSingle(), Decimal.ToSingle(),
System.Diagnostics.CounterSample.Calculate(),
System.Diagnostics.CounterSampleCalculator.ComputeCounterValue(),
System.Diagnostics.PerformanceCounter.NextValue(), IConvertible.ToSingle(),
System.IO.BinaryReader.ReadSingle(), System.Runtime.Serialization.FormatterConverter.ToSingle(),
System.Runtime.Serialization.IFormatterConverter.ToSingle(),
System.Runtime.Serialization.SerializationInfo.GetSingle(), System.Xml.XmlConvert.ToSingle()

Passed To: Multiple types

StackOverflowException

NotInheritable Class

System (mscorlib.dll)

ECMA, serializable

This exception indicates that the .NET runtime environment experienced a stack overflow. This can be caused by pathologically deep recursion.

Public NotInheritable Class **StackOverflowException** : Inherits SystemException
' *Public Constructors*

```
 Public Sub New()
 Public Sub New(ByVal message As String)
 Public Sub New(ByVal message As String, ByVal innerException As Exception)
End Class
```

Hierarchy: Object→ Exception(System.Runtime.Serialization.ISerializable)→ SystemException→ StackOverflowException

STAThreadAttribute   NotInheritable Class

System (mscorlib.dll)

This attribute can be used only on the Main method of an application. It sets the default threading model to STA (single-threaded apartment). Alternatively, you can use the MTAThreadAttribute attribute to use a multithreaded apartment model.

Like its counterpart, MTAThreadAttribute, this attribute has no meaning outside of COM interoperability.

```
Public NotInheritable Class STAThreadAttribute : Inherits Attribute
' Public Constructors
 Public Sub New()
End Class
```

Hierarchy: Object→ Attribute→ STAThreadAttribute

Valid On: Method

String   NotInheritable Class

System (mscorlib.dll)   ECMA, serializable

This class consists of an immutable array of Char characters and built-in helper functions. Methods that appear to modify a string, such as Concat(), actually create and return a new String object. To modify a string directly, use the System.Text.StringBuilder class. This can enhance performance in some routines that make intensive use of string-manipulation operations. In VB.NET, String is aliased as String.

A string is slightly unusual because it is a reference type that behaves like a value type for comparison and assignment operations. Two String objects with the same content but different locations in memory return true when tested for equality. Also, assigning one String to another clones the string itself, rather than just duplicating the reference.

On the other hand, a String is a fully featured object with a Length property and a wide variety of methods for the following: padding or trimming specified characters on either side, converting case, performing inline substitutions (with Replace()), and dividing a string into an array of strings (with Split()). There's also a default indexer that lets you retrieve a single character. Note that strings are zero-based, and the first character is System.String.Chars(0).

You can create a string made up of a single repeated character by using an alternate constructor and supplying a char and the number of repetitions.

```
Public NotInheritable Class String : Implements IComparable, ICloneable, IConvertible, IEnumerable
' Public Constructors
 Public Sub New(ByVal value As Char())
 Public Sub New(ByVal value As Char(), ByVal startIndex As Integer, ByVal length As Integer)
 Public Sub New(ByVal c As Char, ByVal count As Integer)
' Public Shared Fields
 Public Shared ReadOnly Empty As String
' Public Instance Properties
```

Public Default ReadOnly Property **Chars** (ByVal index As Integer) As Char
Public ReadOnly Property **Length** As Integer

' *Public Shared Methods*

Public Shared Function **Compare**(ByVal strA As String, ByVal indexA As Integer, ByVal strB As String, _
ByVal indexB As Integer, ByVal length As Integer) As Integer

Public Shared Function **Compare**(ByVal strA As String, ByVal indexA As Integer, ByVal strB As String, _
ByVal indexB As Integer, ByVal length As Integer, ByVal ignoreCase As Boolean) As Integer

Public Shared Function **Compare**(ByVal strA As String, ByVal indexA As Integer, ByVal strB As String, _
ByVal indexB As Integer, ByVal length As Integer), ByVal ignoreCase As Boolean,   _
ByVal culture As System.Globalization.CultureInfo) As Integer

Public Shared Function **Compare**(ByVal strA As String, ByVal strB As String) As Integer

Public Shared Function **Compare**(ByVal strA As String, ByVal strB As String, ByVal ignoreCase As Boolean) _
As Integer

Public Shared Function **Compare**(ByVal strA As String, ByVal strB As String, ByVal ignoreCase As Boolean, _
ByVal culture As System.Globalization.CultureInfo) As Integer

Public Shared Function **CompareOrdinal**(ByVal strA As String, ByVal indexA As Integer, ByVal strB As String, _
ByVal indexB As Integer, ByVal length As Integer) As Integer

Public Shared Function **CompareOrdinal**(ByVal strA As String, ByVal strB As String) As Integer

Public Shared Function **Concat**(ByVal arg0 As Object) As String

Public Shared Function **Concat**(ParamArray args As Object()) As String

Public Shared Function **Concat**(ByVal arg0 As Object, ByVal arg1 As Object) As String

Public Shared Function **Concat**(ByVal arg0 As Object, ByVal arg1 As Object, ByVal arg2 As Object) As String

Public Shared Function **Concat**(ByVal arg0 As Object, ByVal arg1 As Object, ByVal arg2 As Object, _
ByVal arg3 As Object) As String

Public Shared Function **Concat**(ParamArray values As String()) As String

Public Shared Function **Concat**(ByVal str0 As String, ByVal str1 As String) As String

Public Shared Function **Concat**(ByVal str0 As String, ByVal str1 As String, ByVal str2 As String) As String

Public Shared Function **Concat**(ByVal str0 As String, ByVal str1 As String, ByVal str2 As String, ByVal str3 As String) _
As String

Public Shared Function **Copy**(ByVal str As String) As String

Public Shared Function **Equals**(ByVal a As String, ByVal b As String) As Boolean

Public Shared Function **Format**(ByVal provider As IFormatProvider, ByVal format As String, _
ParamArray args As Object()) As String

Public Shared Function **Format**(ByVal format As String, ByVal arg0 As Object) As String

Public Shared Function **Format**(ByVal format As String, ParamArray args As Object()) As String

Public Shared Function **Format**(ByVal format As String, ByVal arg0 As Object, ByVal arg1 As Object) As String

Public Shared Function **Format**(ByVal format As String, ByVal arg0 As Object, ByVal arg1 As Object, _
ByVal arg2 As Object) As String

Public Shared Function **Intern**(ByVal str As String) As String

Public Shared Function **IsInterned**(ByVal str As String) As String

Public Shared Function **Join**(ByVal separator As String, ByVal value As String()) As String

Public Shared Function **Join**(ByVal separator As String, ByVal value As String(), ByVal startIndex As Integer, _
ByVal count As Integer) As String

Public Shared Boolean operator Sub !=(ByVal a As String, ByVal b As String)

Public Shared Boolean operator Sub ==(ByVal a As String, ByVal b As String)

' *Public Instance Methods*

Public Function **Clone**() As Object Implements ICloneable.Clone

Public Function **CompareTo**(ByVal value As Object) As Integer Implements IComparable.CompareTo

Public Function **CompareTo**(ByVal strB As String) As Integer

Public Sub **CopyTo**(ByVal sourceIndex As Integer, ByVal destination As Char(), ByVal destinationIndex As Integer, _
ByVal count As Integer)

Public Function **EndsWith**(ByVal value As String) As Boolean

Overrides Public Function **Equals**(ByVal obj As Object) As Boolean

Public Function **Equals**(ByVal value As String) As Boolean

Public Function **GetEnumerator**() As CharEnumerator

Overrides Public Function **GetHashCode**() As Integer
Public Function **GetTypeCode**() As TypeCode Implements IConvertible.GetTypeCode
Public Function **IndexOf**(ByVal value As Char) As Integer
Public Function **IndexOf**(ByVal value As Char, ByVal startIndex As Integer) As Integer
Public Function **IndexOf**(ByVal value As Char, ByVal startIndex As Integer, ByVal count As Integer) As Integer
Public Function **IndexOf**(ByVal value As String) As Integer
Public Function **IndexOf**(ByVal value As String, ByVal startIndex As Integer) As Integer
Public Function **IndexOf**(ByVal value As String, ByVal startIndex As Integer, ByVal count As Integer) As Integer
Public Function **IndexOfAny**(ByVal anyOf As Char()) As Integer
Public Function **IndexOfAny**(ByVal anyOf As Char(), ByVal startIndex As Integer) As Integer
Public Function **IndexOfAny**(ByVal anyOf As Char(), ByVal startIndex As Integer, ByVal count As Integer) As Integer
Public Function **Insert**(ByVal startIndex As Integer, ByVal value As String) As String
Public Function **LastIndexOf**(ByVal value As Char) As Integer
Public Function **LastIndexOf**(ByVal value As Char, ByVal startIndex As Integer) As Integer
Public Function **LastIndexOf**(ByVal value As Char, ByVal startIndex As Integer, ByVal count As Integer) As Integer
Public Function **LastIndexOf**(ByVal value As String) As Integer
Public Function **LastIndexOf**(ByVal value As String, ByVal startIndex As Integer) As Integer
Public Function **LastIndexOf**(ByVal value As String, ByVal startIndex As Integer, ByVal count As Integer) As Integer
Public Function **LastIndexOfAny**(ByVal anyOf As Char()) As Integer
Public Function **LastIndexOfAny**(ByVal anyOf As Char(), ByVal startIndex As Integer) As Integer
Public Function **LastIndexOfAny**(ByVal anyOf As Char(), ByVal startIndex As Integer, ByVal count As Integer) _
    As Integer
Public Function **PadLeft**(ByVal totalWidth As Integer) As String
Public Function **PadLeft**(ByVal totalWidth As Integer, ByVal paddingChar As Char) As String
Public Function **PadRight**(ByVal totalWidth As Integer) As String
Public Function **PadRight**(ByVal totalWidth As Integer, ByVal paddingChar As Char) As String
Public Function **Remove**(ByVal startIndex As Integer, ByVal count As Integer) As String
Public Function **Replace**(ByVal oldChar As Char, ByVal newChar As Char) As String
Public Function **Replace**(ByVal oldValue As String, ByVal newValue As String) As String
Public Function **Split**(ParamArray separator As Char()) As String()
Public Function **Split**(ByVal separator As Char(), ByVal count As Integer) As String()
Public Function **StartsWith**(ByVal value As String) As Boolean
Public Function **Substring**(ByVal startIndex As Integer) As String
Public Function **Substring**(ByVal startIndex As Integer, ByVal length As Integer) As String
Public Function **ToCharArray**() As Char()
Public Function **ToCharArray**(ByVal startIndex As Integer, ByVal length As Integer) As Char()
Public Function **ToLower**() As String
Public Function **ToLower**(ByVal culture As System.Globalization.CultureInfo) As String
Overrides Public Function **ToString**() As String
Public Function **ToString**(ByVal provider As IFormatProvider) As String Implements IConvertible.ToString
Public Function **ToUpper**() As String
Public Function **ToUpper**(ByVal culture As System.Globalization.CultureInfo) As String
Public Function **Trim**() As String
Public Function **Trim**(ParamArray trimChars As Char()) As String
Public Function **TrimEnd**(ParamArray trimChars As Char()) As String
Public Function **TrimStart**(ParamArray trimChars As Char()) As String
End Class

Returned By: Multiple types

Passed To: Multiple types

SystemException
Class

System (mscorlib.dll)
ECMA, serializable

This class is the base class of exceptions that represent .NET runtime errors. In contrast, ApplicationException is the base class for user-defined exceptions.

```
Public Class SystemException : Inherits Exception
' Public Constructors
    Public Sub New()
    Public Sub New(ByVal message As String)
    Public Sub New(ByVal message As String, ByVal innerException As Exception)
' Protected Constructors
    Protected Sub New(ByVal info As System.Runtime.Serialization.SerializationInfo, _
        ByVal context As System.Runtime.Serialization.StreamingContext)
End Class
```

Hierarchy: Object→ Exception(System.Runtime.Serialization.ISerializable)→ SystemException

Subclasses: Multiple types

ThreadStaticAttribute
Class

System (mscorlib.dll)
serializable

This attribute designates that a shared field should not be shared between threads. Each thread receives a separate instance of this field and can set and retrieve values for it without causing potential synchronization problems. This also means that each thread has a copy of the shared field that may contain different values.

```
Public Class ThreadStaticAttribute : Inherits Attribute
' Public Constructors
    Public Sub New()
End Class
```

Hierarchy: Object→ Attribute→ ThreadStaticAttribute

Valid On: Field

TimeSpan
Structure

System (mscorlib.dll)
ECMA, serializable

This class encapsulates a positive or negative interval of time that can be used for arithmetic operations and greater-than or less-than comparisons. Internally, the TimeSpan is stored as a number of *ticks*, each of which is equal to 100 nanoseconds. You can convert a string into a TimeSpan using the shared Parse() method.

You can evaluate a time span in terms of days, hours, seconds, and so on, by using the appropriate Total property. The corresponding properties that are not preceded with the word Total return only one component of the time span. (For example, the TotalHours property returns 1.5 for a time span of an hour and a half, while Hours returns 1 for a time span of one hour.)

The TimeSpanshared methods prefixed with From are useful for quickly creating a time span for use as an argument for a method call, as in myApp.SetTimeSpan(TimeSpan.FromMinutes(10)).

```
Public Structure TimeSpan : Implements IComparable
' Public Constructors
    Public Sub New(ByVal hours As Integer, ByVal minutes As Integer, ByVal seconds As Integer)
    Public Sub New(ByVal days As Integer, ByVal hours As Integer, ByVal minutes As Integer, ByVal seconds As Integer)
    Public Sub New(ByVal days As Integer, ByVal hours As Integer, ByVal minutes As Integer, ByVal seconds As Integer, _
        ByVal milliseconds As Integer)
```

```
      Public Sub New(ByVal ticks As Long)
' Public Shared Fields
      Public Shared ReadOnly MaxValue As TimeSpan          =10675199.02:48:05.4775807
      Public Shared ReadOnly MinValue As TimeSpan          =-10675199.02:48:05.4775808
      Public const TicksPerDay As Long                     =864000000000
      Public const TicksPerHour As Long                    =36000000000
      Public const TicksPerMillisecond As Long             =10000
      Public const TicksPerMinute As Long                  =600000000
      Public const TicksPerSecond As Long                  =10000000
      Public Shared ReadOnly Zero As TimeSpan              =00:00:00
' Public Instance Properties
      Public ReadOnly Property Days As Integer
      Public ReadOnly Property Hours As Integer
      Public ReadOnly Property Milliseconds As Integer
      Public ReadOnly Property Minutes As Integer
      Public ReadOnly Property Seconds As Integer
      Public ReadOnly Property Ticks As Long
      Public ReadOnly Property TotalDays As Double
      Public ReadOnly Property TotalHours As Double
      Public ReadOnly Property TotalMilliseconds As Double
      Public ReadOnly Property TotalMinutes As Double
      Public ReadOnly Property TotalSeconds As Double
' Public Shared Methods
      Public Shared Function Compare(ByVal t1 As TimeSpan, ByVal t2 As TimeSpan) As Integer
      Public Shared Function Equals(ByVal t1 As TimeSpan, ByVal t2 As TimeSpan) As Boolean
      Public Shared Function FromDays(ByVal value As Double) As TimeSpan
      Public Shared Function FromHours(ByVal value As Double) As TimeSpan
      Public Shared Function FromMilliseconds(ByVal value As Double) As TimeSpan
      Public Shared Function FromMinutes(ByVal value As Double) As TimeSpan
      Public Shared Function FromSeconds(ByVal value As Double) As TimeSpan
      Public Shared Function FromTicks(ByVal value As Long) As TimeSpan
      Public Shared Function Parse(ByVal s As String) As TimeSpan
      Public Shared TimeSpan operator Sub -(ByVal t As TimeSpan)
      Public Shared TimeSpan operator Sub -(ByVal t1 As TimeSpan, ByVal t2 As TimeSpan)
      Public Shared TimeSpan operator Sub +(ByVal t As TimeSpan)
      Public Shared TimeSpan operator Sub +(ByVal t1 As TimeSpan, ByVal t2 As TimeSpan)
      Public Shared Boolean operator Sub !=(ByVal t1 As TimeSpan, ByVal t2 As TimeSpan)
      Public Shared Boolean operator Sub <(ByVal t1 As TimeSpan, ByVal t2 As TimeSpan)
      Public Shared Boolean operator Sub <=(ByVal t1 As TimeSpan, ByVal t2 As TimeSpan)
      Public Shared Boolean operator Sub ==(ByVal t1 As TimeSpan, ByVal t2 As TimeSpan)
      Public Shared Boolean operator Sub >(ByVal t1 As TimeSpan, ByVal t2 As TimeSpan)
      Public Shared Boolean operator Sub >=(ByVal t1 As TimeSpan, ByVal t2 As TimeSpan)
' Public Instance Methods
      Public Function Add(ByVal ts As TimeSpan) As TimeSpan
      Public Function CompareTo(ByVal value As Object) As Integer Implements  IComparable.CompareTo
      Public Function Duration() As TimeSpan
      Overrides Public Function Equals(ByVal value As Object) As Boolean
      Overrides Public Function GetHashCode() As Integer
      Public Function Negate() As TimeSpan
      Public Function Subtract(ByVal ts As TimeSpan) As TimeSpan
      Overrides Public Function ToString() As String
End Structure
```

Hierarchy: Object→ ValueType→ TimeSpan(IComparable)

Returned By: DateTime.{Subtract(), TimeOfDay},
System.Diagnostics.Process.{PrivilegedProcessorTime, TotalProcessorTime, UserProcessorTime},

System.Diagnostics.ProcessThread.{PrivilegedProcessorTime, TotalProcessorTime, UserProcessorTime},
System.Globalization.DaylightTime.Delta, TimeZone.GetUtcOffset(),
System.Xml.XmlConvert.ToTimeSpan()

Passed To: Multiple types

TimeZone
MustInherit Class

System (mscorlib.dll) | *serializable*

This MustInherit class encapsulates a time zone. You cannot create a TimeZone instance directly because different time zones require different implementations of methods that involve time offsets due to daylight savings time. The most useful member of the Time-Zone class is the shared CurrentTimeZone property, which provides a TimeZone object based on the localization settings of the current system.

```
Public MustInherit Class TimeZone
' Protected Constructors
   Protected Sub New()
' Public Shared Properties
   Public Shared ReadOnly Property CurrentTimeZone As TimeZone
' Public Instance Properties
   MustInherit Public ReadOnly Property DaylightName As String
   MustInherit Public ReadOnly Property StandardName As String
' Public Shared Methods
   Public Shared Function IsDaylightSavingTime(ByVal time As Date, _
      ByVal daylightTimes As System.Globalization.DaylightTime) As Boolean
' Public Instance Methods
   MustInherit Public Function GetDaylightChanges(ByVal year As Integer) As DaylightTime
   MustInherit Public Function GetUtcOffset(ByVal time As Date) As TimeSpan
   Overridable Public Function IsDaylightSavingTime(ByVal time As Date) As Boolean
   Overridable Public Function ToLocalTime(ByVal time As Date) As Date
   Overridable Public Function ToUniversalTime(ByVal time As Date) As Date
End Class
```

Type
MustInherit Class

System (mscorlib.dll) | *ECMA, serializable*

Type is a MustInherit base class that encapsulates the metadata for any .NET type. You can get a Type object by using the System.Object.GetType() method, which is inherited by all .NET types, or by the VB.NET GetType function.

The Type is used most often for reflection. You can get a complete description of an object's metadata, including information about the constructors, methods, fields, properties, and events of a class, as well as the module and the assembly in which the class is deployed by using it. Do this by using the supplied Get methods, such as GetEvents() and GetConstructors(), which return arrays of the appropriate System.Reflection class. You can also use the singular methods, such as GetEvent(), to retrieve a single type object that matches specific criteria. Note that all members can be retrieved, including inherited, private, and protected members.

```
Public MustInherit Class Type : Inherits System.Reflection.MemberInfo : Implements  System.Reflection.IReflect
' Protected Constructors
   Protected Sub New()
' Public Shared Fields
   Public Shared ReadOnly Delimiter As Char                          = [amp  ]H0000002E
   Public Shared ReadOnly EmptyTypes As Type()                       =System.Type()
   Public Shared ReadOnly FilterAttribute As MemberFilter            =System.Reflection.MemberFilter
```

Public Shared ReadOnly **FilterName** As MemberFilter   =*System.Reflection.MemberFilter*
Public Shared ReadOnly **FilterNameIgnoreCase** As MemberFilter   =*System.Reflection.MemberFilter*
Public Shared ReadOnly **Missing** As Object   =*System.Reflection.Missing*

' Public Shared Properties
Public Shared ReadOnly Property **DefaultBinder** As Binder

' Public Instance Properties
MustInherit Public ReadOnly Property **Assembly** As Assembly
MustInherit Public ReadOnly Property **AssemblyQualifiedName** As String
Public ReadOnly Property **Attributes** As TypeAttributes
MustInherit Public ReadOnly Property **BaseType** As Type
Overrides Public ReadOnly Property **DeclaringType** As Type
MustInherit Public ReadOnly Property **FullName** As String
MustInherit Public ReadOnly Property **GUID** As Guid
Public ReadOnly Property **HasElementType** As Boolean
Public ReadOnly Property **IsAbstract** As Boolean
Public ReadOnly Property **IsAnsiClass** As Boolean
Public ReadOnly Property **IsArray** As Boolean
Public ReadOnly Property **IsAutoClass** As Boolean
Public ReadOnly Property **IsAutoLayout** As Boolean
Public ReadOnly Property **IsByRef** As Boolean
Public ReadOnly Property **IsClass** As Boolean
Public ReadOnly Property **IsCOMObject** As Boolean
Public ReadOnly Property **IsContextful** As Boolean
Public ReadOnly Property **IsEnum** As Boolean
Public ReadOnly Property **IsExplicitLayout** As Boolean
Public ReadOnly Property **IsImport** As Boolean
Public ReadOnly Property **IsInterface** As Boolean
Public ReadOnly Property **IsLayoutSequential** As Boolean
Public ReadOnly Property **IsMarshalByRef** As Boolean
Public ReadOnly Property **IsNestedAssembly** As Boolean
Public ReadOnly Property **IsNestedFamANDAssem** As Boolean
Public ReadOnly Property **IsNestedFamily** As Boolean
Public ReadOnly Property **IsNestedFamORAssem** As Boolean
Public ReadOnly Property **IsNestedPrivate** As Boolean
Public ReadOnly Property **IsNestedPublic** As Boolean
Public ReadOnly Property **IsNotPublic** As Boolean
Public ReadOnly Property **IsPointer** As Boolean
Public ReadOnly Property **IsPrimitive** As Boolean
Public ReadOnly Property **IsPublic** As Boolean
Public ReadOnly Property **IsSealed** As Boolean
Public ReadOnly Property **IsSerializable** As Boolean
Public ReadOnly Property **IsSpecialName** As Boolean
Public ReadOnly Property **IsUnicodeClass** As Boolean
Public ReadOnly Property **IsValueType** As Boolean
Overrides Public ReadOnly Property **MemberType** As MemberTypes
MustInherit Public ReadOnly Property **Module** As Module
MustInherit Public ReadOnly Property **Namespace** As String
Overrides Public ReadOnly Property **ReflectedType** As Type
MustInherit Public ReadOnly Property **TypeHandle** As RuntimeTypeHandle
Public ReadOnly Property **TypeInitializer** As ConstructorInfo
MustInherit Public ReadOnly Property **UnderlyingSystemType** As Type _
   Implements IReflect.UnderlyingSystemType

' Public Shared Methods
Public Shared Function **GetType**(ByVal typeName As String) As Type
Public Shared Function **GetType**(ByVal typeName As String, ByVal throwOnError As Boolean) As Type

Public Shared Function **GetType**(ByVal typeName As String, ByVal throwOnError As Boolean, _
ByVal ignoreCase As Boolean) As Type

Public Shared Function **GetTypeArray**(ByVal args As Object()) As Type()

Public Shared Function **GetTypeCode**(ByVal type As Type) As TypeCode

Public Shared Function **GetTypeFromCLSID**(ByVal clsid As Guid) As Type

Public Shared Function **GetTypeFromCLSID**(ByVal clsid As Guid, ByVal throwOnError As Boolean) As Type

Public Shared Function **GetTypeFromCLSID**(ByVal clsid As Guid, ByVal server As String) As Type

Public Shared Function **GetTypeFromCLSID**(ByVal clsid As Guid, ByVal server As String, _
ByVal throwOnError As Boolean) As Type

Public Shared Function **GetTypeFromHandle**(ByVal handle As RuntimeTypeHandle) As Type

Public Shared Function **GetTypeFromProgID**(ByVal progID As String) As Type

Public Shared Function **GetTypeFromProgID**(ByVal progID As String, ByVal throwOnError As Boolean) As Type

Public Shared Function **GetTypeFromProgID**(ByVal progID As String, ByVal server As String) As Type

Public Shared Function **GetTypeFromProgID**(ByVal progID As String, ByVal server As String, _
ByVal throwOnError As Boolean) As Type

Public Shared Function **GetTypeHandle**(ByVal o As Object) As RuntimeTypeHandle

' *Public Instance Methods*

Overrides Public Function **Equals**(ByVal o As Object) As Boolean

Public Function **Equals**(ByVal o As Type) As Boolean

Overridable Public Function **FindInterfaces**(ByVal filter As System.Reflection.TypeFilter, _
ByVal filterCriteria As Object) As Type()

Overridable Public Function **FindMembers**(ByVal memberType As System.Reflection.MemberTypes, _
ByVal bindingAttr As System.Reflection.BindingFlags, ByVal filter As System.Reflection.MemberFilter, _
ByVal filterCriteria As Object) As MemberInfo()

Overridable Public Function **GetArrayRank**() As Integer

Public Function **GetConstructor**(ByVal bindingAttr As System.Reflection.BindingFlags, _
ByVal binder As System.Reflection.Binder, ByVal callConvention As System.Reflection.CallingConventions, _
ByVal types As Type(), ByVal modifiers As System.Reflection.ParameterModifier()) As ConstructorInfo

Public Function **GetConstructor**(ByVal bindingAttr As System.Reflection.BindingFlags, _
ByVal binder As System.Reflection.Binder, ByVal types As Type(), _
ByVal modifiers As System.Reflection.ParameterModifier()) As ConstructorInfo

Public Function **GetConstructor**(ByVal types As Type()) As ConstructorInfo

Public Function **GetConstructors**() As ConstructorInfo()

MustInherit Public Function **GetConstructors**(ByVal bindingAttr As System.Reflection.BindingFlags) _
As ConstructorInfo()

Overridable Public Function **GetDefaultMembers**() As MemberInfo()

MustInherit Public Function **GetElementType**() As Type

Public Function **GetEvent**(ByVal name As String) As EventInfo

MustInherit Public Function **GetEvent**(ByVal name As String, ByVal bindingAttr As System.Reflection.BindingFlags) _
As EventInfo

Overridable Public Function **GetEvents**() As EventInfo()

MustInherit Public Function **GetEvents**(ByVal bindingAttr As System.Reflection.BindingFlags) As EventInfo()

Public Function **GetField**(ByVal name As String) As FieldInfo

MustInherit Public Function **GetField**(ByVal name As String, ByVal bindingAttr As System.Reflection.BindingFlags) _
As FieldInfo Implements IReflect.GetField

Public Function **GetFields**() As FieldInfo()

MustInherit Public Function **GetFields**(ByVal bindingAttr As System.Reflection.BindingFlags) As FieldInfo() _
Implements IReflect.GetFields

Overrides Public Function **GetHashCode**() As Integer

Public Function **GetInterface**(ByVal name As String) As Type

MustInherit Public Function **GetInterface**(ByVal name As String, ByVal ignoreCase As Boolean) As Type

Overridable Public Function **GetInterfaceMap**(ByVal interfaceType As Type) As InterfaceMapping

MustInherit Public Function **GetInterfaces**() As Type()

Public Function **GetMember**(ByVal name As String) As MemberInfo()

Overridable Public Function **GetMember**(ByVal name As String, _
ByVal bindingAttr As System.Reflection.BindingFlags) As MemberInfo() Implements IReflect.GetMember

Overridable Public Function **GetMember**(ByVal name As String, ByVal type As System.Reflection.MemberTypes, _
  ByVal bindingAttr As System.Reflection.BindingFlags) As MemberInfo()
Public Function **GetMembers**() As MemberInfo()
MustInherit Public Function **GetMembers**(ByVal bindingAttr As System.Reflection.BindingFlags) As MemberInfo() _
  Implements IReflect.GetMembers
Public Function **GetMethod**(ByVal name As String) As MethodInfo
Public Function **GetMethod**(ByVal name As String, ByVal bindingAttr As System.Reflection.BindingFlags) _
  As MethodInfo Implements IReflect.GetMethod
Public Function **GetMethod**(ByVal name As String, ByVal bindingAttr As System.Reflection.BindingFlags, _
  ByVal binder As System.Reflection.Binder, ByVal callConvention As System.Reflection.CallingConventions, _
  ByVal types As Type(), ByVal modifiers As System.Reflection.ParameterModifier()) As MethodInfo
Public Function **GetMethod**(ByVal name As String, ByVal bindingAttr As System.Reflection.BindingFlags, _
  ByVal binder As System.Reflection.Binder, ByVal types As Type(), _
  ByVal modifiers As System.Reflection.ParameterModifier()) As MethodInfo Implements IReflect.GetMethod
Public Function **GetMethod**(ByVal name As String, ByVal types As Type()) As MethodInfo
Public Function **GetMethod**(ByVal name As String, ByVal types As Type(), _
  ByVal modifiers As System.Reflection.ParameterModifier()) As MethodInfo
Public Function **GetMethods**() As MethodInfo()
MustInherit Public Function **GetMethods**(ByVal bindingAttr As System.Reflection.BindingFlags) As MethodInfo() _
  Implements IReflect.GetMethods
Public Function **GetNestedType**(ByVal name As String) As Type
MustInherit Public Function **GetNestedType**(ByVal name As String, _
  ByVal bindingAttr As System.Reflection.BindingFlags) As Type
Public Function **GetNestedTypes**() As Type()
MustInherit Public Function **GetNestedTypes**(ByVal bindingAttr As System.Reflection.BindingFlags) As Type()
Public Function **GetProperties**() As PropertyInfo()
MustInherit Public Function **GetProperties**(ByVal bindingAttr As System.Reflection.BindingFlags) _
  As PropertyInfo() Implements IReflect.GetProperties
Public Function **GetProperty**(ByVal name As String) As PropertyInfo
Public Function **GetProperty**(ByVal name As String, ByVal bindingAttr As System.Reflection.BindingFlags) _
  As PropertyInfo Implements IReflect.GetProperty
Public Function **GetProperty**(ByVal name As String, ByVal bindingAttr As System.Reflection.BindingFlags, _
  ByVal binder As System.Reflection.Binder, ByVal returnType As Type, ByVal types As Type(), _
  ByVal modifiers As System.Reflection.ParameterModifier()) As PropertyInfo Implements IReflect.GetProperty
Public Function **GetProperty**(ByVal name As String, ByVal returnType As Type) As PropertyInfo
Public Function **GetProperty**(ByVal name As String, ByVal types As Type()) As PropertyInfo
Public Function **GetProperty**(ByVal name As String, ByVal returnType As Type, ByVal types As Type()) _
  As PropertyInfo
Public Function **GetProperty**(ByVal name As String, ByVal returnType As Type, ByVal types As Type(), _
  ByVal modifiers As System.Reflection.ParameterModifier()) As PropertyInfo
Public Function **InvokeMember**(ByVal name As String, ByVal invokeAttr As System.Reflection.BindingFlags, _
  ByVal binder As System.Reflection.Binder, ByVal target As Object, ByVal args As Object()) As Object
Public Function **InvokeMember**(ByVal name As String, ByVal invokeAttr As System.Reflection.BindingFlags, _
  ByVal binder As System.Reflection.Binder, ByVal target As Object, ByVal args As Object(), _
  ByVal culture As System.Globalization.CultureInfo) As Object
MustInherit Public Function **InvokeMember**(ByVal name As String, _
  ByVal invokeAttr As System.Reflection.BindingFlags, ByVal binder As System.Reflection.Binder, _
  ByVal target As Object, ByVal args As Object(), ByVal modifiers As System.Reflection.ParameterModifier(), _
  ByVal culture As System.Globalization.CultureInfo, ByVal namedParameters As String()) As Object _
  Implements IReflect.InvokeMember
Overridable Public Function **IsAssignableFrom**(ByVal c As Type) As Boolean
Overridable Public Function **IsInstanceOfType**(ByVal o As Object) As Boolean
Overridable Public Function **IsSubclassOf**(ByVal c As Type) As Boolean
Overrides Public Function **ToString**() As String
' *Protected Instance Methods*

MustInherit Protected Function **GetAttributeFlagsImpl**() As TypeAttributes
MustInherit Protected Function **GetConstructorImpl**(ByVal bindingAttr As System.Reflection.BindingFlags, _
   ByVal binder As System.Reflection.Binder, ByVal callConvention As System.Reflection.CallingConventions,   _
   ByVal types As Type(), ByVal modifiers As System.Reflection.ParameterModifier()) As ConstructorInfo
MustInherit Protected Function **GetMethodImpl**(ByVal name As String,   _
   ByVal bindingAttr As System.Reflection.BindingFlags, ByVal binder As System.Reflection.Binder, _
   ByVal callConvention As System.Reflection.CallingConventions, ByVal types As Type(),   _
   ByVal modifiers As System.Reflection.ParameterModifier()) As MethodInfo
MustInherit Protected Function **GetPropertyImpl**(ByVal name As String,   _
   ByVal bindingAttr As System.Reflection.BindingFlags, ByVal binder As System.Reflection.Binder,   _
   ByVal returnType As Type, ByVal types As Type(), ByVal modifiers As System.Reflection.ParameterModifier()) _
   As PropertyInfo
MustInherit Protected Function **HasElementTypeImpl**() As Boolean
MustInherit Protected Function **IsArrayImpl**() As Boolean
MustInherit Protected Function **IsByRefImpl**() As Boolean
MustInherit Protected Function **IsCOMObjectImpl**() As Boolean
Overridable Protected Function **IsContextfulImpl**() As Boolean
Overridable Protected Function **IsMarshalByRefImpl**() As Boolean
MustInherit Protected Function **IsPointerImpl**() As Boolean
MustInherit Protected Function **IsPrimitiveImpl**() As Boolean
Overridable Protected Function **IsValueTypeImpl**() As Boolean
End Class

Hierarchy: Object→ System.Reflection.MemberInfo(System.Reflection.ICustomAttributeProvider)→
Type(System.Reflection.IReflect)

Subclasses: System.Reflection.TypeDelegator, System.Reflection.Emit.{ EnumBuilder, TypeBuilder}

Returned By: Multiple types

Passed To: Multiple types

TypeCode
Enum

System (mscorlib.dll)
serializable

This enumeration specifies the type of an object. It is available for all objects that implement the IConvertible interface. If the object does not implement this interface, use its GetType() method (derived from System.Object) to return an instance of the Type class, which provides a Type.GetTypeCode() method.

The TypeCode enumeration includes members for most simple value types. If you use this method on an object that is not explicitly represented in this enumeration, the catch-all value Object is returned.

Public Enum **TypeCode**
    Empty = 0
    Object = 1
    DBNull = 2
    Boolean = 3
    Char = 4
    SByte = 5
    Byte = 6
    Int16 = 7
    UInt16 = 8
    Int32 = 9
    UInt32 = 10
    Int64 = 11

> | UInt64 = 12 |
> | Single = 13 |
> | Double = 14 |
> | Decimal = 15 |
> | DateTime = 16 |
> | String = 18 |

End Enum

Hierarchy: Object→ ValueType→ Enum(IComparable, IFormattable, IConvertible)→ TypeCode

Returned By: Multiple types

Passed To: Convert.ChangeType(), System.Runtime.Serialization.FormatterConverter.Convert(), System.Runtime.Serialization.IFormatterConverter.Convert()

TypeInitializationException   NotInheritable Class

System (mscorlib.dll)   *ECMA, serializable*

This class provides a wrapper around an exception thrown by the .NET class initializer. The underlying exception is accessible through InnerException.

Public NotInheritable Class **TypeInitializationException** : Inherits SystemException
' *Public Constructors*
   Public Sub **New**(ByVal fullTypeName As String, ByVal innerException As Exception)
' *Public Instance Properties*
   Public ReadOnly Property **TypeName** As String
' *Public Instance Methods*
   Overrides Public Sub **GetObjectData**(ByVal info As System.Runtime.Serialization.SerializationInfo, _
     ByVal context As System.Runtime.Serialization.StreamingContext)
End Class

Hierarchy: Object→ Exception(System.Runtime.Serialization.ISerializable)→ SystemException→ TypeInitializationException

TypeLoadException   Class

System (mscorlib.dll)   *ECMA, serializable*

This exception signals that a class (or its assembly) cannot be found or loaded by the .NET runtime.

Public Class **TypeLoadException** : Inherits SystemException
' *Public Constructors*
   Public Sub **New**()
   Public Sub **New**(ByVal message As String)
   Public Sub **New**(ByVal message As String, ByVal inner As Exception)
' *Protected Constructors*
   Protected Sub **New**(ByVal info As System.Runtime.Serialization.SerializationInfo, _
     ByVal context As System.Runtime.Serialization.StreamingContext)
' *Public Instance Properties*
   Overrides Public ReadOnly Property **Message** As String
   Public ReadOnly Property **TypeName** As String
' *Public Instance Methods*
   Overrides Public Sub **GetObjectData**(ByVal info As System.Runtime.Serialization.SerializationInfo, _
     ByVal context As System.Runtime.Serialization.StreamingContext)
End Class

Hierarchy: Object→ Exception(System.Runtime.Serialization.ISerializable)→ SystemException→ TypeLoadException

Subclasses: DllNotFoundException, EntryPointNotFoundException

TypeUnloadedException   Class

System (mscorlib.dll)   *ECMA, serializable*

This exception signals an attempt to access a Type that has been unloaded.

```
Public Class TypeUnloadedException : Inherits SystemException
' Public Constructors
    Public Sub New()
    Public Sub New(ByVal message As String)
    Public Sub New(ByVal message As String, ByVal innerException As Exception)
' Protected Constructors
    Protected Sub New(ByVal info As System.Runtime.Serialization.SerializationInfo, _
      ByVal context As System.Runtime.Serialization.StreamingContext)
End Class
```

Hierarchy: Object→ Exception(System.Runtime.Serialization.ISerializable)→ SystemException→ TypeUnloadedException

UInt16   Structure

System (mscorlib.dll)   *ECMA, serializable*

This structure is the value type for 16-bit unsigned integers (which range from 0 to 65535). It is not CLS-compliant (although Int16 is).

```
Public Structure UInt16 : Implements IComparable, IFormattable, IConvertible
' Public Shared Fields
    Public const MaxValue As UInt16                                    =65535
    Public const MinValue As UInt16                                        =0
' Public Shared Methods
    Public Shared Function Parse(ByVal s As String) As UInt16
    Public Shared Function Parse(ByVal s As String, ByVal provider As IFormatProvider) As UInt16
    Public Shared Function Parse(ByVal s As String, ByVal style As System.Globalization.NumberStyles) As UInt16
    Public Shared Function Parse(ByVal s As String, ByVal style As System.Globalization.NumberStyles, _
      ByVal provider As IFormatProvider) As UInt16
' Public Instance Methods
    Public Function CompareTo(ByVal value As Object) As Integer Implements IComparable.CompareTo
    Overrides Public Function Equals(ByVal obj As Object) As Boolean
    Overrides Public Function GetHashCode() As Integer
    Public Function GetTypeCode() As TypeCode Implements IConvertible.GetTypeCode
    Overrides Public Function ToString() As String
    Public Function ToString(ByVal provider As IFormatProvider) As String Implements IConvertible.ToString
    Public Function ToString(ByVal format As String) As String
    Public Function ToString(ByVal format As String, ByVal provider As IFormatProvider) As String _
      Implements IFormattable.ToString
End Structure
```

Hierarchy: Object→ ValueType→ UInt16(IComparable, IFormattable, IConvertible)

Returned By: BitConverter.ToUInt16(), Convert.ToUInt16(), Decimal.ToUInt16(), IConvertible.ToUInt16(), System.IO.BinaryReader.ReadUInt16(),

System.Runtime.Serialization.FormatterConverter.ToUInt16(),
System.Runtime.Serialization.IFormatterConverter.ToUInt16(),
System.Runtime.Serialization.SerializationInfo.GetUInt16(), System.Xml.XmlConvert.ToUInt16()

Passed To: Multiple types

UInt32   Structure

System (mscorlib.dll)   *ECMA, serializable*

This structure is the value type for 32-bit unsigned integers (which range from 0 to 4,294,967,295). It is not CLS-compliant (although Int32 is).

Public Structure **UInt32** : Implements IComparable, IFormattable, IConvertible
' Public Shared Fields
  Public const **MaxValue** As UInt32   *=4294967295*
  Public const **MinValue** As UInt32   *=0*
' Public Shared Methods
  Public Shared Function **Parse**(ByVal s As String) As UInt32
  Public Shared Function **Parse**(ByVal s As String, ByVal provider As IFormatProvider) As UInt32
  Public Shared Function **Parse**(ByVal s As String, ByVal style As System.Globalization.NumberStyles) As UInt32
  Public Shared Function **Parse**(ByVal s As String, ByVal style As System.Globalization.NumberStyles, _
    ByVal provider As IFormatProvider) As UInt32
' Public Instance Methods
  Public Function **CompareTo**(ByVal value As Object) As Integer Implements IComparable.CompareTo
  Overrides Public Function **Equals**(ByVal obj As Object) As Boolean
  Overrides Public Function **GetHashCode**() As Integer
  Public Function **GetTypeCode**() As TypeCode Implements IConvertible.GetTypeCode
  Overrides Public Function **ToString**() As String
  Public Function **ToString**(ByVal provider As IFormatProvider) As String Implements IConvertible.ToString
  Public Function **ToString**(ByVal format As String) As String
  Public Function **ToString**(ByVal format As String, ByVal provider As IFormatProvider) As String _
    Implements IFormattable.ToString
End Structure

Hierarchy: Object→ ValueType→ UInt32(IComparable, IFormattable, IConvertible)

Returned By: BitConverter.ToUInt32(), Convert.ToUInt32(), Decimal.ToUInt32(),
IConvertible.ToUInt32(), System.IO.BinaryReader.ReadUInt32(),
System.Reflection.AssemblyAlgorithmIdAttribute.AlgorithmId,
System.Reflection.AssemblyFlagsAttribute.Flags,
System.Runtime.Serialization.FormatterConverter.ToUInt32(),
System.Runtime.Serialization.IFormatterConverter.ToUInt32(),
System.Runtime.Serialization.SerializationInfo.GetUInt32(), UIntPtr.ToUInt32(),
System.Xml.XmlConvert.ToUInt32()

Passed To: Multiple types

UInt64   Structure

System (mscorlib.dll)   *ECMA, serializable*

This structure is the value type for 64-bit unsigned integers (which range from 0 to 1.84×10^{20}). It is not CLS-compliant (although Int64 is).

Public Structure **UInt64** : Implements IComparable, IFormattable, IConvertible
' Public Shared Fields
  Public const **MaxValue** As UInt64   *=18446744073709551615*
  Public const **MinValue** As UInt64   *=0*
' Public Shared Methods

Public Shared Function **Parse**(ByVal s As String) As UInt64
Public Shared Function **Parse**(ByVal s As String, ByVal provider As IFormatProvider) As UInt64
Public Shared Function **Parse**(ByVal s As String, ByVal style As System.Globalization.NumberStyles) As UInt64
Public Shared Function **Parse**(ByVal s As String, ByVal style As System.Globalization.NumberStyles, _
    ByVal provider As IFormatProvider) As UInt64
' *Public Instance Methods*
Public Function **CompareTo**(ByVal value As Object) As Integer Implements IComparable.CompareTo
Overrides Public Function **Equals**(ByVal obj As Object) As Boolean
Overrides Public Function **GetHashCode**() As Integer
Public Function **GetTypeCode**() As TypeCode Implements IConvertible.GetTypeCode
Overrides Public Function **ToString**() As String
Public Function **ToString**(ByVal provider As IFormatProvider) As String Implements IConvertible.ToString
Public Function **ToString**(ByVal format As String) As String
Public Function **ToString**(ByVal format As String, ByVal provider As IFormatProvider) As String _
    Implements IFormattable.ToString
End Structure

Hierarchy: Object→ ValueType→ UInt64(IComparable, IFormattable, IConvertible)

Returned By: BitConverter.ToUInt64(), Convert.ToUInt64(), Decimal.ToUInt64(),
IConvertible.ToUInt64(), System.IO.BinaryReader.ReadUInt64(),
System.IO.IsolatedStorage.IsolatedStorage.{CurrentSize, MaximumSize},
System.Runtime.Serialization.FormatterConverter.ToUInt64(),
System.Runtime.Serialization.IFormatterConverter.ToUInt64(),
System.Runtime.Serialization.SerializationInfo.GetUInt64(), UIntPtr.ToUInt64(),
System.Xml.XmlConvert.ToUInt64()

Passed To: Multiple types

UIntPtr
Structure

System (mscorlib.dll)
ECMA, serializable

This structure is provided mainly for symmetry with IntPtr. Use IntPtr, which is CLS-compliant, instead.

Public Structure **UIntPtr** : Implements System.Runtime.Serialization.ISerializable
' *Public Constructors*
Public Sub **New**(ByVal value As UInt32)
Public Sub **New**(ByVal value As UInt64)
' *Public Shared Fields*
Public Shared ReadOnly **Zero** As UIntPtr   =0
' *Public Shared Properties*
Public Shared ReadOnly Property **Size** As Integer
' *Public Shared Methods*
Public Shared Boolean operator Sub **!=**(ByVal value1 As UIntPtr, ByVal value2 As UIntPtr)
Public Shared Boolean operator Sub **==**(ByVal value1 As UIntPtr, ByVal value2 As UIntPtr)
Public Shared explicit operator Sub **UInt32**(ByVal value As UIntPtr)
Public Shared explicit operator Sub **UInt64**(ByVal value As UIntPtr)
Public Shared explicit operator Sub **UIntPtr**(ByVal value As UInt32)
Public Shared explicit operator Sub **UIntPtr**(ByVal value As UInt64)
' *Public Instance Methods*
Overrides Public Function **Equals**(ByVal obj As Object) As Boolean
Overrides Public Function **GetHashCode**() As Integer
Overrides Public Function **ToString**() As String
Public Function **ToUInt32**() As UInt32

Public Function **ToUInt64**() As UInt64
End Structure

Hierarchy: Object→ ValueType→ UIntPtr(System.Runtime.Serialization.ISerializable)

UnauthorizedAccessException
Class

System (mscorlib.dll)
ECMA, serializable

This exception signals a failed attempt to access a resource (for example, trying to delete a read-only file).

Public Class **UnauthorizedAccessException** : Inherits SystemException
' *Public Constructors*
   Public Sub **New**()
   Public Sub **New**(ByVal message As String)
   Public Sub **New**(ByVal message As String, ByVal inner As Exception)
' *Protected Constructors*
   Protected Sub **New**(ByVal info As System.Runtime.Serialization.SerializationInfo, _
     ByVal context As System.Runtime.Serialization.StreamingContext)
End Class

Hierarchy: Object→ Exception(System.Runtime.Serialization.ISerializable)→ SystemException→
UnauthorizedAccessException

UnhandledExceptionEventArgs
Class

System (mscorlib.dll)
ECMA, serializable

This class is passed as an argument to an UnhandledExceptionEventHandler event handler. Its IsTerminating property specifies whether the CLR is in the process of shutting down.

Public Class **UnhandledExceptionEventArgs** : Inherits EventArgs
' *Public Constructors*
   Public Sub **New**(ByVal exception As Object, ByVal isTerminating As Boolean)
' *Public Instance Properties*
   Public ReadOnly Property **ExceptionObject** As Object
   Public ReadOnly Property **IsTerminating** As Boolean
End Class

Hierarchy: Object→ EventArgs→ UnhandledExceptionEventArgs

Passed To: UnhandledExceptionEventHandler.{BeginInvoke(), Invoke()}

UnhandledExceptionEventHandler
Delegate

System (mscorlib.dll)
ECMA, serializable

This delegate specifies the signature for an event handler that responds to the AppDomain.UnhandledException event. This event is triggered by an exception that is not handled by the application domain.

Public Delegate Sub **UnhandledExceptionEventHandler**(ByVal sender As Object, _
   ByVal e As UnhandledExceptionEventArgs)

Associated Events: AppDomain.UnhandledException()

Uri   **Class**

System (system.dll)   *ECMA, serializable, marshal by reference*

This class encapsulates a complete URI (Uniform Resource Identifier) and provides various parts of it through properties. For example, you can get the Scheme (e.g., http, https, mailto) and the Port number. For http, the default port is 80, if not specified in the Uri (ftp uses port 21, https uses 443, and mailto uses 25). You can also retrieve the query-string arguments—including the initial question mark—from the Query property, or the fragment portion—including the fragment marker (#)—from the Fragment property. Some Boolean properties include IsLoopback, which indicates true if the Uri references the local host, and IsUnc, which indicates true if the Uri is a UNC path (such as *server**folder*).

The Uri constructors perform some basic cleanup of your parameters before creating a Uri, including converting the scheme and hostname to lowercase, removing default and blank port numbers, and removing the trailing slash (/). Instances of Uri have read-only properties. To modify a Uri, use a UriBuilder object.

The Uri class also provides shared helper methods such as EscapeString(), which converts a string to a valid URL by converting all characters with an ASCII value greater than 127 to hexadecimal representation. The CheckHostName() and CheckSchemeName() methods accept a string and check if it is syntactically valid for the given property (although they do not attempt to determine if a host or URI exists).

The Uri class is used by many .NET types, including some in ASP.NET, although you may find many other uses for it as a type-safe way to store and exchange URL information.

```
Public Class Uri : Inherits MarshalByRefObject : Implements System.Runtime.Serialization.ISerializable
' Public Constructors
   Public Sub New(ByVal uriString As String)
   Public Sub New(ByVal uriString As String, ByVal dontEscape As Boolean)
   Public Sub New(ByVal baseUri As Uri, ByVal relativeUri As String)
   Public Sub New(ByVal baseUri As Uri, ByVal relativeUri As String, ByVal dontEscape As Boolean)
' Protected Constructors
   Protected Sub New(ByVal serializationInfo As System.Runtime.Serialization.SerializationInfo, _
      ByVal streamingContext As System.Runtime.Serialization.StreamingContext)
' Public Shared Fields
   Public Shared ReadOnly SchemeDelimiter As String                                  =://
   Public Shared ReadOnly UriSchemeFile As String                                    =file
   Public Shared ReadOnly UriSchemeFtp As String                                     =ftp
   Public Shared ReadOnly UriSchemeGopher As String                                  =gopher
   Public Shared ReadOnly UriSchemeHttp As String                                    =http
   Public Shared ReadOnly UriSchemeHttps As String                                   =https
   Public Shared ReadOnly UriSchemeMailto As String                                  =mailto
   Public Shared ReadOnly UriSchemeNews As String                                    =news
   Public Shared ReadOnly UriSchemeNntp As String                                    =nntp
' Public Instance Properties
   Public ReadOnly Property AbsolutePath As String
   Public ReadOnly Property AbsoluteUri As String
   Public ReadOnly Property Authority As String
   Public ReadOnly Property Fragment As String
   Public ReadOnly Property Host As String
   Public ReadOnly Property HostNameType As UriHostNameType
   Public ReadOnly Property IsDefaultPort As Boolean
   Public ReadOnly Property IsFile As Boolean
   Public ReadOnly Property IsLoopback As Boolean
```

Public ReadOnly Property **IsUnc** As Boolean
Public ReadOnly Property **LocalPath** As String
Public ReadOnly Property **PathAndQuery** As String
Public ReadOnly Property **Port** As Integer
Public ReadOnly Property **Query** As String
Public ReadOnly Property **Scheme** As String
Public ReadOnly Property **Segments** As String()
Public ReadOnly Property **UserEscaped** As Boolean
Public ReadOnly Property **UserInfo** As String
' *Public Shared Methods*
Public Shared Function **CheckHostName**(ByVal name As String) As UriHostNameType
Public Shared Function **CheckSchemeName**(ByVal schemeName As String) As Boolean
Public Shared Function **FromHex**(ByVal digit As Char) As Integer
Public Shared Function **HexEscape**(ByVal character As Char) As String
Public Shared Function **HexUnescape**(ByVal pattern As String, ByRef index As Integer) As Char
Public Shared Function **IsHexDigit**(ByVal character As Char) As Boolean
Public Shared Function **IsHexEncoding**(ByVal pattern As String, ByVal index As Integer) As Boolean
' *Protected Shared Methods*
Shared Protected Function **EscapeString**(ByVal str As String) As String
Shared Protected Function **IsExcludedCharacter**(ByVal character As Char) As Boolean
' *Public Instance Methods*
Overrides Public Function **Equals**(ByVal comparand As Object) As Boolean
Overrides Public Function **GetHashCode**() As Integer
Public Function **GetLeftPart**(ByVal part As UriPartial) As String
Public Function **MakeRelative**(ByVal toUri As Uri) As String
Overrides Public Function **ToString**() As String
' *Protected Instance Methods*
Overridable Protected Sub **Canonicalize**()
Overridable Protected Sub **CheckSecurity**()
Overridable Protected Sub **Escape**()
Overridable Protected Function **IsBadFileSystemCharacter**(ByVal character As Char) As Boolean
Overridable Protected Function **IsReservedCharacter**(ByVal character As Char) As Boolean
Overridable Protected Sub **Parse**()
Overridable Protected Function **Unescape**(ByVal path As String) As String
End Class

Hierarchy: Object→ MarshalByRefObject→ Uri(System.Runtime.Serialization.ISerializable)

Returned By: System.Net.Cookie.CommentUri, System.Net.HttpWebRequest.Address,
System.Net.IWebProxy.GetProxy(), System.Net.ServicePoint.Address, System.Net.WebProxy.{Address,
GetProxy()}, System.Net.WebRequest.RequestUri, System.Net.WebResponse.ResponseUri,
UriBuilder.Uri, System.Xml.XmlResolver.ResolveUri()

Passed To: Multiple types

UriBuilder   Class

System (system.dll)   *ECMA*

Every instance of Uri is immutable. This class wraps a Uri object and allows you to modify some of its properties without needing to create a new Uri. It is analogous to the Sys-
tem.Text.StringBuilder class for strings.

Public Class **UriBuilder**
' *Public Constructors*
Public Sub **New**()
Public Sub **New**(ByVal uri As String)
Public Sub **New**(ByVal schemeName As String, ByVal hostName As String)

```
Public Sub New(ByVal scheme As String, ByVal host As String, ByVal portNumber As Integer)
Public Sub New(ByVal scheme As String, ByVal host As String, ByVal port As Integer, ByVal pathValue As String)
Public Sub New(ByVal scheme As String, ByVal host As String, ByVal port As Integer, ByVal path As String, _
    ByVal extraValue As String)
Public Sub New(ByVal uri As Uri)
' Public Instance Properties
Public Property Fragment As String
Public Property Host As String
Public Property Password As String
Public Property Path As String
Public Property Port As Integer
Public Property Query As String
Public Property Scheme As String
Public ReadOnly Property Uri As Uri
Public Property UserName As String
' Public Instance Methods
Overrides Public Function Equals(ByVal rparam As Object) As Boolean
Overrides Public Function GetHashCode() As Integer
Overrides Public Function ToString() As String
End Class
```

UriFormatException
Class

System (system.dll)   *ECMA, serializable*

This exception indicates that you attempted to use an invalid URI, usually in the Uri constructor. For a description of the URI format, see *http://www.ietf.org/rfc/rfc2396.txt.*

```
Public Class UriFormatException : Inherits FormatException
' Public Constructors
Public Sub New()
Public Sub New(ByVal textString As String)
' Protected Constructors
Protected Sub New(ByVal serializationInfo As System.Runtime.Serialization.SerializationInfo, _
    ByVal streamingContext As System.Runtime.Serialization.StreamingContext)
End Class
```

Hierarchy: Object→ Exception(System.Runtime.Serialization.ISerializable)→ SystemException→ FormatException→ UriFormatException

UriHostNameType
Enum

System (system.dll)   *ECMA, serializable*

This enumeration is used for the Uri.CheckHostName() method. Basic indicates that the host is set, but cannot be determined.

```
Public Enum UriHostNameType
    Unknown = 0
    Basic = 1
    Dns = 2
    IPv4 = 3
    IPv6 = 4
End Enum
```

Hierarchy: Object→ ValueType→ Enum(IComparable, IFormattable, IConvertible)→ UriHostNameType

Returned By: Uri.{CheckHostName(), HostNameType}

UriPartial
Enum

System (system.dll)
ECMA, serializable

This enumeration is used for the Uri.GetLeftPart() method. For example, the URL *http://www.oreilly.com/index.html#toc* has a Scheme of *http://*, an Authority of *http://www.oreilly.com*, and a Path of *http://www.oreilly.com/index.html* (everything up to, but not including, the query delimiter ? or the fragment delimiter #).

```
Public Enum UriPartial
    Scheme = 0
    Authority = 1
    Path = 2
End Enum
```

Hierarchy: Object→ ValueType→ Enum(IComparable, IFormattable, IConvertible)→ UriPartial

Passed To: Uri.GetLeftPart()

ValueType
MustInherit Class

System (mscorlib.dll)
ECMA, serializable

This is the base class for all value types. A value type is a simple data structure, such as UInt32, or an enumeration. It is differentiated from a reference type (or object). Value types are stored on the stack rather than the .NET managed heap and are accessed directly rather than through a reference. Value types also behave differently from reference types, most notably in assignment operations (which create a copy of the data, not a duplicate reference to the same data) and comparison operations (which return true as long as the content of the two value types is the same). To define your own simple value types, use the struct keyword (use the enum keyword to define an enumeration). Value types are implicitly sealed.

```
Public MustInherit Class ValueType
' Protected Constructors
    Protected Sub New()
' Public Instance Methods
    Overrides Public Function Equals(ByVal obj As Object) As Boolean
    Overrides Public Function GetHashCode() As Integer
    Overrides Public Function ToString() As String
End Class
```

Subclasses: Multiple types

Version
NotInheritable Class

System (mscorlib.dll)
ECMA, serializable

This class represents a version number. The .NET framework uses it as the version of assemblies, operating systems, and network protocols. A version number consists of as many as four parts: a major, minor, build, and revision number. For some applications, such as the HTTP protocol, only the first two numbers (major and minor) are used.

```
Public NotInheritable Class Version : Implements ICloneable, IComparable
' Public Constructors
   Public Sub New()
   Public Sub New(ByVal major As Integer, ByVal minor As Integer)
   Public Sub New(ByVal major As Integer, ByVal minor As Integer, ByVal build As Integer)
   Public Sub New(ByVal major As Integer, ByVal minor As Integer, ByVal build As Integer, ByVal revision As Integer)
   Public Sub New(ByVal version As String)
' Public Instance Properties
   Public ReadOnly Property Build As Integer
   Public ReadOnly Property Major As Integer
   Public ReadOnly Property Minor As Integer
   Public ReadOnly Property Revision As Integer
' Public Shared Methods
   Public Shared Boolean operator Sub !=(ByVal v1 As Version, ByVal v2 As Version)
   Public Shared Boolean operator Sub <(ByVal v1 As Version, ByVal v2 As Version)
   Public Shared Boolean operator Sub <=(ByVal v1 As Version, ByVal v2 As Version)
   Public Shared Boolean operator Sub ==(ByVal v1 As Version, ByVal v2 As Version)
   Public Shared Boolean operator Sub >(ByVal v1 As Version, ByVal v2 As Version)
   Public Shared Boolean operator Sub >=(ByVal v1 As Version, ByVal v2 As Version)
' Public Instance Methods
   Public Function Clone() As Object Implements ICloneable.Clone
   Public Function CompareTo(ByVal version As Object) As Integer Implements IComparable.CompareTo
   Overrides Public Function Equals(ByVal obj As Object) As Boolean
   Overrides Public Function GetHashCode() As Integer
   Overrides Public Function ToString() As String
   Public Function ToString(ByVal fieldCount As Integer) As String
End Class
```

Returned By: Environment.Version, System.Net.HttpWebRequest.ProtocolVersion, System.Net.HttpWebResponse.ProtocolVersion, System.Net.ServicePoint.ProtocolVersion, OperatingSystem.Version, System.Reflection.AssemblyName.Version

Passed To: System.Net.HttpWebRequest.ProtocolVersion, OperatingSystem.OperatingSystem(), System.Reflection.Assembly.GetSatelliteAssembly(), System.Reflection.AssemblyName.Version

Void   Structure

System (mscorlib.dll)   *ECMA, serializable*

This structure indicates that a method does not return any information, as in public void Main().

```
Public Structure Void
' No public or protected members
End Structure
```

Hierarchy: Object→ ValueType→ Void

Returned By: Multiple types

Passed To: ArgIterator.ArgIterator(), IntPtr.IntPtr(), System.Reflection.Pointer.Box(), UIntPtr.UIntPtr()

WeakReference   Class

System (mscorlib.dll)   *serializable*

This class encapsulates a *weak reference* to an object. By default, when you instantiate a .NET class, you create a strong reference, which prevents the garbage collector from removing the object and reclaiming memory. A weak reference, however, does not prevent an object from being released.

Objects that are weakly referenced can still be kept alive as long as there is at least one strong reference to them. That means a weak reference allows you to access an object as long as it is in use by another part of your application. For example, objects can be stored in a collection using a weak reference, but not kept alive just because they are in the collection.

To create a weakly referenced object, pass the name of the object to the WeakReference constructor. You can use the IsAlive property to check if the reference is valid, and the Target property to get a reference to the actual object. Assigning the Target property to another variable creates a strong reference.

You can set the TrackResurrection property to true in the constructor to maintain a *long* weak reference, which tracks an object during (or after) finalization.

```
Public Class WeakReference : Implements System.Runtime.Serialization.ISerializable
' Public Constructors
   Public Sub New(ByVal target As Object)
   Public Sub New(ByVal target As Object, ByVal trackResurrection As Boolean)
' Protected Constructors
   Protected Sub New(ByVal info As System.Runtime.Serialization.SerializationInfo, _
      ByVal context As System.Runtime.Serialization.StreamingContext)
' Public Instance Properties
   Overridable Public ReadOnly Property IsAlive As Boolean
   Overridable Public Property Target As Object
   Overridable Public ReadOnly Property TrackResurrection As Boolean
' Public Instance Methods
   Overridable Public Sub GetObjectData(ByVal info As System.Runtime.Serialization.SerializationInfo, _
      ByVal context As System.Runtime.Serialization.StreamingContext)  Implements  ISerializable.GetObjectData
' Protected Instance Methods
   Overrides Protected Sub Finalize()
End Class
```

Passed To: GC.GetGeneration()

CHAPTER 5

System.Collections

The System.Collections namespace provides basic functionality for collections of objects. It defines interfaces, base classes, and implementations for collections such as dictionaries, sorted lists, queues, and stacks. The base classes can also be extended to create specialized collection types. However, the System.Collections.Specialized namespace contains a set of extended collection types based on this namespace, so check there before creating your own types. Figure 5-1 and Figure 5-2 show the types in this namespace.

On first observation, the design of these collections seems somewhat awkward—for example, why does a "list" seem to be broken into two pieces: the IList interface and the ArrayList implementation? On top of this, the namespace defines a number of other interfaces, such as IEnumerable and IEnumerator, that seem unnecessary.

In fact, the design of the collection types in this namespace is quite similar to the designs of other container libraries such as the STL (Standard Template Library) in C++ and the Java Collections library in JDK 1.2. By separating the interface of a collection type (the concept of "list-ness" or "dictionary-ness") from the actual implementation, you are free to assume only the absolute minimum about the actual implementation used, and instead focus only on what is needed in order to carry out the work. For example, VB.NET's For Each construct works by silently using the IEnumerable interface to obtain an object that inherits the IEnumerator interface. Thus, a programmer could, if desired, create a custom type (perhaps modeling a hand of cards) that acts just as any other collection class does. Alternatively, the iterator (the type that inherits from IEnumerator) could be a "smart" iterator, knowing how to walk through (or skip past) types in the container itself. All this is possible solely because the interface is separated from the implementation; it is *decoupled*.

ArrayList   Class
System.Collections (mscorlib.dll)   *ECMA, serializable*

This class is similar to an array, but it can grow or shrink as needed. The Capacity property returns the maximum number of elements the ArrayList can hold. You can reduce the size by setting Capacity explicitly or using the TrimToSize() method. An ArrayList can be

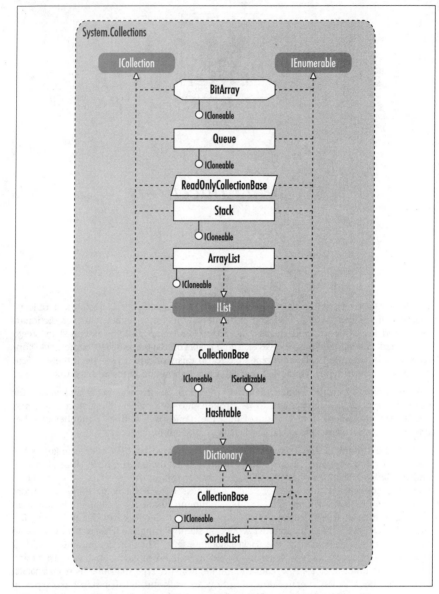

Figure 5–1. Collection types implementing ICollection and IEnumerable

constructed empty or with an integer argument that sets its initial size. You can also pass the constructor an object that implements ICollection to fill the ArrayList with the contents of that object.

A number of methods are provided to modify the contents of the ArrayList. The Add() and AddRange() methods add elements to the end of the list. Insert() and InsertRange() add new elements at a specified location within the list.

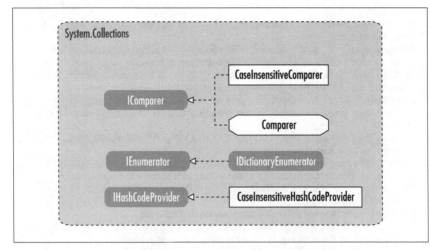

Figure 5-2. More types from the System.Collections namespace

```
Public Class ArrayList : Implements IList, ICollection, IEnumerable, ICloneable
' Public Constructors
  Public Sub New()
  Public Sub New(ByVal c As ICollection)
  Public Sub New(ByVal capacity As Integer)
' Public Instance Properties
  Overridable Public Property Capacity As Integer
  Overridable Public ReadOnly Property Count As Integer Implements ICollection.Count
  Overridable Public ReadOnly Property IsFixedSize As Boolean Implements IList.IsFixedSize
  Overridable Public ReadOnly Property IsReadOnly As Boolean Implements IList.IsReadOnly
  Overridable Public ReadOnly Property IsSynchronized As Boolean Implements ICollection.IsSynchronized
  Overridable Public Default Property Item (ByVal index As Integer) As Object Implements IList.Item
  Overridable Public ReadOnly Property SyncRoot As Object Implements ICollection.SyncRoot
' Public Shared Methods
  Public Shared Function Adapter(ByVal list As IList) As ArrayList
  Public Shared Function FixedSize(ByVal list As ArrayList) As ArrayList
  Public Shared Function FixedSize(ByVal list As IList) As IList
  Public Shared Function ReadOnly(ByVal list As ArrayList) As ArrayList
  Public Shared Function ReadOnly(ByVal list As IList) As IList
  Public Shared Function Repeat(ByVal value As Object, ByVal count As Integer) As ArrayList
  Public Shared Function Synchronized(ByVal list As ArrayList) As ArrayList
  Public Shared Function Synchronized(ByVal list As IList) As IList
' Public Instance Methods
  Overridable Public Function Add(ByVal value As Object) As Integer Implements IList.Add
  Overridable Public Sub AddRange(ByVal c As ICollection)
  Overridable Public Function BinarySearch(ByVal index As Integer, ByVal count As Integer, ByVal value As Object, _
    ByVal comparer As IComparer) As Integer
  Overridable Public Function BinarySearch(ByVal value As Object) As Integer
  Overridable Public Function BinarySearch(ByVal value As Object, ByVal comparer As IComparer) As Integer
  Overridable Public Sub Clear() Implements IList.Clear
  Overridable Public Function Clone() As Object Implements ICloneable.Clone
  Overridable Public Function Contains(ByVal item As Object) As Boolean Implements IList.Contains
  Overridable Public Sub CopyTo(ByVal array As Array)
  Overridable Public Sub CopyTo(ByVal array As Array, ByVal arrayIndex As Integer) Implements ICollection.CopyTo
```

Overridable Public Sub **CopyTo**(ByVal index As Integer, ByVal array As Array, ByVal arrayIndex As Integer, _
  ByVal count As Integer)
Overridable Public Function **GetEnumerator**() As IEnumerator Implements IEnumerable.GetEnumerator
Overridable Public Function **GetEnumerator**(ByVal index As Integer, ByVal count As Integer) As IEnumerator
Overridable Public Function **GetRange**(ByVal index As Integer, ByVal count As Integer) As ArrayList
Overridable Public Function **IndexOf**(ByVal value As Object) As Integer Implements IList.IndexOf
Overridable Public Function **IndexOf**(ByVal value As Object, ByVal startIndex As Integer) As Integer
Overridable Public Function **IndexOf**(ByVal value As Object, ByVal startIndex As Integer, ByVal count As Integer) _
  As Integer
Overridable Public Sub **Insert**(ByVal index As Integer, ByVal value As Object) Implements IList.Insert
Overridable Public Sub **InsertRange**(ByVal index As Integer, ByVal c As ICollection)
Overridable Public Function **LastIndexOf**(ByVal value As Object) As Integer
Overridable Public Function **LastIndexOf**(ByVal value As Object, ByVal startIndex As Integer) As Integer
Overridable Public Function **LastIndexOf**(ByVal value As Object, ByVal startIndex As Integer, _
  ByVal count As Integer) As Integer
Overridable Public Sub **Remove**(ByVal obj As Object) Implements IList.Remove
Overridable Public Sub **RemoveAt**(ByVal index As Integer) Implements IList.RemoveAt
Overridable Public Sub **RemoveRange**(ByVal index As Integer, ByVal count As Integer)
Overridable Public Sub **Reverse**()
Overridable Public Sub **Reverse**(ByVal index As Integer, ByVal count As Integer)
Overridable Public Sub **SetRange**(ByVal index As Integer, ByVal c As ICollection)
Overridable Public Sub **Sort**()
Overridable Public Sub **Sort**(ByVal comparer As IComparer)
Overridable Public Sub **Sort**(ByVal index As Integer, ByVal count As Integer, ByVal comparer As IComparer)
Overridable Public Function **ToArray**(ByVal type As Type) As Array
Overridable Public Function **ToArray**() As Object()
Overridable Public Sub **TrimToSize**()
End Class

Returned By: CollectionBase.InnerList, ReadOnlyCollectionBase.InnerList,
System.Net.WebProxy.BypassArrayList

BitArray   NotInheritable Class

System.Collections (mscorlib.dll)   *serializable*

This class stores a collection of bit values as Boolean types. The constructor takes many
different forms of input to build the initial array, including arguments that specify the
initial values and the size of the array. You can construct the BitArray with an existing
array of Booleans, or with a byte or integer array. With an integer array, each int value
becomes 32 bits of the BitArray, with the least significant bit mapped to the lowest index
value (MyBitArray(0)) of the 32-bit range. A byte array uses 8 bits for each value in a similar fashion. A "bare" array can be constructed by simply providing an integer value for
the number of bits in the BitArray, which are all set to false by default. Provide an additional Boolean value as a second argument to set the default values to either true or
false.

The main functions of the BitArray class allow you to perform bitwise operations with
two BitArrays of the same length. There are methods for And(), Or(), and Xor() that correspond to their respective bitwise operations. The Not() method inverts each bit value in
the BitArray.

Public NotInheritable Class **BitArray** : Implements ICollection, IEnumerable, ICloneable
' Public Constructors
  Public Sub **New**(ByVal bits As BitArray)
  Public Sub **New**(ByVal values As Boolean())
  Public Sub **New**(ByVal bytes As Byte())

```
Public Sub New(ByVal length As Integer)
Public Sub New(ByVal values As Integer())
Public Sub New(ByVal length As Integer, ByVal defaultValue As Boolean)
' Public Instance Properties
Public ReadOnly Property Count As Integer Implements ICollection.Count
Public ReadOnly Property IsReadOnly As Boolean
Public ReadOnly Property IsSynchronized As Boolean Implements ICollection.IsSynchronized
Public Default Property Item (ByVal index As Integer) As Boolean
Public Property Length As Integer
Public ReadOnly Property SyncRoot As Object Implements ICollection.SyncRoot
' Public Instance Methods
Public Function And(ByVal value As BitArray) As BitArray
Public Function Clone() As Object Implements ICloneable.Clone
Public Sub CopyTo(ByVal array As Array, ByVal index As Integer) Implements ICollection.CopyTo
Public Function Get(ByVal index As Integer) As Boolean
Public Function GetEnumerator() As IEnumerator Implements IEnumerable.GetEnumerator
Public Function Not() As BitArray
Public Function Or(ByVal value As BitArray) As BitArray
Public Sub Set(ByVal index As Integer, ByVal value As Boolean)
Public Sub SetAll(ByVal value As Boolean)
Public Function Xor(ByVal value As BitArray) As BitArray
End Class
```

CaseInsensitiveComparer   Class

System.Collections (mscorlib.dll)   *serializable*

This type provides a means for case-insensitive comparison of string objects. This class implements the IComparer.Compare() method.

```
Public Class CaseInsensitiveComparer : Implements IComparer
' Public Constructors
Public Sub New()
Public Sub New(ByVal culture As System.Globalization.CultureInfo)
' Public Shared Properties
Public Shared ReadOnly Property Default As CaseInsensitiveComparer
' Public Instance Methods
Public Function Compare(ByVal a As Object, ByVal b As Object) As Integer Implements IComparer.Compare
End Class
```

CaseInsensitiveHashCodeProvider   Class

System.Collections (mscorlib.dll)   *serializable*

When this object is passed to a Hashtable constructor, it overrides the GetHashCode() method to allow string comparison without regard to case. If you pass an instance of this type into the Hashtable constructor, you should also pass in an instance of CaseInsensitiveComparer to ensure that any comparison operations (such as sorting) are also performed in a case-insensitive fashion.

```
Public Class CaseInsensitiveHashCodeProvider : Implements IHashCodeProvider
' Public Constructors
Public Sub New()
Public Sub New(ByVal culture As System.Globalization.CultureInfo)
' Public Shared Properties
Public Shared ReadOnly Property Default As CaseInsensitiveHashCodeProvider
```

' Public Instance Methods
Public Function **GetHashCode**(ByVal obj As Object) As Integer Implements IHashCodeProvider.GetHashCode
End Class

CollectionBase

MustInherit Class

System.Collections (mscorlib.dll)

serializable

This base collection type must be extended to create strongly typed collection objects. CollectionBase provides a modifiable collection. For a read-only collection of objects, use ReadOnlyCollectionBase. Many special collection types throughout the .NET framework derive from this class.

Public MustInherit Class **CollectionBase** : Implements IList, ICollection , IEnumerable
' Protected Constructors
Protected Sub **New**()
' Public Instance Properties
Public ReadOnly Property **Count** As Integer Implements ICollection.Count
' Protected Instance Properties
Protected Property **InnerList** As ArrayList
Protected Property **List** As IList
' Public Instance Methods
Public Sub **Clear**() Implements IList.Clear
Public Function **GetEnumerator**() As IEnumerator Implements IEnumerable.GetEnumerator
Public Sub **RemoveAt**(ByVal index As Integer) Implements IList.RemoveAt
' Protected Instance Methods
Overridable Protected Sub **OnClear**()
Overridable Protected Sub **OnClearComplete**()
Overridable Protected Sub **OnInsert**(ByVal index As Integer, ByVal value As Object)
Overridable Protected Sub **OnInsertComplete**(ByVal index As Integer, ByVal value As Object)
Overridable Protected Sub **OnRemove**(ByVal index As Integer, ByVal value As Object)
Overridable Protected Sub **OnRemoveComplete**(ByVal index As Integer, ByVal value As Object)
Overridable Protected Sub **OnSet**(ByVal index As Integer, ByVal oldValue As Object, ByVal newValue As Object)
Overridable Protected Sub **OnSetComplete**(ByVal index As Integer, ByVal oldValue As Object, _
ByVal newValue As Object)
Overridable Protected Sub **OnValidate**(ByVal value As Object)
End Class

Subclasses: System.Diagnostics.{ CounterCreationDataCollection, EventLogPermissionEntryCollection, PerformanceCounterPermissionEntryCollection}

Comparer

NotInheritable Class

System.Collections (mscorlib.dll)

ECMA, serializable

The Comparer class is used to compare two objects of the same type. The Compare() method takes two objects. If the first object is less than the second, a negative value is returned. If the first object is greater than the second, a positive value is returned. If the objects are equal, zero is returned. The comparisons of strings are case-sensitive. For case-insensitive string comparisons, use CaseInsensitiveComparer.

Public NotInheritable Class **Comparer** : Implements IComparer
' Public Shared Fields
Public Shared ReadOnly **Default** As Comparer   *=System.Collections.Comparer*
' Public Instance Methods
Public Function **Compare**(ByVal a As Object, ByVal b As Object) As Integer Implements IComparer.Compare
End Class

DictionaryBase

MustInherit Class

System.Collections (mscorlib.dll)

serializable

This MustInherit base class is used to implement specialized dictionary style collections. Classes derived from DictionaryBase allow for strongly typed key and value pairs. A set of protected instance methods is defined to be overridden by derived classes. These methods allow a class to specify customized processes when functions are performed on the derived object. For example, OnSet() lets you perform a function before you set a new element in the dictionary, while OnSetComplete() lets you perform a function after a value is set.

Public MustInherit Class **DictionaryBase** : Implements IDictionary, ICollection, IEnumerable
' Protected Constructors
  Protected Sub **New**()
' Public Instance Properties
  Public ReadOnly Property **Count** As Integer Implements ICollection.Count
' Protected Instance Properties
  Protected Property **Dictionary** As IDictionary
  Protected Property **InnerHashtable** As Hashtable
' Public Instance Methods
  Public Sub **Clear**() Implements IDictionary.Clear
  Public Sub **CopyTo**(ByVal array As Array, ByVal index As Integer) Implements ICollection.CopyTo
  Public Function **GetEnumerator**() As IDictionaryEnumerator Implements IDictionary.GetEnumerator
' Protected Instance Methods
  Overridable Protected Sub **OnClear**()
  Overridable Protected Sub **OnClearComplete**()
  Overridable Protected Function **OnGet**(ByVal key As Object, ByVal currentValue As Object) As Object
  Overridable Protected Sub **OnInsert**(ByVal key As Object, ByVal value As Object)
  Overridable Protected Sub **OnInsertComplete**(ByVal key As Object, ByVal value As Object)
  Overridable Protected Sub **OnRemove**(ByVal key As Object, ByVal value As Object)
  Overridable Protected Sub **OnRemoveComplete**(ByVal key As Object, ByVal value As Object)
  Overridable Protected Sub **OnSet**(ByVal key As Object, ByVal oldValue As Object, ByVal newValue As Object)
  Overridable Protected Sub **OnSetComplete**(ByVal key As Object, ByVal oldValue As Object, _
    ByVal newValue As Object)
  Overridable Protected Sub **OnValidate**(ByVal key As Object, ByVal value As Object)
End Class

Subclasses: System.Diagnostics.{ InstanceDataCollection, InstanceDataCollectionCollection}

DictionaryEntry

Structure

System.Collections (mscorlib.dll)

ECMA, serializable

This structure defines the special value type used for the elements of a dictionary collection. This type consists of a key and a value. A DictionaryEntry is retrieved by the IDictionaryEnumerator.Entry property.

Public Structure **DictionaryEntry**
' Public Constructors
  Public Sub **New**(ByVal key As Object, ByVal value As Object)
' Public Instance Properties
  Public Property **Key** As Object
  Public Property **Value** As Object
End Structure

Hierarchy: System.Object→ System.ValueType→ DictionaryEntry

Returned By: IDictionaryEnumerator.Entry

Hashtable   **Class**

System.Collections (mscorlib.dll)   *ECMA, serializable*

A *hashtable* is an associative array (dictionary) that contains key-value pairs. Each value is identified and retrieved by a specific key that is transformed into an integer value called a *hashcode*.

A hashtable is an efficient way to store and retrieve values in memory. It uses a fast algorithm to convert a hashcode into a hash key. This hash key is used internally to determine which "bucket" a hashtable entry belongs to. Although the algorithm selects a bucket quickly, each bucket may contain more than one value. In this case, a linear search locates the desired value based on its hashcode. However, the fast bucket search offers such an advantage that a subsequent linear search has a negligible impact on the overall performance of the hashtable.

Initially, a 1-to-1 ratio of buckets to values applies (called the *load factor*). However, as more items are added to the hashtable, the load factor is changed, and each bucket ends up holding more elements. Greater load factors reduce the amount of memory required to store the hashtable, but increase lookup time.

The first argument to the Hashtable constructor gives a value for its initial size or provides an existing IDictionary whose values will fill the Hashtable. A Hashtable automatically increases its size when all buckets are full. The loadFactor argument is optionally used to specify the load factor; the default is 1.0. You can also provide references to IHashCodeProvider and IComparer instances in the constructor to provide custom hashcode and key-sorting functionality.

Keys of varying types can be used as in a regular dictionary collection. A hashing algorithm is used to convert the key into the hashcode. This is accomplished by the GetHashCode() method of each key object, which is a virtual method provided by Object. GetHashCode() can be overridden to use a custom algorithm instead of the default hashing algorithm provided by the CLR. (See CaseInsensitiveHashCodeProvider.)

The Keys and Values properties retrieve ICollection objects containing the keys and values, respectively, of the Hashtable.

The Hashtable indexer allows you to get or retrieve a value by specific key. If a key already exists, its value is overwritten. The Add() method can also add a new key and value to a Hashtable, but throws an exception if the key already exists.

```
Public Class Hashtable : Implements IDictionary, ICollection, IEnumerable, System.Runtime.Serialization.ISerializable, _
        System.Runtime.Serialization.IDeserializationCallback, ICloneable
' Public Constructors
   Public Sub New()
   Public Sub New(ByVal d As IDictionary)
   Public Sub New(ByVal d As IDictionary, ByVal hcp As IHashCodeProvider, ByVal comparer As IComparer)
   Public Sub New(ByVal d As IDictionary, ByVal loadFactor As Single)
   Public Sub New(ByVal d As IDictionary, ByVal loadFactor As Single, ByVal hcp As IHashCodeProvider, _
        ByVal comparer As IComparer)
   Public Sub New(ByVal hcp As IHashCodeProvider, ByVal comparer As IComparer)
   Public Sub New(ByVal capacity As Integer)
   Public Sub New(ByVal capacity As Integer, ByVal hcp As IHashCodeProvider, ByVal comparer As IComparer)
   Public Sub New(ByVal capacity As Integer, ByVal loadFactor As Single)
   Public Sub New(ByVal capacity As Integer, ByVal loadFactor As Single, ByVal hcp As IHashCodeProvider, _
        ByVal comparer As IComparer)
' Protected Constructors
   Protected Sub New(ByVal info As System.Runtime.Serialization.SerializationInfo, _
        ByVal context As System.Runtime.Serialization.StreamingContext)
' Public Instance Properties
```

Overridable Public ReadOnly Property **Count** As Integer Implements ICollection.Count
Overridable Public ReadOnly Property **IsFixedSize** As Boolean Implements IDictionary.IsFixedSize
Overridable Public ReadOnly Property **IsReadOnly** As Boolean Implements IDictionary.IsReadOnly
Overridable Public ReadOnly Property **IsSynchronized** As Boolean Implements ICollection.IsSynchronized
Overridable Public Default Property **Item** (ByVal key As Object) As Object Implements IDictionary.Item
Overridable Public ReadOnly Property **Keys** As ICollection Implements IDictionary.Keys
Overridable Public ReadOnly Property **SyncRoot** As Object Implements ICollection.SyncRoot
Overridable Public ReadOnly Property **Values** As ICollection Implements IDictionary.Values
' *Protected Instance Properties*
Protected Property **comparer** As IComparer
Protected Property **hcp** As IHashCodeProvider
' *Public Shared Methods*
Public Shared Function **Synchronized**(ByVal table As Hashtable) As Hashtable
' *Public Instance Methods*
Overridable Public Sub **Add**(ByVal key As Object, ByVal value As Object) Implements IDictionary.Add
Overridable Public Sub **Clear**() Implements IDictionary.Clear
Overridable Public Function **Clone**() As Object Implements ICloneable.Clone
Overridable Public Function **Contains**(ByVal key As Object) As Boolean Implements IDictionary.Contains
Overridable Public Function **ContainsKey**(ByVal key As Object) As Boolean
Overridable Public Function **ContainsValue**(ByVal value As Object) As Boolean
Overridable Public Sub **CopyTo**(ByVal array As Array, ByVal arrayIndex As Integer) Implements ICollection.CopyTo
Overridable Public Function **GetEnumerator**() As IDictionaryEnumerator Implements IDictionary.GetEnumerator
Overridable Public Sub **GetObjectData**(ByVal info As System.Runtime.Serialization.SerializationInfo, _
   ByVal context As System.Runtime.Serialization.StreamingContext) Implements ISerializable.GetObjectData
Overridable Public Sub **OnDeserialization**(ByVal sender As Object) _
   Implements IDeserializationCallback.OnDeserialization
Overridable Public Sub **Remove**(ByVal key As Object) Implements IDictionary.Remove
' *Protected Instance Methods*
Overridable Protected Function **GetHash**(ByVal key As Object) As Integer
Overridable Protected Function **KeyEquals**(ByVal item As Object, ByVal key As Object) As Boolean
End Class

Returned By: DictionaryBase.InnerHashtable,
System.Collections.Specialized.CollectionsUtil.CreateCaseInsensitiveHashtable()

ICollection

Interface

System.Collections (mscorlib.dll)

ECMA

This interface defines the basic characteristics of collection objects and implements three properties. Count gets the number of elements contained in a collection; IsSynchronized indicates whether the collection is thread-safe, and SyncRoot returns an object that synchronizes access to the collection (this is the object itself if the implementing class does not provide a Synchronized() method). ICollection also implements the CopyTo() method for copying elements to an Array object at a specified index.

Public Interface **ICollection** : Implements IEnumerable
' *Public Instance Properties*
Public ReadOnly Property **Count** As Integer
Public ReadOnly Property **IsSynchronized** As Boolean
Public ReadOnly Property **SyncRoot** As Object
' *Public Instance Methods*
Public Sub **CopyTo**(ByVal array As Array, ByVal index As Integer)
End Interface

Implemented By: Multiple types

Returned By: Multiple types

Passed To: ArrayList.{AddRange(), ArrayList(), InsertRange(), SetRange()}, Queue.Queue(), Stack.Stack()

IComparer   Interface
System.Collections (mscorlib.dll)   ECMA

This interface implements a method for comparing objects. Compare() determines whether an object is greater than (positive return value), less than (negative return value), or equal (zero) to another object. This interface is required for classes that need to sort elements or search collections.

```
Public Interface IComparer
' Public Instance Methods
   Public Function Compare(ByVal x As Object, ByVal y As Object) As Integer
End Interface
```

Implemented By: CaseInsensitiveComparer, Comparer

Returned By: Hashtable.comparer

Passed To: System.Array.{BinarySearch(), Sort()}, ArrayList.{BinarySearch(), Sort()}, Hashtable.{comparer, Hashtable()}, SortedList.SortedList(), System.Collections.Specialized.ListDictionary.ListDictionary(), System.Collections.Specialized.NameObjectCollectionBase.NameObjectCollectionBase(), System.Collections.Specialized.NameValueCollection.NameValueCollection(), System.Xml.XPath.XPathExpression.AddSort()

IDictionary   Interface
System.Collections (mscorlib.dll)   ECMA

This base interface for a collection of key/value elements defines the indexer (in C#, the this property—in VB.NET, the property marked as Default), as well as the Keys and Values properties that return collections containing the dictionary's keys or values, respectively. This interface also defines the methods by which the entries may be modified, such as Add(), Clear(), and Remove().

```
Public Interface IDictionary : Implements ICollection, IEnumerable
' Public Instance Properties
   Public ReadOnly Property IsFixedSize As Boolean
   Public ReadOnly Property IsReadOnly As Boolean
   Public Default Property Item (ByVal key As Object) As Object
   Public ReadOnly Property Keys As ICollection
   Public ReadOnly Property Values As ICollection
' Public Instance Methods
   Public Sub Add(ByVal key As Object, ByVal value As Object)
   Public Sub Clear()
   Public Function Contains(ByVal key As Object) As Boolean
   Public Function GetEnumerator() As IDictionaryEnumerator
   Public Sub Remove(ByVal key As Object)
End Interface
```

Implemented By: DictionaryBase, Hashtable, SortedList, System.Collections.Specialized.{ HybridDictionary, ListDictionary}

Returned By: DictionaryBase.Dictionary, System.Environment.GetEnvironmentVariables()

Passed To: Hashtable.Hashtable(), SortedList.SortedList(), System.Collections.Specialized.CollectionsUtil.CreateCaseInsensitiveHashtable(), System.Diagnostics.EventLogInstaller.{Install(), Rollback(), Uninstall()}

IDictionaryEnumerator
Interface

System.Collections (mscorlib.dll) *ECMA*

This interface is an enumerator for Dictionary collections. It defines three read-only properties that can be obtained from the currently selected element of the collection. The Entry property gets an entry (key and value) in the form of a DictionaryEntry object. Key and Value return the key and value of the current element.

```
Public Interface IDictionaryEnumerator : Implements IEnumerator
' Public Instance Properties
   Public ReadOnly Property Entry As DictionaryEntry
   Public ReadOnly Property Key As Object
   Public ReadOnly Property Value As Object
End Interface
```

Returned By: DictionaryBase.GetEnumerator(), Hashtable.GetEnumerator(),
IDictionary.GetEnumerator(), SortedList.GetEnumerator(),
System.Collections.Specialized.HybridDictionary.GetEnumerator(),
System.Collections.Specialized.ListDictionary.GetEnumerator()

IEnumerable
Interface

System.Collections (mscorlib.dll) *ECMA*

This interface exposes an enumerator to iterate over a collection. The GetEnumerator() method returns an IEnumerator for the object.

```
Public Interface IEnumerable
' Public Instance Methods
   Public Function GetEnumerator() As IEnumerator
End Interface
```

Implemented By: Multiple types

IEnumerator
Interface

System.Collections (mscorlib.dll) *ECMA*

This interface provides an enumerator to iterate over the elements of a collection. The Current property gets the current element in the iteration. MoveNext() advances to the next collection element. Reset() returns the position of the iteration to the start of the collection, just before the first element; an initial call to MoveNext() is necessary to retrieve the first element of the collection.

```
Public Interface IEnumerator
' Public Instance Properties
   Public ReadOnly Property Current As Object
' Public Instance Methods
   Public Function MoveNext() As Boolean
   Public Sub Reset()
End Interface
```

Implemented By: IDictionaryEnumerator, System.CharEnumerator,
System.Globalization.TextElementEnumerator, System.Runtime.Serialization.SerializationInfoEnumerator

Returned By: Multiple types

IHashCodeProvider

Interface

System.Collections (mscorlib.dll)

ECMA

This interface implements a custom hash function to supply a hashcode to an object. Normally hashtables use System.Object.GetHashCode() for hash keys. However, if a Hashtable is constructed using an object that implements this interface, GetHashCode() can be used to provide a customized hash function. CaseInsensitiveHashCodeProvider is an example of a custom hash function.

Public Interface **IHashCodeProvider**
' *Public Instance Methods*
   Public Function **GetHashCode**(ByVal obj As Object) As Integer
End Interface

Implemented By: CaseInsensitiveHashCodeProvider

Returned By: Hashtable.hcp

Passed To: Hashtable.{Hashtable(), hcp},
System.Collections.Specialized.NameObjectCollectionBase.NameObjectCollectionBase(),
System.Collections.Specialized.NameValueCollection.NameValueCollection()

IList

Interface

System.Collections (mscorlib.dll)

ECMA

This interface defines the basic characteristics of an indexable collection of objects. All array and collection classes implement this interface. IList defines methods by adding an element to the end of a list (Add()), inserting or removing an element at a specific index (Insert() and RemoveAt()), or removing all elements. Remove() removes the first occurrence of a specific object from a list. Changing the elements of a list requires that the class be resizable and modifiable (see the IsFixedSize property). The Contains() method checks to see if a given value is contained in the list, while IndexOf() returns the index of an existing list value.

Public Interface **IList** : Implements ICollection, IEnumerable
' *Public Instance Properties*
   Public ReadOnly Property **IsFixedSize** As Boolean
   Public ReadOnly Property **IsReadOnly** As Boolean
   Public Default Property **Item** (ByVal index As Integer) As Object
' *Public Instance Methods*
   Public Function **Add**(ByVal value As Object) As Integer
   Public Sub **Clear**()
   Public Function **Contains**(ByVal value As Object) As Boolean
   Public Function **IndexOf**(ByVal value As Object) As Integer
   Public Sub **Insert**(ByVal index As Integer, ByVal value As Object)
   Public Sub **Remove**(ByVal value As Object)
   Public Sub **RemoveAt**(ByVal index As Integer)
End Interface

Implemented By: ArrayList, CollectionBase, System.Array,
System.Collections.Specialized.StringCollection, System.Diagnostics.TraceListenerCollection

Returned By: ArrayList.{FixedSize(), ReadOnly(), Synchronized()}, CollectionBase.List,
SortedList.{GetKeyList(), GetValueList()}

Passed To: ArrayList.{Adapter(), FixedSize(), ReadOnly(), Synchronized()},
System.Net.Sockets.Socket.Select()

Queue
Class

System.Collections (mscorlib.dll)
serializable

This class describes a collection manipulated on a first-in, first-out basis. The newest elements are added to one end with the Enqueue() method, and the oldest are taken off the other end with Dequeue(). A Queue can be constructed as an empty collection or with the elements of an existing collection. The initial capacity can also be specified, although the default for an empty queue is 32. Normally, a Queue automatically increases its capacity when new elements exceed the current capacity, using a default growth factor of 2.0. (The growth factor is multiplied by the current capacity to determine the new capacity.) You may specify your own growth factor when you specify an initial capacity for the Queue.

The Dequeue() method returns the element at the beginning of the Queue, and simultaneously removes it. You can get the first element without removal by using Peek(). The contents of a Queue can be copied to an existing Array object using the CopyTo() method. ToArray() creates a new Array object with the contents of the Queue.

The Queue is not threadsafe. The Synchronize() method provides a wrapper for thread safety.

```
Public Class Queue : Implements ICollection, IEnumerable , ICloneable
' Public Constructors
   Public Sub New()
   Public Sub New(ByVal col As ICollection)
   Public Sub New(ByVal capacity As Integer)
   Public Sub New(ByVal capacity As Integer, ByVal growFactor As Single)
' Public Instance Properties
   Overridable Public ReadOnly Property Count As Integer Implements ICollection.Count
   Overridable Public ReadOnly Property IsSynchronized As Boolean Implements ICollection.IsSynchronized
   Overridable Public ReadOnly Property SyncRoot As Object Implements ICollection.SyncRoot
' Public Shared Methods
   Public Shared Function Synchronized(ByVal queue As Queue) As Queue
' Public Instance Methods
   Overridable Public Sub Clear()
   Overridable Public Function Clone() As Object Implements ICloneable.Clone
   Overridable Public Function Contains(ByVal obj As Object) As Boolean
   Overridable Public Sub CopyTo(ByVal array As Array, ByVal index As Integer)  Implements ICollection.CopyTo
   Overridable Public Function Dequeue() As Object
   Overridable Public Sub Enqueue(ByVal obj As Object)
   Overridable Public Function GetEnumerator() As IEnumerator Implements IEnumerable.GetEnumerator
   Overridable Public Function Peek() As Object
   Overridable Public Function ToArray() As Object()
   Overridable Public Sub TrimToSize()
End Class
```

ReadOnlyCollectionBase
MustInherit Class

System.Collections (mscorlib.dll)
serializable

This MustInherit base class is for read-only collections, similar to CollectionBase.

```
Public MustInherit Class ReadOnlyCollectionBase : Implements ICollection, IEnumerable
' Protected Constructors
   Protected Sub New()
' Public Instance Properties
   Public ReadOnly Property Count As Integer Implements ICollection.Count
' Protected Instance Properties
```

```
    Protected Property InnerList As ArrayList
' Public Instance Methods
    Public Function GetEnumerator() As IEnumerator Implements IEnumerable.GetEnumerator
End Class
```

Subclasses: System.Diagnostics.{ ProcessModuleCollection, ProcessThreadCollection}

SortedList   Class

System.Collections (mscorlib.dll)   *serializable*

This class is a dictionary collection in which values can be retrieved by either associated key or by index (meaning that the elements are specifically ordered). Keys are
sorted based on their object type (e.g., strings are alphabetically sorted). You can override the default key comparison methods by providing your own IComparer-implement-
ing object to the SortedList constructor.

Many methods are defined to allow you to retrieve values by either key name or index
value. The IndexOfKey() and IndexOfValue() methods return the zero-based index value of
the specified key or value. GetByIndex() and SetByIndex() use the index values for their
functionality.

```
Public Class SortedList : Implements IDictionary, ICollection, IEnumerable, ICloneable
' Public Constructors
    Public Sub New()
    Public Sub New(ByVal comparer As IComparer)
    Public Sub New(ByVal comparer As IComparer, ByVal capacity As Integer)
    Public Sub New(ByVal d As IDictionary)
    Public Sub New(ByVal d As IDictionary, ByVal comparer As IComparer)
    Public Sub New(ByVal initialCapacity As Integer)
' Public Instance Properties
    Overridable Public Property Capacity As Integer
    Overridable Public ReadOnly Property Count As Integer Implements ICollection.Count
    Overridable Public ReadOnly Property IsFixedSize As Boolean Implements IDictionary.IsFixedSize
    Overridable Public ReadOnly Property IsReadOnly As Boolean Implements IDictionary.IsReadOnly
    Overridable Public ReadOnly Property IsSynchronized As Boolean Implements ICollection.IsSynchronized
    Overridable Public Default Property Item (ByVal key As Object) As Object Implements IDictionary.Item
    Overridable Public ReadOnly Property Keys As ICollection Implements IDictionary.Keys
    Overridable Public ReadOnly Property SyncRoot As Object Implements ICollection.SyncRoot
    Overridable Public ReadOnly Property Values As ICollection Implements IDictionary.Values
' Public Shared Methods
    Public Shared Function Synchronized(ByVal list As SortedList) As SortedList
' Public Instance Methods
    Overridable Public Sub Add(ByVal key As Object, ByVal value As Object) Implements IDictionary.Add
    Overridable Public Sub Clear() Implements IDictionary.Clear
    Overridable Public Function Clone() As Object Implements ICloneable.Clone
    Overridable Public Function Contains(ByVal key As Object) As Boolean Implements IDictionary.Contains
    Overridable Public Function ContainsKey(ByVal key As Object) As Boolean
    Overridable Public Function ContainsValue(ByVal value As Object) As Boolean
    Overridable Public Sub CopyTo(ByVal array As Array, ByVal arrayIndex As Integer) Implements ICollection.CopyTo
    Overridable Public Function GetByIndex(ByVal index As Integer) As Object
    Overridable Public Function GetEnumerator() As IDictionaryEnumerator Implements IDictionary.GetEnumerator
    Overridable Public Function GetKey(ByVal index As Integer) As Object
    Overridable Public Function GetKeyList() As IList
    Overridable Public Function GetValueList() As IList
    Overridable Public Function IndexOfKey(ByVal key As Object) As Integer
    Overridable Public Function IndexOfValue(ByVal value As Object) As Integer
```

Overridable Public Sub **Remove**(ByVal key As Object) Implements IDictionary.Remove
Overridable Public Sub **RemoveAt**(ByVal index As Integer)
Overridable Public Sub **SetByIndex**(ByVal index As Integer, ByVal value As Object)
Overridable Public Sub **TrimToSize**()
End Class

Returned By: System.Collections.Specialized.CollectionsUtil.CreateCaseInsensitiveSortedList()

Stack   Class

System.Collections (mscorlib.dll)   *serializable*

This class implements a collection of objects manipulated in a last-in, first-out manner.
The primary methods of a Stack are Push() and Pop(). Push() adds an element to the top
of a stack and Pop() removes the top element from the stack. Peek() returns the top element without removing it from the stack.

Public Class **Stack** : Implements ICollection, IEnumerable, ICloneable
' *Public Constructors*
   Public Sub **New**()
   Public Sub **New**(ByVal col As ICollection)
   Public Sub **New**(ByVal initialCapacity As Integer)
' *Public Instance Properties*
   Overridable Public ReadOnly Property **Count** As Integer Implements ICollection.Count
   Overridable Public ReadOnly Property **IsSynchronized** As Boolean Implements ICollection.IsSynchronized
   Overridable Public ReadOnly Property **SyncRoot** As Object Implements ICollection.SyncRoot
' *Public Shared Methods*
   Public Shared Function **Synchronized**(ByVal stack As Stack) As Stack
' *Public Instance Methods*
   Overridable Public Sub **Clear**()
   Overridable Public Function **Clone**() As Object Implements ICloneable.Clone
   Overridable Public Function **Contains**(ByVal obj As Object) As Boolean
   Overridable Public Sub **CopyTo**(ByVal array As Array, ByVal index As Integer) Implements ICollection.CopyTo
   Overridable Public Function **GetEnumerator**() As IEnumerator Implements IEnumerable.GetEnumerator
   Overridable Public Function **Peek**() As Object
   Overridable Public Function **Pop**() As Object
   Overridable Public Sub **Push**(ByVal obj As Object)
   Overridable Public Function **ToArray**() As Object()
End Class

CHAPTER 6

System.Collections.Specialized

The types defined in the System.Collections namespace are fine as general-purpose collection types, but frequently programmers require specialized semantics around a collection class; for example, storing a collection of booleans could be more efficiently stored as a single System.Int64, whereas simply placing System.Boolean instances into a general-purpose collection is far more wasteful, in both memory and processing time.

Additionally, programmers often grow frustrated with the lack of type-safety in the general-purpose containers; not only does a programmer have to typecast any object obtained out of the container, but the container itself holds no intrinsic logic to "screen out" unwanted types being inserted into the container. (This is in marked contrast to C++ template-based collections such as the STL, in which the attempt to put a string into a container of integers causes a compile-time error.)

Container specialization isn't limited to storage type—at times, a programmer desires different processing behavior than the general-purpose container provides. As an example, consider the System.Collections.IDictionary interface. Note that it clearly defines a mapping of keys to values; however, it is only implicitly understood that the exact same key must be produced to obtain the value desired. In most cases, this is exactly what's needed; however, there are times when a less stringent retrieval mechanism is preferred. For example, perhaps a case-insensitive match is wanted instead of doing an exact-match for a string key. The System.Collections.Specialized namespace includes collections designed to address these cases. Figure 6-1 shows the types in this namespace.

BitVector32   Structure
System.Collections.Specialized (system.dll)

This structure defines a lightweight bit vector that can store booleans and 16-bit integers in a 32-bit structure. Sections hold single 16-bit integer values and are the building blocks of a BitVector32. Sections are created with CreateSection(). Each section is constructed with a maximum value for the integer it can hold. Except for the initial section, each subsequent section must provide a reference to the previous section in addition to the maximum value.

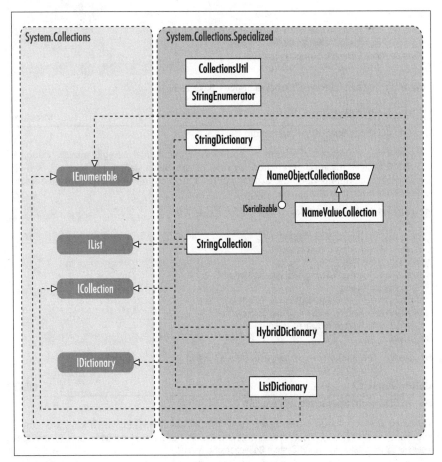

Figure 6–1. The System.Collections.Specialized namespace

The indexer takes two forms. When indexed by a section name, that section's value can be set or retrieved. When indexed by an integer that specifies a bit in the vector, you can determine whether that bit is set or not (true or false).

Public Structure **BitVector32**
' *Public Constructors*
   Public Sub **New**(ByVal value As BitVector32)
   Public Sub **New**(ByVal data As Integer)
' *Public Instance Properties*
   Public ReadOnly Property **Data** As Integer
   Public Default Property **Item** (ByVal section As Section) As Integer
   Public Default Property **Item** (ByVal bit As Integer) As Boolean
' *Public Shared Methods*
   Public Shared Function **CreateMask**() As Integer
   Public Shared Function **CreateMask**(ByVal previous As Integer) As Integer
   Public Shared Function **CreateSection**(ByVal maxValue As Short) As Section
   Public Shared Function **CreateSection**(ByVal maxValue As Short, ByVal previous As Section) As Section
   Public Shared Function **ToString**(ByVal value As BitVector32) As String
' *Public Instance Methods*

```
Overrides Public Function Equals(ByVal o As Object) As Boolean
Overrides Public Function GetHashCode() As Integer
Overrides Public Function ToString() As String
End Structure
```

Hierarchy: System.Object→ System.ValueType→ BitVector32

BitVector32.Section   Structure
System.Collections.Specialized (system.dll)

This structure represents a section of a bit vector that holds a single integer value. A BitVector32.Section instance is created by the BitVector32.CreateSection() method, which specifies the maximum value the Section can hold, and references the preceding Section, unless it is the first Section in the vector.

```
Public Structure BitVector32.Section
' Public Instance Properties
   Public ReadOnly Property Mask As Short
   Public ReadOnly Property Offset As Short
' Public Shared Methods
   Public Shared Function ToString(ByVal value As Section) As String
' Public Instance Methods
   Overrides Public Function Equals(ByVal o As Object) As Boolean
   Overrides Public Function GetHashCode() As Integer
   Overrides Public Function ToString() As String
End Structure
```

Hierarchy: System.Object→ System.ValueType→ Section

CollectionsUtil   Class
System.Collections.Specialized (system.dll)

This class defines shared methods to create special collections in which keys are sorted without respect to case. CreateCaseInsensitiveHashtable() creates a Hashtable, and CreateCase-InsensitiveSortedList() creates a System.Collections.SortedList.

```
Public Class CollectionsUtil
' Public Constructors
   Public Sub New()
' Public Shared Methods
   Public Shared Function CreateCaseInsensitiveHashtable() As Hashtable
   Public Shared Function CreateCaseInsensitiveHashtable(ByVal d As System.Collections.IDictionary) _
      As Hashtable
   Public Shared Function CreateCaseInsensitiveHashtable(ByVal capacity As Integer) As Hashtable
   Public Shared Function CreateCaseInsensitiveSortedList() As SortedList
End Class
```

HybridDictionary   Class
System.Collections.Specialized (system.dll)   *serializable*

This class implements a standard dictionary collection with built-in capability for case-insensitive key comparison. Case-insensitivity can be specified during construction with a Boolean argument.

Public Class **HybridDictionary** : Implements IDictionary, ICollection, IEnumerable
' *Public Constructors*
  Public Sub **New**()
  Public Sub **New**(ByVal caseInsensitive As Boolean)
  Public Sub **New**(ByVal initialSize As Integer)
  Public Sub **New**(ByVal initialSize As Integer, ByVal caseInsensitive As Boolean)
' *Public Instance Properties*
  Public ReadOnly Property **Count** As Integer Implements ICollection.Count
  Public ReadOnly Property **IsFixedSize** As Boolean Implements IDictionary.IsFixedSize
  Public ReadOnly Property **IsReadOnly** As Boolean Implements IDictionary.IsReadOnly
  Public ReadOnly Property **IsSynchronized** As Boolean Implements ICollection.IsSynchronized
  Public Default Property **Item** (ByVal key As Object) As Object Implements IDictionary.Item
  Public ReadOnly Property **Keys** As ICollection Implements IDictionary.Keys
  Public ReadOnly Property **SyncRoot** As Object Implements ICollection.SyncRoot
  Public ReadOnly Property **Values** As ICollection Implements IDictionary.Values
' *Public Instance Methods*
  Public Sub **Add**(ByVal key As Object, ByVal value As Object) Implements IDictionary.Add
  Public Sub **Clear**() Implements IDictionary.Clear
  Public Function **Contains**(ByVal key As Object) As Boolean Implements IDictionary.Contains
  Public Sub **CopyTo**(ByVal array As Array, ByVal index As Integer) Implements ICollection.CopyTo
  Public Function **GetEnumerator**() As IDictionaryEnumerator Implements IDictionary.GetEnumerator
  Public Sub **Remove**(ByVal key As Object) Implements IDictionary.Remove
End Class

ListDictionary   Class

System.Collections.Specialized (system.dll)   *serializable*

This class is a simple implementation of a dictionary collection (System.Collections.IDictionary) for small lists. It implements the IDictionary methods and properties, and it is suggested for use with a small number of elements (less than 10). The overloaded constructor can optionally pass an System.Collections.IComparer reference, which may be used for case-insensitive key comparison or other special key type conversions.

Public Class **ListDictionary** : Implements IDictionary, ICollection , IEnumerable
' *Public Constructors*
  Public Sub **New**()
  Public Sub **New**(ByVal comparer As System.Collections.IComparer)
' *Public Instance Properties*
  Public ReadOnly Property **Count** As Integer Implements ICollection.Count
  Public ReadOnly Property **IsFixedSize** As Boolean Implements IDictionary.IsFixedSize
  Public ReadOnly Property **IsReadOnly** As Boolean Implements IDictionary.IsReadOnly
  Public ReadOnly Property **IsSynchronized** As Boolean Implements ICollection.IsSynchronized
  Public Default Property **Item** (ByVal key As Object) As Object Implements IDictionary.Item
  Public ReadOnly Property **Keys** As ICollection Implements IDictionary.Keys
  Public ReadOnly Property **SyncRoot** As Object Implements ICollection.SyncRoot
  Public ReadOnly Property **Values** As ICollection Implements IDictionary.Values
' *Public Instance Methods*
  Public Sub **Add**(ByVal key As Object, ByVal value As Object) Implements IDictionary.Add
  Public Sub **Clear**() Implements IDictionary.Clear
  Public Function **Contains**(ByVal key As Object) As Boolean Implements IDictionary.Contains
  Public Sub **CopyTo**(ByVal array As Array, ByVal index As Integer) Implements ICollection.CopyTo
  Public Function **GetEnumerator**() As IDictionaryEnumerator Implements IDictionary.GetEnumerator
  Public Sub **Remove**(ByVal key As Object) Implements IDictionary.Remove
End Class

NameObjectCollectionBase
MustInherit Class

System.Collections.Specialized (system.dll)
serializable

This MustInherit base class is for a hashtable-based collection of key/value pairs, in which the key is specifically typed as a string. This class defines methods to be overridden by derived classes that allow for special comparing and sorting of key strings.

Public MustInherit Class **NameObjectCollectionBase** : Implements ICollection, IEnumerable , _
    System.Runtime.Serialization.ISerializable, System.Runtime.Serialization.IDeserializationCallback
' *Protected Constructors*
    Protected Sub **New**()
    Protected Sub **New**(ByVal hashProvider As System.Collections.IHashCodeProvider, _
    ByVal comparer As System.Collections.IComparer)
    Protected Sub **New**(ByVal capacity As Integer)
    Protected Sub **New**(ByVal capacity As Integer, ByVal hashProvider As System.Collections.IHashCodeProvider, _
    ByVal comparer As System.Collections.IComparer)
    Protected Sub **New**(ByVal info As System.Runtime.Serialization.SerializationInfo, _
    ByVal context As System.Runtime.Serialization.StreamingContext)
' *Public Instance Properties*
    Overridable Public ReadOnly Property **Count** As Integer Implements ICollection.Count
    Overridable Public ReadOnly Property **Keys** As KeysCollection
' *Protected Instance Properties*
    Protected Property **IsReadOnly** As Boolean
' *Public Instance Methods*
    Public Function **GetEnumerator**() As IEnumerator Implements IEnumerable.GetEnumerator
    Overridable Public Sub **GetObjectData**(ByVal info As System.Runtime.Serialization.SerializationInfo, _
    ByVal context As System.Runtime.Serialization.StreamingContext) Implements ISerializable.GetObjectData
    Overridable Public Sub **OnDeserialization**(ByVal sender As Object) _
    Implements IDeserializationCallback.OnDeserialization
' *Protected Instance Methods*
    Protected Sub **BaseAdd**(ByVal name As String, ByVal value As Object)
    Protected Sub **BaseClear**()
    Protected Function **BaseGet**(ByVal index As Integer) As Object
    Protected Function **BaseGet**(ByVal name As String) As Object
    Protected Function **BaseGetAllKeys**() As String()
    Protected Function **BaseGetAllValues**() As Object()
    Protected Function **BaseGetAllValues**(ByVal type As Type) As Object()
    Protected Function **BaseGetKey**(ByVal index As Integer) As String
    Protected Function **BaseHasKeys**() As Boolean
    Protected Sub **BaseRemove**(ByVal name As String)
    Protected Sub **BaseRemoveAt**(ByVal index As Integer)
    Protected Sub **BaseSet**(ByVal index As Integer, ByVal value As Object)
    Protected Sub **BaseSet**(ByVal name As String, ByVal value As Object)
End Class

Subclasses: NameValueCollection

NameObjectCollectionBase.KeysCollection
Class

System.Collections.Specialized (system.dll)
serializable

This class is a collection of key strings retrieved by the NameObjectCollectionBase.Keys property.

Public Class **NameObjectCollectionBase.KeysCollection** : Implements ICollection, IEnumerable
' *Public Instance Properties*
    Public ReadOnly Property **Count** As Integer Implements ICollection.Count
    Public Default ReadOnly Property **Item** (ByVal index As Integer) As String

```
' Public Instance Methods
   Overridable Public Function Get(ByVal index As Integer) As String
   Public Function GetEnumerator() As IEnumerator Implements IEnumerable.GetEnumerator
End Class
```

NameValueCollection   Class

System.Collections.Specialized (system.dll)   *ECMA, serializable*

This class is a collection of keys and associated values composed of strings in which a
single key may have multiple values associated with it. A multivalued entry is stored as
a comma-separated list of the string values. Use the Add() method to append new values to existing values of a key. Using Set() or setting the value by key name overwrites
the existing value. You can use a string containing a comma-separated list to assign
multiple values to a key.

The GetValues() method returns a string array containing all the values of the specified
key (or index). An example of how this class is used is System.Net.WebHeaderCollection,
which derives from it. A WebHeaderCollection contains the collection of various HTTP
header names as key strings and their values. HTTP headers such as Accept: often have
multiple values (for example, MIME types for Accept).

```
Public Class NameValueCollection : Inherits NameObjectCollectionBase
' Public Constructors
   Public Sub New()
   Public Sub New(ByVal hashProvider As System.Collections.IHashCodeProvider, _
      ByVal comparer As System.Collections.IComparer)
   Public Sub New(ByVal capacity As Integer)
   Public Sub New(ByVal capacity As Integer, ByVal hashProvider As System.Collections.IHashCodeProvider, _
      ByVal comparer As System.Collections.IComparer)
   Public Sub New(ByVal capacity As Integer, ByVal col As NameValueCollection)
   Public Sub New(ByVal col As NameValueCollection)
' Protected Constructors
   Protected Sub New(ByVal info As System.Runtime.Serialization.SerializationInfo, _
      ByVal context As System.Runtime.Serialization.StreamingContext)
' Public Instance Properties
   Overridable Public ReadOnly Property AllKeys As String()
   Public Default ReadOnly Property Item (ByVal index As Integer) As String
   Public Default Property Item (ByVal name As String) As String
' Public Instance Methods
   Public Sub Add(ByVal c As NameValueCollection)
   Overridable Public Sub Add(ByVal name As String, ByVal value As String)
   Public Sub Clear()
   Public Sub CopyTo(ByVal dest As Array, ByVal index As Integer)  Implements ICollection.CopyTo
   Overridable Public Function Get(ByVal index As Integer) As String
   Overridable Public Function Get(ByVal name As String) As String
   Overridable Public Function GetKey(ByVal index As Integer) As String
   Overridable Public Function GetValues(ByVal index As Integer) As String()
   Overridable Public Function GetValues(ByVal name As String) As String()
   Public Function HasKeys() As Boolean
   Overridable Public Sub Remove(ByVal name As String)
   Overridable Public Sub Set(ByVal name As String, ByVal value As String)
' Protected Instance Methods
   Protected Sub InvalidateCachedArrays()
End Class
```

Hierarchy: System.Object→ NameObjectCollectionBase(System.Collections.ICollection, System.Collections.IEnumerable, System.Runtime.Serialization.ISerializable, System.Runtime.Serialization.IDeserializationCallback)→ NameValueCollection

Subclasses: System.Net.WebHeaderCollection

Returned By: System.Net.WebClient.QueryString

Passed To: System.Net.WebClient.{QueryString, UploadValues()}

StringCollection
Class

System.Collections.Specialized (system.dll)
serializable

This class is a special collection in which the elements are strings.

```
Public Class StringCollection : Implements IList, ICollection, IEnumerable
' Public Constructors
   Public Sub New()
' Public Instance Properties
   Public ReadOnly Property Count As Integer Implements ICollection.Count
   Public ReadOnly Property IsReadOnly As Boolean Implements IList.IsReadOnly
   Public ReadOnly Property IsSynchronized As Boolean Implements ICollection.IsSynchronized
   Public Default Property Item (ByVal index As Integer) As String
   Public ReadOnly Property SyncRoot As Object Implements ICollection.SyncRoot
' Public Instance Methods
   Public Function Add(ByVal value As String) As Integer
   Public Sub AddRange(ByVal value As String())
   Public Sub Clear() Implements IList.Clear
   Public Function Contains(ByVal value As String) As Boolean
   Public Sub CopyTo(ByVal array As String(), ByVal index As Integer)
   Public Function GetEnumerator() As StringEnumerator
   Public Function IndexOf(ByVal value As String) As Integer
   Public Sub Insert(ByVal index As Integer, ByVal value As String)
   Public Sub Remove(ByVal value As String)
   Public Sub RemoveAt(ByVal index As Integer) Implements IList.RemoveAt
End Class
```

StringDictionary
Class

System.Collections.Specialized (system.dll)

This class is a dictionary collection in which keys and values are all strings.

```
Public Class StringDictionary : Implements IEnumerable
' Public Constructors
   Public Sub New()
' Public Instance Properties
   Overridable Public ReadOnly Property Count As Integer
   Overridable Public ReadOnly Property IsSynchronized As Boolean
   Overridable Public Default Property Item (ByVal key As String) As String
   Overridable Public ReadOnly Property Keys As ICollection
   Overridable Public ReadOnly Property SyncRoot As Object
   Overridable Public ReadOnly Property Values As ICollection
' Public Instance Methods
   Overridable Public Sub Add(ByVal key As String, ByVal value As String)
   Overridable Public Sub Clear()
   Overridable Public Function ContainsKey(ByVal key As String) As Boolean
   Overridable Public Function ContainsValue(ByVal value As String) As Boolean
   Overridable Public Sub CopyTo(ByVal array As Array, ByVal index As Integer)
```

Overridable Public Function **GetEnumerator**() As IEnumerator Implements IEnumerable.GetEnumerator
Overridable Public Sub **Remove**(ByVal key As String)
End Class

Returned By: System.Diagnostics.ProcessStartInfo.EnvironmentVariables

StringEnumerator   Class

System.Collections.Specialized (system.dll)

This type implements an enumerator for a StringCollection. This is returned by StringCollection.GetEnumerator().

Public Class **StringEnumerator**
' *Public Instance Properties*
    Public ReadOnly Property **Current** As String
' *Public Instance Methods*
    Public Function **MoveNext**() As Boolean
    Public Sub **Reset**()
End Class

Returned By: StringCollection.GetEnumerator()

CHAPTER 7

System.Diagnostics

Diagnostics are an important part of any software system. In addition to the obvious necessity of debugging the code, diagnostics can keep track of application performance and liveness, thus indicating a problem proactively, rather than waiting for the phone call from the system administrators.

Diagnostics means more than just compiling with debug symbols turned on. Certain code paths might want to execute only when diagnostics are turned on to full power, indicated by a compile-time switch. At other times, particularly in long-running systems (such as WebService-based systems), developers want to keep a log of the system's actions; frequently, debug reports from users are sketchy ("Um, when I clicked the button, it all just crashed"), and having a complete log of the system's actions can be invaluable in tracking the problem down. Not only can the log consist of custom-written messages (usually to a file), but the Windows Event Log is also available for use from within this namespace.

Diagnostics also includes the ability to track the health and performance of the application; under Windows 2000 and XP, this means interaction with the Performance utility. This is a powerful tool that can be launched from the Administrative Tools program group (under Windows NT, it is called Performance Monitor). By creating appropriate performance counters within the application, .NET programmers can give the system support staff (system administrators and production monitoring personnel, among others) the ability to monitor and track the application, even remotely. In addition to its diagnostic facilities, this namespace exposes operating system processes using the Process type. Use this type to launch new processes or take control of processes currently running on the system. The ProcessThread type lets you drill down into each thread that's running within a process for fine-grained control over running applications.

Most of the functionality in this namespace is disabled at runtime unless you've enabled debugging. If you are using command-line compilers, you can pass the /d:DEBUG=True switch to enable debugging (to enable tracing, use /d:TRACE=True). Alternatively, you can use the preprocessor directives #Const TRACE=1 or #Const DEBUG=1. The advantage here is that you can leave all your debugging code in, and it does not affect your release builds. The related /debug switch adds debug symbols to your program. You need the debug symbols to obtain source file and line number information in stack traces or to run your program under the control of a debugger. In Visual Studio .NET, you can enable debugging and debug symbols by creating a debug build of your application.

Some diagnostic settings can be controlled using the application configuration file (appname.exe.config). This lets you control trace and debugging behavior without having to recompile. The root element in an application configuration file is the <configuration> element. Create a <system.diagnostics> element within that root element. All the settings mentioned in this chapter must be contained in that <system.diagnostics> element.

Figure 7-1, Figure 7-2, Figure 7-3, and Figure 7-4 show the types in this namespace.

BooleanSwitch   Class
System.Diagnostics (system.dll)

This class provides a simple on/off switch for debugging and tracing. Consult Enabled to check if the switch has been set. You can configure a Boolean switch using the application configuration file (see Switch). To use a BooleanSwitch, you must enable tracing or debugging at compilation time.

```
Public Class BooleanSwitch : Inherits Switch
' Public Constructors
    Public Sub New(ByVal displayName As String, ByVal description As String)
' Public Instance Properties
    Public Property Enabled As Boolean
End Class
```

Hierarchy: System.Object→ Switch→ BooleanSwitch

ConditionalAttribute   NotInheritable Class
System.Diagnostics (mscorlib.dll)   *ECMA, serializable*

This attribute marks a method as callable only if a compilation variable, given by conditionString, is set. Compilation variables can be set by supplying /define:VARIABLE as a command-line argument to the compiler or by supplying #Const VARIABLE=1 directives in the source code itself. If the compilation variable is not set, calls to the marked method are ignored.

```
Public NotInheritable Class ConditionalAttribute : Inherits Attribute
' Public Constructors
    Public Sub New(ByVal conditionString As String)
' Public Instance Properties
    Public ReadOnly Property ConditionString As String
End Class
```

Hierarchy: System.Object→ System.Attribute→ ConditionalAttribute

Valid On: Method

CounterCreationData   Class
System.Diagnostics (system.dll)   *serializable*

This class is used to specify a type, name, and help string for a custom counter.

```
Public Class CounterCreationData
' Public Constructors
    Public Sub New()
    Public Sub New(ByVal counterName As String, ByVal counterHelp As String, _
        ByVal counterType As PerformanceCounterType)
' Public Instance Properties
    Public Property CounterHelp As String
```

System. Diagnostics

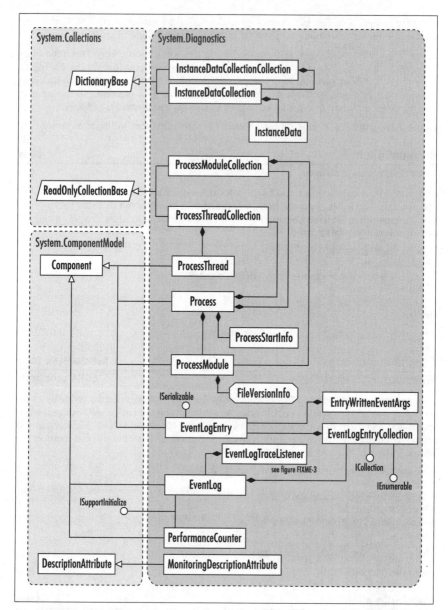

Figure 7–1. Process, EventLog, and related classes

```
Public Property CounterName As String
  Public Property CounterType As PerformanceCounterType
End Class
```

Returned By: CounterCreationDataCollection.this

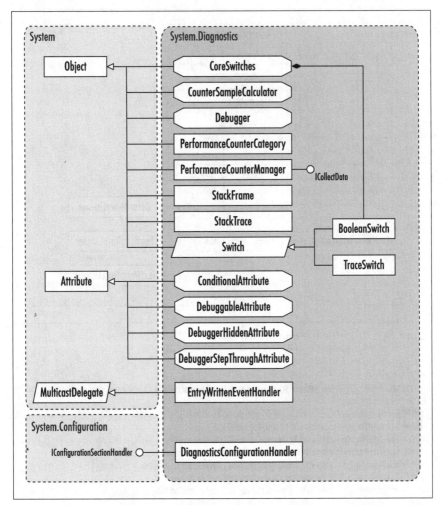

Figure 7–2. More classes from the System.Diagnostics namespace

Passed To: CounterCreationDataCollection.{Add(), AddRange(), Contains(), CopyTo(),
CounterCreationDataCollection(), IndexOf(), Insert(), this, Remove()}

CounterCreationDataCollection   Class

System.Diagnostics (system.dll)   *serializable*

This class is a strongly-typed collection of CounterCreationData objects. Use Add() and
AddRange() to add single or multiple values respectively to the end of the collection.
Insert() allows you to add an item at any position in the collection. Remove() and
RemoveAt() allow you to remove items from the collection.

Public Class **CounterCreationDataCollection** : Inherits CollectionBase
' Public Constructors
    Public Sub **New**()
    Public Sub **New**(ByVal value As CounterCreationData())
    Public Sub **New**(ByVal value As CounterCreationDataCollection)

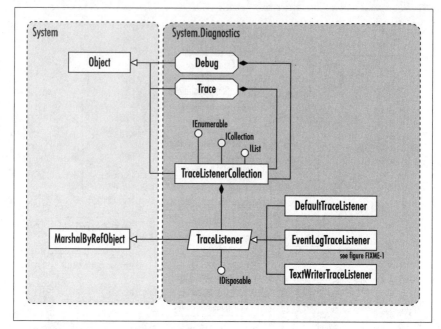

Figure 7–3. TraceListener and related classes

```
' Public Instance Properties
   Public Default Property Item (ByVal index As Integer) As CounterCreationData
' Public Instance Methods
   Public Function Add(ByVal value As CounterCreationData) As Integer
   Public Sub AddRange(ByVal value As CounterCreationData())
   Public Sub AddRange(ByVal value As CounterCreationDataCollection)
   Public Function Contains(ByVal value As CounterCreationData) As Boolean
   Public Sub CopyTo(ByVal array As CounterCreationData(), ByVal index As Integer)
   Public Function IndexOf(ByVal value As CounterCreationData) As Integer
   Public Sub Insert(ByVal index As Integer, ByVal value As CounterCreationData)
   Overridable Public Sub Remove(ByVal value As CounterCreationData)
' Protected Instance Methods
   Overrides Protected Sub OnInsert(ByVal index As Integer, ByVal value As Object)
End Class
```

Hierarchy: System.Object→ System.Collections.CollectionBase(System.Collections.IList, System.Collections.ICollection, System.Collections.IEnumerable)→ CounterCreationDataCollection

Returned By: PerformanceCounterInstaller.Counters

Passed To: PerformanceCounterCategory.Create()

CounterSample   Structure

System.Diagnostics (system.dll)

This structure contains a performance counter's raw data. It represents a sample taken at a particular point in time (the CounterTimeStamp property). Calculate() returns a counter's performance data as a float value. The two-argument form returns values for calculated performance counters, such as averages.

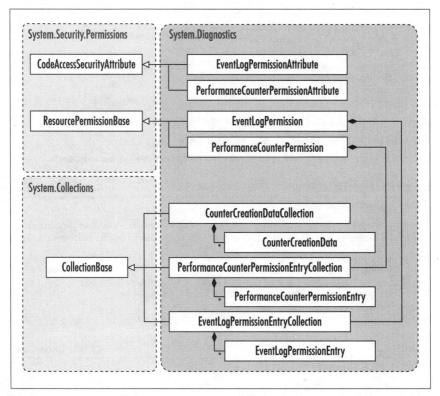

Figure 7-4. CodeAccessSecurityAttributes, collections, and related classes

TimeStamp and TimeStamp100nSec return the system timestamp, with varying degrees of accuracy. (TimeStamp100nSec is the most precise, reporting a timestamp within .1 milliseconds.) BaseValue specifies a base raw value for samples based on multiple counters. RawValue contains the sample's numeric value. SystemFrequency represents how often the system reads the counter, and CounterFrequency represents how often samples are taken by the counter. Both frequencies are represented in milliseconds.

Public Structure **CounterSample**
' Public Constructors
   Public Sub **New**(ByVal rawValue As Long, ByVal baseValue As Long, ByVal counterFrequency As Long, _
     ByVal systemFrequency As Long, ByVal timeStamp As Long), ByVal timeStamp100nSec As Long, _
     ByVal counterType As PerformanceCounterType)
   Public Sub **New**(ByVal rawValue As Long, ByVal baseValue As Long, ByVal counterFrequency As Long, _
     ByVal systemFrequency As Long, ByVal timeStamp As Long, ByVal timeStamp100nSec As Long, _
     ByVal counterType As PerformanceCounterType, ByVal counterTimeStamp As Long)
' Public Shared Fields
   Public Shared **Empty** As CounterSample   *=System.Diagnostics.CounterSample*
' Public Instance Properties
   Public ReadOnly Property **BaseValue** As Long
   Public ReadOnly Property **CounterFrequency** As Long
   Public ReadOnly Property **CounterTimeStamp** As Long
   Public ReadOnly Property **CounterType** As PerformanceCounterType
   Public ReadOnly Property **RawValue** As Long
   Public ReadOnly Property **SystemFrequency** As Long

```
    Public ReadOnly Property TimeStamp As Long
    Public ReadOnly Property TimeStamp100nSec As Long
  ' Public Shared Methods
    Public Shared Function Calculate(ByVal counterSample As CounterSample) As Single
    Public Shared Function Calculate(ByVal counterSample As CounterSample, _
    ByVal nextCounterSample As CounterSample) As Single
End Structure
```

Hierarchy: System.Object→ System.ValueType→ CounterSample

Returned By: InstanceData.Sample, PerformanceCounter.NextSample()

Passed To: CounterSampleCalculator.ComputeCounterValue(), InstanceData.InstanceData()

CounterSampleCalculator   NotInheritable Class
System.Diagnostics (system.dll)

This class provides ComputeCounterValue(), which interprets CounterSample structures. It returns a floating-point value that represents the data contained in one or two samples.

```
Public NotInheritable Class CounterSampleCalculator
  ' Public Shared Methods
    Public Shared Function ComputeCounterValue(ByVal newSample As CounterSample) As Single
    Public Shared Function ComputeCounterValue(ByVal oldSample As CounterSample, _
    ByVal newSample As CounterSample) As Single
End Class
```

Debug   NotInheritable Class
System.Diagnostics (system.dll)

This class provides methods that allow you to print debugging information and use assertions. The Listeners collection contains a set of listeners that are responsible for reporting debugging operations through the user interface or trace log. That collection initially includes an instance of DefaultTraceListener. Add a TraceListener using the Add() method of the Listeners property. Use Close() or Flush() to close or flush all listeners that write output to a file, such as the TextWriterTraceListener. Set AutoFlush to true to automatically flush each listener after a write operation.

Assert() specifies a condition and an optional error message to display if the condition is false. If the DefaultTraceListener's AssertUiEnabled property is true, the error message is displayed as a dialog, and the user has the opportunity to abort the program, retry (test the assertion again), or ignore the failed assertion. Otherwise, the error message is written to DefaultTraceListener.LogFileName. Fail() acts like an assertion in which the condition is always false.

Indent() and Unindent() allow you to set the level of indentation when you call WriteLine(). Use IndentSize to set the number of spaces corresponding to indented text. Write() and WriteLine() send output to each TraceListener in the Listeners collection, and WriteIf() and WriteLineIf() allow you to conditionally output debug information.

You can use the application configuration file to add or remove trace listeners. Look up System.Diagnostics.TraceListener in the .NET Framework SDK Documentation for details.

```
Public NotInheritable Class Debug
  ' Public Shared Properties
    Public Shared Property AutoFlush As Boolean
    Public Shared Property IndentLevel As Integer
    Public Shared Property IndentSize As Integer
```

Public Shared ReadOnly Property **Listeners** As TraceListenerCollection
' *Public Shared Methods*
Public Shared Sub **Assert**(ByVal condition As Boolean)
Public Shared Sub **Assert**(ByVal condition As Boolean, ByVal message As String)
Public Shared Sub **Assert**(ByVal condition As Boolean, ByVal message As String, ByVal detailMessage As String)
Public Shared Sub **Close**()
Public Shared Sub **Fail**(ByVal message As String)
Public Shared Sub **Fail**(ByVal message As String, ByVal detailMessage As String)
Public Shared Sub **Flush**()
Public Shared Sub **Indent**()
Public Shared Sub **Unindent**()
Public Shared Sub **Write**(ByVal value As Object)
Public Shared Sub **Write**(ByVal value As Object, ByVal category As String)
Public Shared Sub **Write**(ByVal message As String)
Public Shared Sub **Write**(ByVal message As String, ByVal category As String)
Public Shared Sub **WriteIf**(ByVal condition As Boolean, ByVal value As Object)
Public Shared Sub **WriteIf**(ByVal condition As Boolean, ByVal value As Object, ByVal category As String)
Public Shared Sub **WriteIf**(ByVal condition As Boolean, ByVal message As String)
Public Shared Sub **WriteIf**(ByVal condition As Boolean, ByVal message As String, ByVal category As String)
Public Shared Sub **WriteLine**(ByVal value As Object)
Public Shared Sub **WriteLine**(ByVal value As Object, ByVal category As String)
Public Shared Sub **WriteLine**(ByVal message As String)
Public Shared Sub **WriteLine**(ByVal message As String, ByVal category As String)
Public Shared Sub **WriteLineIf**(ByVal condition As Boolean, ByVal value As Object)
Public Shared Sub **WriteLineIf**(ByVal condition As Boolean, ByVal value As Object, ByVal category As String)
Public Shared Sub **WriteLineIf**(ByVal condition As Boolean, ByVal message As String)
Public Shared Sub **WriteLineIf**(ByVal condition As Boolean, ByVal message As String, ByVal category As String)
End Class

DebuggableAttribute   NotInheritable Class

System.Diagnostics (mscorlib.dll)

This attribute contains two properties that indicate if code can be debugged. IsJITOptimiz-erDisabled indicates whether optimization has been turned off, and IsJITTrackingEnabled indicates whether debug symbols have been placed in the code. This attribute is auto-matically applied by the compiler, with isJITTrackingEnabled set to false and isJITOptimizerDis-abled set to true. Use the /debug command-line compiler switch to include debug symbols (isJITTrackingEnabled=true), and use /optimize to enable compile-time optimizations (isJITOptimizerDisabled=false).

Public NotInheritable Class **DebuggableAttribute** : Inherits Attribute
' *Public Constructors*
Public Sub **New**(ByVal isJITTrackingEnabled As Boolean, ByVal isJITOptimizerDisabled As Boolean)
' *Public Instance Properties*
Public ReadOnly Property **IsJITOptimizerDisabled** As Boolean
Public ReadOnly Property **IsJITTrackingEnabled** As Boolean
End Class

Hierarchy: System.Object→ System.Attribute→ DebuggableAttribute

Valid On: Assembly, Module

**System.
Diagnostics**

Debugger
NotInheritable Class

System.Diagnostics (mscorlib.dll)

This class enables you to control the debugger from the debugged code. If a debugger is executing your code, IsAttached returns true. Break() sets a breakpoint and causes the debugger to pause. Log() logs output to the debugger window. The Launch() method launches the debugger and attaches it to your process, returning true if successful or if the debugger is already attached. Launch() returns false if the debugger could not be attached.

```
Public NotInheritable Class Debugger
' Public Constructors
    Public Sub New()
' Public Shared Fields
    Public Shared ReadOnly DefaultCategory As String
' Public Shared Properties
    Public Shared ReadOnly Property IsAttached As Boolean
' Public Shared Methods
    Public Shared Sub Break()
    Public Shared Function IsLogging() As Boolean
    Public Shared Function Launch() As Boolean
    Public Shared Sub Log(ByVal level As Integer, ByVal category As String, ByVal message As String)
End Class
```

DebuggerHiddenAttribute
NotInheritable Class

System.Diagnostics (mscorlib.dll)
serializable

This attribute is used by the Visual Studio debugger. Visual Studio does not allow you to set a breakpoint in a method marked with this attribute, nor does it stop inside such a method.

```
Public NotInheritable Class DebuggerHiddenAttribute : Inherits Attribute
' Public Constructors
    Public Sub New()
End Class
```

Hierarchy: System.Object→ System.Attribute→ DebuggerHiddenAttribute

Valid On: Constructor, Method, Property

DebuggerStepThroughAttribute
NotInheritable Class

System.Diagnostics (mscorlib.dll)
serializable

This attribute is used by the Visual Studio debugger. Visual Studio does not stop in a method marked with this attribute, but it does allow you to set a breakpoint in such a method.

```
Public NotInheritable Class DebuggerStepThroughAttribute : Inherits Attribute
' Public Constructors
    Public Sub New()
End Class
```

Hierarchy: System.Object→ System.Attribute→ DebuggerStepThroughAttribute

Valid On: Class, Struct, Constructor, Method

DefaultTraceListener
Class

System.Diagnostics (system.dll)   *marshal by reference, disposable*

This class provides the default TraceListener. By default, an instance of this class is available in the Listeners collection of the Debug and Trace classes. The Write() and WriteLine() methods output to the log and to the active debugger (if any) via the Win32 API function OutputDebugString. The log file is initially unset, so output goes only to the debugger. To specify a log file, set LogFileName. You may also set a logfile in the <assert> element of the application configuration file's <system.diagnostics> section, as in <assert logfile-name="logfile.log"/>.

AssertUiEnabled determines whether to use the user interface for failed assertions. If true, .NET uses a dialog box with the options Abort, Retry, or Fail. Whether this property is set to true or false, .NET always writes messages to the LogFileName, if one is specified. The AssertUiEnabled property can be set using the <assert> element, as in <assert assertui-enabled="false"/> (the default is true).

```
Public Class DefaultTraceListener : Inherits TraceListener
' Public Constructors
   Public Sub New()
' Public Instance Properties
   Public Property AssertUiEnabled As Boolean
   Public Property LogFileName As String
' Public Instance Methods
   Overrides Public Sub Fail(ByVal message As String)
   Overrides Public Sub Fail(ByVal message As String, ByVal detailMessage As String)
   Overrides Public Sub Write(ByVal message As String)
   Overrides Public Sub WriteLine(ByVal message As String)
End Class
```

Hierarchy: System.Object→ System.MarshalByRefObject→ TraceListener(System.IDisposable)→ DefaultTraceListener

EntryWrittenEventArgs
Class

System.Diagnostics (system.dll)

These event arguments are passed by an EventLog.EntryWritten event.

```
Public Class EntryWrittenEventArgs : Inherits EventArgs
' Public Constructors
   Public Sub New()
   Public Sub New(ByVal entry As EventLogEntry)
' Public Instance Properties
   Public ReadOnly Property Entry As EventLogEntry
End Class
```

Hierarchy: System.Object→ System.EventArgs→ EntryWrittenEventArgs

Passed To: EntryWrittenEventHandler.{BeginInvoke(), Invoke()}

EntryWrittenEventHandler
Delegate

System.Diagnostics (system.dll)   *serializable*

This delegate supports the EventLog.EntryWritten event.

```
Public Delegate Sub EntryWrittenEventHandler(ByVal sender As Object, ByVal e As EntryWrittenEventArgs)
```

Associated Events: EventLog.EntryWritten()

EventLog | Class

System.Diagnostics (system.dll) | *marshal by reference, disposable*

This class accesses Windows event logs that are accessible through the *Event Viewer* administrative tool. Windows contains three logs by default: the Application Log, System Log, and Security Log. The Security Log is read-only, so you can't write events to it. Whenever you need to raise an event, you must select a system-wide unique event source. This source can be any keyword, as long as it is unique. To write an event to the Application log, use the shared two-argument version of WriteEntry(), supplying the source name and message as string arguments. If the source does not exist, it is automatically registered.

You can manually register a new event source several ways. First, call CreateEventSource(). If you do not specify a log name, then your events are registered with the generic Application Log. Otherwise, a new *.evt* file is created (in the *%SystemRoot%\system32\config* directory). Alternatively, create a new EventLog object, and set Source, Log, and MachineName to the appropriate values. To delete a source, call DeleteEventSource(). Delete() lets you delete an entire log, but be careful not to delete one of the Windows event logs! GetEventLogs() allows you to find the logs on the system, and LogNameFromSourceName() allows you to determine the log file for a given source.

You can interact with a log in many ways. Add to it using WriteEntry() and remove all log entries by calling Clear(). Examine the Entries property to view the individual log entries. An EventLog can raise the EntryWritten event if you set EnableRaisingEvents to true.

```
Public Class EventLog : Inherits System.ComponentModel.Component : Implements _
     System.ComponentModel.ISupportInitialize
' Public Constructors
   Public Sub New()
   Public Sub New(ByVal logName As String)
   Public Sub New(ByVal logName As String, ByVal machineName As String)
   Public Sub New(ByVal logName As String, ByVal machineName As String, ByVal source As String)
' Public Instance Properties
   Public Property EnableRaisingEvents As Boolean
   Public ReadOnly Property Entries As EventLogEntryCollection
   Public Property Log As String
   Public ReadOnly Property LogDisplayName As String
   Public Property MachineName As String
   Public Property Source As String
   Public Property SynchronizingObject As ISynchronizeInvoke
' Public Shared Methods
   Public Shared Sub CreateEventSource(ByVal source As String, ByVal logName As String)
   Public Shared Sub CreateEventSource(ByVal source As String, ByVal logName As String, _
     ByVal machineName As String)
   Public Shared Sub Delete(ByVal logName As String)
   Public Shared Sub Delete(ByVal logName As String, ByVal machineName As String)
   Public Shared Sub DeleteEventSource(ByVal source As String)
   Public Shared Sub DeleteEventSource(ByVal source As String, ByVal machineName As String)
   Public Shared Function Exists(ByVal logName As String) As Boolean
   Public Shared Function Exists(ByVal logName As String, ByVal machineName As String) As Boolean
   Public Shared Function GetEventLogs() As EventLog()
   Public Shared Function GetEventLogs(ByVal machineName As String) As EventLog()
   Public Shared Function LogNameFromSourceName(ByVal source As String, ByVal machineName As String) _
     As String
   Public Shared Function SourceExists(ByVal source As String) As Boolean
   Public Shared Function SourceExists(ByVal source As String, ByVal machineName As String) As Boolean
   Public Shared Sub WriteEntry(ByVal source As String, ByVal message As String)
```

Public Shared Sub **WriteEntry**(ByVal source As String, ByVal message As String, ByVal type As EventLogEntryType)
Public Shared Sub **WriteEntry**(ByVal source As String, ByVal message As String, ByVal type As EventLogEntryType, _
    ByVal eventID As Integer)
Public Shared Sub **WriteEntry**(ByVal source As String, ByVal message As String, ByVal type As EventLogEntryType, _
    ByVal eventID As Integer, ByVal category As Short)
Public Shared Sub **WriteEntry**(ByVal source As String, ByVal message As String, ByVal type As EventLogEntryType, _
    ByVal eventID As Integer, ByVal category As Short, ByVal rawData As Byte())
' *Public Instance Methods*
Public Sub **BeginInit**() Implements ISupportInitialize.BeginInit
Public Sub **Clear**()
Public Sub **Close**()
Public Sub **EndInit**() Implements ISupportInitialize.EndInit
Public Sub **WriteEntry**(ByVal message As String)
Public Sub **WriteEntry**(ByVal message As String, ByVal type As EventLogEntryType)
Public Sub **WriteEntry**(ByVal message As String, ByVal type As EventLogEntryType, ByVal eventID As Integer)
Public Sub **WriteEntry**(ByVal message As String, ByVal type As EventLogEntryType, ByVal eventID As Integer, _
    ByVal category As Short)
Public Sub **WriteEntry**(ByVal message As String, ByVal type As EventLogEntryType, ByVal eventID As Integer, _
    ByVal category As Short, ByVal rawData As Byte())
' *Protected Instance Methods*
Overrides Protected Sub **Dispose**(ByVal disposing As Boolean)
' *Events*
Public Event **EntryWritten** As EntryWrittenEventHandler
End Class

Hierarchy: System.Object→ System.MarshalByRefObject→
System.ComponentModel.Component(System.ComponentModel.IComponent, System.IDisposable)→
EventLog(System.ComponentModel.ISupportInitialize)

Returned By: EventLogTraceListener.EventLog

Passed To: EventLogTraceListener.{EventLog, EventLogTraceListener()}

EventLogEntry
NotInheritable Class

System.Diagnostics (system.dll)
serializable, marshal by reference, disposable

This class represents an individual entry from an EventLog. A collection of these objects is available through EventLog.Entries. This class exposes all the properties of an event log entry.

Public NotInheritable Class **EventLogEntry** : Inherits System.ComponentModel.Component : Implements _
    System.Runtime.Serialization.ISerializable
' *Public Instance Properties*
Public ReadOnly Property **Category** As String
Public ReadOnly Property **CategoryNumber** As Short
Public ReadOnly Property **Data** As Byte()
Public ReadOnly Property **EntryType** As EventLogEntryType
Public ReadOnly Property **EventID** As Integer
Public ReadOnly Property **Index** As Integer
Public ReadOnly Property **MachineName** As String
Public ReadOnly Property **Message** As String
Public ReadOnly Property **ReplacementStrings** As String()
Public ReadOnly Property **Source** As String
Public ReadOnly Property **TimeGenerated** As Date
Public ReadOnly Property **TimeWritten** As Date
Public ReadOnly Property **UserName** As String
' *Public Instance Methods*

```
    Public Function Equals(ByVal otherEntry As EventLogEntry) As Boolean
End Class
```

Hierarchy: System.Object→ System.MarshalByRefObject→
System.ComponentModel.Component(System.ComponentModel.IComponent, System.IDisposable)→
EventLogEntry(System.Runtime.Serialization.ISerializable)

Returned By: EntryWrittenEventArgs.Entry, EventLogEntryCollection.this

Passed To: EntryWrittenEventArgs.EntryWrittenEventArgs(), EventLogEntryCollection.CopyTo()

EventLogEntryCollection   **Class**

System.Diagnostics (system.dll)

This class is an ICollection implementation for EventLogEntry objects.

```
Public Class EventLogEntryCollection : Implements ICollection, IEnumerable
' Public Instance Properties
    Public ReadOnly Property Count As Integer Implements ICollection.Count
    Overridable Public Default ReadOnly Property Item (ByVal index As Integer) As EventLogEntry
' Public Instance Methods
    Public Sub CopyTo(ByVal entries As EventLogEntry(), ByVal index As Integer)
    Public Function GetEnumerator() As IEnumerator Implements IEnumerable.GetEnumerator
End Class
```

Returned By: EventLog.Entries

EventLogEntryType   **Enum**

System.Diagnostics (system.dll)   *serializable*

This enumeration represents an event log entry's severity level. Error indicates that the message contains an error. SuccessAudit and FailureAudit indicate that an audited access attempt, such as a user logon, has succeeded or failed. Information represents that a significant operation, such as starting or stopping a service, has taken place. Warning indicates that a problem has occurred. Warnings are not as serious as Errors, but they should be investigated and resolved whenever possible, so your log does not fill up with warning messages.

```
Public Enum EventLogEntryType
    Error = 1
    Warning = 2
    Information = 4
    SuccessAudit = 8
    FailureAudit = 16
End Enum
```

Hierarchy: System.Object→ System.ValueType→ System.Enum(System.IComparable,
System.IFormattable, System.IConvertible)→ EventLogEntryType

Returned By: EventLogEntry.EntryType

Passed To: EventLog.WriteEntry()

EventLogInstaller   Class

System.Diagnostics (system.configuration.install.dll)   *marshal by reference, disposable*

This class is a System.Configuration.Install.Installer to install EventLogs. To install a new source, set the appropriate Source and Log properties.

```
Public Class EventLogInstaller : Inherits System.Configuration.Install.ComponentInstaller
' Public Constructors
   Public Sub New()
' Public Instance Properties
   Public Property Log As String
   Public Property Source As String
   Public Property UninstallAction As UninstallAction
' Public Instance Methods
   Overrides Public Sub CopyFromComponent(ByVal component As System.ComponentModel.IComponent)
   Overrides Public Sub Install(ByVal stateSaver As System.Collections.IDictionary)
   Overrides Public Function IsEquivalentInstaller(
      ByVal otherInstaller As System.Configuration.Install.ComponentInstaller) As Boolean
   Overrides Public Sub Rollback(ByVal savedState As System.Collections.IDictionary)
   Overrides Public Sub Uninstall(ByVal savedState As System.Collections.IDictionary)
End Class
```

Hierarchy: System.Object→ System.MarshalByRefObject→
System.ComponentModel.Component(System.ComponentModel.IComponent, System.IDisposable)→
System.Configuration.Install.Installer→ System.Configuration.Install.ComponentInstaller→
EventLogInstaller

EventLogPermission   NotInheritable Class

System.Diagnostics (system.dll)   *serializable*

This class is a System.Security.Permissions.ResourcePermissionBase object, which indicates whether or not the executing code has permission to access the Windows event logs.

```
Public NotInheritable Class EventLogPermission : Inherits System.Security.Permissions.ResourcePermissionBase
' Public Constructors
   Public Sub New()
   Public Sub New(ByVal permissionAccess As EventLogPermissionAccess, ByVal machineName As String)
   Public Sub New(ByVal permissionAccessEntries As EventLogPermissionEntry())
   Public Sub New(ByVal state As System.Security.Permissions.PermissionState)
' Public Instance Properties
   Public ReadOnly Property PermissionEntries As EventLogPermissionEntryCollection
End Class
```

Hierarchy: System.Object→ System.Security.CodeAccessPermission(System.Security.IPermission,
System.Security.ISecurityEncodable, System.Security.IStackWalk)→
System.Security.Permissions.ResourcePermissionBase(System.Security.Permissions.IUnrestrictedPermission)→
EventLogPermission

EventLogPermissionAccess   Enum

System.Diagnostics (system.dll)   *serializable, flag*

This enumeration is used by EventLogPermissionAttribute. None indicates no access, and Browse allows you to read logs. Instrument allows reading and writing. Audit represents the highest level of access. It lets you read logs, clear a log, monitor events, respond to entries, delete logs and event sources, and enumerate a collection of all logs.

```
Public Enum EventLogPermissionAccess
    None = &H000000000
    Browse = &H000000002
    Instrument = &H000000006
    Audit = &H00000000A
End Enum
```

Hierarchy: System.Object→ System.ValueType→ System.Enum(System.IComparable, System.IFormattable, System.IConvertible)→ EventLogPermissionAccess

Returned By: EventLogPermissionAttribute.PermissionAccess, EventLogPermissionEntry.PermissionAccess

Passed To: EventLogPermission.EventLogPermission(), EventLogPermissionAttribute.PermissionAccess, EventLogPermissionEntry.EventLogPermissionEntry()

EventLogPermissionAttribute   Class

System.Diagnostics (system.dll)   *serializable*

This security attribute specifies the EventLogPermissionAccess required by your code.

```
Public Class EventLogPermissionAttribute : Inherits System.Security.Permissions.CodeAccessSecurityAttribute
' Public Constructors
    Public Sub New(ByVal action As System.Security.Permissions.SecurityAction)
' Public Instance Properties
    Public Property MachineName As String
    Public Property PermissionAccess As EventLogPermissionAccess
' Public Instance Methods
    Overrides Public Function CreatePermission() As IPermission
End Class
```

Hierarchy: System.Object→ System.Attribute→ System.Security.Permissions.SecurityAttribute→ System.Security.Permissions.CodeAccessSecurityAttribute→ EventLogPermissionAttribute

Valid On: Assembly, Class, Struct, Constructor, Method, Event

EventLogPermissionEntry   Class

System.Diagnostics (system.dll)   *serializable*

This class represents a single permission from an EventLogPermission's PermissionEntries collection. MachineName checks the machine name the entry is for, and PermissionAccess gets an EventLogPermissionAccess that represents the granted permissions.

```
Public Class EventLogPermissionEntry
' Public Constructors
    Public Sub New(ByVal permissionAccess As EventLogPermissionAccess, ByVal machineName As String)
' Public Instance Properties
    Public ReadOnly Property MachineName As String
    Public ReadOnly Property PermissionAccess As EventLogPermissionAccess
End Class
```

Returned By: EventLogPermissionEntryCollection.this

Passed To: EventLogPermission.EventLogPermission(), EventLogPermissionEntryCollection.{Add(), AddRange(), Contains(), CopyTo(), IndexOf(), Insert(), this, Remove()}

EventLogPermissionEntryCollection

Class

System.Diagnostics (system.dll)

serializable

A strongly typed collection that contains EventLogPermissionEntry objects.

Public Class **EventLogPermissionEntryCollection** : Inherits CollectionBase
' *Public Instance Properties*
   Public Default Property **Item** (ByVal index As Integer) As EventLogPermissionEntry
' *Public Instance Methods*
   Public Function **Add**(ByVal value As EventLogPermissionEntry) As Integer
   Public Sub **AddRange**(ByVal value As EventLogPermissionEntry())
   Public Sub **AddRange**(ByVal value As EventLogPermissionEntryCollection)
   Public Function **Contains**(ByVal value As EventLogPermissionEntry) As Boolean
   Public Sub **CopyTo**(ByVal array As EventLogPermissionEntry(), ByVal index As Integer)
   Public Function **IndexOf**(ByVal value As EventLogPermissionEntry) As Integer
   Public Sub **Insert**(ByVal index As Integer, ByVal value As EventLogPermissionEntry)
   Public Sub **Remove**(ByVal value As EventLogPermissionEntry)
' *Protected Instance Methods*
   Overrides Protected Sub **OnClear**()
   Overrides Protected Sub **OnInsert**(ByVal index As Integer, ByVal value As Object)
   Overrides Protected Sub **OnRemove**(ByVal index As Integer, ByVal value As Object)
   Overrides Protected Sub **OnSet**(ByVal index As Integer, ByVal oldValue As Object, ByVal newValue As Object)
End Class

Hierarchy: System.Object→ System.Collections.CollectionBase(System.Collections.IList,
System.Collections.ICollection, System.Collections.IEnumerable)→ EventLogPermissionEntryCollection

Returned By: EventLogPermission.PermissionEntries

EventLogTraceListener

NotInheritable Class

System.Diagnostics (system.dll)

marshal by reference, disposable

To capture trace and debug output to an EventLog, add an instance of this class to
Debug.Listeners or Trace.Listeners. You can specify an EventLog instance in the constructor or
the name of an event source as a string.

Public NotInheritable Class **EventLogTraceListener** : Inherits TraceListener
' *Public Constructors*
   Public Sub **New**()
   Public Sub **New**(ByVal eventLog As EventLog)
   Public Sub **New**(ByVal source As String)
' *Public Instance Properties*
   Public Property **EventLog** As EventLog
   Overrides Public Property **Name** As String
' *Public Instance Methods*
   Overrides Public Sub **Close**()
   Overrides Public Sub **Write**(ByVal message As String)
   Overrides Public Sub **WriteLine**(ByVal message As String)
' *Protected Instance Methods*
   Overrides Protected Sub **Dispose**(ByVal disposing As Boolean)
End Class

Hierarchy: System.Object→ System.MarshalByRefObject→ TraceListener(System.IDisposable)→
EventLogTraceListener

**System.
Diagnostics**

FileVersionInfo
NotInheritable Class

System.Diagnostics (system.dll)

This class provides access to the attributes specific to binary files. Use GetVersionInfo() to obtain a reference to a file, and then inspect the object's properties to determine information about the file.

```
Public NotInheritable Class FileVersionInfo
' Public Instance Properties
   Public ReadOnly Property Comments As String
   Public ReadOnly Property CompanyName As String
   Public ReadOnly Property FileBuildPart As Integer
   Public ReadOnly Property FileDescription As String
   Public ReadOnly Property FileMajorPart As Integer
   Public ReadOnly Property FileMinorPart As Integer
   Public ReadOnly Property FileName As String
   Public ReadOnly Property FilePrivatePart As Integer
   Public ReadOnly Property FileVersion As String
   Public ReadOnly Property InternalName As String
   Public ReadOnly Property IsDebug As Boolean
   Public ReadOnly Property IsPatched As Boolean
   Public ReadOnly Property IsPreRelease As Boolean
   Public ReadOnly Property IsPrivateBuild As Boolean
   Public ReadOnly Property IsSpecialBuild As Boolean
   Public ReadOnly Property Language As String
   Public ReadOnly Property LegalCopyright As String
   Public ReadOnly Property LegalTrademarks As String
   Public ReadOnly Property OriginalFilename As String
   Public ReadOnly Property PrivateBuild As String
   Public ReadOnly Property ProductBuildPart As Integer
   Public ReadOnly Property ProductMajorPart As Integer
   Public ReadOnly Property ProductMinorPart As Integer
   Public ReadOnly Property ProductName As String
   Public ReadOnly Property ProductPrivatePart As Integer
   Public ReadOnly Property ProductVersion As String
   Public ReadOnly Property SpecialBuild As String
' Public Shared Methods
   Public Shared Function GetVersionInfo(ByVal fileName As String) As FileVersionInfo
' Public Instance Methods
   Overrides Public Function ToString() As String
End Class
```

Returned By: ProcessModule.FileVersionInfo

InstanceData
Class

System.Diagnostics (system.dll)

This type represents the instance data for a performance counter sample. InstanceName returns the InstanceData's name. RawValue returns the sample's raw data. Sample returns the CounterSample responsible for the data.

```
Public Class InstanceData
' Public Constructors
   Public Sub New(ByVal instanceName As String, ByVal sample As CounterSample)
' Public Instance Properties
   Public ReadOnly Property InstanceName As String
   Public ReadOnly Property RawValue As Long
```

Public ReadOnly Property **Sample** As CounterSample
End Class

Returned By: InstanceDataCollection.this

Passed To: InstanceDataCollection.CopyTo()

InstanceDataCollection   Class

System.Diagnostics (system.dll)

This type is a strongly typed collection of InstanceData objects.

Public Class **InstanceDataCollection** : Inherits DictionaryBase
' *Public Constructors*
    Public Sub **New**(ByVal counterName As String)
' *Public Instance Properties*
    Public ReadOnly Property **CounterName** As String
    Public Default ReadOnly Property **Item** (ByVal instanceName As String) As InstanceData
    Public ReadOnly Property **Keys** As ICollection Implements IDictionary.Keys
    Public ReadOnly Property **Values** As ICollection Implements IDictionary.Values
' *Public Instance Methods*
    Public Function **Contains**(ByVal instanceName As String) As Boolean
    Public Sub **CopyTo**(ByVal instances As InstanceData(), ByVal index As Integer)
End Class

Hierarchy: System.Object→ System.Collections.DictionaryBase(System.Collections.IDictionary, System.Collections.ICollection, System.Collections.IEnumerable)→ InstanceDataCollection

Returned By: InstanceDataCollectionCollection.this

Passed To: InstanceDataCollectionCollection.CopyTo()

InstanceDataCollectionCollection   Class

System.Diagnostics (system.dll)

This type is a strongly typed collection of InstanceDataCollection objects (e.g., a collection of collections).

Public Class **InstanceDataCollectionCollection** : Inherits DictionaryBase
' *Public Constructors*
    Public Sub **New**()
' *Public Instance Properties*
    Public Default ReadOnly Property **Item** (ByVal counterName As String) As InstanceDataCollection
    Public ReadOnly Property **Keys** As ICollection Implements IDictionary.Keys
    Public ReadOnly Property **Values** As ICollection Implements IDictionary.Values
' *Public Instance Methods*
    Public Function **Contains**(ByVal counterName As String) As Boolean
    Public Sub **CopyTo**(ByVal counters As InstanceDataCollection(), ByVal index As Integer)
End Class

Hierarchy: System.Object→ System.Collections.DictionaryBase(System.Collections.IDictionary, System.Collections.ICollection, System.Collections.IEnumerable)→ InstanceDataCollectionCollection

Returned By: PerformanceCounterCategory.ReadCategory()

System. Diagnostics

MonitoringDescriptionAttribute   Class
System.Diagnostics (system.dll)

This type is a System.ComponentModel.DescriptionAttribute that holds an informative description of one of the System.Diagnostics monitoring members.

```
Public Class MonitoringDescriptionAttribute : Inherits System.ComponentModel.DescriptionAttribute
' Public Constructors
   Public Sub New(ByVal description As String)
' Public Instance Properties
   Overrides Public ReadOnly Property Description As String
End Class
```

Hierarchy: System.Object→ System.Attribute→ System.ComponentModel.DescriptionAttribute→ MonitoringDescriptionAttribute

Valid On: All

PerformanceCounter   NotInheritable Class
System.Diagnostics (system.dll)   *marshal by reference, disposable*

This class represents a Windows NT, 2000, or XP performance counter that can be accessed using the Performance Administrative Tool. PerformanceCounters already exist for system devices, such as processor, disk, or memory usage, as well as for system resources, such as processes or threads. Using the PerformanceCounter class, you can both read from and write performance data to existing custom counters.

To create your own custom performance counters, use PerformanceCounterCategory.Create(). You can write to a performance counter by using one of the PerformanceCounter constructors that takes the boolean readonly argument. Set that argument to false to create a performance counter that you can write to. To set the value of a performance counter, call IncrementBy(), Increment(), Decrement(), or set the RawValue to the desired value.

To access an existing performance counter, create an instance of PerformanceCounter with the CategoryName and CounterName set to that of an available category and an existing performance counter. The category and counter names are case-insensitive, so you could sample the available memory by calling the constructor as Performance-Counter("memory", "available mbytes"). Consult the Performance Administrative Tool for the available performance counters. You can explicitly set the CategoryName and CounterName (and the optional InstanceName and MachineName) properties, if you choose not to set these using the constructor.

To obtain a new data sample for a counter, call either NextValue() or NextSample(). NextSample() returns a CounterSample structure that represents the raw captured performance data. NextValue() fetches the next sample and calculates its value based on the raw data it contains. To permanently remove a counter, call RemoveInstance(). If you attempt to modify or remove a counter in which the ReadOnly property is set to true, an InvalidOperationException is returned.

```
Public NotInheritable Class PerformanceCounter : Inherits System.ComponentModel.Component : Implements _
      System.ComponentModel.ISupportInitialize
' Public Constructors
   Public Sub New()
   Public Sub New(ByVal categoryName As String, ByVal counterName As String)
   Public Sub New(ByVal categoryName As String, ByVal counterName As String, ByVal readOnly As Boolean)
   Public Sub New(ByVal categoryName As String, ByVal counterName As String, ByVal instanceName As String)
   Public Sub New(ByVal categoryName As String, ByVal counterName As String, ByVal instanceName As String, _
      ByVal readOnly As Boolean)
```

```
Public Sub New(ByVal categoryName As String, ByVal counterName As String, ByVal instanceName As String, _
   ByVal machineName As String)
' Public Shared Fields
   Public Shared DefaultFileMappingSize As Integer                              =524288
' Public Instance Properties
   Public Property CategoryName As String
   Public ReadOnly Property CounterHelp As String
   Public Property CounterName As String
   Public ReadOnly Property CounterType As PerformanceCounterType
   Public Property InstanceName As String
   Public Property MachineName As String
   Public Property RawValue As Long
   Public Property ReadOnly As Boolean
' Public Shared Methods
   Public Shared Sub CloseSharedResources()
' Public Instance Methods
   Public Sub BeginInit() Implements ISupportInitialize.BeginInit
   Public Sub Close()
   Public Function Decrement() As Long
   Public Sub EndInit() Implements ISupportInitialize.EndInit
   Public Function Increment() As Long
   Public Function IncrementBy(ByVal value As Long) As Long
   Public Function NextSample() As CounterSample
   Public Function NextValue() As Single
   Public Sub RemoveInstance()
' Protected Instance Methods
   Overrides Protected Sub Dispose(ByVal disposing As Boolean)
End Class
```

Hierarchy: System.Object→ System.MarshalByRefObject→
System.ComponentModel.Component(System.ComponentModel.IComponent, System.IDisposable)→
PerformanceCounter(System.ComponentModel.ISupportInitialize)

Returned By: PerformanceCounterCategory.GetCounters()

PerformanceCounterCategory   NotInheritable Class
System.Diagnostics (system.dll)

This class allows you to create and manage categories of performance counters. You can see the categories recognized by your system when you use the Performance Administrative Tool. When you attempt to add a counter, you'll see the categories listed in the Performance object drop-list, such as Processor, Memory, Thread, and Network Interface.

Use Create() to add a new category. The three-argument form lets you supply a category name, a description of the category, and a collection of CounterCreationData objects. Each CounterCreationData object describes a counter to create in the new category. Use the four-argument form of Create() to create a new category with only a single counter.

Delete() removes a counter category, and Exists() checks whether a given category exists. If you want to check if a specific counter exists in a category, call CounterExists(). To check for an instance in a category, use InstanceExists(). GetCategories() returns all the categories recognized by the system.

The CategoryHelp, CategoryName, and MachineName properties provide access to the name, help text, and machine name for a given category. You can use the nonshared versions of CounterExists() and InstanceExists() to check if a specified counter or instance exists in the inspected category. GetCounters() and GetInstanceNames() retrieve a list of the counters and instances in a category.

Public NotInheritable Class **PerformanceCounterCategory**
' Public Constructors
  Public Sub **New**()
  Public Sub **New**(ByVal categoryName As String)
  Public Sub **New**(ByVal categoryName As String, ByVal machineName As String)
' Public Instance Properties
  Public ReadOnly Property **CategoryHelp** As String
  Public Property **CategoryName** As String
  Public Property **MachineName** As String
' Public Shared Methods
  Public Shared Function **CounterExists**(ByVal counterName As String, ByVal categoryName As String) As Boolean
  Public Shared Function **CounterExists**(ByVal counterName As String, ByVal categoryName As String, _
    ByVal machineName As String) As Boolean
  Public Shared Function **Create**(ByVal categoryName As String, ByVal categoryHelp As String, _
    ByVal counterData As CounterCreationDataCollection) As PerformanceCounterCategory
  Public Shared Function **Create**(ByVal categoryName As String, ByVal categoryHelp As String, _
    ByVal counterName As String, ByVal counterHelp As String) As PerformanceCounterCategory
  Public Shared Sub **Delete**(ByVal categoryName As String)
  Public Shared Function **Exists**(ByVal categoryName As String) As Boolean
  Public Shared Function **Exists**(ByVal categoryName As String, ByVal machineName As String) As Boolean
  Public Shared Function **GetCategories**() As PerformanceCounterCategory()
  Public Shared Function **GetCategories**(ByVal machineName As String) As PerformanceCounterCategory()
  Public Shared Function **InstanceExists**(ByVal instanceName As String, ByVal categoryName As String) _
    As Boolean
  Public Shared Function **InstanceExists**(ByVal instanceName As String, ByVal categoryName As String, _
    ByVal machineName As String) As Boolean
' Public Instance Methods
  Public Function **CounterExists**(ByVal counterName As String) As Boolean
  Public Function **GetCounters**() As PerformanceCounter()
  Public Function **GetCounters**(ByVal instanceName As String) As PerformanceCounter()
  Public Function **GetInstanceNames**() As String()
  Public Function **InstanceExists**(ByVal instanceName As String) As Boolean
  Public Function **ReadCategory**() As InstanceDataCollectionCollection
End Class

PerformanceCounterInstaller   Class

System.Diagnostics (system.configuration.install.dll)   *marshal by reference, disposable*

This is an installer for a PerformanceCounter component. CategoryName and CategoryHelp contain the name and help text pertinent to the category to install the counters into, and Counters contains the counters that will be installed.

Public Class **PerformanceCounterInstaller** : Inherits System.Configuration.Install.ComponentInstaller
' Public Constructors
  Public Sub **New**()
' Public Instance Properties
  Public Property **CategoryHelp** As String
  Public Property **CategoryName** As String
  Public ReadOnly Property **Counters** As CounterCreationDataCollection
  Public Property **UninstallAction** As UninstallAction
' Public Instance Methods
  Overrides Public Sub **CopyFromComponent**(ByVal component As System.ComponentModel.IComponent)
  Overrides Public Sub **Install**(ByVal stateSaver As System.Collections.IDictionary)
  Overrides Public Sub **Rollback**(ByVal savedState As System.Collections.IDictionary)

```
Overrides Public Sub Uninstall(ByVal savedState As System.Collections.IDictionary)
End Class
```

Hierarchy: System.Object→ System.MarshalByRefObject→
System.ComponentModel.Component(System.ComponentModel.IComponent, System.IDisposable)→
System.Configuration.Install.Installer→ System.Configuration.Install.ComponentInstaller→
PerformanceCounterInstaller

PerformanceCounterPermission
NotInheritable Class

System.Diagnostics (system.dll)
serializable

This class is a System.Security.CodeAccessPermission object that specifies code access to PerformanceCounter instances. The PermissionEntries property returns a collection of PerformanceCounterPermissionEntry objects representing the specific permissions granted.

```
Public NotInheritable Class PerformanceCounterPermission : Inherits _
    System.Security.Permissions.ResourcePermissionBase
' Public Constructors
    Public Sub New()
    Public Sub New(ByVal permissionAccess As PerformanceCounterPermissionAccess, ByVal machineName As String, _
    ByVal categoryName As String)
    Public Sub New(ByVal permissionAccessEntries As PerformanceCounterPermissionEntry())
    Public Sub New(ByVal state As System.Security.Permissions.PermissionState)
' Public Instance Properties
    Public ReadOnly Property PermissionEntries As PerformanceCounterPermissionEntryCollection
End Class
```

Hierarchy: System.Object→ System.Security.CodeAccessPermission(System.Security.IPermission,
System.Security.ISecurityEncodable, System.Security.IStackWalk)→
System.Security.Permissions.ResourcePermissionBase(System.Security.Permissions.IUnrestrictedPermission)→
PerformanceCounterPermission

PerformanceCounterPermissionAccess
Enum

System.Diagnostics (system.dll)
serializable, flag

This enumeration represents the different types of access that can be granted to executing code. Administer allows full control over a PerformanceCounter, while Browse allows you to view, but not modify PerformanceCounter data. Instrument allows the code to act as a performance counter (you may read and write, but not create, categories). None explicitly denies access to a PerformanceCounterCategory.

```
Public Enum PerformanceCounterPermissionAccess
    None = &H00000000
    Browse = &H00000002
    Instrument = &H00000006
    Administer = &H0000000E
End Enum
```

Hierarchy: System.Object→ System.ValueType→ System.Enum(System.IComparable,
System.IFormattable, System.IConvertible)→ PerformanceCounterPermissionAccess

Returned By: PerformanceCounterPermissionAttribute.PermissionAccess,
PerformanceCounterPermissionEntry.PermissionAccess

Passed To: PerformanceCounterPermission.PerformanceCounterPermission(),
PerformanceCounterPermissionAttribute.PermissionAccess,
PerformanceCounterPermissionEntry.PerformanceCounterPermissionEntry()

PerformanceCounterPermissionAttribute   Class

System.Diagnostics (system.dll)   *serializable*

This class is a System.Security.Permissions.SecurityAttribute that explicitly allows you to set required or denied performance counter permissions. You can use the CategoryName, MachineName, and PermissionAccess properties to indicate the required permissions for a specific PerformanceCounter.

```
Public Class PerformanceCounterPermissionAttribute : Inherits _
      System.Security.Permissions.CodeAccessSecurityAttribute
' Public Constructors
   Public Sub New(ByVal action As System.Security.Permissions.SecurityAction)
' Public Instance Properties
   Public Property CategoryName As String
   Public Property MachineName As String
   Public Property PermissionAccess As PerformanceCounterPermissionAccess
' Public Instance Methods
   Overrides Public Function CreatePermission() As IPermission
End Class
```

Hierarchy: System.Object→ System.Attribute→ System.Security.Permissions.SecurityAttribute→ System.Security.Permissions.CodeAccessSecurityAttribute→ PerformanceCounterPermissionAttribute

Valid On: Assembly, Class, Struct, Constructor, Method, Event

PerformanceCounterPermissionEntry   Class

System.Diagnostics (system.dll)   *serializable*

This class holds the necessary information for a given permission. The PermissionAccess property sets the PerformanceCounterPermissionAccess level for a specific CategoryName and MachineName.

```
Public Class PerformanceCounterPermissionEntry
' Public Constructors
   Public Sub New(ByVal permissionAccess As PerformanceCounterPermissionAccess, ByVal machineName As String, _
      ByVal categoryName As String)
' Public Instance Properties
   Public ReadOnly Property CategoryName As String
   Public ReadOnly Property MachineName As String
   Public ReadOnly Property PermissionAccess As PerformanceCounterPermissionAccess
End Class
```

Returned By: PerformanceCounterPermissionEntryCollection.this

Passed To: PerformanceCounterPermission.PerformanceCounterPermission(), PerformanceCounterPermissionEntryCollection.{Add(), AddRange(), Contains(), CopyTo(), IndexOf(), Insert(), this, Remove()}

PerformanceCounterPermissionEntryCollection   Class

System.Diagnostics (system.dll)   *serializable*

This strongly typed collection contains PerformanceCounterPermissionEntry objects.

```
Public Class PerformanceCounterPermissionEntryCollection : Inherits CollectionBase
' Public Instance Properties
   Public Default Property Item (ByVal index As Integer) As PerformanceCounterPermissionEntry
' Public Instance Methods
   Public Function Add(ByVal value As PerformanceCounterPermissionEntry) As Integer
   Public Sub AddRange(ByVal value As PerformanceCounterPermissionEntry())
```

Public Sub **AddRange**(ByVal value As PerformanceCounterPermissionEntryCollection)
Public Function **Contains**(ByVal value As PerformanceCounterPermissionEntry) As Boolean
Public Sub **CopyTo**(ByVal array As PerformanceCounterPermissionEntry(), ByVal index As Integer)
Public Function **IndexOf**(ByVal value As PerformanceCounterPermissionEntry) As Integer
Public Sub **Insert**(ByVal index As Integer, ByVal value As PerformanceCounterPermissionEntry)
Public Sub **Remove**(ByVal value As PerformanceCounterPermissionEntry)
' Protected Instance Methods
Overrides Protected Sub **OnClear**()
Overrides Protected Sub **OnInsert**(ByVal index As Integer, ByVal value As Object)
Overrides Protected Sub **OnRemove**(ByVal index As Integer, ByVal value As Object)
Overrides Protected Sub **OnSet**(ByVal index As Integer, ByVal oldValue As Object, ByVal newValue As Object)
End Class

Hierarchy: System.Object→ System.Collections.CollectionBase(System.Collections.IList,
System.Collections.ICollection, System.Collections.IEnumerable) →
PerformanceCounterPermissionEntryCollection

Returned By: PerformanceCounterPermission.PermissionEntries

PerformanceCounterType　　　　　　　　　　　　　　　　　　　　**Enum**

System.Diagnostics (system.dll)　　　　　　　　　　　　　　　　*serializable*

This enumeration represents the different types of performance counters available.
Look up System.Diagnostics.PerformanceCounterType in the .NET Framework SDK Documentation for complete details.

Public Enum **PerformanceCounterType**
　　NumberOfItemsHEX32 = 0
　　NumberOfItemsHEX64 = 256
　　NumberOfItems32 = 65536
　　NumberOfItems64 = 65792
　　CounterDelta32 = 4195328
　　CounterDelta64 = 4195584
　　SampleCounter = 4260864
　　CountPerTimeInterval32 = 4523008
　　CountPerTimeInterval64 = 4523264
　　RateOfCountsPerSecond32 = 272696320
　　RateOfCountsPerSecond64 = 272696576
　　RawFraction = 537003008
　　CounterTimer = 541132032
　　Timer100Ns = 542180608
　　SampleFraction = 549585920
　　CounterTimerInverse = 557909248
　　Timer100NsInverse = 558957824
　　CounterMultiTimer = 574686464
　　CounterMultiTimer100Ns = 575735040
　　CounterMultiTimerInverse = 591463680
　　CounterMultiTimer100NsInverse = 592512256
　　AverageTimer32 = 805438464
　　ElapsedTime = 807666944
　　AverageCount64 = 1073874176
　　SampleBase = 1073939457
　　AverageBase = 1073939458
　　RawBase = 1073939459
　　CounterMultiBase = 1107494144
End Enum

System. Diagnostics

Hierarchy: System.Object→ System.ValueType→ System.Enum(System.IComparable, System.IFormattable, System.IConvertible)→ PerformanceCounterType

Returned By: CounterCreationData.CounterType, CounterSample.CounterType, PerformanceCounter.CounterType

Passed To: CounterCreationData.{CounterCreationData(), CounterType}, CounterSample.CounterSample()

Process   Class
System.Diagnostics (system.dll)   *marshal by reference, disposable*

This class represents a system process. Use it to start, stop, and interact with a process. To launch a new process, create an instance of ProcessStartInfo, set its properties, and pass it to the single-argument form of the sharedStart() method. This offers a great deal of control over process creation. To launch a process without customizing its StartInfo, simply call the one-string or two-string argument form of the sharedStart() method. The first string argument is the name of the program, batch file, or document to start, and the optional second argument contains any command-line arguments. You can also explicitly create a new instance of Process, set its StartInfo property, and call the Start() method to start the process.

GetCurrentProcess() creates a Process instance that represents the current process. Enumerate all running processes on the system by using GetProcesses(). Use GetProcessesByName() to get all processes for a given program. GetProcessById() retrieves a Process given its process ID.

Use CloseMainWindow() to shut down a process that has a user interface. You can terminate a process with Kill(), but this forces an abnormal termination, which may result in data corruption. If you would like to raise an event when the process finishes executing, use Exited (EnableRaisingEvents must be set to true).

Most of the properties allow you to access general information about the running process. However, this information is populated at the time you associate a Process object with a running process. You can call Refresh() each time you need to update this information. Modules allows you to inspect the code modules the process has loaded into memory, and MainModule returns the module that started the process. StandardInput, StandardOutput, and StandardError allow access to the default I/O streams (see the ProcessStartInfo.Redirect* methods). Threads returns the threads in use by the process, and WorkingSet returns the physical memory usage of the process.

```
Public Class Process : Inherits System.ComponentModel.Component
' Public Constructors
   Public Sub New()
' Public Instance Properties
   Public ReadOnly Property BasePriority As Integer
   Public Property EnableRaisingEvents As Boolean
   Public ReadOnly Property ExitCode As Integer
   Public ReadOnly Property ExitTime As Date
   Public ReadOnly Property Handle As IntPtr
   Public ReadOnly Property HandleCount As Integer
   Public ReadOnly Property HasExited As Boolean
   Public ReadOnly Property Id As Integer
   Public ReadOnly Property MachineName As String
   Public ReadOnly Property MainModule As ProcessModule
   Public ReadOnly Property MainWindowHandle As IntPtr
   Public ReadOnly Property MainWindowTitle As String
   Public Property MaxWorkingSet As IntPtr
```

Public Property **MinWorkingSet** As IntPtr
Public ReadOnly Property **Modules** As ProcessModuleCollection
Public ReadOnly Property **NonpagedSystemMemorySize** As Integer
Public ReadOnly Property **PagedMemorySize** As Integer
Public ReadOnly Property **PagedSystemMemorySize** As Integer
Public ReadOnly Property **PeakPagedMemorySize** As Integer
Public ReadOnly Property **PeakVirtualMemorySize** As Integer
Public ReadOnly Property **PeakWorkingSet** As Integer
Public Property **PriorityBoostEnabled** As Boolean
Public Property **PriorityClass** As ProcessPriorityClass
Public ReadOnly Property **PrivateMemorySize** As Integer
Public ReadOnly Property **PrivilegedProcessorTime** As TimeSpan
Public ReadOnly Property **ProcessName** As String
Public Property **ProcessorAffinity** As IntPtr
Public ReadOnly Property **Responding** As Boolean
Public ReadOnly Property **StandardError** As StreamReader
Public ReadOnly Property **StandardInput** As StreamWriter
Public ReadOnly Property **StandardOutput** As StreamReader
Public Property **StartInfo** As ProcessStartInfo
Public ReadOnly Property **StartTime** As Date
Public Property **SynchronizingObject** As ISynchronizeInvoke
Public ReadOnly Property **Threads** As ProcessThreadCollection
Public ReadOnly Property **TotalProcessorTime** As TimeSpan
Public ReadOnly Property **UserProcessorTime** As TimeSpan
Public Property **VirtualMemorySize** As Integer
Public ReadOnly Property **WorkingSet** As Integer
' *Public Shared Methods*
Public Shared Sub **EnterDebugMode**()
Public Shared Function **GetCurrentProcess**() As Process
Public Shared Function **GetProcessById**(ByVal processId As Integer) As Process
Public Shared Function **GetProcessById**(ByVal processId As Integer, ByVal machineName As String) As Process
Public Shared Function **GetProcesses**() As Process()
Public Shared Function **GetProcesses**(ByVal machineName As String) As Process()
Public Shared Function **GetProcessesByName**(ByVal processName As String) As Process()
Public Shared Function **GetProcessesByName**(ByVal processName As String, ByVal machineName As String) _
    As Process()
Public Shared Sub **LeaveDebugMode**()
Public Shared Function **Start**(ByVal startInfo As ProcessStartInfo) As Process
Public Shared Function **Start**(ByVal fileName As String) As Process
Public Shared Function **Start**(ByVal fileName As String, ByVal arguments As String) As Process
' *Public Instance Methods*
Public Sub **Close**()
Public Function **CloseMainWindow**() As Boolean
Public Sub **Kill**()
Public Sub **Refresh**()
Public Function **Start**() As Boolean
Overrides Public Function **ToString**() As String
Public Function **WaitForExit**(ByVal milliseconds As Integer) As Boolean
Public Sub **WaitForExit**()
Public Function **WaitForInputIdle**() As Boolean
Public Function **WaitForInputIdle**(ByVal milliseconds As Integer) As Boolean
' *Protected Instance Methods*
Overrides Protected Sub **Dispose**(ByVal disposing As Boolean)
Protected Sub **OnExited**()
' *Events*

```
    Public Event Exited As EventHandler
End Class
```

Hierarchy: System.Object→ System.MarshalByRefObject→
System.ComponentModel.Component(System.ComponentModel.IComponent, System.IDisposable)→
Process

ProcessModule   Class
System.Diagnostics (system.dll)   *marshal by reference, disposable*

This class represents a DLL or EXE file loaded by a process. BaseAddress returns the starting memory address of the loaded module and EntryPointAddress returns the memory
address of the module's entry point (such as Main(), WinMain(), or DllMain()). You can also
check the size of the loaded module by checking ModuleMemorySize. FileName returns the
full path to the file of a loaded module and FileVersionInfo allows you to access the version information of a file. Lastly, you can view the name of the module with Module-
Name.

```
Public Class ProcessModule : Inherits System.ComponentModel.Component
' Public Instance Properties
    Public ReadOnly Property BaseAddress As IntPtr
    Public ReadOnly Property EntryPointAddress As IntPtr
    Public ReadOnly Property FileName As String
    Public ReadOnly Property FileVersionInfo As FileVersionInfo
    Public ReadOnly Property ModuleMemorySize As Integer
    Public ReadOnly Property ModuleName As String
' Public Instance Methods
    Overrides Public Function ToString() As String
End Class
```

Hierarchy: System.Object→ System.MarshalByRefObject→
System.ComponentModel.Component(System.ComponentModel.IComponent, System.IDisposable)→
ProcessModule

Returned By: Process.MainModule, ProcessModuleCollection.this

Passed To: ProcessModuleCollection.{Contains(), CopyTo(), IndexOf(), ProcessModuleCollection()}

ProcessModuleCollection   Class
System.Diagnostics (system.dll)

This class is a strongly typed collection that contains ProcessModule objects.

```
Public Class ProcessModuleCollection : Inherits ReadOnlyCollectionBase
' Public Constructors
    Public Sub New(ByVal processModules As ProcessModule())
' Protected Constructors
    Protected Sub New()
' Public Instance Properties
    Public Default ReadOnly Property Item (ByVal index As Integer) As ProcessModule
' Public Instance Methods
    Public Function Contains(ByVal module As ProcessModule) As Boolean
    Public Sub CopyTo(ByVal array As ProcessModule(), ByVal index As Integer)
    Public Function IndexOf(ByVal module As ProcessModule) As Integer
End Class
```

Hierarchy: System.Object→
System.Collections.ReadOnlyCollectionBase(System.Collections.ICollection,
System.Collections.IEnumerable)→ ProcessModuleCollection

Returned By: Process.Modules

ProcessPriorityClass   Enum
System.Diagnostics (system.dll)   *serializable*

This enumeration represents the different priorities given to a process. Process priorities, along with thread priorities, determine how processor time is allocated. Most processes run with Normal priority. Use Idle to specify that processor time should be allocated to a process only when the processor is idle. AboveNormal and BelowNormal allow you to set priorities slightly above or below Normal, but are not supported by Windows 95, 98, or Me. An exception is thrown if you attempt to use them.

High should be used only for time-critical tasks, but use care in choosing this priority because little time will be available to other applications. RealTime is the maximum allowable priority. When this priority is used, the process runs with higher priority than even the operating system. Assigning High and RealTime to a process will almost certainly make your system's user interface unresponsive. For this reason, be careful when using these.

```
Public Enum ProcessPriorityClass
    Normal = 32
    Idle = 64
    High = 128
    RealTime = 256
    BelowNormal = 16384
    AboveNormal = 32768
End Enum
```

Hierarchy: System.Object→ System.ValueType→ System.Enum(System.IComparable,
System.IFormattable, System.IConvertible)→ ProcessPriorityClass

Returned By: Process.PriorityClass

Passed To: Process.PriorityClass

ProcessStartInfo   NotInheritable Class
System.Diagnostics (system.dll)

This class is used to configure how a process is started or to view the settings a process was started with. To start a process, set FileName to the full path of the application or file, then pass the ProcessStartInfo instance to Process.Start(). FileName is the only property you must set. Use the other properties for more control. (Use Arguments to specify the command-line arguments.)

In Windows, each document type has a verb that you can use to do different things with (for example, a Microsoft Word document has an open and a print verb). To consult the possible verbs for a specific file, enumerate the Verbs property after you set FileName. To start a process with a specific verb, set Verb.

To change the standard error, input, or output source or targets (usually the system console) set one or more of RedirectStandardError, RedirectStandardInput or RedirectStandardOutput to true. This enables the Process.StandardError, Process.StandardInput, and Process.StandardOutput properties, which you can then set as needed. Set the EnvironmentVariables and WorkingDirectory to change the default process start behavior. If the process cannot be started, you can display an error dialog window by setting ErrorDialog (set the handle of

*System.
Diagnostics*

the dialog's parent window with ErrorDialogParentHandle). If you set CreateNoWindow, a new window is not created to start the new process. However, if you want a window, set its style by setting WindowStyle. You can also specify that the file should be executed from a Windows command prompt with UseShellExecute.

```
Public NotInheritable Class ProcessStartInfo
' Public Constructors
   Public Sub New()
   Public Sub New(ByVal fileName As String)
   Public Sub New(ByVal fileName As String, ByVal arguments As String)
' Public Instance Properties
   Public Property Arguments As String
   Public Property CreateNoWindow As Boolean
   Public ReadOnly Property EnvironmentVariables As StringDictionary
   Public Property ErrorDialog As Boolean
   Public Property ErrorDialogParentHandle As IntPtr
   Public Property FileName As String
   Public Property RedirectStandardError As Boolean
   Public Property RedirectStandardInput As Boolean
   Public Property RedirectStandardOutput As Boolean
   Public Property UseShellExecute As Boolean
   Public Property Verb As String
   Public ReadOnly Property Verbs As String()
   Public Property WindowStyle As ProcessWindowStyle
   Public Property WorkingDirectory As String
End Class
```

Returned By: Process.StartInfo

Passed To: Process.{Start(), StartInfo}

ProcessThread   Class

System.Diagnostics (system.dll)   *marshal by reference, disposable*

This class represents a thread, the smallest unit of execution under Win32. Use Process.Threads to get an array of all the threads contained within a given process. As with processes, a thread runs with a given priority. BasePriority represents the base priority for a thread. From time to time, the operating system changes a thread's priority; a thread's current priority is available from CurrentPriority. Threads in background applications run with a lower priority, as do threads that are sleeping. BasePriorityPriorityLevel specifies a range of appropriate priorities for a thread.

If a process is ProcessPriorityClass.Normal, ProcessPriorityClass.High, or ProcessPriorityClass.Real-Time, you can set a thread's PriorityBoostEnabled to true. This gives the thread an extra boost whenever the user is interacting with the program's user interface. You can make a thread prefer one processor over another by setting the value of IdealProcessor. ProcessorAffinity allows you to set up a bitfield that represents one or more preferred processors. Bit 0 represents the first processor, bit 1 the second, and so on. For example, a ProcessorAffinity of 0x0005 (bits 0 and 2 on) indicates that the first and third processor are preferred. Use ResetIdealProcessor() to tell the thread that it can run on any processor, leaving the processor choice up to the operating system.

The current state of a thread is returned by ThreadState. If a thread is waiting, you can retrieve the reason the thread is waiting via WaitReason. PrivilegedProcessorTime and UserProcessorTime return the privileged and user processor time, and TotalProcessorTime returns the sum of those two.

The ProcessThread class differs from the System.Threading.Thread type. ProcessThread represents the view of a thread from an administrative viewpoint, while

System.Threading.Thread represents a thread from its creator's viewpoint. When you want to enumerate and interact with the threads of an external process, use ProcessThread. When you need to create a new thread in your own program, use System.Threading.Thread.

```
Public Class ProcessThread : Inherits System.ComponentModel.Component
' Public Instance Properties
    Public ReadOnly Property BasePriority As Integer
    Public ReadOnly Property CurrentPriority As Integer
    Public ReadOnly Property Id As Integer
    Public WriteOnly Property IdealProcessor As Integer
    Public Property PriorityBoostEnabled As Boolean
    Public Property PriorityLevel As ThreadPriorityLevel
    Public ReadOnly Property PrivilegedProcessorTime As TimeSpan
    Public WriteOnly Property ProcessorAffinity As IntPtr
    Public ReadOnly Property StartAddress As IntPtr
    Public ReadOnly Property StartTime As Date
    Public ReadOnly Property ThreadState As ThreadState
    Public ReadOnly Property TotalProcessorTime As TimeSpan
    Public ReadOnly Property UserProcessorTime As TimeSpan
    Public ReadOnly Property WaitReason As ThreadWaitReason
' Public Instance Methods
    Public Sub ResetIdealProcessor()
End Class
```

Hierarchy: System.Object→ System.MarshalByRefObject→
System.ComponentModel.Component(System.ComponentModel.IComponent, System.IDisposable)→
ProcessThread

Returned By: ProcessThreadCollection.this

Passed To: ProcessThreadCollection.{Add(), Contains(), CopyTo(), IndexOf(), Insert(),
ProcessThreadCollection(), Remove()}

ProcessThreadCollection   Class

System.Diagnostics (system.dll)

This strongly typed collection contains ProcessThread objects.

```
Public Class ProcessThreadCollection : Inherits ReadOnlyCollectionBase
' Public Constructors
    Public Sub New(ByVal processThreads As ProcessThread())
' Protected Constructors
    Protected Sub New()
' Public Instance Properties
    Public Default ReadOnly Property Item (ByVal index As Integer) As ProcessThread
' Public Instance Methods
    Public Function Add(ByVal thread As ProcessThread) As Integer
    Public Function Contains(ByVal thread As ProcessThread) As Boolean
    Public Sub CopyTo(ByVal array As ProcessThread(), ByVal index As Integer)
    Public Function IndexOf(ByVal thread As ProcessThread) As Integer
    Public Sub Insert(ByVal index As Integer, ByVal thread As ProcessThread)
    Public Sub Remove(ByVal thread As ProcessThread)
End Class
```

Hierarchy: System.Object→
System.Collections.ReadOnlyCollectionBase(System.Collections.ICollection,
System.Collections.IEnumerable)→ ProcessThreadCollection

Returned By: Process.Threads

ProcessWindowStyle   Enum
System.Diagnostics (system.dll)   *serializable*

This enumeration contains the window states you can choose from when starting a Process.

```
Public Enum ProcessWindowStyle
    Normal = 0
    Hidden = 1
    Minimized = 2
    Maximized = 3
End Enum
```

Hierarchy: System.Object→ System.ValueType→ System.Enum(System.IComparable,
System.IFormattable, System.IConvertible)→ ProcessWindowStyle

Returned By: ProcessStartInfo.WindowStyle

Passed To: ProcessStartInfo.WindowStyle

StackFrame   Class
System.Diagnostics (mscorlib.dll)   *serializable*

A stack frame is an abstraction of the current state of an executing method. Use StackTrace to enumerate all the stack frames that led up to the current process. Use GetMethod() to obtain information about the method represented by a stack frame. Use GetFileName() to retrieve the name of the module that contains the method. The column and line numbers of the method, which are determined from debugging symbols, can be accessed with GetFileColumnNumber() and GetFileLineNumber(). To obtain the location in memory of the StackFrame, use GetNativeOffset(), or, alternatively, for the offset of IL code, call GetILOffset(). If the JIT compiler is not generating debugging symbols, this number is approximated by the runtime.

```
Public Class StackFrame
' Public Constructors
    Public Sub New()
    Public Sub New(ByVal fNeedFileInfo As Boolean)
    Public Sub New(ByVal skipFrames As Integer)
    Public Sub New(ByVal skipFrames As Integer, ByVal fNeedFileInfo As Boolean)
    Public Sub New(ByVal fileName As String, ByVal lineNumber As Integer)
    Public Sub New(ByVal fileName As String, ByVal lineNumber As Integer, ByVal colNumber As Integer)
' Public Shared Fields
    Public const OFFSET_UNKNOWN As Integer                                    =-1
' Public Instance Methods
    Overridable Public Function GetFileColumnNumber() As Integer
    Overridable Public Function GetFileLineNumber() As Integer
    Overridable Public Function GetFileName() As String
    Overridable Public Function GetILOffset() As Integer
    Overridable Public Function GetMethod() As MethodBase
    Overridable Public Function GetNativeOffset() As Integer
    Overrides Public Function ToString() As String
End Class
```

Returned By: StackTrace.GetFrame()

Passed To: StackTrace.StackTrace()

StackTrace   Class

System.Diagnostics (mscorlib.dll)   *serializable*

A stack trace is an ordered list of StackFrame objects. Call the constructor to create a stack trace that starts with a StackFrame corresponding to the current method. The optional boolean argument fNeedFileInfo indicates that the stack trace should include the filename as well as the line and column number. (The program must have been compiled with /debug to get this information.)

When one method calls another, a new stack frame is created and FrameCount is incremented. To get a specific StackFrame, use GetFrame(). The shared constant METHODS_TO_SKIP returns the number of methods skipped at the beginning of the StackTrace.

```
Public Class StackTrace
' Public Constructors
   Public Sub New()
   Public Sub New(ByVal fNeedFileInfo As Boolean)
   Public Sub New(ByVal e As Exception)
   Public Sub New(ByVal e As Exception, ByVal fNeedFileInfo As Boolean)
   Public Sub New(ByVal e As Exception, ByVal skipFrames As Integer)
   Public Sub New(ByVal e As Exception, ByVal skipFrames As Integer, ByVal fNeedFileInfo As Boolean)
   Public Sub New(ByVal skipFrames As Integer)
   Public Sub New(ByVal skipFrames As Integer, ByVal fNeedFileInfo As Boolean)
   Public Sub New(ByVal frame As StackFrame)
   Public Sub New(ByVal targetThread As System.Threading.Thread, ByVal needFileInfo As Boolean)
' Public Shared Fields
   Public const METHODS_TO_SKIP As Integer                                    =0
' Public Instance Properties
   Overridable Public ReadOnly Property FrameCount As Integer
' Public Instance Methods
   Overridable Public Function GetFrame(ByVal index As Integer) As StackFrame
   Overrides Public Function ToString() As String
End Class
```

Switch   MustInherit Class

System.Diagnostics (system.dll)

Consult this class in a conditional statement to execute special tracing or debugging code. To use a switch you must have debugging enabled. Each Switch has a DisplayName and Description. SwitchSetting contains the current setting.

Specify the value of a switch in the application configuration file. Under the <system.diagnostics> element, add an element <switches> to hold all the switches. Within the <switches> element, define each switch you want with <add name="switchname" value="value"/>. For a BooleanSwitch, any nonzero value sets BooleanSwitch.Enabled to true. For a TraceSwitch, use a value from the TraceLevel enumeration.

```
Public MustInherit Class Switch
' Protected Constructors
   Protected Sub New(ByVal displayName As String, ByVal description As String)
' Public Instance Properties
   Public ReadOnly Property Description As String
   Public ReadOnly Property DisplayName As String
' Protected Instance Properties
```

Protected Property **SwitchSetting** As Integer
' *Protected Instance Methods*
Overridable Protected Sub **OnSwitchSettingChanged**()
End Class

Subclasses: BooleanSwitch, TraceSwitch

TextWriterTraceListener   Class

System.Diagnostics (system.dll)   *marshal by reference, disposable*

This class writes to a System.IO.TextWriter. Use Writer to set or change the TextWriter.

Public Class **TextWriterTraceListener** : Inherits TraceListener
' *Public Constructors*
Public Sub **New**()
Public Sub **New**(ByVal stream As System.IO.Stream)
Public Sub **New**(ByVal stream As System.IO.Stream, ByVal name As String)
Public Sub **New**(ByVal fileName As String)
Public Sub **New**(ByVal fileName As String, ByVal name As String)
Public Sub **New**(ByVal writer As System.IO.TextWriter)
Public Sub **New**(ByVal writer As System.IO.TextWriter, ByVal name As String)
' *Public Instance Properties*
Public Property **Writer** As TextWriter
' *Public Instance Methods*
Overrides Public Sub **Close**()
Overrides Public Sub **Flush**()
Overrides Public Sub **Write**(ByVal message As String)
Overrides Public Sub **WriteLine**(ByVal message As String)
' *Protected Instance Methods*
Overrides Protected Sub **Dispose**(ByVal disposing As Boolean)
End Class

Hierarchy: System.Object→ System.MarshalByRefObject→ TraceListener(System.IDisposable)→
TextWriterTraceListener

ThreadPriorityLevel   Enum

System.Diagnostics (system.dll)   *serializable*

This enumeration represents the different thread priority levels. A thread's priority level
is computed relative to the process priority level using ProcessThread.PriorityLevel.

Public Enum **ThreadPriorityLevel**
    Normal = 0
    AboveNormal = 1
    Highest = 2
    TimeCritical = 15
    Idle = -15
    Lowest = -2
    BelowNormal = -1
End Enum

Hierarchy: System.Object→ System.ValueType→ System.Enum(System.IComparable,
System.IFormattable, System.IConvertible)→ ThreadPriorityLevel

Returned By: ProcessThread.PriorityLevel

Passed To: ProcessThread.PriorityLevel

ThreadState

Enum

System.Diagnostics (system.dll)   *serializable*

This enumeration represents the different thread states as recognized by the operating system. They mostly correspond to the states defined by System.Threading.ThreadState, but also include Transition for when a thread is waiting on something other than the CPU (it might be waiting on disk I/O, for example).

```
Public Enum ThreadState
    Initialized = 0
    Ready = 1
    Running = 2
    Standby = 3
    Terminated = 4
    Wait = 5
    Transition = 6
    Unknown = 7
End Enum
```

Hierarchy: System.Object→ System.ValueType→ System.Enum(System.IComparable, System.IFormattable, System.IConvertible)→ ThreadState

Returned By: ProcessThread.ThreadState

ThreadWaitReason

Enum

System.Diagnostics (system.dll)   *serializable*

This enumeration specifies the reason a thread is waiting. VirtualMemory indicates that a thread is waiting for virtual memory to be allocated, and PageIn and PageOut indicate that a thread is waiting for virtual memory to page in or out, respectively. FreePage is for threads waiting for a free virtual memory page. EventPairHigh and EventPairLow signal that the thread is waiting on events. LpcReceive indicates that a thread is waiting for a local procedure call, and LpcReply means that it is waiting for a reply to a local procedure call. If thread execution has been suspended or delayed, you will see either Suspended or ExecutionDelay. SystemAllocation means that the thread is waiting for a system allocation, and Executive indicates that it is waiting for the scheduler. Unknown is for when the operating system cannot report why a thread is waiting.

```
Public Enum ThreadWaitReason
    Executive = 0
    FreePage = 1
    PageIn = 2
    SystemAllocation = 3
    ExecutionDelay = 4
    Suspended = 5
    UserRequest = 6
    EventPairHigh = 7
    EventPairLow = 8
    LpcReceive = 9
    LpcReply = 10
    VirtualMemory = 11
    PageOut = 12
    Unknown = 13
End Enum
```

Hierarchy: System.Object→ System.ValueType→ System.Enum(System.IComparable, System.IFormattable, System.IConvertible)→ ThreadWaitReason

Returned By: ProcessThread.WaitReason

Trace

NotInheritable Class

System.Diagnostics (system.dll)

This class supplies shared methods and properties to provide tracing ability. The calls to the Trace methods and properties are executed only if tracing is enabled. (See the introduction to this chapter for instructions on enabling tracing.)

The shared properties allow you to adjust the settings that are used when you call the methods. You can specify that output be indented a certain amount with IndentLevel or increase or decrease the IndentLevel by one using Indent() and Unindent(). You can also adjust the number of spaces each indent level adds using IndentSize. AutoFlush makes sure that after each use of a Trace method, the Listeners are flushed.

Write() and WriteLine() simply write to each TraceListener in the Listeners collection (by default, this collection includes an instance of DefaultTraceListener). WriteIf() and WriteLineIf() do the same, but only if the specified condition evaluates to true. Assert() emits an error message if a condition evaluates to false, and Fail() always emits an error message.

One possible point of confusion is that Listeners is read-only. This means that you may not point Listeners to a different collection. You can, however, add new TraceListener objects to the TraceListenerCollection with the TraceListenerCollection.Add() method.

You can use the application configuration file to configure this class. Under the <system.diagnostics> element, add a <trace> element. You can set attributes for this element that correspond to Trace properties, as in <trace autoflush="true" indentsize="4"/>.

```
Public NotInheritable Class Trace
' Public Shared Properties
   Public Shared Property AutoFlush As Boolean
   Public Shared Property IndentLevel As Integer
   Public Shared Property IndentSize As Integer
   Public Shared ReadOnly Property Listeners As TraceListenerCollection
' Public Shared Methods
   Public Shared Sub Assert(ByVal condition As Boolean)
   Public Shared Sub Assert(ByVal condition As Boolean, ByVal message As String)
   Public Shared Sub Assert(ByVal condition As Boolean, ByVal message As String, ByVal detailMessage As String)
   Public Shared Sub Close()
   Public Shared Sub Fail(ByVal message As String)
   Public Shared Sub Fail(ByVal message As String, ByVal detailMessage As String)
   Public Shared Sub Flush()
   Public Shared Sub Indent()
   Public Shared Sub Unindent()
   Public Shared Sub Write(ByVal value As Object)
   Public Shared Sub Write(ByVal value As Object, ByVal category As String)
   Public Shared Sub Write(ByVal message As String)
   Public Shared Sub Write(ByVal message As String, ByVal category As String)
   Public Shared Sub WriteIf(ByVal condition As Boolean, ByVal value As Object)
   Public Shared Sub WriteIf(ByVal condition As Boolean, ByVal value As Object, ByVal category As String)
   Public Shared Sub WriteIf(ByVal condition As Boolean, ByVal message As String)
   Public Shared Sub WriteIf(ByVal condition As Boolean, ByVal message As String, ByVal category As String)
   Public Shared Sub WriteLine(ByVal value As Object)
   Public Shared Sub WriteLine(ByVal value As Object, ByVal category As String)
   Public Shared Sub WriteLine(ByVal message As String)
```

Public Shared Sub **WriteLine**(ByVal message As String, ByVal category As String)
Public Shared Sub **WriteLineIf**(ByVal condition As Boolean, ByVal value As Object)
Public Shared Sub **WriteLineIf**(ByVal condition As Boolean, ByVal value As Object, ByVal category As String)
Public Shared Sub **WriteLineIf**(ByVal condition As Boolean, ByVal message As String)
Public Shared Sub **WriteLineIf**(ByVal condition As Boolean, ByVal message As String, ByVal category As String)
End Class

TraceLevel   Enum
System.Diagnostics (system.dll)   *serializable*

This enumeration represents the possible levels for a trace. Use a TraceSwitch to inspect a switch's current level. Error indicates that tracing code should emit messages for error conditions, while Warning indicates that tracing code should emit both warnings and error messages. Info adds to Warning by including informational messages along with warnings and errors. Verbose indicates that *all* trace messages should be emitted. Turn tracing messages off with Off.

Public Enum **TraceLevel**
    Off = 0
    Error = 1
    Warning = 2
    Info = 3
    Verbose = 4
End Enum

Hierarchy: System.Object→ System.ValueType→ System.Enum(System.IComparable, System.IFormattable, System.IConvertible)→ TraceLevel

Returned By: TraceSwitch.Level

Passed To: TraceSwitch.Level

TraceListener   MustInherit Class
System.Diagnostics (system.dll)   *marshal by reference, disposable*

This MustInherit class TraceListener is associated with a trace through inclusion in the Trace.Listeners collection. Each TraceListener is responsible for sending trace output somewhere. For example, when you call Trace.WriteLine(), each TraceListener sends the same output to its respective output destination. Use Name to give a name to your TraceListener instances.

Use IndentLevel to control the level of indentation in the output. IndentSize specifies the number of spaces in each level of indent. NeedIndent toggles whether to indent the output at all. Use Write() and WriteLine() to send output to the TraceListener's destination. WriteIndent() emits whitespace according to the current IndentLevel and IndentSize. It has the side effect of setting NeedIndent to false, so the next time you call one of the Write* methods, it will not emit extra indentation.

You can use the application configuration file to add or remove TraceListeners. Look up System.Diagnostics.TraceListener in the .NET Framework SDK Documentation for details.

Public MustInherit Class **TraceListener** : Inherits MarshalByRefObject : Implements IDisposable
' Protected Constructors
    Protected Sub **New**()
    Protected Sub **New**(ByVal name As String)
' Public Instance Properties
    Public Property **IndentLevel** As Integer

Public Property **IndentSize** As Integer
Overridable Public Property **Name** As String
' *Protected Instance Properties*
Protected Property **NeedIndent** As Boolean
' *Public Instance Methods*
Overridable Public Sub **Close**()
Public Sub **Dispose**() Implements IDisposable.Dispose
Overridable Public Sub **Fail**(ByVal message As String)
Overridable Public Sub **Fail**(ByVal message As String, ByVal detailMessage As String)
Overridable Public Sub **Flush**()
Overridable Public Sub **Write**(ByVal o As Object)
Overridable Public Sub **Write**(ByVal o As Object, ByVal category As String)
MustInherit Public Sub **Write**(ByVal message As String)
Overridable Public Sub **Write**(ByVal message As String, ByVal category As String)
Overridable Public Sub **WriteLine**(ByVal o As Object)
Overridable Public Sub **WriteLine**(ByVal o As Object, ByVal category As String)
MustInherit Public Sub **WriteLine**(ByVal message As String)
Overridable Public Sub **WriteLine**(ByVal message As String, ByVal category As String)
' *Protected Instance Methods*
Overridable Protected Sub **Dispose**(ByVal disposing As Boolean)
Overridable Protected Sub **WriteIndent**()
End Class

Hierarchy: System.Object→ System.MarshalByRefObject→ TraceListener(System.IDisposable)

Subclasses: DefaultTraceListener, EventLogTraceListener, TextWriterTraceListener

Returned By: TraceListenerCollection.this

Passed To: TraceListenerCollection.{Add(), AddRange(), Contains(), CopyTo(), IndexOf(), Insert(), this, Remove()}

TraceListenerCollection   Class

System.Diagnostics (system.dll)

This class is a strongly typed, thread-safe collection that contains TraceListener objects.

Public Class **TraceListenerCollection** : Implements IList, ICollection, IEnumerable
' *Public Instance Properties*
Public ReadOnly Property **Count** As Integer Implements ICollection.Count
Public Default ReadOnly Property **Item** (ByVal name As String) As TraceListener
Public Default Property **Item** (ByVal i As Integer) As TraceListener
' *Public Instance Methods*
Public Function **Add**(ByVal listener As TraceListener) As Integer
Public Sub **AddRange**(ByVal value As TraceListener())
Public Sub **AddRange**(ByVal value As TraceListenerCollection)
Public Sub **Clear**() Implements IList.Clear
Public Function **Contains**(ByVal listener As TraceListener) As Boolean
Public Sub **CopyTo**(ByVal listeners As TraceListener(), ByVal index As Integer)
Public Function **GetEnumerator**() As IEnumerator Implements IEnumerable.GetEnumerator
Public Function **IndexOf**(ByVal listener As TraceListener) As Integer
Public Sub **Insert**(ByVal index As Integer, ByVal listener As TraceListener)
Public Sub **Remove**(ByVal name As String)
Public Sub **Remove**(ByVal listener As TraceListener)
Public Sub **RemoveAt**(ByVal index As Integer) Implements IList.RemoveAt
End Class

Returned By: Debug.Listeners, Trace.Listeners

TraceSwitch   Class

System.Diagnostics (system.dll)

This class provides a switch that can be set to one of the values in the TraceLevel enumeration. These values are inclusive and cumulative (for example, if Level is set to TraceLevel.Info, then TraceInfo, TraceWarning, and TraceError are true). See TraceLevel for more details. You can configure a trace switch using the application configuration file (see Switch).

Public Class **TraceSwitch** : Inherits Switch
' Public Constructors
   Public Sub **New**(ByVal displayName As String, ByVal description As String)
' Public Instance Properties
   Public Property **Level** As TraceLevel
   Public ReadOnly Property **TraceError** As Boolean
   Public ReadOnly Property **TraceInfo** As Boolean
   Public ReadOnly Property **TraceVerbose** As Boolean
   Public ReadOnly Property **TraceWarning** As Boolean
' Protected Instance Methods
   Overrides Protected Sub **OnSwitchSettingChanged**()
End Class

Hierarchy: System.Object→ Switch→ TraceSwitch

CHAPTER 8

System.Globalization

The System.Globalization namespace provides classes that assist in localization of applications based on language and culture. The CultureInfo class is the primary container for a set of resources that is used for a specified language and culture implementation. It describes how strings are sorted, the specifics of calendars and date and time formats, as well as language and dialect code pages. An application obtains its culture information based on either the CultureInfo specified by the current thread or from the user or local machine's preferences. Specific cultural information is contained in resource files deployed in satellite assemblies. System.Resources.ResourceManager marshals these resource files into System.Resources.ResourceSets that provide the objects and methods specific to a localization.

The System.Globalization namespace provides a base Calendar class, as well as specific calendar implementations for major cultures. CompareInfo defines how string comparison and sorting are handled. DateTimeFormatInfo defines how DateTime values are formatted, and NumberFormatInfo defines various formatting styles, such as currency symbols and decimal and grouping separators. Figure 8-1 shows the types in this namespace.

Calendar   MustInherit Class
System.Globalization (mscorlib.dll)   serializable

This MustInherit class determines the division and measurement of time in units, such as day, months, years, and eras. It is a MustInherit base class for culture-specific calendar implementations included in this namespace. Derived classes store the specific information about a calendar's eras, lengths of years and months, and the sometimes esoteric rules for calculating leap years. These properties get used by DateTimeFormatInfo to properly display a date and time string from a specific DateTime value.

```
Public MustInherit Class Calendar
' Protected Constructors
    Protected Sub New()
' Public Shared Fields
    Public const CurrentEra As Integer                                       =0
' Public Instance Properties
    MustInherit Public ReadOnly Property Eras As Integer()
```

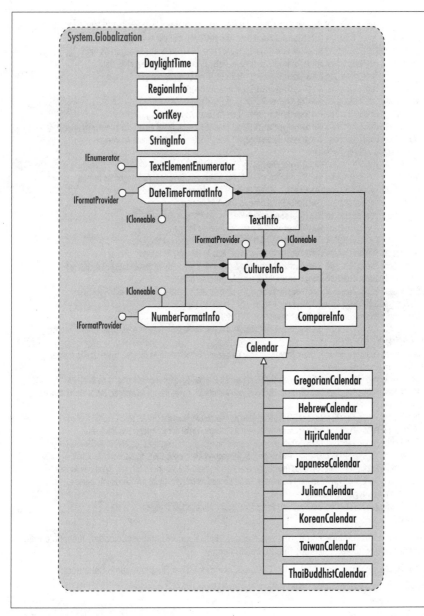

Figure 8–1. The System.Globalization namespace

Overridable Public Property **TwoDigitYearMax** As Integer
' Public Instance Methods
Overridable Public Function **AddDays**(ByVal time As Date, ByVal days As Integer) As Date
Overridable Public Function **AddHours**(ByVal time As Date, ByVal hours As Integer) As Date
Overridable Public Function **AddMilliseconds**(ByVal time As Date, ByVal milliseconds As Double) As Date

Overridable Public Function **AddMinutes**(ByVal time As Date, ByVal minutes As Integer) As Date
MustInherit Public Function **AddMonths**(ByVal time As Date, ByVal months As Integer) As Date
Overridable Public Function **AddSeconds**(ByVal time As Date, ByVal seconds As Integer) As Date
Overridable Public Function **AddWeeks**(ByVal time As Date, ByVal weeks As Integer) As Date
MustInherit Public Function **AddYears**(ByVal time As Date, ByVal years As Integer) As Date
MustInherit Public Function **GetDayOfMonth**(ByVal time As Date) As Integer
MustInherit Public Function **GetDayOfWeek**(ByVal time As Date) As DayOfWeek
MustInherit Public Function **GetDayOfYear**(ByVal time As Date) As Integer
Overridable Public Function **GetDaysInMonth**(ByVal year As Integer, ByVal month As Integer) As Integer
MustInherit Public Function **GetDaysInMonth**(ByVal year As Integer, ByVal month As Integer, _
   ByVal era As Integer) As Integer
Overridable Public Function **GetDaysInYear**(ByVal year As Integer) As Integer
MustInherit Public Function **GetDaysInYear**(ByVal year As Integer, ByVal era As Integer) As Integer
MustInherit Public Function **GetEra**(ByVal time As Date) As Integer
Overridable Public Function **GetHour**(ByVal time As Date) As Integer
Overridable Public Function **GetMilliseconds**(ByVal time As Date) As Double
Overridable Public Function **GetMinute**(ByVal time As Date) As Integer
MustInherit Public Function **GetMonth**(ByVal time As Date) As Integer
Overridable Public Function **GetMonthsInYear**(ByVal year As Integer) As Integer
MustInherit Public Function **GetMonthsInYear**(ByVal year As Integer, ByVal era As Integer) As Integer
Overridable Public Function **GetSecond**(ByVal time As Date) As Integer
Overridable Public Function **GetWeekOfYear**(ByVal time As Date, ByVal rule As CalendarWeekRule, _
   ByVal firstDayOfWeek As DayOfWeek) As Integer
MustInherit Public Function **GetYear**(ByVal time As Date) As Integer
Overridable Public Function **IsLeapDay**(ByVal year As Integer, ByVal month As Integer, ByVal day As Integer) _
   As Boolean
MustInherit Public Function **IsLeapDay**(ByVal year As Integer, ByVal month As Integer, ByVal day As Integer, _
   ByVal era As Integer) As Boolean
Overridable Public Function **IsLeapMonth**(ByVal year As Integer, ByVal month As Integer) As Boolean
MustInherit Public Function **IsLeapMonth**(ByVal year As Integer, ByVal month As Integer, ByVal era As Integer) _
   As Boolean
Overridable Public Function **IsLeapYear**(ByVal year As Integer) As Boolean
MustInherit Public Function **IsLeapYear**(ByVal year As Integer, ByVal era As Integer) As Boolean
Overridable Public Function **ToDateTime**(ByVal year As Integer, ByVal month As Integer, ByVal day As Integer, _
   ByVal hour As Integer, ByVal minute As Integer), ByVal second As Integer, ByVal millisecond As Integer) As Date
MustInherit Public Function **ToDateTime**(ByVal year As Integer, ByVal month As Integer, ByVal day As Integer, _
   ByVal hour As Integer, ByVal minute As Integer, ByVal second As Integer, ByVal millisecond As Integer, _
   ByVal era As Integer) As Date
Overridable Public Function **ToFourDigitYear**(ByVal year As Integer) As Integer
End Class

Subclasses: GregorianCalendar, HebrewCalendar, HijriCalendar, JapaneseCalendar, JulianCalendar, KoreanCalendar, TaiwanCalendar, ThaiBuddhistCalendar

Returned By: CultureInfo.{Calendar, OptionalCalendars}, DateTimeFormatInfo.Calendar

Passed To: System.DateTime.DateTime(), DateTimeFormatInfo.Calendar

CalendarWeekRule   Enum

System.Globalization (mscorlib.dll)   *serializable*

This enumeration contains values that specify how the first week of a calendar year is determined. Each calendar requires that the starting day of a week is designated (i.e., Sunday in the Gregorian calendar). The value FirstDay designates that the first calendar week begins on the first day of the year regardless of the number of days left in the week. The FirstFourDayWeek specifies the first week that has at least four days in it. First-FullWeek uses the first complete week as the first in the calendar.

```
Public Enum CalendarWeekRule
    FirstDay = 0
    FirstFullWeek = 1
    FirstFourDayWeek = 2
End Enum
```

Hierarchy: System.Object→ System.ValueType→ System.Enum(System.IComparable, System.IFormattable, System.IConvertible)→ CalendarWeekRule

Returned By: DateTimeFormatInfo.CalendarWeekRule

Passed To: Calendar.GetWeekOfYear(), DateTimeFormatInfo.CalendarWeekRule

CompareInfo   Class

System.Globalization (mscorlib.dll)   *serializable*

This class defines methods of string comparison that follow culture-specific rules. The CultureInfo.CompareInfo property contains an instance of this class. The Compare() method and other string searching methods, such as IndexOf() and IsPrefix(), can be passed a set of CompareOptions, which provide culture-specific flags related to strings. The GetCompare-Info() method is used instead of a public constructor to retrieve an instance of this class.

```
Public Class CompareInfo : Implements System.Runtime.Serialization.IDeserializationCallback
' Public Instance Properties
    Public ReadOnly Property LCID As Integer
' Public Shared Methods
    Public Shared Function GetCompareInfo(ByVal culture As Integer) As CompareInfo
    Public Shared Function GetCompareInfo(ByVal culture As Integer, _
        ByVal assembly As System.Reflection.Assembly) As CompareInfo
    Public Shared Function GetCompareInfo(ByVal name As String) As CompareInfo
    Public Shared Function GetCompareInfo(ByVal name As String, ByVal assembly As System.Reflection.Assembly) _
        As CompareInfo
' Public Instance Methods
    Overridable Public Function Compare(ByVal string1 As String, ByVal offset1 As Integer, ByVal length1 As Integer, _
        ByVal string2 As String, ByVal offset2 As Integer, ByVal length2 As Integer) As Integer
    Overridable Public Function Compare(ByVal string1 As String, ByVal offset1 As Integer, ByVal length1 As Integer, _
        ByVal string2 As String, ByVal offset2 As Integer, ByVal length2 As Integer, ByVal options As CompareOptions) _
        As Integer
    Overridable Public Function Compare(ByVal string1 As String, ByVal offset1 As Integer, ByVal string2 As String, _
        ByVal offset2 As Integer) As Integer
    Overridable Public Function Compare(ByVal string1 As String, ByVal offset1 As Integer, ByVal string2 As String, _
        ByVal offset2 As Integer, ByVal options As CompareOptions) As Integer
    Overridable Public Function Compare(ByVal string1 As String, ByVal string2 As String) As Integer
    Overridable Public Function Compare(ByVal string1 As String, ByVal string2 As String, _
        ByVal options As CompareOptions) As Integer
    Overrides Public Function Equals(ByVal value As Object) As Boolean
    Overrides Public Function GetHashCode() As Integer
    Overridable Public Function GetSortKey(ByVal source As String) As SortKey
    Overridable Public Function GetSortKey(ByVal source As String, ByVal options As CompareOptions) As SortKey
    Overridable Public Function IndexOf(ByVal source As String, ByVal value As Char) As Integer
    Overridable Public Function IndexOf(ByVal source As String, ByVal value As Char, _
        ByVal options As CompareOptions) As Integer
    Overridable Public Function IndexOf(ByVal source As String, ByVal value As Char, ByVal startIndex As Integer) _
        As Integer
    Overridable Public Function IndexOf(ByVal source As String, ByVal value As Char, ByVal startIndex As Integer, _
        ByVal options As CompareOptions) As Integer
    Overridable Public Function IndexOf(ByVal source As String, ByVal value As Char, ByVal startIndex As Integer, _
        ByVal count As Integer) As Integer
```

Overridable Public Function **IndexOf**(ByVal source As String, ByVal value As Char, ByVal startIndex As Integer, _
ByVal count As Integer, ByVal options As CompareOptions) As Integer

Overridable Public Function **IndexOf**(ByVal source As String, ByVal value As String) As Integer

Overridable Public Function **IndexOf**(ByVal source As String, ByVal value As String, _
ByVal options As CompareOptions) As Integer

Overridable Public Function **IndexOf**(ByVal source As String, ByVal value As String, ByVal startIndex As Integer) _
As Integer

Overridable Public Function **IndexOf**(ByVal source As String, ByVal value As String, ByVal startIndex As Integer, _
ByVal options As CompareOptions) As Integer

Overridable Public Function **IndexOf**(ByVal source As String, ByVal value As String, ByVal startIndex As Integer, _
ByVal count As Integer) As Integer

Overridable Public Function **IndexOf**(ByVal source As String, ByVal value As String, ByVal startIndex As Integer, _
ByVal count As Integer, ByVal options As CompareOptions) As Integer

Overridable Public Function **IsPrefix**(ByVal source As String, ByVal prefix As String) As Boolean

Overridable Public Function **IsPrefix**(ByVal source As String, ByVal prefix As String, _
ByVal options As CompareOptions) As Boolean

Overridable Public Function **IsSuffix**(ByVal source As String, ByVal suffix As String) As Boolean

Overridable Public Function **IsSuffix**(ByVal source As String, ByVal suffix As String, _
ByVal options As CompareOptions) As Boolean

Overridable Public Function **LastIndexOf**(ByVal source As String, ByVal value As Char) As Integer

Overridable Public Function **LastIndexOf**(ByVal source As String, ByVal value As Char, _
ByVal options As CompareOptions) As Integer

Overridable Public Function **LastIndexOf**(ByVal source As String, ByVal value As Char, ByVal startIndex As Integer) _
As Integer

Overridable Public Function **LastIndexOf**(ByVal source As String, ByVal value As Char, ByVal startIndex As Integer, _
ByVal options As CompareOptions) As Integer

Overridable Public Function **LastIndexOf**(ByVal source As String, ByVal value As Char, ByVal startIndex As Integer, _
ByVal count As Integer) As Integer

Overridable Public Function **LastIndexOf**(ByVal source As String, ByVal value As Char, ByVal startIndex As Integer, _
ByVal count As Integer, ByVal options As CompareOptions) As Integer

Overridable Public Function **LastIndexOf**(ByVal source As String, ByVal value As String) As Integer

Overridable Public Function **LastIndexOf**(ByVal source As String, ByVal value As String, _
ByVal options As CompareOptions) As Integer

Overridable Public Function **LastIndexOf**(ByVal source As String, ByVal value As String, _
ByVal startIndex As Integer) As Integer

Overridable Public Function **LastIndexOf**(ByVal source As String, ByVal value As String, ByVal startIndex As Integer _
, ByVal options As CompareOptions) As Integer

Overridable Public Function **LastIndexOf**(ByVal source As String, ByVal value As String, ByVal startIndex As Integer _
, ByVal count As Integer) As Integer

Overridable Public Function **LastIndexOf**(ByVal source As String, ByVal value As String, ByVal startIndex As Integer _
, ByVal count As Integer, ByVal options As CompareOptions) As Integer

Overrides Public Function **ToString**() As String

End Class

Returned By: CultureInfo.CompareInfo

CompareOptions
Enum

System.Globalization (mscorlib.dll)
serializable, flag

This enumeration defines a set of constants that set culture-specific behavior on string comparisons in the CompareInfo class. IgnoreKanaType treats phonetic Japanese symbols the same whether they are in hiragana or katagana characters. IgnoreNonSpace disregards nonspacing characters such as diacritics. Ordinal specifies that comparison is done with Unicode values.

```
Public Enum CompareOptions
    None = &H000000000
    IgnoreCase = &H000000001
    IgnoreNonSpace = &H000000002
    IgnoreSymbols = &H000000004
    IgnoreKanaType = &H000000008
    IgnoreWidth = &H000000010
    StringSort = &H020000000
    Ordinal = &H040000000
End Enum
```

Hierarchy: System.Object→ System.ValueType→ System.Enum(System.IComparable, System.IFormattable, System.IConvertible)→ CompareOptions

Passed To: CompareInfo.{Compare(), GetSortKey(), IndexOf(), IsPrefix(), IsSuffix(), LastIndexOf()}

CultureInfo   Class

System.Globalization (mscorlib.dll)   *ECMA, serializable*

The CultureInfo class encapsulates information about handling information according to the special requirements of a particular culture and language. Culture information is identified by language and country/region codes as specified in RFC 1766. For example, U.S. English is identified as en-US. The two-letter, lowercase language codes are defined in ISO 639-1. The two-letter, uppercase region codes are defined in ISO 3166.

The specific CultureInfo to use at runtime can be found in a number of ways. The class provides four public properties that return the current CultureInfo instance. CurrentCulture returns the value of Thread.CurrentCulture, which is the CultureInfo used by the current thread. CurrentUICulture returns the CultureInfo used by the System.Resources.ResourceManager. This can be a user, machine, or application-based locale setting. It is set in Thread.CurrentUICulture. InstalledUICulture gets the default CultureInfo used by the ResourceManager and represents the locale of the operating system. InvariantCulture returns the CultureInfo for the invariant locale, which is nonculture-specific, as well as in the default OS language. This is used with nonculture-specific functions such as system-level calls.

The instance properties of the class provide a number of ways to retrieve the culture name. For example, NativeName gets the culture name in the language of that culture. LCID gets the NLS-specified number for a culture name. Other properties get or set the various class instances used for localization. Calendar, CompareInfo, DateTimeFormat, Number-Format, and TextInfo return instances of the analogous classes that set their functionality.

```
Public Class CultureInfo : Implements ICloneable, IFormatProvider
' Public Constructors
    Public Sub New(ByVal culture As Integer)
    Public Sub New(ByVal culture As Integer, ByVal useUserOverride As Boolean)
    Public Sub New(ByVal name As String)
    Public Sub New(ByVal name As String, ByVal useUserOverride As Boolean)
' Public Shared Properties
    Public Shared ReadOnly Property CurrentCulture As CultureInfo
    Public Shared ReadOnly Property CurrentUICulture As CultureInfo
    Public Shared ReadOnly Property InstalledUICulture As CultureInfo
    Public Shared ReadOnly Property InvariantCulture As CultureInfo
' Public Instance Properties
    Overridable Public ReadOnly Property Calendar As Calendar
    Overridable Public ReadOnly Property CompareInfo As CompareInfo
    Overridable Public Property DateTimeFormat As DateTimeFormatInfo
    Overridable Public ReadOnly Property DisplayName As String
```

```
Overridable Public ReadOnly Property EnglishName As String
Overridable Public ReadOnly Property IsNeutralCulture As Boolean
Public ReadOnly Property IsReadOnly As Boolean
Overridable Public ReadOnly Property LCID As Integer
Overridable Public ReadOnly Property Name As String
Overridable Public ReadOnly Property NativeName As String
Overridable Public Property NumberFormat As NumberFormatInfo
Overridable Public ReadOnly Property OptionalCalendars As Calendar()
Overridable Public ReadOnly Property Parent As CultureInfo
Overridable Public ReadOnly Property TextInfo As TextInfo
Overridable Public ReadOnly Property ThreeLetterISOLanguageName As String
Overridable Public ReadOnly Property ThreeLetterWindowsLanguageName As String
Overridable Public ReadOnly Property TwoLetterISOLanguageName As String
Public ReadOnly Property UseUserOverride As Boolean
' Public Shared Methods
Public Shared Function CreateSpecificCulture(ByVal name As String) As CultureInfo
Public Shared Function GetCultures(ByVal types As CultureTypes) As CultureInfo()
Public Shared Function ReadOnly(ByVal ci As CultureInfo) As CultureInfo
' Public Instance Methods
Public Sub ClearCachedData()
Overridable Public Function Clone() As Object Implements ICloneable.Clone
Overrides Public Function Equals(ByVal value As Object) As Boolean
Overridable Public Function GetFormat(ByVal formatType As Type) As Object _
    Implements  IFormatProvider.GetFormat
Overrides Public Function GetHashCode() As Integer
Overrides Public Function ToString() As String
End Class
```

Returned By: System.Reflection.AssemblyName.CultureInfo,
System.Threading.Thread.{CurrentCulture, CurrentUICulture}

Passed To: Multiple types

CultureTypes   Enum

System.Globalization (mscorlib.dll)   *serializable, flag*

The values of this enumeration determine which cultures are returned by CultureInfo.GetCultures(). NeutralCultures specifies language-specific cultures without any regional or country association. SpecificCultures specifies cultures that are identified by both language and region.

```
Public Enum CultureTypes
    NeutralCultures = &H000000001
    SpecificCultures = &H000000002
    InstalledWin32Cultures = &H000000004
    AllCultures = &H000000007
End Enum
```

Hierarchy: System.Object→ System.ValueType→ System.Enum(System.IComparable,
System.IFormattable, System.IConvertible)→ CultureTypes

Passed To: CultureInfo.GetCultures()

DateTimeFormatInfo	**NotInheritable Class**
System.Globalization (mscorlib.dll)	*ECMA, serializable*

This class defines how DateTime values are formatted for a culture. Several standard patterns are defined with the default property values. These standard patterns are designated by a format character. The format character provides a shortcut to specify the format of a DateTime with the ToString() method. You can create custom formats using a set of format pattern characters. These characters represent different styles of day and time representations and allow you to build customized pattern strings. To create custom patterns, first you need to construct a writable instance of DateTimeFormatInfo by using its constructor. Use InvariantInfo to fetch a culture-independent, read-only instance of this class.

```
Public NotInheritable Class DateTimeFormatInfo : Implements ICloneable, IFormatProvider
' Public Constructors
   Public Sub New()
' Public Shared Properties
   Public Shared ReadOnly Property CurrentInfo As DateTimeFormatInfo
   Public Shared ReadOnly Property InvariantInfo As DateTimeFormatInfo
' Public Instance Properties
   Public Property AbbreviatedDayNames As String()
   Public Property AbbreviatedMonthNames As String()
   Public Property AMDesignator As String
   Public Property Calendar As Calendar
   Public Property CalendarWeekRule As CalendarWeekRule
   Public Property DateSeparator As String
   Public Property DayNames As String()
   Public Property FirstDayOfWeek As DayOfWeek
   Public Property FullDateTimePattern As String
   Public ReadOnly Property IsReadOnly As Boolean
   Public Property LongDatePattern As String
   Public Property LongTimePattern As String
   Public Property MonthDayPattern As String
   Public Property MonthNames As String()
   Public Property PMDesignator As String
   Public ReadOnly Property RFC1123Pattern As String
   Public Property ShortDatePattern As String
   Public Property ShortTimePattern As String
   Public ReadOnly Property SortableDateTimePattern As String
   Public Property TimeSeparator As String
   Public ReadOnly Property UniversalSortableDateTimePattern As String
   Public Property YearMonthPattern As String
' Public Shared Methods
   Public Shared Function GetInstance(ByVal provider As IFormatProvider) As DateTimeFormatInfo
   Public Shared Function ReadOnly(ByVal dtfi As DateTimeFormatInfo) As DateTimeFormatInfo
' Public Instance Methods
   Public Function Clone() As Object Implements ICloneable.Clone
   Public Function GetAbbreviatedDayName(ByVal dayofweek As DayOfWeek) As String
   Public Function GetAbbreviatedEraName(ByVal era As Integer) As String
   Public Function GetAbbreviatedMonthName(ByVal month As Integer) As String
   Public Function GetAllDateTimePatterns() As String()
   Public Function GetAllDateTimePatterns(ByVal format As Char) As String()
   Public Function GetDayName(ByVal dayofweek As DayOfWeek) As String
   Public Function GetEra(ByVal eraName As String) As Integer
   Public Function GetEraName(ByVal era As Integer) As String
   Public Function GetFormat(ByVal formatType As Type) As Object Implements IFormatProvider.GetFormat
```

System. Globalization

```
    Public Function GetMonthName(ByVal month As Integer) As String
End Class
```

Returned By: CultureInfo.DateTimeFormat

Passed To: CultureInfo.DateTimeFormat

DateTimeStyles   Enum
System.Globalization (mscorlib.dll)   *ECMA, serializable, flag*

This enumeration provides several formatting options for the DateTime.Parse() and Date-Time.ParseExact() methods to use. The values supplied mostly determine how whitespace is dealt with when a string is parsed into a DateTime value by ParseExact(). When the string is compared to a format pattern, some whitespace can be disregarded if it is not exactly aligned with the pattern. Parse() ignores whitespace by default, so AdjustToUniversal and NoCurrentDateDefault are the only relevant values for that method. If the string to parse does not include a date with NoCurrentDateDefault, its result is created with day, month, and year values all set to 1. The date and time are converted to coordinated universal time (UTC) with AdjustToUniversal.

```
Public Enum DateTimeStyles
    None = &H000000000
    AllowLeadingWhite = &H000000001
    AllowTrailingWhite = &H000000002
    AllowInnerWhite = &H000000004
    AllowWhiteSpaces = &H000000007
    NoCurrentDateDefault = &H000000008
    AdjustToUniversal = &H000000010
End Enum
```

Hierarchy: System.Object→ System.ValueType→ System.Enum(System.IComparable, System.IFormattable, System.IConvertible)→ DateTimeStyles

Passed To: System.DateTime.{Parse(), ParseExact()}

DaylightTime   Class
System.Globalization (mscorlib.dll)   *serializable*

This setting defines when daylight saving time begins and ends. It uses three properties: Start is the time when daylight saving time begins; End is when standard time resumes; and Delta is the length of time (measured in ticks) that the clock is adjusted from standard time during this period. Delta is a System.TimeSpan value measured in "ticks" or 100 nanosecond periods.

```
Public Class DaylightTime
' Public Constructors
    Public Sub New(ByVal start As Date, ByVal end As Date, ByVal delta As TimeSpan)
' Public Instance Properties
    Public ReadOnly Property Delta As TimeSpan
    Public ReadOnly Property End As Date
    Public ReadOnly Property Start As Date
End Class
```

Returned By: System.TimeZone.GetDaylightChanges()

Passed To: System.TimeZone.IsDaylightSavingTime()

GregorianCalendar

Class

System.Globalization (mscorlib.dll)   *serializable*

This class implements the standard Western calendar, and also the default culture-invariant calendar. It defines two eras (B.C./B.C.E. and A.D./C.E.), 12 months per year. A leap year occurs every four years except for years divisible by 100. However, years divisible by 400 are leap years. Only the current era (A.D./C.E.) is recognized by .NET's implementation of the Gregorian calendar.

```
Public Class GregorianCalendar : Inherits Calendar
' Public Constructors
   Public Sub New()
   Public Sub New(ByVal type As GregorianCalendarTypes)
' Public Shared Fields
   Public const ADEra As Integer                                                          =1
' Public Instance Properties
   Overridable Public Property CalendarType As GregorianCalendarTypes
   Overrides Public ReadOnly Property Eras As Integer()
   Overrides Public Property TwoDigitYearMax As Integer
' Public Instance Methods
   Overrides Public Function AddMonths(ByVal time As Date, ByVal months As Integer) As Date
   Overrides Public Function AddWeeks(ByVal time As Date, ByVal weeks As Integer) As Date
   Overrides Public Function AddYears(ByVal time As Date, ByVal years As Integer) As Date
   Overrides Public Function GetDayOfMonth(ByVal time As Date) As Integer
   Overrides Public Function GetDayOfWeek(ByVal time As Date) As DayOfWeek
   Overrides Public Function GetDayOfYear(ByVal time As Date) As Integer
   Overrides Public Function GetDaysInMonth(ByVal year As Integer, ByVal month As Integer, ByVal era As Integer) _
      As Integer
   Overrides Public Function GetDaysInYear(ByVal year As Integer, ByVal era As Integer) As Integer
   Overrides Public Function GetEra(ByVal time As Date) As Integer
   Overrides Public Function GetMonth(ByVal time As Date) As Integer
   Overrides Public Function GetMonthsInYear(ByVal year As Integer, ByVal era As Integer) As Integer
   Overrides Public Function GetYear(ByVal time As Date) As Integer
   Overrides Public Function IsLeapDay(ByVal year As Integer, ByVal month As Integer, ByVal day As Integer, _
      ByVal era As Integer)  As Boolean
   Overrides Public Function IsLeapMonth(ByVal year As Integer, ByVal month As Integer, ByVal era As Integer) _
      As Boolean
   Overrides Public Function IsLeapYear(ByVal year As Integer, ByVal era As Integer) As Boolean
   Overrides Public Function ToDateTime(ByVal year As Integer, ByVal month As Integer, ByVal day As Integer, _
      ByVal hour As Integer, ByVal minute As Integer, ByVal second As Integer, ByVal millisecond As Integer,   _
      ByVal era As Integer) As Date
   Overrides Public Function ToFourDigitYear(ByVal year As Integer) As Integer
End Class
```

Hierarchy: System.Object→ Calendar→ GregorianCalendar

GregorianCalendarTypes

Enum

System.Globalization (mscorlib.dll)   *serializable*

This enumeration specifies some language-specific variations of the Gregorian calendar that can be set with the GregorianCalendar.CalendarType property.

```
Public Enum GregorianCalendarTypes
      Localized = 1
      USEnglish = 2
      MiddleEastFrench = 9
      Arabic = 10
```

        TransliteratedEnglish = 11
        TransliteratedFrench = 12
End Enum

Hierarchy: System.Object→ System.ValueType→ System.Enum(System.IComparable, System.IFormattable, System.IConvertible)→ GregorianCalendarTypes

Returned By: GregorianCalendar.CalendarType

Passed To: GregorianCalendar.{CalendarType, GregorianCalendar()}

HebrewCalendar   Class

System.Globalization (mscorlib.dll)   *serializable*

This calendar class implements the Hebrew calendar. This complicated calendar determines leap years within a 19-year cycle. The 3rd, 6th, 8th, 11th, 14th, 17th, and 19th years are leap years. Regular years have 12 months and between 353 to 355 days, leap years have 13 months and between 383 to 385 days; the variance is determined by the placement of Jewish holidays. This implementation recognizes the years 5343 to 6000 (A.M.), which is equivalent to the Gregorian years 1582 to 2240.

Public Class **HebrewCalendar** : Inherits Calendar
' *Public Constructors*
    Public Sub **New**()
' *Public Shared Fields*
    Public Shared ReadOnly **HebrewEra** As Integer   *=1*
' *Public Instance Properties*
    Overrides Public ReadOnly Property **Eras** As Integer()
    Overrides Public Property **TwoDigitYearMax** As Integer
' *Public Instance Methods*
    Overrides Public Function **AddMonths**(ByVal time As Date, ByVal months As Integer) As Date
    Overrides Public Function **AddYears**(ByVal time As Date, ByVal years As Integer) As Date
    Overrides Public Function **GetDayOfMonth**(ByVal time As Date) As Integer
    Overrides Public Function **GetDayOfWeek**(ByVal time As Date) As DayOfWeek
    Overrides Public Function **GetDayOfYear**(ByVal time As Date) As Integer
    Overrides Public Function **GetDaysInMonth**(ByVal year As Integer, ByVal month As Integer, ByVal era As Integer) _
        As Integer
    Overrides Public Function **GetDaysInYear**(ByVal year As Integer, ByVal era As Integer) As Integer
    Overrides Public Function **GetEra**(ByVal time As Date) As Integer
    Overrides Public Function **GetMonth**(ByVal time As Date) As Integer
    Overrides Public Function **GetMonthsInYear**(ByVal year As Integer, ByVal era As Integer) As Integer
    Overrides Public Function **GetYear**(ByVal time As Date) As Integer
    Overrides Public Function **IsLeapDay**(ByVal year As Integer, ByVal month As Integer, ByVal day As Integer, _
        ByVal era As Integer) As Boolean
    Overrides Public Function **IsLeapMonth**(ByVal year As Integer, ByVal month As Integer, ByVal era As Integer) _
        As Boolean
    Overrides Public Function **IsLeapYear**(ByVal year As Integer, ByVal era As Integer) As Boolean
    Overrides Public Function **ToDateTime**(ByVal year As Integer, ByVal month As Integer, ByVal day As Integer, _
        ByVal hour As Integer, ByVal minute As Integer, ByVal second As Integer, ByVal millisecond As Integer,   _
        ByVal era As Integer) As Date
    Overrides Public Function **ToFourDigitYear**(ByVal year As Integer) As Integer
End Class

Hierarchy: System.Object→ Calendar→ HebrewCalendar

HijriCalendar
Class

System.Globalization (mscorlib.dll)
serializable

This calendar class implements the Islamic Hijri calendar. This calendar is based from the time of Mohammed's migration from Mecca (denoted as A.H.). Regular years have 12 months and 354 days. Leap years have 355 days. Leap years are calculated in 30-year cycles, occurring in the 2nd, 5th, 7th, 10th, 13th, 16th, 18th, 21st, 24th, 26th, and 29th years.

```
Public Class HijriCalendar : Inherits Calendar
' Public Constructors
   Public Sub New()
' Public Shared Fields
   Public Shared ReadOnly HijriEra As Integer                                          =1
' Public Instance Properties
   Overrides Public ReadOnly Property Eras As Integer()
   Overrides Public Property TwoDigitYearMax As Integer
' Public Instance Methods
   Overrides Public Function AddMonths(ByVal time As Date, ByVal months As Integer) As Date
   Overrides Public Function AddYears(ByVal time As Date, ByVal years As Integer) As Date
   Overrides Public Function GetDayOfMonth(ByVal time As Date) As Integer
   Overrides Public Function GetDayOfWeek(ByVal time As Date) As DayOfWeek
   Overrides Public Function GetDayOfYear(ByVal time As Date) As Integer
   Overrides Public Function GetDaysInMonth(ByVal year As Integer, ByVal month As Integer, ByVal era As Integer) _
      As Integer
   Overrides Public Function GetDaysInYear(ByVal year As Integer, ByVal era As Integer) As Integer
   Overrides Public Function GetEra(ByVal time As Date) As Integer
   Overrides Public Function GetMonth(ByVal time As Date) As Integer
   Overrides Public Function GetMonthsInYear(ByVal year As Integer, ByVal era As Integer) As Integer
   Overrides Public Function GetYear(ByVal time As Date) As Integer
   Overrides Public Function IsLeapDay(ByVal year As Integer, ByVal month As Integer, ByVal day As Integer, _
      ByVal era As Integer)  As Boolean
   Overrides Public Function IsLeapMonth(ByVal year As Integer, ByVal month As Integer, ByVal era As Integer) _
      As Boolean
   Overrides Public Function IsLeapYear(ByVal year As Integer, ByVal era As Integer) As Boolean
   Overrides Public Function ToDateTime(ByVal year As Integer, ByVal month As Integer, ByVal day As Integer, _
      ByVal hour As Integer, ByVal minute As Integer, ByVal second As Integer, ByVal millisecond As Integer,   _
      ByVal era As Integer) As Date
   Overrides Public Function ToFourDigitYear(ByVal year As Integer) As Integer
End Class
```

Hierarchy: System.Object→ Calendar→ HijriCalendar

JapaneseCalendar
Class

System.Globalization (mscorlib.dll)
serializable

This calendar class implements the Japanese or Wareki calendar. This calendar follows the same rules and settings as the Gregorian calendar, except that it is divided into eras based on the reign of each Japanese Emperor.

```
Public Class JapaneseCalendar : Inherits Calendar
' Public Constructors
   Public Sub New()
' Public Instance Properties
   Overrides Public ReadOnly Property Eras As Integer()
   Overrides Public Property TwoDigitYearMax As Integer
' Public Instance Methods
```

Overrides Public Function **AddMonths**(ByVal time As Date, ByVal months As Integer) As Date
Overrides Public Function **AddYears**(ByVal time As Date, ByVal years As Integer) As Date
Overrides Public Function **GetDayOfMonth**(ByVal time As Date) As Integer
Overrides Public Function **GetDayOfWeek**(ByVal time As Date) As DayOfWeek
Overrides Public Function **GetDayOfYear**(ByVal time As Date) As Integer
Overrides Public Function **GetDaysInMonth**(ByVal year As Integer, ByVal month As Integer, ByVal era As Integer) _
  As Integer
Overrides Public Function **GetDaysInYear**(ByVal year As Integer, ByVal era As Integer) As Integer
Overrides Public Function **GetEra**(ByVal time As Date) As Integer
Overrides Public Function **GetMonth**(ByVal time As Date) As Integer
Overrides Public Function **GetMonthsInYear**(ByVal year As Integer, ByVal era As Integer) As Integer
Overrides Public Function **GetYear**(ByVal time As Date) As Integer
Overrides Public Function **IsLeapDay**(ByVal year As Integer, ByVal month As Integer, ByVal day As Integer, _
  ByVal era As Integer) As Boolean
Overrides Public Function **IsLeapMonth**(ByVal year As Integer, ByVal month As Integer, ByVal era As Integer) _
  As Boolean
Overrides Public Function **IsLeapYear**(ByVal year As Integer, ByVal era As Integer) As Boolean
Overrides Public Function **ToDateTime**(ByVal year As Integer, ByVal month As Integer, ByVal day As Integer, _
  ByVal hour As Integer, ByVal minute As Integer, ByVal second As Integer, ByVal millisecond As Integer, _
  ByVal era As Integer) As Date
Overrides Public Function **ToFourDigitYear**(ByVal year As Integer) As Integer
End Class

Hierarchy: System.Object→ Calendar→ JapaneseCalendar

JulianCalendar
Class

System.Globalization (mscorlib.dll)
serializable

This calendar class implements the calendar created by a decree from Julius Caesar in 45 B.C.E. The calendar recognizes a leap year every four years without exception, but in all other respects is the same as the Gregorian calendar, which replaced it in 1582 C.E. Due to the difference in leap-year calculation, the Julian calendar is currently 12 days behind the Gregorian calendar.

Public Class **JulianCalendar** : Inherits Calendar
' *Public Constructors*
  Public Sub **New**()
' *Public Shared Fields*
  Public Shared ReadOnly **JulianEra** As Integer
                                                =1
' *Public Instance Properties*
  Overrides Public ReadOnly Property **Eras** As Integer()
  Overrides Public Property **TwoDigitYearMax** As Integer
' *Public Instance Methods*
  Overrides Public Function **AddMonths**(ByVal time As Date, ByVal months As Integer) As Date
  Overrides Public Function **AddYears**(ByVal time As Date, ByVal years As Integer) As Date
  Overrides Public Function **GetDayOfMonth**(ByVal time As Date) As Integer
  Overrides Public Function **GetDayOfWeek**(ByVal time As Date) As DayOfWeek
  Overrides Public Function **GetDayOfYear**(ByVal time As Date) As Integer
  Overrides Public Function **GetDaysInMonth**(ByVal year As Integer, ByVal month As Integer, ByVal era As Integer) _
    As Integer
  Overrides Public Function **GetDaysInYear**(ByVal year As Integer, ByVal era As Integer) As Integer
  Overrides Public Function **GetEra**(ByVal time As Date) As Integer
  Overrides Public Function **GetMonth**(ByVal time As Date) As Integer
  Overrides Public Function **GetMonthsInYear**(ByVal year As Integer, ByVal era As Integer) As Integer
  Overrides Public Function **GetYear**(ByVal time As Date) As Integer
  Overrides Public Function **IsLeapDay**(ByVal year As Integer, ByVal month As Integer, ByVal day As Integer, _
    ByVal era As Integer) As Boolean

Overrides Public Function **IsLeapMonth**(ByVal year As Integer, ByVal month As Integer, ByVal era As Integer) _
  As Boolean
Overrides Public Function **IsLeapYear**(ByVal year As Integer, ByVal era As Integer) As Boolean
Overrides Public Function **ToDateTime**(ByVal year As Integer, ByVal month As Integer, ByVal day As Integer, _
  ByVal hour As Integer, ByVal minute As Integer, ByVal second As Integer, ByVal millisecond As Integer,   _
  ByVal era As Integer) As Date
Overrides Public Function **ToFourDigitYear**(ByVal year As Integer) As Integer
End Class

Hierarchy: System.Object→ Calendar→ JulianCalendar

KoreanCalendar   **Class**

System.Globalization (mscorlib.dll)   *serializable*

This calendar class implements the Korean calendar. The Korean calendar is the same as the Gregorian calendar except that the eras are defined differently. 01 January, 2001 on the Gregorian calendar is 01 January, 4334 on the Korean calendar.

Public Class **KoreanCalendar** : Inherits Calendar
' Public Constructors
  Public Sub **New**()
' Public Shared Fields
  Public const **KoreanEra** As Integer   *=1*
' Public Instance Properties
  Overrides Public ReadOnly Property **Eras** As Integer()
  Overrides Public Property **TwoDigitYearMax** As Integer
' Public Instance Methods
  Overrides Public Function **AddMonths**(ByVal time As Date, ByVal months As Integer) As Date
  Overrides Public Function **AddYears**(ByVal time As Date, ByVal years As Integer) As Date
  Overrides Public Function **GetDayOfMonth**(ByVal time As Date) As Integer
  Overrides Public Function **GetDayOfWeek**(ByVal time As Date) As DayOfWeek
  Overrides Public Function **GetDayOfYear**(ByVal time As Date) As Integer
  Overrides Public Function **GetDaysInMonth**(ByVal year As Integer, ByVal month As Integer, ByVal era As Integer) _
    As Integer
  Overrides Public Function **GetDaysInYear**(ByVal year As Integer, ByVal era As Integer) As Integer
  Overrides Public Function **GetEra**(ByVal time As Date) As Integer
  Overrides Public Function **GetMonth**(ByVal time As Date) As Integer
  Overrides Public Function **GetMonthsInYear**(ByVal year As Integer, ByVal era As Integer) As Integer
  Overrides Public Function **GetYear**(ByVal time As Date) As Integer
  Overrides Public Function **IsLeapDay**(ByVal year As Integer, ByVal month As Integer, ByVal day As Integer, _
    ByVal era As Integer) As Boolean
  Overrides Public Function **IsLeapMonth**(ByVal year As Integer, ByVal month As Integer, ByVal era As Integer) _
    As Boolean
  Overrides Public Function **IsLeapYear**(ByVal year As Integer, ByVal era As Integer) As Boolean
  Overrides Public Function **ToDateTime**(ByVal year As Integer, ByVal month As Integer, ByVal day As Integer, _
    ByVal hour As Integer, ByVal minute As Integer, ByVal second As Integer, ByVal millisecond As Integer,   _
    ByVal era As Integer) As Date
  Overrides Public Function **ToFourDigitYear**(ByVal year As Integer) As Integer
End Class

Hierarchy: System.Object→ Calendar→ KoreanCalendar

NumberFormatInfo

NotInheritable Class

System.Globalization (mscorlib.dll)

ECMA, serializable

This class defines how numbers are displayed according to culture and language. Formats for currency and its symbols and types of numeric formats, such as scientific and hexadecimal notations and their separators, are described by the properties of this class. As with DateTimeFormatInfo, a set of standard numeric formats is predefined and specified by format characters.

The default property values apply to the invariant culture settings. The culture-specific NumberFormatInfo instance is retrieved by CurrentInfo, which is determined by the CultureInfo of the current thread or environment.

```
Public NotInheritable Class NumberFormatInfo : Implements ICloneable, IFormatProvider
' Public Constructors
   Public Sub New()
' Public Shared Properties
   Public Shared ReadOnly Property CurrentInfo As NumberFormatInfo
   Public Shared ReadOnly Property InvariantInfo As NumberFormatInfo
' Public Instance Properties
   Public Property CurrencyDecimalDigits As Integer
   Public Property CurrencyDecimalSeparator As String
   Public Property CurrencyGroupSeparator As String
   Public Property CurrencyGroupSizes As Integer()
   Public Property CurrencyNegativePattern As Integer
   Public Property CurrencyPositivePattern As Integer
   Public Property CurrencySymbol As String
   Public ReadOnly Property IsReadOnly As Boolean
   Public Property NaNSymbol As String
   Public Property NegativeInfinitySymbol As String
   Public Property NegativeSign As String
   Public Property NumberDecimalDigits As Integer
   Public Property NumberDecimalSeparator As String
   Public Property NumberGroupSeparator As String
   Public Property NumberGroupSizes As Integer()
   Public Property NumberNegativePattern As Integer
   Public Property PercentDecimalDigits As Integer
   Public Property PercentDecimalSeparator As String
   Public Property PercentGroupSeparator As String
   Public Property PercentGroupSizes As Integer()
   Public Property PercentNegativePattern As Integer
   Public Property PercentPositivePattern As Integer
   Public Property PercentSymbol As String
   Public Property PerMilleSymbol As String
   Public Property PositiveInfinitySymbol As String
   Public Property PositiveSign As String
' Public Shared Methods
   Public Shared Function GetInstance(ByVal formatProvider As IFormatProvider) As NumberFormatInfo
   Public Shared Function ReadOnly(ByVal nfi As NumberFormatInfo) As NumberFormatInfo
' Public Instance Methods
   Public Function Clone() As Object Implements ICloneable.Clone
   Public Function GetFormat(ByVal formatType As Type) As Object Implements  IFormatProvider.GetFormat
End Class
```

Returned By: CultureInfo.NumberFormat

Passed To: CultureInfo.NumberFormat

NumberStyles   Enum

System.Globalization (mscorlib.dll)   *ECMA, serializable, flag*

This enumeration specifies a number of style rules that may be used when a numeric type uses the Parse() method to convert a string into a number.

```
Public Enum NumberStyles
    None = &H000000000
    AllowLeadingWhite = &H000000001
    AllowTrailingWhite = &H000000002
    AllowLeadingSign = &H000000004
    Integer = &H000000007
    AllowTrailingSign = &H000000008
    AllowParentheses = &H000000010
    AllowDecimalPoint = &H000000020
    AllowThousands = &H000000040
    Number = &H00000006F
    AllowExponent = &H000000080
    Float = &H0000000A7
    AllowCurrencySymbol = &H000000100
    Currency = &H00000017F
    Any = &H0000001FF
    AllowHexSpecifier = &H000000200
    HexNumber = &H000000203
End Enum
```

Hierarchy: System.Object→ System.ValueType→ System.Enum(System.IComparable, System.IFormattable, System.IConvertible)→ NumberStyles

Passed To: System.Byte.Parse(), System.Decimal.Parse(), System.Double.{Parse(), TryParse()}, System.Int16.Parse(), System.Int32.Parse(), System.Int64.Parse(), System.SByte.Parse(), System.Single.Parse(), System.UInt16.Parse(), System.UInt32.Parse(), System.UInt64.Parse()

RegionInfo   Class

System.Globalization (mscorlib.dll)   *serializable*

This class contains properties for the selected region or country settings. It stores information on the name and standard letter codes for the region, the currency symbol, and whether the metric system is used or not. The region names are the two- and three-letter codes defined in ISO 3166. Currency strings are defined by ISO 4217.

```
Public Class RegionInfo
' Public Constructors
    Public Sub New(ByVal culture As Integer)
    Public Sub New(ByVal name As String)
' Public Shared Properties
    Public Shared ReadOnly Property CurrentRegion As RegionInfo
' Public Instance Properties
    Overridable Public ReadOnly Property CurrencySymbol As String
    Overridable Public ReadOnly Property DisplayName As String
    Overridable Public ReadOnly Property EnglishName As String
    Overridable Public ReadOnly Property IsMetric As Boolean
    Overridable Public ReadOnly Property ISOCurrencySymbol As String
    Overridable Public ReadOnly Property Name As String
    Overridable Public ReadOnly Property ThreeLetterISORegionName As String
    Overridable Public ReadOnly Property ThreeLetterWindowsRegionName As String
    Overridable Public ReadOnly Property TwoLetterISORegionName As String
```

' *Public Instance Methods*
Overrides Public Function **Equals**(ByVal value As Object) As Boolean
Overrides Public Function **GetHashCode**() As Integer
Overrides Public Function **ToString**() As String
End Class

SortKey
Class

System.Globalization (mscorlib.dll)
serializable

This class represents a set of weighted classifications used to sort individual elements of a string.

Public Class **SortKey**
' *Public Instance Properties*
Overridable Public ReadOnly Property **KeyData** As Byte()
Overridable Public ReadOnly Property **OriginalString** As String
' *Public Shared Methods*
Public Shared Function **Compare**(ByVal sortkey1 As SortKey, ByVal sortkey2 As SortKey) As Integer
' *Public Instance Methods*
Overrides Public Function **Equals**(ByVal value As Object) As Boolean
Overrides Public Function **GetHashCode**() As Integer
Overrides Public Function **ToString**() As String
End Class

Returned By: CompareInfo.GetSortKey()

StringInfo
Class

System.Globalization (mscorlib.dll)
serializable

This class allows you to manipulate a string by its individual elements. Each separately displayed character is considered a text element. This includes base characters and the Unicode-defined surrogate pairs and combining character sequences. The class provides enumeration of the elements in the string, as well as a means of further identifying combining characters. ParseCombiningCharacters() returns only the indexes of the base characters, high surrogates, and combined characters within a string.

Public Class **StringInfo**
' *Public Constructors*
Public Sub **New**()
' *Public Shared Methods*
Public Shared Function **GetNextTextElement**(ByVal str As String) As String
Public Shared Function **GetNextTextElement**(ByVal str As String, ByVal index As Integer) As String
Public Shared Function **GetTextElementEnumerator**(ByVal str As String) As TextElementEnumerator
Public Shared Function **GetTextElementEnumerator**(ByVal str As String, ByVal index As Integer) _
    As TextElementEnumerator
Public Shared Function **ParseCombiningCharacters**(ByVal str As String) As Integer()
End Class

TaiwanCalendar
Class

System.Globalization (mscorlib.dll)
serializable

This class implements the Taiwanese calendar. This calendar works like the Gregorian calendar, except for difference in the year and era. 2001 in the Gregorian calendar is the year 90 in the Taiwanese calendar.

Public Class **TaiwanCalendar** : Inherits Calendar

```
' Public Constructors
  Public Sub New()
' Public Instance Properties
  Overrides Public ReadOnly Property Eras As Integer()
  Overrides Public Property TwoDigitYearMax As Integer
' Public Instance Methods
  Overrides Public Function AddMonths(ByVal time As Date, ByVal months As Integer) As Date
  Overrides Public Function AddYears(ByVal time As Date, ByVal years As Integer) As Date
  Overrides Public Function GetDayOfMonth(ByVal time As Date) As Integer
  Overrides Public Function GetDayOfWeek(ByVal time As Date) As DayOfWeek
  Overrides Public Function GetDayOfYear(ByVal time As Date) As Integer
  Overrides Public Function GetDaysInMonth(ByVal year As Integer, ByVal month As Integer, ByVal era As Integer) _
    As Integer
  Overrides Public Function GetDaysInYear(ByVal year As Integer, ByVal era As Integer) As Integer
  Overrides Public Function GetEra(ByVal time As Date) As Integer
  Overrides Public Function GetMonth(ByVal time As Date) As Integer
  Overrides Public Function GetMonthsInYear(ByVal year As Integer, ByVal era As Integer) As Integer
  Overrides Public Function GetYear(ByVal time As Date) As Integer
  Overrides Public Function IsLeapDay(ByVal year As Integer, ByVal month As Integer, ByVal day As Integer, _
    ByVal era As Integer) As Boolean
  Overrides Public Function IsLeapMonth(ByVal year As Integer, ByVal month As Integer, ByVal era As Integer) _
    As Boolean
  Overrides Public Function IsLeapYear(ByVal year As Integer, ByVal era As Integer) As Boolean
  Overrides Public Function ToDateTime(ByVal year As Integer, ByVal month As Integer, ByVal day As Integer, _
    ByVal hour As Integer, ByVal minute As Integer, ByVal second As Integer, ByVal millisecond As Integer, _
    ByVal era As Integer) As Date
  Overrides Public Function ToFourDigitYear(ByVal year As Integer) As Integer
End Class
```

Hierarchy: System.Object→ Calendar→ TaiwanCalendar

TextElementEnumerator   Class

System.Globalization (mscorlib.dll)   *serializable*

This class provides enumeration for individual text elements in a string composed of complex characters. This enumerator is retrieved by StringInfo.GetTextElementEnumerator().

```
Public Class TextElementEnumerator : Implements IEnumerator
' Public Instance Properties
  Public ReadOnly Property Current As Object Implements IEnumerator.Current
  Public ReadOnly Property ElementIndex As Integer
' Public Instance Methods
  Public Function GetTextElement() As String
  Public Function MoveNext() As Boolean Implements IEnumerator.MoveNext
  Public Sub Reset() Implements IEnumerator.Reset
End Class
```

Returned By: StringInfo.GetTextElementEnumerator()

TextInfo   Class

System.Globalization (mscorlib.dll)   *serializable*

This class is used to describe certain properties of the writing system in use by a culture. The properties of this class specify system-specific and standardized code pages for text, as well as the ListSeparator string (a "," for the invariant culture). TextInfo defines methods that determine casing semantics per culture. For example, ToLower() returns the lowercase version of the specified character or string. The ToTitleCase() method capitalizes the first letter of each word in a string.

```
Public Class TextInfo : Implements System.Runtime.Serialization.IDeserializationCallback
' Public Instance Properties
   Overridable Public ReadOnly Property ANSICodePage As Integer
   Overridable Public ReadOnly Property EBCDICCodePage As Integer
   Overridable Public ReadOnly Property ListSeparator As String
   Overridable Public ReadOnly Property MacCodePage As Integer
   Overridable Public ReadOnly Property OEMCodePage As Integer
' Public Instance Methods
   Overrides Public Function Equals(ByVal obj As Object) As Boolean
   Overrides Public Function GetHashCode() As Integer
   Overridable Public Function ToLower(ByVal c As Char) As Char
   Overridable Public Function ToLower(ByVal str As String) As String
   Overrides Public Function ToString() As String
   Public Function ToTitleCase(ByVal str As String) As String
   Overridable Public Function ToUpper(ByVal c As Char) As Char
   Overridable Public Function ToUpper(ByVal str As String) As String
End Class
```

Returned By: CultureInfo.TextInfo

ThaiBuddhistCalendar   Class

System.Globalization (mscorlib.dll)   *serializable*

This class implements the Thai Buddhist calendar. This calendar works like the Gregorian calendar except for the year and era. 2001 in the Gregorian calendar is the year 2544 in the Thai Buddhist calendar.

```
Public Class ThaiBuddhistCalendar : Inherits Calendar
' Public Constructors
   Public Sub New()
' Public Shared Fields
   Public const ThaiBuddhistEra As Integer                                    =1
' Public Instance Properties
   Overrides Public ReadOnly Property Eras As Integer()
   Overrides Public Property TwoDigitYearMax As Integer
' Public Instance Methods
   Overrides Public Function AddMonths(ByVal time As Date, ByVal months As Integer) As Date
   Overrides Public Function AddYears(ByVal time As Date, ByVal years As Integer) As Date
   Overrides Public Function GetDayOfMonth(ByVal time As Date) As Integer
   Overrides Public Function GetDayOfWeek(ByVal time As Date) As DayOfWeek
   Overrides Public Function GetDayOfYear(ByVal time As Date) As Integer
   Overrides Public Function GetDaysInMonth(ByVal year As Integer, ByVal month As Integer, ByVal era As Integer) _
      As Integer
   Overrides Public Function GetDaysInYear(ByVal year As Integer, ByVal era As Integer) As Integer
   Overrides Public Function GetEra(ByVal time As Date) As Integer
   Overrides Public Function GetMonth(ByVal time As Date) As Integer
   Overrides Public Function GetMonthsInYear(ByVal year As Integer, ByVal era As Integer) As Integer
   Overrides Public Function GetYear(ByVal time As Date) As Integer
   Overrides Public Function IsLeapDay(ByVal year As Integer, ByVal month As Integer, ByVal day As Integer, _
      ByVal era As Integer)  As Boolean
   Overrides Public Function IsLeapMonth(ByVal year As Integer, ByVal month As Integer, ByVal era As Integer) _
      As Boolean
   Overrides Public Function IsLeapYear(ByVal year As Integer, ByVal era As Integer) As Boolean
   Overrides Public Function ToDateTime(ByVal year As Integer, ByVal month As Integer, ByVal day As Integer, _
      ByVal hour As Integer, ByVal minute As Integer, ByVal second As Integer, ByVal millisecond As Integer,   _
```

ByVal era As Integer) As Date
Overrides Public Function **ToFourDigitYear**(ByVal year As Integer) As Integer
End Class

Hierarchy: System.Object→ Calendar→ ThaiBuddhistCalendar

UnicodeCategory   Enum

System.Globalization (mscorlib.dll)   *ECMA, serializable*

The values of this enumeration specify the specific category of a character defined by
the Unicode standard. This enumeration supports the System.Char class in determining
properties of Unicode characters such as case with regard to the CultureInfo setting.

```
Public Enum UnicodeCategory
      UppercaseLetter = 0
      LowercaseLetter = 1
      TitlecaseLetter = 2
      ModifierLetter = 3
      OtherLetter = 4
      NonSpacingMark = 5
      SpacingCombiningMark = 6
      EnclosingMark = 7
      DecimalDigitNumber = 8
      LetterNumber = 9
      OtherNumber = 10
      SpaceSeparator = 11
      LineSeparator = 12
      ParagraphSeparator = 13
      Control = 14
      Format = 15
      Surrogate = 16
      PrivateUse = 17
      ConnectorPunctuation = 18
      DashPunctuation = 19
      OpenPunctuation = 20
      ClosePunctuation = 21
      InitialQuotePunctuation = 22
      FinalQuotePunctuation = 23
      OtherPunctuation = 24
      MathSymbol = 25
      CurrencySymbol = 26
      ModifierSymbol = 27
      OtherSymbol = 28
      OtherNotAssigned = 29
End Enum
```

Hierarchy: System.Object→ System.ValueType→ System.Enum(System.IComparable,
System.IFormattable, System.IConvertible)→ UnicodeCategory

Returned By: System.Char.GetUnicodeCategory()

CHAPTER 9

System.IO

The System.IO types serve as the primary means for stream-oriented I/O—files, principally, although the MustInherit types defined here serve as base classes for other forms of I/O, such as the XML stack in System.Xml. The System.IO namespace is shown in Figure 9-1 and Figure 9-2.

The System.IO namespace can be seen as two distinct partitions: a set of utility types for using and working with the local machine's filesystem, and a protocol stack for working with bytestream-oriented input and output. The former partition is the collection of classes such as Directory and FileSystemWatcher, whereas the latter partition is the set of Stream and Reader/Writer types.

The Stream types in System.IO follow a basic object model, similar to the I/O model used by the C/C++ runtime library: all serial byte access is a stream, and there are different sources and sinks for this serialized byte data. In the System.IO package, this is represented directly by the MustInherit base type Stream; its concrete subtypes represent the actual I/O access: FileStream represents I/O to a file, and MemoryStream represents I/O to a literal array of bytes (whose size is dynamically managed) in memory. Other packages within the .NET Framework Class Library offer up their own Stream-derived types. For example, in the System.Net namespace, socket connections and HTTP responses are offered up as Stream-derived types, giving .NET programmers the ability to treat any sort of input or output data as "just a Stream."

Simply reading and writing to these streams is not enough of an abstraction, however. In particular, programmers often need to perform one of two sorts of I/O: binary I/O, which is writing actual binary representations of objects or data to disk, or text I/O, which is writing the textual representations of that data. These operations are fundamentally different—writing the text representation of the integer value 5 produces the literal text "5" within the stream, whereas writing the binary value generates the hex value 0x00000005 (represented as four bytes, 05 00 00 00, in the file). In the .NET libraries, because these types of I/O operations are different from one another, these operations are abstracted out into two sets of MustInherit base types. BinaryReader and BinaryWriter are for reading and writing binary values to streams, and TextReader and TextWriter are for reading and writing character-based data.

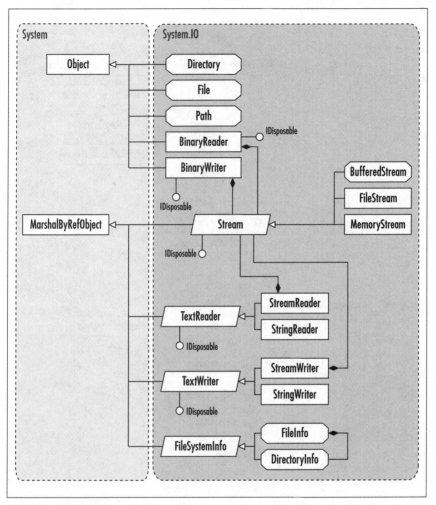

Figure 9–1. The System.IO namespace

Note that the System.IO namespace also offers some interesting stream-on-stream options. Like the Java java.io package, Stream types can layer on top of other Stream types to offer additional functionality—this is the Decorator pattern (from the Design Patterns book). The sole example of this in the System.IO namespace is the Buffered-Stream, which maintains a buffer on top of the Stream object passed to it in its constructor.

All of these types work together to provide some powerful abstraction and composite behaviors. For example, when working with random-access data, create a BinaryReader around a BufferedStream, which in turn wraps around a FileStream. If you decide later to store the random-access data in memory for optimization's sake, change the Buffered-Stream/ FileStream pair to a MemoryStream. When reading a configuration file, choose to declare the ReadConfiguration method you have written to take an arbitrary TextReader, rather than ask for a string containing the filename. This allows for flexibility later—perhaps the configuration wants to be stored into a CLOB field in an RDBMS. Simply change the actual Stream instance passed into the TextReader, and start reading the

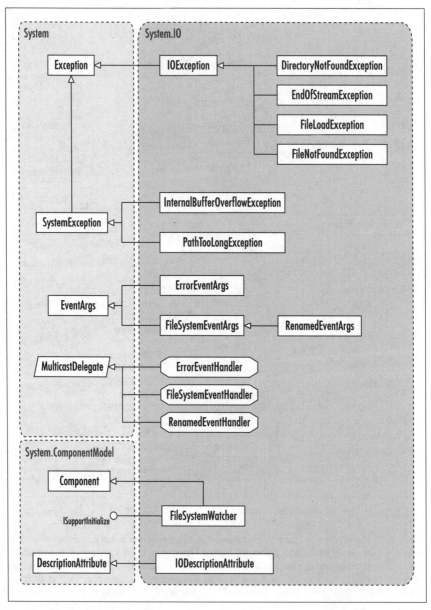

Figure 9-2. Exceptions, delegates, event arguments, and components in the System.IO namespace

configuration out of the RDBMS, off of a socket request, or out of the HTTP response sent to a web server. Similarly, when planning to extend the System.IO namespace's capabilities, try to follow this same model. If you want to add compression to save on a configuration file's size just build a CompressingStream that wraps another Stream in the manner BufferedStream does. If you want to have some interprocess communication with an existing "legacy" Win32 app (perhaps communicate over an NT Named Pipe), simply build a NamedPipeStream. In general, there is no particular reason to take specific derivatives of Stream as parameters—by limiting expected parameters to be of type Stream, .NET programmers can gain an incredible amount of flexibility regarding where and how data lives.

All this notwithstanding, certain programmatic tasks simply require access to the filesystem. The underlying filesystem is a hierarchical one, and there will be times there is simply no escaping that fact. For these tasks, the .NET System.IO namespace provides the filesystem types: Directory, DirectoryInfo, File, FileInfo and its associated enumerations, FileSystemInfo, FileSystemWatcher, and Path (finally, a class that understands directory paths in all their various incarnations!). These classes should be used for mostly "meta-file" operations (enumerating files, discovering attributes about a file, creating or destroying a directory, and so on) rather than for operations on the contents of the file (for which the Stream-based types described earlier are more appropriate).

BinaryReader   Class
System.IO (mscorlib.dll)   *disposable*

This class allows you to read data from a Stream. When using a BinaryReader, the data represented by a Stream is regarded as a binary format, and bits are merely read from the stream and copied into the appropriate types. The methods prefixed with Read() allow you to grab data of a specific type from the front of the Stream and advance the current position. The next table shows how many bytes each of these methods reads in from a stream.

Method	*Bytes read*
Read	variable
ReadBoolean	1
ReadByte	1
ReadBytes	variable
ReadChar	2
ReadChars	variable
ReadDecimal	16
ReadDouble	8
ReadInt16	2
ReadInt32	4
ReadInt64	8
ReadSByte	1
ReadSingle	4
ReadString	variable
ReadUInt16	2
ReadUInt32	4
ReadUInt64	8

ReadString() uses the current encoding of the BinaryReader, which can be set when you call the constructor. Strings are prefixed with their length. PeekChar() allows you to look at the first character of a stream (a System.Char, which is two bytes) without advancing the position of the Stream. Because a binary reader may hold on to resources that should be freed when not needed, the BinaryReader must be closed using Close() or by calling the protected Dispose() method to do the cleanup.

Public Class **BinaryReader** : Implements IDisposable
' *Public Constructors*
   Public Sub **New**(ByVal input As Stream)
   Public Sub **New**(ByVal input As Stream, ByVal encoding As System.Text.Encoding)
' *Public Instance Properties*
   Overridable Public ReadOnly Property **BaseStream** As Stream
' *Public Instance Methods*
   Overridable Public Sub **Close**()
   Overridable Public Function **PeekChar**() As Integer
   Overridable Public Function **Read**() As Integer
   Overridable Public Function **Read**(ByVal buffer As Byte(), ByVal index As Integer, ByVal count As Integer) As Integer
   Overridable Public Function **Read**(ByVal buffer As Char(), ByVal index As Integer, ByVal count As Integer) As Integer
   Overridable Public Function **ReadBoolean**() As Boolean
   Overridable Public Function **ReadByte**() As Byte
   Overridable Public Function **ReadBytes**(ByVal count As Integer) As Byte()
   Overridable Public Function **ReadChar**() As Char
   Overridable Public Function **ReadChars**(ByVal count As Integer) As Char()
   Overridable Public Function **ReadDecimal**() As Decimal
   Overridable Public Function **ReadDouble**() As Double
   Overridable Public Function **ReadInt16**() As Short
   Overridable Public Function **ReadInt32**() As Integer
   Overridable Public Function **ReadInt64**() As Long
   Overridable Public Function **ReadSByte**() As SByte
   Overridable Public Function **ReadSingle**() As Single
   Overridable Public Function **ReadString**() As String
   Overridable Public Function **ReadUInt16**() As UInt16
   Overridable Public Function **ReadUInt32**() As UInt32
   Overridable Public Function **ReadUInt64**() As UInt64
' *Protected Instance Methods*
   Overridable Protected Sub **Dispose**(ByVal disposing As Boolean)
   Overridable Protected Sub **FillBuffer**(ByVal numBytes As Integer)
   Protected Function **Read7BitEncodedInt**() As Integer
End Class

BinaryWriter
Class

System.IO (mscorlib.dll)
serializable, disposable

This class complements BinaryReader. To write binary data, simply call Write() and pass data of the desired type; the method is overloaded for all "primitive types" (but not the generic System.Object type—that is the subject of the System.Runtime.Serialization namespaces). Be aware, however, that because BinaryWriter is not the actual destination of the data (the wrapped Stream object is) the data may be cached in a buffer somewhere between the BinaryWriter and the sink. To ensure data is completely written, call the Flush() method. When working with a BinaryWriter in a sensitive code area, consider placing it in a using block to ensure cleanup (in this case, release of the Stream it wraps after flushing the data).

Public Class **BinaryWriter** : Implements IDisposable
' *Public Constructors*
   Public Sub **New**(ByVal output As Stream)
   Public Sub **New**(ByVal output As Stream, ByVal encoding As System.Text.Encoding)
' *Protected Constructors*
   Protected Sub **New**()
' *Public Shared Fields*
   Public Shared ReadOnly **Null** As BinaryWriter   *=System.IO.BinaryWriter*

```
' Protected Instance Fields
    protected OutStream As Stream
' Public Instance Properties
    Overridable Public ReadOnly Property BaseStream As Stream
' Public Instance Methods
    Overridable Public Sub Close()
    Overridable Public Sub Flush()
    Overridable Public Function Seek(ByVal offset As Integer, ByVal origin As SeekOrigin) As Long
    Overridable Public Sub Write(ByVal value As Boolean)
    Overridable Public Sub Write(ByVal value As Byte)
    Overridable Public Sub Write(ByVal buffer As Byte())
    Overridable Public Sub Write(ByVal buffer As Byte(), ByVal index As Integer, ByVal count As Integer)
    Overridable Public Sub Write(ByVal ch As Char)
    Overridable Public Sub Write(ByVal chars As Char())
    Overridable Public Sub Write(ByVal chars As Char(), ByVal index As Integer, ByVal count As Integer)
    Overridable Public Sub Write(ByVal value As Decimal)
    Overridable Public Sub Write(ByVal value As Double)
    Overridable Public Sub Write(ByVal value As Short)
    Overridable Public Sub Write(ByVal value As Integer)
    Overridable Public Sub Write(ByVal value As Long)
    Overridable Public Sub Write(ByVal value As SByte)
    Overridable Public Sub Write(ByVal value As Single)
    Overridable Public Sub Write(ByVal value As String)
    Overridable Public Sub Write(ByVal value As UInt16)
    Overridable Public Sub Write(ByVal value As UInt32)
    Overridable Public Sub Write(ByVal value As UInt64)
' Protected Instance Methods
    Overridable Protected Sub Dispose(ByVal disposing As Boolean)
    Protected Sub Write7BitEncodedInt(ByVal value As Integer)
End Class
```

BufferedStream   NotInheritable Class

System.IO (mscorlib.dll)   *marshal by reference, disposable*

These buffers read and write operations to a stream. Because the I/O devices are usually the slowest part of the machine, it usually makes sense to write larger amounts of data at a time, so buffering can improve I/O performance dramatically.

Note that many of the Stream-based types automatically buffer data or represent resources that also buffer data, not only in the System.IO namespace, but also in other namespaces. For example, the filesystem usually has several buffers in place at various levels. This type, however, offers some optimization capabilities, since data won't be sent to the underlying Stream until this object's buffer is full. This can help with accidental flushing in the middle of sensitive operations, such as a tightly executing loop.

```
Public NotInheritable Class BufferedStream : Inherits Stream
' Public Constructors
    Public Sub New(ByVal stream As Stream)
    Public Sub New(ByVal stream As Stream, ByVal bufferSize As Integer)
' Public Instance Properties
    Overrides Public ReadOnly Property CanRead As Boolean
    Overrides Public ReadOnly Property CanSeek As Boolean
    Overrides Public ReadOnly Property CanWrite As Boolean
    Overrides Public ReadOnly Property Length As Long
    Overrides Public Property Position As Long
' Public Instance Methods
```

Overrides Public Sub **Close**()
Overrides Public Sub **Flush**()
Overrides Public Function **Read**(ByRef array As Byte(), ByVal offset As Integer, ByVal count As Integer) As Integer
Overrides Public Function **ReadByte**() As Integer
Overrides Public Function **Seek**(ByVal offset As Long, ByVal origin As SeekOrigin) As Long
Overrides Public Sub **SetLength**(ByVal value As Long)
Overrides Public Sub **Write**(ByVal array As Byte(), ByVal offset As Integer, ByVal count As Integer)
Overrides Public Sub **WriteByte**(ByVal value As Byte)
End Class

Hierarchy: System.Object→ System.MarshalByRefObject→ Stream(System.IDisposable)→
BufferedStream

Directory   NotInheritable Class

System.IO (mscorlib.dll)   *ECMA*

This class provides many shared methods for working with filesystem directories. Most
of the methods behave as expected. GetLogicalDrives() returns an array of all of the drives
of a system in the format "k:", in which "k" is the drive letter. GetParent() returns the parent path of the specified path, and GetDirectoryRoot() returns the root directory of the
specified path.

Public NotInheritable Class **Directory**
' Public Shared Methods
   Public Shared Function **CreateDirectory**(ByVal path As String) As DirectoryInfo
   Public Shared Sub **Delete**(ByVal path As String)
   Public Shared Sub **Delete**(ByVal path As String, ByVal recursive As Boolean)
   Public Shared Function **Exists**(ByVal path As String) As Boolean
   Public Shared Function **GetCreationTime**(ByVal path As String) As Date
   Public Shared Function **GetCurrentDirectory**() As String
   Public Shared Function **GetDirectories**(ByVal path As String) As String()
   Public Shared Function **GetDirectories**(ByVal path As String, ByVal searchPattern As String) As String()
   Public Shared Function **GetDirectoryRoot**(ByVal path As String) As String
   Public Shared Function **GetFiles**(ByVal path As String) As String()
   Public Shared Function **GetFiles**(ByVal path As String, ByVal searchPattern As String) As String()
   Public Shared Function **GetFileSystemEntries**(ByVal path As String) As String()
   Public Shared Function **GetFileSystemEntries**(ByVal path As String, ByVal searchPattern As String) As String()
   Public Shared Function **GetLastAccessTime**(ByVal path As String) As Date
   Public Shared Function **GetLastWriteTime**(ByVal path As String) As Date
   Public Shared Function **GetLogicalDrives**() As String()
   Public Shared Function **GetParent**(ByVal path As String) As DirectoryInfo
   Public Shared Sub **Move**(ByVal sourceDirName As String, ByVal destDirName As String)
   Public Shared Sub **SetCreationTime**(ByVal path As String, ByVal creationTime As Date)
   Public Shared Sub **SetCurrentDirectory**(ByVal path As String)
   Public Shared Sub **SetLastAccessTime**(ByVal path As String, ByVal lastAccessTime As Date)
   Public Shared Sub **SetLastWriteTime**(ByVal path As String, ByVal lastWriteTime As Date)
End Class

DirectoryInfo   NotInheritable Class

System.IO (mscorlib.dll)   *serializable, marshal by reference*

This class provides the same functionality as Directory, but in a strongly typed, object-oriented manner. An instance of this type represents a single directory. This class extends
FileSystemInfo and implements all its methods. In addition, it adds Parent and Root properties to return the parent and root directories, respectively. Similarly, it also supplies Get-
Directories() and GetFiles(), to retrieve its subdirectories and files, as well as

GetFileSystemInfos(), which returns both the files and subdirectories contained by the current directory. MoveTo() allows you to move a directory from one place to another.

Given the similarity between this type and the Directory type, it may not be clear when one should be used in place of the other. The key difference is the Directory class is a collection of shared utility functions, whereas a DirectoryInfo object is an actual object, maintaining state and identity in the classic style of all objects. (In fact, the DirectoryInfo methods often map over to use the corresponding Directory methods.)

```
Public NotInheritable Class DirectoryInfo : Inherits FileSystemInfo
' Public Constructors
   Public Sub New(ByVal path As String)
' Public Instance Properties
   Overrides Public ReadOnly Property Exists As Boolean
   Overrides Public ReadOnly Property Name As String
   Public ReadOnly Property Parent As DirectoryInfo
   Public ReadOnly Property Root As DirectoryInfo
' Public Instance Methods
   Public Sub Create()
   Public Function CreateSubdirectory(ByVal path As String) As DirectoryInfo
   Overrides Public Sub Delete()
   Public Sub Delete(ByVal recursive As Boolean)
   Public Function GetDirectories() As DirectoryInfo()
   Public Function GetDirectories(ByVal searchPattern As String) As DirectoryInfo()
   Public Function GetFiles() As FileInfo()
   Public Function GetFiles(ByVal searchPattern As String) As FileInfo()
   Public Function GetFileSystemInfos() As FileSystemInfo()
   Public Function GetFileSystemInfos(ByVal searchPattern As String) As FileSystemInfo()
   Public Sub MoveTo(ByVal destDirName As String)
   Overrides Public Function ToString() As String
End Class
```

Hierarchy: System.Object→ System.MarshalByRefObject→ FileSystemInfo→ DirectoryInfo

Returned By: Directory.{CreateDirectory(), GetParent()}, FileInfo.Directory

DirectoryNotFoundException   Class

System.IO (mscorlib.dll)   *ECMA, serializable*

This exception is thrown if you attempt to access a directory that does not exist.

```
Public Class DirectoryNotFoundException : Inherits IOException
' Public Constructors
   Public Sub New()
   Public Sub New(ByVal message As String)
   Public Sub New(ByVal message As String, ByVal innerException As Exception)
' Protected Constructors
   Protected Sub New(ByVal info As System.Runtime.Serialization.SerializationInfo, _
      ByVal context As System.Runtime.Serialization.StreamingContext)
End Class
```

Hierarchy: System.Object→ System.Exception(System.Runtime.Serialization.ISerializable)→ System.SystemException→ IOException→ DirectoryNotFoundException

EndOfStreamException   Class

System.IO (mscorlib.dll)   *ECMA, serializable*

This exception is thrown if you attempt to read data from a stream at its end position.

Public Class **EndOfStreamException** : Inherits IOException
' *Public Constructors*
   Public Sub **New**()
   Public Sub **New**(ByVal message As String)
   Public Sub **New**(ByVal message As String, ByVal innerException As Exception)
' *Protected Constructors*
   Protected Sub **New**(ByVal info As System.Runtime.Serialization.SerializationInfo, _
     ByVal context As System.Runtime.Serialization.StreamingContext)
End Class

Hierarchy: System.Object→ System.Exception(System.Runtime.Serialization.ISerializable)→
System.SystemException→ IOException→ EndOfStreamException

ErrorEventArgs   Class

System.IO (system.dll)

This type defines the event arguments that are passed when a FileSystemWatcher.Error
event occurs. It contains the exception that was raised by the error, which you can
access by calling GetException().

Public Class **ErrorEventArgs** : Inherits EventArgs
' *Public Constructors*
   Public Sub **New**(ByVal exception As Exception)
' *Public Instance Methods*
   Overridable Public Function **GetException**() As Exception
End Class

Hierarchy: System.Object→ System.EventArgs→ ErrorEventArgs

Passed To: ErrorEventHandler.{BeginInvoke(), Invoke()}, FileSystemWatcher.OnError()

ErrorEventHandler   Delegate

System.IO (system.dll)   *serializable*

This is a delegate for the FileSystemWatcher.Error event.

Public Delegate Sub **ErrorEventHandler**(ByVal sender As Object, ByVal e As ErrorEventArgs)

Associated Events: FileSystemWatcher.Error()

File   NotInheritable Class

System.IO (mscorlib.dll)   *ECMA*

Like the Directory type, this type offers a collection of shared utility methods for working
with files on the filesystem. In most cases, these methods are simply shortcuts for working with the System.IO types directly; for example, the AppendText() method returns a
StreamWriter that can append text to the file specified in the path argument. This could
be accomplished just as easily by creating a StreamWriter around a FileStream opened to
the same file, with the FileMode.Append flag passed into the constructor.

That stated, there are methods on this type that aren't available through the Stream-
based API. For example, the file's creation time, last-accessed time, last-modified times,
and attributes, are all available via this type, whereas no such corresponding call exists
on the Stream type.

Public NotInheritable Class **File**
' *Public Shared Methods*
   Public Shared Function **AppendText**(ByVal path As String) As StreamWriter
   Public Shared Sub **Copy**(ByVal sourceFileName As String, ByVal destFileName As String)
   Public Shared Sub **Copy**(ByVal sourceFileName As String, ByVal destFileName As String, _
     ByVal overwrite As Boolean)
   Public Shared Function **Create**(ByVal path As String) As FileStream
   Public Shared Function **Create**(ByVal path As String, ByVal bufferSize As Integer) As FileStream
   Public Shared Function **CreateText**(ByVal path As String) As StreamWriter
   Public Shared Sub **Delete**(ByVal path As String)
   Public Shared Function **Exists**(ByVal path As String) As Boolean
   Public Shared Function **GetAttributes**(ByVal path As String) As FileAttributes
   Public Shared Function **GetCreationTime**(ByVal path As String) As Date
   Public Shared Function **GetLastAccessTime**(ByVal path As String) As Date
   Public Shared Function **GetLastWriteTime**(ByVal path As String) As Date
   Public Shared Sub **Move**(ByVal sourceFileName As String, ByVal destFileName As String)
   Public Shared Function **Open**(ByVal path As String, ByVal mode As FileMode) As FileStream
   Public Shared Function **Open**(ByVal path As String, ByVal mode As FileMode, ByVal access As FileAccess) _
     As FileStream
   Public Shared Function **Open**(ByVal path As String, ByVal mode As FileMode, ByVal access As FileAccess, _
     ByVal share As FileShare) As FileStream
   Public Shared Function **OpenRead**(ByVal path As String) As FileStream
   Public Shared Function **OpenText**(ByVal path As String) As StreamReader
   Public Shared Function **OpenWrite**(ByVal path As String) As FileStream
   Public Shared Sub **SetAttributes**(ByVal path As String, ByVal fileAttributes As FileAttributes)
   Public Shared Sub **SetCreationTime**(ByVal path As String, ByVal creationTime As Date)
   Public Shared Sub **SetLastAccessTime**(ByVal path As String, ByVal lastAccessTime As Date)
   Public Shared Sub **SetLastWriteTime**(ByVal path As String, ByVal lastWriteTime As Date)
End Class

FileAccess
Enum

System.IO (mscorlib.dll)
ECMA, serializable, flag

This enumeration represents the various access levels a program can exercise on a file. Programs can either read, write, or do both.

Public Enum **FileAccess**
     Read = &H000000001
     Write = &H000000002
     ReadWrite = &H000000003
End Enum

Hierarchy: System.Object→ System.ValueType→ System.Enum(System.IComparable, System.IFormattable, System.IConvertible)→ FileAccess

Passed To: File.Open(), FileInfo.Open(), FileStream.FileStream(), System.IO.IsolatedStorage.IsolatedStorageFileStream.IsolatedStorageFileStream(), System.Net.Sockets.NetworkStream.NetworkStream()

FileAttributes

Enum

System.IO (mscorlib.dll)

serializable, flag

This enumeration represents the various attributes a file can have in the .NET environment; many, if not most, of these attributes parallel the standard Win32 filesystem attributes of the same name.

Public Enum **FileAttributes**
   ReadOnly = &H000000001
   Hidden = &H000000002
   System = &H000000004
   Directory = &H000000010
   Archive = &H000000020
   Device = &H000000040
   Normal = &H000000080
   Temporary = &H000000100
   SparseFile = &H000000200
   ReparsePoint = &H000000400
   Compressed = &H000000800
   Offline = &H000001000
   NotContentIndexed = &H000002000
   Encrypted = &H000004000
End Enum

Hierarchy: System.Object→ System.ValueType→ System.Enum(System.IComparable, System.IFormattable, System.IConvertible)→ FileAttributes

Returned By: File.GetAttributes(), FileSystemInfo.Attributes

Passed To: File.SetAttributes(), FileSystemInfo.Attributes

FileInfo

NotInheritable Class

System.IO (mscorlib.dll)

serializable, marshal by reference

Like the parallels between Directory and DirectoryInfo, this class offers an object-centric spin on the shared functions offered in the File type.

Public NotInheritable Class **FileInfo** : Inherits FileSystemInfo
' Public Constructors
   Public Sub **New**(ByVal fileName As String)
' Public Instance Properties
   Public ReadOnly Property **Directory** As DirectoryInfo
   Public ReadOnly Property **DirectoryName** As String
   Overrides Public ReadOnly Property **Exists** As Boolean
   Public ReadOnly Property **Length** As Long
   Overrides Public ReadOnly Property **Name** As String
' Public Instance Methods
   Public Function **AppendText**() As StreamWriter
   Public Function **CopyTo**(ByVal destFileName As String) As FileInfo
   Public Function **CopyTo**(ByVal destFileName As String, ByVal overwrite As Boolean) As FileInfo
   Public Function **Create**() As FileStream
   Public Function **CreateText**() As StreamWriter
   Overrides Public Sub **Delete**()
   Public Sub **MoveTo**(ByVal destFileName As String)
   Public Function **Open**(ByVal mode As FileMode) As FileStream
   Public Function **Open**(ByVal mode As FileMode, ByVal access As FileAccess) As FileStream
   Public Function **Open**(ByVal mode As FileMode, ByVal access As FileAccess, ByVal share As FileShare) _
     As FileStream

```
   Public Function OpenRead() As FileStream
   Public Function OpenText() As StreamReader
   Public Function OpenWrite() As FileStream
   Overrides Public Function ToString() As String
End Class
```

Hierarchy: System.Object→ System.MarshalByRefObject→ FileSystemInfo→ FileInfo

Returned By: DirectoryInfo.GetFiles()

FileLoadException   Class

System.IO (mscorlib.dll)   *ECMA, serializable*

This exception is thrown when a file cannot be loaded.

```
Public Class FileLoadException : Inherits IOException
' Public Constructors
   Public Sub New()
   Public Sub New(ByVal message As String)
   Public Sub New(ByVal message As String, ByVal inner As Exception)
   Public Sub New(ByVal message As String, ByVal fileName As String)
   Public Sub New(ByVal message As String, ByVal fileName As String, ByVal inner As Exception)
' Protected Constructors
   Protected Sub New(ByVal info As System.Runtime.Serialization.SerializationInfo, _
      ByVal context As System.Runtime.Serialization.StreamingContext)
' Public Instance Properties
   Public ReadOnly Property FileName As String
   Public ReadOnly Property FusionLog As String
   Overrides Public ReadOnly Property Message As String
' Public Instance Methods
   Overrides Public Sub GetObjectData(ByVal info As System.Runtime.Serialization.SerializationInfo, _
      ByVal context As System.Runtime.Serialization.StreamingContext)
   Overrides Public Function ToString() As String
End Class
```

Hierarchy: System.Object→ System.Exception(System.Runtime.Serialization.ISerializable)→
System.SystemException→ IOException→ FileLoadException

FileMode   Enum

System.IO (mscorlib.dll)   *ECMA, serializable*

This enumeration allows you to specify how you want to open a file. If you use Create,
and the file already exists, an IOException is thrown. If you use CreateNew, any file that
currently exists is overwritten. OpenOrCreate indicates that if a file already exists, it must
be opened, otherwise, a new file must be created. Similarly, Truncate indicates that the
file must be opened and all its data erased (writing then begins at the first byte in the
file). Append indicates that the file must be opened and the "file position" set to the end
of the file (the opposite of Truncate).

```
Public Enum FileMode
   CreateNew = 1
   Create = 2
   Open = 3
   OpenOrCreate = 4
   Truncate = 5
   Append = 6
End Enum
```

Hierarchy: System.Object→ System.ValueType→ System.Enum(System.IComparable, System.IFormattable, System.IConvertible)→ FileMode

Passed To: File.Open(), FileInfo.Open(), FileStream.FileStream(), System.IO.IsolatedStorage.IsolatedStorageFileStream.IsolatedStorageFileStream()

FileNotFoundException   Class

System.IO (mscorlib.dll)   *ECMA, serializable*

This exception is thrown when you attempt to access a file that does not exist.

```
Public Class FileNotFoundException : Inherits IOException
' Public Constructors
    Public Sub New()
    Public Sub New(ByVal message As String)
    Public Sub New(ByVal message As String, ByVal innerException As Exception)
    Public Sub New(ByVal message As String, ByVal fileName As String)
    Public Sub New(ByVal message As String, ByVal fileName As String, ByVal innerException As Exception)
' Protected Constructors
    Protected Sub New(ByVal info As System.Runtime.Serialization.SerializationInfo, _
        ByVal context As System.Runtime.Serialization.StreamingContext)
' Public Instance Properties
    Public ReadOnly Property FileName As String
    Public ReadOnly Property FusionLog As String
    Overrides Public ReadOnly Property Message As String
' Public Instance Methods
    Overrides Public Sub GetObjectData(ByVal info As System.Runtime.Serialization.SerializationInfo, _
        ByVal context As System.Runtime.Serialization.StreamingContext)
    Overrides Public Function ToString() As String
End Class
```

Hierarchy: System.Object→ System.Exception(System.Runtime.Serialization.ISerializable)→ System.SystemException→ IOException→ FileNotFoundException

FileShare   Enum

System.IO (mscorlib.dll)   *ECMA, serializable, flag*

This enumeration defines how two different processes can access the same file. If one process is using ReadWrite or Write, no other process can use the file. Similarly, if another process is using Read, then other processes can read from the file, but not write to it.

```
Public Enum FileShare
        None = &H000000000
        Read = &H000000001
        Write = &H000000002
        ReadWrite = &H000000003
        Inheritable = &H000000010
End Enum
```

Hierarchy: System.Object→ System.ValueType→ System.Enum(System.IComparable, System.IFormattable, System.IConvertible)→ FileShare

Passed To: File.Open(), FileInfo.Open(), FileStream.FileStream(), System.IO.IsolatedStorage.IsolatedStorageFileStream.IsolatedStorageFileStream()

FileStream

Class

System.IO (mscorlib.dll)

ECMA, marshal by reference, disposable

This class is the basic implementation of Stream for files. It implements Stream, and adds a few methods specifically for working with files. Handle allows you to grab the underlying system handle to the file resource. IsAsync tells you if the file was opened asynchronously or synchronously. If you want to prevent other processes from accessing parts (or all) of the file, call Lock(). Subsequently, to free the lock, call Unlock().

Note that using the Lock() or Unlock() methods is not the same as using the SyncLock keyword in VB.NET. The SyncLock action locks only for this process, whereas the file-range locks used in the Lock/Unlock methods are implemented at the filesystem level and are therefore a cross-process mechanism.

```
Public Class FileStream : Inherits Stream
' Public Constructors
   Public Sub New(ByVal handle As IntPtr, ByVal access As FileAccess)
   Public Sub New(ByVal handle As IntPtr, ByVal access As FileAccess, ByVal ownsHandle As Boolean)
   Public Sub New(ByVal handle As IntPtr, ByVal access As FileAccess, ByVal ownsHandle As Boolean, _
      ByVal bufferSize As Integer)
   Public Sub New(ByVal handle As IntPtr, ByVal access As FileAccess, ByVal ownsHandle As Boolean, _
      ByVal bufferSize As Integer, ByVal isAsync As Boolean)
   Public Sub New(ByVal path As String, ByVal mode As FileMode)
   Public Sub New(ByVal path As String, ByVal mode As FileMode, ByVal access As FileAccess)
   Public Sub New(ByVal path As String, ByVal mode As FileMode, ByVal access As FileAccess, _
      ByVal share As FileShare)
   Public Sub New(ByVal path As String, ByVal mode As FileMode, ByVal access As FileAccess, _
      ByVal share As FileShare, ByVal bufferSize As Integer)
   Public Sub New(ByVal path As String, ByVal mode As FileMode, ByVal access As FileAccess, _
      ByVal share As FileShare, ByVal bufferSize As Integer, ByVal useAsync As Boolean)
' Public Instance Properties
   Overrides Public ReadOnly Property CanRead As Boolean
   Overrides Public ReadOnly Property CanSeek As Boolean
   Overrides Public ReadOnly Property CanWrite As Boolean
   Overridable Public ReadOnly Property Handle As IntPtr
   Overridable Public ReadOnly Property IsAsync As Boolean
   Overrides Public ReadOnly Property Length As Long
   Public ReadOnly Property Name As String
   Overrides Public Property Position As Long
' Public Instance Methods
   Overrides Public Function BeginRead(ByVal array As Byte(), ByVal offset As Integer, ByVal numBytes As Integer, _
      ByVal userCallback As AsyncCallback, ByVal stateObject As Object) As IAsyncResult
   Overrides Public Function BeginWrite(ByVal array As Byte(), ByVal offset As Integer, ByVal numBytes As Integer, _
      ByVal userCallback As AsyncCallback, ByVal stateObject As Object) As IAsyncResult
   Overrides Public Sub Close()
   Overrides Public Function EndRead(ByVal asyncResult As IAsyncResult) As Integer
   Overrides Public Sub EndWrite(ByVal asyncResult As IAsyncResult)
   Overrides Public Sub Flush()
   Overridable Public Sub Lock(ByVal position As Long, ByVal length As Long)
   Overrides Public Function Read(ByRef array As Byte(), ByVal offset As Integer, ByVal count As Integer) As Integer
   Overrides Public Function ReadByte() As Integer
   Overrides Public Function Seek(ByVal offset As Long, ByVal origin As SeekOrigin) As Long
   Overrides Public Sub SetLength(ByVal value As Long)
   Overridable Public Sub Unlock(ByVal position As Long, ByVal length As Long)
   Overrides Public Sub Write(ByVal array As Byte(), ByVal offset As Integer, ByVal count As Integer)
   Overrides Public Sub WriteByte(ByVal value As Byte)
' Protected Instance Methods
```

```
     Overridable Protected Sub Dispose(ByVal disposing As Boolean)
     Overrides Protected Sub Finalize()
End Class
```

Hierarchy: System.Object→ System.MarshalByRefObject→ Stream(System.IDisposable)→ FileStream

Subclasses: System.IO.IsolatedStorage.IsolatedStorageFileStream

Returned By: File.{Create(), Open(), OpenRead(), OpenWrite()}, FileInfo.{Create(), Open(), OpenRead(), OpenWrite()}, System.Reflection.Assembly.{GetFile(), GetFiles()}

Passed To: System.Reflection.StrongNameKeyPair.StrongNameKeyPair()

FileSystemEventArgs   Class

System.IO (system.dll)

This class offers the arguments for a FileSystemEventHandler.

```
Public Class FileSystemEventArgs : Inherits EventArgs
' Public Constructors
    Public Sub New(ByVal changeType As WatcherChangeTypes, ByVal directory As String, ByVal name As String)
' Public Instance Properties
    Public ReadOnly Property ChangeType As WatcherChangeTypes
    Public ReadOnly Property FullPath As String
    Public ReadOnly Property Name As String
End Class
```

Hierarchy: System.Object→ System.EventArgs→ FileSystemEventArgs

Subclasses: RenamedEventArgs

Passed To: FileSystemEventHandler.{BeginInvoke(), Invoke()}, FileSystemWatcher.{OnChanged(), OnCreated(), OnDeleted()}

FileSystemEventHandler   Delegate

System.IO (system.dll)   *serializable*

This delegate is for the FileSystemWatcher.Changed, FileSystemWatcher.Created, and FileSystemWatcher.Deleted events.

```
Public Delegate Sub FileSystemEventHandler(ByVal sender As Object, ByVal e As FileSystemEventArgs)
```

Associated Events: FileSystemWatcher.{Changed(), Created(), Deleted()}

FileSystemInfo   MustInherit Class

System.IO (mscorlib.dll)   *serializable, marshal by reference*

This serves as the base class for both FileInfo and DirectoryInfo, and allows access to the basic filesystem information relating to both.

```
Public MustInherit Class FileSystemInfo : Inherits MarshalByRefObject
' Protected Constructors
    Protected Sub New()
' Protected Instance Fields
    protected FullPath As String
    protected OriginalPath As String
' Public Instance Properties
    Public Property Attributes As FileAttributes
    Public Property CreationTime As Date
```

```
MustInherit Public ReadOnly Property Exists As Boolean
Public ReadOnly Property Extension As String
Overridable Public ReadOnly Property FullName As String
Public Property LastAccessTime As Date
Public Property LastWriteTime As Date
MustInherit Public ReadOnly Property Name As String
' Public Instance Methods
MustInherit Public Sub Delete()
Public Sub Refresh()
End Class
```

Hierarchy: System.Object→ System.MarshalByRefObject→ FileSystemInfo

Subclasses: DirectoryInfo, FileInfo

Returned By: DirectoryInfo.GetFileSystemInfos()

FileSystemWatcher   Class

System.IO (system.dll)   *marshal by reference, disposable*

This class allows you to listen to the filesystem and respond to different operations on
it. To register a watch on files or directories, first set Path to the path you wish to watch.
Next, set the Filter property. If you want to respond to all file changes, set it to an
empty ("") string. To watch an individual file, set Filter to the filename. You can also use
wildcards (such as *) in the filename. You must then also set NotifyFilter to register the
types of events you wish to be notified of. If you want to monitor the subdirectories as
well, set IncludeSubdirectories. EnableRaisingEvents allows you to enable or disable the
FileSystemWatcher. The watcher then exposes the following events: Changed, Created,
Deleted, Disposed, Error and Renamed. An Error is raised if too many events occur on a
filesystem for the watcher to correctly monitor it.

```
Public Class FileSystemWatcher : Inherits System.ComponentModel.Component : Implements _
    System.ComponentModel.ISupportInitialize
' Public Constructors
Public Sub New()
Public Sub New(ByVal path As String)
Public Sub New(ByVal path As String, ByVal filter As String)
' Public Instance Properties
Public Property EnableRaisingEvents As Boolean
Public Property Filter As String
Public Property IncludeSubdirectories As Boolean
Public Property InternalBufferSize As Integer
Public Property NotifyFilter As NotifyFilters
Public Property Path As String
Overrides Public Property Site As ISite
Public Property SynchronizingObject As ISynchronizeInvoke
' Public Instance Methods
Public Sub BeginInit() Implements ISupportInitialize.BeginInit
Public Sub EndInit() Implements ISupportInitialize.EndInit
Public Function WaitForChanged(ByVal changeType As WatcherChangeTypes) As WaitForChangedResult
Public Function WaitForChanged(ByVal changeType As WatcherChangeTypes, ByVal timeout As Integer) _
    As WaitForChangedResult
' Protected Instance Methods
Overrides Protected Sub Dispose(ByVal disposing As Boolean)
Protected Sub OnChanged(ByVal e As FileSystemEventArgs)
Protected Sub OnCreated(ByVal e As FileSystemEventArgs)
Protected Sub OnDeleted(ByVal e As FileSystemEventArgs)
```

```
Protected Sub OnError(ByVal e As ErrorEventArgs)
Protected Sub OnRenamed(ByVal e As RenamedEventArgs)
' Events
Public Event Changed As FileSystemEventHandler
Public Event Created As FileSystemEventHandler
Public Event Deleted As FileSystemEventHandler
Public Event Error As ErrorEventHandler
Public Event Renamed As RenamedEventHandler
End Class
```

Hierarchy: System.Object→ System.MarshalByRefObject→
System.ComponentModel.Component(System.ComponentModel.IComponent, System.IDisposable)→
FileSystemWatcher(System.ComponentModel.ISupportInitialize)

InternalBufferOverflowException   •   Class

System.IO (system.dll)   *serializable*

This exception is passed by a FileSystemWatcher.Error event. This occurs when the internal buffer of a FileSystemWatcher overflows because too many events have occurred.

```
Public Class InternalBufferOverflowException : Inherits SystemException
' Public Constructors
Public Sub New()
Public Sub New(ByVal message As String)
Public Sub New(ByVal message As String, ByVal inner As Exception)
' Protected Constructors
Protected Sub New(ByVal info As System.Runtime.Serialization.SerializationInfo, _
    ByVal context As System.Runtime.Serialization.StreamingContext)
End Class
```

Hierarchy: System.Object→ System.Exception(System.Runtime.Serialization.ISerializable)→
System.SystemException→ InternalBufferOverflowException

IODescriptionAttribute   Class

System.IO (system.dll)

This custom attribute describes an I/O property or event.

```
Public Class IODescriptionAttribute : Inherits System.ComponentModel.DescriptionAttribute
' Public Constructors
Public Sub New(ByVal description As String)
' Public Instance Properties
Overrides Public ReadOnly Property Description As String
End Class
```

Hierarchy: System.Object→ System.Attribute→ System.ComponentModel.DescriptionAttribute→
IODescriptionAttribute

Valid On: All

IOException   Class

System.IO (mscorlib.dll)   *ECMA, serializable*

This is the base class of all the I/O related exceptions.

```
Public Class IOException : Inherits SystemException
' Public Constructors
Public Sub New()
```

```
  Public Sub New(ByVal message As String)
  Public Sub New(ByVal message As String, ByVal innerException As Exception)
  Public Sub New(ByVal message As String, ByVal hresult As Integer)
' Protected Constructors
  Protected Sub New(ByVal info As System.Runtime.Serialization.SerializationInfo, _
    ByVal context As System.Runtime.Serialization.StreamingContext)
End Class
```

Hierarchy: System.Object→ System.Exception(System.Runtime.Serialization.ISerializable)→
System.SystemException→ IOException

Subclasses: DirectoryNotFoundException, EndOfStreamException, FileLoadException,
FileNotFoundException, PathTooLongException

MemoryStream   Class

System.IO (mscorlib.dll)   *ECMA, serializable, marshal by reference, disposable*

This class is a stream that keeps its data in memory as opposed to on the disk (as a
FileStream does). In addition to the Stream methods, ToArray() writes the entire stream to a
byte array, and WriteTo() dumps the contents of this stream to a different one.

```
Public Class MemoryStream : Inherits Stream
' Public Constructors
  Public Sub New()
  Public Sub New(ByVal buffer As Byte())
  Public Sub New(ByVal buffer As Byte(), ByVal writable As Boolean)
  Public Sub New(ByVal buffer As Byte(), ByVal index As Integer, ByVal count As Integer)
  Public Sub New(ByVal buffer As Byte(), ByVal index As Integer, ByVal count As Integer, ByVal writable As Boolean)
  Public Sub New(ByVal buffer As Byte(), ByVal index As Integer, ByVal count As Integer, ByVal writable As Boolean, _
    ByVal publiclyVisible As Boolean)
  Public Sub New(ByVal capacity As Integer)
' Public Instance Properties
  Overrides Public ReadOnly Property CanRead As Boolean
  Overrides Public ReadOnly Property CanSeek As Boolean
  Overrides Public ReadOnly Property CanWrite As Boolean
  Overridable Public Property Capacity As Integer
  Overrides Public ReadOnly Property Length As Long
  Overrides Public Property Position As Long
' Public Instance Methods
  Overrides Public Sub Close()
  Overrides Public Sub Flush()
  Overridable Public Function GetBuffer() As Byte()
  Overrides Public Function Read(ByRef buffer As Byte(), ByVal offset As Integer, ByVal count As Integer) As Integer
  Overrides Public Function ReadByte() As Integer
  Overrides Public Function Seek(ByVal offset As Long, ByVal loc As SeekOrigin) As Long
  Overrides Public Sub SetLength(ByVal value As Long)
  Overridable Public Function ToArray() As Byte()
  Overrides Public Sub Write(ByVal buffer As Byte(), ByVal offset As Integer, ByVal count As Integer)
  Overrides Public Sub WriteByte(ByVal value As Byte)
  Overridable Public Sub WriteTo(ByVal stream As Stream)
End Class
```

Hierarchy: System.Object→ System.MarshalByRefObject→ Stream(System.IDisposable)→
MemoryStream

NotifyFilters   Enum

System.IO (system.dll)   *serializable, flag*

This type represents the different types of filesystem events you can use a FileSystemWatcher to look for. NotifyFilters allows you to indicate what kind of changes a FileSystemWatcher should respond to.

Public Enum **NotifyFilters**
    FileName = &H000000001
    DirectoryName = &H000000002
    Attributes = &H000000004
    Size = &H000000008
    LastWrite = &H000000010
    LastAccess = &H000000020
    CreationTime = &H000000040
    Security = &H000000100
End Enum

Hierarchy: System.Object→ System.ValueType→ System.Enum(System.IComparable, System.IFormattable, System.IConvertible)→ NotifyFilters

Returned By: FileSystemWatcher.NotifyFilter

Passed To: FileSystemWatcher.NotifyFilter

Path   NotInheritable Class

System.IO (mscorlib.dll)   *ECMA*

This class provides many shared methods for processing strings representing file paths in a platform-independent manner. The shared properties allow you to inspect the file conventions of the system on which the software is running. The shared methods supply an implementation of the frequently performed path manipulations. ChangeExtension() allows you to change the extension of a file and GetExtension() allows you to retrieve it. Combine() combines two file paths (the second argument cannot contain a UNC or a drive letter). GetTempPath() returns the current system temporary storage folder, and the infinitely cooler GetTempFileName() creates a unique temporary filename, then creates a zero-byte file there. IsPathRooted() checks to see if a path contains a root, which can also be retrieved by calling GetPathRoot().

Public NotInheritable Class **Path**
' *Public Shared Fields*
  Public Shared ReadOnly **AltDirectorySeparatorChar** As Char   *= [amp] H00000002F*
  Public Shared ReadOnly **DirectorySeparatorChar** As Char   *= [amp] H00000005C*
  Public Shared ReadOnly **InvalidPathChars** As Char()   *=System.Char()*
  Public Shared ReadOnly **PathSeparator** As Char   *= [amp] H00000003B*
  Public Shared ReadOnly **VolumeSeparatorChar** As Char   *= [amp] H00000003A*
' *Public Shared Methods*
  Public Shared Function **ChangeExtension**(ByVal path As String, ByVal extension As String) As String
  Public Shared Function **Combine**(ByVal path1 As String, ByVal path2 As String) As String
  Public Shared Function **GetDirectoryName**(ByVal path As String) As String
  Public Shared Function **GetExtension**(ByVal path As String) As String
  Public Shared Function **GetFileName**(ByVal path As String) As String
  Public Shared Function **GetFileNameWithoutExtension**(ByVal path As String) As String
  Public Shared Function **GetFullPath**(ByVal path As String) As String
  Public Shared Function **GetPathRoot**(ByVal path As String) As String
  Public Shared Function **GetTempFileName**() As String
  Public Shared Function **GetTempPath**() As String

```
Public Shared Function HasExtension(ByVal path As String) As Boolean
Public Shared Function IsPathRooted(ByVal path As String) As Boolean
End Class
```

PathTooLongException   Class

System.IO (mscorlib.dll)   *ECMA, serializable*

This exception is thrown when you attempt to access or create a file with a name that is too long for the filesystem.

```
Public Class PathTooLongException : Inherits IOException
' Public Constructors
   Public Sub New()
   Public Sub New(ByVal message As String)
   Public Sub New(ByVal message As String, ByVal innerException As Exception)
' Protected Constructors
   Protected Sub New(ByVal info As System.Runtime.Serialization.SerializationInfo, _
      ByVal context As System.Runtime.Serialization.StreamingContext)
End Class
```

Hierarchy: System.Object→ System.Exception(System.Runtime.Serialization.ISerializable)→ System.SystemException→ IOException→ PathTooLongException

RenamedEventArgs   Class

System.IO (system.dll)

This type represents the arguments passed by a FileSystemWatcher.Renamed event.

```
Public Class RenamedEventArgs : Inherits FileSystemEventArgs
' Public Constructors
   Public Sub New(ByVal changeType As WatcherChangeTypes, ByVal directory As String, ByVal name As String, _
      ByVal oldName As String)
' Public Instance Properties
   Public ReadOnly Property OldFullPath As String
   Public ReadOnly Property OldName As String
End Class
```

Hierarchy: System.Object→ System.EventArgs→ FileSystemEventArgs→ RenamedEventArgs

Passed To: FileSystemWatcher.OnRenamed(), RenamedEventHandler.{BeginInvoke(), Invoke()}

RenamedEventHandler   Delegate

System.IO (system.dll)   *serializable*

This delegate is for the FileSystemWatcher.Renamed event.

```
Public Delegate Sub RenamedEventHandler(ByVal sender As Object, ByVal e As RenamedEventArgs)
```

Associated Events: FileSystemWatcher.Renamed()

SeekOrigin   Enum

System.IO (mscorlib.dll)   *ECMA, serializable*

This enumeration is used by the Stream.Seek() method. You can specify that you want to seek either from the beginning with Begin, from the current position with Current, or end with End.

```
Public Enum SeekOrigin
    Begin = 0
    Current = 1
    End = 2
End Enum
```

Hierarchy: System.Object→ System.ValueType→ System.Enum(System.IComparable, System.IFormattable, System.IConvertible)→ SeekOrigin

Passed To: BinaryWriter.Seek(), Stream.Seek()

Stream   MustInherit Class

System.IO (mscorlib.dll)   *ECMA, serializable, marshal by reference, disposable*

This class is the basic building block of I/O in the .NET Framework. Many types of application use a Stream in one way or another. When calling System.Console.WriteLine(), you use a TextWriter, which contains a StreamWriter. When you design an ASP.NET application, the System.Web.UI.Page uses a System.Net.Sockets.NetworkStream. In fact, whenever you access a remote database server you are using a NetworkStream.

To determine whether a given Stream can read, write, or seek, check CanRead, CanWrite, or CanSeek respectively. If your stream can seek, you may seek forward or backward using Seek(). Length reveals the length of the stream, which can also be set by calling SetLength(), and Position allows you to check your current position in the stream.

To perform asynchronous I/O, call BeginRead() or BeginWrite(). Notification of an asynchronous operation comes in two ways: either via an System.AsyncCallback delegate callback passed in as part of the BeginRead()/BeginWrite() call, or else by calling the EndRead() or EndWrite() method explicitly, which blocks the calling thread until the async operation completes.

Streams usually hold on to a precious resource (a network connection or a file handle), which should be freed as soon as it is not needed any more. Because destruction is completely nondeterministic with garbage collection, be sure to call Close() at the end of the Stream's useful lifetime. (Alternatively, call Dispose()—which in turn calls Close()—when you've finished with the Stream.)

```
Public MustInherit Class Stream : Inherits MarshalByRefObject : Implements IDisposable
' Protected Constructors
    Protected Sub New()
' Public Shared Fields
    Public Shared ReadOnly Null As Stream                          =System.IO.Stream+NullStream
' Public Instance Properties
    MustInherit Public ReadOnly Property CanRead As Boolean
    MustInherit Public ReadOnly Property CanSeek As Boolean
    MustInherit Public ReadOnly Property CanWrite As Boolean
    MustInherit Public ReadOnly Property Length As Long
    MustInherit Public Property Position As Long
' Public Instance Methods
    Overridable Public Function BeginRead(ByVal buffer As Byte(), ByVal offset As Integer, ByVal count As Integer, _
        ByVal callback As AsyncCallback, ByVal state As Object) As IAsyncResult
    Overridable Public Function BeginWrite(ByVal buffer As Byte(), ByVal offset As Integer, ByVal count As Integer, _
        ByVal callback As AsyncCallback, ByVal state As Object) As IAsyncResult
    Overridable Public Sub Close()
    Overridable Public Function EndRead(ByVal asyncResult As IAsyncResult) As Integer
    Overridable Public Sub EndWrite(ByVal asyncResult As IAsyncResult)
    MustInherit Public Sub Flush()
```

MustInherit Public Function **Read**(ByRef buffer As Byte(), ByVal offset As Integer, ByVal count As Integer) As Integer
Overridable Public Function **ReadByte**() As Integer
MustInherit Public Function **Seek**(ByVal offset As Long, ByVal origin As SeekOrigin) As Long
MustInherit Public Sub **SetLength**(ByVal value As Long)
MustInherit Public Sub **Write**(ByVal buffer As Byte(), ByVal offset As Integer, ByVal count As Integer)
Overridable Public Sub **WriteByte**(ByVal value As Byte)
' Protected Instance Methods
Overridable Protected Function **CreateWaitHandle**() As WaitHandle
End Class

Hierarchy: System.Object→ System.MarshalByRefObject→ Stream(System.IDisposable)

Subclasses: BufferedStream, FileStream, MemoryStream, System.Net.Sockets.NetworkStream

Returned By: Multiple types

Passed To: Multiple types

StreamReader   Class

System.IO (mscorlib.dll)   *ECMA, serializable, marshal by reference, disposable*

This class is an extension of a TextReader and provides implementations for all its methods. CurrentEncoding returns the current encoding the StreamReader is using. If you would like to discard the buffered data (so it isn't written to a disk or other resource), call DiscardBufferedData().

This class is a quick way to open a file for reading. Simply call the constructor with a string containing the filename, and you can immediately begin reading from the file with methods such as Read(), ReadLine(), or ReadToEnd().

Public Class **StreamReader** : Inherits TextReader
' Public Constructors
Public Sub **New**(ByVal stream As Stream)
Public Sub **New**(ByVal stream As Stream, ByVal detectEncodingFromByteOrderMarks As Boolean)
Public Sub **New**(ByVal stream As Stream, ByVal encoding As System.Text.Encoding)
Public Sub **New**(ByVal stream As Stream, ByVal encoding As System.Text.Encoding, _
  ByVal detectEncodingFromByteOrderMarks As Boolean)
Public Sub **New**(ByVal stream As Stream, ByVal encoding As System.Text.Encoding, _
  ByVal detectEncodingFromByteOrderMarks As Boolean, ByVal bufferSize As Integer)
Public Sub **New**(ByVal path As String)
Public Sub **New**(ByVal path As String, ByVal detectEncodingFromByteOrderMarks As Boolean)
Public Sub **New**(ByVal path As String, ByVal encoding As System.Text.Encoding)
Public Sub **New**(ByVal path As String, ByVal encoding As System.Text.Encoding, _
  ByVal detectEncodingFromByteOrderMarks As Boolean)
Public Sub **New**(ByVal path As String, ByVal encoding As System.Text.Encoding, _
  ByVal detectEncodingFromByteOrderMarks As Boolean, ByVal bufferSize As Integer)
' Public Shared Fields
Public Shared ReadOnly **Null** As StreamReader   *=System.IO.StreamReader+NullStreamReader*
' Public Instance Properties
Overridable Public ReadOnly Property **BaseStream** As Stream
Overridable Public ReadOnly Property **CurrentEncoding** As Encoding
' Public Instance Methods
Overrides Public Sub **Close**()
Public Sub **DiscardBufferedData**()
Overrides Public Function **Peek**() As Integer
Overrides Public Function **Read**() As Integer
Overrides Public Function **Read**(ByRef buffer As Char(), ByVal index As Integer, ByVal count As Integer) As Integer
Overrides Public Function **ReadLine**() As String

System.

Overrides Public Function **ReadToEnd**() As String
' Protected Instance Methods
Overrides Protected Sub **Dispose**(ByVal disposing As Boolean)
End Class

Hierarchy: System.Object→ System.MarshalByRefObject→ TextReader(System.IDisposable)→
StreamReader

Returned By: System.Diagnostics.Process.{StandardError, StandardOutput}, File.OpenText(),
FileInfo.OpenText()

StreamWriter   Class

System.IO (mscorlib.dll)   *ECMA, serializable, marshal by reference, disposable*

This class implements TextWriter and provides all its methods. If you set the AutoFlush
property, every call to Write() or WriteLine() flushes the buffer.

This class is a quick way to open a file for writing. Call the constructor with a string
containing the filename, and you can immediately begin writing to the file with Write()
or WriteLine().

Public Class **StreamWriter** : Inherits TextWriter
' Public Constructors
Public Sub **New**(ByVal stream As Stream)
Public Sub **New**(ByVal stream As Stream, ByVal encoding As System.Text.Encoding)
Public Sub **New**(ByVal stream As Stream, ByVal encoding As System.Text.Encoding, ByVal bufferSize As Integer)
Public Sub **New**(ByVal path As String)
Public Sub **New**(ByVal path As String, ByVal append As Boolean)
Public Sub **New**(ByVal path As String, ByVal append As Boolean, ByVal encoding As System.Text.Encoding)
Public Sub **New**(ByVal path As String, ByVal append As Boolean, ByVal encoding As System.Text.Encoding, _
   ByVal bufferSize As Integer)
' Public Shared Fields
Public Shared ReadOnly **Null** As StreamWriter   =*System.IO.StreamWriter*
' Public Instance Properties
Overridable Public Property **AutoFlush** As Boolean
Overridable Public ReadOnly Property **BaseStream** As Stream
Overrides Public ReadOnly Property **Encoding** As Encoding
' Public Instance Methods
Overrides Public Sub **Close**()
Overrides Public Sub **Flush**()
Overrides Public Sub **Write**(ByVal value As Char)
Overrides Public Sub **Write**(ByVal buffer As Char())
Overrides Public Sub **Write**(ByVal buffer As Char(), ByVal index As Integer, ByVal count As Integer)
Overrides Public Sub **Write**(ByVal value As String)
' Protected Instance Methods
Overrides Protected Sub **Dispose**(ByVal disposing As Boolean)
Overrides Protected Sub **Finalize**()
End Class

Hierarchy: System.Object→ System.MarshalByRefObject→ TextWriter(System.IDisposable)→
StreamWriter

Returned By: System.Diagnostics.Process.StandardInput, File.{AppendText(), CreateText()},
FileInfo.{AppendText(), CreateText()}

StringReader **Class**

System.IO (mscorlib.dll) *ECMA, serializable, marshal by reference, disposable*

This class implements TextReader and provides all its methods. It is useful when you would like to deal with a System.String in the same way you would work with a Text-Reader.

Public Class **StringReader** : Inherits TextReader
' *Public Constructors*
 Public Sub **New**(ByVal s As String)
' *Public Instance Methods*
 Overrides Public Sub **Close**()
 Overrides Public Function **Peek**() As Integer
 Overrides Public Function **Read**() As Integer
 Overrides Public Function **Read**(ByRef buffer As Char(), ByVal index As Integer, ByVal count As Integer) As Integer
 Overrides Public Function **ReadLine**() As String
 Overrides Public Function **ReadToEnd**() As String
' *Protected Instance Methods*
 Overrides Protected Sub **Dispose**(ByVal disposing As Boolean)
End Class

Hierarchy: System.Object→ System.MarshalByRefObject→ TextReader(System.IDisposable)→ StringReader

StringWriter **Class**

System.IO (mscorlib.dll) *ECMA, serializable, marshal by reference, disposable*

This class provides an alternative to using a System.Text.StringBuilder to create a string. This allows you to create a string in the exact same manner you would create a text file, which can be very useful. It implements all of the TextWriter methods.

Public Class **StringWriter** : Inherits TextWriter
' *Public Constructors*
 Public Sub **New**()
 Public Sub **New**(ByVal formatProvider As IFormatProvider)
 Public Sub **New**(ByVal sb As System.Text.StringBuilder)
 Public Sub **New**(ByVal sb As System.Text.StringBuilder, ByVal formatProvider As IFormatProvider)
' *Public Instance Properties*
 Overrides Public ReadOnly Property **Encoding** As Encoding
' *Public Instance Methods*
 Overrides Public Sub **Close**()
 Overridable Public Function **GetStringBuilder**() As StringBuilder
 Overrides Public Function **ToString**() As String
 Overrides Public Sub **Write**(ByVal value As Char)
 Overrides Public Sub **Write**(ByVal buffer As Char(), ByVal index As Integer, ByVal count As Integer)
 Overrides Public Sub **Write**(ByVal value As String)
' *Protected Instance Methods*
 Overrides Protected Sub **Dispose**(ByVal disposing As Boolean)
End Class

Hierarchy: System.Object→ System.MarshalByRefObject→ TextWriter(System.IDisposable)→ StringWriter

TextReader

MustInherit Class

System.IO (mscorlib.dll)   *ECMA, serializable, marshal by reference, disposable*

This class is optimized to read a stream of sequential characters. The Read() methods read data from the front of a stream, and Peek() looks at the first character without advancing the position of an associated stream. If you need a thread-safe TextReader, use Synchronized() to create a thread-safe copy of a TextReader.

```
Public MustInherit Class TextReader : Inherits MarshalByRefObject : Implements IDisposable
' Protected Constructors
   Protected Sub New()
' Public Shared Fields
   Public Shared ReadOnly Null As TextReader                              =System.IO.TextReader+NullTextReader
' Public Shared Methods
   Public Shared Function Synchronized(ByVal reader As TextReader) As TextReader
' Public Instance Methods
   Overridable Public Sub Close()
   Overridable Public Function Peek() As Integer
   Overridable Public Function Read() As Integer
   Overridable Public Function Read(ByRef buffer As Char(), ByVal index As Integer, ByVal count As Integer) As Integer
   Overridable Public Function ReadBlock(ByRef buffer As Char(), ByVal index As Integer, ByVal count As Integer) _
      As Integer
   Overridable Public Function ReadLine() As String
   Overridable Public Function ReadToEnd() As String
' Protected Instance Methods
   Overridable Protected Sub Dispose(ByVal disposing As Boolean)
End Class
```

Hierarchy: System.Object→ System.MarshalByRefObject→ TextReader(System.IDisposable)

Subclasses: StreamReader, StringReader

Returned By: System.Console.In, System.Xml.XmlTextReader.GetRemainder()

Passed To: System.Console.SetIn(), System.Xml.XmlDocument.Load(), System.Xml.XmlTextReader.XmlTextReader(), System.Xml.XPath.XPathDocument.XPathDocument()

TextWriter

MustInherit Class

System.IO (mscorlib.dll)   *ECMA, serializable, marshal by reference, disposable*

This class writes strings of characters to a stream. Encoding sets the encoding of the produced text; change the object that provides formatting by setting FormatProvider. To change the newline character produced in your text, set the NewLine property. To write to a stream, call either Write() or WriteLine(). To clear the current buffer of characters, use Flush(). As always, Close() allows you to free the resources in use by the TextWriter.

```
Public MustInherit Class TextWriter : Inherits MarshalByRefObject : Implements IDisposable
' Protected Constructors
   Protected Sub New()
   Protected Sub New(ByVal formatProvider As IFormatProvider)
' Public Shared Fields
   Public Shared ReadOnly Null As TextWriter                              =System.IO.TextWriter+NullTextWriter
' Protected Instance Fields
   protected CoreNewLine As Char()
' Public Instance Properties
   MustInherit Public ReadOnly Property Encoding As Encoding
   Overridable Public ReadOnly Property FormatProvider As IFormatProvider
   Overridable Public Property NewLine As String
' Public Shared Methods
```

Public Shared Function **Synchronized**(ByVal writer As TextWriter) As TextWriter
' *Public Instance Methods*
Overridable Public Sub **Close**()
Overridable Public Sub **Flush**()
Overridable Public Sub **Write**(ByVal value As Boolean)
Overridable Public Sub **Write**(ByVal value As Char)
Overridable Public Sub **Write**(ByVal buffer As Char())
Overridable Public Sub **Write**(ByVal buffer As Char(), ByVal index As Integer, ByVal count As Integer)
Overridable Public Sub **Write**(ByVal value As Decimal)
Overridable Public Sub **Write**(ByVal value As Double)
Overridable Public Sub **Write**(ByVal value As Integer)
Overridable Public Sub **Write**(ByVal value As Long)
Overridable Public Sub **Write**(ByVal value As Object)
Overridable Public Sub **Write**(ByVal value As Single)
Overridable Public Sub **Write**(ByVal value As String)
Overridable Public Sub **Write**(ByVal format As String, ByVal arg0 As Object)
Overridable Public Sub **Write**(ByVal format As String, ParamArray arg As Object())
Overridable Public Sub **Write**(ByVal format As String, ByVal arg0 As Object, ByVal arg1 As Object)
Overridable Public Sub **Write**(ByVal format As String, ByVal arg0 As Object, ByVal arg1 As Object, _
   ByVal arg2 As Object)
Overridable Public Sub **Write**(ByVal value As UInt32)
Overridable Public Sub **Write**(ByVal value As UInt64)
Overridable Public Sub **WriteLine**()
Overridable Public Sub **WriteLine**(ByVal value As Boolean)
Overridable Public Sub **WriteLine**(ByVal value As Char)
Overridable Public Sub **WriteLine**(ByVal buffer As Char())
Overridable Public Sub **WriteLine**(ByVal buffer As Char(), ByVal index As Integer, ByVal count As Integer)
Overridable Public Sub **WriteLine**(ByVal value As Decimal)
Overridable Public Sub **WriteLine**(ByVal value As Double)
Overridable Public Sub **WriteLine**(ByVal value As Integer)
Overridable Public Sub **WriteLine**(ByVal value As Long)
Overridable Public Sub **WriteLine**(ByVal value As Object)
Overridable Public Sub **WriteLine**(ByVal value As Single)
Overridable Public Sub **WriteLine**(ByVal value As String)
Overridable Public Sub **WriteLine**(ByVal format As String, ByVal arg0 As Object)
Overridable Public Sub **WriteLine**(ByVal format As String, ParamArray arg As Object())
Overridable Public Sub **WriteLine**(ByVal format As String, ByVal arg0 As Object, ByVal arg1 As Object)
Overridable Public Sub **WriteLine**(ByVal format As String, ByVal arg0 As Object, ByVal arg1 As Object, _
   ByVal arg2 As Object)
Overridable Public Sub **WriteLine**(ByVal value As UInt32)
Overridable Public Sub **WriteLine**(ByVal value As UInt64)
' *Protected Instance Methods*
Overridable Protected Sub **Dispose**(ByVal disposing As Boolean)
End Class

Hierarchy: System.Object→ System.MarshalByRefObject→ TextWriter(System.IDisposable)

Subclasses: StreamWriter, StringWriter

Returned By: System.Console.{Error, Out}, System.Diagnostics.TextWriterTraceListener.Writer

Passed To: System.Console.{SetError(), SetOut()},
System.Diagnostics.TextWriterTraceListener.{TextWriterTraceListener(), Writer},
System.Xml.XmlDocument.Save(), System.Xml.XmlTextWriter.XmlTextWriter(),
System.Xml.Xsl.XslTransform.Transform()

WaitForChangedResult   Structure

System.IO (system.dll)

This structure contains the changes on a file. This is used to construct FileSystemEventArgs and RenamedEventArgs.

Public Structure **WaitForChangedResult**
' Public Instance Properties
   Public Property **ChangeType** As WatcherChangeTypes
   Public Property **Name** As String
   Public Property **OldName** As String
   Public Property **TimedOut** As Boolean
End Structure

Hierarchy: System.Object→ System.ValueType→ WaitForChangedResult

Returned By: FileSystemWatcher.WaitForChanged()

WatcherChangeTypes   Enum

System.IO (system.dll)   *serializable, flag*

This enumeration represents the different types of changes that can occur on a file. It is used by FileSystemEventArgs.

Public Enum **WatcherChangeTypes**
     Created = &H000000001
     Deleted = &H000000002
     Changed = &H000000004
     Renamed = &H000000008
     All = &H00000000F
End Enum

Hierarchy: System.Object→ System.ValueType→ System.Enum(System.IComparable, System.IFormattable, System.IConvertible)→ WatcherChangeTypes

Returned By: FileSystemEventArgs.ChangeType, WaitForChangedResult.ChangeType

Passed To: FileSystemEventArgs.FileSystemEventArgs(), FileSystemWatcher.WaitForChanged(), RenamedEventArgs.RenamedEventArgs(), WaitForChangedResult.ChangeType

CHAPTER 10

System.IO.IsolatedStorage

System.IO.IsolatedStorage allows you to access an isolated area of a filesystem for your application. This is useful when access to the System.IO classes is not possible. The security settings of the .NET Framework prohibit web applications and downloaded controls from accessing the local filesystem directly, but those settings allow them to use System.IO.IsolatedStorage. Applications' storage areas are isolated from one another, so anything in isolated storage is protected from untrusted applications. The size of isolated storage is limited, so an untrusted application cannot create a denial-of-service condition by filling your hard disk with data.

When you use isolated storage, the runtime sets aside disk space for a given level of isolation (specified using IsolatedStorageScope). If you use Windows 2000 or XP, *<SYSTEMDRIVE>\Documents and Settings\<user>\Application Data* contains the isolated storage area if roaming is turned on, and *<SYSTEMDRIVE>\Documents and Settings\<user>\Local Settings\Application Data* contains the storage area if roaming is not on. Applications can use this area as a data store for their particular persistence needs. Figure 10-1 shows the inheritance diagram for this namespace.

INormalizeForIsolatedStorage   Interface
System.IO.IsolatedStorage (mscorlib.dll)

This interface exposes Normalize(), which returns a normalized copy of the object on which it is called. You usually use this method if you are inheriting from IsolatedStorage and you want to see if a store already exists.

```
Public Interface INormalizeForIsolatedStorage
' Public Instance Methods
   Public Function Normalize() As Object
End Interface
```

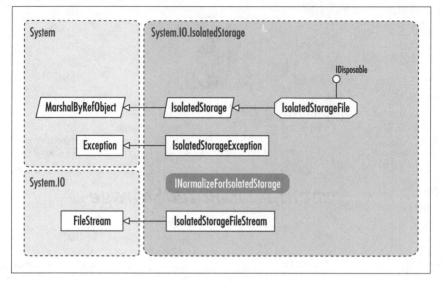

Figure 10–1. The System.IO.IsolatedStorage namespace

IsolatedStorage

MustInherit Class

System.IO.IsolatedStorage (mscorlib.dll)

marshal by reference

This is the MustInherit base class from which all isolated storage classes must inherit. AssemblyIdentity returns the assembly identity associated with the isolated store, and DomainIdentity returns the domain associated with the store. Use CurrentSize to detect how much space the store takes up on the disk, and use MaximumSize to detect the maximum storage allowed. Scope returns an IsolatedStorageScope enumeration for the store. If you wish to delete the isolated store and all its contents completely, call Remove().

```
Public MustInherit Class IsolatedStorage : Inherits MarshalByRefObject
' Protected Constructors
    Protected Sub New()
' Public Instance Properties
    Public ReadOnly Property AssemblyIdentity As Object
    Overridable Public ReadOnly Property CurrentSize As UInt64
    Public ReadOnly Property DomainIdentity As Object
    Overridable Public ReadOnly Property MaximumSize As UInt64
    Public ReadOnly Property Scope As IsolatedStorageScope
' Protected Instance Properties
    Overridable Protected Property SeparatorExternal As Char
    Overridable Protected Property SeparatorInternal As Char
' Public Instance Methods
    MustInherit Public Sub Remove()
' Protected Instance Methods
    MustInherit Protected Function GetPermission(ByVal ps As System.Security.PermissionSet) _
        As IsolatedStoragePermission
    Protected Sub InitStore(ByVal scope As IsolatedStorageScope, ByVal domainEvidenceType As Type, _
        ByVal assemblyEvidenceType As Type)
End Class
```

Hierarchy: System.Object→ System.MarshalByRefObject→ IsolatedStorage

Subclasses: IsolatedStorageFile

IsolatedStorageException   **Class**

System.IO.IsolatedStorage (mscorlib.dll)   *serializable*

This exception represents isolated storage errors.

Public Class **IsolatedStorageException** : Inherits Exception
' *Public Constructors*
    Public Sub **New**()
    Public Sub **New**(ByVal message As String)
    Public Sub **New**(ByVal message As String, ByVal inner As Exception)
' *Protected Constructors*
    Protected Sub **New**(ByVal info As System.Runtime.Serialization.SerializationInfo, _
        ByVal context As System.Runtime.Serialization.StreamingContext)
End Class

Hierarchy: System.Object→ System.Exception(System.Runtime.Serialization.ISerializable)→
IsolatedStorageException

IsolatedStorageFile   **NotInheritable Class**

System.IO.IsolatedStorage (mscorlib.dll)   *marshal by reference, disposable*

This class represents an isolated-storage filesystem area that can contain files and directories. The sharedGetStore() returns a reference to the current store. Call GetStore() only
with the proper IsolatedStorageScope enumerations set. There are two shortcuts for this
method: GetUserStoreForAssembly() returns the same store as GetStore() with IsolatedStor-
ageScope.User | IsolatedStorageScope.Assembly as its first argument, and GetUserStoreForDo-
main() returns as though GetStore() was called with IsolatedStorageScope.User |
IsolatedStorageScope.Assembly | IsolatedStorageScope.Domain. GetEnumerator() returns all valid
types of storage isolation for the specified assembly and domain.

The rest of the methods for this class allow you to work with files and directories. Cre-
ateDirectory() and DeleteDirectory() allow you to create and delete directories, just as Delete-
File() allows you to delete files (use an IsolatedStorageFileStream to create them). Close()
allows you to close a store opened with GetStore(). GetFileNames() returns an array of filenames matching a given filter.

Public NotInheritable Class **IsolatedStorageFile** : Inherits IsolatedStorage : Implements IDisposable
' *Public Instance Properties*
    Overrides Public ReadOnly Property **CurrentSize** As UInt64
    Overrides Public ReadOnly Property **MaximumSize** As UInt64
' *Public Shared Methods*
    Public Shared Function **GetEnumerator**(ByVal scope As IsolatedStorageScope) As IEnumerator
    Public Shared Function **GetStore**(ByVal scope As IsolatedStorageScope,   _
        ByVal domainEvidence As System.Security.Policy.Evidence, ByVal domainEvidenceType As Type,   _
        ByVal assemblyEvidence As System.Security.Policy.Evidence, ByVal assemblyEvidenceType As Type) _
        As IsolatedStorageFile
    Public Shared Function **GetStore**(ByVal scope As IsolatedStorageScope, ByVal domainIdentity As Object, _
        ByVal assemblyIdentity As Object) As IsolatedStorageFile
    Public Shared Function **GetStore**(ByVal scope As IsolatedStorageScope, ByVal domainEvidenceType As Type, _
        ByVal assemblyEvidenceType As Type) As IsolatedStorageFile
    Public Shared Function **GetUserStoreForAssembly**() As IsolatedStorageFile
    Public Shared Function **GetUserStoreForDomain**() As IsolatedStorageFile
    Public Shared Sub **Remove**(ByVal scope As IsolatedStorageScope)
' *Public Instance Methods*

Public Sub **Close**()
Public Sub **CreateDirectory**(ByVal dir As String)
Public Sub **DeleteDirectory**(ByVal dir As String)
Public Sub **DeleteFile**(ByVal file As String)
Public Sub **Dispose**() Implements IDisposable.Dispose
Public Function **GetDirectoryNames**(ByVal searchPattern As String) As String()
Public Function **GetFileNames**(ByVal searchPattern As String) As String()
Overrides Public Sub **Remove**()
' *Protected Instance Methods*
Overrides Protected Sub **Finalize**()
Overrides Protected Function **GetPermission**(ByVal ps As System.Security.PermissionSet) _
   As IsolatedStoragePermission
End Class

Hierarchy: System.Object→ System.MarshalByRefObject→ IsolatedStorage→
IsolatedStorageFile(System.IDisposable)

Passed To: IsolatedStorageFileStream.IsolatedStorageFileStream()

IsolatedStorageFileStream   Class

System.IO.IsolatedStorage (mscorlib.dll)   *marshal by reference, disposable*

This class is simply a System.IO.FileStream implementation for isolated storage. Use it to
create and modify isolated storage files.

Public Class **IsolatedStorageFileStream** : Inherits System.IO.FileStream
' *Public Constructors*
Public Sub **New**(ByVal path As String, ByVal mode As System.IO.FileMode)
Public Sub **New**(ByVal path As String, ByVal mode As System.IO.FileMode, ByVal access As System.IO.FileAccess)
Public Sub **New**(ByVal path As String, ByVal mode As System.IO.FileMode, ByVal access As System.IO.FileAccess, _
   ByVal share As System.IO.FileShare)
Public Sub **New**(ByVal path As String, ByVal mode As System.IO.FileMode, ByVal access As System.IO.FileAccess, _
   ByVal share As System.IO.FileShare, ByVal bufferSize As Integer)
Public Sub **New**(ByVal path As String, ByVal mode As System.IO.FileMode, ByVal access As System.IO.FileAccess, _
   ByVal share As System.IO.FileShare, ByVal bufferSize As Integer, ByVal isf As IsolatedStorageFile)
Public Sub **New**(ByVal path As String, ByVal mode As System.IO.FileMode, ByVal access As System.IO.FileAccess, _
   ByVal share As System.IO.FileShare, ByVal isf As IsolatedStorageFile)
Public Sub **New**(ByVal path As String, ByVal mode As System.IO.FileMode, ByVal access As System.IO.FileAccess, _
   ByVal isf As IsolatedStorageFile)
Public Sub **New**(ByVal path As String, ByVal mode As System.IO.FileMode, ByVal isf As IsolatedStorageFile)
' *Public Instance Properties*
Overrides Public ReadOnly Property **CanRead** As Boolean
Overrides Public ReadOnly Property **CanSeek** As Boolean
Overrides Public ReadOnly Property **CanWrite** As Boolean
Overrides Public ReadOnly Property **Handle** As IntPtr
Overrides Public ReadOnly Property **IsAsync** As Boolean
Overrides Public ReadOnly Property **Length** As Long
Overrides Public Property **Position** As Long
' *Public Instance Methods*
Overrides Public Function **BeginRead**(ByVal buffer As Byte(), ByVal offset As Integer, ByVal numBytes As Integer, _
   ByVal userCallback As AsyncCallback, ByVal stateObject As Object) As IAsyncResult
Overrides Public Function **BeginWrite**(ByVal buffer As Byte(), ByVal offset As Integer, ByVal numBytes As Integer, _
   ByVal userCallback As AsyncCallback, ByVal stateObject As Object) As IAsyncResult
Overrides Public Sub **Close**()
Overrides Public Function **EndRead**(ByVal asyncResult As IAsyncResult) As Integer
Overrides Public Sub **EndWrite**(ByVal asyncResult As IAsyncResult)
Overrides Public Sub **Flush**()

Overrides Public Function **Read**(ByVal buffer As Byte(), ByVal offset As Integer, ByVal count As Integer) As Integer
Overrides Public Function **ReadByte**() As Integer
Overrides Public Function **Seek**(ByVal offset As Long, ByVal origin As System.IO.SeekOrigin) As Long
Overrides Public Sub **SetLength**(ByVal value As Long)
Overrides Public Sub **Write**(ByVal buffer As Byte(), ByVal offset As Integer, ByVal count As Integer)
Overrides Public Sub **WriteByte**(ByVal value As Byte)
' *Protected Instance Methods*
Overrides Protected Sub **Dispose**(ByVal disposing As Boolean)
End Class

Hierarchy: System.Object→ System.MarshalByRefObject→
System.IO.Stream(System.IDisposable)→ System.IO.FileStream→ IsolatedStorageFileStream

IsolatedStorageScope   Enum

System.IO.IsolatedStorage (mscorlib.dll)   *serializable, flag*

This enumeration allows you to specify the levels of isolation an IsolatedStorageFile store should have. For example, if you call IsolatedStorageFile.GetStore() with Assembly, the isolated storage cannot be accessed by code from another assembly. Roaming allows the isolated store to be placed in a roaming profile; without it, the store does not roam with the user.

Public Enum **IsolatedStorageScope**
    None = &H000000000
    User = &H000000001
    Domain = &H000000002
    Assembly = &H000000004
    Roaming = &H000000008
End Enum

Hierarchy: System.Object→ System.ValueType→ System.Enum(System.IComparable,
System.IFormattable, System.IConvertible)→ IsolatedStorageScope

Returned By: IsolatedStorage.Scope

Passed To: IsolatedStorage.InitStore(), IsolatedStorageFile.{GetEnumerator(), GetStore(), Remove()}

CHAPTER 11

System.Net

System.Net supports a high-level API for working with common Internet protocols (HTTP being the principal example) without having to deal with low-level details (such as the actual protocol format). In addition, this namespace provides some high-level constructs for working with networks—TCP/IP in particular.

Most .NET programmers will work with either the WebClient type, which provides the most high-level view of doing HTTP-style request/response communications over a TCP/IP network (such as the Internet), or else the slightly lower-level WebRequest and WebResponse types. The choice between the two is really not all that difficult—for most high-level, protocol-agnostic work, WebClient will likely be the preferred choice. If protocol-specific actions need to be taken (such as specifying additional headers as part of an HTTP request, for example), then likely the .NET programmer will want to work with WebRequest and WebResponse. To be specific, the .NET programmer will work with the concrete derived types HttpWebRequest and HttpWebResponse.

As shipped, the .NET Framework Class Library provides implementations for three URI protocol schemes: HTTP, HTTPS, and files (http:, https:, and file:, respectively). For support of other URI types (such as FTP, NNTP, or POP3), a new derivative of WebRequest and WebResponse must be written, an Abstract Factory type implementing the IWebRequestCreate interface must be created, and an instance of it (along with the protocol scheme prefix) must be registered with WebRequest.RegisterPrefix(). Figure 11-1 shows the collaborations between the concrete classes HttpWebRequest, HttpWebResponse, FileWebRequest, and FileWebResponse.

Figure 11-2 shows the composition of the ServicePoint class, and Figure 11-3 shows the remaining types in this namespace.

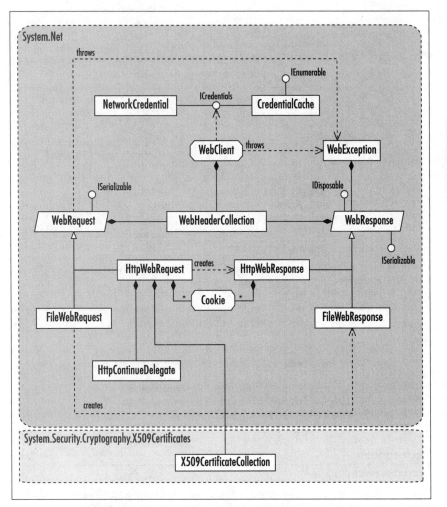

Figure 11–1. The MustInherit WebRequest, WebResponse, and related concrete types

AuthenticationManager   Class

System.Net (system.dll)   *ECMA*

This class is responsible for finding an authentication module to authorize access to network resources. You do not need to use this class unless you have defined your own authentication scheme. By default, Basic, Digest, NTLM, and Kerberos authentication schemes are supported. This, for the most part, covers the needs of 99.9% of all .NET programmers in the world. Kerberos is not supported on Windows 95/98 or on Windows ME.

Public Class **AuthenticationManager**
' Public Shared Properties
   Public Shared ReadOnly Property **RegisteredModules** As IEnumerator
' Public Shared Methods
   Public Shared Function **Authenticate**(ByVal challenge As String, ByVal request As WebRequest, _

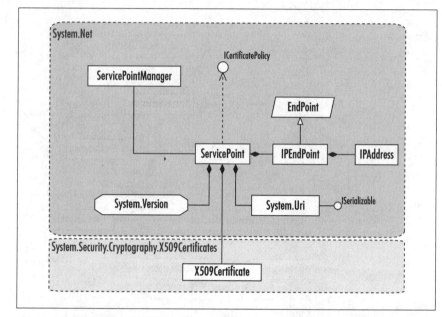

Figure 11-2. Endpoints, service points, and associated types

```
       ByVal credentials As ICredentials) As Authorization
       Public Shared Function PreAuthenticate(ByVal request As WebRequest, ByVal credentials As ICredentials) _
          As Authorization
       Public Shared Sub Register(ByVal authenticationModule As IAuthenticationModule)
       Public Shared Sub Unregister(ByVal authenticationModule As IAuthenticationModule)
       Public Shared Sub Unregister(ByVal authenticationScheme As String)
    End Class
```

Authorization   Class

System.Net (system.dll)   *ECMA*

This class encapsulates an authentication message that AuthenticationManager sends to a
remote server. The Message property contains the string that is sent to the server in
response to its authentication challenge.

The Authorization class is used by implementations of IAuthenticationModule and by AuthenticationManager. You should not need to use it directly unless you have implemented your
own authentication scheme.

```
Public Class Authorization
' Public Constructors
   Public Sub New(ByVal token As String)
   Public Sub New(ByVal token As String, ByVal finished As Boolean)
   Public Sub New(ByVal token As String, ByVal finished As Boolean, ByVal connectionGroupId As String)
' Public Instance Properties
   Public ReadOnly Property Complete As Boolean
   Public ReadOnly Property ConnectionGroupId As String
   Public ReadOnly Property Message As String
   Public Property ProtectionRealm As String()
End Class
```

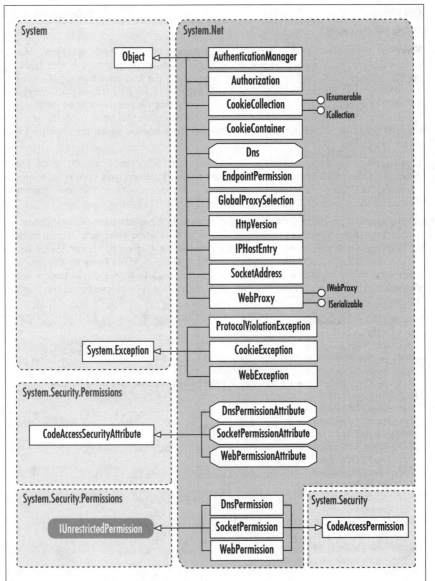

Figure 11–3. Other classes in the System.Net namespace

Returned By: AuthenticationManager.{Authenticate(), PreAuthenticate()},
IAuthenticationModule.{Authenticate(), PreAuthenticate()}

Cookie

NotInheritable Class

System.Net (system.dll)

serializable

This class represents an HTTP cookie, as standardized by RFC 2965 (*ftp://ftp.isi.edu/in-notes/rfc2965.txt*). A cookie represents a simple name-value pair that is sent back by the HTTP User-Agent on each subsequent request to the URL host that set the cookie. The rules governing the visibility, scope, and lifetime of cookies is well documented in the RFC; see that document for details. The Cookie has properties defined on it corresponding to the settable values in the RFC—principally, the Value property sets the value of the cookie, and the Name property sets the name by which the cookie's value can be retrieved.

As a User-Agent, adding a Cookie to an HttpWebRequest is as simple as adding the Cookie instance to the HttpWebRequest.CookieContainer property. When you receive a response from an HTTP server, it may contain one or more cookies. Use the HttpWebResponse.Cookies collection to obtain the cookies that the HTTP server sent you.

Note that, as a User-Agent (the client), it is the .NET programmer's responsibility for maintaining all the semantics of the RFC—that is, the cookie must only be sent back to the host that set it, the cookie can only be sent back if it obeys the "path" prefix set on the cookie, and so forth. Failure to do so could result in different hosts viewing cookies that they didn't set, which is a potential security hole (albeit only if a host puts sensitive material into the cookie in the first place). None of this is implemented in the HttpWebRequest or Cookie types.

Public NotInheritable Class **Cookie**
' *Public Constructors*
   Public Sub **New**()
   Public Sub **New**(ByVal name As String, ByVal value As String)
   Public Sub **New**(ByVal name As String, ByVal value As String, ByVal path As String)
   Public Sub **New**(ByVal name As String, ByVal value As String, ByVal path As String, ByVal domain As String)
' *Public Instance Properties*
   Public Property **Comment** As String
   Public Property **CommentUri** As Uri
   Public Property **Discard** As Boolean
   Public Property **Domain** As String
   Public Property **Expired** As Boolean
   Public Property **Expires** As Date
   Public Property **Name** As String
   Public Property **Path** As String
   Public Property **Port** As String
   Public Property **Secure** As Boolean
   Public ReadOnly Property **TimeStamp** As Date
   Public Property **Value** As String
   Public Property **Version** As Integer
' *Public Instance Methods*
   Overrides Public Function **Equals**(ByVal comparand As Object) As Boolean
   Overrides Public Function **GetHashCode**() As Integer
   Overrides Public Function **ToString**() As String
End Class

Returned By: CookieCollection.this

Passed To: CookieCollection.Add(), CookieContainer.Add()

CookieCollection   Class

System.Net (system.dll)   *serializable*

This class is a specialized collection for holding cookies. It's used by HttpWebResponse to represent a set of cookies returned by a server. By default, the IsReadOnly property is set to true.

```
Public Class CookieCollection : Implements ICollection, IEnumerable
' Public Constructors
   Public Sub New()
' Public Instance Properties
   Public ReadOnly Property Count As Integer Implements ICollection.Count
   Public ReadOnly Property IsReadOnly As Boolean
   Public ReadOnly Property IsSynchronized As Boolean Implements ICollection.IsSynchronized
   Public Default ReadOnly Property Item (ByVal index As Integer) As Cookie
   Public Default ReadOnly Property Item (ByVal name As String) As Cookie
   Public ReadOnly Property SyncRoot As Object Implements ICollection.SyncRoot
' Public Instance Methods
   Public Sub Add(ByVal cookie As Cookie)
   Public Sub Add(ByVal cookies As CookieCollection)
   Public Sub CopyTo(ByVal array As Array, ByVal index As Integer)  Implements ICollection.CopyTo
   Public Function GetEnumerator() As IEnumerator Implements IEnumerable.GetEnumerator
End Class
```

Returned By: CookieContainer.GetCookies(), HttpWebResponse.Cookies

Passed To: CookieContainer.Add(), HttpWebResponse.Cookies

CookieContainer   Class

System.Net (system.dll)   *serializable*

This class is a container that holds cookies and organizes them by URI. You can add a Cookie or CookieCollection to a container using the simplest forms of the Add() method, or you can use the forms of the Add() method that take a System.Uri argument. You can retrieve all the cookies for a given URI using the GetCookies() method.

```
Public Class CookieContainer
' Public Constructors
   Public Sub New()
   Public Sub New(ByVal capacity As Integer)
   Public Sub New(ByVal capacity As Integer, ByVal perDomainCapacity As Integer, ByVal maxCookieSize As Integer)
' Public Shared Fields
   Public const DefaultCookieLengthLimit As Integer                               =4096
   Public const DefaultCookieLimit As Integer                                     =300
   Public const DefaultPerDomainCookieLimit As Integer                            =20
' Public Instance Properties
   Public Property Capacity As Integer
   Public ReadOnly Property Count As Integer
   Public Property MaxCookieSize As Integer
   Public Property PerDomainCapacity As Integer
' Public Instance Methods
   Public Sub Add(ByVal cookie As Cookie)
   Public Sub Add(ByVal cookies As CookieCollection)
   Public Sub Add(ByVal uri As Uri, ByVal cookie As Cookie)
   Public Sub Add(ByVal uri As Uri, ByVal cookies As CookieCollection)
   Public Function GetCookieHeader(ByVal uri As Uri) As String
   Public Function GetCookies(ByVal uri As Uri) As CookieCollection
```

```
Public Sub SetCookies(ByVal uri As Uri, ByVal cookieHeader As String)
End Class
```

Returned By: HttpWebRequest.CookieContainer

Passed To: HttpWebRequest.CookieContainer

CookieException
Class

System.Net (system.dll)
serializable

This exception signals an error encountered during a cookie-related operation.

```
Public Class CookieException : Inherits FormatException
' Public Constructors
   Public Sub New()
' Protected Constructors
   Protected Sub New(ByVal serializationInfo As System.Runtime.Serialization.SerializationInfo, _
      ByVal streamingContext As System.Runtime.Serialization.StreamingContext)
End Class
```

Hierarchy: System.Object→ System.Exception(System.Runtime.Serialization.ISerializable)→
System.SystemException→ System.FormatException→ CookieException

CredentialCache
Class

System.Net (system.dll)
ECMA

This class maintains credentials for multiple network resources. If you are developing a client application that needs to authenticate itself to more than one server, you can store an instance of this class in the WebRequest.Credentials property.

After you create an instance of this class, use the Add() method to associate NetworkCredential objects with a URI and authentication type (using a string such as "Basic" or "Digest"). Then you can assign the CredentialCache instance to the WebRequest.Credentials property to use the credentials for future web requests.

```
Public Class CredentialCache : Implements ICredentials, IEnumerable
' Public Constructors
   Public Sub New()
' Public Shared Properties
   Public Shared ReadOnly Property DefaultCredentials As ICredentials
' Public Instance Methods
   Public Sub Add(ByVal uriPrefix As Uri, ByVal authType As String, ByVal cred As NetworkCredential)
   Public Function GetCredential(ByVal uriPrefix As Uri, ByVal authType As String) As NetworkCredential _
      Implements ICredentials.GetCredential
   Public Function GetEnumerator() As IEnumerator Implements IEnumerable.GetEnumerator
   Public Sub Remove(ByVal uriPrefix As Uri, ByVal authType As String)
End Class
```

Dns
NotInheritable Class

System.Net (system.dll)
ECMA

This type offers up a collection of shared methods for resolving DNS (Domain Name Service) operations. Because raw IP addresses (such as 192.168.0.1) can be difficult for humans to remember, DNS servers take human-friendly names (such as "www.oreilly.com") and in turn translate them into IP addresses and/or back again. This ability can be useful in a variety of scenarios, including the simple logging of clients who have visited a web site recently. (Note that this is not a secure way of tracking usage—even a simple attacker can spoof the return address of an IP packet, so don't rely on this mechanism for any kind of security validation or audit trail.)

The GetHostByName() method takes a hostname (such as "www.oreilly.com") and returns the corresponding IPHostEntry instance—this IPHostEntry instance is used later in several of the System.Net and System.Net.Sockets types. This method (along with the paired method Resolve()) can be invoked asynchronously using the BeginGetHostByName() or BeginResolve() methods. Like all async methods in the .NET Framework, they take two additional parameters: an AsyncCallback object, and a generic object parameter that is passed to the AsyncCallback when the call completes.

At the surface, there would appear to be no difference between calling Resolve() or GetHostByName(); in fact, the Resolve() method calls into GetHostByName() after doing a small amount of preprocessing to check if the string passed is either a standard host name ("www.oreilly.com") or a dotted-quad IP address ("192.168.0.1"); GetHostByName() requires a hostname. (For those familiar with the Berkeley sockets API, the GetHostBy-Name() method is a wrapper around the native BSD gethostbyname function.)

Public NotInheritable Class **Dns**
' Public Shared Methods
  Public Shared Function **BeginGetHostByName**(ByVal hostName As String, _
    ByVal requestCallback As AsyncCallback, ByVal stateObject As Object) As IAsyncResult
  Public Shared Function **BeginResolve**(ByVal hostName As String, ByVal requestCallback As AsyncCallback, _
    ByVal stateObject As Object) As IAsyncResult
  Public Shared Function **EndGetHostByName**(ByVal asyncResult As IAsyncResult) As IPHostEntry
  Public Shared Function **EndResolve**(ByVal asyncResult As IAsyncResult) As IPHostEntry
  Public Shared Function **GetHostByAddress**(ByVal address As IPAddress) As IPHostEntry
  Public Shared Function **GetHostByAddress**(ByVal address As String) As IPHostEntry
  Public Shared Function **GetHostByName**(ByVal hostName As String) As IPHostEntry
  Public Shared Function **GetHostName**() As String
  Public Shared Function **Resolve**(ByVal hostName As String) As IPHostEntry
End Class

DnsPermission   NotInheritable Class

System.Net (system.dll)   *ECMA, serializable*

This class controls access to DNS services. The constructor accepts one argument, either System.Security.Permissions.PermissionState.None (no access to DNS services) or System.Security.Permissions.PermissionState.Unrestricted (all access).

This permission is Demand()ed by all of the methods on the Dns class.

Public NotInheritable Class **DnsPermission** : Inherits System.Security.CodeAccessPermission : Implements _
    System.Security.Permissions.IUnrestrictedPermission
' Public Constructors
  Public Sub **New**(ByVal state As System.Security.Permissions.PermissionState)
' Public Instance Methods
  Overrides Public Function **Copy**() As IPermission
  Overrides Public Sub **FromXml**(ByVal securityElement As System.Security.SecurityElement)
  Overrides Public Function **Intersect**(ByVal target As System.Security.IPermission) As IPermission
  Overrides Public Function **IsSubsetOf**(ByVal target As System.Security.IPermission) As Boolean
  Public Function **IsUnrestricted**() As Boolean Implements IUnrestrictedPermission.IsUnrestricted
  Overrides Public Function **ToXml**() As SecurityElement
  Overrides Public Function **Union**(ByVal target As System.Security.IPermission) As IPermission
End Class

Hierarchy: System.Object→ System.Security.CodeAccessPermission(System.Security.IPermission, System.Security.ISecurityEncodable, System.Security.IStackWalk)→ DnsPermission(System.Security.Permissions.IUnrestrictedPermission)

DnsPermissionAttribute

NotInheritable Class

System.Net (system.dll)

ECMA, serializable

This attribute is used to declare in metadata that the attributed method or class requires DnsPermission of the declared form.

```
Public NotInheritable Class DnsPermissionAttribute : Inherits _
     System.Security.Permissions.CodeAccessSecurityAttribute
' Public Constructors
   Public Sub New(ByVal action As System.Security.Permissions.SecurityAction)
' Public Instance Methods
   Overrides Public Function CreatePermission() As IPermission
End Class
```

Hierarchy: System.Object→ System.Attribute→ System.Security.Permissions.SecurityAttribute→ System.Security.Permissions.CodeAccessSecurityAttribute→ DnsPermissionAttribute

Valid On: Assembly, Class, Struct, Constructor, Method

EndPoint

MustInherit Class

System.Net (system.dll)

ECMA, serializable

This MustInherit class represents a network address. It is extended by IPEndPoint, which represents an IP network address. It could later be extended to represent other kinds of networking endpoints for other protocol stacks beyond TCP/IP.

```
Public MustInherit Class EndPoint
' Protected Constructors
   Protected Sub New()
' Public Instance Properties
   Overridable Public ReadOnly Property AddressFamily As AddressFamily
' Public Instance Methods
   Overridable Public Function Create(ByVal socketAddress As SocketAddress) As EndPoint
   Overridable Public Function Serialize() As SocketAddress
End Class
```

Subclasses: IPEndPoint

Returned By: IPEndPoint.Create(), System.Net.Sockets.Socket.{LocalEndPoint, RemoteEndPoint}, System.Net.Sockets.TcpListener.LocalEndpoint

Passed To: System.Net.Sockets.Socket.{BeginConnect(), BeginReceiveFrom(), BeginSendTo(), Bind(), Connect(), EndReceiveFrom(), ReceiveFrom(), SendTo()}

EndpointPermission

Class

System.Net (system.dll)

serializable

This permission is Demand()ed by all of the methods on the EndPoint class.

```
Public Class EndpointPermission
' Public Instance Properties
   Public ReadOnly Property Hostname As String
   Public ReadOnly Property Port As Integer
   Public ReadOnly Property Transport As TransportType
' Public Instance Methods
   Overrides Public Function Equals(ByVal obj As Object) As Boolean
   Overrides Public Function GetHashCode() As Integer
   Overrides Public Function ToString() As String
End Class
```

FileWebRequest
Class

System.Net (system.dll)
serializable, marshal by reference

This subclass of WebRequest provides access to resources that use the file URL scheme (such as a file on your local filesystem). Use WebRequest.Create() with a *file://* URL to create an instance of this class. The WebRequest.Create() method returns an instance of this class as a reference of type WebRequest.

You may feel a small sense of confusion regarding this type and the "file:" protocol scheme; if a program needs access to a file on the filesystem, why not simply open a System.IO.FileStream instead of using WebRequest.Create("file:/...")? In terms of straight functionality, the System.IO.FileStream call more closely represents the fact that this resource is coming from disk; however, due to the ubiquity of HTTP servers growing within the enterprise, there are often times when a system wishes to equally represent HTTP URLs and filesystem paths within an arbitrary context. For example, a configuration file might be used to indicate where to retrieve user preferences; by specifying the location as an URL rather than an absolute file location, storage of user preferences is permitted on a centralized server without any additional code. (This allows a kind of "roaming preferences" capability within the system.) Many of the .NET tools also use this approach to identify "files" to act upon via command-line parameters.

```
Public Class FileWebRequest : Inherits WebRequest
' Protected Constructors
    Protected Sub New(ByVal serializationInfo As System.Runtime.Serialization.SerializationInfo, _
      ByVal streamingContext As System.Runtime.Serialization.StreamingContext)
' Public Instance Properties
    Overrides Public Property ConnectionGroupName As String
    Overrides Public Property ContentLength As Long
    Overrides Public Property ContentType As String
    Overrides Public Property Credentials As ICredentials
    Overrides Public ReadOnly Property Headers As WebHeaderCollection
    Overrides Public Property Method As String
    Overrides Public Property PreAuthenticate As Boolean
    Overrides Public Property Proxy As IWebProxy
    Overrides Public ReadOnly Property RequestUri As Uri
    Overrides Public Property Timeout As Integer
' Public Instance Methods
    Overrides Public Function BeginGetRequestStream(ByVal callback As AsyncCallback, ByVal state As Object) _
      As IAsyncResult
    Overrides Public Function BeginGetResponse(ByVal callback As AsyncCallback, ByVal state As Object) _
      As IAsyncResult
    Overrides Public Function EndGetRequestStream(ByVal asyncResult As IAsyncResult) As Stream
    Overrides Public Function EndGetResponse(ByVal asyncResult As IAsyncResult) As WebResponse
    Overrides Public Function GetRequestStream() As Stream
    Overrides Public Function GetResponse() As WebResponse
End Class
```

Hierarchy: System.Object→ System.MarshalByRefObject→ WebRequest(System.Runtime.Serialization.ISerializable)→ FileWebRequest

FileWebResponse
Class

System.Net (system.dll)
serializable, marshal by reference, disposable

This subclass of WebResponse is returned by WebRequest.GetResponse() when you request access to a file URI. Since this subclass does not add any new methods, there's no need to cast the return value to a FileWebResponse; the GetResponseStream() method returns a System.IO.Stream from which the file's contents can be retrieved.

```
Public Class FileWebResponse : Inherits WebResponse
' Protected Constructors
   Protected Sub New(ByVal serializationInfo As System.Runtime.Serialization.SerializationInfo, _
      ByVal streamingContext As System.Runtime.Serialization.StreamingContext)
' Public Instance Properties
   Overrides Public ReadOnly Property ContentLength As Long
   Overrides Public ReadOnly Property ContentType As String
   Overrides Public ReadOnly Property Headers As WebHeaderCollection
   Overrides Public ReadOnly Property ResponseUri As Uri
' Public Instance Methods
   Overrides Public Sub Close()
   Overrides Public Function GetResponseStream() As Stream
' Protected Instance Methods
   Overridable Protected Sub Dispose(ByVal disposing As Boolean)
End Class
```

Hierarchy: System.Object→ System.MarshalByRefObject→
WebResponse(System.Runtime.Serialization.ISerializable, System.IDisposable)→ FileWebResponse

GlobalProxySelection   Class

System.Net (system.dll)   *ECMA*

This class holds the default IWebProxy object used by all HTTP requests. To change it, set
the Select property to an instance of WebProxy.

```
Public Class GlobalProxySelection
' Public Constructors
   Public Sub New()
' Public Shared Properties
   Public Shared Property Select As IWebProxy
' Public Shared Methods
   Public Shared Function GetEmptyWebProxy() As IWebProxy
End Class
```

HttpContinueDelegate   Delegate

System.Net (system.dll)   *ECMA, serializable*

The HttpWebRequest.ContinueDelegate property uses this class to handle HttpStatusCode.Con-
tinue responses. These responses are sent when the server receives the HTTP request, is
able to process it, and wishes to notify the client that the request was successfully
received. (Most HTTP servers will send this only if the request processing would take
longer than expected.)

```
Public Delegate Sub HttpContinueDelegate(ByVal StatusCode As Integer, _
   ByVal httpHeaders As WebHeaderCollection)
```

Returned By: HttpWebRequest.ContinueDelegate

Passed To: HttpWebRequest.ContinueDelegate

HttpStatusCode   Enum

System.Net (system.dll)   *ECMA, serializable*

This enumeration contains HTTP 1.1 status codes as defined in RFC 2616
(*ftp://ftp.isi.edu/in-notes/rfc2616.txt*).

```
Public Enum HttpStatusCode
        Continue = 100
        SwitchingProtocols = 101
        OK = 200
        Created = 201
        Accepted = 202
        NonAuthoritativeInformation = 203
        NoContent = 204
        ResetContent = 205
        PartialContent = 206
        MultipleChoices = 300
        Ambiguous = 300
        MovedPermanently = 301
        Moved = 301
        Found = 302
        Redirect = 302
        SeeOther = 303
        RedirectMethod = 303
        NotModified = 304
        UseProxy = 305
        Unused = 306
        TemporaryRedirect = 307
        RedirectKeepVerb = 307
        BadRequest = 400
        Unauthorized = 401
        PaymentRequired = 402
        Forbidden = 403
        NotFound = 404
        MethodNotAllowed = 405
        NotAcceptable = 406
        ProxyAuthenticationRequired = 407
        RequestTimeout = 408
        Conflict = 409
        Gone = 410
        LengthRequired = 411
        PreconditionFailed = 412
        RequestEntityTooLarge = 413
        RequestUriTooLong = 414
        UnsupportedMediaType = 415
        RequestedRangeNotSatisfiable = 416
        ExpectationFailed = 417
        InternalServerError = 500
        NotImplemented = 501
        BadGateway = 502
        ServiceUnavailable = 503
        GatewayTimeout = 504
        HttpVersionNotSupported = 505
End Enum
```

System.Net

Hierarchy: System.Object→ System.ValueType→ System.Enum(System.IComparable, System.IFormattable, System.IConvertible)→ HttpStatusCode

Returned By: HttpWebResponse.StatusCode

HttpVersion   Class

System.Net (system.dll)   *ECMA*

This class contains System.Version values that represent versions for HTTP 1.0 and 1.1.

```
Public Class HttpVersion
' Public Constructors
    Public Sub New()
' Public Shared Fields
    Public Shared ReadOnly Version10 As Version                                =1.0
    Public Shared ReadOnly Version11 As Version                                =1.1
End Class
```

HttpWebRequest   Class

System.Net (system.dll)   *ECMA, serializable, marshal by reference*

This is a subclass of WebRequest. .NET uses this subclass to request documents from the http and https URI schemes (RFC's 2616 and 2818, respectively). An instance of this type is returned by WebRequest.Create() when a URI starting with the *http://* or *https://* prefix is passed in. Since that method's return value is WebRequest, cast it to HttpWebRequest if you need access to any of the methods or properties that are unique to this class (and the HTTP or HTTPS protocol).

The properties on this type correspond directly to the headers documented in the RFC standard documentation; see that document for details regarding their contents. Note that because these headers are sent as part of the HTTP request, any modification of the headers must be done before the request is sent to the remote host. (Calling either the GetResponse() or the BeginGetResponse(), the asynchronous version of GetResponse(), sends the request.)

When a WebRequest encounters an error, a WebException is thrown.

```
Public Class HttpWebRequest : Inherits WebRequest
' Protected Constructors
    Protected Sub New(ByVal serializationInfo As System.Runtime.Serialization.SerializationInfo, _
        ByVal streamingContext As System.Runtime.Serialization.StreamingContext)
' Public Instance Properties
    Public Property Accept As String
    Public ReadOnly Property Address As Uri
    Public Property AllowAutoRedirect As Boolean
    Public Property AllowWriteStreamBuffering As Boolean
    Public ReadOnly Property ClientCertificates As X509CertificateCollection
    Public Property Connection As String
    Overrides Public Property ConnectionGroupName As String
    Overrides Public Property ContentLength As Long
    Overrides Public Property ContentType As String
    Public Property ContinueDelegate As HttpContinueDelegate
    Public Property CookieContainer As CookieContainer
    Overrides Public Property Credentials As ICredentials
    Public Property Expect As String
    Public ReadOnly Property HaveResponse As Boolean
    Overrides Public Property Headers As WebHeaderCollection
    Public Property IfModifiedSince As Date
```

Public Property **KeepAlive** As Boolean
Public Property **MaximumAutomaticRedirections** As Integer
Public Property **MediaType** As String
Overrides Public Property **Method** As String
Public Property **Pipelined** As Boolean
Overrides Public Property **PreAuthenticate** As Boolean
Public Property **ProtocolVersion** As Version
Overrides Public Property **Proxy** As IWebProxy
Public Property **Referer** As String
Overrides Public ReadOnly Property **RequestUri** As Uri
Public Property **SendChunked** As Boolean
Public ReadOnly Property **ServicePoint** As ServicePoint
Overrides Public Property **Timeout** As Integer
Public Property **TransferEncoding** As String
Public Property **UserAgent** As String
' *Public Instance Methods*
Overrides Public Sub **Abort**()
Public Sub **AddRange**(ByVal range As Integer)
Public Sub **AddRange**(ByVal from As Integer, ByVal to As Integer)
Public Sub **AddRange**(ByVal rangeSpecifier As String, ByVal range As Integer)
Public Sub **AddRange**(ByVal rangeSpecifier As String, ByVal from As Integer, ByVal to As Integer)
Overrides Public Function **BeginGetRequestStream**(ByVal callback As AsyncCallback, ByVal state As Object) _
  As IAsyncResult
Overrides Public Function **BeginGetResponse**(ByVal callback As AsyncCallback, ByVal state As Object) _
  As IAsyncResult
Overrides Public Function **EndGetRequestStream**(ByVal asyncResult As IAsyncResult) As Stream
Overrides Public Function **EndGetResponse**(ByVal asyncResult As IAsyncResult) As WebResponse
Overrides Public Function **GetHashCode**() As Integer
Overrides Public Function **GetRequestStream**() As Stream
Overrides Public Function **GetResponse**() As WebResponse
End Class

Hierarchy: System.Object→ System.MarshalByRefObject→
WebRequest(System.Runtime.Serialization.ISerializable)→ HttpWebRequest

HttpWebResponse   Class

System.Net (system.dll)   *ECMA, serializable, marshal by reference, disposable*

This class represents a response from an HTTP server. This is usually returned from
WebRequest.GetResponse() or WebRequest.EndGetResponse(). Use GetResponseStream() to obtain
a System.IO.Stream object containing the response body. Use GetResponseHeader() to fetch
a specific HTTP header.

Public Class **HttpWebResponse** : Inherits WebResponse
' *Protected Constructors*
Protected Sub **New**(ByVal serializationInfo As System.Runtime.Serialization.SerializationInfo, _
  ByVal streamingContext As System.Runtime.Serialization.StreamingContext)
' *Public Instance Properties*
Public ReadOnly Property **CharacterSet** As String
Public ReadOnly Property **ContentEncoding** As String
Overrides Public ReadOnly Property **ContentLength** As Long
Overrides Public ReadOnly Property **ContentType** As String
Public Property **Cookies** As CookieCollection
Overrides Public ReadOnly Property **Headers** As WebHeaderCollection
Public ReadOnly Property **LastModified** As Date
Public ReadOnly Property **Method** As String

```
Public ReadOnly Property ProtocolVersion As Version
Overrides Public ReadOnly Property ResponseUri As Uri
Public ReadOnly Property Server As String
Public ReadOnly Property StatusCode As HttpStatusCode
Public ReadOnly Property StatusDescription As String
' Public Instance Methods
Overrides Public Sub Close()
Overrides Public Function GetHashCode() As Integer
Public Function GetResponseHeader(ByVal headerName As String) As String
Overrides Public Function GetResponseStream() As Stream
' Protected Instance Methods
Overridable Protected Sub Dispose(ByVal disposing As Boolean)
End Class
```

Hierarchy: System.Object→ System.MarshalByRefObject→
WebResponse(System.Runtime.Serialization.ISerializable, System.IDisposable)→ HttpWebResponse

IAuthenticationModule   Interface

System.Net (system.dll)   *ECMA*

This interface is implemented by all authentication modules. If you develop a custom authentication module, you must implement this interface and register an instance of your module with AuthenticationManager.Register().

```
Public Interface IAuthenticationModule
' Public Instance Properties
Public ReadOnly Property AuthenticationType As String
Public ReadOnly Property CanPreAuthenticate As Boolean
' Public Instance Methods
Public Function Authenticate(ByVal challenge As String, ByVal request As WebRequest, _
   ByVal credentials As ICredentials) As Authorization
Public Function PreAuthenticate(ByVal request As WebRequest, ByVal credentials As ICredentials) _
   As Authorization
End Interface
```

Passed To: AuthenticationManager.{Register(), Unregister()}

ICertificatePolicy   Interface

System.Net (system.dll)

This interface validates the certificates that web servers present to your applications. If you create a web request that uses the https protocol, the .NET Framework uses the default certificate policy to validate the server's certificate.

You can implement this interface to create your own custom certificate policy. Unlike authentication modules, only one certificate policy may be active at a time. To set this, create an instance of your implementation and assign it to ServicePointManager.CertificatePolicy.

```
Public Interface ICertificatePolicy
' Public Instance Methods
Public Function CheckValidationResult(ByVal srvPoint As ServicePoint, _
   ByVal certificate As System.Security.Cryptography.X509Certificates.X509Certificate, ByVal request As WebRequest, _
   ByVal certificateProblem As Integer)  As Boolean
End Interface
```

Returned By: ServicePointManager.CertificatePolicy

Passed To: ServicePointManager.CertificatePolicy

ICredentials
Interface

System.Net (system.dll)
ECMA

This interface is implemented by all web-client credentials. The class NetworkCredential works with authentication schemes such as Basic and Digest authentication, NTLM, and Kerberos. If you need to implement a client authentication scheme not supported by .NET (such as SSL client certificates), you need to implement ICredentials and add a new instance of your implementation to your application's credential cache. For more information on using a credential cache, see CredentialCache.

Public Interface **ICredentials**
' Public Instance Methods
   Public Function **GetCredential**(ByVal uri As Uri, ByVal authType As String) As NetworkCredential
End Interface

Implemented By: CredentialCache, NetworkCredential

Returned By: CredentialCache.DefaultCredentials, IWebProxy.Credentials, WebClient.Credentials, WebProxy.Credentials, WebRequest.Credentials

Passed To: AuthenticationManager.{Authenticate(), PreAuthenticate()}, IAuthenticationModule.{Authenticate(), PreAuthenticate()}, IWebProxy.Credentials, WebClient.Credentials, WebProxy.{Credentials, WebProxy()}, WebRequest.Credentials, System.Xml.XmlResolver.Credentials

IPAddress
Class

System.Net (system.dll)
ECMA, serializable

This class represents an IP address. Use the Parse() method to turn a dotted-quad string (such as "192.168.0.1") into an IPAddress. Use the ToString() method to convert an IPAddress into a string.

Public Class **IPAddress**
' Public Constructors
   Public Sub **New**(ByVal newAddress As Long)
' Public Shared Fields
   Public Shared ReadOnly **Any** As IPAddress   =0.0.0.0
   Public Shared ReadOnly **Broadcast** As IPAddress   =255.255.255.255
   Public Shared ReadOnly **Loopback** As IPAddress   =127.0.0.1
   Public Shared ReadOnly **None** As IPAddress   =255.255.255.255
' Public Instance Properties
   Public Property **Address** As Long
   Public ReadOnly Property **AddressFamily** As AddressFamily
' Public Shared Methods
   Public Shared Function **HostToNetworkOrder**(ByVal host As Short) As Short
   Public Shared Function **HostToNetworkOrder**(ByVal host As Integer) As Integer
   Public Shared Function **HostToNetworkOrder**(ByVal host As Long) As Long
   Public Shared Function **IsLoopback**(ByVal address As IPAddress) As Boolean
   Public Shared Function **NetworkToHostOrder**(ByVal network As Short) As Short
   Public Shared Function **NetworkToHostOrder**(ByVal network As Integer) As Integer
   Public Shared Function **NetworkToHostOrder**(ByVal network As Long) As Long
   Public Shared Function **Parse**(ByVal ipString As String) As IPAddress
' Public Instance Methods
   Overrides Public Function **Equals**(ByVal comparand As Object) As Boolean

Overrides Public Function **GetHashCode**() As Integer
Overrides Public Function **ToString**() As String
End Class

Returned By: IPEndPoint.Address, IPHostEntry.AddressList,
System.Net.Sockets.MulticastOption.{Group, LocalAddress}

Passed To: Dns.GetHostByAddress(), IPEndPoint.{Address, IPEndPoint()}, IPHostEntry.AddressList,
System.Net.Sockets.MulticastOption.{Group, LocalAddress, MulticastOption()},
System.Net.Sockets.TcpClient.Connect(), System.Net.Sockets.TcpListener.TcpListener(),
System.Net.Sockets.UdpClient.{Connect(), DropMulticastGroup(), JoinMulticastGroup()}

IPEndPoint
Class

System.Net (system.dll)
ECMA, serializable

This class represents a network endpoint as a combination of IPAddress and an integer
port number. The shared fields MinPort and MaxPort represent the minimum and maximum acceptable values for Port. These values are operating system–dependent.

This class does not represent an open socket connection, which contains two endpoints (local and remote). To create a socket, use System.Net.Sockets.Socket.

Public Class **IPEndPoint** : Inherits EndPoint
' Public Constructors
   Public Sub **New**(ByVal address As Long, ByVal port As Integer)
   Public Sub **New**(ByVal address As IPAddress, ByVal port As Integer)
' Public Shared Fields
   Public const **MaxPort** As Integer   =65535
   Public const **MinPort** As Integer   =0
' Public Instance Properties
   Public Property **Address** As IPAddress
   Overrides Public ReadOnly Property **AddressFamily** As AddressFamily
   Public Property **Port** As Integer
' Public Instance Methods
   Overrides Public Function **Create**(ByVal socketAddress As SocketAddress) As EndPoint
   Overrides Public Function **Equals**(ByVal comparand As Object) As Boolean
   Overrides Public Function **GetHashCode**() As Integer
   Overrides Public Function **Serialize**() As SocketAddress
   Overrides Public Function **ToString**() As String
End Class

Hierarchy: System.Object→ EndPoint→ IPEndPoint

Passed To: System.Net.Sockets.TcpClient.{Connect(), TcpClient()},
System.Net.Sockets.TcpListener.TcpListener(), System.Net.Sockets.UdpClient.{Connect(), Receive(),
Send(), UdpClient()}

IPHostEntry
Class

System.Net (system.dll)
ECMA

The Dns class uses this class to represent hosts. A host is named by its HostName property, and its aliases are stored in the Aliases property. The AddressList property contains
all the IP addresses for that host.

Public Class **IPHostEntry**
' Public Constructors
   Public Sub **New**()
' Public Instance Properties

```
Public Property AddressList As IPAddress()
Public Property Aliases As String()
Public Property HostName As String
End Class
```

Returned By: Dns.{EndGetHostByName(), EndResolve(), GetHostByAddress(), GetHostByName(), Resolve()}

IWebProxy   Interface
System.Net (system.dll)   *ECMA*

IWebProxy defines the interface used by the WebProxy class. Parties interested in creating customized proxy handlers would implement this interface to do so, but the WebProxy implementation is sufficient for most HTTP access purposes.

To use an implementation of IWebProxy, see the GlobalProxySelection class or the WebRequest.Proxy property.

```
Public Interface IWebProxy
' Public Instance Properties
    Public Property Credentials As ICredentials
' Public Instance Methods
    Public Function GetProxy(ByVal destination As Uri) As Uri
    Public Function IsBypassed(ByVal host As Uri) As Boolean
End Interface
```

Implemented By: WebProxy

Returned By: GlobalProxySelection.{GetEmptyWebProxy(), Select}, WebRequest.Proxy

Passed To: GlobalProxySelection.Select, ServicePointManager.FindServicePoint(), WebRequest.Proxy

IWebRequestCreate   Interface
System.Net (system.dll)   *ECMA*

This interface is for objects that create protocol-specific instances of WebRequest. For example, the private class HttpRequestCreator is the underlying class that implements this interface. WebRequest uses that class under the hood to create instances of HttpWebRequest when an application connects to an http or https URI.

If you create your own protocol-specific implementation of this interface, you can register it with the WebRequest.RegisterPrefix()shared method.

```
Public Interface IWebRequestCreate
' Public Instance Methods
    Public Function Create(ByVal uri As Uri) As WebRequest
End Interface
```

Passed To: WebRequest.RegisterPrefix()

NetworkAccess   Enum
System.Net (system.dll)   *ECMA, serializable*

This enumeration specifies network access permissions. Accept indicates that an application has permission to accept network connections. Connect indicates that the application can connect to network hosts.

Both WebPermission and SocketPermission use this enumeration.

```
Public Enum NetworkAccess
    Connect = 64
    Accept = 128
End Enum
```

Hierarchy: System.Object→ System.ValueType→ System.Enum(System.IComparable, System.IFormattable, System.IConvertible)→ NetworkAccess

Passed To: SocketPermission.{AddPermission(), SocketPermission()}, WebPermission.{AddPermission(), WebPermission()}

NetworkCredential   Class

System.Net (system.dll)   *ECMA*

This class is an implementation of ICredentials for authentication schemes that use passwords, such as basic and digest authentication, NTLM, and Kerberos. See CredentialCache for more details.

```
Public Class NetworkCredential : Implements ICredentials
' Public Constructors
    Public Sub New()
    Public Sub New(ByVal userName As String, ByVal password As String)
    Public Sub New(ByVal userName As String, ByVal password As String, ByVal domain As String)
' Public Instance Properties
    Public Property Domain As String
    Public Property Password As String
    Public Property UserName As String
' Public Instance Methods
    Public Function GetCredential(ByVal uri As Uri, ByVal authType As String) As NetworkCredential _
        Implements ICredentials.GetCredential
End Class
```

Returned By: CredentialCache.GetCredential(), ICredentials.GetCredential()

Passed To: CredentialCache.Add()

ProtocolViolationException   Class

System.Net (system.dll)   *ECMA, serializable*

This exception is thrown when a network protocol error occurs.

```
Public Class ProtocolViolationException : Inherits InvalidOperationException
' Public Constructors
    Public Sub New()
    Public Sub New(ByVal message As String)
' Protected Constructors
    Protected Sub New(ByVal serializationInfo As System.Runtime.Serialization.SerializationInfo, _
        ByVal streamingContext As System.Runtime.Serialization.StreamingContext)
End Class
```

Hierarchy: System.Object→ System.Exception(System.Runtime.Serialization.ISerializable)→ System.SystemException→ System.InvalidOperationException→ ProtocolViolationException

ServicePoint
Class

System.Net (system.dll)
ECMA

This class is used by ServicePointManager to manage connections to remote hosts. The .NET Framework reuses service points for all requests to a given URI. The lifetime of a given ServicePoint is governed by its MaxIdleTime property.

The ServicePoint class is a high-level abstraction of the underlying implementation. Details of the implementation, such as the sockets used for HTTP transport, are not publicly exposed.

```
Public Class ServicePoint
' Public Instance Properties
   Public ReadOnly Property Address As Uri
   Public ReadOnly Property Certificate As X509Certificate
   Public ReadOnly Property ClientCertificate As X509Certificate
   Public Property ConnectionLimit As Integer
   Public ReadOnly Property ConnectionName As String
   Public ReadOnly Property CurrentConnections As Integer
   Public ReadOnly Property IdleSince As Date
   Public Property MaxIdleTime As Integer
   Overridable Public ReadOnly Property ProtocolVersion As Version
   Public ReadOnly Property SupportsPipelining As Boolean
' Public Instance Methods
   Overrides Public Function GetHashCode() As Integer
End Class
```

Returned By: HttpWebRequest.ServicePoint, ServicePointManager.FindServicePoint()

Passed To: ICertificatePolicy.CheckValidationResult()

ServicePointManager
Class

System.Net (system.dll)
ECMA

This class is responsible for managing ServicePoint instances. As your applications make HTTP connections to network resources, this class is working behind the scenes to maintain the connections. When your application makes many connections to the same server, this class eliminates the overhead of making a new connection each time you connect.

The ServicePointManager also sets the default certificate policy for new connections. In most cases, the default certificate policy should suit your needs. If you need to change it, see ICertificatePolicy for more details.

```
Public Class ServicePointManager
' Public Shared Fields
   Public const DefaultNonPersistentConnectionLimit As Integer          =4
   Public const DefaultPersistentConnectionLimit As Integer             =2
' Public Shared Properties
   Public Shared Property CertificatePolicy As ICertificatePolicy
   Public Shared Property DefaultConnectionLimit As Integer
   Public Shared Property MaxServicePointIdleTime As Integer
   Public Shared Property MaxServicePoints As Integer
' Public Shared Methods
   Public Shared Function FindServicePoint(ByVal uriString As String, ByVal proxy As IWebProxy) As ServicePoint
   Public Shared Function FindServicePoint(ByVal address As Uri) As ServicePoint
   Public Shared Function FindServicePoint(ByVal address As Uri, ByVal proxy As IWebProxy) As ServicePoint
End Class
```

SocketAddress   **Class**

System.Net (system.dll)   *ECMA*

This type defines an address of a particular socket; in particular, it defines the family of networking protocols to which the address belongs (for example, IP or IPv6), as well as the size of the address itself. This type can be safely ignored for most high-level (and, arguably, most low-level) networking operations.

```
Public Class SocketAddress
' Public Constructors
    Public Sub New(ByVal family As System.Net.Sockets.AddressFamily)
    Public Sub New(ByVal family As System.Net.Sockets.AddressFamily, ByVal size As Integer)
' Public Instance Properties
    Public ReadOnly Property Family As AddressFamily
    Public Default Property Item (ByVal offset As Integer) As Byte
    Public ReadOnly Property Size As Integer
' Public Instance Methods
    Overrides Public Function Equals(ByVal comparand As Object) As Boolean
    Overrides Public Function GetHashCode() As Integer
    Overrides Public Function ToString() As String
End Class
```

Returned By: EndPoint.Serialize()

Passed To: EndPoint.Create()

SocketPermission   **NotInheritable Class**

System.Net (system.dll)   *ECMA, serializable*

This permission controls whether code can make or accept socket connections for a given NetworkAccess, TransportType, hostname, and port number (see the four-argument form of the constructor). The shared field AllPorts is a constant that represents permission to all ports and can be used as the port argument to the constructor.

```
Public NotInheritable Class SocketPermission : Inherits System.Security.CodeAccessPermission : Implements _
        System.Security.Permissions.IUnrestrictedPermission
' Public Constructors
    Public Sub New(ByVal access As NetworkAccess, ByVal transport As TransportType, ByVal hostName As String, _
        ByVal portNumber As Integer)
    Public Sub New(ByVal state As System.Security.Permissions.PermissionState)
' Public Shared Fields
    Public const AllPorts As Integer                                                                =-1
' Public Instance Properties
    Public ReadOnly Property AcceptList As IEnumerator
    Public ReadOnly Property ConnectList As IEnumerator
' Public Instance Methods
    Public Sub AddPermission(ByVal access As NetworkAccess, ByVal transport As TransportType, _
        ByVal hostName As String, ByVal portNumber As Integer)
    Overrides Public Function Copy() As IPermission
    Overrides Public Sub FromXml(ByVal securityElement As System.Security.SecurityElement)
    Overrides Public Function Intersect(ByVal target As System.Security.IPermission) As IPermission
    Overrides Public Function IsSubsetOf(ByVal target As System.Security.IPermission) As Boolean
    Public Function IsUnrestricted() As Boolean Implements IUnrestrictedPermission.IsUnrestricted
    Overrides Public Function ToXml() As SecurityElement
    Overrides Public Function Union(ByVal target As System.Security.IPermission) As IPermission
End Class
```

Hierarchy: System.Object→ System.Security.CodeAccessPermission(System.Security.IPermission,
System.Security.ISecurityEncodable, System.Security.IStackWalk)→
SocketPermission(System.Security.Permissions.IUnrestrictedPermission)

SocketPermissionAttribute

NotInheritable Class

System.Net (system.dll)   *ECMA, serializable*

This attribute is used to declare in metadata that the attributed method or class requires
SocketPermission of the declared form.

```
Public NotInheritable Class SocketPermissionAttribute : Inherits _
      System.Security.Permissions.CodeAccessSecurityAttribute
' Public Constructors
   Public Sub New(ByVal action As System.Security.Permissions.SecurityAction)
' Public Instance Properties
   Public Property Access As String
   Public Property Host As String
   Public Property Port As String
   Public Property Transport As String
' Public Instance Methods
   Overrides Public Function CreatePermission() As IPermission
End Class
```

Hierarchy: System.Object→ System.Attribute→ System.Security.Permissions.SecurityAttribute→
System.Security.Permissions.CodeAccessSecurityAttribute→ SocketPermissionAttribute

Valid On: Assembly, Class, Struct, Constructor, Method

TransportType

Enum

System.Net (system.dll)   *ECMA, serializable*

This enumeration defines the transport protocols that can be used to communicate over
a socket.

```
Public Enum TransportType
   Udp = 1
   Connectionless = 1
   Tcp = 2
   ConnectionOriented = 2
   All = 3
End Enum
```

Hierarchy: System.Object→ System.ValueType→ System.Enum(System.IComparable,
System.IFormattable, System.IConvertible)→ TransportType

Returned By: EndpointPermission.Transport

Passed To: SocketPermission.{AddPermission(), SocketPermission()}

WebClient

NotInheritable Class

System.Net (system.dll)   *ECMA, marshal by reference, disposable*

This class is a simple HTTP User-Agent. Use DownloadData() to fetch a document as an
array of bytes. The DownloadFile() method fetches a document and stores it in a file. You
can upload data to a URI using UploadFile() or UploadData() (which uploads the contents
of a byte array).

Before connecting to a URI, invoke the Add() method of the QueryString or Headers properties to add a key/value pair to the HTTP query string or HTTP request headers. Set
the credentials property to authenticate the WebClient to the remote server, if necessary.

Public NotInheritable Class **WebClient** : Inherits System.ComponentModel.Component
' *Public Constructors*
  Public Sub **New**()
' *Public Instance Properties*
  Public Property **BaseAddress** As String
  Public Property **Credentials** As ICredentials
  Public Property **Headers** As WebHeaderCollection
  Public Property **QueryString** As NameValueCollection
  Public ReadOnly Property **ResponseHeaders** As WebHeaderCollection
' *Public Instance Methods*
  Public Function **DownloadData**(ByVal address As String) As Byte()
  Public Sub **DownloadFile**(ByVal address As String, ByVal fileName As String)
  Public Function **OpenRead**(ByVal address As String) As Stream
  Public Function **OpenWrite**(ByVal address As String) As Stream
  Public Function **OpenWrite**(ByVal address As String, ByVal method As String) As Stream
  Public Function **UploadData**(ByVal address As String, ByVal data As Byte()) As Byte()
  Public Function **UploadData**(ByVal address As String, ByVal method As String, ByVal data As Byte()) As Byte()
  Public Function **UploadFile**(ByVal address As String, ByVal fileName As String) As Byte()
  Public Function **UploadFile**(ByVal address As String, ByVal method As String, ByVal fileName As String) As Byte()
  Public Function **UploadValues**(ByVal address As String, _
    ByVal data As System.Collections.Specialized.NameValueCollection) As Byte()
  Public Function **UploadValues**(ByVal address As String, ByVal method As String, _
    ByVal data As System.Collections.Specialized.NameValueCollection) As Byte()
End Class

Hierarchy: System.Object→ System.MarshalByRefObject→
System.ComponentModel.Component(System.ComponentModel.IComponent, System.IDisposable)→
WebClient

WebException   **Class**

System.Net (system.dll)   *ECMA, serializable*

This exception represents an error that occurred while using a protocol-specific implementation of WebRequest. In the case of some protocols, such as HTTP, the exception's Response property contains information about the error that occurred.

Public Class **WebException** : Inherits InvalidOperationException
' *Public Constructors*
  Public Sub **New**()
  Public Sub **New**(ByVal message As String)
  Public Sub **New**(ByVal message As String, ByVal innerException As Exception)
  Public Sub **New**(ByVal message As String, ByVal innerException As Exception, ByVal status As WebExceptionStatus, _
    ByVal response As WebResponse)
  Public Sub **New**(ByVal message As String, ByVal status As WebExceptionStatus)
' *Protected Constructors*
  Protected Sub **New**(ByVal serializationInfo As System.Runtime.Serialization.SerializationInfo, _
    ByVal streamingContext As System.Runtime.Serialization.StreamingContext)
' *Public Instance Properties*
  Public ReadOnly Property **Response** As WebResponse
  Public ReadOnly Property **Status** As WebExceptionStatus
End Class

Hierarchy: System.Object→ System.Exception(System.Runtime.Serialization.ISerializable)→
System.SystemException→ System.InvalidOperationException→ WebException

WebExceptionStatus

Enum

System.Net (system.dll)   *ECMA, serializable*

This enumeration defines constants for the status codes used in WebException.Status.

Public Enum **WebExceptionStatus**
    Success = 0
    NameResolutionFailure = 1
    ConnectFailure = 2
    ReceiveFailure = 3
    SendFailure = 4
    PipelineFailure = 5
    RequestCanceled = 6
    ProtocolError = 7
    ConnectionClosed = 8
    TrustFailure = 9
    SecureChannelFailure = 10
    ServerProtocolViolation = 11
    KeepAliveFailure = 12
    Pending = 13
    Timeout = 14
    ProxyNameResolutionFailure = 15
End Enum

Hierarchy: System.Object→ System.ValueType→ System.Enum(System.IComparable, System.IFormattable, System.IConvertible)→ WebExceptionStatus

Returned By: WebException.Status

Passed To: WebException.WebException()

WebHeaderCollection

Class

System.Net (system.dll)   *ECMA, serializable*

This class contains the headers that are part of a WebRequest or WebResponse. Some headers should not be accessed through this collection. Instead, use the corresponding properties of the WebRequest or WebResponse (or the HTTP-specific subclasses). These headers are Accept, Connection, Content-Length, Content-Type, Date, Expect, Host, Range, Referer, Transfer-Encoding, and User-Agent.

Public Class **WebHeaderCollection** : Inherits System.Collections.Specialized.NameValueCollection
' Public Constructors
    Public Sub **New**()
' Protected Constructors
    Protected Sub **New**(ByVal serializationInfo As System.Runtime.Serialization.SerializationInfo, _
        ByVal streamingContext As System.Runtime.Serialization.StreamingContext)
' Public Shared Methods
    Public Shared Function **IsRestricted**(ByVal headerName As String) As Boolean
' Public Instance Methods
    Public Sub **Add**(ByVal header As String)
    Overrides Public Sub **Add**(ByVal name As String, ByVal value As String)
    Overrides Public Function **GetValues**(ByVal header As String) As String()
    Overrides Public Sub **OnDeserialization**(ByVal sender As Object)
    Overrides Public Sub **Remove**(ByVal name As String)
    Overrides Public Sub **Set**(ByVal name As String, ByVal value As String)
    Public Function **ToByteArray**() As Byte()
    Overrides Public Function **ToString**() As String
' Protected Instance Methods

```
    Protected Sub AddWithoutValidate(ByVal headerName As String, ByVal headerValue As String)
End Class
```

Hierarchy: System.Object→
System.Collections.Specialized.NameObjectCollectionBase(System.Collections.ICollection,
System.Collections.IEnumerable, System.Runtime.Serialization.ISerializable,
System.Runtime.Serialization.IDeserializationCallback)→
System.Collections.Specialized.NameValueCollection→ WebHeaderCollection

Returned By: WebClient.{Headers, ResponseHeaders}, WebRequest.Headers, WebResponse.Headers

Passed To: HttpContinueDelegate.{BeginInvoke(), Invoke()}, WebClient.Headers, WebRequest.Headers

WebPermission   NotInheritable Class

System.Net (system.dll)   *ECMA, serializable*

This permission controls which connections an application can make or accept.

```
Public NotInheritable Class WebPermission : Inherits System.Security.CodeAccessPermission : Implements _
    System.Security.Permissions.IUnrestrictedPermission
' Public Constructors
    Public Sub New()
    Public Sub New(ByVal access As NetworkAccess, ByVal uriRegex As System.Text.RegularExpressions.Regex)
    Public Sub New(ByVal access As NetworkAccess, ByVal uriString As String)
    Public Sub New(ByVal state As System.Security.Permissions.PermissionState)
' Public Instance Properties
    Public ReadOnly Property AcceptList As IEnumerator
    Public ReadOnly Property ConnectList As IEnumerator
' Public Instance Methods
    Public Sub AddPermission(ByVal access As NetworkAccess, _
      ByVal uriRegex As System.Text.RegularExpressions.Regex)
    Public Sub AddPermission(ByVal access As NetworkAccess, ByVal uriString As String)
    Overrides Public Function Copy() As IPermission
    Overrides Public Sub FromXml(ByVal securityElement As System.Security.SecurityElement)
    Overrides Public Function Intersect(ByVal target As System.Security.IPermission) As IPermission
    Overrides Public Function IsSubsetOf(ByVal target As System.Security.IPermission) As Boolean
    Public Function IsUnrestricted() As Boolean Implements IUnrestrictedPermission.IsUnrestricted
    Overrides Public Function ToXml() As SecurityElement
    Overrides Public Function Union(ByVal target As System.Security.IPermission) As IPermission
End Class
```

Hierarchy: System.Object→ System.Security.CodeAccessPermission(System.Security.IPermission,
System.Security.ISecurityEncodable, System.Security.IStackWalk)→
WebPermission(System.Security.Permissions.IUnrestrictedPermission)

WebPermissionAttribute   NotInheritable Class

System.Net (system.dll)   *ECMA, serializable*

This attribute is used to declare in metadata that the attributed method or class requires
WebPermission of the declared form.

```
Public NotInheritable Class WebPermissionAttribute : Inherits _
    System.Security.Permissions.CodeAccessSecurityAttribute
' Public Constructors
    Public Sub New(ByVal action As System.Security.Permissions.SecurityAction)
' Public Instance Properties
    Public Property Accept As String
    Public Property AcceptPattern As String
```

```
  Public Property Connect As String
  Public Property ConnectPattern As String
' Public Instance Methods
  Overrides Public Function CreatePermission() As IPermission
End Class
```

Hierarchy: System.Object→ System.Attribute→ System.Security.Permissions.SecurityAttribute→
System.Security.Permissions.CodeAccessSecurityAttribute→ WebPermissionAttribute

Valid On: Assembly, Class, Struct, Constructor, Method

WebProxy   Class

System.Net (system.dll)   *ECMA, serializable*

This implementation of IWebProxy supports HTTP proxies. Use the one-argument form of
the constructor to specify the URI of the proxy server. The second argument BypassOnLo-
cal, if set to true, bypasses the proxy server for local (intranet) addresses. Other forms
of the constructor allow you to specify an array that lists servers for which you should
bypass the proxy (this list can contain regular expression strings containing URI patterns to match). You can also supply network credentials to authenticate your application to the proxy server.

See GlobalProxySelection or the WebRequest.Proxy property for details on configuring a
proxy.

```
Public Class WebProxy : Implements IWebProxy, System.Runtime.Serialization.ISerializable
' Public Constructors
  Public Sub New()
  Public Sub New(ByVal Address As String)
  Public Sub New(ByVal Address As String, ByVal BypassOnLocal As Boolean)
  Public Sub New(ByVal Address As String, ByVal BypassOnLocal As Boolean, ByVal BypassList As String())
  Public Sub New(ByVal Address As String, ByVal BypassOnLocal As Boolean, ByVal BypassList As String(), _
      ByVal Credentials As ICredentials)
  Public Sub New(ByVal Host As String, ByVal Port As Integer)
  Public Sub New(ByVal Address As Uri)
  Public Sub New(ByVal Address As Uri, ByVal BypassOnLocal As Boolean)
  Public Sub New(ByVal Address As Uri, ByVal BypassOnLocal As Boolean, ByVal BypassList As String())
  Public Sub New(ByVal Address As Uri, ByVal BypassOnLocal As Boolean, ByVal BypassList As String(), _
      ByVal Credentials As ICredentials)
' Protected Constructors
  Protected Sub New(ByVal serializationInfo As System.Runtime.Serialization.SerializationInfo, _
      ByVal streamingContext As System.Runtime.Serialization.StreamingContext)
' Public Instance Properties
  Public Property Address As Uri
  Public ReadOnly Property BypassArrayList As ArrayList
  Public Property BypassList As String()
  Public Property BypassProxyOnLocal As Boolean
  Public Property Credentials As ICredentials Implements IWebProxy.Credentials
' Public Shared Methods
  Public Shared Function GetDefaultProxy() As WebProxy
' Public Instance Methods
  Public Function GetProxy(ByVal destination As Uri) As Uri Implements  IWebProxy.GetProxy
  Public Function IsBypassed(ByVal host As Uri) As Boolean Implements  IWebProxy.IsBypassed
End Class
```

WebRequest

MustInherit Class

System.Net (system.dll)   *ECMA, serializable, marshal by reference*

Because many Internet protocols are request-response synchronous protocols, this class serves as a base type for any and all request-response style of network communication. As such, a .NET programmer will never create a WebRequest type directly—instead, a shared method on this class, Create(), is used as a "virtual constructor" to create a subtype of WebRequest that matches the protocol scheme requested. For example, if the string *http://www.oreilly.com* is passed to Create(), an instance of HttpWebRequest is handed back. Out of the box, only "http", "https", and "file" are supported.

Once obtained, a .NET programmer can manipulate the common properties of the WebRequest type to control various aspects of the request. Alternatively, downcast the generic WebRequest reference to the concrete type returned to access protocol-specific aspects of that protocol—for example, the returned object from WebRequest.Create("http://www.oreilly.com") will be a HttpWebRequest, so it is safe to cast it as such. This allows access to the Accept and SendChunked properties/headers in the request. Be sure to manipulate these properties before the request is sent, or the modifications will have no effect.

Use the GetResponse() method to obtain a WebResponse object corresponding to the response that the remote server sent. This means that the request is sent, and the response harvested. The methods BeginGetResponse() and EndGetResponse() are asynchronous versions of GetResponse().

By default, WebRequest uses the proxy server specified in GlobalProxySelection.Select. Override that setting by assigning an IWebProxy implementation to the Proxy property.

```
Public MustInherit Class WebRequest : Inherits MarshalByRefObject : Implements _
      System.Runtime.Serialization.ISerializable
' Protected Constructors
   Protected Sub New()
   Protected Sub New(ByVal serializationInfo As System.Runtime.Serialization.SerializationInfo, _
      ByVal streamingContext As System.Runtime.Serialization.StreamingContext)
' Public Instance Properties
   Overridable Public Property ConnectionGroupName As String
   Overridable Public Property ContentLength As Long
   Overridable Public Property ContentType As String
   Overridable Public Property Credentials As ICredentials
   Overridable Public Property Headers As WebHeaderCollection
   Overridable Public Property Method As String
   Overridable Public Property PreAuthenticate As Boolean
   Overridable Public Property Proxy As IWebProxy
   Overridable Public ReadOnly Property RequestUri As Uri
   Overridable Public Property Timeout As Integer
' Public Shared Methods
   Public Shared Function Create(ByVal requestUriString As String) As WebRequest
   Public Shared Function Create(ByVal requestUri As Uri) As WebRequest
   Public Shared Function CreateDefault(ByVal requestUri As Uri) As WebRequest
   Public Shared Function RegisterPrefix(ByVal prefix As String, ByVal creator As IWebRequestCreate) As Boolean
' Public Instance Methods
   Overridable Public Sub Abort()
   Overridable Public Function BeginGetRequestStream(ByVal callback As AsyncCallback, ByVal state As Object) _
      As IAsyncResult
   Overridable Public Function BeginGetResponse(ByVal callback As AsyncCallback, ByVal state As Object) _
      As IAsyncResult
   Overridable Public Function EndGetRequestStream(ByVal asyncResult As IAsyncResult) As Stream
```

Overridable Public Function **EndGetResponse**(ByVal asyncResult As IAsyncResult) As WebResponse
Overridable Public Function **GetRequestStream**() As Stream
Overridable Public Function **GetResponse**() As WebResponse
End Class

Hierarchy: System.Object→ System.MarshalByRefObject→
WebRequest(System.Runtime.Serialization.ISerializable)

Subclasses: FileWebRequest, HttpWebRequest

Returned By: IWebRequestCreate.Create()

Passed To: AuthenticationManager.{Authenticate(), PreAuthenticate()},
IAuthenticationModule.{Authenticate(), PreAuthenticate()}, ICertificatePolicy.CheckValidationResult()

WebResponse   MustInherit Class

System.Net (system.dll)   *ECMA, serializable, marshal by reference, disposable*

This class represents a response received from a WebRequest. A response consists of
headers (stored as key/value pairs in the Headers property) and a response body. You
can obtain the response body as a System.IO.Stream using the GetResponseStream()
method.

When you are finished with the response, call its Close() method; this releases any open
resources still held by the WebResponse without having to wait for garbage collection to
do so (which could take longer than desired).

Public MustInherit Class **WebResponse** : Inherits MarshalByRefObject: Implements _
        System.Runtime.Serialization.ISerializable, IDisposable
' *Protected Constructors*
    Protected Sub **New**()
    Protected Sub **New**(ByVal serializationInfo As System.Runtime.Serialization.SerializationInfo, _
        ByVal streamingContext As System.Runtime.Serialization.StreamingContext)
' *Public Instance Properties*
    Overridable Public Property **ContentLength** As Long
    Overridable Public Property **ContentType** As String
    Overridable Public ReadOnly Property **Headers** As WebHeaderCollection
    Overridable Public ReadOnly Property **ResponseUri** As Uri
' *Public Instance Methods*
    Overridable Public Sub **Close**()
    Overridable Public Function **GetResponseStream**() As Stream
End Class

Hierarchy: System.Object→ System.MarshalByRefObject→
WebResponse(System.Runtime.Serialization.ISerializable, System.IDisposable)

Subclasses: FileWebResponse, HttpWebResponse

Returned By: WebException.Response, WebRequest.{EndGetResponse(), GetResponse()}

Passed To: WebException.WebException()

CHAPTER 12

System.Net.Sockets

The System.Net.Sockets namespace classes implement standard Berkeley sockets APIs for cross-process/cross-host communication. Sockets are low-level objects (abstractions, really) that provide the foundation for most Internet networking. A socket binds to a local address and port, and either waits for a connection from a remote address or connects to a remote address and exchanges data across the network. Two socket implementations are made available in this namespace, TCP/IP and UDP/IP. Most Internet applications, such as FTP clients and web browsers, are built upon socket connections.

Although many system-level programmers feel a close kinship with these types, .NET programmers are greatly encouraged to consider using higher-level constructs, such as HTTP (see the System.Net namespace) or the System.Runtime.Remoting types, to facilitate remote communications. If you need to work at the socket level, consider using Tcp-Client or TcpListener. These are high-level abstractions of the socket API that support client and server functionality.

For more details regarding many of the options mentioned in this namespace, consult a low-level sockets reference, such as W. Richard Stevens' "Network Programming in the Unix Environment" (Volumes 1 and 2) or "TCP/IP Illustrated" (Volumes 1, 2, and 3). Although the books were written for a Unix environment, .NET faithfully mirrors much, if not all, of the Berkeley sockets API (which originally came from Unix). Figure 12-1 shows the types in this namespace.

AddressFamily   Enum
System.Net.Sockets (system.dll)   *ECMA, serializable*

This enumeration contains values to specify the address family used by a socket. This indicates to which family of addressing schemes the address of the socket belongs. Note that the standard four-digit IP scheme falls under the enumeration InterNetwork, and its successor, IPv6, under the enumeration InterNetworkV6.

```
Public Enum AddressFamily
      Unspecified = 0
      Unix = 1
      InterNetwork = 2
```

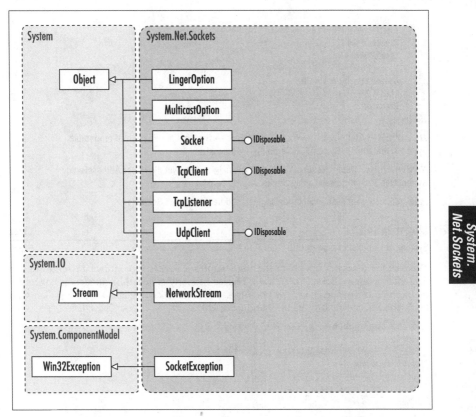

Figure 12-1. The System.Net.Sockets namespace

ImpLink = 3
Pup = 4
Chaos = 5
Ipx = 6
NS = 6
Iso = 7
Osi = 7
Ecma = 8
DataKit = 9
Ccitt = 10
Sna = 11
DecNet = 12
DataLink = 13
Lat = 14
HyperChannel = 15
AppleTalk = 16
NetBios = 17
VoiceView = 18
FireFox = 19
Banyan = 21
Atm = 22

```
      InterNetworkV6 = 23
      Cluster = 24
      Ieee12844 = 25
      Irda = 26
      NetworkDesigners = 28
      Max = 29
      Unknown = -1
End Enum
```

Hierarchy: System.Object→ System.ValueType→ System.Enum(System.IComparable, System.IFormattable, System.IConvertible)→ AddressFamily

Returned By: System.Net.EndPoint.AddressFamily, System.Net.IPAddress.AddressFamily, System.Net.SocketAddress.Family, Socket.AddressFamily

Passed To: System.Net.SocketAddress.SocketAddress(), Socket.Socket()

LingerOption   Class
System.Net.Sockets (system.dll)   *ECMA*

This class is a socket option object that enables a socket to continue to send queued data after a call to Socket.Close(). If the Enabled property is True, the connection lingers for the number of seconds given by LingerTime. The LingerOption object is set on a socket with the Socket.SetSocketOption() method and a SocketOptionName of SocketOptionName.Linger.

```
Public Class LingerOption
' Public Constructors
   Public Sub New(ByVal enable As Boolean, ByVal seconds As Integer)
' Public Instance Properties
   Public Property Enabled As Boolean
   Public Property LingerTime As Integer
End Class
```

Returned By: TcpClient.LingerState

Passed To: TcpClient.LingerState

MulticastOption   Class
System.Net.Sockets (system.dll)   *ECMA*

This class specifies an IP address for IP-multicast packets. IP-multicast addresses must be in the range of 224.0.0.0 to 239.255.255.255. The MulticastOption is set on a socket using the SocketOptionName.AddMembership value with Socket.SetSocketOption(). You can drop multicast with SocketOptionName.DropMembership.

```
Public Class MulticastOption
' Public Constructors
   Public Sub New(ByVal group As System.Net.IPAddress)
   Public Sub New(ByVal group As System.Net.IPAddress, ByVal mcint As System.Net.IPAddress)
' Public Instance Properties
   Public Property Group As IPAddress
   Public Property LocalAddress As IPAddress
End Class
```

NetworkStream

Class

System.Net.Sockets (system.dll)   *ECMA, marshal by reference, disposable*

This class creates a basic network stream from an underlying socket. It allows for simple data access to the stream and supports permissions settings.

```
Public Class NetworkStream : Inherits System.IO.Stream
' Public Constructors
   Public Sub New(ByVal socket As Socket)
   Public Sub New(ByVal socket As Socket, ByVal ownsSocket As Boolean)
   Public Sub New(ByVal socket As Socket, ByVal access As System.IO.FileAccess)
   Public Sub New(ByVal socket As Socket, ByVal access As System.IO.FileAccess, ByVal ownsSocket As Boolean)
' Public Instance Properties
   Overrides Public ReadOnly Property CanRead As Boolean
   Overrides Public ReadOnly Property CanSeek As Boolean
   Overrides Public ReadOnly Property CanWrite As Boolean
   Overridable Public ReadOnly Property DataAvailable As Boolean
   Overrides Public ReadOnly Property Length As Long
   Overrides Public Property Position As Long
' Protected Instance Properties
   Protected Property Readable As Boolean
   Protected Property Socket As Socket
   Protected Property Writeable As Boolean
' Public Instance Methods
   Overrides Public Function BeginRead(ByVal buffer As Byte(), ByVal offset As Integer, ByVal size As Integer, _
      ByVal callback As AsyncCallback, ByVal state As Object) As IAsyncResult
   Overrides Public Function BeginWrite(ByVal buffer As Byte(), ByVal offset As Integer, ByVal size As Integer, _
      ByVal callback As AsyncCallback, ByVal state As Object) As IAsyncResult
   Overrides Public Sub Close()
   Overrides Public Function EndRead(ByVal asyncResult As IAsyncResult) As Integer
   Overrides Public Sub EndWrite(ByVal asyncResult As IAsyncResult)
   Overrides Public Sub Flush()
   Overrides Public Function Read(ByRef buffer As Byte(), ByVal offset As Integer, ByVal size As Integer) As Integer
   Overrides Public Function Seek(ByVal offset As Long, ByVal origin As System.IO.SeekOrigin) As Long
   Overrides Public Sub SetLength(ByVal value As Long)
   Overrides Public Sub Write(ByVal buffer As Byte(), ByVal offset As Integer, ByVal size As Integer)
' Protected Instance Methods
   Overridable Protected Sub Dispose(ByVal disposing As Boolean)
   Overrides Protected Sub Finalize()
End Class
```

Hierarchy: System.Object→ System.MarshalByRefObject→
System.IO.Stream(System.IDisposable)→ NetworkStream

Returned By: TcpClient.GetStream()

ProtocolFamily

Enum

System.Net.Sockets (system.dll)   *serializable*

This enumeration contains settings for the protocol family of a socket.

```
Public Enum ProtocolFamily
     Unspecified = 0
     Unix = 1
     InterNetwork = 2
     ImpLink = 3
     Pup = 4
```

```
        Chaos = 5
        Ipx = 6
        NS = 6
        Iso = 7
        Osi = 7
        Ecma = 8
        DataKit = 9
        Ccitt = 10
        Sna = 11
        DecNet = 12
        DataLink = 13
        Lat = 14
        HyperChannel = 15
        AppleTalk = 16
        NetBios = 17
        VoiceView = 18
        FireFox = 19
        Banyan = 21
        Atm = 22
        InterNetworkV6 = 23
        Cluster = 24
        Ieee12844 = 25
        Irda = 26
        NetworkDesigners = 28
        Max = 29
        Unknown = -1
End Enum
```

Hierarchy: System.Object→ System.ValueType→ System.Enum(System.IComparable, System.IFormattable, System.IConvertible)→ ProtocolFamily

ProtocolType   Enum

System.Net.Sockets (system.dll)   *ECMA, serializable*

This enumeration contains settings for the protocol type of a socket. A protocol type must be specified for every Socket instance.

```
Public Enum ProtocolType
        Unspecified = 0
        IP = 0
        Icmp = 1
        Igmp = 2
        Ggp = 3
        Tcp = 6
        Pup = 12
        Udp = 17
        Idp = 22
        ND = 77
        Raw = 255
        Ipx = 1000
        Spx = 1256
        SpxII = 1257
        Unknown = -1
End Enum
```

Hierarchy: System.Object→ System.ValueType→ System.Enum(System.IComparable, System.IFormattable, System.IConvertible)→ ProtocolType

Returned By: Socket.ProtocolType

Passed To: Socket.Socket()

SelectMode

Enum

System.Net.Sockets (system.dll)

ECMA, serializable

This enumeration contains the settings for polling modes used by Socket.Poll().

```
Public Enum SelectMode
    SelectRead = 0
    SelectWrite = 1
    SelectError = 2
End Enum
```

Hierarchy: System.Object→ System.ValueType→ System.Enum(System.IComparable, System.IFormattable, System.IConvertible)→ SelectMode

Passed To: Socket.Poll()

Socket

Class

System.Net.Sockets (system.dll)

ECMA, disposable

This class implements a standard Berkeley socket. Each socket is constructed with the address family to use, the socket type (datagram or stream), and the protocol that the socket will use. Every socket must be bound to a local endpoint before you can use it. The Bind() method takes a System.Net.IPEndPoint object that contains the local IP address and port number to bind the socket to. Bind() must be called before any connection can be made through the socket. To establish a connection to a remote address, use Connect().

To listen for connections from remote clients, use Listen() to set the socket in listening mode where it waits for incoming connections. The integer argument to Listen() specifies how many remote connection requests can be queued at one time, waiting for a socket connection. A call to Accept() returns a new socket that connects to the first pending connection request in the listening queue. This new socket exists only for this connection and is destroyed once the connection is closed.

Data is written to a socket using Send(). Data from a specified buffer is sent through the socket to its remote endpoint. Data is read from a socket using Receive(). Receive() gets data from the socket connection and stores it in a specified receive buffer.

You can set several socket options to control the behavior of a socket with SetSocketOption(). This method requires a SocketOptionLevel value, which determines the type of socket option to set. For example, SocketOptionLevel.IP is used for options related to an IP socket. The SocketOptionName value gives the specific option, which must be applicable to the SocketOptionLevel. The last argument to SetSocketOption() provides the value of the option. SetSocketOption() enables features such as SocketOptionName.KeepAlive, in which a connection is maintained even when no data transfer is occurring, or SocketOptionName.MaxConnections, which sets the maximum permitted size of a listen queue.

When a session is finished, the connection can be gracefully closed with Shutdown(). When send or receive options are called with a SocketShutdown value, they are no longer allowed on the socket. A call to Close() terminates the socket connection.

```
Public Class Socket : Implements IDisposable
' Public Constructors
   Public Sub New(ByVal addressFamily As AddressFamily, ByVal socketType As SocketType, _
      ByVal protocolType As ProtocolType)
' Public Instance Properties
   Public ReadOnly Property AddressFamily As AddressFamily
   Public ReadOnly Property Available As Integer
   Public Property Blocking As Boolean
   Public ReadOnly Property Connected As Boolean
   Public ReadOnly Property Handle As IntPtr
   Public ReadOnly Property LocalEndPoint As EndPoint
   Public ReadOnly Property ProtocolType As ProtocolType
   Public ReadOnly Property RemoteEndPoint As EndPoint
   Public ReadOnly Property SocketType As SocketType
' Public Shared Methods
   Public Shared Sub Select(ByVal checkRead As System.Collections.IList,          _
      ByVal checkWrite As System.Collections.IList, ByVal checkError As System.Collections.IList, _
      ByVal microSeconds As Integer)
' Public Instance Methods
   Public Function Accept() As Socket
   Public Function BeginAccept(ByVal callback As AsyncCallback, ByVal state As Object) As IAsyncResult
   Public Function BeginConnect(ByVal remoteEP As System.Net.EndPoint, ByVal callback As AsyncCallback, _
      ByVal state As Object) As IAsyncResult
   Public Function BeginReceive(ByVal buffer As Byte(), ByVal offset As Integer, ByVal size As Integer,     _
      ByVal socketFlags As SocketFlags, ByVal callback As AsyncCallback, ByVal state As Object) As IAsyncResult
   Public Function BeginReceiveFrom(ByVal buffer As Byte(), ByVal offset As Integer, ByVal size As Integer, _
      ByVal socketFlags As SocketFlags, ByRef remoteEP As System.Net.EndPoint), ByVal callback As AsyncCallback, _
      ByVal state As Object)  As IAsyncResult
   Public Function BeginSend(ByVal buffer As Byte(), ByVal offset As Integer, ByVal size As Integer,       _
      ByVal socketFlags As SocketFlags, ByVal callback As AsyncCallback, ByVal state As Object) As IAsyncResult
   Public Function BeginSendTo(ByVal buffer As Byte(), ByVal offset As Integer, ByVal size As Integer,    _
      ByVal socketFlags As SocketFlags, ByVal remoteEP As System.Net.EndPoint), ByVal callback As AsyncCallback, _
      ByVal state As Object) As IAsyncResult
   Public Sub Bind(ByVal localEP As System.Net.EndPoint)
   Public Sub Close()
   Public Sub Connect(ByVal remoteEP As System.Net.EndPoint)
   Public Function EndAccept(ByVal asyncResult As IAsyncResult) As Socket
   Public Sub EndConnect(ByVal asyncResult As IAsyncResult)
   Public Function EndReceive(ByVal asyncResult As IAsyncResult) As Integer
   Public Function EndReceiveFrom(ByVal asyncResult As IAsyncResult, ByRef endPoint As System.Net.EndPoint) _
      As Integer
   Public Function EndSend(ByVal asyncResult As IAsyncResult) As Integer
   Public Function EndSendTo(ByVal asyncResult As IAsyncResult) As Integer
   Overrides Public Function GetHashCode() As Integer
   Public Function GetSocketOption(ByVal optionLevel As SocketOptionLevel,          _
      ByVal optionName As SocketOptionName, ByVal optionLength As Integer) As Byte()
   Public Function GetSocketOption(ByVal optionLevel As SocketOptionLevel, _
      ByVal optionName As SocketOptionName) As Object
   Public Sub GetSocketOption(ByVal optionLevel As SocketOptionLevel, ByVal optionName As SocketOptionName _
      , ByVal optionValue As Byte())
   Public Function IOControl(ByVal ioControlCode As Integer, ByVal optionInValue As Byte(), _
      ByVal optionOutValue As Byte()) As Integer
   Public Sub Listen(ByVal backlog As Integer)
   Public Function Poll(ByVal microSeconds As Integer, ByVal mode As SelectMode) As Boolean
   Public Function Receive(ByVal buffer As Byte()) As Integer
```

Public Function **Receive**(ByVal buffer As Byte(), ByVal offset As Integer, ByVal size As Integer, _
  ByVal socketFlags As SocketFlags) As Integer
Public Function **Receive**(ByVal buffer As Byte(), ByVal size As Integer, ByVal socketFlags As SocketFlags) As Integer
Public Function **Receive**(ByVal buffer As Byte(), ByVal socketFlags As SocketFlags) As Integer
Public Function **ReceiveFrom**(ByVal buffer As Byte(), ByRef remoteEP As System.Net.EndPoint) As Integer
Public Function **ReceiveFrom**(ByVal buffer As Byte(), ByVal offset As Integer, ByVal size As Integer, _
  ByVal socketFlags As SocketFlags, ByRef remoteEP As System.Net.EndPoint) As Integer
Public Function **ReceiveFrom**(ByVal buffer As Byte(), ByVal size As Integer, ByVal socketFlags As SocketFlags, _
  ByRef remoteEP As System.Net.EndPoint) As Integer
Public Function **ReceiveFrom**(ByVal buffer As Byte(), ByVal socketFlags As SocketFlags, _
  ByRef remoteEP As System.Net.EndPoint) As Integer
Public Function **Send**(ByVal buffer As Byte()) As Integer
Public Function **Send**(ByVal buffer As Byte(), ByVal offset As Integer, ByVal size As Integer, _
  ByVal socketFlags As SocketFlags) As Integer
Public Function **Send**(ByVal buffer As Byte(), ByVal size As Integer, ByVal socketFlags As SocketFlags) As Integer
Public Function **Send**(ByVal buffer As Byte(), ByVal socketFlags As SocketFlags) As Integer
Public Function **SendTo**(ByVal buffer As Byte(), ByVal remoteEP As System.Net.EndPoint) As Integer
Public Function **SendTo**(ByVal buffer As Byte(), ByVal offset As Integer, ByVal size As Integer, _
  ByVal socketFlags As SocketFlags, ByVal remoteEP As System.Net.EndPoint) As Integer
Public Function **SendTo**(ByVal buffer As Byte(), ByVal size As Integer, ByVal socketFlags As SocketFlags, _
  ByVal remoteEP As System.Net.EndPoint) As Integer
Public Function **SendTo**(ByVal buffer As Byte(), ByVal socketFlags As SocketFlags, _
  ByVal remoteEP As System.Net.EndPoint) As Integer
Public Sub **SetSocketOption**(ByVal optionLevel As SocketOptionLevel, ByVal optionName As SocketOptionName, _
  ByVal optionValue As Byte())
Public Sub **SetSocketOption**(ByVal optionLevel As SocketOptionLevel, ByVal optionName As SocketOptionName, _
  ByVal optionValue As Integer)
Public Sub **SetSocketOption**(ByVal optionLevel As SocketOptionLevel, ByVal optionName As SocketOptionName, _
  ByVal optionValue As Object)
Public Sub **Shutdown**(ByVal how As SocketShutdown)
' *Protected Instance Methods*
Overridable Protected Sub **Dispose**(ByVal disposing As Boolean)
Overrides Protected Sub **Finalize**()
End Class

Returned By: NetworkStream.Socket, TcpClient.Client, TcpListener.{AcceptSocket(), Server},
UdpClient.Client

Passed To: NetworkStream.NetworkStream(), TcpClient.Client, UdpClient.Client

SocketException   **Class**

System.Net.Sockets (system.dll)   *ECMA, serializable*

This exception represents a socket-related error.

Public Class **SocketException** : Inherits System.ComponentModel.Win32Exception
' *Public Constructors*
Public Sub **New**()
Public Sub **New**(ByVal errorCode As Integer)
' *Protected Constructors*
Protected Sub **New**(ByVal serializationInfo As System.Runtime.Serialization.SerializationInfo, _
  ByVal streamingContext As System.Runtime.Serialization.StreamingContext)
' *Public Instance Properties*
Overrides Public ReadOnly Property **ErrorCode** As Integer
End Class

Hierarchy: System.Object→ System.Exception(System.Runtime.Serialization.ISerializable)→ System.SystemException→ System.Runtime.InteropServices.ExternalException→ System.ComponentModel.Win32Exception→ SocketException

SocketFlags   Enum

System.Net.Sockets (system.dll)   *ECMA, serializable, flag*

This enumeration contains values for setting flags for socket messages. SocketFlags are provided to Socket.Send() and Socket.Receive() to specify parameters for how data is transferred. The OutOfBand flag tells the socket to process out-of-band data in the stream. DontRoute tells the socket to send data to the remote endpoint without using routing tables.

```
Public Enum SocketFlags
    None = &H000000000
    OutOfBand = &H000000001
    Peek = &H000000002
    DontRoute = &H000000004
    MaxIOVectorLength = &H000000010
    Partial = &H000008000
End Enum
```

Hierarchy: System.Object→ System.ValueType→ System.Enum(System.IComparable, System.IFormattable, System.IConvertible)→ SocketFlags

Passed To: Socket.{BeginReceive(), BeginReceiveFrom(), BeginSend(), BeginSendTo(), Receive(), ReceiveFrom(), Send(), SendTo()}

SocketOptionLevel   Enum

System.Net.Sockets (system.dll)   *ECMA, serializable*

This enumeration contains values for the type of socket option specified in Socket.SetSocketOption().

```
Public Enum SocketOptionLevel
    IP = 0
    Tcp = 6
    Udp = 17
    Socket = 65535
End Enum
```

Hierarchy: System.Object→ System.ValueType→ System.Enum(System.IComparable, System.IFormattable, System.IConvertible)→ SocketOptionLevel

Passed To: Socket.{GetSocketOption(), SetSocketOption()}

SocketOptionName   Enum

System.Net.Sockets (system.dll)   *ECMA, serializable*

This enumeration contains the names of socket options set by Socket.SetSocketOption(). The socket option named must be applicable to the option level from SocketOptionLevel.

```
Public Enum SocketOptionName
    IPOptions = 1
    Debug = 1
    NoDelay = 1
    NoChecksum = 1
```

```
    HeaderIncluded = 2
    AcceptConnection = 2
    Expedited = 2
    BsdUrgent = 2
    TypeOfService = 3
    ReuseAddress = 4
    IpTimeToLive = 4
    KeepAlive = 8
    MulticastInterface = 9
    MulticastTimeToLive = 10
    MulticastLoopback = 11
    AddMembership = 12
    DropMembership = 13
    DontFragment = 14
    AddSourceMembership = 15
    DropSourceMembership = 16
    DontRoute = 16
    BlockSource = 17
    UnblockSource = 18
    PacketInformation = 19
    ChecksumCoverage = 20
    Broadcast = 32
    UseLoopback = 64
    Linger = 128
    OutOfBandInline = 256
    SendBuffer = 4097
    ReceiveBuffer = 4098
    SendLowWater = 4099
    ReceiveLowWater = 4100
    SendTimeout = 4101
    ReceiveTimeout = 4102
    Error = 4103
    Type = 4104
    MaxConnections = 2147483647
    DontLinger = -129
    ExclusiveAddressUse = -5
End Enum
```

Hierarchy: System.Object→ System.ValueType→ System.Enum(System.IComparable, System.IFormattable, System.IConvertible)→ SocketOptionName

Passed To: Socket.{GetSocketOption(), SetSocketOption()}

SocketShutdown   Enum

System.Net.Sockets (system.dll)   *ECMA, serializable*

This enumeration provides values used by Socket.Shutdown(). Receive specifies that receiving will be disabled on a socket. Send specifies that sending will be disabled. Both disables sending and receiving.

```
Public Enum SocketShutdown
    Receive = 0
    Send = 1
    Both = 2
End Enum
```

Hierarchy: System.Object→ System.ValueType→ System.Enum(System.IComparable, System.IFormattable, System.IConvertible)→ SocketShutdown

Passed To: Socket.Shutdown()

SocketType   Enum

System.Net.Sockets (system.dll)   *ECMA, serializable*

This enumeration contains the names for the type of socket that is created.

```
Public Enum SocketType
    Stream = 1
    Dgram = 2
    Raw = 3
    Rdm = 4
    Seqpacket = 5
    Unknown = -1
End Enum
```

Hierarchy: System.Object→ System.ValueType→ System.Enum(System.IComparable, System.IFormattable, System.IConvertible)→ SocketType

Returned By: Socket.SocketType

Passed To: Socket.Socket()

TcpClient   Class

System.Net.Sockets (system.dll)   *disposable*

This class provides a client-side abstraction of the sockets API. The zero-argument form of the constructor creates the client. Connect to a remote server with the Connect() method (you must specify an existing System.Net.IPEndPoint or a remote IP address and port number). Alternatively, use an overloaded form of the constructor to simultaneously create the client and make the connection.

This class completely obscures the underlying socket. However, the GetStream() method returns a NetworkStream that you can use to send and receive data across the network.

```
Public Class TcpClient : Implements IDisposable
' Public Constructors
    Public Sub New()
    Public Sub New(ByVal localEP As System.Net.IPEndPoint)
    Public Sub New(ByVal hostname As String, ByVal port As Integer)
' Public Instance Properties
    Public Property LingerState As LingerOption
    Public Property NoDelay As Boolean
    Public Property ReceiveBufferSize As Integer
    Public Property ReceiveTimeout As Integer
    Public Property SendBufferSize As Integer
    Public Property SendTimeout As Integer
' Protected Instance Properties
    Protected Property Active As Boolean
    Protected Property Client As Socket
' Public Instance Methods
    Public Sub Close()
    Public Sub Connect(ByVal address As System.Net.IPAddress, ByVal port As Integer)
    Public Sub Connect(ByVal remoteEP As System.Net.IPEndPoint)
    Public Sub Connect(ByVal hostname As String, ByVal port As Integer)
    Public Function GetStream() As NetworkStream
```

' Protected Instance Methods
Overridable Protected Sub **Dispose**(ByVal disposing As Boolean)
Overrides Protected Sub **Finalize**()
End Class

Returned By: TcpListener.AcceptTcpClient()

TcpListener
Class

System.Net.Sockets (system.dll)

This class provides a server-side abstraction of the sockets API. The TcpListener is constructed with a local address and port to which it is automatically bound. A call to Start() initiates listening for connection requests. When a request is received, either AcceptSocket() or AcceptTcpClient() accepts the connection and returns a Socket or a TcpClient you can use to exchange data with the remote.

Public Class **TcpListener**
' Public Constructors
Public Sub **New**(ByVal port As Integer)
Public Sub **New**(ByVal localaddr As System.Net.IPAddress, ByVal port As Integer)
Public Sub **New**(ByVal localEP As System.Net.IPEndPoint)
' Public Instance Properties
Public ReadOnly Property **LocalEndpoint** As EndPoint
' Protected Instance Properties
Protected Property **Active** As Boolean
Protected Property **Server** As Socket
' Public Instance Methods
Public Function **AcceptSocket**() As Socket
Public Function **AcceptTcpClient**() As TcpClient
Public Function **Pending**() As Boolean
Public Sub **Start**()
Public Sub **Stop**()
' Protected Instance Methods
Overrides Protected Sub **Finalize**()
End Class

UdpClient
Class

System.Net.Sockets (system.dll)
disposable

This class is used to create UDP client sockets. UDP-based clients transmit messages called datagrams across a connection. Unlike TCP, control data is not sent to ensure the integrity and order of the data (so UDP is faster than TCP, but not as reliable). UDP is often used to broadcast media streams, such as video, and to support multicasting. The UdpClient can be constructed with a binding to a local address and port, or it can be constructed given the IP address and port number of the remote server to which it connects.

The JoinMulticastGroup() method sets the address of an IP-multicast group to join. DropMulticastGroup() drops the client from the group.

Public Class **UdpClient** : Implements IDisposable
' Public Constructors
Public Sub **New**()
Public Sub **New**(ByVal port As Integer)
Public Sub **New**(ByVal localEP As System.Net.IPEndPoint)
Public Sub **New**(ByVal hostname As String, ByVal port As Integer)

```
' Protected Instance Properties
    Protected Property Active As Boolean
    Protected Property Client As Socket
' Public Instance Methods
    Public Sub Close()
    Public Sub Connect(ByVal addr As System.Net.IPAddress, ByVal port As Integer)
    Public Sub Connect(ByVal endPoint As System.Net.IPEndPoint)
    Public Sub Connect(ByVal hostname As String, ByVal port As Integer)
    Public Sub DropMulticastGroup(ByVal multicastAddr As System.Net.IPAddress)
    Public Sub JoinMulticastGroup(ByVal multicastAddr As System.Net.IPAddress)
    Public Sub JoinMulticastGroup(ByVal multicastAddr As System.Net.IPAddress, ByVal timeToLive As Integer)
    Public Function Receive(ByRef remoteEP As System.Net.IPEndPoint) As Byte()
    Public Function Send(ByVal dgram As Byte(), ByVal bytes As Integer) As Integer
    Public Function Send(ByVal dgram As Byte(), ByVal bytes As Integer, ByVal endPoint As System.Net.IPEndPoint) _
        As Integer
    Public Function Send(ByVal dgram As Byte(), ByVal bytes As Integer, ByVal hostname As String, _
        ByVal port As Integer)  As Integer
End Class
```

CHAPTER 13

System.Reflection

System.Reflection is the API that exposes the full-fidelity metadata of the .NET environment to the .NET programmer. In short, it permits complete access to compile-time data at runtime. Everything is available, including fields, methods, constructors, properties, delegate types, and events. The reflection API (as exposed by the System.Reflection namespace) offers some truly unique capabilities unavailable in other compile-time bound languages such as C++. The closest the average COM programmer has come to using reflection is the IDispatch interface and/or type libraries. Reflection, fortunately, is at once both easier to use and far more powerful.

Reflection offers up a number of possible approaches to use. Introspection is the act of using the reflection APIs to discover information about a component assembly (and its constituent types) at runtime without any prior (compile-time) knowledge of it. This approach was first popularized by tools such as Visual Basic and numerous Java IDEs that offered GUI-based construction of visual interfaces. The third-party component was dropped into some well-known location, and the IDE "discovered" it and offered it on a toolbar the next time the IDE was started.

Along similar lines, reflection is often used as part of development tools; for example, the .NET utility *xsd.exe* uses metadata to generate XML Schema documents that correspond to .NET declared types. A .NET programmer could use reflection to generate SQL (Structured Query Language) statements for storing object instances into a relational database, or even into the SQL DDL (Data Definition Language) itself. Other tools could produce remoting proxies, transparently adding the necessary code to marshal and unmarshal parameters and return values across a network connection, even for types that weren't designed to be remoted in the first place.

Lastly, reflection isn't just a read-only view of a type's construction; the reflective APIs in .NET also allow for manipulation of methods and state (although not the rewriting of code—once loaded, a type's methods remain exactly as they were defined). The most prevalent example of this sort of usage of reflection is in the .NET Object Serialization code (in the System.Runtime.Serialization namespace). Serialization takes an existing object instance, uses reflection to suck out the object's state, transforms it into a binary representation, and stores that representation (a stream of bytes) to some source, such as a file on disk, a socket, a binary column in a database, and so on. Later, serialization can also take that same stream of bytes and rehydrate the serialized object back into existence.

Careful readers will note that last sentence and wonder, if only for a moment, how it could be possible for code to reach into an object and directly manipulate its state; after all, any object-oriented developer worthy of the name knows to mark all fields as "private," which should make said fields completely inaccessible. The fact is, reflection can violate even these most sacrosanct of boundaries—it can reach in and manipulate any private member it finds—thus it is highly sensitive to any changes in the definition of fields inside of a type.

Figure 13-1 shows the inheritance diagram for this namespace. Figure 13-2 shows the exceptions, delegates, and attributes from this namespace.

AmbiguousMatchException   NotInheritable Class

System.Reflection (mscorlib.dll)   *ECMA, serializable*

This exception is thrown when you attempt to bind to a method with the Binder and the given criteria matches more than one method; this is the case, for example, when binding against an overloaded method solely by its name.

```
Public NotInheritable Class AmbiguousMatchException : Inherits SystemException
' Public Constructors
   Public Sub New()
   Public Sub New(ByVal message As String)
   Public Sub New(ByVal message As String, ByVal inner As Exception)
End Class
```

Hierarchy: System.Object→ System.Exception(System.Runtime.Serialization.ISerializable)→ System.SystemException→ AmbiguousMatchException

Assembly   Class

System.Reflection (mscorlib.dll)   *ECMA, serializable*

In the .NET environment, assemblies are the fundamental units of development and deployment; although the various languages allow the .NET programmer to work with elements as fine-grained as classes or functions, these types must belong as part of an assembly in order to be loaded and used. Consequently, the assembly is the core of the component model in .NET.

The Assembly type is the Reflection API object representing the assembly. An assembly (either a .DLL or .EXE—to the CLR, there is no difference) consists of one or more modules; most assemblies are in fact single-module assemblies. (Multimodule assemblies are certainly possible, but usually not necessary for most developers' needs. As such, they are not discussed here.) .NET programmers can use the object model in the Assembly class to discover information about a particular assembly—for example, an assembly knows the modules contained within it, and each module knows the types defined and bound to that module. Thus, for any random assembly, a .NET program can enumerate each type defined inside that assembly. This is, in fact, what the *WinCV.exe* sample program (see the .NET SDK, in the *bin* subdirectory) does. (The *ILDasm.exe* application provides similar results, but uses unmanaged APIs to view into an assembly, rather than Reflection.)

The Assembly API can be broken into two collections: those representing operations against a particular assembly (indicated by a particular Assembly instance), and those

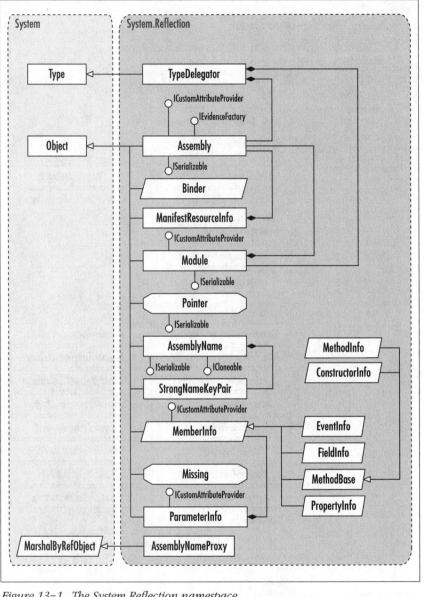

Figure 13-1. The System.Reflection namespace

that work independently of a particular instance—loading an assembly into the CLR, for example.

The instance-specific methods of Assembly are, for the most part, self-describing. The properties of Assembly, in particular, are straightforward. CodeBase describes the URL from which this assembly was loaded, EntryPoint describes the entry point (the Main()) of the assembly, if it has one, Evidence is the security information regarding this particular assembly, and FullName is the fully qualified (name, culture, version info, and public key token) for this assembly. The remaining two properties are a bit more obscure:

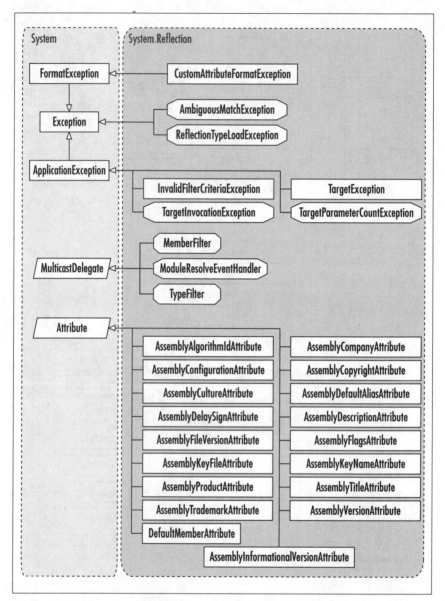

Figure 13-2. Exceptions, delegates, and attributes from System.Reflection

GlobalAssemblyCache is a simple boolean value indicating whether this assembly was loaded out of the global assembly cache or not, and Location describes the location of the manifest file (which may be in a different file if this is a multimodule assembly).

Some instance methods of Assembly require a bit more in the way of explanation. Get-Name() returns the fully qualified for this assembly; note that this is an AssemblyName instance, rather than a string. Because an Assembly is also a producer of custom attribute types (such as AssemblyVersionAttribute or AssemblyKeyFileAttribute), Assembly also has the Get-CustomAttributes() method. In addition, the IsDefined() method can be used to find a particular attribute type defined in this assembly; it simply returns a boolean true/false value, whereas GetCustomAttributes() returns the instance(s) of the attribute itself. A list (an array of AssemblyName instances) of all assemblies that this assembly references can be found by calling GetReferencedAssemblies().

In addition to code, assemblies can contain arbitrary "resources." (Here the term "resource" means "anything that's not code.") These resources are contained as .file references in the assembly's manifest file and can be discovered from an Assembly instance by calling GetManifestResourceNames(). Information about the persistence scheme used for the resources is available via the GetManifestResourceInfo(). The actual resource itself can be obtained by calling GetManifestResourceStream(), which returns a System.IO.Stream object containing or pointing to the file's contents. In addition, a list of all files (both resources and code) can be obtained by calling GetFiles(), and a particular file can be opened by calling GetFile().

An assembly consists of one or more modules; the list of modules bound to this assembly are available via the GetModules() call. A particular module can be obtained as a Module instance by calling GetModule() against the assembly. Because the CLR delays loading modules until required, Assembly also provides the GetLoadedModules() to list the modules of this assembly that have been loaded into the CLR. Going the other direction, the LoadModule() call forces the CLR to load the given module name into memory, rather than waiting for the usual on-demand loading policy of the CLR. Should a module-load fail for some reason, the CLR signals event handlers bound against the Assembly instance's ModuleResolve event.

Frequently, a .NET programmer will not be interested in the modules that comprise the assembly, only the types defined within it. Towards that end, the Assembly type has a couple of "shortcut" methods to get the types. GetTypes() returns a list of all the types defined in this assembly as an array of System.Type references. GetType() returns a particular System.Type, or optionally (depending on which overload is used) throws an exception if the type cannot be found. Take note that the parameterless version of GetType() is the inherited method from System.Object; it returns the System.Type reference for Assembly, not any types defined within the assembly itself. Note that the GetTypes() call returns a list of all types defined in the assembly, even those declared as private to the assembly (which normally should not be seen by assembly consumers); to see a list of only the "public" types, call GetExportedTypes() instead.

Once a particular type within the assembly has been located, an instance of that type can be created by calling CreateInstance(). This uses the system activator (see System.Activator) to create an instance of that type and hand it back as a generic object reference. For example, calling Dim o As Object = GetType(Object).Assembly.CreateInstance("DateTime") is a roundabout way to create an instance of a System.DateTime; the typeof(Object) returns the System.Type for System.Object. That type lives in the mscorlib.dll assembly, and calling CreateInstance("DateTime") succeeds because DateTime is defined within that assembly. .NET programmers typically only use this method when building a container application (such as ASP.NET) that will be creating instances of objects not known at compile-time.

The Assembly type also contains a number of shared methods for use in referencing assemblies as a collective whole; for example, the GetAssembly() call returns the Assembly in which a particular Type is defined. (Knowing this, we could change the example in the last paragraph to read Dim o As Object = Assembly.GetAssembly(GetType(Object)).CreateInstance("DateTime"), which is a bit clearer if a bit longer.) Likewise, the GetExecutingAssembly() returns the assembly in which the current code is executing from and GetCallingAssembly() returns the assembly whose code called the methods in this assembly. (These methods by themselves may seem less than useful, until the idea of walking the call-stack, as Code Access Security does, is considered.)

However, the two most important shared methods on the Assembly class by far are Load() and LoadFrom(). Both load an assembly into the CLR, but in drastically different ways. LoadFrom() is the simpler of the two, taking a filename and loading it as an assembly into the CLR—no questions asked. Load() goes through the assembly-load algorithm and checks the private probe path and the Global Assembly Cache before giving up on finding the assembly. (Note that if an assembly-load request fails, the appropriate events on the containing AppDomain instance are signaled.)

```
Public Class Assembly : Implements System.Security.IEvidenceFactory, ICustomAttributeProvider, _
    System.Runtime.Serialization.ISerializable
' Public Instance Properties
    Overridable Public ReadOnly Property CodeBase As String
    Overridable Public ReadOnly Property EntryPoint As MethodInfo
    Overridable Public ReadOnly Property EscapedCodeBase As String
    Overridable Public ReadOnly Property Evidence As Evidence Implements IEvidenceFactory.Evidence
    Overridable Public ReadOnly Property FullName As String
    Public ReadOnly Property GlobalAssemblyCache As Boolean
    Overridable Public ReadOnly Property Location As String
' Public Shared Methods
    Public Shared Function CreateQualifiedName(ByVal assemblyName As String, ByVal typeName As String) _
        As String
    Public Shared Function GetAssembly(ByVal type As Type) As Assembly
    Public Shared Function GetCallingAssembly() As Assembly
    Public Shared Function GetEntryAssembly() As Assembly
    Public Shared Function GetExecutingAssembly() As Assembly
    Public Shared Function Load(ByVal assemblyRef As AssemblyName) As Assembly
    Public Shared Function Load(ByVal assemblyRef As AssemblyName,    _
        ByVal assemblySecurity As System.Security.Policy.Evidence) As Assembly
    Public Shared Function Load(ByVal rawAssembly As Byte()) As Assembly
    Public Shared Function Load(ByVal rawAssembly As Byte(), ByVal rawSymbolStore As Byte()) As Assembly
    Public Shared Function Load(ByVal rawAssembly As Byte(), ByVal rawSymbolStore As Byte(), _
        ByVal securityEvidence As System.Security.Policy.Evidence) As Assembly
    Public Shared Function Load(ByVal assemblyString As String) As Assembly
    Public Shared Function Load(ByVal assemblyString As String,    _
        ByVal assemblySecurity As System.Security.Policy.Evidence) As Assembly
    Public Shared Function LoadFrom(ByVal assemblyFile As String) As Assembly
    Public Shared Function LoadFrom(ByVal assemblyFile As String,    _
        ByVal securityEvidence As System.Security.Policy.Evidence) As Assembly
    Public Shared Function LoadWithPartialName(ByVal partialName As String) As Assembly
    Public Shared Function LoadWithPartialName(ByVal partialName As String, _
        ByVal securityEvidence As System.Security.Policy.Evidence) As Assembly
' Public Instance Methods
    Public Function CreateInstance(ByVal typeName As String) As Object
    Public Function CreateInstance(ByVal typeName As String, ByVal ignoreCase As Boolean) As Object
    Public Function CreateInstance(ByVal typeName As String, ByVal ignoreCase As Boolean,    _
        ByVal bindingAttr As BindingFlags, ByVal binder As Binder, ByVal args As Object()),    _
        ByVal culture As System.Globalization.CultureInfo, ByVal activationAttributes As Object())  As Object
    Overridable Public Function GetCustomAttributes(ByVal inherit As Boolean) As Object() _
        Implements ICustomAttributeProvider.GetCustomAttributes
    Overridable Public Function GetCustomAttributes(ByVal attributeType As Type, ByVal inherit As Boolean) _
        As Object() Implements ICustomAttributeProvider.GetCustomAttributes
    Overridable Public Function GetExportedTypes() As Type()
    Overridable Public Function GetFile(ByVal name As String) As FileStream
    Overridable Public Function GetFiles() As FileStream()
    Overridable Public Function GetFiles(ByVal getResourceModules As Boolean) As FileStream()
    Public Function GetLoadedModules() As Module()
```

Public Function **GetLoadedModules**(ByVal getResourceModules As Boolean) As Module()
Overridable Public Function **GetManifestResourceInfo**(ByVal resourceName As String) _
    As ManifestResourceInfo
Overridable Public Function **GetManifestResourceNames**() As String()
Overridable Public Function **GetManifestResourceStream**(ByVal name As String) As Stream
Overridable Public Function **GetManifestResourceStream**(ByVal type As Type, ByVal name As String) _
    As Stream
Public Function **GetModule**(ByVal name As String) As Module
Public Function **GetModules**() As Module()
Public Function **GetModules**(ByVal getResourceModules As Boolean) As Module()
Overridable Public Function **GetName**() As AssemblyName
Overridable Public Function **GetName**(ByVal copiedName As Boolean) As AssemblyName
Overridable Public Sub **GetObjectData**(ByVal info As System.Runtime.Serialization.SerializationInfo, _
    ByVal context As System.Runtime.Serialization.StreamingContext) Implements ISerializable.GetObjectData
Public Function **GetReferencedAssemblies**() As AssemblyName()
Public Function **GetSatelliteAssembly**(ByVal culture As System.Globalization.CultureInfo) As Assembly
Public Function **GetSatelliteAssembly**(ByVal culture As System.Globalization.CultureInfo, _
    ByVal version As Version) As Assembly
Overridable Public Function **GetType**(ByVal name As String) As Type
Overridable Public Function **GetType**(ByVal name As String, ByVal throwOnError As Boolean) As Type
Public Function **GetType**(ByVal name As String, ByVal throwOnError As Boolean, ByVal ignoreCase As Boolean) _
    As Type
Overridable Public Function **GetTypes**() As Type()
Overridable Public Function **IsDefined**(ByVal attributeType As Type, ByVal inherit As Boolean) As Boolean _
    Implements ICustomAttributeProvider.IsDefined
Public Function **LoadModule**(ByVal moduleName As String, ByVal rawModule As Byte()) As Module
Public Function **LoadModule**(ByVal moduleName As String, ByVal rawModule As Byte(), _
    ByVal rawSymbolStore As Byte()) As Module
Overrides Public Function **ToString**() As String
' Events
    Public Event **ModuleResolve** As ModuleResolveEventHandler
End Class

Subclasses: System.Reflection.Emit.AssemblyBuilder

Returned By: System.AppDomain.{GetAssemblies(), Load()},
System.AssemblyLoadEventArgs.LoadedAssembly, ManifestResourceInfo.ReferencedAssembly,
Module.Assembly, System.ResolveEventHandler.{EndInvoke(), Invoke()}, System.Type.Assembly

Passed To: Multiple types

AssemblyAlgorithmIdAttribute   NotInheritable Class

System.Reflection (mscorlib.dll)

The assembly manifest contains a hash of all of the files in the assembly. This attribute
allows you to specify and change which hashing algorithm is used to hash these files.

Public NotInheritable Class **AssemblyAlgorithmIdAttribute** : Inherits Attribute
' Public Constructors
    Public Sub **New**(ByVal algorithmId As System.Configuration.Assemblies.AssemblyHashAlgorithm)
    Public Sub **New**(ByVal algorithmId As UInt32)
' Public Instance Properties
    Public ReadOnly Property **AlgorithmId** As UInt32
End Class

Hierarchy: System.Object→ System.Attribute→ AssemblyAlgorithmIdAttribute

Valid On: Assembly

AssemblyCompanyAttribute   **NotInheritable Class**

System.Reflection (mscorlib.dll)

This custom attribute is applied on an assembly that allows you to specify the company
that created the assembly.

```
Public NotInheritable Class AssemblyCompanyAttribute : Inherits Attribute
' Public Constructors
    Public Sub New(ByVal company As String)
' Public Instance Properties
    Public ReadOnly Property Company As String
End Class
```

Hierarchy: System.Object→ System.Attribute→ AssemblyCompanyAttribute

Valid On: Assembly

AssemblyConfigurationAttribute   **NotInheritable Class**

System.Reflection (mscorlib.dll)

This custom attribute allows you to specify a configuration for the assembly (such as
debug, release, beta, etc.).

```
Public NotInheritable Class AssemblyConfigurationAttribute : Inherits Attribute
' Public Constructors
    Public Sub New(ByVal configuration As String)
' Public Instance Properties
    Public ReadOnly Property Configuration As String
End Class
```

Hierarchy: System.Object→ System.Attribute→ AssemblyConfigurationAttribute

Valid On: Assembly

AssemblyCopyrightAttribute   **NotInheritable Class**

System.Reflection (mscorlib.dll)

This custom attribute string contains copyright information.

```
Public NotInheritable Class AssemblyCopyrightAttribute : Inherits Attribute
' Public Constructors
    Public Sub New(ByVal copyright As String)
' Public Instance Properties
    Public ReadOnly Property Copyright As String
End Class
```

Hierarchy: System.Object→ System.Attribute→ AssemblyCopyrightAttribute

Valid On: Assembly

AssemblyCultureAttribute   **NotInheritable Class**

System.Reflection (mscorlib.dll)

This custom attribute specifies the supported culture of an assembly.

```
Public NotInheritable Class AssemblyCultureAttribute : Inherits Attribute
' Public Constructors
    Public Sub New(ByVal culture As String)
```

```
' Public Instance Properties
   Public ReadOnly Property Culture As String
End Class
```

Hierarchy: System.Object→ System.Attribute→ AssemblyCultureAttribute

Valid On: Assembly

AssemblyDefaultAliasAttribute   NotInheritable Class

System.Reflection (mscorlib.dll)

This custom attribute specifies a friendly name for an assembly. This is useful when assemblies have cryptic names such as GUIDs, as COM components do.

```
Public NotInheritable Class AssemblyDefaultAliasAttribute : Inherits Attribute
' Public Constructors
   Public Sub New(ByVal defaultAlias As String)
' Public Instance Properties
   Public ReadOnly Property DefaultAlias As String
End Class
```

Hierarchy: System.Object→ System.Attribute→ AssemblyDefaultAliasAttribute

Valid On: Assembly

AssemblyDelaySignAttribute   NotInheritable Class

System.Reflection (mscorlib.dll)

When an assembly designer does not have access to a key-pair to sign a component, this attribute reserves space in the manifest to be filled by a signing utility. The framework's sn.exe utility has a command-line switch (-R or -Rc) just for this purpose.

```
Public NotInheritable Class AssemblyDelaySignAttribute : Inherits Attribute
' Public Constructors
   Public Sub New(ByVal delaySign As Boolean)
' Public Instance Properties
   Public ReadOnly Property DelaySign As Boolean
End Class
```

Hierarchy: System.Object→ System.Attribute→ AssemblyDelaySignAttribute

Valid On: Assembly

AssemblyDescriptionAttribute   NotInheritable Class

System.Reflection (mscorlib.dll)

This custom attribute allows a description to be stored with an assembly.

```
Public NotInheritable Class AssemblyDescriptionAttribute : Inherits Attribute
' Public Constructors
   Public Sub New(ByVal description As String)
' Public Instance Properties
   Public ReadOnly Property Description As String
End Class
```

Hierarchy: System.Object→ System.Attribute→ AssemblyDescriptionAttribute

Valid On: Assembly

AssemblyFileVersionAttribute   NotInheritable Class

System.Reflection (mscorlib.dll)

This custom attribute stores a given version number in the assembly's Win32 VERSION-INFO resource. This is not the same as the assembly's version (given by the AssemblyVersionAttribute).

Public NotInheritable Class **AssemblyFileVersionAttribute** : Inherits Attribute
' *Public Constructors*
   Public Sub **New**(ByVal version As String)
' *Public Instance Properties*
   Public ReadOnly Property **Version** As String
End Class

Hierarchy: System.Object→ System.Attribute→ AssemblyFileVersionAttribute

Valid On: Assembly

AssemblyFlagsAttribute   NotInheritable Class

System.Reflection (mscorlib.dll)

Use this attribute to specify the side-by-side execution behavior of this assembly. The flags parameter may take one of the following values: 0x0000 (side-by-side compatible), 0x0010 (side-by-side operation is prohibited within the same application domain), 0x0020 (side-by-side operation prohibited within same process), or 0x0030 (side-by-side operation prohibited within the same machine boundary).

Public NotInheritable Class **AssemblyFlagsAttribute** : Inherits Attribute
' *Public Constructors*
   Public Sub **New**(ByVal flags As UInt32)
' *Public Instance Properties*
   Public ReadOnly Property **Flags** As UInt32
End Class

Hierarchy: System.Object→ System.Attribute→ AssemblyFlagsAttribute

Valid On: Assembly

AssemblyInformationalVersionAttribute   NotInheritable Class

System.Reflection (mscorlib.dll)

This custom attribute allows a version number to be stored. This stored version is purely for documentation and is not used by the runtime.

Public NotInheritable Class **AssemblyInformationalVersionAttribute** : Inherits Attribute
' *Public Constructors*
   Public Sub **New**(ByVal informationalVersion As String)
' *Public Instance Properties*
   Public ReadOnly Property **InformationalVersion** As String
End Class

Hierarchy: System.Object→ System.Attribute→ AssemblyInformationalVersionAttribute

Valid On: Assembly

AssemblyKeyFileAttribute

NotInheritable Class

System.Reflection (mscorlib.dll)

To create a strong-named assembly, use this attribute, specifying a file containing a key-pair. Alternatively, you could use an AssemblyDelaySignAttribute or an AssemblyKeyNameAttribute.

Public NotInheritable Class **AssemblyKeyFileAttribute** : Inherits Attribute
' *Public Constructors*
   Public Sub **New**(ByVal keyFile As String)
' *Public Instance Properties*
   Public ReadOnly Property **KeyFile** As String
End Class

Hierarchy: System.Object→ System.Attribute→ AssemblyKeyFileAttribute

Valid On: Assembly

AssemblyKeyNameAttribute

NotInheritable Class

System.Reflection (mscorlib.dll)

This attribute serves the same purpose as an AssemblyKeyFileAttribute, but allows you to specify a key container instead of a file.

Public NotInheritable Class **AssemblyKeyNameAttribute** : Inherits Attribute
' *Public Constructors*
   Public Sub **New**(ByVal keyName As String)
' *Public Instance Properties*
   Public ReadOnly Property **KeyName** As String
End Class

Hierarchy: System.Object→ System.Attribute→ AssemblyKeyNameAttribute

Valid On: Assembly

AssemblyName

NotInheritable Class

System.Reflection (mscorlib.dll)

serializable

This class represents an assembly's fully qualified name, which makes it unique. An assembly's identity consists of a simple name (the Name property), supported culture (CultureInfo), version number, and key pair. The version number itself has four parts: major version, minor version, build number and revision number. The Flags property allows you to set the flags for an assembly (see the AssemblyNameFlags enumeration). Use HashAlgorithm to access the hash algorithm used with the manifest to verify that the files of an assembly are correct. VersionCompatibility is a System.Configuration.Assemblies.AssemblyVersionCompatibility enumeration, which allows specification of the compatibility between versions.

Both FullName and ToString() return a comma-delimited string formatted, such as: Name, Culture = CultureInfo, Version = Version Number, SN = StrongName, PK = Public Key Token. Any of the parameters except Name are optional. SetPublicKey() and SetPublicKeyToken() allow you to specify a public key for an originator or the strong name respectively, and the complementary Get methods allow you to retrieve the same information.

Public NotInheritable Class **AssemblyName** : Implements ICloneable, System.Runtime.Serialization.ISerializable, _
   System.Runtime.Serialization.IDeserializationCallback
' *Public Constructors*
   Public Sub **New**()
' *Public Instance Properties*

Public Property **CodeBase** As String
Public Property **CultureInfo** As CultureInfo
Public ReadOnly Property **EscapedCodeBase** As String
Public Property **Flags** As AssemblyNameFlags
Public ReadOnly Property **FullName** As String
Public Property **HashAlgorithm** As AssemblyHashAlgorithm
Public Property **KeyPair** As StrongNameKeyPair
Public Property **Name** As String
Public Property **Version** As Version
Public Property **VersionCompatibility** As AssemblyVersionCompatibility
' *Public Shared Methods*
Public Shared Function **GetAssemblyName**(ByVal assemblyFile As String) As AssemblyName
' *Public Instance Methods*
Public Function **Clone**() As Object Implements ICloneable.Clone
Public Sub **GetObjectData**(ByVal info As System.Runtime.Serialization.SerializationInfo,
    ByVal context As System.Runtime.Serialization.StreamingContext) Implements ISerializable.GetObjectData
Public Function **GetPublicKey**() As Byte()
Public Function **GetPublicKeyToken**() As Byte()
Public Sub **OnDeserialization**(ByVal sender As Object) Implements IDeserializationCallback.OnDeserialization
Public Sub **SetPublicKey**(ByVal publicKey As Byte())
Public Sub **SetPublicKeyToken**(ByVal publicKeyToken As Byte())
Overrides Public Function **ToString**() As String
End Class

Returned By: Assembly.{GetName(), GetReferencedAssemblies()},
AssemblyNameProxy.GetAssemblyName()

Passed To: System.AppDomain.{DefineDynamicAssembly(), Load()}, Assembly.Load(),
System.Text.RegularExpressions.Regex.CompileToAssembly()

AssemblyNameFlags   Enum

System.Reflection (mscorlib.dll)   *serializable, flag*

This enumeration represents the possible flags for an AssemblyName. AssemblyName.Flags
can either be set to None or PublicKey. PublicKey specifies that the originator is fully given
by the public key, rather than by a token.

Public Enum **AssemblyNameFlags**
    None = &H000000000
    PublicKey = &H000000001
End Enum

Hierarchy: System.Object→ System.ValueType→ System.Enum(System.IComparable,
System.IFormattable, System.IConvertible)→ AssemblyNameFlags

Returned By: AssemblyName.Flags

Passed To: AssemblyName.Flags

AssemblyNameProxy   Class

System.Reflection (mscorlib.dll)   *marshal by reference*

This class is a remotable wrapper around AssemblyName. To access the underlying AssemblyName, call AssemblyName.GetAssemblyName().

Public Class **AssemblyNameProxy** : Inherits MarshalByRefObject
' *Public Constructors*
    Public Sub **New**()

```
' Public Instance Methods
   Public Function GetAssemblyName(ByVal assemblyFile As String) As AssemblyName
End Class
```

Hierarchy: System.Object→ System.MarshalByRefObject→ AssemblyNameProxy

AssemblyProductAttribute   NotInheritable Class
System.Reflection (mscorlib.dll)

This class is a custom attribute for the product name.

```
Public NotInheritable Class AssemblyProductAttribute : Inherits Attribute
' Public Constructors
   Public Sub New(ByVal product As String)
' Public Instance Properties
   Public ReadOnly Property Product As String
End Class
```

Hierarchy: System.Object→ System.Attribute→ AssemblyProductAttribute

Valid On: Assembly

AssemblyTitleAttribute   NotInheritable Class
System.Reflection (mscorlib.dll)

This class is a custom attribute for an assembly title.

```
Public NotInheritable Class AssemblyTitleAttribute : Inherits Attribute
' Public Constructors
   Public Sub New(ByVal title As String)
' Public Instance Properties
   Public ReadOnly Property Title As String
End Class
```

Hierarchy: System.Object→ System.Attribute→ AssemblyTitleAttribute

Valid On: Assembly

AssemblyTrademarkAttribute   NotInheritable Class
System.Reflection (mscorlib.dll)

This custom attribute is used to add a trademark.

```
Public NotInheritable Class AssemblyTrademarkAttribute : Inherits Attribute
' Public Constructors
   Public Sub New(ByVal trademark As String)
' Public Instance Properties
   Public ReadOnly Property Trademark As String
End Class
```

Hierarchy: System.Object→ System.Attribute→ AssemblyTrademarkAttribute

Valid On: Assembly

AssemblyVersionAttribute
NotInheritable Class

System.Reflection (mscorlib.dll)

This attribute is the version of the assembly. This version is used by the framework to check compatibility and determine if side-by-side execution is needed.

Public NotInheritable Class **AssemblyVersionAttribute** : Inherits Attribute
' *Public Constructors*
    Public Sub **New**(ByVal version As String)
' *Public Instance Properties*
    Public ReadOnly Property **Version** As String
End Class

Hierarchy: System.Object→ System.Attribute→ AssemblyVersionAttribute

Valid On: Assembly

Binder
MustInherit Class

System.Reflection (mscorlib.dll)
ECMA, serializable

This type is used by the .NET runtime for method argument conversion. It is responsible for such things as determining whether it is permissible to pass a short to a method that takes a long parameter. If you need to override .NET's default conversion rules, you could subclass this type (however, most programmers will never need to do this). For more details, see the .NET Framework SDK documentation on this type.

Public MustInherit Class **Binder**
' *Protected Constructors*
    Protected Sub **New**()
' *Public Instance Methods*
    MustInherit Public Function **BindToField**(ByVal bindingAttr As BindingFlags, ByVal match As FieldInfo(), _
      ByVal value As Object, ByVal culture As System.Globalization.CultureInfo) As FieldInfo
    MustInherit Public Function **BindToMethod**(ByVal bindingAttr As BindingFlags, ByVal match As MethodBase(), _
      ByRef args As Object(), ByVal modifiers As ParameterModifier(), ByVal culture As System.Globalization.CultureInfo) _
      , ByVal names As String(), ByRef state As Object) As MethodBase
    MustInherit Public Function **ChangeType**(ByVal value As Object, ByVal type As Type, _
      ByVal culture As System.Globalization.CultureInfo) As Object
    MustInherit Public Sub **ReorderArgumentArray**(ByRef args As Object(), ByVal state As Object)
    MustInherit Public Function **SelectMethod**(ByVal bindingAttr As BindingFlags, ByVal match As MethodBase(), _
      ByVal types As Type(), ByVal modifiers As ParameterModifier()) As MethodBase
    MustInherit Public Function **SelectProperty**(ByVal bindingAttr As BindingFlags, ByVal match As PropertyInfo(), _
      ByVal returnType As Type, ByVal indexes As Type(), ByVal modifiers As ParameterModifier()) As PropertyInfo
End Class

Returned By: System.Type.DefaultBinder

Passed To: Multiple types

BindingFlags
Enum

System.Reflection (mscorlib.dll)
ECMA, serializable, flag

This enumeration specifies how reflection searches for members. It is used by many types in the System and System.Reflection namespaces. The following list describes each enumeration member:

CreateInstance
    Tells reflection to call a constructor that matches the specified arguments. If a member name is supplied, it is ignored.

DeclaredOnly
> Specifies to search only from the declared methods, and not from the inherited ones.

Default
> Specifies that all the default search parameters should be used.

ExactBinding
> Ensures that arguments must match exactly (no downcasting is performed).

Static
> Allows shared members to match.

FlattenHierarchy
> Allows matching of shared methods from inherited classes.

GetField
GetProperty
> Specify that the value of a specified field or property should be returned.

SetField
SetProperty
> Allow you to set fields and properties.

IgnoreCase
> Causes the search to be case-insensitive.

IgnoreReturn
> Tells the search to ignore the return value. This is used primarily for COM Interop.

Public
> Allows public members to be searched.

Instance
> Specifies that instance members must be searched.

NonPublic
> Allows nonpublic members to be searched.

InvokeMethod
> Says that a method that is not a constructor should be invoked.

OptionalParamBinding
> Allows matching based on the number of parameters for methods with optional arguments.

SuppressChangeType
> Specifies that the CLR should not perform type coercions to invoke a method (as of this writing, SuppressChangeType is unimplemented).

PutDispProperty
PutRefDispProperty
> Allow you to call the COM accessors. If the put method expects a COM intrinsic type, use PutDispProperty; if the put method expects a COM object, use PutRefDisp-Property.

```
Public Enum BindingFlags
    Default = &H000000000
    IgnoreCase = &H000000001
    DeclaredOnly = &H000000002
    Instance = &H000000004
    Static = &H000000008
    Public = &H000000010
    NonPublic = &H000000020
    FlattenHierarchy = &H000000040
    InvokeMethod = &H000000100
    CreateInstance = &H000000200
    GetField = &H000000400
    SetField = &H000000800
    GetProperty = &H000001000
    SetProperty = &H000002000
    PutDispProperty = &H000004000
    PutRefDispProperty = &H000008000
    ExactBinding = &H000010000
    SuppressChangeType = &H000020000
    OptionalParamBinding = &H000040000
    IgnoreReturn = &H001000000
End Enum
```

Hierarchy: System.Object→ System.ValueType→ System.Enum(System.IComparable, System.IFormattable, System.IConvertible)→ BindingFlags

Passed To: Multiple types

CallingConventions   Enum

System.Reflection (mscorlib.dll)   *serializable, flag*

Calling conventions are the rules that govern the semantics of how method arguments and return values are passed. They also specify which registers to use, and designate what this method does with the stack. The following list describes each enumeration member:

Standard
    Designates the default CLR conventions.

VarArgs
    Allows variable arguments.

Any
    Allows either convention.

HasThis
    Passes the target method the this (or Me) reference as the first argument and cannot be used for shared methods.

ExplicitThis
    Represents a call to a nonshared method and is a function pointer (for delegates). If ExplicitThis is set, HasThis must also be set.

```
Public Enum CallingConventions
    Standard = &H000000001
    VarArgs = &H000000002
```

```
   Any = &H000000003
   HasThis = &H000000020
   ExplicitThis = &H000000040
End Enum
```

Hierarchy: System.Object→ System.ValueType→ System.Enum(System.IComparable, System.IFormattable, System.IConvertible)→ CallingConventions

Returned By: MethodBase.CallingConvention

Passed To: Multiple types

ConstructorInfo
System.Reflection (mscorlib.dll)

MustInherit Class

ECMA, serializable

This class is an implementation of MethodBase explicitly for constructors. It adds the two shared read-only properties ConstructorName and TypeConstructorName, which are defined in metadata as methods of the name .ctor and .cctor respectively. (Recall that a "type constructor" is executed as soon as the type is loaded into the CLR; hence the name "class constructor,"—"cctor" for short.)

```
Public MustInherit Class ConstructorInfo : Inherits MethodBase
' Protected Constructors
   Protected Sub New()
' Public Shared Fields
   Public Shared ReadOnly ConstructorName As String                        =.ctor
   Public Shared ReadOnly TypeConstructorName As String                    =.cctor
' Public Instance Properties
   Overrides Public ReadOnly Property MemberType As MemberTypes
' Public Instance Methods
   MustInherit Public Function Invoke(ByVal invokeAttr As BindingFlags, ByVal binder As Binder, _
      ByVal parameters As Object(), ByVal culture As System.Globalization.CultureInfo)  As Object
   Public Function Invoke(ByVal parameters As Object()) As Object
End Class
```

Hierarchy: System.Object→ MemberInfo(ICustomAttributeProvider)→ MethodBase→ ConstructorInfo

Subclasses: System.Reflection.Emit.ConstructorBuilder

Returned By: System.Type.{GetConstructor(), GetConstructorImpl(), GetConstructors(), TypeInitializer}

Passed To: Multiple types

CustomAttributeFormatException
System.Reflection (mscorlib.dll)

Class

serializable

This exception is thrown when the binary format of an attribute of a type cannot be read. This can occur when custom attributes and types are created at runtime.

```
Public Class CustomAttributeFormatException : Inherits FormatException
' Public Constructors
   Public Sub New()
   Public Sub New(ByVal message As String)
   Public Sub New(ByVal message As String, ByVal inner As Exception)
' Protected Constructors
   Protected Sub New(ByVal info As System.Runtime.Serialization.SerializationInfo, _
      ByVal context As System.Runtime.Serialization.StreamingContext)
End Class
```

System.Reflection

Hierarchy: System.Object→ System.Exception(System.Runtime.Serialization.ISerializable)→ System.SystemException→ System.FormatException→ CustomAttributeFormatException

DefaultMemberAttribute NotInheritable Class
System.Reflection (mscorlib.dll) *ECMA, serializable*

This attribute allows you to specify the default member of a class. It corresponds to the VB.NET Default keyword. C# does not permit the use of default members as part of the language, although other .NET languages (most notably VB.NET) do.

```
Public NotInheritable Class DefaultMemberAttribute : Inherits Attribute
' Public Constructors
    Public Sub New(ByVal memberName As String)
' Public Instance Properties
    Public ReadOnly Property MemberName As String
End Class
```

Hierarchy: System.Object→ System.Attribute→ DefaultMemberAttribute

Valid On: Class, Struct, Interface

EventAttributes Enum
System.Reflection (mscorlib.dll) *ECMA, serializable*

This is an enumeration of the attributes that can be placed on events. None specifies no attributes. ReservedMask is a reserved flag for use only by the runtime. SpecialName indicates that the event is described by the name. RTSpecialName is similar, but states that the runtime should check the encoding of the name.

```
Public Enum EventAttributes
    None = 0
    SpecialName = 512
    ReservedMask = 1024
    RTSpecialName = 1024
End Enum
```

Hierarchy: System.Object→ System.ValueType→ System.Enum(System.IComparable, System.IFormattable, System.IConvertible)→ EventAttributes

Returned By: EventInfo.Attributes

Passed To: System.Reflection.Emit.TypeBuilder.DefineEvent()

EventInfo MustInherit Class
System.Reflection (mscorlib.dll) *ECMA*

This class allows you to access events through reflection and is, itself, an implementation of MemberInfo. Attributes gets the EventAttributes object, and EventHandlerType gets the System.Type of the event-handler delegate for the event. IsMulticast returns true if the event is multicast, and IsSpecialName indicates whether this has special meaning. AddEventHandler() adds the passed delegate to the event handler, and GetAddMethod(), GetRaiseMethod(), and GetRemoveMethod() return a MethodInfo for the method used to add an event handler, raise an event, or remove an event handler, respectively.

```
Public MustInherit Class EventInfo : Inherits MemberInfo
' Protected Constructors
    Protected Sub New()
' Public Instance Properties
    MustInherit Public ReadOnly Property Attributes As EventAttributes
```

```
Public ReadOnly Property EventHandlerType As Type
Public ReadOnly Property IsMulticast As Boolean
Public ReadOnly Property IsSpecialName As Boolean
Overrides Public ReadOnly Property MemberType As MemberTypes
' Public Instance Methods
Public Sub AddEventHandler(ByVal target As Object, ByVal handler As Delegate)
Public Function GetAddMethod() As MethodInfo
MustInherit Public Function GetAddMethod(ByVal nonPublic As Boolean) As MethodInfo
Public Function GetRaiseMethod() As MethodInfo
MustInherit Public Function GetRaiseMethod(ByVal nonPublic As Boolean) As MethodInfo
Public Function GetRemoveMethod() As MethodInfo
MustInherit Public Function GetRemoveMethod(ByVal nonPublic As Boolean) As MethodInfo
Public Sub RemoveEventHandler(ByVal target As Object, ByVal handler As Delegate)
End Class
```

Hierarchy: System.Object→ MemberInfo(ICustomAttributeProvider)→ EventInfo

Returned By: System.Type.{GetEvent(), GetEvents()}

FieldAttributes   Enum

System.Reflection (mscorlib.dll)   *ECMA, serializable*

This is an enumeration of the attributes that can be specified on a field. Assembly means that the field is internal (that is, private to the assembly); Family indicates that the field is protected. Private, Public, and Static are self-explanatory. If the field has a default value, HasDefault is marked; if a field is constant, Literal is marked. InitOnly indicates that the field can only be set on object initialization. To exclude a field from being serialized, NotSerialized should be asserted. HasFieldMarshal specifies that the field has special marshaling information.

```
Public Enum FieldAttributes
    PrivateScope = 0
    Private = 1
    FamANDAssem = 2
    Assembly = 3
    Family = 4
    FamORAssem = 5
    Public = 6
    FieldAccessMask = 7
    Static = 16
    InitOnly = 32
    Literal = 64
    NotSerialized = 128
    HasFieldRVA = 256
    SpecialName = 512
    RTSpecialName = 1024
    HasFieldMarshal = 4096
    PinvokeImpl = 8192
    HasDefault = 32768
    ReservedMask = 38144
End Enum
```

Hierarchy: System.Object→ System.ValueType→ System.Enum(System.IComparable, System.IFormattable, System.IConvertible)→ FieldAttributes

Returned By: FieldInfo.Attributes

Passed To: System.Reflection.Emit.ModuleBuilder.{DefineInitializedData(), DefineUninitializedData()}, System.Reflection.Emit.TypeBuilder.{DefineField(), DefineInitializedData(), DefineUninitializedData()}

FieldInfo   MustInherit Class

System.Reflection (mscorlib.dll)   *ECMA, serializable*

This class is an implementation of MemberInfo and allows access to an instance field. Note that, like all reflective objects, the FieldInfo instance refers to the metadata concept of the field within the type, not a particular field within a particular instance of that type. (This is important when working with or manipulating the value stored in object instance fields.)

IsAssembly, IsFamily, IsFamilyAndAssembly, IsFamilyOrAssembly, IsPublic, and IsPrivate allow you to check the visibility of the field. FieldType returns the declared type of this field. Field-Handle is a System.RuntimeFieldHandle. Use Attributes to retrieve the attributes. To see if the FieldInfo has the NotSerialized or PinvokeImpl FieldAttributes set, inspect the IsNotSerialized and IsPinvokeImpl properties. If the field is shared, IsStatic is true. The Set and Get methods allow you set the values, and the ones with Direct in their name take a typed reference as opposed to an object.

```
Public MustInherit Class FieldInfo : Inherits MemberInfo
' Protected Constructors
    Protected Sub New()
' Public Instance Properties
    MustInherit Public ReadOnly Property Attributes As FieldAttributes
    MustInherit Public ReadOnly Property FieldHandle As RuntimeFieldHandle
    MustInherit Public ReadOnly Property FieldType As Type
    Public ReadOnly Property IsAssembly As Boolean
    Public ReadOnly Property IsFamily As Boolean
    Public ReadOnly Property IsFamilyAndAssembly As Boolean
    Public ReadOnly Property IsFamilyOrAssembly As Boolean
    Public ReadOnly Property IsInitOnly As Boolean
    Public ReadOnly Property IsLiteral As Boolean
    Public ReadOnly Property IsNotSerialized As Boolean
    Public ReadOnly Property IsPinvokeImpl As Boolean
    Public ReadOnly Property IsPrivate As Boolean
    Public ReadOnly Property IsPublic As Boolean
    Public ReadOnly Property IsSpecialName As Boolean
    Public ReadOnly Property IsStatic As Boolean
    Overrides Public ReadOnly Property MemberType As MemberTypes
' Public Shared Methods
    Public Shared Function GetFieldFromHandle(ByVal handle As RuntimeFieldHandle) As FieldInfo
' Public Instance Methods
    MustInherit Public Function GetValue(ByVal obj As Object) As Object
    Overridable Public Function GetValueDirect(ByVal obj As TypedReference) As Object
    Public Sub SetValue(ByVal obj As Object, ByVal value As Object)
    MustInherit Public Sub SetValue(ByVal obj As Object, ByVal value As Object, ByVal invokeAttr As BindingFlags, _
        ByVal binder As Binder, ByVal culture As System.Globalization.CultureInfo)
    Overridable Public Sub SetValueDirect(ByVal obj As TypedReference, ByVal value As Object)
End Class
```

Hierarchy: System.Object→ MemberInfo(ICustomAttributeProvider)→ FieldInfo

Subclasses: System.Reflection.Emit.FieldBuilder

Returned By: Binder.BindToField(), IReflect.{GetField(), GetFields()}, Module.{GetField(), GetFields()}, System.Runtime.InteropServices.Expando.IExpando.AddField(), System.Type.{GetField(), GetFields()}

Passed To: Binder.BindToField(),
System.Reflection.Emit.CustomAttributeBuilder.CustomAttributeBuilder(),
System.Reflection.Emit.ILGenerator.{Emit(), EmitWriteLine()},
System.Reflection.Emit.ModuleBuilder.GetFieldToken()

ICustomAttributeProvider   Interface

System.Reflection (mscorlib.dll)

This interface is implemented if an object supports custom attributes. GetCustomAttributes() returns the custom attributes, and IsDefined() returns true if an attribute of a passed System.Type is defined on this member.

```
Public Interface ICustomAttributeProvider
' Public Instance Methods
    Public Function GetCustomAttributes(ByVal inherit As Boolean) As Object()
    Public Function GetCustomAttributes(ByVal attributeType As Type, ByVal inherit As Boolean) As Object()
    Public Function IsDefined(ByVal attributeType As Type, ByVal inherit As Boolean) As Boolean
End Interface
```

Implemented By: Assembly, MemberInfo, Module, ParameterInfo

Returned By: MethodInfo.ReturnTypeCustomAttributes

InterfaceMapping   Structure

System.Reflection (mscorlib.dll)

This value type allows you to retrieve information about interfaces. To access the Type for an interface, use InterfaceType. TargetType contains the Type of the implementing class. Similarly, InterfaceMethods and TargetMethods return the methods of the interface and the implementing class respectively.

```
Public Structure InterfaceMapping
' Public Instance Fields
    Public InterfaceMethods As MethodInfo()
    Public InterfaceType As Type
    Public TargetMethods As MethodInfo()
    Public TargetType As Type
End Structure
```

Hierarchy: System.Object→ System.ValueType→ InterfaceMapping

Returned By: System.Type.GetInterfaceMap()

InvalidFilterCriteriaException   Class

System.Reflection (mscorlib.dll)   *serializable*

This exception is thrown when the filter criteria passed to System.Type.FindMembers() is invalid.

```
Public Class InvalidFilterCriteriaException : Inherits ApplicationException
' Public Constructors
    Public Sub New()
    Public Sub New(ByVal message As String)
    Public Sub New(ByVal message As String, ByVal inner As Exception)
' Protected Constructors
    Protected Sub New(ByVal info As System.Runtime.Serialization.SerializationInfo, _
        ByVal context As System.Runtime.Serialization.StreamingContext)
End Class
```

Hierarchy: System.Object→ System.Exception(System.Runtime.Serialization.ISerializable)→
System.ApplicationException→ InvalidFilterCriteriaException

IReflect Interface

System.Reflection (mscorlib.dll)

This interface defines how types are reflected and provides all the relevant information about the members of a class (methods, fields, and properties). The Get methods allow access to these members. The methods GetField(), GetMethod(), GetProperty(), and GetMember() return single members of the specified type by name. The methods GetFields(), GetMethods(), GetProperties(), and GetMembers() return all of the specified type of members contained by the class.

```
Public Interface IReflect
' Public Instance Properties
   Public ReadOnly Property UnderlyingSystemType As Type
' Public Instance Methods
   Public Function GetField(ByVal name As String, ByVal bindingAttr As BindingFlags) As FieldInfo
   Public Function GetFields(ByVal bindingAttr As BindingFlags) As FieldInfo()
   Public Function GetMember(ByVal name As String, ByVal bindingAttr As BindingFlags) As MemberInfo()
   Public Function GetMembers(ByVal bindingAttr As BindingFlags) As MemberInfo()
   Public Function GetMethod(ByVal name As String, ByVal bindingAttr As BindingFlags) As MethodInfo
   Public Function GetMethod(ByVal name As String, ByVal bindingAttr As BindingFlags, ByVal binder As Binder, _
      ByVal types As Type(), ByVal modifiers As ParameterModifier()) As MethodInfo
   Public Function GetMethods(ByVal bindingAttr As BindingFlags) As MethodInfo()
   Public Function GetProperties(ByVal bindingAttr As BindingFlags) As PropertyInfo()
   Public Function GetProperty(ByVal name As String, ByVal bindingAttr As BindingFlags) As PropertyInfo
   Public Function GetProperty(ByVal name As String, ByVal bindingAttr As BindingFlags, ByVal binder As Binder, _
      ByVal returnType As Type, ByVal types As Type(), ByVal modifiers As ParameterModifier()) As PropertyInfo
   Public Function InvokeMember(ByVal name As String, ByVal invokeAttr As BindingFlags, ByVal binder As Binder, _
      ByVal target As Object, ByVal args As Object(), ByVal modifiers As ParameterModifier(),
      ByVal culture As System.Globalization.CultureInfo, ByVal namedParameters As String()) As Object    _
End Interface
```

Implemented By: System.Type, System.Runtime.InteropServices.Expando.IExpando

ManifestResourceInfo Class

System.Reflection (mscorlib.dll)

This class represents a resource from an assembly manifest. As assemblies can span multiple files, this resource represents one file from an assembly. The FileName returns the name of the file containing the resource if it is not the same as the file containing the manifest. ResourceLocation allows you to inspect the ResourceLocation enumeration for this resource, telling you whether the resource is contained in the same file as the manifest. ReferencedAssembly returns the Assembly object representing the specified assembly.

```
Public Class ManifestResourceInfo
' Public Instance Properties
   Overridable Public ReadOnly Property FileName As String
   Overridable Public ReadOnly Property ReferencedAssembly As Assembly
   Overridable Public ReadOnly Property ResourceLocation As ResourceLocation
End Class
```

Returned By: Assembly.GetManifestResourceInfo()

MemberFilter   Delegate

System.Reflection (mscorlib.dll)   *serializable*

This delegate defines a function that is used to filter an array of MemberInfo objects. This method is run for each MemberInfo and should return true to include the MemberInfo. The second parameter, filterCriteria, is an arbitrary argument that you may specify to be passed to the filter.

This delegate is used from the System.Type.FindMembers() method and is designed to allow for high-level "searches" of a type's members (fields, methods, properties, and so on) without having to code the actual looping logic itself.

Public Delegate Function **MemberFilter**(ByVal m As MemberInfo, ByVal filterCriteria As Object) As Boolean

Passed To: System.Type.FindMembers()

MemberInfo   MustInherit Class

System.Reflection (mscorlib.dll)   *ECMA, serializable*

This class is the base type for all reflective types defined in the .NET environment; it defines the basic data associated with any member (field, method, property, event, nested type) of a given type. Note that even System.Type itself inherits from this class.

By itself, MemberInfo is a fairly simple type. It consists of four properties: DeclaringType (a reference to the System.Type in which this member was declared, which might be a base type to the class being reflected over), MemberType (an enumeration describing the type of the member), Name, and ReflectedType (the System.Type instance from which this MemberInfo object was received in the first place). MemberInfo also consists of two methods, GetCustomAttributes() and IsDefined(), both of which deal with any custom attributes defined on this member.

Public MustInherit Class **MemberInfo** : Implements ICustomAttributeProvider
' Protected Constructors
  Protected Sub **New**()
' Public Instance Properties
  MustInherit Public ReadOnly Property **DeclaringType** As Type
  MustInherit Public ReadOnly Property **MemberType** As MemberTypes
  MustInherit Public ReadOnly Property **Name** As String
  MustInherit Public ReadOnly Property **ReflectedType** As Type
' Public Instance Methods
  MustInherit Public Function **GetCustomAttributes**(ByVal inherit As Boolean) As Object() _
    Implements ICustomAttributeProvider.GetCustomAttributes
  MustInherit Public Function **GetCustomAttributes**(ByVal attributeType As Type, ByVal inherit As Boolean) _
    As Object() Implements ICustomAttributeProvider.GetCustomAttributes
  MustInherit Public Function **IsDefined**(ByVal attributeType As Type, ByVal inherit As Boolean) As Boolean _
    Implements ICustomAttributeProvider.IsDefined
End Class

Subclasses: EventInfo, FieldInfo, MethodBase, PropertyInfo, System.Type

Returned By: IReflect.{GetMember(), GetMembers()}, ParameterInfo.Member,
System.Runtime.InteropServices.Marshal.GetMethodInfoForComSlot(),
System.Runtime.Serialization.FormatterServices.GetSerializableMembers(),
System.Type.{FindMembers(), GetDefaultMembers(), GetMember(), GetMembers()}

Passed To: System.Attribute.{GetCustomAttribute(), GetCustomAttributes(), IsDefined()},
MemberFilter.{BeginInvoke(), Invoke()},
System.Runtime.InteropServices.Expando.IExpando.RemoveMember(),

System.Runtime.InteropServices.Marshal.GetComSlotForMethodInfo(),
System.Runtime.Serialization.FormatterServices.{GetObjectData(), PopulateObjectMembers()},
System.Runtime.Serialization.ObjectManager.{RecordFixup(), RegisterObject()}

MemberTypes   Enum

System.Reflection (mscorlib.dll)   *serializable*

This enumeration represents the different types of MemberInfo objects. All specifies all
member types, and Custom specifies a custom member type. All of the other enumerated values specify the type of the MemberInfo object. For example, Field designates that
the MemberInfo object is actually a FieldInfo object.

```
Public Enum MemberTypes
      Constructor = 1
      Event = 2
      Field = 4
      Method = 8
      Property = 16
      TypeInfo = 32
      Custom = 64
      NestedType = 128
      All = 191
End Enum
```

Hierarchy: System.Object→ System.ValueType→ System.Enum(System.IComparable,
System.IFormattable, System.IConvertible)→ MemberTypes

Returned By: MemberInfo.MemberType

Passed To: System.Type.{FindMembers(), GetMember()}

MethodAttributes   Enum

System.Reflection (mscorlib.dll)   *ECMA, serializable*

These attributes can be placed on methods. The behavior of most of these is obvious
and the same as for FieldAttributes. The others are used for specifying the structure of the
object vTable.

```
Public Enum MethodAttributes
      ReuseSlot = 0
      PrivateScope = 0
      Private = 1
      FamANDAssem = 2
      Assembly = 3
      Family = 4
      FamORAssem = 5
      Public = 6
      MemberAccessMask = 7
      UnmanagedExport = 8
      Static = 16
      Final = 32
      Virtual = 64
      HideBySig = 128
      VtableLayoutMask = 256
      NewSlot = 256
      Abstract = 1024
      SpecialName = 2048
```

```
    RTSpecialName = 4096
    PinvokeImpl = 8192
    HasSecurity = 16384
    RequireSecObject = 32768
    ReservedMask = 53248
End Enum
```

Hierarchy: System.Object→ System.ValueType→ System.Enum(System.IComparable, System.IFormattable, System.IConvertible)→ MethodAttributes

Returned By: MethodBase.Attributes

Passed To: System.Reflection.Emit.ModuleBuilder.{DefineGlobalMethod(), DefinePInvokeMethod()}, System.Reflection.Emit.TypeBuilder.{DefineConstructor(), DefineDefaultConstructor(), DefineMethod(), DefinePInvokeMethod()}

MethodBase   MustInherit Class

System.Reflection (mscorlib.dll)   *ECMA, serializable*

This is a MustInherit base class representing executable method calls, which fall into two categories: regular methods and constructors. GetCurrentMethod() and GetMethodFromHandle() are shared methods that return the currently executing method and a method represented by a System.RuntimeMethodHandle object, respectively. The MethodHandle returns the handle for a specific method instance.

The properties prefixed by Is return boolean values, allowing inspection of the modifiers of the reflected method. Only some require explanation: IsAssembly returns true if the method is internal, and IsFamily returns true for protected methods. If a member of exactly the same name and signature is hidden by a derived class, IsHideBySig is true. IsSpecialName indicates if this method has a special name, such as a property accessor, get_PropertyName or set_PropertyName.

Similarly, the attributes on a given method can be inspected from the Attributes property. GetParameters() returns the parameters of a method or constructor, and GetMethodImplementationFlags() returns the MethodImplAttributes flags set on the method.

In addition to introspecting on a method, the MethodBase also allows for reflective invocation of a method, using the Invoke() method. Note that Invoke() requires both the object instance against which to invoke the method (or null if the method is declared shared), as well as an array of object references containing the arguments to the method, in their proper order. Should the argument array mismatch in any way (wrong number of arguments, wrong type of arguments, wrong order of arguments, and so on), an exception is thrown and the method call is not even attempted. Method invocation in this manner is much slower than direct compile-time-bound method execution.

```
Public MustInherit Class MethodBase : Inherits MemberInfo
' Protected Constructors
    Protected Sub New()
' Public Instance Properties
    MustInherit Public ReadOnly Property Attributes As MethodAttributes
    Overridable Public ReadOnly Property CallingConvention As CallingConventions
    Public ReadOnly Property IsAbstract As Boolean
    Public ReadOnly Property IsAssembly As Boolean
    Public ReadOnly Property IsConstructor As Boolean
    Public ReadOnly Property IsFamily As Boolean
    Public ReadOnly Property IsFamilyAndAssembly As Boolean
    Public ReadOnly Property IsFamilyOrAssembly As Boolean
    Public ReadOnly Property IsFinal As Boolean
```

Public ReadOnly Property **IsHideBySig** As Boolean
Public ReadOnly Property **IsPrivate** As Boolean
Public ReadOnly Property **IsPublic** As Boolean
Public ReadOnly Property **IsSpecialName** As Boolean
Public ReadOnly Property **IsStatic** As Boolean
Public ReadOnly Property **IsVirtual** As Boolean
MustInherit Public ReadOnly Property **MethodHandle** As RuntimeMethodHandle
' Public Shared Methods
Public Shared Function **GetCurrentMethod**() As MethodBase
Public Shared Function **GetMethodFromHandle**(ByVal handle As RuntimeMethodHandle) As MethodBase
' Public Instance Methods
MustInherit Public Function **GetMethodImplementationFlags**() As MethodImplAttributes
MustInherit Public Function **GetParameters**() As ParameterInfo()
MustInherit Public Function **Invoke**(ByVal obj As Object, ByVal invokeAttr As BindingFlags, ByVal binder As Binder, _
    ByVal parameters As Object(), ByVal culture As System.Globalization.CultureInfo) As Object
Public Function **Invoke**(ByVal obj As Object, ByVal parameters As Object()) As Object
End Class

Hierarchy: System.Object→ MemberInfo(ICustomAttributeProvider)→ MethodBase

Subclasses: ConstructorInfo, MethodInfo

Returned By: System.Diagnostics.StackFrame.GetMethod(), System.Exception.TargetSite,
Binder.{BindToMethod(), SelectMethod()}

Passed To: Binder.{BindToMethod(), SelectMethod()}

MethodImplAttributes Enum

System.Reflection (mscorlib.dll) *serializable*

These flags specify how a method has been implemented. Managed, Unmanaged, and
ManagedMask indicate whether the method is managed or unmanaged code. If a method
allows only one thread to execute it at a time, then its Synchronized flag is set. ForwardRef
specifies that the method has not been defined, and InternalCall indicates that the
method is an internal call. IL and OPTIL specify that the code is IL or optimized IL. If the
method is provided by the runtime, Runtime should be set, and if the method implementation is native, Native is marked. When a method should not be inlined during optimization, NoInlining is set. When the method signature should be exported exactly as
specified, PreserveSig is set.

Public Enum **MethodImplAttributes**
    Managed = 0
    IL = 0
    Native = 1
    OPTIL = 2
    Runtime = 3
    CodeTypeMask = 3
    Unmanaged = 4
    ManagedMask = 4
    NoInlining = 8
    ForwardRef = 16
    Synchronized = 32
    PreserveSig = 128
    InternalCall = 4096
    MaxMethodImplVal = 65535
End Enum

Hierarchy: System.Object→ System.ValueType→ System.Enum(System.IComparable, System.IFormattable, System.IConvertible)→ MethodImplAttributes

Returned By: MethodBase.GetMethodImplementationFlags()

Passed To: System.Reflection.Emit.ConstructorBuilder.SetImplementationFlags(), System.Reflection.Emit.MethodBuilder.SetImplementationFlags()

MethodInfo   MustInherit Class
System.Reflection (mscorlib.dll)   *ECMA, serializable*

This class is an implementation of MethodBase for methods (ConstructorInfo is the other implementation for constructors). It adds two properties: ReturnType and ReturnTypeCustom-Attributes, which allow access to the System.Type object of the value returned and to the custom attributes set on that value. If the method is overridden from a base class, then GetBaseDefinition() returns the MethodInfo for the overridden method.

```
Public MustInherit Class MethodInfo : Inherits MethodBase
' Protected Constructors
   Protected Sub New()
' Public Instance Properties
   Overrides Public ReadOnly Property MemberType As MemberTypes
   MustInherit Public ReadOnly Property ReturnType As Type
   MustInherit Public ReadOnly Property ReturnTypeCustomAttributes As ICustomAttributeProvider
' Public Instance Methods
   MustInherit Public Function GetBaseDefinition() As MethodInfo
End Class
```

Hierarchy: System.Object→ MemberInfo(ICustomAttributeProvider)→ MethodBase→ MethodInfo

Subclasses: System.Reflection.Emit.MethodBuilder

Returned By: Multiple types

Passed To: System.Delegate.CreateDelegate(), System.Reflection.Emit.AssemblyBuilder.SetEntryPoint(), System.Reflection.Emit.ILGenerator.{Emit(), EmitCall()}, System.Reflection.Emit.ModuleBuilder.{GetMethodToken(), SetUserEntryPoint()}, System.Reflection.Emit.TypeBuilder.DefineMethodOverride(), System.Runtime.InteropServices.Marshal.{NumParamBytes(), Prelink()}

Missing   NotInheritable Class
System.Reflection (mscorlib.dll)

Because C# (as well as some other languages) does not allow optional parameters, Missing allows those languages to pass this value to indicate that a value will not be specified for those optional parameters. The only way to access an instance of this class—there can only be one—is by the return value of the shared field, called Value.

```
Public NotInheritable Class Missing
' Public Shared Fields
   Public Shared ReadOnly Value As Missing                    =System.Reflection.Missing
End Class
```

Module
Class

System.Reflection (mscorlib.dll)
ECMA, serializable

Modules are .NET executable files (either .EXE or .DLL files) consisting of classes or interfaces. One or more modules and other resources (such as graphics) make up an assembly. The Module class allows reflection of these executables. FilterTypeName and FilterTypeNameIgnoreCase are shared properties that return a TypeFilter delegate that filters types by name. The first is case-sensitive, and the second is case-insensitive. Assembly returns the appropriate Assembly object that this is part of. Name returns the filename of this module and FullyQualifiedName returns that filename as well as the full path. Use Find-Types() to return a list of types from a module accepted by a TypeFilter delegate. The methods prefixed with Get return the specific methods, types, or fields contained in this module, and IsDefined() checks whether a specific attribute is defined on the module.

```
Public Class Module : Implements System.Runtime.Serialization.ISerializable, ICustomAttributeProvider
' Public Shared Fields
   Public Shared ReadOnly FilterTypeName As TypeFilter                           =System.Reflection.TypeFilter
   Public Shared ReadOnly FilterTypeNameIgnoreCase As TypeFilter                 =System.Reflection.TypeFilter
' Public Instance Properties
   Public ReadOnly Property Assembly As Assembly
   Overridable Public ReadOnly Property FullyQualifiedName As String
   Public ReadOnly Property Name As String
   Public ReadOnly Property ScopeName As String
' Public Instance Methods
   Overridable Public Function FindTypes(ByVal filter As TypeFilter, ByVal filterCriteria As Object) As Type()
   Overridable Public Function GetCustomAttributes(ByVal inherit As Boolean) As Object() _
      Implements ICustomAttributeProvider.GetCustomAttributes
   Overridable Public Function GetCustomAttributes(ByVal attributeType As Type, ByVal inherit As Boolean) _
      As Object() Implements ICustomAttributeProvider.GetCustomAttributes
   Public Function GetField(ByVal name As String) As FieldInfo
   Public Function GetField(ByVal name As String, ByVal bindingAttr As BindingFlags) As FieldInfo
   Public Function GetFields() As FieldInfo()
   Public Function GetMethod(ByVal name As String) As MethodInfo
   Public Function GetMethod(ByVal name As String, ByVal bindingAttr As BindingFlags, ByVal binder As Binder, _
      ByVal callConvention As CallingConventions, ByVal types As Type(), ByVal modifiers As ParameterModifier()) _
      As MethodInfo
   Public Function GetMethod(ByVal name As String, ByVal types As Type()) As MethodInfo
   Public Function GetMethods() As MethodInfo()
   Overridable Public Sub GetObjectData(ByVal info As System.Runtime.Serialization.SerializationInfo, _
      ByVal context As System.Runtime.Serialization.StreamingContext) Implements ISerializable.GetObjectData
   Public Function GetSignerCertificate() As X509Certificate
   Overridable Public Function GetType(ByVal className As String) As Type
   Overridable Public Function GetType(ByVal className As String, ByVal ignoreCase As Boolean) As Type
   Overridable Public Function GetType(ByVal className As String, ByVal throwOnError As Boolean, _
      ByVal ignoreCase As Boolean) As Type
   Overridable Public Function GetTypes() As Type()
   Overridable Public Function IsDefined(ByVal attributeType As Type, ByVal inherit As Boolean) As Boolean _
      Implements ICustomAttributeProvider.IsDefined
   Public Function IsResource() As Boolean
   Overrides Public Function ToString() As String
' Protected Instance Methods
   Overridable Protected Function GetMethodImpl(ByVal name As String, ByVal bindingAttr As BindingFlags, _
      ByVal binder As Binder, ByVal callConvention As CallingConventions, ByVal types As Type(), _
      ByVal modifiers As ParameterModifier()) As MethodInfo
End Class
```

Subclasses: System.Reflection.Emit.ModuleBuilder

Returned By: Assembly.{GetLoadedModules(), GetModule(), GetModules(), LoadModule()},
System.Reflection.Emit.ConstructorBuilder.GetModule(),
System.Reflection.Emit.MethodBuilder.GetModule(), ModuleResolveEventHandler.{EndInvoke(),
Invoke()}, System.Type.Module

Passed To: System.Attribute.{GetCustomAttribute(), GetCustomAttributes(), IsDefined()},
System.Reflection.Emit.SignatureHelper.{GetFieldSigHelper(), GetLocalVarSigHelper(),
GetMethodSigHelper(), GetPropertySigHelper()},
System.Runtime.InteropServices.Marshal.GetHINSTANCE()

ModuleResolveEventHandler   Delegate

System.Reflection (mscorlib.dll)   *serializable*

This delegate is used as an event handler by Assembly when it cannot resolve a reference to a module that is part of an assembly. One instance in which this might occur is
if one resource is not present.

```
Public Delegate Function ModuleResolveEventHandler(ByVal sender As Object, ByVal e As ResolveEventArgs) _
    As Module
```

Associated Events: Assembly.ModuleResolve(),
System.Reflection.Emit.AssemblyBuilder.ModuleResolve()

ParameterAttributes   Enum

System.Reflection (mscorlib.dll)   *ECMA, serializable, flag*

These attributes are specified on a parameter. When the parameter has a default value,
HasDefault is asserted. Optional, Out, In, and Retval all behave as you would expect them
to. If a parameter has no attribute, None must be marked alone. If the parameter contains locale identifying information, Lcid should be set. Lastly, if the parameter is for
marshaling information, HasFieldMarshal is asserted.

```
Public Enum ParameterAttributes
    None = &H000000000
    In = &H000000001
    Out = &H000000002
    Lcid = &H000000004
    Retval = &H000000008
    Optional = &H000000010
    HasDefault = &H000001000
    HasFieldMarshal = &H000002000
    Reserved3 = &H000004000
    Reserved4 = &H000008000
    ReservedMask = &H00000F000
End Enum
```

Hierarchy: System.Object→ System.ValueType→ System.Enum(System.IComparable,
System.IFormattable, System.IConvertible)→ ParameterAttributes

Returned By: ParameterInfo.Attributes

Passed To: System.Reflection.Emit.ConstructorBuilder.DefineParameter(),
System.Reflection.Emit.MethodBuilder.DefineParameter()

ParameterInfo
System.Reflection (mscorlib.dll)

Class

ECMA, serializable

This class allows the inspection of the type and behavior of a method parameter. Because parameters can have custom attributes on them, the class implements ICustomAttributeProvider. Attributes returns the attributes defined on this parameter. If the parameter has a default, it is stored in DefaultValue. Retrieve the name, type, and member the parameter is from by inspecting Name, ParameterType, and Member. Position returns the ordinal position of this parameter. IsOptional returns true if the parameter is optional, and IsLcid indicates when the parameter is a locale identifier.

A parameter is passed by reference if the IsByRef property of its ParameterType property is true and the IsOut property is false (*out* parameters have IsByRef and IsOut set to true). A parameter that has been marked as (In) has IsOut set to false and IsIn set to true.

```
Public Class ParameterInfo : Implements ICustomAttributeProvider
' Protected Constructors
    Protected Sub New()
' Protected Instance Fields
    protected AttrsImpl As ParameterAttributes
    protected ClassImpl As Type
    protected DefaultValueImpl As Object
    protected MemberImpl As MemberInfo
    protected NameImpl As String
    protected PositionImpl As Integer
' Public Instance Properties
    Overridable Public ReadOnly Property Attributes As ParameterAttributes
    Overridable Public ReadOnly Property DefaultValue As Object
    Public ReadOnly Property IsIn As Boolean
    Public ReadOnly Property IsLcid As Boolean
    Public ReadOnly Property IsOptional As Boolean
    Public ReadOnly Property IsOut As Boolean
    Public ReadOnly Property IsRetval As Boolean
    Overridable Public ReadOnly Property Member As MemberInfo
    Overridable Public ReadOnly Property Name As String
    Overridable Public ReadOnly Property ParameterType As Type
    Overridable Public ReadOnly Property Position As Integer
' Public Instance Methods
    Overridable Public Function GetCustomAttributes(ByVal inherit As Boolean) As Object() _
        Implements ICustomAttributeProvider.GetCustomAttributes
    Overridable Public Function GetCustomAttributes(ByVal attributeType As Type, ByVal inherit As Boolean) _
        As Object() Implements ICustomAttributeProvider.GetCustomAttributes
    Overridable Public Function IsDefined(ByVal attributeType As Type, ByVal inherit As Boolean) As Boolean _
        Implements ICustomAttributeProvider.IsDefined
End Class
```

Returned By: MethodBase.GetParameters(), PropertyInfo.GetIndexParameters()

Passed To: System.Attribute.{GetCustomAttribute(), GetCustomAttributes(), IsDefined()}

ParameterModifier
System.Reflection (mscorlib.dll)

Structure

ECMA

This value type acts much like an array of boolean values. It can be constructed to a certain size, and then each index can be set or retrieved.

```
Public Structure ParameterModifier
' Public Constructors
```

```
  Public Sub New(ByVal paramaterCount As Integer)
' Public Instance Properties
  Public Default Property Item (ByVal index As Integer) As Boolean
End Structure
```

Hierarchy: System.Object→ System.ValueType→ ParameterModifier

Passed To: Multiple types

Pointer   NotInheritable Class

System.Reflection (mscorlib.dll)

This class allows access to direct pointers to .NET objects through two shared methods. Unbox() returns a void* pointer to the passed object and pins it, not allowing the garbage collector to move its place in memory, and Box() returns control over the object to the .NET runtime.

```
Public NotInheritable Class Pointer : Implements System.Runtime.Serialization.ISerializable
' No public or protected members
End Class
```

PropertyAttributes   Enum

System.Reflection (mscorlib.dll)   *ECMA, serializable, flag*

Specifies the attributes that can be placed on properties. The important ones that you will encounter are None and HasDefault, which specify either the absence of attributes or that there is a default.

```
Public Enum PropertyAttributes
  None = &H000000000
  SpecialName = &H000000200
  RTSpecialName = &H000000400
  HasDefault = &H000001000
  Reserved2 = &H000002000
  Reserved3 = &H000004000
  Reserved4 = &H000008000
  ReservedMask = &H00000F400
End Enum
```

Hierarchy: System.Object→ System.ValueType→ System.Enum(System.IComparable, System.IFormattable, System.IConvertible)→ PropertyAttributes

Returned By: PropertyInfo.Attributes

Passed To: System.Reflection.Emit.TypeBuilder.DefineProperty()

PropertyInfo   MustInherit Class

System.Reflection (mscorlib.dll)   *ECMA, serializable*

This class implements MemberInfo and represents a declared property on a type. CanRead and CanWrite check whether this property has get or set behaviors defined. These methods can be inspected directly (as MethodInfo instances) by calling GetGetMethod() and Get-SetMethod(), or together by calling GetAccessors(), which returns an array of all defined accessors. If the property is an indexer, GetIndexParameters() returns parameters to access the indexer. GetValue() and SetValue() allow the instance of this property to be set or retrieved; these act as a shortcut to calling Invoke on the methods returned from GetGet-Method() or GetSetMethod().

```
Public MustInherit Class PropertyInfo : Inherits MemberInfo
' Protected Constructors
   Protected Sub New()
' Public Instance Properties
   MustInherit Public ReadOnly Property Attributes As PropertyAttributes
   MustInherit Public ReadOnly Property CanRead As Boolean
   MustInherit Public ReadOnly Property CanWrite As Boolean
   Public ReadOnly Property IsSpecialName As Boolean
   Overrides Public ReadOnly Property MemberType As MemberTypes
   MustInherit Public ReadOnly Property PropertyType As Type
' Public Instance Methods
   Public Function GetAccessors() As MethodInfo()
   MustInherit Public Function GetAccessors(ByVal nonPublic As Boolean) As MethodInfo()
   Public Function GetGetMethod() As MethodInfo
   MustInherit Public Function GetGetMethod(ByVal nonPublic As Boolean) As MethodInfo
   MustInherit Public Function GetIndexParameters() As ParameterInfo()
   Public Function GetSetMethod() As MethodInfo
   MustInherit Public Function GetSetMethod(ByVal nonPublic As Boolean) As MethodInfo
   MustInherit Public Function GetValue(ByVal obj As Object, ByVal invokeAttr As BindingFlags, _
      ByVal binder As Binder, ByVal index As Object(), ByVal culture As System.Globalization.CultureInfo) As Object
   Overridable Public Function GetValue(ByVal obj As Object, ByVal index As Object()) As Object
   MustInherit Public Sub SetValue(ByVal obj As Object, ByVal value As Object, ByVal invokeAttr As BindingFlags, _
      ByVal binder As Binder, ByVal index As Object(), ByVal culture As System.Globalization.CultureInfo)
   Overridable Public Sub SetValue(ByVal obj As Object, ByVal value As Object, ByVal index As Object())
End Class
```

Hierarchy: System.Object→ MemberInfo(ICustomAttributeProvider)→ PropertyInfo

Subclasses: System.Reflection.Emit.PropertyBuilder

Returned By: Binder.SelectProperty(), IReflect.{GetProperties(), GetProperty()}, System.Runtime.InteropServices.Expando.IExpando.AddProperty(), System.Type.{GetProperties(), GetProperty(), GetPropertyImpl()}

Passed To: Binder.SelectProperty(), System.Reflection.Emit.CustomAttributeBuilder.CustomAttributeBuilder()

ReflectionTypeLoadException   **NotInheritable Class**

System.Reflection (mscorlib.dll)   *serializable*

This exception is thrown if any of the types from a module cannot be loaded when Module.GetTypes() is called. This exception provides access to the correctly loaded classes via Types.

```
Public NotInheritable Class ReflectionTypeLoadException : Inherits SystemException
' Public Constructors
   Public Sub New(ByVal classes As Type(), ByVal exceptions As Exception())
   Public Sub New(ByVal classes As Type(), ByVal exceptions As Exception(), ByVal message As String)
' Public Instance Properties
   Public ReadOnly Property LoaderExceptions As Exception()
   Public ReadOnly Property Types As Type()
' Public Instance Methods
   Overrides Public Sub GetObjectData(ByVal info As System.Runtime.Serialization.SerializationInfo, _
      ByVal context As System.Runtime.Serialization.StreamingContext)
End Class
```

Hierarchy: System.Object→ System.Exception(System.Runtime.Serialization.ISerializable)→ System.SystemException→ ReflectionTypeLoadException

---

ResourceAttributes
Enum

System.Reflection (mscorlib.dll)
serializable, flag

This enumeration includes the only two flags that can be placed on resources: Public and Private.

```
Public Enum ResourceAttributes
    Public = &H000000001
    Private = &H000000002
End Enum
```

Hierarchy: System.Object→ System.ValueType→ System.Enum(System.IComparable, System.IFormattable, System.IConvertible)→ ResourceAttributes

Passed To: System.Reflection.Emit.AssemblyBuilder.{AddResourceFile(), DefineResource()}, System.Reflection.Emit.ModuleBuilder.DefineResource()

ResourceLocation
Enum

System.Reflection (mscorlib.dll)
serializable, flag

This enumeration returns the location of a resource relative to the assembly.

```
Public Enum ResourceLocation
    Embedded = &H000000001
    ContainedInAnotherAssembly = &H000000002
    ContainedInManifestFile = &H000000004
End Enum
```

Hierarchy: System.Object→ System.ValueType→ System.Enum(System.IComparable, System.IFormattable, System.IConvertible)→ ResourceLocation

Returned By: ManifestResourceInfo.ResourceLocation

StrongNameKeyPair
Class

System.Reflection (mscorlib.dll)
serializable

This property allows reflection of an assembly's strong name. Use PublicKey to decrypt the encrypted name to verify the authenticity of the assembly.

```
Public Class StrongNameKeyPair
' Public Constructors
    Public Sub New(ByVal keyPairArray As Byte())
    Public Sub New(ByVal keyPairFile As System.IO.FileStream)
    Public Sub New(ByVal keyPairContainer As String)
' Public Instance Properties
    Public ReadOnly Property PublicKey As Byte()
End Class
```

Returned By: AssemblyName.KeyPair

Passed To: AssemblyName.KeyPair

TargetException
Class

System.Reflection (mscorlib.dll)
ECMA, serializable

This exception is thrown when you attempt to invoke a nonshared method on a null object reference. (Note that in Beta1 of the .NET SDK, it was permissible to call a non-virtual method against a null reference, so long as that method didn't access any of the fields in the type. In Beta2 and beyond, this "feature" has been closed and removed.)

```
Public Class TargetException : Inherits ApplicationException
' Public Constructors
   Public Sub New()
   Public Sub New(ByVal message As String)
   Public Sub New(ByVal message As String, ByVal inner As Exception)
' Protected Constructors
   Protected Sub New(ByVal info As System.Runtime.Serialization.SerializationInfo, _
      ByVal context As System.Runtime.Serialization.StreamingContext)
End Class
```

Hierarchy: System.Object→ System.Exception(System.Runtime.Serialization.ISerializable)→
System.ApplicationException→ TargetException

TargetInvocationException   NotInheritable Class
System.Reflection (mscorlib.dll)   *ECMA, serializable*

This exception is thrown by methods invoked via Reflection when they raise exceptions. Check InnerException to view the actual exception raised.

```
Public NotInheritable Class TargetInvocationException : Inherits ApplicationException
' Public Constructors
   Public Sub New(ByVal inner As Exception)
   Public Sub New(ByVal message As String, ByVal inner As Exception)
End Class
```

Hierarchy: System.Object→ System.Exception(System.Runtime.Serialization.ISerializable)→
System.ApplicationException→ TargetInvocationException

TargetParameterCountException   NotInheritable Class
System.Reflection (mscorlib.dll)   *ECMA, serializable*

This exception is thrown when a method is invoked with an incorrect number of parameters. Note that this can only come when invoking methods via reflection, since the compiler detects any normal parameter count errors.

```
Public NotInheritable Class TargetParameterCountException : Inherits ApplicationException
' Public Constructors
   Public Sub New()
   Public Sub New(ByVal message As String)
   Public Sub New(ByVal message As String, ByVal inner As Exception)
End Class
```

Hierarchy: System.Object→ System.Exception(System.Runtime.Serialization.ISerializable)→
System.ApplicationException→ TargetParameterCountException

TypeAttributes   Enum
System.Reflection (mscorlib.dll)   *ECMA, serializable, flag*

These attributes can be applied to a type. A type is either a class or interface, so either Class or Interface must be set. Most of the modifiers share the same keywords with C# and VB.NET, so they are easy to understand. The values prefixed with Nested indicate a class that is nested as well as its visibility.

```
Public Enum TypeAttributes
      Class = &H000000000
      AutoLayout = &H000000000
      AnsiClass = &H000000000
```

```
     NotPublic = &H000000000
     Public = &H000000001
     NestedPublic = &H000000002
     NestedPrivate = &H000000003
     NestedFamily = &H000000004
     NestedAssembly = &H000000005
     NestedFamANDAssem = &H000000006
     VisibilityMask = &H000000007
     NestedFamORAssem = &H000000007
     SequentialLayout = &H000000008
     ExplicitLayout = &H000000010
     LayoutMask = &H000000018
     Interface = &H000000020
     ClassSemanticsMask = &H000000020
     Abstract = &H000000080
     Sealed = &H000000100
     SpecialName = &H000000400
     RTSpecialName = &H000000800
     Import = &H000001000
     Serializable = &H000002000
     UnicodeClass = &H000010000
     AutoClass = &H000020000
     StringFormatMask = &H000030000
     HasSecurity = &H000040000
     ReservedMask = &H000040800
     BeforeFieldInit = &H000100000
End Enum
```

Hierarchy: System.Object→ System.ValueType→ System.Enum(System.IComparable, System.IFormattable, System.IConvertible)→ TypeAttributes

Returned By: System.Type.{Attributes, GetAttributeFlagsImpl()}

Passed To: System.Reflection.Emit.ModuleBuilder.{DefineEnum(), DefineType()}, System.Reflection.Emit.TypeBuilder.DefineNestedType()

TypeDelegator   Class

System.Reflection (mscorlib.dll)   *serializable*

Because System.Type is a MustInherit class, TypeDelegator simply wraps System.Type methods and provides the necessary implementations.

```
Public Class TypeDelegator : Inherits Type
' Public Constructors
   Public Sub New(ByVal delegatingType As Type)
' Protected Constructors
   Protected Sub New()
' Protected Instance Fields
   protected typeImpl As Type
' Public Instance Properties
   Overrides Public ReadOnly Property Assembly As Assembly
   Overrides Public ReadOnly Property AssemblyQualifiedName As String
   Overrides Public ReadOnly Property BaseType As Type
   Overrides Public ReadOnly Property FullName As String
   Overrides Public ReadOnly Property GUID As Guid
   Overrides Public ReadOnly Property Module As Module
   Overrides Public ReadOnly Property Name As String
```

Overrides Public ReadOnly Property **Namespace** As String
Overrides Public ReadOnly Property **TypeHandle** As RuntimeTypeHandle
Overrides Public ReadOnly Property **UnderlyingSystemType** As Type
' Public Instance Methods
Overrides Public Function **GetConstructors**(ByVal bindingAttr As BindingFlags) As ConstructorInfo()
Overrides Public Function **GetCustomAttributes**(ByVal inherit As Boolean) As Object()
Overrides Public Function **GetCustomAttributes**(ByVal attributeType As Type, ByVal inherit As Boolean) _
  As Object()
Overrides Public Function **GetElementType**() As Type
Overrides Public Function **GetEvent**(ByVal name As String, ByVal bindingAttr As BindingFlags) As EventInfo
Overrides Public Function **GetEvents**() As EventInfo()
Overrides Public Function **GetEvents**(ByVal bindingAttr As BindingFlags) As EventInfo()
Overrides Public Function **GetField**(ByVal name As String, ByVal bindingAttr As BindingFlags) As FieldInfo
Overrides Public Function **GetFields**(ByVal bindingAttr As BindingFlags) As FieldInfo()
Overrides Public Function **GetInterface**(ByVal name As String, ByVal ignoreCase As Boolean) As Type
Overrides Public Function **GetInterfaceMap**(ByVal interfaceType As Type) As InterfaceMapping
Overrides Public Function **GetInterfaces**() As Type()
Overrides Public Function **GetMember**(ByVal name As String, ByVal type As MemberTypes, _
  ByVal bindingAttr As BindingFlags) As MemberInfo()
Overrides Public Function **GetMembers**(ByVal bindingAttr As BindingFlags) As MemberInfo()
Overrides Public Function **GetMethods**(ByVal bindingAttr As BindingFlags) As MethodInfo()
Overrides Public Function **GetNestedType**(ByVal name As String, ByVal bindingAttr As BindingFlags) As Type
Overrides Public Function **GetNestedTypes**(ByVal bindingAttr As BindingFlags) As Type()
Overrides Public Function **GetProperties**(ByVal bindingAttr As BindingFlags) As PropertyInfo()
Overrides Public Function **InvokeMember**(ByVal name As String, ByVal invokeAttr As BindingFlags,   _
  ByVal binder As Binder, ByVal target As Object, ByVal args As Object(), ByVal modifiers As ParameterModifier(), _
  ByVal culture As System.Globalization.CultureInfo, ByVal namedParameters As String()) As Object
Overrides Public Function **IsDefined**(ByVal attributeType As Type, ByVal inherit As Boolean) As Boolean
' Protected Instance Methods
Overrides Protected Function **GetAttributeFlagsImpl**() As TypeAttributes
Overrides Protected Function **GetConstructorImpl**(ByVal bindingAttr As BindingFlags, ByVal binder As Binder, _
  ByVal callConvention As CallingConventions, ByVal types As Type(), ByVal modifiers As ParameterModifier())   _
  As ConstructorInfo
Overrides Protected Function **GetMethodImpl**(ByVal name As String, ByVal bindingAttr As BindingFlags, _
  ByVal binder As Binder, ByVal callConvention As CallingConventions, ByVal types As Type(),   _
  ByVal modifiers As ParameterModifier()) As MethodInfo
Overrides Protected Function **GetPropertyImpl**(ByVal name As String, ByVal bindingAttr As BindingFlags,   _
  ByVal binder As Binder, ByVal returnType As Type, ByVal types As Type(), ByVal modifiers As ParameterModifier()) _
  As PropertyInfo
Overrides Protected Function **HasElementTypeImpl**() As Boolean
Overrides Protected Function **IsArrayImpl**() As Boolean
Overrides Protected Function **IsByRefImpl**() As Boolean
Overrides Protected Function **IsCOMObjectImpl**() As Boolean
Overrides Protected Function **IsPointerImpl**() As Boolean
Overrides Protected Function **IsPrimitiveImpl**() As Boolean
Overrides Protected Function **IsValueTypeImpl**() As Boolean
End Class

Hierarchy: System.Object→ MemberInfo(ICustomAttributeProvider)→ System.Type(IReflect)→
TypeDelegator

TypeFilter

	Delegate
System.Reflection (mscorlib.dll)	*serializable*

This delegate maps to a function that will be applied individually to a list of System.Type objects. A filter runs through the list, and if this delegate returns true, the filtered list includes this object, otherwise it is excluded.

Public Delegate Function **TypeFilter**(ByVal m As Type, ByVal filterCriteria As Object) As Boolean

Passed To: Module.FindTypes(), System.Type.FindInterfaces()

CHAPTER 14

System.Reflection.Emit

There are several ways to use reflection in .NET. Reflection can be used for runtime-type inspection and late-bound object creation using the types in the System.Reflection namespace. Reflection can also be used for dynamic code creation, which is supported by the types in this namespace, System.Reflection.Emit. Dynamic code creation means a programmer can programmatically create code constructs such as methods and events from within code, using the appropriate corresponding type (for example, MethodBuilder and EventBuilder). These code elements are all ingredients that can be added to a dynamic assembly, represented by an AssemblyBuilder object. Dynamic assemblies can be saved to disk as PE (Portable Executable) files, typically in DLL form. Or, alternatively, emit it directly to memory for immediate use, at the expense of persistence (memory-only types disappear when the containing AppDomain terminates).

The ILGenerator class allows you to emit the MSIL (Microsoft Intermediate Language) for your code, using the corresponding GetILGenerator() method from a *builder* class. This process (sometimes known as "baking") allows you to convert the information in the builder object into a legitimate .NET type. You can then instantiate this newly created type on the spot.

The primary use of the System.Reflection.Emit namespace is to create compilers and script hosts, although many other uses are possible, including programs that dynamically create code that is fine-tuned to process a specific regular expression (see System.Text.RegularExpressions.Regex.CompileToAssembly()). When creating dynamic types, you generally begin by creating an AssemblyBuilder, which contains one or more ModuleBuilder objects. This in turn contains TypeBuilder instances. TypeBuilder objects contain most of the other ingredients in this namespace, including classes for building events, properties, methods, and enumerations.

Many of the builder classes in this namespace use similar methods and properties for retrieving information about the containing module (for example, ConstructorBuilder.GetModule()), getting an internal handle to the metadata (for example, EnumBuilder.TypeHandle()), and retrieving attributes (MethodBuilder.Attributes). Also note that though the builder classes derive from the corresponding "-Info" class (for example, MethodBuilder derives from System.Reflection.MethodInfo), not all of the inherited properties are currently supported. This includes methods such as Invoke(). To use these methods, you may

342

need to reflect on the object with System.Type.GetType(). Figure 14-1 shows the types in this namespace.

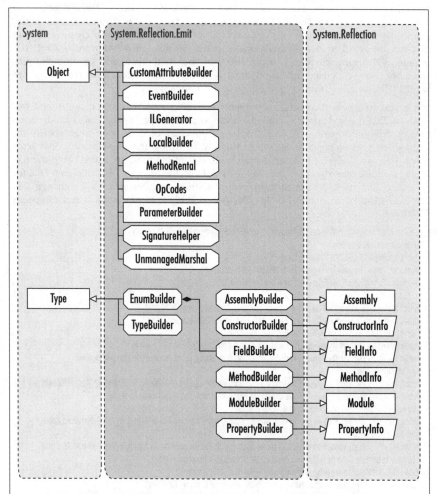

Figure 14–1. The System.Reflection.Emit namespace

AssemblyBuilder

NotInheritable Class

System.Reflection.Emit (mscorlib.dll)

This class represents a dynamic assembly. A dynamic assembly is the root container for all the builder objects in the System.Reflection.Emit namespace. You can create an AssemblyBuilder object by using the DefineDynamicAssembly() method of the System.AppDomain class. When you create a dynamic assembly, specify a name and the access mode, using the AssemblyBuilderAccess enumeration. If you plan to save the assembly to disk using the the Save() method, be sure to specify AssemblyBuilderAccess.Save or Assembly-BuilderAccess.RunAndSave.

A dynamic assembly can contain one or more modules, which are defined by Module-Builder objects. Use the DefineDynamicModule() method to define, create, and return a ModuleBuilder object, as in Dim myModB As ModuleBuilder = myAssemblyB.DefineDynamicModule("ModuleName"). By default, this is a transient module that cannot be saved, regardless of the AssemblyBuilderAccess specified. To create a module that can be saved to disk, use a version of the overloaded DefineDynamicModule() that requires a fileName argument. You can also use other methods to add an attribute to the assembly, add or create managed and unmanaged resources, and retrieve a System.IO.FileStream object for any of the files in the assembly.

When you are finished creating an assembly and all its members, you can use the Save() method. This method takes a simple filename as a parameter, which can't include directory or drive information. To use a different directory or drive, you must specify the path when you create the dynamic assembly by using the appropriate constructor. When you save a dynamic assembly, all nontransient modules are saved using the filename specified when you created them. By default, the assembly is saved as a DLL file (as if you had used the /target:library command-line compiler switch). To change this, use the SetEntryPoint() method to specify the assembly's startup method and to specify PEFileKinds.

```
Public NotInheritable Class AssemblyBuilder : Inherits System.Reflection.Assembly
' Public Instance Properties
   Overrides Public ReadOnly Property CodeBase As String
   Overrides Public ReadOnly Property EntryPoint As MethodInfo
   Overrides Public ReadOnly Property Location As String
' Public Instance Methods
   Public Sub AddResourceFile(ByVal name As String, ByVal fileName As String)
   Public Sub AddResourceFile(ByVal name As String, ByVal fileName As String, _
      ByVal attribute As System.Reflection.ResourceAttributes)
   Public Function DefineDynamicModule(ByVal name As String) As ModuleBuilder
   Public Function DefineDynamicModule(ByVal name As String, ByVal emitSymbolInfo As Boolean) _
      As ModuleBuilder
   Public Function DefineDynamicModule(ByVal name As String, ByVal fileName As String) As ModuleBuilder
   Public Function DefineDynamicModule(ByVal name As String, ByVal fileName As String, _
      ByVal emitSymbolInfo As Boolean) As ModuleBuilder
   Public Function DefineResource(ByVal name As String, ByVal description As String, ByVal fileName As String) _
      As IResourceWriter
   Public Function DefineResource(ByVal name As String, ByVal description As String, ByVal fileName As String, _
      ByVal attribute As System.Reflection.ResourceAttributes)  As IResourceWriter
   Public Sub DefineUnmanagedResource(ByVal resource As Byte())
   Public Sub DefineUnmanagedResource(ByVal resourceFileName As String)
   Public Sub DefineVersionInfoResource()
   Public Sub DefineVersionInfoResource(ByVal product As String, ByVal productVersion As String, _
      ByVal company As String, ByVal copyright As String, ByVal trademark As String)
   Public Function GetDynamicModule(ByVal name As String) As ModuleBuilder
   Overrides Public Function GetExportedTypes() As Type()
   Overrides Public Function GetFile(ByVal name As String) As FileStream
   Overrides Public Function GetFiles(ByVal getResourceModules As Boolean) As FileStream()
   Overrides Public Function GetManifestResourceInfo(ByVal resourceName As String) As ManifestResourceInfo
   Overrides Public Function GetManifestResourceNames() As String()
   Overrides Public Function GetManifestResourceStream(ByVal name As String) As Stream
   Overrides Public Function GetManifestResourceStream(ByVal type As Type, ByVal name As String) As Stream
   Public Sub Save(ByVal assemblyFileName As String)
   Public Sub SetCustomAttribute(ByVal con As System.Reflection.ConstructorInfo, ByVal binaryAttribute As Byte())
   Public Sub SetCustomAttribute(ByVal customBuilder As CustomAttributeBuilder)
   Public Sub SetEntryPoint(ByVal entryMethod As System.Reflection.MethodInfo)
```

```
Public Sub SetEntryPoint(ByVal entryMethod As System.Reflection.MethodInfo, ByVal fileKind As PEFileKinds)
End Class
```

Hierarchy: System.Object→ System.Reflection.Assembly(System.Security.IEvidenceFactory, System.Reflection.ICustomAttributeProvider, System.Runtime.Serialization.ISerializable)→ AssemblyBuilder

Returned By: System.AppDomain.DefineDynamicAssembly()

AssemblyBuilderAccess

Enum

System.Reflection.Emit (mscorlib.dll)
serializable

This enumeration is used by the System.AppDomain.DefineDynamicAssembly() method. It specifies whether a dynamic assembly will support dynamic execution only (Run), save to disk only (Save), or both (RunAndSave).

```
Public Enum AssemblyBuilderAccess
    Run = 1
    Save = 2
    RunAndSave = 3
End Enum
```

Hierarchy: System.Object→ System.ValueType→ System.Enum(System.IComparable, System.IFormattable, System.IConvertible)→ AssemblyBuilderAccess

Passed To: System.AppDomain.DefineDynamicAssembly()

ConstructorBuilder

NotInheritable Class

System.Reflection.Emit (mscorlib.dll)

This class represents a dynamically created constructor method. Create a constructor and add it to a type using either the TypeBuilder.DefineConstructor() method or the Type-Builder.DefineDefaultConstructor() method. The default constructor accepts no parameters, and just calls the constructor of the parent class. You cannot use the ILGenerator class with a default constructor, because its code is provided by the runtime. Generally, a default constructor does not need to be created, as the CLR provides it for you.

If you create a custom constructor with TypeBuilder.DefineConstructor(), you can specify the constructor's parameters as an array of System.Type objects. Alternatively, you can use the DefineParameter() method to create a ParameterBuilder. You can also add MSIL code to the constructor using the GetILGenerator() method.

```
Public NotInheritable Class ConstructorBuilder : Inherits System.Reflection.ConstructorInfo
' Public Instance Properties
    Overrides Public ReadOnly Property Attributes As MethodAttributes
    Overrides Public ReadOnly Property DeclaringType As Type
    Public Property InitLocals As Boolean
    Overrides Public ReadOnly Property MethodHandle As RuntimeMethodHandle
    Overrides Public ReadOnly Property Name As String
    Overrides Public ReadOnly Property ReflectedType As Type
    Public ReadOnly Property ReturnType As Type
    Public ReadOnly Property Signature As String
' Public Instance Methods
    Public Sub AddDeclarativeSecurity(ByVal action As System.Security.Permissions.SecurityAction, _
        ByVal pset As System.Security.PermissionSet)
    Public Function DefineParameter(ByVal iSequence As Integer,                              _
        ByVal attributes As System.Reflection.ParameterAttributes, ByVal strParamName As String) As ParameterBuilder
```

Overrides Public Function **GetCustomAttributes**(ByVal inherit As Boolean) As Object()
Overrides Public Function **GetCustomAttributes**(ByVal attributeType As Type, ByVal inherit As Boolean) _
  As Object()
Public Function **GetILGenerator**() As ILGenerator
Overrides Public Function **GetMethodImplementationFlags**() As MethodImplAttributes
Public Function **GetModule**() As Module
Overrides Public Function **GetParameters**() As ParameterInfo()
Public Function **GetToken**() As MethodToken
Overrides Public Function **Invoke**(ByVal invokeAttr As System.Reflection.BindingFlags, _
  ByVal binder As System.Reflection.Binder, ByVal parameters As Object(),   _
  ByVal culture As System.Globalization.CultureInfo) As Object
Overrides Public Function **Invoke**(ByVal obj As Object, ByVal invokeAttr As System.Reflection.BindingFlags, _
  ByVal binder As System.Reflection.Binder, ByVal parameters As Object(),
  ByVal culture As System.Globalization.CultureInfo) As Object
Overrides Public Function **IsDefined**(ByVal attributeType As Type, ByVal inherit As Boolean) As Boolean
Public Sub **SetCustomAttribute**(ByVal con As System.Reflection.ConstructorInfo, ByVal binaryAttribute As Byte())
Public Sub **SetCustomAttribute**(ByVal customBuilder As CustomAttributeBuilder)
Public Sub **SetImplementationFlags**(ByVal attributes As System.Reflection.MethodImplAttributes)
Public Sub **SetSymCustomAttribute**(ByVal name As String, ByVal data As Byte())
Overrides Public Function **ToString**() As String
End Class

Hierarchy: System.Object→
System.Reflection.MemberInfo(System.Reflection.ICustomAttributeProvider)→
System.Reflection.MethodBase→ System.Reflection.ConstructorInfo→ ConstructorBuilder

Returned By: TypeBuilder.{DefineConstructor(), DefineDefaultConstructor(), DefineTypeInitializer()}

CustomAttributeBuilder   Class

System.Reflection.Emit (mscorlib.dll)

This class represents a dynamically created custom attribute. To apply a custom attribute, pass an instance of this type to the SetCustomAttribute() method for the appropriate builder (for example, PropertyBuilder.SetCustomAttribute() or MethodBuilder.SetCustomAttribute()). The constructor allows you to specify the custom attribute's named properties and fields, their values, and a constructor.

Public Class **CustomAttributeBuilder**
' *Public Constructors*
  Public Sub **New**(ByVal con As System.Reflection.ConstructorInfo, ByVal constructorArgs As Object())
  Public Sub **New**(ByVal con As System.Reflection.ConstructorInfo, ByVal constructorArgs As Object(), _
    ByVal namedFields As System.Reflection.FieldInfo(), ByVal fieldValues As Object())
  Public Sub **New**(ByVal con As System.Reflection.ConstructorInfo, ByVal constructorArgs As Object(), _
    ByVal namedProperties As System.Reflection.PropertyInfo(), ByVal propertyValues As Object())
  Public Sub **New**(ByVal con As System.Reflection.ConstructorInfo, ByVal constructorArgs As Object(), _
    ByVal namedProperties As System.Reflection.PropertyInfo(), ByVal propertyValues As Object(),   _
    ByVal namedFields As System.Reflection.FieldInfo(), ByVal fieldValues As Object())
End Class

Passed To: AssemblyBuilder.SetCustomAttribute(), ConstructorBuilder.SetCustomAttribute(),
EnumBuilder.SetCustomAttribute(), EventBuilder.SetCustomAttribute(),
FieldBuilder.SetCustomAttribute(), MethodBuilder.SetCustomAttribute(),
ModuleBuilder.SetCustomAttribute(), ParameterBuilder.SetCustomAttribute(),
PropertyBuilder.SetCustomAttribute(), TypeBuilder.SetCustomAttribute(),
System.Text.RegularExpressions.Regex.CompileToAssembly()

EnumBuilder

System.Reflection.Emit (mscorlib.dll)

This class represents a dynamically created enumeration. Enumerations are created at module scope using the ModuleBuilder.DefineEnum() method. Before using a dynamically created enumeration, you must use the CreateType() method to complete it.

Public NotInheritable Class **EnumBuilder** : Inherits Type
' *Public Instance Properties*
  Overrides Public ReadOnly Property **Assembly** As Assembly
  Overrides Public ReadOnly Property **AssemblyQualifiedName** As String
  Overrides Public ReadOnly Property **BaseType** As Type
  Overrides Public ReadOnly Property **DeclaringType** As Type
  Overrides Public ReadOnly Property **FullName** As String
  Overrides Public ReadOnly Property **GUID** As Guid
  Overrides Public ReadOnly Property **Module** As Module
  Overrides Public ReadOnly Property **Name** As String
  Overrides Public ReadOnly Property **Namespace** As String
  Overrides Public ReadOnly Property **ReflectedType** As Type
  Overrides Public ReadOnly Property **TypeHandle** As RuntimeTypeHandle
  Public ReadOnly Property **TypeToken** As TypeToken
  Public ReadOnly Property **UnderlyingField** As FieldBuilder
  Overrides Public ReadOnly Property **UnderlyingSystemType** As Type
' *Public Instance Methods*
  Public Function **CreateType**() As Type
  Public Function **DefineLiteral**(ByVal literalName As String, ByVal literalValue As Object) As FieldBuilder
  Overrides Public Function **GetConstructors**(ByVal bindingAttr As System.Reflection.BindingFlags) _
    As ConstructorInfo()
  Overrides Public Function **GetCustomAttributes**(ByVal inherit As Boolean) As Object()
  Overrides Public Function **GetCustomAttributes**(ByVal attributeType As Type, ByVal inherit As Boolean) _
    As Object()
  Overrides Public Function **GetElementType**() As Type
  Overrides Public Function **GetEvent**(ByVal name As String, ByVal bindingAttr As System.Reflection.BindingFlags) _
    As EventInfo
  Overrides Public Function **GetEvents**() As EventInfo()
  Overrides Public Function **GetEvents**(ByVal bindingAttr As System.Reflection.BindingFlags) As EventInfo()
  Overrides Public Function **GetField**(ByVal name As String, ByVal bindingAttr As System.Reflection.BindingFlags) _
    As FieldInfo
  Overrides Public Function **GetFields**(ByVal bindingAttr As System.Reflection.BindingFlags) As FieldInfo()
  Overrides Public Function **GetInterface**(ByVal name As String, ByVal ignoreCase As Boolean) As Type
  Overrides Public Function **GetInterfaceMap**(ByVal interfaceType As Type) As InterfaceMapping
  Overrides Public Function **GetInterfaces**() As Type()
  Overrides Public Function **GetMember**(ByVal name As String, ByVal type As System.Reflection.MemberTypes, _
    ByVal bindingAttr As System.Reflection.BindingFlags) As MemberInfo()
  Overrides Public Function **GetMembers**(ByVal bindingAttr As System.Reflection.BindingFlags) As MemberInfo()
  Overrides Public Function **GetMethods**(ByVal bindingAttr As System.Reflection.BindingFlags) As MethodInfo()
  Overrides Public Function **GetNestedType**(ByVal name As String, _
    ByVal bindingAttr As System.Reflection.BindingFlags) As Type
  Overrides Public Function **GetNestedTypes**(ByVal bindingAttr As System.Reflection.BindingFlags) As Type()
  Overrides Public Function **GetProperties**(ByVal bindingAttr As System.Reflection.BindingFlags) As PropertyInfo()
  Overrides Public Function **InvokeMember**(ByVal name As String, _
    ByVal invokeAttr As System.Reflection.BindingFlags, ByVal binder As System.Reflection.Binder, _
    ByVal target As Object, ByVal args As Object(), ByVal modifiers As System.Reflection.ParameterModifier(), _
    ByVal culture As System.Globalization.CultureInfo, ByVal namedParameters As String()) As Object
  Overrides Public Function **IsDefined**(ByVal attributeType As Type, ByVal inherit As Boolean) As Boolean
  Public Sub **SetCustomAttribute**(ByVal con As System.Reflection.ConstructorInfo, ByVal binaryAttribute As Byte())
  Public Sub **SetCustomAttribute**(ByVal customBuilder As CustomAttributeBuilder)

' Protected Instance Methods

Overrides Protected Function **GetAttributeFlagsImpl**() As TypeAttributes

Overrides Protected Function **GetConstructorImpl**(ByVal bindingAttr As System.Reflection.BindingFlags, _
ByVal binder As System.Reflection.Binder, ByVal callConvention As System.Reflection.CallingConventions, _
ByVal types As Type(), ByVal modifiers As System.Reflection.ParameterModifier()) As ConstructorInfo

Overrides Protected Function **GetMethodImpl**(ByVal name As String, _
ByVal bindingAttr As System.Reflection.BindingFlags, ByVal binder As System.Reflection.Binder, _
ByVal callConvention As System.Reflection.CallingConventions, ByVal types As Type(), _
ByVal modifiers As System.Reflection.ParameterModifier()) As MethodInfo

Overrides Protected Function **GetPropertyImpl**(ByVal name As String, _
ByVal bindingAttr As System.Reflection.BindingFlags, ByVal binder As System.Reflection.Binder, _
ByVal returnType As Type, ByVal types As Type(), ByVal modifiers As System.Reflection.ParameterModifier()) _
As PropertyInfo

Overrides Protected Function **HasElementTypeImpl**() As Boolean

Overrides Protected Function **IsArrayImpl**() As Boolean

Overrides Protected Function **IsByRefImpl**() As Boolean

Overrides Protected Function **IsCOMObjectImpl**() As Boolean

Overrides Protected Function **IsPointerImpl**() As Boolean

Overrides Protected Function **IsPrimitiveImpl**() As Boolean

Overrides Protected Function **IsValueTypeImpl**() As Boolean

End Class

Hierarchy: System.Object→
System.Reflection.MemberInfo(System.Reflection.ICustomAttributeProvider)→
System.Type(System.Reflection.IReflect)→ EnumBuilder

Returned By: ModuleBuilder.DefineEnum()

EventBuilder   NotInheritable Class

System.Reflection.Emit (mscorlib.dll)

This class represents a dynamically created event. Events are created with the Type-Builder.DefineEvent() method. You can then attach a MethodBuilder object to represent one of three methods: the method used to raise the event (SetRaiseMethod()), the method used to subscribe to the event (SetAddOnMethod()), and the method used to unsubscribe (SetRemoveOnMethod()).

Public NotInheritable Class **EventBuilder**

' Public Instance Methods

Public Sub **AddOtherMethod**(ByVal mdBuilder As MethodBuilder)

Public Function **GetEventToken**() As EventToken

Public Sub **SetAddOnMethod**(ByVal mdBuilder As MethodBuilder)

Public Sub **SetCustomAttribute**(ByVal con As System.Reflection.ConstructorInfo, ByVal binaryAttribute As Byte())

Public Sub **SetCustomAttribute**(ByVal customBuilder As CustomAttributeBuilder)

Public Sub **SetRaiseMethod**(ByVal mdBuilder As MethodBuilder)

Public Sub **SetRemoveOnMethod**(ByVal mdBuilder As MethodBuilder)

End Class

Returned By: TypeBuilder.DefineEvent()

EventToken

Structure

System.Reflection.Emit (mscorlib.dll)

serializable

This class represents the token for an event. A token is a 4-byte number that points to the metadata description of a program element in MSIL. The first byte in the token identifies the metadata table, which depends on the type of program element. The remaining 3 bytes specify the row in the metadata table. For example, the token 0x06000004 specifies that the corresponding metadata is stored in the fourth row of table 0x06 (the MethodDef table).

```
Public Structure EventToken
' Public Shared Fields
   Public Shared ReadOnly Empty As EventToken                    =System.Reflection.Emit.EventToken
' Public Instance Properties
   Public ReadOnly Property Token As Integer
' Public Instance Methods
   Overrides Public Function Equals(ByVal obj As Object) As Boolean
   Overrides Public Function GetHashCode() As Integer
End Structure
```

Hierarchy: System.Object→ System.ValueType→ EventToken

Returned By: EventBuilder.GetEventToken()

FieldBuilder

NotInheritable Class

System.Reflection.Emit (mscorlib.dll)

This class represents a dynamically created field. Fields are created with the TypeBuilder.DefineField() method, which allows you to specify the field's characteristics using the System.Reflection.FieldAttributes enumeration. The TypeBuilder.DefineField() method also determines the name and type of the field. Fields must be a simple data type such as a string or integer. Use SetConstant() to set the default value of the field.

```
Public NotInheritable Class FieldBuilder : Inherits System.Reflection.FieldInfo
' Public Instance Properties
   Overrides Public ReadOnly Property Attributes As FieldAttributes
   Overrides Public ReadOnly Property DeclaringType As Type
   Overrides Public ReadOnly Property FieldHandle As RuntimeFieldHandle
   Overrides Public ReadOnly Property FieldType As Type
   Overrides Public ReadOnly Property Name As String
   Overrides Public ReadOnly Property ReflectedType As Type
' Public Instance Methods
   Overrides Public Function GetCustomAttributes(ByVal inherit As Boolean) As Object()
   Overrides Public Function GetCustomAttributes(ByVal attributeType As Type, ByVal inherit As Boolean) _
      As Object()
   Public Function GetToken() As FieldToken
   Overrides Public Function GetValue(ByVal obj As Object) As Object
   Overrides Public Function IsDefined(ByVal attributeType As Type, ByVal inherit As Boolean) As Boolean
   Public Sub SetConstant(ByVal defaultValue As Object)
   Public Sub SetCustomAttribute(ByVal con As System.Reflection.ConstructorInfo, ByVal binaryAttribute As Byte())
   Public Sub SetCustomAttribute(ByVal customBuilder As CustomAttributeBuilder)
   Public Sub SetMarshal(ByVal unmanagedMarshal As UnmanagedMarshal)
   Public Sub SetOffset(ByVal iOffset As Integer)
   Overrides Public Sub SetValue(ByVal obj As Object, ByVal val As Object,                              _
      ByVal invokeAttr As System.Reflection.BindingFlags, ByVal binder As System.Reflection.Binder, _
      ByVal culture As System.Globalization.CultureInfo)
End Class
```

System. Reflection

Hierarchy: System.Object→
System.Reflection.MemberInfo(System.Reflection.ICustomAttributeProvider)→
System.Reflection.FieldInfo→ FieldBuilder

Returned By: EnumBuilder.{DefineLiteral(), UnderlyingField}, ModuleBuilder.{DefineInitializedData(),
DefineUninitializedData()}, TypeBuilder.{DefineField(), DefineInitializedData(), DefineUninitializedData()}

FieldToken   Structure

System.Reflection.Emit (mscorlib.dll)   *serializable*

This class represents the token for a field. See EventToken for more details on tokens.

Public Structure **FieldToken**
' *Public Shared Fields*
   Public Shared ReadOnly **Empty** As FieldToken   =*System.Reflection.Emit.FieldToken*
' *Public Instance Properties*
   Public ReadOnly Property **Token** As Integer
' *Public Instance Methods*
   Overrides Public Function **Equals**(ByVal obj As Object) As Boolean
   Overrides Public Function **GetHashCode**() As Integer
End Structure

Hierarchy: System.Object→ System.ValueType→ FieldToken

Returned By: FieldBuilder.GetToken(), ModuleBuilder.GetFieldToken()

FlowControl   Enum

System.Reflection.Emit (mscorlib.dll)   *serializable*

This enumeration is used by the OpCode.FlowControl property. It describes how the
instruction alters the flow of control. Next indicates a normal flow of control, while
Cond_Branch indicates a conditional branch instruction. The Meta value provides information about a subsequent instruction.

Public Enum **FlowControl**
     Branch = 0
     Break = 1
     Call = 2
     Cond_Branch = 3
     Meta = 4
     Next = 5
     Phi = 6
     Return = 7
     Throw = 8
End Enum

Hierarchy: System.Object→ System.ValueType→ System.Enum(System.IComparable,
System.IFormattable, System.IConvertible)→ FlowControl

Returned By: OpCode.FlowControl

ILGenerator   Class

System.Reflection.Emit (mscorlib.dll)

This class generates MSIL (Microsoft Intermediate Language) instructions. You receive
an ILGenerator object from a GetILGenerator method in a builder class. For example, you
can use the ConstructorBuilder.GetILGenerator() to create MSIL instructions for a constructor,
or MethodBuilder.GetILGenerator() to create MSIL instructions for a method. Use BeginScope()
and EndScope() to start and stop a lexical scope.

To emit instructions, use the Emit() method. The Emit() method requires an OpCode object. The easiest way to supply this is by using one of the constant fields from OpCodes, as in myGenerator.Emit(OpCodes.Ret);. EmitWriteLine() creates the MSIL code required to call System.Console.WriteLine() with the supplied variable. You can also define and mark labels in the instruction stream (DefineLabel() and MarkLabel()), emit an instruction for throwing an exception (ThrowException()), and define local variables (DeclareLocal()).

Emit error handling blocks with BeginExceptionBlock() and EndExceptionBlock() (which emits the equivalent of a VB.NET Try statement), BeginCatchBlock() (which emits the equivalent of the Catch statement), and BeginFinallyBlock() (which emits the equivalent of the Finally statement). You must end the exception block using EndExceptionBlock().

```
Public Class ILGenerator
' Public Instance Methods
   Overridable Public Sub BeginCatchBlock(ByVal exceptionType As Type)
   Overridable Public Sub BeginExceptFilterBlock()
   Overridable Public Function BeginExceptionBlock() As Label
   Overridable Public Sub BeginFaultBlock()
   Overridable Public Sub BeginFinallyBlock()
   Overridable Public Sub BeginScope()
   Public Function DeclareLocal(ByVal localType As Type) As LocalBuilder
   Overridable Public Function DefineLabel() As Label
   Overridable Public Sub Emit(ByVal opcode As OpCode)
   Overridable Public Sub Emit(ByVal opcode As OpCode, ByVal arg As Byte)
   Overridable Public Sub Emit(ByVal opcode As OpCode, ByVal con As System.Reflection.ConstructorInfo)
   Overridable Public Sub Emit(ByVal opcode As OpCode, ByVal arg As Double)
   Overridable Public Sub Emit(ByVal opcode As OpCode, ByVal field As System.Reflection.FieldInfo)
   Overridable Public Sub Emit(ByVal opcode As OpCode, ByVal arg As Short)
   Overridable Public Sub Emit(ByVal opcode As OpCode, ByVal arg As Integer)
   Overridable Public Sub Emit(ByVal opcode As OpCode, ByVal arg As Long)
   Overridable Public Sub Emit(ByVal opcode As OpCode, ByVal label As Label)
   Overridable Public Sub Emit(ByVal opcode As OpCode, ByVal labels As Label())
   Overridable Public Sub Emit(ByVal opcode As OpCode, ByVal local As LocalBuilder)
   Overridable Public Sub Emit(ByVal opcode As OpCode, ByVal meth As System.Reflection.MethodInfo)
   Public Sub Emit(ByVal opcode As OpCode, ByVal arg As SByte)
   Overridable Public Sub Emit(ByVal opcode As OpCode, ByVal signature As SignatureHelper)
   Overridable Public Sub Emit(ByVal opcode As OpCode, ByVal arg As Single)
   Overridable Public Sub Emit(ByVal opcode As OpCode, ByVal str As String)
   Overridable Public Sub Emit(ByVal opcode As OpCode, ByVal cls As Type)
   Public Sub EmitCall(ByVal opcode As OpCode, ByVal methodInfo As System.Reflection.MethodInfo, _
      ByVal optionalParameterTypes As Type())
   Public Sub EmitCalli(ByVal opcode As OpCode, ByVal callingConvention As System.Reflection.CallingConventions, _
      ByVal returnType As Type, ByVal parameterTypes As Type(), ByVal optionalParameterTypes As Type())
   Public Sub EmitCalli(ByVal opcode As OpCode,                                                    _
      ByVal unmanagedCallConv As System.Runtime.InteropServices.CallingConvention, ByVal returnType As Type, _
      ByVal parameterTypes As Type())
   Overridable Public Sub EmitWriteLine(ByVal fld As System.Reflection.FieldInfo)
   Overridable Public Sub EmitWriteLine(ByVal localBuilder As LocalBuilder)
   Overridable Public Sub EmitWriteLine(ByVal value As String)
   Overridable Public Sub EndExceptionBlock()
   Overridable Public Sub EndScope()
   Overridable Public Sub MarkLabel(ByVal loc As Label)
   Overridable Public Sub MarkSequencePoint(                                                        _
      ByVal document As System.Diagnostics.SymbolStore.ISymbolDocumentWriter, ByVal startLine As Integer, _
      ByVal startColumn As Integer, ByVal endLine As Integer, ByVal endColumn As Integer)
   Overridable Public Sub ThrowException(ByVal excType As Type)
```

```
    Public Sub UsingNamespace(ByVal usingNamespace As String)
End Class
```

Returned By: ConstructorBuilder.GetILGenerator(), MethodBuilder.GetILGenerator()

Label   Structure

System.Reflection.Emit (mscorlib.dll)   *serializable*

This class represents a label in the MSIL instruction stream. You can create a label with ILGenerator.DefineLabel() and place it in the stream with ILGenerator.MarkLabel().

```
Public Structure Label
' Public Instance Methods
    Overrides Public Function Equals(ByVal obj As Object) As Boolean
    Overrides Public Function GetHashCode() As Integer
End Structure
```

Hierarchy: System.Object→ System.ValueType→ Label

Returned By: ILGenerator.{BeginExceptionBlock(), DefineLabel()}

Passed To: ILGenerator.{Emit(), MarkLabel()}

LocalBuilder   NotInheritable Class

System.Reflection.Emit (mscorlib.dll)

This class represents a dynamically created local variable. Local variables are created for methods and constructors through the ILGenerator object, using the ILGenerator.DeclareLocal().

```
Public NotInheritable Class LocalBuilder
' Public Instance Properties
    Public ReadOnly Property LocalType As Type
' Public Instance Methods
    Public Sub SetLocalSymInfo(ByVal name As String)
    Public Sub SetLocalSymInfo(ByVal name As String, ByVal startOffset As Integer, ByVal endOffset As Integer)
End Class
```

Returned By: ILGenerator.DeclareLocal()

Passed To: ILGenerator.{Emit(), EmitWriteLine()}

MethodBuilder   NotInheritable Class

System.Reflection.Emit (mscorlib.dll)

This class represents a dynamically created method. Methods are created with Type-Builder.DefineMethod(). When creating a method, specify the name, parameters, and return type. You can also specify other characteristics of the method, such as whether it is shared, MustInherit, or overridable, by using the System.Reflection.MethodAttributes enumeration. After creating a method, you can specify how the return value will be marshaled to unmanaged code using SetMarshal(), and add declarative security using AddDeclarativeSecurity(). You must specify the security action (such as Demand, Assert, Deny) using the System.Security.Permissions.SecurityAction enumeration and the permissions required using the System.Security.PermissionSet collection class. You can call AddDeclarativeSecurity() several times to specify different security actions.

To create a global method builder, use ModuleBuilder.DefineGlobalMethod(). You must also use ModuleBuilder.CreateGlobalFunctions() to finish creating global methods before you persist or use the dynamic module. Global methods must be shared. You can also create a global native method using ModuleBuilder.DefinePInvokeMethod(). PInvoke methods cannot be MustInherit or overridable.

```
Public NotInheritable Class MethodBuilder : Inherits System.Reflection.MethodInfo
' Public Instance Properties
   Overrides Public ReadOnly Property Attributes As MethodAttributes
   Overrides Public ReadOnly Property CallingConvention As CallingConventions
   Overrides Public ReadOnly Property DeclaringType As Type
   Public Property InitLocals As Boolean
   Overrides Public ReadOnly Property MethodHandle As RuntimeMethodHandle
   Overrides Public ReadOnly Property Name As String
   Overrides Public ReadOnly Property ReflectedType As Type
   Overrides Public ReadOnly Property ReturnType As Type
   Overrides Public ReadOnly Property ReturnTypeCustomAttributes As ICustomAttributeProvider
   Public ReadOnly Property Signature As String
' Public Instance Methods
   Public Sub AddDeclarativeSecurity(ByVal action As System.Security.Permissions.SecurityAction, _
      ByVal pset As System.Security.PermissionSet)
   Public Sub CreateMethodBody(ByVal il As Byte(), ByVal count As Integer)
   Public Function DefineParameter(ByVal position As Integer, _
      ByVal attributes As System.Reflection.ParameterAttributes, ByVal strParamName As String) As ParameterBuilder
   Overrides Public Function Equals(ByVal obj As Object) As Boolean
   Overrides Public Function GetBaseDefinition() As MethodInfo
   Overrides Public Function GetCustomAttributes(ByVal inherit As Boolean) As Object()
   Overrides Public Function GetCustomAttributes(ByVal attributeType As Type, ByVal inherit As Boolean) _
      As Object()
   Overrides Public Function GetHashCode() As Integer
   Public Function GetILGenerator() As ILGenerator
   Public Function GetILGenerator(ByVal size As Integer) As ILGenerator
   Overrides Public Function GetMethodImplementationFlags() As MethodImplAttributes
   Public Function GetModule() As Module
   Overrides Public Function GetParameters() As ParameterInfo()
   Public Function GetToken() As MethodToken
   Overrides Public Function Invoke(ByVal obj As Object, ByVal invokeAttr As System.Reflection.BindingFlags, _
      ByVal binder As System.Reflection.Binder, ByVal parameters As Object(), _
      ByVal culture As System.Globalization.CultureInfo) As Object
   Overrides Public Function IsDefined(ByVal attributeType As Type, ByVal inherit As Boolean) As Boolean
   Public Sub SetCustomAttribute(ByVal con As System.Reflection.ConstructorInfo, ByVal binaryAttribute As Byte())
   Public Sub SetCustomAttribute(ByVal customBuilder As CustomAttributeBuilder)
   Public Sub SetImplementationFlags(ByVal attributes As System.Reflection.MethodImplAttributes)
   Public Sub SetMarshal(ByVal unmanagedMarshal As UnmanagedMarshal)
   Public Sub SetSymCustomAttribute(ByVal name As String, ByVal data As Byte())
   Overrides Public Function ToString() As String
End Class
```

Hierarchy: System.Object→
System.Reflection.MemberInfo(System.Reflection.ICustomAttributeProvider)→
System.Reflection.MethodBase→ System.Reflection.MethodInfo→ MethodBuilder

Returned By: ModuleBuilder.{DefineGlobalMethod(), DefinePInvokeMethod()},
TypeBuilder.{DefineMethod(), DefinePInvokeMethod()}

Passed To: EventBuilder.{AddOtherMethod(), SetAddOnMethod(), SetRaiseMethod(),
SetRemoveOnMethod()}, PropertyBuilder.{AddOtherMethod(), SetGetMethod(), SetSetMethod()}

MethodRental

NotInheritable Class

System.Reflection.Emit (mscorlib.dll)

This class can be used to swap a method "body" (the MSIL code inside the method). To do this, use the shared SwapMethodBody() method and specify the target Type, the token of the method that should receive the new body, a pointer to the new method, the size of the new method, and a flag specifying the type of compilation using the appropriate field constant (either JitImmediate or JitOnDemand). The IntPtr to the new method body should point to an array of bytes that contain the IL for the method's header and body.

```
Public NotInheritable Class MethodRental
' Public Shared Fields
   Public const JitImmediate As Integer                                    =1
   Public const JitOnDemand As Integer                                     =0
' Public Shared Methods
   Public Shared Sub SwapMethodBody(ByVal cls As Type, ByVal methodtoken As Integer, ByVal rgIL As IntPtr, _
      ByVal methodSize As Integer, ByVal flags As Integer)
End Class
```

MethodToken

Structure

System.Reflection.Emit (mscorlib.dll)

serializable

This class represents the token for a method. See EventToken for more details on tokens.

```
Public Structure MethodToken
' Public Shared Fields
   Public Shared ReadOnly Empty As MethodToken                  =System.Reflection.Emit.MethodToken
' Public Instance Properties
   Public ReadOnly Property Token As Integer
' Public Instance Methods
   Overrides Public Function Equals(ByVal obj As Object) As Boolean
   Overrides Public Function GetHashCode() As Integer
End Structure
```

Hierarchy: System.Object→ System.ValueType→ MethodToken

Returned By: ConstructorBuilder.GetToken(), MethodBuilder.GetToken(), ModuleBuilder.{GetArrayMethodToken(), GetConstructorToken(), GetMethodToken()}

ModuleBuilder

Class

System.Reflection.Emit (mscorlib.dll)

This class represents a dynamically created module inside a dynamic assembly. Dynamic modules are created with the AssemblyBuilder.DefineDynamicModule() method. A dynamic module can be either transient or persistable, which means you can save it to disk as part of a PE file. To create a persistable module, use a version of the Assembly-Builder.DefineDynamicModule() method that allows you to specify a filename.

You can use the methods that begin with Define to create types, managed and unmanaged resources, global methods, and PInvoke (global native) methods.

```
Public Class ModuleBuilder : Inherits System.Reflection.Module
' Public Instance Properties
   Overrides Public ReadOnly Property FullyQualifiedName As String
' Public Instance Methods
   Public Sub CreateGlobalFunctions()
   Public Function DefineDocument(ByVal url As String, ByVal language As Guid, ByVal languageVendor As Guid, _
      ByVal documentType As Guid)  As ISymbolDocumentWriter
```

Public Function **DefineEnum**(ByVal name As String, ByVal visibility As System.Reflection.TypeAttributes, _
ByVal underlyingType As Type) As EnumBuilder

Public Function **DefineGlobalMethod**(ByVal name As String, _
ByVal attributes As System.Reflection.MethodAttributes, _
ByVal callingConvention As System.Reflection.CallingConventions, ByVal returnType As Type, _
ByVal parameterTypes As Type()) As MethodBuilder

Public Function **DefineGlobalMethod**(ByVal name As String, _
ByVal attributes As System.Reflection.MethodAttributes, ByVal returnType As Type, ByVal parameterTypes As Type()) _
As MethodBuilder

Public Function **DefineInitializedData**(ByVal name As String, ByVal data As Byte(), _
ByVal attributes As System.Reflection.FieldAttributes) As FieldBuilder

Public Function **DefinePInvokeMethod**(ByVal name As String, ByVal dllName As String, _
ByVal attributes As System.Reflection.MethodAttributes, _
ByVal callingConvention As System.Reflection.CallingConventions, ByVal returnType As Type, _
ByVal parameterTypes As Type(), ByVal nativeCallConv As System.Runtime.InteropServices.CallingConvention, _
ByVal nativeCharSet As System.Runtime.InteropServices.CharSet) As MethodBuilder

Public Function **DefinePInvokeMethod**(ByVal name As String, ByVal dllName As String, _
ByVal entryName As String, ByVal attributes As System.Reflection.MethodAttributes, _
ByVal callingConvention As System.Reflection.CallingConventions, ByVal returnType As Type, _
ByVal parameterTypes As Type(), ByVal nativeCallConv As System.Runtime.InteropServices.CallingConvention, _
ByVal nativeCharSet As System.Runtime.InteropServices.CharSet) As MethodBuilder

Public Function **DefineResource**(ByVal name As String, ByVal description As String) As IResourceWriter

Public Function **DefineResource**(ByVal name As String, ByVal description As String, _
ByVal attribute As System.Reflection.ResourceAttributes) As IResourceWriter

Public Function **DefineType**(ByVal name As String) As TypeBuilder

Public Function **DefineType**(ByVal name As String, ByVal attr As System.Reflection.TypeAttributes) As TypeBuilder

Public Function **DefineType**(ByVal name As String, ByVal attr As System.Reflection.TypeAttributes, _
ByVal parent As Type) As TypeBuilder

Public Function **DefineType**(ByVal name As String, ByVal attr As System.Reflection.TypeAttributes, _
ByVal parent As Type, ByVal typesize As Integer) As TypeBuilder

Public Function **DefineType**(ByVal name As String, ByVal attr As System.Reflection.TypeAttributes, _
ByVal parent As Type, ByVal packsize As PackingSize) As TypeBuilder

Public Function **DefineType**(ByVal name As String, ByVal attr As System.Reflection.TypeAttributes, _
ByVal parent As Type, ByVal packingSize As PackingSize, ByVal typesize As Integer) As TypeBuilder

Public Function **DefineType**(ByVal name As String, ByVal attr As System.Reflection.TypeAttributes, _
ByVal parent As Type, ByVal interfaces As Type()) As TypeBuilder

Public Function **DefineUninitializedData**(ByVal name As String, ByVal size As Integer, _
ByVal attributes As System.Reflection.FieldAttributes) As FieldBuilder

Public Sub **DefineUnmanagedResource**(ByVal resource As Byte())

Public Sub **DefineUnmanagedResource**(ByVal resourceFileName As String)

Public Function **GetArrayMethod**(ByVal arrayClass As Type, ByVal methodName As String, _
ByVal callingConvention As System.Reflection.CallingConventions, ByVal returnType As Type, _
ByVal parameterTypes As Type()) As MethodInfo

Public Function **GetArrayMethodToken**(ByVal arrayClass As Type, ByVal methodName As String, _
ByVal callingConvention As System.Reflection.CallingConventions, ByVal returnType As Type, _
ByVal parameterTypes As Type()) As MethodToken

Public Function **GetConstructorToken**(ByVal con As System.Reflection.ConstructorInfo) As MethodToken

Public Function **GetFieldToken**(ByVal field As System.Reflection.FieldInfo) As FieldToken

Public Function **GetMethodToken**(ByVal method As System.Reflection.MethodInfo) As MethodToken

Public Function **GetSignatureToken**(ByVal sigBytes As Byte(), ByVal sigLength As Integer) As SignatureToken

Public Function **GetSignatureToken**(ByVal sigHelper As SignatureHelper) As SignatureToken

Public Function **GetStringConstant**(ByVal str As String) As StringToken

Public Function **GetSymWriter**() As ISymbolWriter

Overrides Public Function **GetType**(ByVal className As String) As Type

Overrides Public Function **GetType**(ByVal className As String, ByVal ignoreCase As Boolean) As Type

Overrides Public Function **GetType**(ByVal className As String, ByVal throwOnError As Boolean, _
  ByVal ignoreCase As Boolean) As Type
Overrides Public Function **GetTypes**() As Type()
Public Function **GetTypeToken**(ByVal name As String) As TypeToken
Public Function **GetTypeToken**(ByVal type As Type) As TypeToken
Public Function **IsTransient**() As Boolean
Public Sub **SetCustomAttribute**(ByVal con As System.Reflection.ConstructorInfo, ByVal binaryAttribute As Byte())
Public Sub **SetCustomAttribute**(ByVal customBuilder As CustomAttributeBuilder)
Public Sub **SetSymCustomAttribute**(ByVal name As String, ByVal data As Byte())
Public Sub **SetUserEntryPoint**(ByVal entryPoint As System.Reflection.MethodInfo)
End Class

Hierarchy: System.Object→ System.Reflection.Module(System.Runtime.Serialization.ISerializable,
System.Reflection.ICustomAttributeProvider)→ ModuleBuilder

Returned By: AssemblyBuilder.{DefineDynamicModule(), GetDynamicModule()}

OpCode
Structure

System.Reflection.Emit (mscorlib.dll)

This structure describes a single MSIL instruction. It is used by the ILGenerator.Emit()
method. Alternatively, use a field from the OpCodes class to supply a specific instruction
without needing to create an OpCode object. Instructions are characterized by several
pieces of information, represented as properties, such as OpCode, Operand, and flow control.

Public Structure **OpCode**
' *Public Instance Properties*
  Public ReadOnly Property **FlowControl** As FlowControl
  Public ReadOnly Property **Name** As String
  Public ReadOnly Property **OpCodeType** As OpCodeType
  Public ReadOnly Property **OperandType** As OperandType
  Public ReadOnly Property **Size** As Integer
  Public ReadOnly Property **StackBehaviourPop** As StackBehaviour
  Public ReadOnly Property **StackBehaviourPush** As StackBehaviour
  Public ReadOnly Property **Value** As Short
' *Public Instance Methods*
  Overrides Public Function **Equals**(ByVal obj As Object) As Boolean
  Overrides Public Function **GetHashCode**() As Integer
  Overrides Public Function **ToString**() As String
End Structure

Hierarchy: System.Object→ System.ValueType→ OpCode

Passed To: ILGenerator.{Emit(), EmitCall(), EmitCalli()}, OpCodes.TakesSingleByteArgument()

OpCodes
Class

System.Reflection.Emit (mscorlib.dll)

This class provides the set of MSIL instructions through shared fields. Each field returns
the OpCode object that represents the corresponding instruction, and can be used in the
ILGenerator.Emit() method. For a detailed description of these opcodes, see *Partition III,
CIL* of the ECMA CLI specification (*http://msdn.microsoft.com/net/ecma*).

Public Class **OpCodes**
' *Public Shared Fields*
  Public Shared ReadOnly **Add** As OpCode   *=add*
  Public Shared ReadOnly **Add_Ovf** As OpCode   *=add.ovf*

Public Shared ReadOnly **Add_Ovf_Un** As OpCode	*=add.ovf.un*
Public Shared ReadOnly **And** As OpCode	*=and*
Public Shared ReadOnly **Arglist** As OpCode	*=arglist*
Public Shared ReadOnly **Beq** As OpCode	*=beq*
Public Shared ReadOnly **Beq_S** As OpCode	*=beq.s*
Public Shared ReadOnly **Bge** As OpCode	*=bge*
Public Shared ReadOnly **Bge_S** As OpCode	*=bge.s*
Public Shared ReadOnly **Bge_Un** As OpCode	*=bge.un*
Public Shared ReadOnly **Bge_Un_S** As OpCode	*=bge.un.s*
Public Shared ReadOnly **Bgt** As OpCode	*=bgt*
Public Shared ReadOnly **Bgt_S** As OpCode	*=bgt.s*
Public Shared ReadOnly **Bgt_Un** As OpCode	*=bgt.un*
Public Shared ReadOnly **Bgt_Un_S** As OpCode	*=bgt.un.s*
Public Shared ReadOnly **Ble** As OpCode	*=ble*
Public Shared ReadOnly **Ble_S** As OpCode	*=ble.s*
Public Shared ReadOnly **Ble_Un** As OpCode	*=ble.un*
Public Shared ReadOnly **Ble_Un_S** As OpCode	*=ble.un.s*
Public Shared ReadOnly **Blt** As OpCode	*=blt*
Public Shared ReadOnly **Blt_S** As OpCode	*=blt.s*
Public Shared ReadOnly **Blt_Un** As OpCode	*=blt.un*
Public Shared ReadOnly **Blt_Un_S** As OpCode	*=blt.un.s*
Public Shared ReadOnly **Bne_Un** As OpCode	*=bne.un*
Public Shared ReadOnly **Bne_Un_S** As OpCode	*=bne.un.s*
Public Shared ReadOnly **Box** As OpCode	*=box*
Public Shared ReadOnly **Br** As OpCode	*=br*
Public Shared ReadOnly **Br_S** As OpCode	*=br.s*
Public Shared ReadOnly **Break** As OpCode	*=break*
Public Shared ReadOnly **Brfalse** As OpCode	*=brfalse*
Public Shared ReadOnly **Brfalse_S** As OpCode	*=brfalse.s*
Public Shared ReadOnly **Brtrue** As OpCode	*=brtrue*
Public Shared ReadOnly **Brtrue_S** As OpCode	*=brtrue.s*
Public Shared ReadOnly **Call** As OpCode	*=call*
Public Shared ReadOnly **Calli** As OpCode	*=calli*
Public Shared ReadOnly **Callvirt** As OpCode	*=callvirt*
Public Shared ReadOnly **Castclass** As OpCode	*=castclass*
Public Shared ReadOnly **Ceq** As OpCode	*=ceq*
Public Shared ReadOnly **Cgt** As OpCode	*=cgt*
Public Shared ReadOnly **Cgt_Un** As OpCode	*=cgt.un*
Public Shared ReadOnly **Ckfinite** As OpCode	*=ckfinite*
Public Shared ReadOnly **Clt** As OpCode	*=clt*
Public Shared ReadOnly **Clt_Un** As OpCode	*=clt.un*
Public Shared ReadOnly **Conv_I** As OpCode	*=conv.i*
Public Shared ReadOnly **Conv_I1** As OpCode	*=conv.i1*
Public Shared ReadOnly **Conv_I2** As OpCode	*=conv.i2*
Public Shared ReadOnly **Conv_I4** As OpCode	*=conv.i4*
Public Shared ReadOnly **Conv_I8** As OpCode ·	*=conv.i8*
Public Shared ReadOnly **Conv_Ovf_I** As OpCode	*=conv.ovf.i*
Public Shared ReadOnly **Conv_Ovf_I_Un** As OpCode	*=conv.ovf.i.un*
Public Shared ReadOnly **Conv_Ovf_I1** As OpCode	*=conv.ovf.i1*
Public Shared ReadOnly **Conv_Ovf_I1_Un** As OpCode	*=conv.ovf.i1.un*
Public Shared ReadOnly **Conv_Ovf_I2** As OpCode	*=conv.ovf.i2*
Public Shared ReadOnly **Conv_Ovf_I2_Un** As OpCode	*=conv.ovf.i2.un*
Public Shared ReadOnly **Conv_Ovf_I4** As OpCode	*=conv.ovf.i4*
Public Shared ReadOnly **Conv_Ovf_I4_Un** As OpCode	*=conv.ovf.i4.un*
Public Shared ReadOnly **Conv_Ovf_I8** As OpCode	*=conv.ovf.i8*

**System.
Reflection**

Public Shared ReadOnly **Conv_Ovf_I8_Un** As OpCode	=conv.ovf.i8.un
Public Shared ReadOnly **Conv_Ovf_U** As OpCode	=conv.ovf.u
Public Shared ReadOnly **Conv_Ovf_U_Un** As OpCode	=conv.ovf.u.un
Public Shared ReadOnly **Conv_Ovf_U1** As OpCode	=conv.ovf.u1
Public Shared ReadOnly **Conv_Ovf_U1_Un** As OpCode	=conv.ovf.u1.un
Public Shared ReadOnly **Conv_Ovf_U2** As OpCode	=conv.ovf.u2
Public Shared ReadOnly **Conv_Ovf_U2_Un** As OpCode	=conv.ovf.u2.un
Public Shared ReadOnly **Conv_Ovf_U4** As OpCode	=conv.ovf.u4
Public Shared ReadOnly **Conv_Ovf_U4_Un** As OpCode	=conv.ovf.u4.un
Public Shared ReadOnly **Conv_Ovf_U8** As OpCode	=conv.ovf.u8
Public Shared ReadOnly **Conv_Ovf_U8_Un** As OpCode	=conv.ovf.u8.un
Public Shared ReadOnly **Conv_R_Un** As OpCode	=conv.r.un
Public Shared ReadOnly **Conv_R4** As OpCode	=conv.r4
Public Shared ReadOnly **Conv_R8** As OpCode	=conv.r8
Public Shared ReadOnly **Conv_U** As OpCode	=conv.u
Public Shared ReadOnly **Conv_U1** As OpCode	=conv.u1
Public Shared ReadOnly **Conv_U2** As OpCode	=conv.u2
Public Shared ReadOnly **Conv_U4** As OpCode	=conv.u4
Public Shared ReadOnly **Conv_U8** As OpCode	=conv.u8
Public Shared ReadOnly **Cpblk** As OpCode	=cpblk
Public Shared ReadOnly **Cpobj** As OpCode	=cpobj
Public Shared ReadOnly **Div** As OpCode	=div
Public Shared ReadOnly **Div_Un** As OpCode	=div.un
Public Shared ReadOnly **Dup** As OpCode	=dup
Public Shared ReadOnly **Endfilter** As OpCode	=endfilter
Public Shared ReadOnly **Endfinally** As OpCode	=endfinally
Public Shared ReadOnly **Initblk** As OpCode	=initblk
Public Shared ReadOnly **Initobj** As OpCode	=initobj
Public Shared ReadOnly **Isinst** As OpCode	=isinst
Public Shared ReadOnly **Jmp** As OpCode	=jmp
Public Shared ReadOnly **Ldarg** As OpCode	=ldarg
Public Shared ReadOnly **Ldarg_0** As OpCode	=ldarg.0
Public Shared ReadOnly **Ldarg_1** As OpCode	=ldarg.1
Public Shared ReadOnly **Ldarg_2** As OpCode	=ldarg.2
Public Shared ReadOnly **Ldarg_3** As OpCode	=ldarg.3
Public Shared ReadOnly **Ldarg_S** As OpCode	=ldarg.s
Public Shared ReadOnly **Ldarga** As OpCode	=ldarga
Public Shared ReadOnly **Ldarga_S** As OpCode	=ldarga.s
Public Shared ReadOnly **Ldc_I4** As OpCode	=ldc.i4
Public Shared ReadOnly **Ldc_I4_0** As OpCode	=ldc.i4.0
Public Shared ReadOnly **Ldc_I4_1** As OpCode	=ldc.i4.1
Public Shared ReadOnly **Ldc_I4_2** As OpCode	=ldc.i4.2
Public Shared ReadOnly **Ldc_I4_3** As OpCode	=ldc.i4.3
Public Shared ReadOnly **Ldc_I4_4** As OpCode	=ldc.i4.4
Public Shared ReadOnly **Ldc_I4_5** As OpCode	=ldc.i4.5
Public Shared ReadOnly **Ldc_I4_6** As OpCode	=ldc.i4.6
Public Shared ReadOnly **Ldc_I4_7** As OpCode	=ldc.i4.7
Public Shared ReadOnly **Ldc_I4_8** As OpCode	=ldc.i4.8
Public Shared ReadOnly **Ldc_I4_M1** As OpCode	=ldc.i4.m1
Public Shared ReadOnly **Ldc_I4_S** As OpCode	=ldc.i4.s
Public Shared ReadOnly **Ldc_I8** As OpCode	=ldc.i8
Public Shared ReadOnly **Ldc_R4** As OpCode	=ldc.r4
Public Shared ReadOnly **Ldc_R8** As OpCode	=ldc.r8
Public Shared ReadOnly **Ldelem_I** As OpCode	=ldelem.i
Public Shared ReadOnly **Ldelem_I1** As OpCode	=ldelem.i1

Public Shared ReadOnly **Ldelem_I2** As OpCode	=*ldelem.i2*
Public Shared ReadOnly **Ldelem_I4** As OpCode	=*ldelem.i4*
Public Shared ReadOnly **Ldelem_I8** As OpCode	=*ldelem.i8*
Public Shared ReadOnly **Ldelem_R4** As OpCode	=*ldelem.r4*
Public Shared ReadOnly **Ldelem_R8** As OpCode	=*ldelem.r8*
Public Shared ReadOnly **Ldelem_Ref** As OpCode	=*ldelem.ref*
Public Shared ReadOnly **Ldelem_U1** As OpCode	=*ldelem.u1*
Public Shared ReadOnly **Ldelem_U2** As OpCode	=*ldelem.u2*
Public Shared ReadOnly **Ldelem_U4** As OpCode	=*ldelem.u4*
Public Shared ReadOnly **Ldelema** As OpCode	=*ldelema*
Public Shared ReadOnly **Ldfld** As OpCode	=*ldfld*
Public Shared ReadOnly **Ldflda** As OpCode	=*ldflda*
Public Shared ReadOnly **Ldftn** As OpCode	=*ldftn*
Public Shared ReadOnly **Ldind_I** As OpCode	=*ldind.i*
Public Shared ReadOnly **Ldind_I1** As OpCode	=*ldind.i1*
Public Shared ReadOnly **Ldind_I2** As OpCode	=*ldind.i2*
Public Shared ReadOnly **Ldind_I4** As OpCode	=*ldind.i4*
Public Shared ReadOnly **Ldind_I8** As OpCode	=*ldind.i8*
Public Shared ReadOnly **Ldind_R4** As OpCode	=*ldind.r4*
Public Shared ReadOnly **Ldind_R8** As OpCode	=*ldind.r8*
Public Shared ReadOnly **Ldind_Ref** As OpCode	=*ldind.ref*
Public Shared ReadOnly **Ldind_U1** As OpCode	=*ldind.u1*
Public Shared ReadOnly **Ldind_U2** As OpCode	=*ldind.u2*
Public Shared ReadOnly **Ldind_U4** As OpCode	=*ldind.u4*
Public Shared ReadOnly **Ldlen** As OpCode	=*ldlen*
Public Shared ReadOnly **Ldloc** As OpCode	=*ldloc*
Public Shared ReadOnly **Ldloc_0** As OpCode	=*ldloc.0*
Public Shared ReadOnly **Ldloc_1** As OpCode	=*ldloc.1*
Public Shared ReadOnly **Ldloc_2** As OpCode	=*ldloc.2*
Public Shared ReadOnly **Ldloc_3** As OpCode	=*ldloc.3*
Public Shared ReadOnly **Ldloc_S** As OpCode	=*ldloc.s*
Public Shared ReadOnly **Ldloca** As OpCode	=*ldloca*
Public Shared ReadOnly **Ldloca_S** As OpCode	=*ldloca.s*
Public Shared ReadOnly **Ldnull** As OpCode	=*ldnull*
Public Shared ReadOnly **Ldobj** As OpCode	=*ldobj*
Public Shared ReadOnly **Ldsfld** As OpCode	=*ldsfld*
Public Shared ReadOnly **Ldsflda** As OpCode	=*ldsflda*
Public Shared ReadOnly **Ldstr** As OpCode	=*ldstr*
Public Shared ReadOnly **Ldtoken** As OpCode	=*ldtoken*
Public Shared ReadOnly **Ldvirtftn** As OpCode	=*ldvirtftn*
Public Shared ReadOnly **Leave** As OpCode	=*leave*
Public Shared ReadOnly **Leave_S** As OpCode	=*leave.s*
Public Shared ReadOnly **Localloc** As OpCode	=*localloc*
Public Shared ReadOnly **Mkrefany** As OpCode	=*mkrefany*
Public Shared ReadOnly **Mul** As OpCode	=*mul*
Public Shared ReadOnly **Mul_Ovf** As OpCode	=*mul.ovf*
Public Shared ReadOnly **Mul_Ovf_Un** As OpCode	=*mul.ovf.un*
Public Shared ReadOnly **Neg** As OpCode	=*neg*
Public Shared ReadOnly **Newarr** As OpCode	=*newarr*
Public Shared ReadOnly **Newobj** As OpCode	=*newobj*
Public Shared ReadOnly **Nop** As OpCode	=*nop*
Public Shared ReadOnly **Not** As OpCode	=*not*
Public Shared ReadOnly **Or** As OpCode	=*or*
Public Shared ReadOnly **Pop** As OpCode	=*pop*
Public Shared ReadOnly **Prefix1** As OpCode	=*prefix1*

System. Reflection

Public Shared ReadOnly **Prefix2** As OpCode	*=prefix2*
Public Shared ReadOnly **Prefix3** As OpCode	*=prefix3*
Public Shared ReadOnly **Prefix4** As OpCode	*=prefix4*
Public Shared ReadOnly **Prefix5** As OpCode	*=prefix5*
Public Shared ReadOnly **Prefix6** As OpCode	*=prefix6*
Public Shared ReadOnly **Prefix7** As OpCode	*=prefix7*
Public Shared ReadOnly **Prefixref** As OpCode	*=prefixref*
Public Shared ReadOnly **Refanytype** As OpCode	*=refanytype*
Public Shared ReadOnly **Refanyval** As OpCode	*=refanyval*
Public Shared ReadOnly **Rem** As OpCode	*=rem*
Public Shared ReadOnly **Rem_Un** As OpCode	*=rem.un*
Public Shared ReadOnly **Ret** As OpCode	*=ret*
Public Shared ReadOnly **Rethrow** As OpCode	*=rethrow*
Public Shared ReadOnly **Shl** As OpCode	*=shl*
Public Shared ReadOnly **Shr** As OpCode	*=shr*
Public Shared ReadOnly **Shr_Un** As OpCode	*=shr.un*
Public Shared ReadOnly **Sizeof** As OpCode	*=sizeof*
Public Shared ReadOnly **Starg** As OpCode	*=starg*
Public Shared ReadOnly **Starg_S** As OpCode	*=starg.s*
Public Shared ReadOnly **Stelem_I** As OpCode	*=stelem.i*
Public Shared ReadOnly **Stelem_I1** As OpCode	*=stelem.i1*
Public Shared ReadOnly **Stelem_I2** As OpCode	*=stelem.i2*
Public Shared ReadOnly **Stelem_I4** As OpCode	*=stelem.i4*
Public Shared ReadOnly **Stelem_I8** As OpCode	*=stelem.i8*
Public Shared ReadOnly **Stelem_R4** As OpCode	*=stelem.r4*
Public Shared ReadOnly **Stelem_R8** As OpCode	*=stelem.r8*
Public Shared ReadOnly **Stelem_Ref** As OpCode	*=stelem.ref*
Public Shared ReadOnly **Stfld** As OpCode	*=stfld*
Public Shared ReadOnly **Stind_I** As OpCode	*=stind.i*
Public Shared ReadOnly **Stind_I1** As OpCode	*=stind.i1*
Public Shared ReadOnly **Stind_I2** As OpCode	*=stind.i2*
Public Shared ReadOnly **Stind_I4** As OpCode	*=stind.i4*
Public Shared ReadOnly **Stind_I8** As OpCode	*=stind.i8*
Public Shared ReadOnly **Stind_R4** As OpCode	*=stind.r4*
Public Shared ReadOnly **Stind_R8** As OpCode	*=stind.r8*
Public Shared ReadOnly **Stind_Ref** As OpCode	*=stind.ref*
Public Shared ReadOnly **Stloc** As OpCode	*=stloc*
Public Shared ReadOnly **Stloc_0** As OpCode	*=stloc.0*
Public Shared ReadOnly **Stloc_1** As OpCode	*=stloc.1*
Public Shared ReadOnly **Stloc_2** As OpCode	*=stloc.2*
Public Shared ReadOnly **Stloc_3** As OpCode	*=stloc.3*
Public Shared ReadOnly **Stloc_S** As OpCode	*=stloc.s*
Public Shared ReadOnly **Stobj** As OpCode	*=stobj*
Public Shared ReadOnly **Stsfld** As OpCode	*=stsfld*
Public Shared ReadOnly **Sub** As OpCode	*=sub*
Public Shared ReadOnly **Sub_Ovf** As OpCode	*=sub.ovf*
Public Shared ReadOnly **Sub_Ovf_Un** As OpCode	*=sub.ovf.un*
Public Shared ReadOnly **Switch** As OpCode	*=switch*
Public Shared ReadOnly **Tailcall** As OpCode	*=tail.*
Public Shared ReadOnly **Throw** As OpCode	*=throw*
Public Shared ReadOnly **Unaligned** As OpCode	*=unaligned.*
Public Shared ReadOnly **Unbox** As OpCode	*=unbox*
Public Shared ReadOnly **Volatile** As OpCode	*=volatile.*
Public Shared ReadOnly **Xor** As OpCode	*=xor*

' Public Shared Methods

Public Shared Function **TakesSingleByteArgument**(ByVal *inst* As OpCode) As Boolean
End Class

OpCodeType   Enum

System.Reflection.Emit (mscorlib.dll)   *serializable*

This enumeration specifies the type of an MSIL OpCode, which is provided through the OpCode.OpCodeType property. These types include Annotation (an instruction that carries extra information for specific MSIL processors, but can usually be ignored), Macro (a synonym for another MSIL instruction), Nternal (a reserved instruction), Objmodel (an instruction that applies to objects), Prefix (an instruction that specifies an action that must be taken before the next instruction is executed), and Primitive (a built-in instruction).

```
Public Enum OpCodeType
    Annotation = 0
    Macro = 1
    Nternal = 2
    Objmodel = 3
    Prefix = 4
    Primitive = 5
End Enum
```

Hierarchy: System.Object→ System.ValueType→ System.Enum(System.IComparable, System.IFormattable, System.IConvertible)→ OpCodeType

Returned By: OpCode.OpCodeType

OperandType   Enum

System.Reflection.Emit (mscorlib.dll)   *serializable*

This enumeration specifies the operand type of an MSIL OpCode, which is provided through the OpCode.OperandType property. Operands include tokens (InlineField, InlineMethod, InlineType, and InlineTok) and integers (InlineI8, InlineI8, ShortInlineI, and ShortInlineR).

```
Public Enum OperandType
    InlineBrTarget = 0
    InlineField = 1
    InlineI = 2
    InlineI8 = 3
    InlineMethod = 4
    InlineNone = 5
    InlinePhi = 6
    InlineR = 7
    InlineSig = 9
    InlineString = 10
    InlineSwitch = 11
    InlineTok = 12
    InlineType = 13
    InlineVar = 14
    ShortInlineBrTarget = 15
    ShortInlineI = 16
    ShortInlineR = 17
    ShortInlineVar = 18
End Enum
```

System.Reflection

Hierarchy: System.Object→ System.ValueType→ System.Enum(System.IComparable, System.IFormattable, System.IConvertible)→ OperandType

Returned By: OpCode.OperandType

PackingSize
Enum

System.Reflection.Emit (mscorlib.dll)
serializable

This enumeration defines the packing size for a type and is set in the Module-Builder.DefineType() and TypeBuilder.DefineNestedType() methods. The digit at the end of each value name in this enumeration specifies a number of bytes.

```
Public Enum PackingSize
    Unspecified = 0
    Size1 = 1
    Size2 = 2
    Size4 = 4
    Size8 = 8
    Size16 = 16
End Enum
```

Hierarchy: System.Object→ System.ValueType→ System.Enum(System.IComparable, System.IFormattable, System.IConvertible)→ PackingSize

Returned By: TypeBuilder.PackingSize

Passed To: ModuleBuilder.DefineType(), TypeBuilder.DefineNestedType()

ParameterBuilder
Class

System.Reflection.Emit (mscorlib.dll)

This class represents a dynamically created parameter, which is created through the MethodBuilder.DefineParameter() or ConstructorBuilder.DefineParameter() method. When creating a ParameterBuilder with these methods, specify the name of the parameter and its position in the list of arguments. This list is 1-based, so the first parameter is given an index of 1. Use the SetMarshal() method to specify how the parameter is marshaled from unmanaged code. The SetConstant() method specifies the default value for a parameter.

```
Public Class ParameterBuilder
' Public Instance Properties
    Overridable Public ReadOnly Property Attributes As Integer
    Public ReadOnly Property IsIn As Boolean
    Public ReadOnly Property IsOptional As Boolean
    Public ReadOnly Property IsOut As Boolean
    Overridable Public ReadOnly Property Name As String
    Overridable Public ReadOnly Property Position As Integer
' Public Instance Methods
    Overridable Public Function GetToken() As ParameterToken
    Overridable Public Sub SetConstant(ByVal defaultValue As Object)
    Public Sub SetCustomAttribute(ByVal con As System.Reflection.ConstructorInfo, ByVal binaryAttribute As Byte())
    Public Sub SetCustomAttribute(ByVal customBuilder As CustomAttributeBuilder)
    Overridable Public Sub SetMarshal(ByVal unmanagedMarshal As UnmanagedMarshal)
End Class
```

Returned By: ConstructorBuilder.DefineParameter(), MethodBuilder.DefineParameter()

ParameterToken

Structure

System.Reflection.Emit (mscorlib.dll)

serializable

This class represents the token for a parameter. See EventToken for more details on tokens.

```
Public Structure ParameterToken
' Public Shared Fields
   Public Shared ReadOnly Empty As ParameterToken              =System.Reflection.Emit.ParameterToken
' Public Instance Properties
   Public ReadOnly Property Token As Integer
' Public Instance Methods
   Overrides Public Function Equals(ByVal obj As Object) As Boolean
   Overrides Public Function GetHashCode() As Integer
End Structure
```

Hierarchy: System.Object→ System.ValueType→ ParameterToken

Returned By: ParameterBuilder.GetToken()

PEFileKinds

Enum

System.Reflection.Emit (mscorlib.dll)

serializable

This enumeration is used by the AssemblyBuilder.SetEntryPoint() method. It specifies the type of PE file that will be created by the AssemblyBuilder.

```
Public Enum PEFileKinds
   Dll = 1
   ConsoleApplication = 2
   WindowApplication = 3
End Enum
```

Hierarchy: System.Object→ System.ValueType→ System.Enum(System.IComparable, System.IFormattable, System.IConvertible)→ PEFileKinds

Passed To: AssemblyBuilder.SetEntryPoint()

PropertyBuilder

NotInheritable Class

System.Reflection.Emit (mscorlib.dll)

This class represents a dynamically created property. To create a PropertyBuilder object, use the TypeBuilder.DefineProperty() method and specify the parameter types, return value type, and any additional special settings through the System.Reflection.PropertyAttributes enumeration. You can specify MethodBuilder objects for the property get and property set methods using SetGetMethod() and SetSetMethod(). You can also set the property's default value using the SetConstant() method.

```
Public NotInheritable Class PropertyBuilder : Inherits System.Reflection.PropertyInfo
' Public Instance Properties
   Overrides Public ReadOnly Property Attributes As PropertyAttributes
   Overrides Public ReadOnly Property CanRead As Boolean
   Overrides Public ReadOnly Property CanWrite As Boolean
   Overrides Public ReadOnly Property DeclaringType As Type
   Overrides Public ReadOnly Property Name As String
   Public ReadOnly Property PropertyToken As PropertyToken
   Overrides Public ReadOnly Property PropertyType As Type
   Overrides Public ReadOnly Property ReflectedType As Type
' Public Instance Methods
```

```
Public Sub AddOtherMethod(ByVal mdBuilder As MethodBuilder)
Overrides Public Function GetAccessors(ByVal nonPublic As Boolean) As MethodInfo()
Overrides Public Function GetCustomAttributes(ByVal inherit As Boolean) As Object()
Overrides Public Function GetCustomAttributes(ByVal attributeType As Type, ByVal inherit As Boolean) _
    As Object()
Overrides Public Function GetGetMethod(ByVal nonPublic As Boolean) As MethodInfo
Overrides Public Function GetIndexParameters() As ParameterInfo()
Overrides Public Function GetSetMethod(ByVal nonPublic As Boolean) As MethodInfo
Overrides Public Function GetValue(ByVal obj As Object, ByVal invokeAttr As System.Reflection.BindingFlags, _
    ByVal binder As System.Reflection.Binder, ByVal index As Object(), _
    ByVal culture As System.Globalization.CultureInfo) As Object
Overrides Public Function GetValue(ByVal obj As Object, ByVal index As Object()) As Object
Overrides Public Function IsDefined(ByVal attributeType As Type, ByVal inherit As Boolean) As Boolean
Public Sub SetConstant(ByVal defaultValue As Object)
Public Sub SetCustomAttribute(ByVal con As System.Reflection.ConstructorInfo, ByVal binaryAttribute As Byte())
Public Sub SetCustomAttribute(ByVal customBuilder As CustomAttributeBuilder)
Public Sub SetGetMethod(ByVal mdBuilder As MethodBuilder)
Public Sub SetSetMethod(ByVal mdBuilder As MethodBuilder)
Overrides Public Sub SetValue(ByVal obj As Object, ByVal value As Object, _
    ByVal invokeAttr As System.Reflection.BindingFlags, ByVal binder As System.Reflection.Binder, _
    ByVal index As Object(), ByVal culture As System.Globalization.CultureInfo)
Overrides Public Sub SetValue(ByVal obj As Object, ByVal value As Object, ByVal index As Object())
End Class
```

Hierarchy: System.Object→
System.Reflection.MemberInfo(System.Reflection.ICustomAttributeProvider)→
System.Reflection.PropertyInfo→ PropertyBuilder

Returned By: TypeBuilder.DefineProperty()

PropertyToken   Structure

System.Reflection.Emit (mscorlib.dll)   *serializable*

This class represents the token for a property. See EventToken for more details on tokens.

```
Public Structure PropertyToken
' Public Shared Fields
    Public Shared ReadOnly Empty As PropertyToken              =System.Reflection.Emit.PropertyToken
' Public Instance Properties
    Public ReadOnly Property Token As Integer
' Public Instance Methods
    Overrides Public Function Equals(ByVal obj As Object) As Boolean
    Overrides Public Function GetHashCode() As Integer
End Structure
```

Hierarchy: System.Object→ System.ValueType→ PropertyToken

Returned By: PropertyBuilder.PropertyToken

SignatureHelper   NotInheritable Class

System.Reflection.Emit (mscorlib.dll)

This class contains helper functions that allow you to build a signature for a method,
such as AddArgument(). Use one of the shared methods to get a SignatureHelper, which you
can pass to ILGenerator.Emit().

```
Public NotInheritable Class SignatureHelper
' Public Shared Methods
```

Public Shared Function **GetFieldSigHelper**(ByVal mod As System.Reflection.Module) As SignatureHelper
Public Shared Function **GetLocalVarSigHelper**(ByVal mod As System.Reflection.Module) As SignatureHelper
Public Shared Function **GetMethodSigHelper**(ByVal mod As System.Reflection.Module, _
  ByVal callingConvention As System.Reflection.CallingConventions, ByVal returnType As Type) As SignatureHelper
Public Shared Function **GetMethodSigHelper**(ByVal mod As System.Reflection.Module, _
  ByVal unmanagedCallConv As System.Runtime.InteropServices.CallingConvention, ByVal returnType As Type) _
  As SignatureHelper
Public Shared Function **GetMethodSigHelper**(ByVal mod As System.Reflection.Module, _
  ByVal returnType As Type, ByVal parameterTypes As Type()) As SignatureHelper
Public Shared Function **GetPropertySigHelper**(ByVal mod As System.Reflection.Module, _
  ByVal returnType As Type, ByVal parameterTypes As Type()) As SignatureHelper
' Public Instance Methods
Public Sub **AddArgument**(ByVal clsArgument As Type)
Public Sub **AddSentinel**()
Overrides Public Function **Equals**(ByVal obj As Object) As Boolean
Overrides Public Function **GetHashCode**() As Integer
Public Function **GetSignature**() As Byte()
Overrides Public Function **ToString**() As String
End Class

Passed To: ILGenerator.Emit(), ModuleBuilder.GetSignatureToken()

SignatureToken   Structure

System.Reflection.Emit (mscorlib.dll)   *serializable*

This class represents the token for a method signature. See EventToken for more details on tokens.

Public Structure **SignatureToken**
' Public Shared Fields
  Public Shared ReadOnly **Empty** As SignatureToken   =*System.Reflection.Emit.SignatureToken*
' Public Instance Properties
  Public ReadOnly Property **Token** As Integer
' Public Instance Methods
  Overrides Public Function **Equals**(ByVal obj As Object) As Boolean
  Overrides Public Function **GetHashCode**() As Integer
End Structure

Hierarchy: System.Object→ System.ValueType→ SignatureToken

Returned By: ModuleBuilder.GetSignatureToken()

StackBehaviour   Enum

System.Reflection.Emit (mscorlib.dll)   *serializable*

This enumeration is used to set the OpCode.StackBehaviourPush() and OpCode.StackBehaviour-Pop() methods, which determine how an MSIL instruction pushes an operand onto the stack and pops it off.

Public Enum **StackBehaviour**
    Pop0 = 0
    Pop1 = 1
    Pop1_pop1 = 2
    Popi = 3
    Popi_pop1 = 4
    Popi_popi = 5
    Popi_popi8 = 6

```
   Popi_popi_popi = 7
   Popi_popr4 = 8
   Popi_popr8 = 9
   Popref = 10
   Popref_pop1 = 11
   Popref_popi = 12
   Popref_popi_popi = 13
   Popref_popi_popi8 = 14
   Popref_popi_popr4 = 15
   Popref_popi_popr8 = 16
   Popref_popi_popref = 17
   Push0 = 18
   Push1 = 19
   Push1_push1 = 20
   Pushi = 21
   Pushi8 = 22
   Pushr4 = 23
   Pushr8 = 24
   Pushref = 25
   Varpop = 26
   Varpush = 27
End Enum
```

Hierarchy: System.Object→ System.ValueType→ System.Enum(System.IComparable, System.IFormattable, System.IConvertible)→ StackBehaviour

Returned By: OpCode.{StackBehaviourPop, StackBehaviourPush}

StringToken   Structure
System.Reflection.Emit (mscorlib.dll)   *serializable*

This class represents the token for a string constant in a module's constant pool. See EventToken for more details on tokens.

```
Public Structure StringToken
' Public Instance Properties
   Public ReadOnly Property Token As Integer
' Public Instance Methods
   Overrides Public Function Equals(ByVal obj As Object) As Boolean
   Overrides Public Function GetHashCode() As Integer
End Structure
```

Hierarchy: System.Object→ System.ValueType→ StringToken

Returned By: ModuleBuilder.GetStringConstant()

TypeBuilder   NotInheritable Class
System.Reflection.Emit (mscorlib.dll)

This class represents a dynamically created type in a dynamic module (ModuleBuilder object). Generally, a type is either a class or an interface. To create a TypeBuilder, use the overloaded ModuleBuilder.DefineType() method. Depending on which overload you use, you can specify different information including the type name, superclass, and implemented interfaces. You can also use the System.Reflection.TypeAttributes enumeration to specify other options, such as making a class sealed, MustInherit, or public, or defining it as an interface. Once the type is created, you can add members such as constructors, events, fields, properties, methods, and other nested types, using the corresponding Define method.

Before using a type you created, you must use the CreateType() method to get a Type object. After that, you can instantiate the Type with the System.Activator.CreateInstance() method, and invoke members of the type with the System.Type.InvokeMember() method. After creating a type, you can no longer use TypeBuilder methods that would change the type, such as a Define method.

Public NotInheritable Class **TypeBuilder** : Inherits Type
' Public Shared Fields
   Public const **UnspecifiedTypeSize** As Integer   =0
' Public Instance Properties
   Overrides Public ReadOnly Property **Assembly** As Assembly
   Overrides Public ReadOnly Property **AssemblyQualifiedName** As String
   Overrides Public ReadOnly Property **BaseType** As Type
   Overrides Public ReadOnly Property **DeclaringType** As Type
   Overrides Public ReadOnly Property **FullName** As String
   Overrides Public ReadOnly Property **GUID** As Guid
   Overrides Public ReadOnly Property **Module** As Module
   Overrides Public ReadOnly Property **Name** As String
   Overrides Public ReadOnly Property **Namespace** As String
   Public ReadOnly Property **PackingSize** As PackingSize
   Overrides Public ReadOnly Property **ReflectedType** As Type
   Public ReadOnly Property **Size** As Integer
   Overrides Public ReadOnly Property **TypeHandle** As RuntimeTypeHandle
   Public ReadOnly Property **TypeToken** As TypeToken
   Overrides Public ReadOnly Property **UnderlyingSystemType** As Type
' Public Instance Methods
   Public Sub **AddDeclarativeSecurity**(ByVal action As System.Security.Permissions.SecurityAction, _
      ByVal pset As System.Security.PermissionSet)
   Public Sub **AddInterfaceImplementation**(ByVal interfaceType As Type)
   Public Function **CreateType**() As Type
   Public Function **DefineConstructor**(ByVal attributes As System.Reflection.MethodAttributes, _
      ByVal callingConvention As System.Reflection.CallingConventions, ByVal parameterTypes As Type()) _
      As ConstructorBuilder
   Public Function **DefineDefaultConstructor**(ByVal attributes As System.Reflection.MethodAttributes) _
      As ConstructorBuilder
   Public Function **DefineEvent**(ByVal name As String, ByVal attributes As System.Reflection.EventAttributes, _
      ByVal eventtype As Type) As EventBuilder
   Public Function **DefineField**(ByVal fieldName As String, ByVal type As Type, _
      ByVal attributes As System.Reflection.FieldAttributes) As FieldBuilder
   Public Function **DefineInitializedData**(ByVal name As String, ByVal data As Byte(), _
      ByVal attributes As System.Reflection.FieldAttributes) As FieldBuilder
   Public Function **DefineMethod**(ByVal name As String, ByVal attributes As System.Reflection.MethodAttributes, _
      ByVal callingConvention As System.Reflection.CallingConventions, ByVal returnType As Type, _
      ByVal parameterTypes As Type()) As MethodBuilder
   Public Function **DefineMethod**(ByVal name As String, ByVal attributes As System.Reflection.MethodAttributes, _
      ByVal returnType As Type, ByVal parameterTypes As Type()) As MethodBuilder
   Public Sub **DefineMethodOverride**(ByVal methodInfoBody As System.Reflection.MethodInfo, _
      ByVal methodInfoDeclaration As System.Reflection.MethodInfo)
   Public Function **DefineNestedType**(ByVal name As String) As TypeBuilder
   Public Function **DefineNestedType**(ByVal name As String, ByVal attr As System.Reflection.TypeAttributes) _
      As TypeBuilder
   Public Function **DefineNestedType**(ByVal name As String, ByVal attr As System.Reflection.TypeAttributes, _
      ByVal parent As Type) As TypeBuilder
   Public Function **DefineNestedType**(ByVal name As String, ByVal attr As System.Reflection.TypeAttributes, _
      ByVal parent As Type, ByVal typeSize As Integer) As TypeBuilder
   Public Function **DefineNestedType**(ByVal name As String, ByVal attr As System.Reflection.TypeAttributes, _
      ByVal parent As Type, ByVal packSize As PackingSize) As TypeBuilder

**System.
Reflection**

Public Function **DefineNestedType**(ByVal name As String, ByVal attr As System.Reflection.TypeAttributes, _
    ByVal parent As Type, ByVal interfaces As Type()) As TypeBuilder
Public Function **DefinePInvokeMethod**(ByVal name As String, ByVal dllName As String, _
    ByVal attributes As System.Reflection.MethodAttributes, _
    ByVal callingConvention As System.Reflection.CallingConventions, ByVal returnType As Type, _
    ByVal parameterTypes As Type(), ByVal nativeCallConv As System.Runtime.InteropServices.CallingConvention, _
    ByVal nativeCharSet As System.Runtime.InteropServices.CharSet) As MethodBuilder
Public Function **DefinePInvokeMethod**(ByVal name As String, ByVal dllName As String, _
    ByVal entryName As String, ByVal attributes As System.Reflection.MethodAttributes, _
    ByVal callingConvention As System.Reflection.CallingConventions, ByVal returnType As Type, _
    ByVal parameterTypes As Type(), ByVal nativeCallConv As System.Runtime.InteropServices.CallingConvention, _
    ByVal nativeCharSet As System.Runtime.InteropServices.CharSet) As MethodBuilder
Public Function **DefineProperty**(ByVal name As String, ByVal attributes As System.Reflection.PropertyAttributes, _
    ByVal returnType As Type, ByVal parameterTypes As Type()) As PropertyBuilder
Public Function **DefineTypeInitializer**() As ConstructorBuilder
Public Function **DefineUninitializedData**(ByVal name As String, ByVal size As Integer, _
    ByVal attributes As System.Reflection.FieldAttributes) As FieldBuilder
Overrides Public Function **GetConstructors**(ByVal bindingAttr As System.Reflection.BindingFlags) _
    As ConstructorInfo()
Overrides Public Function **GetCustomAttributes**(ByVal inherit As Boolean) As Object()
Overrides Public Function **GetCustomAttributes**(ByVal attributeType As Type, ByVal inherit As Boolean) _
    As Object()
Overrides Public Function **GetElementType**() As Type
Overrides Public Function **GetEvent**(ByVal name As String, ByVal bindingAttr As System.Reflection.BindingFlags) _
    As EventInfo
Overrides Public Function **GetEvents**() As EventInfo()
Overrides Public Function **GetEvents**(ByVal bindingAttr As System.Reflection.BindingFlags) As EventInfo()
Overrides Public Function **GetField**(ByVal name As String, ByVal bindingAttr As System.Reflection.BindingFlags) _
    As FieldInfo
Overrides Public Function **GetFields**(ByVal bindingAttr As System.Reflection.BindingFlags) As FieldInfo()
Overrides Public Function **GetInterface**(ByVal name As String, ByVal ignoreCase As Boolean) As Type
Overrides Public Function **GetInterfaceMap**(ByVal interfaceType As Type) As InterfaceMapping
Overrides Public Function **GetInterfaces**() As Type()
Overrides Public Function **GetMember**(ByVal name As String, ByVal type As System.Reflection.MemberTypes, _
    ByVal bindingAttr As System.Reflection.BindingFlags) As MemberInfo()
Overrides Public Function **GetMembers**(ByVal bindingAttr As System.Reflection.BindingFlags) As MemberInfo()
Overrides Public Function **GetMethods**(ByVal bindingAttr As System.Reflection.BindingFlags) As MethodInfo()
Overrides Public Function **GetNestedType**(ByVal name As String, _
    ByVal bindingAttr As System.Reflection.BindingFlags) As Type
Overrides Public Function **GetNestedTypes**(ByVal bindingAttr As System.Reflection.BindingFlags) As Type()
Overrides Public Function **GetProperties**(ByVal bindingAttr As System.Reflection.BindingFlags) As PropertyInfo()
Overrides Public Function **InvokeMember**(ByVal name As String, _
    ByVal invokeAttr As System.Reflection.BindingFlags, ByVal binder As System.Reflection.Binder, _
    ByVal target As Object, ByVal args As Object(), ByVal modifiers As System.Reflection.ParameterModifier(), _
    ByVal culture As System.Globalization.CultureInfo, ByVal namedParameters As String()) As Object
Overrides Public Function **IsAssignableFrom**(ByVal c As Type) As Boolean
Overrides Public Function **IsDefined**(ByVal attributeType As Type, ByVal inherit As Boolean) As Boolean
Overrides Public Function **IsSubclassOf**(ByVal c As Type) As Boolean
Public Sub **SetCustomAttribute**(ByVal con As System.Reflection.ConstructorInfo, ByVal binaryAttribute As Byte())
Public Sub **SetCustomAttribute**(ByVal customBuilder As CustomAttributeBuilder)
Public Sub **SetParent**(ByVal parent As Type)
Overrides Public Function **ToString**() As String
' *Protected Instance Methods*
Overrides Protected Function **GetAttributeFlagsImpl**() As TypeAttributes
Overrides Protected Function **GetConstructorImpl**(ByVal bindingAttr As System.Reflection.BindingFlags, _
    ByVal binder As System.Reflection.Binder, ByVal callConvention As System.Reflection.CallingConventions, _

ByVal types As Type(), ByVal modifiers As System.Reflection.ParameterModifier()) As ConstructorInfo
Overrides Protected Function **GetMethodImpl**(ByVal name As String,   _
    ByVal bindingAttr As System.Reflection.BindingFlags, ByVal binder As System.Reflection.Binder, _
    ByVal callConvention As System.Reflection.CallingConventions, ByVal types As Type(),   _
    ByVal modifiers As System.Reflection.ParameterModifier()) As MethodInfo
Overrides Protected Function **GetPropertyImpl**(ByVal name As String,   _
    ByVal bindingAttr As System.Reflection.BindingFlags, ByVal binder As System.Reflection.Binder, _
    ByVal returnType As Type, ByVal types As Type(), ByVal modifiers As System.Reflection.ParameterModifier()) _
    As PropertyInfo
Overrides Protected Function **HasElementTypeImpl**() As Boolean
Overrides Protected Function **IsArrayImpl**() As Boolean
Overrides Protected Function **IsByRefImpl**() As Boolean
Overrides Protected Function **IsCOMObjectImpl**() As Boolean
Overrides Protected Function **IsPointerImpl**() As Boolean
Overrides Protected Function **IsPrimitiveImpl**() As Boolean
End Class

Hierarchy: System.Object→
System.Reflection.MemberInfo(System.Reflection.ICustomAttributeProvider) →
System.Type(System.Reflection.IReflect)→ TypeBuilder

Returned By: ModuleBuilder.DefineType()

TypeToken · Structure
System.Reflection.Emit (mscorlib.dll) *serializable*

This class represents the token for a type. See EventToken for more details on tokens.

Public Structure **TypeToken**
' *Public Shared Fields*
    Public Shared ReadOnly **Empty** As TypeToken   =*System.Reflection.Emit.TypeToken*
' *Public Instance Properties*
    Public ReadOnly Property **Token** As Integer
' *Public Instance Methods*
    Overrides Public Function **Equals**(ByVal obj As Object) As Boolean
    Overrides Public Function **GetHashCode**() As Integer
End Structure

Hierarchy: System.Object→ System.ValueType→ TypeToken

Returned By: EnumBuilder.TypeToken, ModuleBuilder.GetTypeToken(), TypeBuilder.TypeToken

UnmanagedMarshal NotInheritable Class
System.Reflection.Emit (mscorlib.dll) *serializable*

This class defines how parameters or fields should be marshaled in function calls to unmanaged code. By default, the CLR applies certain format conversions automatically during this marshaling (for example, it might change a System.String object to an unmanaged BSTR). Use this class to override this default behavior.

To create an instance of this class, use one of the shared methods to define the unmanaged type you want. Typically, you will use DefineUnmanagedMarshal() for this purpose and specify the unmanaged type using the System.Runtime.InteropServices.UnmanagedType enumeration. Alternatively, use DefineByValTStr() to specify marshaling to a string in a fixed array buffer, and specify the other methods for various types of unmanaged arrays. These shared methods all return an UnmanagedMarshal object, with its read-only properties set accordingly. Lastly, associate the UnmanagedMarshal with the appropriate type using the SetMarshal() method for the ParameterBuilder, MethodBuilder, or FieldBuilder class.

```
Public NotInheritable Class UnmanagedMarshal
' Public Instance Properties
   Public ReadOnly Property BaseType As UnmanagedType
   Public ReadOnly Property ElementCount As Integer
   Public ReadOnly Property GetUnmanagedType As UnmanagedType
   Public ReadOnly Property IIDGuid As Guid
' Public Shared Methods
   Public Shared Function DefineByValArray(ByVal elemCount As Integer) As UnmanagedMarshal
   Public Shared Function DefineByValTStr(ByVal elemCount As Integer) As UnmanagedMarshal
   Public Shared Function DefineLPArray(ByVal elemType As System.Runtime.InteropServices.UnmanagedType) _
      As UnmanagedMarshal
   Public Shared Function DefineSafeArray(ByVal elemType As System.Runtime.InteropServices.UnmanagedType) _
      As UnmanagedMarshal
   Public Shared Function DefineUnmanagedMarshal(                                                        _
      ByVal unmanagedType As System.Runtime.InteropServices.UnmanagedType) As UnmanagedMarshal
End Class
```

Passed To: FieldBuilder.SetMarshal(), MethodBuilder.SetMarshal(), ParameterBuilder.SetMarshal()

CHAPTER 15

System.Runtime.InteropServices

The types in this namespace work with unmanaged code using either PInvoke or COM. PInvoke (short for Platform Invoke) lets you access functions that reside in underlying operating system–specific shared libraries (on Win32, these are DLLs). COM (Component Object Model) is a Win32 legacy component architecture that is used throughout Windows and Windows applications. Many programmers experience COM through the object models of applications such as Microsoft Office, Exchange, and SQL Server. The COM support in .NET lets you access COM components as though they were native .NET classes.

We have omitted some of the more esoteric parts of this namespace, so there are some classes that aren't discussed here. For the most part, you will not need those classes unless you are developing specialized code that handles marshaling data types between managed and unmanaged code. If so, you should consult the MSDN .NET reference materials. Figure 15-1 and Figure 15-2 show the types in this namespace.

ArrayWithOffset   Structure
System.Runtime.InteropServices (mscorlib.dll)

This class converts an array of value type instances to an unmanaged array. Your unmanaged code accesses this array as a pointer that initially points to the first array element. Each time the pointer increments, it points to the next element in the array. The constructor takes a mandatory **offset** argument that specifies which element should be the first element in the unmanaged array. If you want to pass the whole array, specify an offset of zero.

```
Public Structure ArrayWithOffset
' Public Constructors
   Public Sub New(ByVal array As Object, ByVal offset As Integer)
' Public Instance Methods
   Overrides Public Function Equals(ByVal obj As Object) As Boolean
   Public Function GetArray() As Object
   Overrides Public Function GetHashCode() As Integer
   Public Function GetOffset() As Integer
End Structure
```

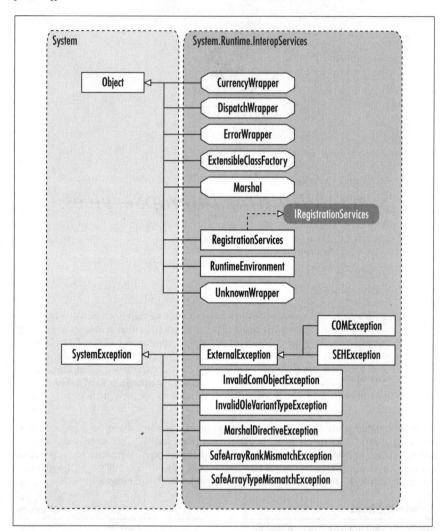

Figure 15–1. The System.Runtime.InteropServices namespace

Hierarchy: System.Object→ System.ValueType→ ArrayWithOffset

AssemblyRegistrationFlags   Enum

System.Runtime.InteropServices (mscorlib.dll)   *serializable, flag*

This enumeration specifies the flags you can use with IRegistrationServices.RegisterAssembly().

```
Public Enum AssemblyRegistrationFlags
      None = &H000000000
      SetCodeBase = &H000000001
End Enum
```

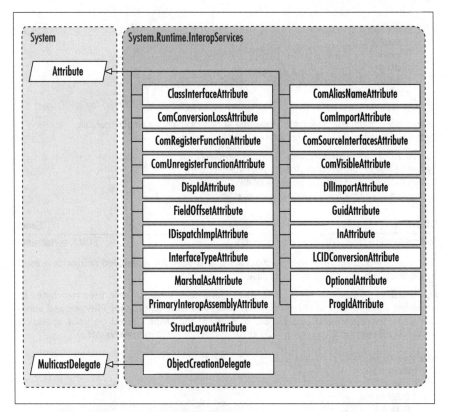

Figure 15-2. Attributes and delegates from System.Runtime.InteropServices

Hierarchy: System.Object→ System.ValueType→ System.Enum(System.IComparable, System.IFormattable, System.IConvertible)→ AssemblyRegistrationFlags

Passed To: IRegistrationServices.RegisterAssembly(), RegistrationServices.RegisterAssembly()

CallingConvention   Enum

System.Runtime.InteropServices (mscorlib.dll)   *ECMA, serializable*

This enumeration specifies the calling convention to use when you invoke a function. DllImportAttribute uses this in its CallingConvention parameter.

Cdecl specifies the standard calling convention used by C++ and C programs. This is required for functions that take a variable number of arguments, such as printf(). FastCall attempts to put function arguments into registers. StdCall is the convention used for calling Win32 API functions. ThisCall is the calling convention used by C++ member functions taking fixed arguments. Use the Winapi calling convention for function calls that use PASCAL or _ _far _ _pascal.

```
Public Enum CallingConvention
    Winapi = 1
    Cdecl = 2
    StdCall = 3
    ThisCall = 4
    FastCall = 5
End Enum
```

Hierarchy: System.Object→ System.ValueType→ System.Enum(System.IComparable, System.IFormattable, System.IConvertible)→ CallingConvention

Passed To: System.Reflection.Emit.ILGenerator.EmitCalli(), System.Reflection.Emit.ModuleBuilder.DefinePInvokeMethod(), System.Reflection.Emit.SignatureHelper.GetMethodSigHelper(), System.Reflection.Emit.TypeBuilder.DefinePInvokeMethod()

CharSet   Enum

System.Runtime.InteropServices (mscorlib.dll)   *ECMA, serializable*

This enumeration specifies the character set that is used for marshaled strings. It is used by DllImportAttribute and StructLayoutAttribute.

Ansi marshals strings using one byte ANSI characters, while Unicode uses two bytes to represent a single Unicode character. The Auto value is used only for PInvoke and specifies that PInvoke should decide how to marshal the strings based on your operating system (Unicode for Windows NT/2000/XP and ANSI for Windows 9x/ME).

```
Public Enum CharSet
    None = 1
    Ansi = 2
    Unicode = 3
    Auto = 4
End Enum
```

Hierarchy: System.Object→ System.ValueType→ System.Enum(System.IComparable, System.IFormattable, System.IConvertible)→ CharSet

Passed To: System.Reflection.Emit.ModuleBuilder.DefinePInvokeMethod(), System.Reflection.Emit.TypeBuilder.DefinePInvokeMethod()

ClassInterfaceAttribute   NotInheritable Class

System.Runtime.InteropServices (mscorlib.dll)

This attribute specifies the interface that should be exposed to COM when you generate a type library. See ClassInterfaceType for the possible arguments to this attribute.

```
Public NotInheritable Class ClassInterfaceAttribute : Inherits Attribute
' Public Constructors
    Public Sub New(ByVal classInterfaceType As ClassInterfaceType)
    Public Sub New(ByVal classInterfaceType As Short)
' Public Instance Properties
    Public ReadOnly Property Value As ClassInterfaceType
End Class
```

Hierarchy: System.Object→ System.Attribute→ ClassInterfaceAttribute

Valid On: Assembly, Class

ClassInterfaceType   Enum

System.Runtime.InteropServices (mscorlib.dll)   *serializable*

This enumeration contains values to use as arguments for ClassInterfaceAttribute. AutoDispatch specifies that a dispatch-only interface should be generated. AutoDual specifies that a dual interface should be generated, and None specifies that no interface should be generated.

```
Public Enum ClassInterfaceType
    None = 0
    AutoDispatch = 1
    AutoDual = 2
End Enum
```

Hierarchy: System.Object→ System.ValueType→ System.Enum(System.IComparable, System.IFormattable, System.IConvertible)→ ClassInterfaceType

Returned By: ClassInterfaceAttribute.Value

Passed To: ClassInterfaceAttribute.ClassInterfaceAttribute()

CoClassAttribute   NotInheritable Class

System.Runtime.InteropServices (mscorlib.dll)

This attribute describes the class ID of a coclass that was imported from a type library.

```
Public NotInheritable Class CoClassAttribute : Inherits  Attribute
' Public Constructors
    Public Sub New(ByVal coClass As Type)
' Public Instance Properties
    Public ReadOnly Property CoClass As Type
End Class
```

Hierarchy: System.Object→ System.Attribute→ CoClassAttribute

Valid On: Interface

ComAliasNameAttribute   NotInheritable Class

System.Runtime.InteropServices (mscorlib.dll)

This attribute is automatically added when COM type libraries are imported into the .NET runtime. COM uses alias names for various data types (such as typedef [public] int SHOE_SIZE). When you import a COM object that uses such an alias, .NET automatically decorates each parameter, property, field, and return value with this attribute. If you need to know the name of the COM alias, use the System.Reflection API to see if this custom attribute has been attached to the parameter, property, field, or return value you are interested in.

Since .NET automatically converts COM aliases to the underlying .NET types when it imports a type library, you do not need to use this attribute for typical applications (tool developers will find this attribute useful, though).

System. Runtime

```
Public NotInheritable Class ComAliasNameAttribute : Inherits Attribute
' Public Constructors
   Public Sub New(ByVal alias As String)
' Public Instance Properties
   Public ReadOnly Property Value As String
End Class
```

Hierarchy: System.Object→ System.Attribute→ ComAliasNameAttribute

Valid On: Property, Field, Parameter, ReturnValue

ComConversionLossAttribute   NotInheritable Class

System.Runtime.InteropServices (mscorlib.dll)

The presence of this attribute indicates that information about a type was lost as it was imported from a type library.

```
Public NotInheritable Class ComConversionLossAttribute : Inherits Attribute
' Public Constructors
   Public Sub New()
End Class
```

Hierarchy: System.Object→ System.Attribute→ ComConversionLossAttribute

Valid On: All

COMException   Class

System.Runtime.InteropServices (mscorlib.dll)   *serializable*

When a COM error occurs, .NET tries to map it to an exception in the .NET Framework and throws that exception. If the COM error does not map to any exception in the .NET Framework, this exception is thrown instead. It's the "couldn't find an exception" exception.

```
Public Class COMException : Inherits ExternalException
' Public Constructors
   Public Sub New()
   Public Sub New(ByVal message As String)
   Public Sub New(ByVal message As String, ByVal inner As Exception)
   Public Sub New(ByVal message As String, ByVal errorCode As Integer)
' Protected Constructors
   Protected Sub New(ByVal info As System.Runtime.Serialization.SerializationInfo, _
      ByVal context As System.Runtime.Serialization.StreamingContext)
' Public Instance Methods
   Overrides Public Function ToString() As String
End Class
```

Hierarchy: System.Object→ System.Exception(System.Runtime.Serialization.ISerializable)→ System.SystemException→ ExternalException→ COMException

ComImportAttribute   NotInheritable Class

System.Runtime.InteropServices (mscorlib.dll)

This attribute indicates that the type decorated by this attribute is in fact an unmanaged type defined in a previously published type library and should be treated differently internally to support that.

This attribute is necessary only if the .NET type definition—the class definition in VB.NET—is merely a "shim" for interacting with the unmanaged version. In most cases,

.NET programmers only use this type when interacting with existing COM APIs, such as when building Explorer Shell Extensions.

```
Public NotInheritable Class ComImportAttribute : Inherits Attribute
' Public Constructors
   Public Sub New()
End Class
```

Hierarchy: System.Object→ System.Attribute→ ComImportAttribute

Valid On: Class, Interface

ComInterfaceType   Enum

System.Runtime.InteropServices (mscorlib.dll)   *serializable*

This enumeration specifies the COM interface type. Use this attribute with InterfaceTypeAttribute to specify how your .NET interfaces are exposed to COM.

```
Public Enum ComInterfaceType
   InterfaceIsDual = 0
   InterfaceIsIUnknown = 1
   InterfaceIsIDispatch = 2
End Enum
```

Hierarchy: System.Object→ System.ValueType→ System.Enum(System.IComparable, System.IFormattable, System.IConvertible)→ ComInterfaceType

Returned By: InterfaceTypeAttribute.Value

Passed To: InterfaceTypeAttribute.InterfaceTypeAttribute()

ComMemberType   Enum

System.Runtime.InteropServices (mscorlib.dll)   *serializable*

This enumeration describes a COM member. Method indicates that the member is an ordinary method. PropGet and PropSet identify methods that get and set the values of properties (getters and setters).

```
Public Enum ComMemberType
   Method = 0
   PropGet = 1
   PropSet = 2
End Enum
```

Hierarchy: System.Object→ System.ValueType→ System.Enum(System.IComparable, System.IFormattable, System.IConvertible)→ ComMemberType

Passed To: Marshal.GetMethodInfoForComSlot()

ComRegisterFunctionAttribute   NotInheritable Class

System.Runtime.InteropServices (mscorlib.dll)

This attribute is attached to a shared method to indicate that it should be invoked when the enclosing assembly is registered with COM. The method should take two string arguments. The first is the name of the registry key being updated and the second is the namespace-qualified name of the type being registered (such as System.String). There can only be one registration function in each assembly.

Microsoft suggests that you do not use this feature and includes it only for backward compatibility. If you use this feature to specify a registration method, you must also specify an unregistration method (see ComUnregisterFunctionAttribute) that reverses all changes you made in the registration function.

```
Public NotInheritable Class ComRegisterFunctionAttribute : Inherits Attribute
' Public Constructors
   Public Sub New()
End Class
```

Hierarchy: System.Object→ System.Attribute→ ComRegisterFunctionAttribute

Valid On: Method

ComSourceInterfacesAttribute   NotInheritable Class

System.Runtime.InteropServices (mscorlib.dll)

This attribute indicates the unmanaged event (using the COM IConnectionPoint architecture) interfaces that are available on the decorated type. For each method defined in the COM interface, the type must provide a corresponding "event" instance that the COM architecture will plug into.

This attribute is only necessary when building .NET objects for plugging into COM event-aware systems, such as ActiveX control containers.

```
Public NotInheritable Class ComSourceInterfacesAttribute : Inherits Attribute
' Public Constructors
   Public Sub New(ByVal sourceInterfaces As String)
   Public Sub New(ByVal sourceInterface As Type)
   Public Sub New(ByVal sourceInterface1 As Type, ByVal sourceInterface2 As Type)
   Public Sub New(ByVal sourceInterface1 As Type, ByVal sourceInterface2 As Type, ByVal sourceInterface3 As Type)
   Public Sub New(ByVal sourceInterface1 As Type, ByVal sourceInterface2 As Type, ByVal sourceInterface3 As Type, _
      ByVal sourceInterface4 As Type)
' Public Instance Properties
   Public ReadOnly Property Value As String
End Class
```

Hierarchy: System.Object→ System.Attribute→ ComSourceInterfacesAttribute

Valid On: Class

ComUnregisterFunctionAttribute   NotInheritable Class

System.Runtime.InteropServices (mscorlib.dll)

This attribute is attached to a shared method to indicate that it should be invoked when the enclosing assembly is unregistered from COM. There can only be one unregistration function in each assembly.

For more details, see ComRegisterFunctionAttribute.

```
Public NotInheritable Class ComUnregisterFunctionAttribute : Inherits Attribute
' Public Constructors
   Public Sub New()
End Class
```

Hierarchy: System.Object→ System.Attribute→ ComUnregisterFunctionAttribute

Valid On: Method

ComVisibleAttribute   NotInheritable Class
System.Runtime.InteropServices (mscorlib.dll)

By default, all public assemblies, types, and members that are registered with COM are visible to COM. This attribute is used with a false argument to hide an assembly, type, or member from COM. This attribute has a cascading effect: if you hide an assembly, all the public types in that assembly are hidden as well.

You can override this attribute on individual types. If, for example, you want to make only one public type visible from an assembly, add the attribute false)> to the assembly, but also add true)> to the one type that you want to expose.

Public NotInheritable Class **ComVisibleAttribute** : Inherits Attribute
' Public Constructors
   Public Sub **New**(ByVal visibility As Boolean)
' Public Instance Properties
   Public ReadOnly Property **Value** As Boolean
End Class

Hierarchy: System.Object→ System.Attribute→ ComVisibleAttribute

Valid On: Assembly, Class, Struct, Enum, Method, Property, Field, Interface, Delegate

CurrencyWrapper   NotInheritable Class
System.Runtime.InteropServices (mscorlib.dll)

This class is used to create a wrapper around a decimal value. Then, when you pass the newly created CurrencyWrapper to an unmanaged method, the object is marshaled as the VT_CURRENCY type.

Public NotInheritable Class **CurrencyWrapper**
' Public Constructors
   Public Sub **New**(ByVal obj As Decimal)
   Public Sub **New**(ByVal obj As Object)
' Public Instance Properties
   Public ReadOnly Property **WrappedObject** As Decimal
End Class

DispatchWrapper   NotInheritable Class
System.Runtime.InteropServices (mscorlib.dll)

By default, objects are passed to unmanaged methods as the VT_UNKNOWN type. This wrapper is used to send an object as type VT_DISPATCH.

Public NotInheritable Class **DispatchWrapper**
' Public Constructors
   Public Sub **New**(ByVal obj As Object)
' Public Instance Properties
   Public ReadOnly Property **WrappedObject** As Object
End Class

DispIdAttribute   NotInheritable Class
System.Runtime.InteropServices (mscorlib.dll)

Specifies a member's DispId when it is exposed to COM.

Public NotInheritable Class **DispIdAttribute** : Inherits Attribute
' Public Constructors
   Public Sub **New**(ByVal dispId As Integer)

```
' Public Instance Properties
   Public ReadOnly Property Value As Integer
End Class
```

Hierarchy: System.Object→ System.Attribute→ DispIdAttribute

Valid On: Method, Property, Field, Event

DllImportAttribute   NotInheritable Class

System.Runtime.InteropServices (mscorlib.dll)   *ECMA*

This attribute (and, in VB.NET, the Declare statement) specifies that a method definition is implemented externally (usually in a DLL). Apply this attribute to a method that has been declared (but not defined) to specify the DLL name and entry point in which the method can be found.

The attribute can be customized in a number of different ways to help control the binding against the external method. The CallingConvention value dictates how the parameters to the call (and return value coming back) should be sent to the function. CallingConvention.StdCall (used for calling into _stdcall-declared functions, which is most of the Win32 API set) and CallingConvention.Cdecl (used for calling functions declared directly from C or C++) are the two most common values. The CharSet value indicates which character set parameters to the call are expected to be, either two-byte Unicode or one-byte ANSI. EntryPoint indicates the name of the exported function from the DLL to bind to (normally this is guessed from the name of the .NET-declared method), and ExactSpelling indicates whether the .NET compiler should attempt to "best match" a declared DllImport method against a possible set of exported functions. The PreserveSig value indicates how .NET should treat [out]-declared and [retval]-declared parameters. By default, the .NET compilers ignore the HRESULT return value on IDL-declared methods and use the [retval]-declared parameter as the return value; setting PreserveSig to true turns this off. Lastly, because many Win32 APIs use the GetLastError API call to note the exact reason a call fails, the SetLastError value indicates whether the caller should use that API to discover the reason for failures.

```
Public NotInheritable Class DllImportAttribute : Inherits  Attribute
' Public Constructors
   Public Sub New(ByVal dllName As String)
' Public Instance Fields
   Public CallingConvention As CallingConvention
   Public CharSet As CharSet
   Public EntryPoint As String
   Public ExactSpelling As Boolean
   Public PreserveSig As Boolean
   Public SetLastError As Boolean
' Public Instance Properties
   Public ReadOnly Property Value As String
End Class
```

Hierarchy: System.Object→ System.Attribute→ DllImportAttribute

Valid On: Method

ErrorWrapper
NotInheritable Class

System.Runtime.InteropServices (mscorlib.dll)

This wrapper is used to force an integer, Exception, or other object to be marshaled as type VT_ERROR.

```
Public NotInheritable Class ErrorWrapper
' Public Constructors
   Public Sub New(ByVal e As Exception)
   Public Sub New(ByVal errorCode As Integer)
   Public Sub New(ByVal errorCode As Object)
' Public Instance Properties
   Public ReadOnly Property ErrorCode As Integer
End Class
```

ExtensibleClassFactory
NotInheritable Class

System.Runtime.InteropServices (mscorlib.dll)

This class exposes the method RegisterObjectCreationCallback(), which specifies a delegate that manufactures instances of a managed type. Use this to build managed types that extend unmanaged types. Since a managed type cannot directly inherit from an unmanaged type, the managed type needs to aggregate an instance of the unmanaged type. The delegate that you register with RegisterObjectCreationCallback() takes care of creating the unmanaged type.

```
Public NotInheritable Class ExtensibleClassFactory
' Public Shared Methods
   Public Shared Sub RegisterObjectCreationCallback(ByVal callback As ObjectCreationDelegate)
End Class
```

ExternalException
Class

System.Runtime.InteropServices (mscorlib.dll)
serializable

This is the base class for COM interop and SEH (Structured Exception Handler) exceptions.

```
Public Class ExternalException : Inherits SystemException
' Public Constructors
   Public Sub New()
   Public Sub New(ByVal message As String)
   Public Sub New(ByVal message As String, ByVal inner As Exception)
   Public Sub New(ByVal message As String, ByVal errorCode As Integer)
' Protected Constructors
   Protected Sub New(ByVal info As System.Runtime.Serialization.SerializationInfo, _
      ByVal context As System.Runtime.Serialization.StreamingContext)
' Public Instance Properties
   Overridable Public ReadOnly Property ErrorCode As Integer
End Class
```

Hierarchy: System.Object→ System.Exception(System.Runtime.Serialization.ISerializable)→ System.SystemException→ ExternalException

Subclasses: COMException, SEHException

FieldOffsetAttribute   NotInheritable Class

System.Runtime.InteropServices (mscorlib.dll)   *ECMA*

This attribute controls the offset, in bytes, of a field. Use it to match your .NET types to the layout of C and C++ structures exactly. This attribute can be used only within classes that have the StructLayoutAttribute attribute where LayoutKind.Explicit was used.

Public NotInheritable Class **FieldOffsetAttribute** : Inherits Attribute
' Public Constructors
   Public Sub **New**(ByVal offset As Integer)
' Public Instance Properties
   Public ReadOnly Property **Value** As Integer
End Class

Hierarchy: System.Object→ System.Attribute→ FieldOffsetAttribute

Valid On: Field

GCHandle   Structure

System.Runtime.InteropServices (mscorlib.dll)   *ECMA*

This class is used when you need to pass a managed object to unmanaged code. To use this class, pass an instance of a .NET-managed type to the Alloc() method. The single-argument form of Alloc() creates the GCHandle with GCHandleType.Normal, which ensures that the object will not be freed by the garbage collector. (This means that some kind of user code must also call the Free() method in order to release the object.) Managed code can use the Target property to access the underlying object.

Public Structure **GCHandle**
' Public Instance Properties
   Public ReadOnly Property **IsAllocated** As Boolean
   Public Property **Target** As Object
' Public Shared Methods
   Public Shared Function **Alloc**(ByVal value As Object) As GCHandle
   Public Shared Function **Alloc**(ByVal value As Object, ByVal type As GCHandleType) As GCHandle
   Public Shared explicit operator Sub **GCHandle**(ByVal value As IntPtr)
   Public Shared explicit operator Sub **IntPtr**(ByVal value As GCHandle)
' Public Instance Methods
   Public Function **AddrOfPinnedObject**() As IntPtr
   Public Sub **Free**()
End Structure

Hierarchy: System.Object→ System.ValueType→ GCHandle

GCHandleType   Enum

System.Runtime.InteropServices (mscorlib.dll)   *ECMA, serializable*

This enumeration contains values for the two-argument form of GCHandle.Alloc(). Normal protects the object from being garbage collected, and Pinned does the same (but it also enables the GCHandle.AddrOfPinnedObject() method). Weak and WeakTrackResurrection both allow the object to be garbage collected. However, Weak causes the object to be zeroed out before the finalizer runs, but WeakTrackResurrection does not zero the object, so the object's finalizer can safely resurrect it.

```
Public Enum GCHandleType
    Weak = 0
    WeakTrackResurrection = 1
    Normal = 2
    Pinned = 3
End Enum
```

Hierarchy: System.Object→ System.ValueType→ System.Enum(System.IComparable, System.IFormattable, System.IConvertible)→ GCHandleType

Passed To: GCHandle.Alloc()

GuidAttribute   NotInheritable Class
System.Runtime.InteropServices (mscorlib.dll)

This attribute is used to specify the GUID of assemblies, modules, or types you expose to COM. If you don't use this attribute to specify a GUID, one is automatically generated. When you apply this attribute, use its full name ()> rather than [Guid()]) to avoid clashes with the System.Guid type.

```
Public NotInheritable Class GuidAttribute : Inherits Attribute
' Public Constructors
    Public Sub New(ByVal guid As String)
' Public Instance Properties
    Public ReadOnly Property Value As String
End Class
```

Hierarchy: System.Object→ System.Attribute→ GuidAttribute

Valid On: Assembly, Class, Struct, Enum, Interface, Delegate

HandleRef   Structure
System.Runtime.InteropServices (mscorlib.dll)

When you pass a managed object into unmanaged code using PInvoke, there is a chance that the garbage collector will finalize the object before the unmanaged code is finished with it. This can only happen when your managed code does not reference the object after the PInvoke call. Because the garbage collector's reach does not extend into unmanaged code, this fools the garbage collector into thinking that you are finished with it.

This class is used to wrap your managed object before passing it into unmanaged code, and you are guaranteed that the garbage collector will not touch it until the PInvoke call returns.

```
Public Structure HandleRef
' Public Constructors
    Public Sub New(ByVal wrapper As Object, ByVal handle As IntPtr)
' Public Instance Properties
    Public ReadOnly Property Handle As IntPtr
    Public ReadOnly Property Wrapper As Object
' Public Shared Methods
    Public Shared explicit operator Sub IntPtr(ByVal value As HandleRef)
End Structure
```

Hierarchy: System.Object→ System.ValueType→ HandleRef

IDispatchImplAttribute
NotInheritable Class

System.Runtime.InteropServices (mscorlib.dll)

There are multiple implementations of IDispatch available for you to expose dual interfaces and dispinterfaces to COM. Attach this attribute to a class or an assembly to specify which IDispatch implementation to use. If you apply this attribute to an assembly, it applies to all classes within that assembly. For a list of available IDispatch implementations, see IDispatchImplType.

```
Public NotInheritable Class IDispatchImplAttribute : Inherits Attribute
' Public Constructors
   Public Sub New(ByVal implType As IDispatchImplType)
   Public Sub New(ByVal implType As Short)
' Public Instance Properties
   Public ReadOnly Property Value As IDispatchImplType
End Class
```

Hierarchy: System.Object→ System.Attribute→ IDispatchImplAttribute

Valid On: Assembly, Class

IDispatchImplType
Enum

System.Runtime.InteropServices (mscorlib.dll)
serializable

This enumeration contains the values used by IDispatchImplAttribute. SystemDefinedImpl tells the runtime to decide which IDispatch implementation to use. InternalImpl tells .NET to use its own IDispatch implementation, and CompatibleImpl uses an IDispatch implementation that is compatible with OLE automation. If you use this last implementation, it requires static type information. Because this information is automatically generated at runtime, CompatibleImpl may have an adverse impact on performance.

```
Public Enum IDispatchImplType
   SystemDefinedImpl = 0
   InternalImpl = 1
   CompatibleImpl = 2
End Enum
```

Hierarchy: System.Object→ System.ValueType→ System.Enum(System.IComparable, System.IFormattable, System.IConvertible)→ IDispatchImplType

Returned By: IDispatchImplAttribute.Value

Passed To: IDispatchImplAttribute.IDispatchImplAttribute()

InAttribute
NotInheritable Class

System.Runtime.InteropServices (mscorlib.dll)
ECMA

This attribute is attached to a parameter to marshal it as an in parameter. By default, parameters are marshaled based on their modifiers, so this attribute is only necessary if you want to override the defaults. Parameters with no modifiers are marshaled as [In]. Parameters with the ref modifier are marshaled as [In, Out]. Parameters with the out modifier are marshaled as [Out].

```
Public NotInheritable Class InAttribute : Inherits Attribute
' Public Constructors
   Public Sub New()
End Class
```

Hierarchy: System.Object→ System.Attribute→ InAttribute

Valid On: Parameter

InterfaceTypeAttribute   NotInheritable Class

System.Runtime.InteropServices (mscorlib.dll)

This attribute is used to create a .NET interface that maps a COM interface into your managed application. See ComInterfaceType for the available values.

```
Public NotInheritable Class InterfaceTypeAttribute : Inherits Attribute
' Public Constructors
   Public Sub New(ByVal interfaceType As ComInterfaceType)
   Public Sub New(ByVal interfaceType As Short)
' Public Instance Properties
   Public ReadOnly Property Value As ComInterfaceType
End Class
```

Hierarchy: System.Object→ System.Attribute→ InterfaceTypeAttribute

Valid On: Interface

InvalidComObjectException   Class

System.Runtime.InteropServices (mscorlib.dll)   *serializable*

This exception signals that an invalid COM object has been used.

```
Public Class InvalidComObjectException : Inherits SystemException
' Public Constructors
   Public Sub New()
   Public Sub New(ByVal message As String)
   Public Sub New(ByVal message As String, ByVal inner As Exception)
' Protected Constructors
   Protected Sub New(ByVal info As System.Runtime.Serialization.SerializationInfo, _
      ByVal context As System.Runtime.Serialization.StreamingContext)
End Class
```

Hierarchy: System.Object→ System.Exception(System.Runtime.Serialization.ISerializable)→ System.SystemException→ InvalidComObjectException

InvalidOleVariantTypeException   Class

System.Runtime.InteropServices (mscorlib.dll)   *serializable*

This exception signals that the marshaler failed in an attempt to marshal a variant to managed code.

```
Public Class InvalidOleVariantTypeException : Inherits SystemException
' Public Constructors
   Public Sub New()
   Public Sub New(ByVal message As String)
   Public Sub New(ByVal message As String, ByVal inner As Exception)
' Protected Constructors
   Protected Sub New(ByVal info As System.Runtime.Serialization.SerializationInfo, _
      ByVal context As System.Runtime.Serialization.StreamingContext)
End Class
```

Hierarchy: System.Object→ System.Exception(System.Runtime.Serialization.ISerializable)→ System.SystemException→ InvalidOleVariantTypeException

System. Runtime

IRegistrationServices
Interface

System.Runtime.InteropServices (mscorlib.dll)

This interface defines the interface used by classes that register and unregister assemblies with COM.

```
Public Interface IRegistrationServices
' Public Instance Methods
    Public Function GetManagedCategoryGuid() As Guid
    Public Function GetProgIdForType(ByVal type As Type) As String
    Public Function GetRegistrableTypesInAssembly(ByVal assembly As System.Reflection.Assembly) As Type()
    Public Function RegisterAssembly(ByVal assembly As System.Reflection.Assembly, _
        ByVal flags As AssemblyRegistrationFlags) As Boolean
    Public Sub RegisterTypeForComClients(ByVal type As Type, ByRef g As Guid)
    Public Function TypeRepresentsComType(ByVal type As Type) As Boolean
    Public Function TypeRequiresRegistration(ByVal type As Type) As Boolean
    Public Function UnregisterAssembly(ByVal assembly As System.Reflection.Assembly) As Boolean
End Interface
```

Implemented By: RegistrationServices

LayoutKind
Enum

System.Runtime.InteropServices (mscorlib.dll)
ECMA, serializable

This enumeration is used to specify how objects are laid out when they are passed to unmanaged code. Auto specifies that .NET should choose the best method to lay out the objects. Explicit gives you complete control over how the object's data members are laid out. You must use FieldOffsetAttribute with each member if you specify Explicit. Sequential lays out the object's members one after the other, in the same order that they are defined in the class definition.

```
Public Enum LayoutKind
    Sequential = 0
    Explicit = 2
    Auto = 3
End Enum
```

Hierarchy: System.Object→ System.ValueType→ System.Enum(System.IComparable, System.IFormattable, System.IConvertible)→ LayoutKind

Returned By: StructLayoutAttribute.Value

Passed To: StructLayoutAttribute.StructLayoutAttribute()

LCIDConversionAttribute
NotInheritable Class

System.Runtime.InteropServices (mscorlib.dll)

This attribute indicates that a parameter within the method's unmanaged signature expects an [lcid] argument. Pass an integer value to the constructor to specify which parameter, starting with 0 for the first parameter.

```
Public NotInheritable Class LCIDConversionAttribute : Inherits Attribute
' Public Constructors
    Public Sub New(ByVal lcid As Integer)
' Public Instance Properties
    Public ReadOnly Property Value As Integer
End Class
```

Hierarchy: System.Object→ System.Attribute→ LCIDConversionAttribute

Valid On: Method

Marshal
NotInheritable Class

System.Runtime.InteropServices (mscorlib.dll)

This class offers a collection of shared methods for working with unmanaged memory and converting managed types to unmanaged types. Unless you are developing specialized code for marshaling types between managed and unmanaged code, you probably do not need to use any of these methods.

GetHRForException() converts a .NET exception to a COM HResult. If you are curious about the platform you are running on, you can find out the size of a character with the SystemDefaultCharSize field, which is 1 on an ANSI platform (Windows 9x/ME) and 2 on a Unicode platform (Windows NT, 2000, and XP).

Use the IsComObject() method to determine whether an object is actually an unmanaged COM object. The AddRef() method increments a COM object's reference count.

Public NotInheritable Class **Marshal**
' Public Shared Fields
   Public Shared ReadOnly **SystemDefaultCharSize** As Integer   =2
   Public Shared ReadOnly **SystemMaxDBCSCharSize** As Integer   =1
' Public Shared Methods
   Public Shared Function **AddRef**(ByVal pUnk As IntPtr) As Integer
   Public Shared Function **AllocCoTaskMem**(ByVal cb As Integer) As IntPtr
   Public Shared Function **AllocHGlobal**(ByVal cb As Integer) As IntPtr
   Public Shared Function **AllocHGlobal**(ByVal cb As IntPtr) As IntPtr
   Public Shared Function **BindToMoniker**(ByVal monikerName As String) As Object
   Public Shared Sub **ChangeWrapperHandleStrength**(ByVal otp As Object, ByVal flsWeak As Boolean)
   Public Shared Sub **Copy**(ByVal source As Byte(), ByVal startIndex As Integer, ByVal destination As IntPtr, _
      ByVal length As Integer)
   Public Shared Sub **Copy**(ByVal source As Char(), ByVal startIndex As Integer, ByVal destination As IntPtr, _
      ByVal length As Integer)
   Public Shared Sub **Copy**(ByVal source As Double(), ByVal startIndex As Integer, ByVal destination As IntPtr, _
      ByVal length As Integer)
   Public Shared Sub **Copy**(ByVal source As Short(), ByVal startIndex As Integer, ByVal destination As IntPtr, _
      ByVal length As Integer)
   Public Shared Sub **Copy**(ByVal source As Integer(), ByVal startIndex As Integer, ByVal destination As IntPtr, _
      ByVal length As Integer)
   Public Shared Sub **Copy**(ByVal source As Long(), ByVal startIndex As Integer, ByVal destination As IntPtr, _
      ByVal length As Integer)
   Public Shared Sub **Copy**(ByVal source As IntPtr, ByVal destination As Byte(), ByVal startIndex As Integer, _
      ByVal length As Integer)
   Public Shared Sub **Copy**(ByVal source As IntPtr, ByVal destination As Char(), ByVal startIndex As Integer, _
      ByVal length As Integer)
   Public Shared Sub **Copy**(ByVal source As IntPtr, ByVal destination As Double(), ByVal startIndex As Integer, _
      ByVal length As Integer)
   Public Shared Sub **Copy**(ByVal source As IntPtr, ByVal destination As Short(), ByVal startIndex As Integer, _
      ByVal length As Integer)
   Public Shared Sub **Copy**(ByVal source As IntPtr, ByVal destination As Integer(), ByVal startIndex As Integer, _
      ByVal length As Integer)
   Public Shared Sub **Copy**(ByVal source As IntPtr, ByVal destination As Long(), ByVal startIndex As Integer, _
      ByVal length As Integer)
   Public Shared Sub **Copy**(ByVal source As IntPtr, ByVal destination As Single(), ByVal startIndex As Integer, _
      ByVal length As Integer)
   Public Shared Sub **Copy**(ByVal source As Single(), ByVal startIndex As Integer, ByVal destination As IntPtr, _
      ByVal length As Integer)

*System.
Runtime*

Public Shared Function **CreateWrapperOfType**(ByVal o As Object, ByVal t As Type) As Object

Public Shared Sub **DestroyStructure**(ByVal ptr As IntPtr, ByVal structuretype As Type)

Public Shared Sub **FreeBSTR**(ByVal ptr As IntPtr)

Public Shared Sub **FreeCoTaskMem**(ByVal ptr As IntPtr)

Public Shared Sub **FreeHGlobal**(ByVal hglobal As IntPtr)

Public Shared Function **GenerateGuidForType**(ByVal type As Type) As Guid

Public Shared Function **GenerateProgIdForType**(ByVal type As Type) As String

Public Shared Function **GetActiveObject**(ByVal progID As String) As Object

Public Shared Function **GetComInterfaceForObject**(ByVal o As Object, ByVal T As Type) As IntPtr

Public Shared Function **GetComObjectData**(ByVal obj As Object, ByVal key As Object) As Object

Public Shared Function **GetComSlotForMethodInfo**(ByVal m As System.Reflection.MemberInfo) As Integer

Public Shared Function **GetEndComSlot**(ByVal t As Type) As Integer

Public Shared Function **GetExceptionCode**() As Integer

Public Shared Function **GetExceptionPointers**() As IntPtr

Public Shared Function **GetHINSTANCE**(ByVal m As System.Reflection.Module) As IntPtr

Public Shared Function **GetHRForException**(ByVal e As Exception) As Integer

Public Shared Function **GetHRForLastWin32Error**() As Integer

Public Shared Function **GetIDispatchForObject**(ByVal o As Object) As IntPtr

Public Shared Function **GetITypeInfoForType**(ByVal t As Type) As IntPtr

Public Shared Function **GetIUnknownForObject**(ByVal o As Object) As IntPtr

Public Shared Function **GetLastWin32Error**() As Integer

Public Shared Function **GetManagedThunkForUnmanagedMethodPtr**(ByVal pfnMethodToWrap As IntPtr, _
ByVal pbSignature As IntPtr, ByVal cbSignature As Integer) As IntPtr

Public Shared Function **GetMethodInfoForComSlot**(ByVal t As Type, ByVal slot As Integer, _
ByRef memberType As ComMemberType) As MemberInfo

Public Shared Sub **GetNativeVariantForObject**(ByVal obj As Object, ByVal pDstNativeVariant As IntPtr)

Public Shared Function **GetObjectForIUnknown**(ByVal pUnk As IntPtr) As Object

Public Shared Function **GetObjectForNativeVariant**(ByVal pSrcNativeVariant As IntPtr) As Object

Public Shared Function **GetObjectsForNativeVariants**(ByVal aSrcNativeVariant As IntPtr, _
ByVal cVars As Integer) As Object()

Public Shared Function **GetStartComSlot**(ByVal t As Type) As Integer

Public Shared Function **GetThreadFromFiberCookie**(ByVal cookie As Integer) As Thread

Public Shared Function **GetTypedObjectForIUnknown**(ByVal pUnk As IntPtr, ByVal t As Type) As Object

Public Shared Function **GetTypeForITypeInfo**(ByVal piTypeInfo As IntPtr) As Type

Public Shared Function **GetTypeInfoName**(ByVal pTI As UCOMITypeInfo) As String

Public Shared Function **GetTypeLibGuid**(ByVal pTLB As UCOMITypeLib) As Guid

Public Shared Function **GetTypeLibGuidForAssembly**(ByVal asm As System.Reflection.Assembly) As Guid

Public Shared Function **GetTypeLibLcid**(ByVal pTLB As UCOMITypeLib) As Integer

Public Shared Function **GetTypeLibName**(ByVal pTLB As UCOMITypeLib) As String

Public Shared Function **GetUnmanagedThunkForManagedMethodPtr**(ByVal pfnMethodToWrap As IntPtr, _
ByVal pbSignature As IntPtr, ByVal cbSignature As Integer) As IntPtr

Public Shared Function **IsComObject**(ByVal o As Object) As Boolean

Public Shared Function **IsTypeVisibleFromCom**(ByVal t As Type) As Boolean

Public Shared Function **NumParamBytes**(ByVal m As System.Reflection.MethodInfo) As Integer

Public Shared Function **OffsetOf**(ByVal t As Type, ByVal fieldName As String) As IntPtr

Public Shared Sub **Prelink**(ByVal m As System.Reflection.MethodInfo)

Public Shared Sub **PrelinkAll**(ByVal c As Type)

Public Shared Function **PtrToStringAnsi**(ByVal ptr As IntPtr) As String

Public Shared Function **PtrToStringAnsi**(ByVal ptr As IntPtr, ByVal len As Integer) As String

Public Shared Function **PtrToStringAuto**(ByVal ptr As IntPtr) As String

Public Shared Function **PtrToStringAuto**(ByVal ptr As IntPtr, ByVal len As Integer) As String

Public Shared Function **PtrToStringBSTR**(ByVal ptr As IntPtr) As String

Public Shared Function **PtrToStringUni**(ByVal ptr As IntPtr) As String

Public Shared Function **PtrToStringUni**(ByVal ptr As IntPtr, ByVal len As Integer) As String

Public Shared Function **PtrToStructure**(ByVal ptr As IntPtr, ByVal structureType As Type) As Object

Public Shared Sub **PtrToStructure**(ByVal ptr As IntPtr, ByVal structure As Object)

Public Shared Function **QueryInterface**(ByVal pUnk As IntPtr, ByRef iid As Guid, ByRef ppv As IntPtr) As Integer

Public Shared Function **ReadByte**(ByVal ptr As IntPtr) As Byte

Public Shared Function **ReadByte**(ByVal ptr As IntPtr, ByVal ofs As Integer) As Byte

Public Shared Function **ReadByte**(ByVal ptr As Object, ByVal ofs As Integer) As Byte

Public Shared Function **ReadInt16**(ByVal ptr As IntPtr) As Short

Public Shared Function **ReadInt16**(ByVal ptr As IntPtr, ByVal ofs As Integer) As Short

Public Shared Function **ReadInt16**(ByVal ptr As Object, ByVal ofs As Integer) As Short

Public Shared Function **ReadInt32**(ByVal ptr As IntPtr) As Integer

Public Shared Function **ReadInt32**(ByVal ptr As IntPtr, ByVal ofs As Integer) As Integer

Public Shared Function **ReadInt32**(ByVal ptr As Object, ByVal ofs As Integer) As Integer

Public Shared Function **ReadInt64**(ByVal ptr As IntPtr) As Long

Public Shared Function **ReadInt64**(ByVal ptr As IntPtr, ByVal ofs As Integer) As Long

Public Shared Function **ReadInt64**(ByVal ptr As Object, ByVal ofs As Integer) As Long

Public Shared Function **ReadIntPtr**(ByVal ptr As IntPtr) As IntPtr

Public Shared Function **ReadIntPtr**(ByVal ptr As IntPtr, ByVal ofs As Integer) As IntPtr

Public Shared Function **ReadIntPtr**(ByVal ptr As Object, ByVal ofs As Integer) As IntPtr

Public Shared Function **ReAllocCoTaskMem**(ByVal pv As IntPtr, ByVal cb As Integer) As IntPtr

Public Shared Function **ReAllocHGlobal**(ByVal pv As IntPtr, ByVal cb As IntPtr) As IntPtr

Public Shared Function **Release**(ByVal pUnk As IntPtr) As Integer

Public Shared Function **ReleaseComObject**(ByVal o As Object) As Integer

Public Shared Sub **ReleaseThreadCache**()

Public Shared Function **SetComObjectData**(ByVal obj As Object, ByVal key As Object, ByVal data As Object) _
As Boolean

Public Shared Function **SizeOf**(ByVal structure As Object) As Integer

Public Shared Function **SizeOf**(ByVal t As Type) As Integer

Public Shared Function **StringToBSTR**(ByVal s As String) As IntPtr

Public Shared Function **StringToCoTaskMemAnsi**(ByVal s As String) As IntPtr

Public Shared Function **StringToCoTaskMemAuto**(ByVal s As String) As IntPtr

Public Shared Function **StringToCoTaskMemUni**(ByVal s As String) As IntPtr

Public Shared Function **StringToHGlobalAnsi**(ByVal s As String) As IntPtr

Public Shared Function **StringToHGlobalAuto**(ByVal s As String) As IntPtr

Public Shared Function **StringToHGlobalUni**(ByVal s As String) As IntPtr

Public Shared Sub **StructureToPtr**(ByVal structure As Object, ByVal ptr As IntPtr, ByVal fDeleteOld As Boolean)

Public Shared Sub **ThrowExceptionForHR**(ByVal errorCode As Integer)

Public Shared Sub **ThrowExceptionForHR**(ByVal errorCode As Integer, ByVal errorInfo As IntPtr)

Public Shared Function **UnsafeAddrOfPinnedArrayElement**(ByVal arr As Array, ByVal index As Integer) _
As IntPtr

Public Shared Sub **WriteByte**(ByVal ptr As IntPtr, ByVal val As Byte)

Public Shared Sub **WriteByte**(ByVal ptr As IntPtr, ByVal ofs As Integer, ByVal val As Byte)

Public Shared Sub **WriteByte**(ByRef ptr As Object, ByVal ofs As Integer, ByVal val As Byte)

Public Shared Sub **WriteInt16**(ByVal ptr As IntPtr, ByVal val As Char)

Public Shared Sub **WriteInt16**(ByVal ptr As IntPtr, ByVal val As Short)

Public Shared Sub **WriteInt16**(ByVal ptr As IntPtr, ByVal ofs As Integer, ByVal val As Char)

Public Shared Sub **WriteInt16**(ByVal ptr As IntPtr, ByVal ofs As Integer, ByVal val As Short)

Public Shared Sub **WriteInt16**(ByRef ptr As Object, ByVal ofs As Integer, ByVal val As Char)

Public Shared Sub **WriteInt16**(ByRef ptr As Object, ByVal ofs As Integer, ByVal val As Short)

Public Shared Sub **WriteInt32**(ByVal ptr As IntPtr, ByVal val As Integer)

Public Shared Sub **WriteInt32**(ByVal ptr As IntPtr, ByVal ofs As Integer, ByVal val As Integer)

Public Shared Sub **WriteInt32**(ByRef ptr As Object, ByVal ofs As Integer, ByVal val As Integer)

Public Shared Sub **WriteInt64**(ByVal ptr As IntPtr, ByVal ofs As Integer, ByVal val As Long)

Public Shared Sub **WriteInt64**(ByVal ptr As IntPtr, ByVal val As Long)

Public Shared Sub **WriteInt64**(ByRef ptr As Object, ByVal ofs As Integer, ByVal val As Long)

Public Shared Sub **WriteIntPtr**(ByVal ptr As IntPtr, ByVal ofs As Integer, ByVal val As IntPtr)

Public Shared Sub **WriteIntPtr**(ByVal ptr As IntPtr, ByVal val As IntPtr)

System. Runtime

Public Shared Sub **WriteIntPtr**(ByRef ptr As Object, ByVal ofs As Integer, ByVal val As IntPtr)
End Class

MarshalAsAttribute

NotInheritable Class

System.Runtime.InteropServices (mscorlib.dll)   *ECMA*

This optional attribute is used to explicitly specify the unmanaged type a parameter, field, or return value should be marshaled to. If you do not specify this attribute, .NET uses the type's default marshaler. The UnmanagedType enumeration contains the unmanaged types you can marshal to with this attribute.

Public NotInheritable Class **MarshalAsAttribute** : Inherits Attribute
' *Public Constructors*
   Public Sub **New**(ByVal unmanagedType As Short)
   Public Sub **New**(ByVal unmanagedType As UnmanagedType)
' *Public Instance Fields*
   Public **ArraySubType** As UnmanagedType
   Public **MarshalCookie** As String
   Public **MarshalType** As String
   Public **MarshalTypeRef** As Type
   Public **SafeArraySubType** As VarEnum
   Public **SafeArrayUserDefinedSubType** As Type
   Public **SizeConst** As Integer
   Public **SizeParamIndex** As Short
' *Public Instance Properties*
   Public ReadOnly Property **Value** As UnmanagedType
End Class

Hierarchy: System.Object→ System.Attribute→ MarshalAsAttribute

Valid On: Field, Parameter, ReturnValue

MarshalDirectiveException

Class

System.Runtime.InteropServices (mscorlib.dll)   *serializable*

This exception is thrown when the marshaler encounters an unsupported MarshalAsAttribute.

Public Class **MarshalDirectiveException** : Inherits SystemException
' *Public Constructors*
   Public Sub **New**()
   Public Sub **New**(ByVal message As String)
   Public Sub **New**(ByVal message As String, ByVal inner As Exception)
' *Protected Constructors*
   Protected Sub **New**(ByVal info As System.Runtime.Serialization.SerializationInfo, _
     ByVal context As System.Runtime.Serialization.StreamingContext)
End Class

Hierarchy: System.Object→ System.Exception(System.Runtime.Serialization.ISerializable)→
System.SystemException→ MarshalDirectiveException

ObjectCreationDelegate   Delegate

System.Runtime.InteropServices (mscorlib.dll)   *serializable*

Use this delegate with the ExtensibleClassFactory.RegisterObjectCreationCallback() method to create a COM object.

Public Delegate Function **ObjectCreationDelegate**(ByVal aggregator As IntPtr) As IntPtr

Passed To: ExtensibleClassFactory.RegisterObjectCreationCallback()

OptionalAttribute   NotInheritable Class

System.Runtime.InteropServices (mscorlib.dll)

This attribute is attached to a parameter to indicate that it is optional.

Public NotInheritable Class **OptionalAttribute** : Inherits Attribute
' *Public Constructors*
  Public Sub **New**()
End Class

Hierarchy: System.Object→ System.Attribute→ OptionalAttribute

Valid On: Parameter

OutAttribute   NotInheritable Class

System.Runtime.InteropServices (mscorlib.dll)   *ECMA*

This attribute is attached to a parameter to cause it to be marshaled as an out parameter. See InAttribute for more details, including information on the default behavior.

Public NotInheritable Class **OutAttribute** : Inherits Attribute
' *Public Constructors*
  Public Sub **New**()
End Class

Hierarchy: System.Object→ System.Attribute→ OutAttribute

Valid On: Parameter

PreserveSigAttribute   NotInheritable Class

System.Runtime.InteropServices (mscorlib.dll)

When .NET converts a managed method signature to an unmanaged signature, it changes the return value to a parameter that has the out and retval COM attributes. Instead of the original return value, the unmanaged method returns a COM HRESULT. If you want to override this behavior, attach the PreserveSigAttribute to the method.

Something similar happens when you call unmanaged methods from managed code. In that case, the [out, retval] parameter on the COM side becomes the return value, and an HRESULT that indicates an error condition is translated into a .NET exception. If you want to be able to access the HRESULT as a long return value, use the PreserveSigAttribute on the methods in your COM interface declaration (see InterfaceTypeAttribute).

Public NotInheritable Class **PreserveSigAttribute** : Inherits Attribute
' *Public Constructors*
  Public Sub **New**()
End Class

Hierarchy: System.Object→ System.Attribute→ PreserveSigAttribute

Valid On: Method

*System.
Runtime*

ProgIdAttribute

System.Runtime.InteropServices (mscorlib.dll)

This attribute is attached to a class to specify its COM ProgID.

```
Public NotInheritable Class ProgIdAttribute : Inherits Attribute
' Public Constructors
   Public Sub New(ByVal progId As String)
' Public Instance Properties
   Public ReadOnly Property Value As String
End Class
```

Hierarchy: System.Object→ System.Attribute→ ProgIdAttribute

Valid On: Class

RegistrationServices

System.Runtime.InteropServices (mscorlib.dll)

This class is responsible for registering and unregistering assemblies with COM.

```
Public Class RegistrationServices : Implements IRegistrationServices
' Public Constructors
   Public Sub New()
' Public Instance Methods
   Overridable Public Function GetManagedCategoryGuid() As Guid _
      Implements IRegistrationServices.GetManagedCategoryGuid
   Overridable Public Function GetProgIdForType(ByVal type As Type) As String _
      Implements IRegistrationServices.GetProgIdForType
   Overridable Public Function GetRegistrableTypesInAssembly(ByVal assembly As System.Reflection.Assembly) _
      As Type() Implements IRegistrationServices.GetRegistrableTypesInAssembly
   Overridable Public Function RegisterAssembly(ByVal assembly As System.Reflection.Assembly, _
      ByVal flags As AssemblyRegistrationFlags) As Boolean Implements IRegistrationServices.RegisterAssembly
   Overridable Public Sub RegisterTypeForComClients(ByVal type As Type, ByRef g As Guid) _
      Implements IRegistrationServices.RegisterTypeForComClients
   Overridable Public Function TypeRepresentsComType(ByVal type As Type) As Boolean _
      Implements IRegistrationServices.TypeRepresentsComType
   Overridable Public Function TypeRequiresRegistration(ByVal type As Type) As Boolean _
      Implements IRegistrationServices.TypeRequiresRegistration
   Overridable Public Function UnregisterAssembly(ByVal assembly As System.Reflection.Assembly) As Boolean _
      Implements IRegistrationServices.UnregisterAssembly
End Class
```

RuntimeEnvironment

System.Runtime.InteropServices (mscorlib.dll)

This type exposes shared methods you can use to get information about the CLR's environment.

```
Public Class RuntimeEnvironment
' Public Constructors
   Public Sub New()
' Public Shared Properties
   Public Shared ReadOnly Property SystemConfigurationFile As String
```

' *Public Shared Methods*
   Public Shared Function **FromGlobalAccessCache**(ByVal a As System.Reflection.Assembly) As Boolean
   Public Shared Function **GetRuntimeDirectory**() As String
   Public Shared Function **GetSystemVersion**() As String
End Class

SafeArrayRankMismatchException
               Class

System.Runtime.InteropServices (mscorlib.dll)   *serializable*

This exception signals that a SAFEARRAY's rank does not match the rank in the method signature; it might be thrown when invoking a managed method.

Public Class **SafeArrayRankMismatchException** : Inherits SystemException
' *Public Constructors*
   Public Sub **New**()
   Public Sub **New**(ByVal message As String)
   Public Sub **New**(ByVal message As String, ByVal inner As Exception)
' *Protected Constructors*
   Protected Sub **New**(ByVal info As System.Runtime.Serialization.SerializationInfo, _
     ByVal context As System.Runtime.Serialization.StreamingContext)
End Class

Hierarchy: System.Object→ System.Exception(System.Runtime.Serialization.ISerializable)→
System.SystemException→ SafeArrayRankMismatchException

SafeArrayTypeMismatchException
               Class

System.Runtime.InteropServices (mscorlib.dll)   *serializable*

This exception signals that a SAFEARRAY's type does not match the type in the method signature; it might be thrown when invoking a managed method.

Public Class **SafeArrayTypeMismatchException** : Inherits SystemException
' *Public Constructors*
   Public Sub **New**()
   Public Sub **New**(ByVal message As String)
   Public Sub **New**(ByVal message As String, ByVal inner As Exception)
' *Protected Constructors*
   Protected Sub **New**(ByVal info As System.Runtime.Serialization.SerializationInfo, _
     ByVal context As System.Runtime.Serialization.StreamingContext)
End Class

Hierarchy: System.Object→ System.Exception(System.Runtime.Serialization.ISerializable)→
System.SystemException→ SafeArrayTypeMismatchException

SEHException
               Class

System.Runtime.InteropServices (mscorlib.dll)   *serializable*

This class is used as a wrapper for an unmanaged C++ exception that was thrown.

Public Class **SEHException** : Inherits ExternalException
' *Public Constructors*
   Public Sub **New**()
   Public Sub **New**(ByVal message As String)
   Public Sub **New**(ByVal message As String, ByVal inner As Exception)
' *Protected Constructors*
   Protected Sub **New**(ByVal info As System.Runtime.Serialization.SerializationInfo, _
     ByVal context As System.Runtime.Serialization.StreamingContext)

*System.
Runtime*

```
' Public Instance Methods
   Overridable Public Function CanResume() As Boolean
End Class
```

Hierarchy: System.Object→ System.Exception(System.Runtime.Serialization.ISerializable)→ System.SystemException→ ExternalException→ SEHException

StructLayoutAttribute   NotInheritable Class

System.Runtime.InteropServices (mscorlib.dll)   *ECMA*

Use this attribute to control how the members of a class are laid out in memory. See LayoutKind for the possible values you can use with this attribute.

```
Public NotInheritable Class StructLayoutAttribute : Inherits Attribute
' Public Constructors
   Public Sub New(ByVal layoutKind As Short)
   Public Sub New(ByVal layoutKind As LayoutKind)
' Public Instance Fields
   Public CharSet As CharSet
   Public Pack As Integer
   Public Size As Integer
' Public Instance Properties
   Public ReadOnly Property Value As LayoutKind
End Class
```

Hierarchy: System.Object→ System.Attribute→ StructLayoutAttribute

Valid On: Class, Struct

UnknownWrapper   NotInheritable Class

System.Runtime.InteropServices (mscorlib.dll)

Use this wrapper to pass a managed object into unmanaged code as type VT_UNKNOWN.

```
Public NotInheritable Class UnknownWrapper
' Public Constructors
   Public Sub New(ByVal obj As Object)
' Public Instance Properties
   Public ReadOnly Property WrappedObject As Object
End Class
```

UnmanagedType   Enum

System.Runtime.InteropServices (mscorlib.dll)   *ECMA, serializable*

This enumeration contains constant values that represent various unmanaged types.

```
Public Enum UnmanagedType
         Bool = 2
         I1 = 3
         U1 = 4
         I2 = 5
         U2 = 6
         I4 = 7
         U4 = 8
         I8 = 9
         U8 = 10
         R4 = 11
```

```
        R8 = 12
        Currency = 15
        BStr = 19
        LPStr = 20
        LPWStr = 21
        LPTStr = 22
        ByValTStr = 23
        IUnknown = 25
        IDispatch = 26
        Struct = 27
        Interface = 28
        SafeArray = 29
        ByValArray = 30
        SysInt = 31
        SysUInt = 32
        VBByRefStr = 34
        AnsiBStr = 35
        TBStr = 36
        VariantBool = 37
        FunctionPtr = 38
        AsAny = 40
        LPArray = 42
        LPStruct = 43
        CustomMarshaler = 44
        Error = 45
End Enum
```

Hierarchy: System.Object→ System.ValueType→ System.Enum(System.IComparable, System.IFormattable, System.IConvertible)→ UnmanagedType

Returned By: System.Reflection.Emit.UnmanagedMarshal.{BaseType, GetUnmanagedType}, MarshalAsAttribute.Value

Passed To: System.Reflection.Emit.UnmanagedMarshal.{DefineLPArray(), DefineSafeArray(), DefineUnmanagedMarshal()}, MarshalAsAttribute.MarshalAsAttribute()

VarEnum   Enum

System.Runtime.InteropServices (mscorlib.dll)   *serializable*

This enumeration contains constants that can be used with MarshalAsAttribute.SafeArraySub-Type to specify how to marshal arrays that are passed from managed to unmanaged code.

```
Public Enum VarEnum
        VT_EMPTY = 0
        VT_NULL = 1
        VT_I2 = 2
        VT_I4 = 3
        VT_R4 = 4
        VT_R8 = 5
        VT_CY = 6
        VT_DATE = 7
        VT_BSTR = 8
        VT_DISPATCH = 9
        VT_ERROR = 10
        VT_BOOL = 11
```

```
      VT_VARIANT = 12
      VT_UNKNOWN = 13
      VT_DECIMAL = 14
      VT_I1 = 16
      VT_UI1 = 17
      VT_UI2 = 18
      VT_UI4 = 19
      VT_I8 = 20
      VT_UI8 = 21
      VT_INT = 22
      VT_UINT = 23
      VT_VOID = 24
      VT_HRESULT = 25
      VT_PTR = 26
      VT_SAFEARRAY = 27
      VT_CARRAY = 28
      VT_USERDEFINED = 29
      VT_LPSTR = 30
      VT_LPWSTR = 31
      VT_RECORD = 36
      VT_FILETIME = 64
      VT_BLOB = 65
      VT_STREAM = 66
      VT_STORAGE = 67
      VT_STREAMED_OBJECT = 68
      VT_STORED_OBJECT = 69
      VT_BLOB_OBJECT = 70
      VT_CF = 71
      VT_CLSID = 72
      VT_VECTOR = 4096
      VT_ARRAY = 8192
      VT_BYREF = 16384
End Enum
```

Hierarchy: System.Object→ System.ValueType→ System.Enum(System.IComparable, System.IFormattable, System.IConvertible)→ VarEnum

IExpando   Interface

System.Runtime.InteropServices.Expando (mscorlib.dll)

This interface indicates a type whose members can be removed or added. The members are represented as System.Reflection.MemberInfo objects.

```
Public Interface IExpando : Implements System.Reflection.IReflect
' Public Instance Methods
   Public Function AddField(ByVal name As String) As FieldInfo
   Public Function AddMethod(ByVal name As String, ByVal method As Delegate) As MethodInfo
   Public Function AddProperty(ByVal name As String) As PropertyInfo
   Public Sub RemoveMember(ByVal m As System.Reflection.MemberInfo)
End Interface
```

CHAPTER 16

System.Runtime.Serialization

The act of serialization transforms an object (and all of its associated objects and/or data elements) into a stream of bytes, suitable for storage or transmission across a network. The reverse of this act, called deserialization, is to take the same stream of bytes and reconstitute the objects exactly as they were at the time of serialization.

This act, which sounds simple in theory, encompasses a number of points that must be addressed. For starters, the serialization libraries must provide complete reference semantics—that is, if an object holds two references to other objects, both of which happen to point to the same object, then the serialization mechanism needs to keep that in place. Therefore, when the stream is deserialized, both references point to the same object again.

In addition, the actual format of the stream of bytes may be different from application to application. For example, for storage into a binary column in a database, the serialized representation must be as compact and succinct as possible—no "wasted" bytes. But if we want to send the serialized data over an HTTP link to a non-.NET process, then a binary format is entirely inappropriate, and an XML-based one is more useful.

The System.Runtime.Serialization namespace and its child namespace, System.Runtime.Serialization.Formatters (with its own two child namespaces, System.Runtime.Serialization.Formatters.Binary, and System.Runtime.Serialization.Formatters.Soap), directly addresses these needs. System.Runtime.Serialization contains the types necessary to perform the serialization of an object into a stream of bytes, using an alternative object (which implements the IFormatter interface) to actually format the bytes into either binary or XML form. While it is certainly feasible to write your own custom formatters, most .NET programmers have no real practical need to do so, since a binary format and an XML format cover most needs.

Serialization does not necessarily come for free, however—there are a few things a .NET programmer must do in order to take advantage of the Serialization mechanism. For starters, a type must be marked as serializable in order to be eligible for serialization; this requires adding the System.SerializableAttribute to the type's declaration. By default, when a type becomes Serializable, all nonshared fields within that type are transformed into bytes when serialized. If a field is itself nonSerializable, an exception is thrown; fields that wish to remain unserialized (that is, remain empty during the

397

serialization process) must be marked with the System.NonSerializedAttribute in the type declaration.

It is possible to take greater control over the serialization process by implementing the ISerializable interface and providing definitions for the methods declared there; however, most .NET programmers are generally satisfied with the default serialization behavior.

Figure 16-1 shows the types in this namespace.

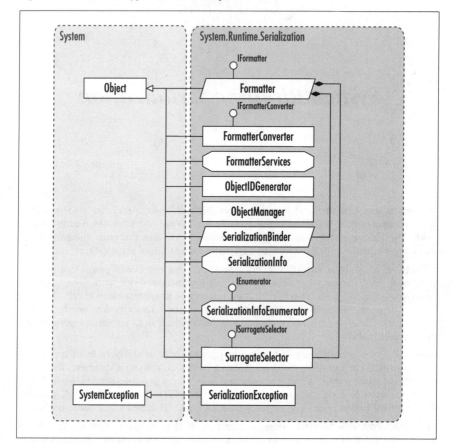

Figure 16–1. The System.Runtime.Serialization namespace

Formatter

MustInherit Class

System.Runtime.Serialization (mscorlib.dll)

serializable

This is the MustInherit base class for all runtime serialization formatters. It implements the IFormatter interface, which provides the properties that select the binder, surrogates, and streaming context of the formatter. This interface also implements the Serialize() and Deserialize() methods.

Additionally, the Formatter manages the queue of objects to serialize and provides a set of Write* methods for writing types to the stream.

```
Public MustInherit Class Formatter : Implements IFormatter
' Protected Constructors
   Protected Sub New()
' Protected Instance Fields
   protected m_idGenerator As ObjectIDGenerator
   protected m_objectQueue As Queue
' Public Instance Properties
   MustInherit Public Property Binder As SerializationBinder Implements  IFormatter.Binder
   MustInherit Public Property Context As StreamingContext Implements  IFormatter.Context
   MustInherit Public Property SurrogateSelector As ISurrogateSelector Implements  IFormatter.SurrogateSelector
' Public Instance Methods
   MustInherit Public Function Deserialize(ByVal serializationStream As System.IO.Stream) As Object _
      Implements  IFormatter.Deserialize
   MustInherit Public Sub Serialize(ByVal serializationStream As System.IO.Stream, ByVal graph As Object) _
      Implements  IFormatter.Serialize
' Protected Instance Methods
   Overridable Protected Function GetNext(ByRef objID As Long) As Object
   Overridable Protected Function Schedule(ByVal obj As Object) As Long
   MustInherit Protected Sub WriteArray(ByVal obj As Object, ByVal name As String, ByVal memberType As Type)
   MustInherit Protected Sub WriteBoolean(ByVal val As Boolean, ByVal name As String)
   MustInherit Protected Sub WriteByte(ByVal val As Byte, ByVal name As String)
   MustInherit Protected Sub WriteChar(ByVal val As Char, ByVal name As String)
   MustInherit Protected Sub WriteDateTime(ByVal val As Date, ByVal name As String)
   MustInherit Protected Sub WriteDecimal(ByVal val As Decimal, ByVal name As String)
   MustInherit Protected Sub WriteDouble(ByVal val As Double, ByVal name As String)
   MustInherit Protected Sub WriteInt16(ByVal val As Short, ByVal name As String)
   MustInherit Protected Sub WriteInt32(ByVal val As Integer, ByVal name As String)
   MustInherit Protected Sub WriteInt64(ByVal val As Long, ByVal name As String)
   Overridable Protected Sub WriteMember(ByVal memberName As String, ByVal data As Object)
   MustInherit Protected Sub WriteObjectRef(ByVal obj As Object, ByVal name As String, _
      ByVal memberType As Type)
   MustInherit Protected Sub WriteSByte(ByVal val As SByte, ByVal name As String)
   MustInherit Protected Sub WriteSingle(ByVal val As Single, ByVal name As String)
   MustInherit Protected Sub WriteTimeSpan(ByVal val As TimeSpan, ByVal name As String)
   MustInherit Protected Sub WriteUInt16(ByVal val As UInt16, ByVal name As String)
   MustInherit Protected Sub WriteUInt32(ByVal val As UInt32, ByVal name As String)
   MustInherit Protected Sub WriteUInt64(ByVal val As UInt64, ByVal name As String)
   MustInherit Protected Sub WriteValueType(ByVal obj As Object, ByVal name As String, _
      ByVal memberType As Type)
End Class
```

FormatterConverter   Class

System.Runtime.Serialization (mscorlib.dll)

This class is a basic implementation of the IFormatterConverter interface. It provides a formatter with a means to convert values to different base types. The generic Convert()
method converts a value into a specified type. The various To* methods convert values
into specific types.

```
Public Class FormatterConverter : Implements IFormatterConverter
' Public Constructors
   Public Sub New()
' Public Instance Methods
   Public Function Convert(ByVal value As Object, ByVal type As Type) As Object _
      Implements  IFormatterConverter.Convert
```

```
      Public Function Convert(ByVal value As Object, ByVal typeCode As TypeCode) As Object _
        Implements IFormatterConverter.Convert
      Public Function ToBoolean(ByVal value As Object) As Boolean Implements IFormatterConverter.ToBoolean
      Public Function ToByte(ByVal value As Object) As Byte Implements IFormatterConverter.ToByte
      Public Function ToChar(ByVal value As Object) As Char Implements IFormatterConverter.ToChar
      Public Function ToDateTime(ByVal value As Object) As Date Implements IFormatterConverter.ToDateTime
      Public Function ToDecimal(ByVal value As Object) As Decimal Implements IFormatterConverter.ToDecimal
      Public Function ToDouble(ByVal value As Object) As Double Implements IFormatterConverter.ToDouble
      Public Function ToInt16(ByVal value As Object) As Short Implements IFormatterConverter.ToInt16
      Public Function ToInt32(ByVal value As Object) As Integer Implements IFormatterConverter.ToInt32
      Public Function ToInt64(ByVal value As Object) As Long Implements IFormatterConverter.ToInt64
      Public Function ToSByte(ByVal value As Object) As SByte Implements IFormatterConverter.ToSByte
      Public Function ToSingle(ByVal value As Object) As Single Implements IFormatterConverter.ToSingle
      Public Function ToString(ByVal value As Object) As String Implements IFormatterConverter.ToString
      Public Function ToUInt16(ByVal value As Object) As UInt16 Implements IFormatterConverter.ToUInt16
      Public Function ToUInt32(ByVal value As Object) As UInt32 Implements IFormatterConverter.ToUInt32
      Public Function ToUInt64(ByVal value As Object) As UInt64 Implements IFormatterConverter.ToUInt64
End Class
```

FormatterServices   NotInheritable Class

System.Runtime.Serialization (mscorlib.dll)

The methods of this noninheritable class provide some background functionality to a
formatter when serializing and deserializing objects. For example, GetObjectData() creates
an array of System.Reflection.MemberInfo object data. GetSerializableMembers() retrieves all the
serializable members of a given class. PopulateObjectMembers() is the basic deserialization
method, using a MemberInfo array of member names and an array of corresponding data
values to repopulate a specified object.

```
Public NotInheritable Class FormatterServices
    ' Public Shared Methods
      Public Shared Function GetObjectData(ByVal obj As Object, ByVal members As System.Reflection.MemberInfo()) _
        As Object()
      Public Shared Function GetSerializableMembers(ByVal type As Type) As MemberInfo()
      Public Shared Function GetSerializableMembers(ByVal type As Type, ByVal context As StreamingContext) _
        As MemberInfo()
      Public Shared Function GetTypeFromAssembly(ByVal assem As System.Reflection.Assembly, _
        ByVal name As String) As Type
      Public Shared Function GetUninitializedObject(ByVal type As Type) As Object
      Public Shared Function PopulateObjectMembers(ByVal obj As Object,                    _
        ByVal members As System.Reflection.MemberInfo(), ByVal data As Object()) As Object
End Class
```

IDeserializationCallback   Interface

System.Runtime.Serialization (mscorlib.dll)

This interface implements a notification triggered when deserialization of an object is
completed. Specify callback functionality with the OnDeserialization() method. This class is
useful for restoring members that can be computed after deserialization, instead of serializing them and using more storage resources.

```
Public Interface IDeserializationCallback
    ' Public Instance Methods
      Public Sub OnDeserialization(ByVal sender As Object)
End Interface
```

Implemented By: System.Collections.Hashtable,
System.Collections.Specialized.NameObjectCollectionBase, System.Globalization.{ CompareInfo,
TextInfo}, System.Reflection.AssemblyName

IFormatter   Interface

System.Runtime.Serialization (mscorlib.dll)

This interface defines the basic serialization and deserialization functionality for a formatter. Its three properties determine the SerializationBinder, StreamingContext, and Surrogate-Selector of the formatter. It also defines the two basic methods of Serialize() and Deserialize().

```
Public Interface IFormatter
' Public Instance Properties
    Public Property Binder As SerializationBinder
    Public Property Context As StreamingContext
    Public Property SurrogateSelector As ISurrogateSelector
' Public Instance Methods
    Public Function Deserialize(ByVal serializationStream As System.IO.Stream) As Object
    Public Sub Serialize(ByVal serializationStream As System.IO.Stream, ByVal graph As Object)
End Interface
```

Implemented By: Formatter, System.Runtime.Serialization.Formatters.Binary.BinaryFormatter,
System.Runtime.Serialization.Formatters.Soap.SoapFormatter

IFormatterConverter   Interface

System.Runtime.Serialization (mscorlib.dll)

This interface defines the basic methods that convert serializable data into base class types. These conversion methods are used to parse the data contained in SerializationInfo instances.

```
Public Interface IFormatterConverter
' Public Instance Methods
    Public Function Convert(ByVal value As Object, ByVal type As Type) As Object
    Public Function Convert(ByVal value As Object, ByVal typeCode As TypeCode) As Object
    Public Function ToBoolean(ByVal value As Object) As Boolean
    Public Function ToByte(ByVal value As Object) As Byte
    Public Function ToChar(ByVal value As Object) As Char
    Public Function ToDateTime(ByVal value As Object) As Date
    Public Function ToDecimal(ByVal value As Object) As Decimal
    Public Function ToDouble(ByVal value As Object) As Double
    Public Function ToInt16(ByVal value As Object) As Short
    Public Function ToInt32(ByVal value As Object) As Integer
    Public Function ToInt64(ByVal value As Object) As Long
    Public Function ToSByte(ByVal value As Object) As SByte
    Public Function ToSingle(ByVal value As Object) As Single
    Public Function ToString(ByVal value As Object) As String
    Public Function ToUInt16(ByVal value As Object) As UInt16
    Public Function ToUInt32(ByVal value As Object) As UInt32
    Public Function ToUInt64(ByVal value As Object) As UInt64
End Interface
```

Implemented By: FormatterConverter

Passed To: SerializationInfo.SerializationInfo()

IObjectReference
Interface

System.Runtime.Serialization (mscorlib.dll)

This interface indicates that an object references another object. Use of this interface means that during deserialization, the object must be dereferenced during fixup so the "real" object is placed in the object graph.

Public Interface **IObjectReference**
' Public Instance Methods
   Public Function **GetRealObject**(ByVal context As StreamingContext) As Object
End Interface

ISerializable
Interface

System.Runtime.Serialization (mscorlib.dll)

Indicates that an object is serializable and provides serialization information to the formatter. This interface defines GetObjectData(), which specifies the member information that will be provided to a SerializationInfo instance in a specific StreamingContext. Classes that implement ISerializable must also provide a constructor that takes the same arguments as GetObjectData(). The constructor must use those arguments to deserialize an instance of the class.

Public Interface **ISerializable**
' Public Instance Methods
   Public Sub **GetObjectData**(ByVal info As SerializationInfo, ByVal context As StreamingContext)
End Interface

Implemented By: Multiple types

ISerializationSurrogate
Interface

System.Runtime.Serialization (mscorlib.dll)

Objects that implement this interface can be delegated to perform the serialization and deserialization of another object by providing customized methods for GetObjectData() and SetObjectData(). GetObjectData() gets the member information to create a SerializationInfo instance, while SetObjectData() uses information from a SerializationInfo instance to recreate an object.

Public Interface **ISerializationSurrogate**
' Public Instance Methods
   Public Sub **GetObjectData**(ByVal obj As Object, ByVal info As SerializationInfo, _
     ByVal context As StreamingContext)
   Public Function **SetObjectData**(ByVal obj As Object, ByVal info As SerializationInfo, _
     ByVal context As StreamingContext, ByVal selector As ISurrogateSelector) As Object
End Interface

Returned By: ISurrogateSelector.GetSurrogate(), SurrogateSelector.GetSurrogate()

Passed To: SurrogateSelector.AddSurrogate()

ISurrogateSelector
Interface

System.Runtime.Serialization (mscorlib.dll)

This interface is implemented by classes that help the formatter decide the appropriate surrogate to serialize or deserialize a particular type.

Public Interface **ISurrogateSelector**
' Public Instance Methods
   Public Sub **ChainSelector**(ByVal selector As ISurrogateSelector)

Public Function **GetNextSelector**() As ISurrogateSelector
Public Function **GetSurrogate**(ByVal type As Type, ByVal context As StreamingContext, _
   ByRef selector As ISurrogateSelector) As ISerializationSurrogate
End Interface

Implemented By: SurrogateSelector

Returned By: Formatter.SurrogateSelector,
System.Runtime.Serialization.Formatters.Binary.BinaryFormatter.SurrogateSelector,
System.Runtime.Serialization.Formatters.Soap.SoapFormatter.SurrogateSelector,
IFormatter.SurrogateSelector, SurrogateSelector.GetNextSelector()

Passed To: Formatter.SurrogateSelector,
System.Runtime.Serialization.Formatters.Binary.BinaryFormatter.{BinaryFormatter(), SurrogateSelector},
System.Runtime.Serialization.Formatters.Soap.SoapFormatter.{SoapFormatter(), SurrogateSelector},
IFormatter.SurrogateSelector, ISerializationSurrogate.SetObjectData(), ObjectManager.ObjectManager(),
SurrogateSelector.{ChainSelector(), GetSurrogate()}

ObjectIDGenerator Class

System.Runtime.Serialization (mscorlib.dll)   *serializable*

This class is used by formatters to identify objects within a serialized stream in order to track object references. The IDs are 64-bit numbers that are generated when an object is referenced or is referencing another. (An ID with a zero value is a null reference.) The GetId() method creates and returns an ID for an object if it does not already have one.

Public Class **ObjectIDGenerator**
  ' Public Constructors
    Public Sub **New**()
  ' Public Instance Methods
    Overridable Public Function **GetId**(ByVal obj As Object, ByRef firstTime As Boolean) As Long
    Overridable Public Function **HasId**(ByVal obj As Object, ByRef firstTime As Boolean) As Long
End Class

ObjectManager Class

System.Runtime.Serialization (mscorlib.dll)

This class is used by a formatter to manage object references during deserialization. Objects in the stream can refer to already deserialized objects. This causes the formatter to ask the ObjectManager to complete the reference after the deserialization is completed (i.e., on "fixup").

Public Class **ObjectManager**
  ' Public Constructors
    Public Sub **New**(ByVal selector As ISurrogateSelector, ByVal context As StreamingContext)
  ' Public Instance Methods
    Overridable Public Sub **DoFixups**()
    Overridable Public Function **GetObject**(ByVal objectID As Long) As Object
    Overridable Public Sub **RaiseDeserializationEvent**()
    Overridable Public Sub **RecordArrayElementFixup**(ByVal arrayToBeFixed As Long, ByVal indices As Integer(), _
      ByVal objectRequired As Long)
    Overridable Public Sub **RecordArrayElementFixup**(ByVal arrayToBeFixed As Long, ByVal index As Integer, _
      ByVal objectRequired As Long)
    Overridable Public Sub **RecordDelayedFixup**(ByVal objectToBeFixed As Long, ByVal memberName As String, _
      ByVal objectRequired As Long)
    Overridable Public Sub **RecordFixup**(ByVal objectToBeFixed As Long, _
      ByVal member As System.Reflection.MemberInfo, ByVal objectRequired As Long)

Overridable Public Sub **RegisterObject**(ByVal obj As Object, ByVal objectID As Long)
  Public Sub **RegisterObject**(ByVal obj As Object, ByVal objectID As Long, ByVal info As SerializationInfo)
  Public Sub **RegisterObject**(ByVal obj As Object, ByVal objectID As Long, ByVal info As SerializationInfo, _
    ByVal idOfContainingObj As Long, ByVal member As System.Reflection.MemberInfo)
    Public Sub **RegisterObject**(ByVal obj As Object, ByVal objectID As Long, ByVal info As SerializationInfo, _
    ByVal idOfContainingObj As Long, ByVal member As System.Reflection.MemberInfo, ByVal arrayIndex As Integer())
End Class

SerializationBinder **MustInherit Class**

System.Runtime.Serialization (mscorlib.dll) *serializable*

This MustInherit base class provides a binder to a formatter that controls which classes
are loaded during deserialization according to assembly information.

Public MustInherit Class **SerializationBinder**
' *Protected Constructors*
  Protected Sub **New**()
' *Public Instance Methods*
  MustInherit Public Function **BindToType**(ByVal assemblyName As String, ByVal typeName As String) As Type
End Class

Returned By: Formatter.Binder,
System.Runtime.Serialization.Formatters.Binary.BinaryFormatter.Binder,
System.Runtime.Serialization.Formatters.Soap.SoapFormatter.Binder, IFormatter.Binder

Passed To: Formatter.Binder, System.Runtime.Serialization.Formatters.Binary.BinaryFormatter.Binder,
System.Runtime.Serialization.Formatters.Soap.SoapFormatter.Binder, IFormatter.Binder

SerializationEntry **Structure**

System.Runtime.Serialization (mscorlib.dll)

This class encapsulates the information used for a single member stored within SerializationInfo. This object stores the Name of the object, its Value, and the ObjectType. Serialization-
Entry instances are the elements returned via the SerializationInfoEnumerator.

Public Structure **SerializationEntry**
' *Public Instance Properties*
  Public ReadOnly Property **Name** As String
  Public ReadOnly Property **ObjectType** As Type
  Public ReadOnly Property **Value** As Object
End Structure

Hierarchy: System.Object→ System.ValueType→ SerializationEntry

Returned By: SerializationInfoEnumerator.Current

SerializationException **Class**

System.Runtime.Serialization (mscorlib.dll) *serializable*

This class contains the exceptions thrown on serialization and deserialization errors.

Public Class **SerializationException** : Inherits SystemException
' *Public Constructors*
  Public Sub **New**()
  Public Sub **New**(ByVal message As String)
  Public Sub **New**(ByVal message As String, ByVal innerException As Exception)

' Protected Constructors
  Protected Sub **New**(ByVal info As SerializationInfo, ByVal context As StreamingContext)
End Class

Hierarchy: System.Object→ System.Exception(ISerializable)→ System.SystemException→
SerializationException

SerializationInfo   NotInheritable Class

System.Runtime.Serialization (mscorlib.dll)

SerializationInfo objects are used by classes that customize serialization behavior. The data
required for each member is the name of the member, its type, and its value. Within a
class's ISerializable.GetObjectData() block, the AddValue() method is used to add member
data. Deserialization is defined within a deserialization constructor (see ISerializable). It is
specified by retrieving member data with GetValue(), or one of the many other Get*
methods, and assigning the data to the appropriate members.

Public NotInheritable Class **SerializationInfo**
' Public Constructors
  Public Sub **New**(ByVal type As Type, ByVal converter As IFormatterConverter)
' Public Instance Properties
  Public Property **AssemblyName** As String
  Public Property **FullTypeName** As String
  Public ReadOnly Property **MemberCount** As Integer
' Public Instance Methods
  Public Sub **AddValue**(ByVal name As String, ByVal value As Boolean)
  Public Sub **AddValue**(ByVal name As String, ByVal value As Byte)
  Public Sub **AddValue**(ByVal name As String, ByVal value As Char)
  Public Sub **AddValue**(ByVal name As String, ByVal value As Date)
  Public Sub **AddValue**(ByVal name As String, ByVal value As Decimal)
  Public Sub **AddValue**(ByVal name As String, ByVal value As Double)
  Public Sub **AddValue**(ByVal name As String, ByVal value As Short)
  Public Sub **AddValue**(ByVal name As String, ByVal value As Integer)
  Public Sub **AddValue**(ByVal name As String, ByVal value As Long)
  Public Sub **AddValue**(ByVal name As String, ByVal value As Object)
  Public Sub **AddValue**(ByVal name As String, ByVal value As Object, ByVal type As Type)
  Public Sub **AddValue**(ByVal name As String, ByVal value As SByte)
  Public Sub **AddValue**(ByVal name As String, ByVal value As Single)
  Public Sub **AddValue**(ByVal name As String, ByVal value As UInt16)
  Public Sub **AddValue**(ByVal name As String, ByVal value As UInt32)
  Public Sub **AddValue**(ByVal name As String, ByVal value As UInt64)
  Public Function **GetBoolean**(ByVal name As String) As Boolean
  Public Function **GetByte**(ByVal name As String) As Byte
  Public Function **GetChar**(ByVal name As String) As Char
  Public Function **GetDateTime**(ByVal name As String) As Date
  Public Function **GetDecimal**(ByVal name As String) As Decimal
  Public Function **GetDouble**(ByVal name As String) As Double
  Public Function **GetEnumerator**() As SerializationInfoEnumerator
  Public Function **GetInt16**(ByVal name As String) As Short
  Public Function **GetInt32**(ByVal name As String) As Integer
  Public Function **GetInt64**(ByVal name As String) As Long
  Public Function **GetSByte**(ByVal name As String) As SByte
  Public Function **GetSingle**(ByVal name As String) As Single
  Public Function **GetString**(ByVal name As String) As String
  Public Function **GetUInt16**(ByVal name As String) As UInt16
  Public Function **GetUInt32**(ByVal name As String) As UInt32

Sys.Runtime.Serialization

```
      Public Function GetUInt64(ByVal name As String) As UInt64
      Public Function GetValue(ByVal name As String, ByVal type As Type) As Object
      Public Sub SetType(ByVal type As Type)
   End Class
```

Passed To: Multiple types

SerializationInfoEnumerator   NotInheritable Class

System.Runtime.Serialization (mscorlib.dll)

This class provides an enumerator to iterate over the elements contained in the SerializationInfo. Each element is of type SerializationEntry.

```
Public NotInheritable Class SerializationInfoEnumerator : Implements IEnumerator
' Public Instance Properties
   Public ReadOnly Property Current As SerializationEntry
   Public ReadOnly Property Name As String
   Public ReadOnly Property ObjectType As Type
   Public ReadOnly Property Value As Object
' Public Instance Methods
   Public Function MoveNext() As Boolean Implements IEnumerator.MoveNext
   Public Sub Reset() Implements IEnumerator.Reset
End Class
```

Returned By: SerializationInfo.GetEnumerator()

StreamingContext   Structure

System.Runtime.Serialization (mscorlib.dll)   *serializable*

This class describes the source or destination of a serialized stream. The context can determine how classes are serialized and require special parsing during deserialization. The State property holds a value from StreamingContextStates that indicates the destination of object data during serialization and the source of data during deserialization. This could indicate that you are serializing data to a file, for example, or deserializing data that came from another process.

```
Public Structure StreamingContext
' Public Constructors
   Public Sub New(ByVal state As StreamingContextStates)
   Public Sub New(ByVal state As StreamingContextStates, ByVal additional As Object)
' Public Instance Properties
   Public ReadOnly Property Context As Object
   Public ReadOnly Property State As StreamingContextStates
' Public Instance Methods
   Overrides Public Function Equals(ByVal obj As Object) As Boolean
   Overrides Public Function GetHashCode() As Integer
End Structure
```

Hierarchy: System.Object→ System.ValueType→ StreamingContext

Returned By: Formatter.Context,
System.Runtime.Serialization.Formatters.Binary.BinaryFormatter.Context,
System.Runtime.Serialization.Formatters.Soap.SoapFormatter.Context, IFormatter.Context

Passed To: Multiple types

StreamingContextStates Enum

System.Runtime.Serialization (mscorlib.dll) *serializable, flag*

This enumeration contains values that describe types of streams that serialized data derives from or targets.

```
Public Enum StreamingContextStates
        CrossProcess = &H000000001
        CrossMachine = &H000000002
        File = &H000000004
        Persistence = &H000000008
        Remoting = &H000000010
        Other = &H000000020
        Clone = &H000000040
        CrossAppDomain = &H000000080
        All = &H0000000FF
End Enum
```

Hierarchy: System.Object→ System.ValueType→ System.Enum(System.IComparable, System.IFormattable, System.IConvertible)→ StreamingContextStates

Returned By: StreamingContext.State

Passed To: StreamingContext.StreamingContext()

SurrogateSelector Class

System.Runtime.Serialization (mscorlib.dll)

This class is the basic implementation of the ISurrogateSelector interface. A formatter uses this class to find the appropriate surrogate object to serialize or deserialize an object of a specific type, assembly, or context.

```
Public Class SurrogateSelector : Implements ISurrogateSelector
' Public Constructors
    Public Sub New()
' Public Instance Methods
    Overridable Public Sub AddSurrogate(ByVal type As Type, ByVal context As StreamingContext, _
        ByVal surrogate As ISerializationSurrogate)
    Overridable Public Sub ChainSelector(ByVal selector As ISurrogateSelector) _
        Implements ISurrogateSelector.ChainSelector
    Overridable Public Function GetNextSelector() As ISurrogateSelector _
        Implements ISurrogateSelector.GetNextSelector
    Overridable Public Function GetSurrogate(ByVal type As Type, ByVal context As StreamingContext, _
        ByRef selector As ISurrogateSelector) As ISerializationSurrogate Implements ISurrogateSelector.GetSurrogate
    Overridable Public Sub RemoveSurrogate(ByVal type As Type, ByVal context As StreamingContext)
End Class
```

CHAPTER 17

System.Runtime.Serialization.Formatters

This chapter covers the System.Runtime.Serialization.Formatters namespace, which contains a number of types that are used by serialization formatters. Figure 17-1 shows the types in this namespace. This chapter also features the BinaryFormatter and SoapFormatter, two formatters that live in their own namespace and rely on the types in the System.Runtime.Serialization.Formatters namespace.

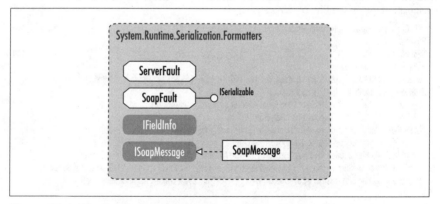

Figure 17-1. The System.Runtime.Serialization.Formatters namespace

BinaryFormatter   **NotInheritable Class**

System.Runtime.Serialization.Formatters.Binary (mscorlib.dll)

This formatter uses a binary format to serialize or deserialize a single object or an object graph.

```
Public NotInheritable Class BinaryFormatter : Implements System.Runtime.Remoting.Messaging.IRemotingFormatter, _
    System.Runtime.Serialization.IFormatter
' Public Constructors
    Public Sub New()
    Public Sub New(ByVal selector As System.Runtime.Serialization.ISurrogateSelector, _
       ByVal context As System.Runtime.Serialization.StreamingContext)
' Public Instance Properties
    Public Property AssemblyFormat As FormatterAssemblyStyle
    Public Property Binder As SerializationBinder Implements IFormatter.Binder
    Public Property Context As StreamingContext Implements IFormatter.Context
    Public Property SurrogateSelector As ISurrogateSelector Implements IFormatter.SurrogateSelector
    Public Property TypeFormat As FormatterTypeStyle
' Public Instance Methods
    Public Function Deserialize(ByVal serializationStream As System.IO.Stream) As Object _
       Implements IFormatter.Deserialize
    Public Function Deserialize(ByVal serializationStream As System.IO.Stream, _
       ByVal handler As System.Runtime.Remoting.Messaging.HeaderHandler) As Object _
       Implements IRemotingFormatter.Deserialize
    Public Function DeserializeMethodResponse(ByVal serializationStream As System.IO.Stream, _
       ByVal handler As System.Runtime.Remoting.Messaging.HeaderHandler, _
       ByVal methodCallMessage As System.Runtime.Remoting.Messaging.IMethodCallMessage) As Object
    Public Sub Serialize(ByVal serializationStream As System.IO.Stream, ByVal graph As Object) _
       Implements IFormatter.Serialize
    Public Sub Serialize(ByVal serializationStream As System.IO.Stream, ByVal graph As Object, _
       ByVal headers As System.Runtime.Remoting.Messaging.Header()) Implements IRemotingFormatter.Serialize
End Class
```

FormatterAssemblyStyle   **Enum**

System.Runtime.Serialization.Formatters (mscorlib.dll)   *serializable*

This enumeration controls how assembly names are serialized. Simple serializes assemblies using only the assembly name. The default, Full, includes the assembly name, its culture, public key token, and version.

```
Public Enum FormatterAssemblyStyle
    Simple = 0
    Full = 1
End Enum
```

Hierarchy: System.Object→ System.ValueType→ System.Enum(System.IComparable, System.IFormattable, System.IConvertible)→ FormatterAssemblyStyle

Returned By: System.Runtime.Serialization.Formatters.Binary.BinaryFormatter.AssemblyFormat, System.Runtime.Serialization.Formatters.Soap.SoapFormatter.AssemblyFormat

Passed To: System.Runtime.Serialization.Formatters.Binary.BinaryFormatter.AssemblyFormat, System.Runtime.Serialization.Formatters.Soap.SoapFormatter.AssemblyFormat

*Sys.Run.Ser.
Formatters*

FormatterTypeStyle   **Enum**

System.Runtime.Serialization.Formatters (mscorlib.dll)   *serializable*

This enumeration controls how type information is specified for members. TypesAlways specifies that type information be placed in the serialization stream for all object members. The default, TypesWhenNeeded, places type information in the stream for the following: object arrays, members of type System.Object, and nonprimitive value types (such as structs and enums) that implement the ISerializable interface. XsdString can be bitwise-ORed with another option to specify that strings are represented with the XSD format instead of the SOAP format.

```
Public Enum FormatterTypeStyle
    TypesWhenNeeded = 0
    TypesAlways = 1
    XsdString = 2
End Enum
```

Hierarchy: System.Object→ System.ValueType→ System.Enum(System.IComparable, System.IFormattable, System.IConvertible)→ FormatterTypeStyle

Returned By: System.Runtime.Serialization.Formatters.Binary.BinaryFormatter.TypeFormat, System.Runtime.Serialization.Formatters.Soap.SoapFormatter.TypeFormat

Passed To: System.Runtime.Serialization.Formatters.Binary.BinaryFormatter.TypeFormat, System.Runtime.Serialization.Formatters.Soap.SoapFormatter.TypeFormat

IFieldInfo   **Interface**

System.Runtime.Serialization.Formatters (mscorlib.dll)

This interface can expose the field names and types of serialized objects. It is used to supply parameter type information to the SoapFormatter when deserializing in SOAP RPC format.

```
Public Interface IFieldInfo
' Public Instance Properties
    Public Property FieldNames As String()
    Public Property FieldTypes As Type()
End Interface
```

ISoapMessage   **Interface**

System.Runtime.Serialization.Formatters (mscorlib.dll)

This type defines the interface used by SoapMessage. This interface is used to serialize and deserialize SOAP in RPC format.

```
Public Interface ISoapMessage
' Public Instance Properties
    Public Property Headers As Header()
    Public Property MethodName As String
    Public Property ParamNames As String()
    Public Property ParamTypes As Type()
    Public Property ParamValues As Object()
    Public Property XmlNameSpace As String
End Interface
```

Implemented By: SoapMessage

Returned By: System.Runtime.Serialization.Formatters.Soap.SoapFormatter.TopObject

Passed To: System.Runtime.Serialization.Formatters.Soap.SoapFormatter.TopObject

ServerFault   NotInheritable Class

System.Runtime.Serialization.Formatters (mscorlib.dll)   *serializable*

This class represents an error that was thrown from a remote server to the client. It is placed in the Detail section of a SoapFault object.

```
Public NotInheritable Class ServerFault
' Public Constructors
    Public Sub New(ByVal exceptionType As String, ByVal message As String, ByVal stackTrace As String)
' Public Instance Properties
    Public Property ExceptionMessage As String
    Public Property ExceptionType As String
    Public Property StackTrace As String
End Class
```

Passed To: SoapFault.SoapFault()

SoapFault   NotInheritable Class

System.Runtime.Serialization.Formatters (mscorlib.dll)   *serializable*

This class represents a SOAP fault.

```
Public NotInheritable Class SoapFault : Implements System.Runtime.Serialization.ISerializable
' Public Constructors
    Public Sub New()
    Public Sub New(ByVal faultCode As String, ByVal faultString As String, ByVal faultActor As String, _
        ByVal serverFault As ServerFault)
' Public Instance Properties
    Public Property Detail As Object
    Public Property FaultActor As String
    Public Property FaultCode As String
    Public Property FaultString As String
' Public Instance Methods
    Public Sub GetObjectData(ByVal info As System.Runtime.Serialization.SerializationInfo, _
        ByVal context As System.Runtime.Serialization.StreamingContext) Implements ISerializable.GetObjectData
End Class
```

SoapFormatter   NotInheritable Class

System.Runtime.Serialization.Formatters.Soap (system.runtime.serialization.formatters.soap.dll)

This formatter performs SOAP serialization or deserialization on a single object or an object graph.

```
Public NotInheritable Class SoapFormatter : Implements System.Runtime.Remoting.Messaging.IRemotingFormatter, _
        System.Runtime.Serialization.IFormatter
' Public Constructors
    Public Sub New()
    Public Sub New(ByVal selector As System.Runtime.Serialization.ISurrogateSelector, _
        ByVal context As System.Runtime.Serialization.StreamingContext)
' Public Instance Properties
    Public Property AssemblyFormat As FormatterAssemblyStyle
    Public Property Binder As SerializationBinder Implements IFormatter.Binder
    Public Property Context As StreamingContext Implements IFormatter.Context
```

Sys. Run. Ser.
Formatters

Public Property **SurrogateSelector** As ISurrogateSelector Implements IFormatter.SurrogateSelector
Public Property **TopObject** As ISoapMessage
Public Property **TypeFormat** As FormatterTypeStyle
' *Public Instance Methods*
Public Function **Deserialize**(ByVal serializationStream As System.IO.Stream) As Object _
   Implements IFormatter.Deserialize
Public Function **Deserialize**(ByVal serializationStream As System.IO.Stream, _
   ByVal handler As System.Runtime.Remoting.Messaging.HeaderHandler) As Object _
   Implements IRemotingFormatter.Deserialize
Public Sub **Serialize**(ByVal serializationStream As System.IO.Stream, ByVal graph As Object) _
   Implements IFormatter.Serialize
Public Sub **Serialize**(ByVal serializationStream As System.IO.Stream, ByVal graph As Object, _
   ByVal headers As System.Runtime.Remoting.Messaging.Header()) Implements IRemotingFormatter.Serialize
End Class

SoapMessage

Class

System.Runtime.Serialization.Formatters (mscorlib.dll)   *serializable*

This type encapsulates a message sent as part of a SOAP RPC (Remote Procedure Call).

Public Class **SoapMessage** : Implements ISoapMessage
' *Public Constructors*
Public Sub **New**()
' *Public Instance Properties*
Public Property **Headers** As Header() Implements ISoapMessage.Headers
Public Property **MethodName** As String Implements ISoapMessage.MethodName
Public Property **ParamNames** As String() Implements ISoapMessage.ParamNames
Public Property **ParamTypes** As Type() Implements ISoapMessage.ParamTypes
Public Property **ParamValues** As Object() Implements ISoapMessage.ParamValues
Public Property **XmlNameSpace** As String Implements ISoapMessage.XmlNameSpace
End Class

CHAPTER 18

System.Text

The **System.Text** namespace provides encoding and decoding capabilities for arrays of bytes and characters. These classes allow you to convert characters easily from different subsets of Unicode encodings, such as ASCII, UTF-8, and UTF-16. Additionally, a string-building class allows you to modify strings without creating intermediate string objects. Figure 18-1 shows the types in this namespace.

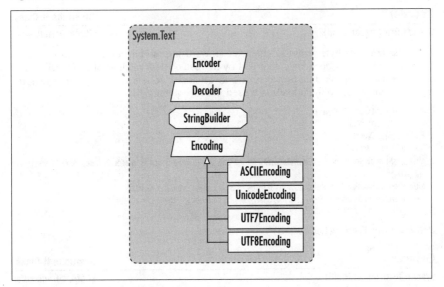

Figure 18–1. The System.Text namespace

ASCIIEncoding

Class

System.Text (mscorlib.dll)

ECMA, serializable

This class is a character encoding that encodes Unicode characters as 7-bit ASCII characters. ASCII uses the first 128 characters of a Unicode encoding.

```
Public Class ASCIIEncoding : Inherits Encoding
' Public Constructors
   Public Sub New()
' Public Instance Methods
   Overrides Public Function GetByteCount(ByVal chars As Char(), ByVal index As Integer, ByVal count As Integer) _
      As Integer
   Overrides Public Function GetByteCount(ByVal chars As String) As Integer
   Overrides Public Function GetBytes(ByVal chars As Char(), ByVal charIndex As Integer, ByVal charCount As Integer, _
      ByVal bytes As Byte(), ByVal byteIndex As Integer) As Integer
   Overrides Public Function GetBytes(ByVal chars As String, ByVal charIndex As Integer, ByVal charCount As Integer, _
      ByVal bytes As Byte(), ByVal byteIndex As Integer) As Integer
   Overrides Public Function GetCharCount(ByVal bytes As Byte(), ByVal index As Integer, ByVal count As Integer) _
      As Integer
   Overrides Public Function GetChars(ByVal bytes As Byte(), ByVal byteIndex As Integer, ByVal byteCount As Integer, _
      ByVal chars As Char(), ByVal charIndex As Integer) As Integer
   Overrides Public Function GetMaxByteCount(ByVal charCount As Integer) As Integer
   Overrides Public Function GetMaxCharCount(ByVal byteCount As Integer) As Integer
   Overrides Public Function GetString(ByVal bytes As Byte()) As String
   Overrides Public Function GetString(ByVal bytes As Byte(), ByVal byteIndex As Integer, ByVal byteCount As Integer) _
      As String
End Class
```

Hierarchy: System.Object→ Encoding→ ASCIIEncoding

Decoder

MustInherit Class

System.Text (mscorlib.dll)

ECMA, serializable

This class converts byte arrays to character arrays using the encoding class from which it was constructed (a decoder is returned by the GetDecoder() method of an Encoding subclass). Decoder saves its state between calls to GetChars(), so leftover bytes from previous input byte arrays are remembered and used in subsequent calls.

```
Public MustInherit Class Decoder
' Protected Constructors
   Protected Sub New()
' Public Instance Methods
   MustInherit Public Function GetCharCount(ByVal bytes As Byte(), ByVal index As Integer, ByVal count As Integer) _
      As Integer
   MustInherit Public Function GetChars(ByVal bytes As Byte(), ByVal byteIndex As Integer, _
      ByVal byteCount As Integer, ByVal chars As Char(), ByVal charIndex As Integer) As Integer
End Class
```

Returned By: Encoding.GetDecoder()

Encoder

MustInherit Class

System.Text (mscorlib.dll)

ECMA, serializable

Encoding.GetEncoder() returns an instance of this type, which converts character arrays to byte arrays using the encoding subclass from which it was constructed. This class exposes the GetBytes() method, which converts a sequence of character blocks into a sequence of byte blocks. Since Encoder maintains state between calls to GetBytes(), it can deal with partial sequences that occur at block boundaries.

The last argument to GetBytes() is a boolean that specifies whether the internal buffer is flushed after the method is called. If true, state information on the object is lost between blocks. If false (the default), the buffer is maintained. A call with flushing set to true is needed on the final call to Encoding.GetBytes() to close the byte array properly.

```
Public MustInherit Class Encoder
' Protected Constructors
   Protected Sub New()
' Public Instance Methods
   MustInherit Public Function GetByteCount(ByVal chars As Char(), ByVal index As Integer, ByVal count As Integer, _
      ByVal flush As Boolean)  As Integer
   MustInherit Public Function GetBytes(ByVal chars As Char(), ByVal charIndex As Integer,                  _
      ByVal charCount As Integer, ByVal bytes As Byte(), ByVal byteIndex As Integer, ByVal flush As Boolean) As Integer
End Class
```

Returned By: Encoding.GetEncoder()

Encoding
System.Text (mscorlib.dll)

MustInherit Class
ECMA, serializable

This class converts strings of Unicode characters to and from byte arrays. Derived classes implement specific encoding types. The GetBytes() method takes an array of characters and returns the corresponding array of bytes. The GetChars() method does the opposite conversion. GetByteCount() and GetCharCount() allow you to get the exact size of the encoding or decoding to size the output buffer appropriately.

The GetEncoder() and GetDecoder() methods create Encoder and Decoder instances that allow you to do encoding across sequential blocks in which partial byte codes may remain in the buffer.

```
Public MustInherit Class Encoding
' Protected Constructors
   Protected Sub New()
   Protected Sub New(ByVal codePage As Integer)
' Public Shared Properties
   Public Shared ReadOnly Property ASCII As Encoding
   Public Shared ReadOnly Property BigEndianUnicode As Encoding
   Public Shared ReadOnly Property Default As Encoding
   Public Shared ReadOnly Property Unicode As Encoding
   Public Shared ReadOnly Property UTF7 As Encoding
   Public Shared ReadOnly Property UTF8 As Encoding
' Public Instance Properties
   Overridable Public ReadOnly Property BodyName As String
   Overridable Public ReadOnly Property CodePage As Integer
   Overridable Public ReadOnly Property EncodingName As String
   Overridable Public ReadOnly Property HeaderName As String
   Overridable Public ReadOnly Property IsBrowserDisplay As Boolean
   Overridable Public ReadOnly Property IsBrowserSave As Boolean
   Overridable Public ReadOnly Property IsMailNewsDisplay As Boolean
   Overridable Public ReadOnly Property IsMailNewsSave As Boolean
   Overridable Public ReadOnly Property WebName As String
   Overridable Public ReadOnly Property WindowsCodePage As Integer
' Public Shared Methods
   Public Shared Function Convert(ByVal srcEncoding As Encoding, ByVal dstEncoding As Encoding, _
      ByVal bytes As Byte()) As Byte()
   Public Shared Function Convert(ByVal srcEncoding As Encoding, ByVal dstEncoding As Encoding, _
      ByVal bytes As Byte(), ByVal index As Integer, ByVal count As Integer) As Byte()
   Public Shared Function GetEncoding(ByVal codepage As Integer) As Encoding
```

Public Shared Function **GetEncoding**(ByVal name As String) As Encoding
' *Public Instance Methods*
Overrides Public Function **Equals**(ByVal value As Object) As Boolean
Overridable Public Function **GetByteCount**(ByVal chars As Char()) As Integer
MustInherit Public Function **GetByteCount**(ByVal chars As Char(), ByVal index As Integer, ByVal count As Integer) _
   As Integer
Overridable Public Function **GetByteCount**(ByVal s As String) As Integer
Overridable Public Function **GetBytes**(ByVal chars As Char()) As Byte()
Overridable Public Function **GetBytes**(ByVal chars As Char(), ByVal index As Integer, ByVal count As Integer) _
   As Byte()
Overridable Public Function **GetBytes**(ByVal s As String) As Byte()
MustInherit Public Function **GetBytes**(ByVal chars As Char(), ByVal charIndex As Integer, _
   ByVal charCount As Integer, ByVal bytes As Byte(), ByVal byteIndex As Integer) As Integer
Overridable Public Function **GetBytes**(ByVal s As String, ByVal charIndex As Integer, ByVal charCount As Integer, _
   ByVal bytes As Byte(), ByVal byteIndex As Integer) As Integer
Overridable Public Function **GetCharCount**(ByVal bytes As Byte()) As Integer
MustInherit Public Function **GetCharCount**(ByVal bytes As Byte(), ByVal index As Integer, ByVal count As Integer) _
   As Integer
Overridable Public Function **GetChars**(ByVal bytes As Byte()) As Char()
Overridable Public Function **GetChars**(ByVal bytes As Byte(), ByVal index As Integer, ByVal count As Integer) _
   As Char()
MustInherit Public Function **GetChars**(ByVal bytes As Byte(), ByVal byteIndex As Integer, _
   ByVal byteCount As Integer, ByVal chars As Char(), ByVal charIndex As Integer) As Integer
Overridable Public Function **GetDecoder**() As Decoder
Overridable Public Function **GetEncoder**() As Encoder
Overrides Public Function **GetHashCode**() As Integer
MustInherit Public Function **GetMaxByteCount**(ByVal charCount As Integer) As Integer
MustInherit Public Function **GetMaxCharCount**(ByVal byteCount As Integer) As Integer
Overridable Public Function **GetPreamble**() As Byte()
Overridable Public Function **GetString**(ByVal bytes As Byte()) As String
Overridable Public Function **GetString**(ByVal bytes As Byte(), ByVal index As Integer, ByVal count As Integer) _
   As String
End Class

Subclasses: ASCIIEncoding, UnicodeEncoding, UTF7Encoding, UTF8Encoding

Returned By: System.IO.StreamReader.CurrentEncoding, System.IO.TextWriter.Encoding,
System.Xml.XmlParserContext.Encoding, System.Xml.XmlTextReader.Encoding,
System.Xml.XmlValidatingReader.Encoding

Passed To: System.IO.BinaryReader.BinaryReader(), System.IO.BinaryWriter.BinaryWriter(),
System.IO.StreamReader.StreamReader(), System.IO.StreamWriter.StreamWriter(),
System.String.String(), System.Xml.XmlParserContext.{Encoding, XmlParserContext()},
System.Xml.XmlTextWriter.XmlTextWriter()

StringBuilder
NotInheritable Class

System.Text (mscorlib.dll)
ECMA, serializable

This String helper class enables in-place modification of a string without having to create
new string instances. Since strings are immutable, their values cannot change once set.
(Attempts to assign a new value to an existing string succeed, but at the expense of
destroying and re-creating the original string.) The StringBuilder constructor allows you to
set the size of the StringBuilder and specify the initial string it contains. The Insert() methods put new data (of varying types) into the StringBuilder at a specified position. Append()
adds data to the end of a StringBuilder. The ToString() method converts the StringBuilder into
a real string.

Public NotInheritable Class **StringBuilder**
' *Public Constructors*
  Public Sub **New**()
  Public Sub **New**(ByVal capacity As Integer)
  Public Sub **New**(ByVal capacity As Integer, ByVal maxCapacity As Integer)
  Public Sub **New**(ByVal value As String)
  Public Sub **New**(ByVal value As String, ByVal capacity As Integer)
  Public Sub **New**(ByVal value As String, ByVal startIndex As Integer, ByVal length As Integer, _
    ByVal capacity As Integer)
' *Public Instance Properties*
  Public Property **Capacity** As Integer
  Public Default Property **Chars** (ByVal index As Integer) As Char
  Public Property **Length** As Integer
  Public ReadOnly Property **MaxCapacity** As Integer
' *Public Instance Methods*
  Public Function **Append**(ByVal value As Boolean) As StringBuilder
  Public Function **Append**(ByVal value As Byte) As StringBuilder
  Public Function **Append**(ByVal value As Char) As StringBuilder
  Public Function **Append**(ByVal value As Char()) As StringBuilder
  Public Function **Append**(ByVal value As Char(), ByVal startIndex As Integer, ByVal charCount As Integer) _
    As StringBuilder
  Public Function **Append**(ByVal value As Char, ByVal repeatCount As Integer) As StringBuilder
  Public Function **Append**(ByVal value As Decimal) As StringBuilder
  Public Function **Append**(ByVal value As Double) As StringBuilder
  Public Function **Append**(ByVal value As Short) As StringBuilder
  Public Function **Append**(ByVal value As Integer) As StringBuilder
  Public Function **Append**(ByVal value As Long) As StringBuilder
  Public Function **Append**(ByVal value As Object) As StringBuilder
  Public Function **Append**(ByVal value As SByte) As StringBuilder
  Public Function **Append**(ByVal value As Single) As StringBuilder
  Public Function **Append**(ByVal value As String) As StringBuilder
  Public Function **Append**(ByVal value As String, ByVal startIndex As Integer, ByVal count As Integer) As StringBuilder
  Public Function **Append**(ByVal value As UInt16) As StringBuilder
  Public Function **Append**(ByVal value As UInt32) As StringBuilder
  Public Function **Append**(ByVal value As UInt64) As StringBuilder
  Public Function **AppendFormat**(ByVal provider As IFormatProvider, ByVal format As String, _
    ParamArray args As Object()) As StringBuilder
  Public Function **AppendFormat**(ByVal format As String, ByVal arg0 As Object) As StringBuilder
  Public Function **AppendFormat**(ByVal format As String, ParamArray args As Object()) As StringBuilder
  Public Function **AppendFormat**(ByVal format As String, ByVal arg0 As Object, ByVal arg1 As Object) _
    As StringBuilder
  Public Function **AppendFormat**(ByVal format As String, ByVal arg0 As Object, ByVal arg1 As Object, _
    ByVal arg2 As Object) As StringBuilder
  Public Function **EnsureCapacity**(ByVal capacity As Integer) As Integer
  Public Function **Equals**(ByVal sb As StringBuilder) As Boolean
  Public Function **Insert**(ByVal index As Integer, ByVal value As Boolean) As StringBuilder
  Public Function **Insert**(ByVal index As Integer, ByVal value As Byte) As StringBuilder
  Public Function **Insert**(ByVal index As Integer, ByVal value As Char) As StringBuilder
  Public Function **Insert**(ByVal index As Integer, ByVal value As Char()) As StringBuilder
  Public Function **Insert**(ByVal index As Integer, ByVal value As Char(), ByVal startIndex As Integer, _
    ByVal charCount As Integer) As StringBuilder
  Public Function **Insert**(ByVal index As Integer, ByVal value As Decimal) As StringBuilder
  Public Function **Insert**(ByVal index As Integer, ByVal value As Double) As StringBuilder
  Public Function **Insert**(ByVal index As Integer, ByVal value As Short) As StringBuilder
  Public Function **Insert**(ByVal index As Integer, ByVal value As Integer) As StringBuilder

Public Function **Insert**(ByVal index As Integer, ByVal value As Long) As StringBuilder
Public Function **Insert**(ByVal index As Integer, ByVal value As Object) As StringBuilder
Public Function **Insert**(ByVal index As Integer, ByVal value As SByte) As StringBuilder
Public Function **Insert**(ByVal index As Integer, ByVal value As Single) As StringBuilder
Public Function **Insert**(ByVal index As Integer, ByVal value As String) As StringBuilder
Public Function **Insert**(ByVal index As Integer, ByVal value As String, ByVal count As Integer) As StringBuilder
Public Function **Insert**(ByVal index As Integer, ByVal value As UInt16) As StringBuilder
Public Function **Insert**(ByVal index As Integer, ByVal value As UInt32) As StringBuilder
Public Function **Insert**(ByVal index As Integer, ByVal value As UInt64) As StringBuilder
Public Function **Remove**(ByVal startIndex As Integer, ByVal length As Integer) As StringBuilder
Public Function **Replace**(ByVal oldChar As Char, ByVal newChar As Char) As StringBuilder
Public Function **Replace**(ByVal oldChar As Char, ByVal newChar As Char, ByVal startIndex As Integer, _
  ByVal count As Integer) As StringBuilder
Public Function **Replace**(ByVal oldValue As String, ByVal newValue As String) As StringBuilder
Public Function **Replace**(ByVal oldValue As String, ByVal newValue As String, ByVal startIndex As Integer, _
  ByVal count As Integer) As StringBuilder
Overrides Public Function **ToString**() As String
Public Function **ToString**(ByVal startIndex As Integer, ByVal length As Integer) As String
End Class

Returned By: System.IO.StringWriter.GetStringBuilder()

Passed To: System.IO.StringWriter.StringWriter()

UnicodeEncoding   Class
System.Text (mscorlib.dll)   *ECMA, serializable*

This class encodes Unicode characters as UTF-16, two-byte characters. This class supports little-endian and big-endian encodings. With zero arguments, the overloaded constructor for this class uses little-endian byte order by default. The two-argument constructor can use a boolean true as the first argument to specify big-endian byte order. If set to true, the second boolean argument specifies the inclusion of the Unicode byte-order mark in the resulting string. A UnicodeEncoding can also be obtained from two Encoding properties. A little-endian encoding is returned by Encoding.Unicode. A big-endian encoding is returned by Encoding.BigEndianUnicode.

Public Class **UnicodeEncoding** : Inherits Encoding
' Public Constructors
  Public Sub **New**()
  Public Sub **New**(ByVal bigEndian As Boolean, ByVal byteOrderMark As Boolean)
' Public Shared Fields
  Public const **CharSize** As Integer   =2
' Public Instance Methods
  Overrides Public Function **Equals**(ByVal value As Object) As Boolean
  Overrides Public Function **GetByteCount**(ByVal chars As Char(), ByVal index As Integer, ByVal count As Integer) _
    As Integer
  Overrides Public Function **GetByteCount**(ByVal s As String) As Integer
  Overrides Public Function **GetBytes**(ByVal s As String) As Byte()
  Overrides Public Function **GetBytes**(ByVal chars As Char(), ByVal charIndex As Integer, ByVal charCount As Integer, _
    ByVal bytes As Byte(), ByVal byteIndex As Integer) As Integer
  Overrides Public Function **GetBytes**(ByVal s As String, ByVal charIndex As Integer, ByVal charCount As Integer, _
    ByVal bytes As Byte(), ByVal byteIndex As Integer) As Integer
  Overrides Public Function **GetCharCount**(ByVal bytes As Byte(), ByVal index As Integer, ByVal count As Integer) _
    As Integer
  Overrides Public Function **GetChars**(ByVal bytes As Byte(), ByVal byteIndex As Integer, ByVal byteCount As Integer, _
    ByVal chars As Char(), ByVal charIndex As Integer) As Integer

```
Overrides Public Function GetDecoder() As Decoder
Overrides Public Function GetHashCode() As Integer
Overrides Public Function GetMaxByteCount(ByVal charCount As Integer) As Integer
Overrides Public Function GetMaxCharCount(ByVal byteCount As Integer) As Integer
Overrides Public Function GetPreamble() As Byte()
End Class
```

Hierarchy: System.Object→ Encoding→ UnicodeEncoding

UTF7Encoding   Class

System.Text (mscorlib.dll)   *serializable*

This class encodes Unicode characters as UTF-7, 7-bit characters. UTF-7 is a Unicode Transformation of the US-ASCII character set, designed for safe use over common Internet mail and news gateways. RFC 2152, which defines UTF-7, specifies an optional set of characters in the character set, which may or may not be encoded, because they may interfere with mail-transfer header fields. The overloaded constructor has two forms that take this into account. With no arguments, the encoding object disallows the use of optional characters (such as exclamation points and dollar signs). With a single boolean argument set to true, these optional characters are allowed in the encoding.

```
Public Class UTF7Encoding : Inherits Encoding
' Public Constructors
   Public Sub New()
   Public Sub New(ByVal allowOptionals As Boolean)
' Public Instance Methods
   Overrides Public Function GetByteCount(ByVal chars As Char(), ByVal index As Integer, ByVal count As Integer) _
      As Integer
   Overrides Public Function GetBytes(ByVal chars As Char(), ByVal charIndex As Integer, ByVal charCount As Integer, _
      ByVal bytes As Byte(), ByVal byteIndex As Integer) As Integer
   Overrides Public Function GetCharCount(ByVal bytes As Byte(), ByVal index As Integer, ByVal count As Integer) _
      As Integer
   Overrides Public Function GetChars(ByVal bytes As Byte(), ByVal byteIndex As Integer, ByVal byteCount As Integer, _
      ByVal chars As Char(), ByVal charIndex As Integer) As Integer
   Overrides Public Function GetDecoder() As Decoder
   Overrides Public Function GetEncoder() As Encoder
   Overrides Public Function GetMaxByteCount(ByVal charCount As Integer) As Integer
   Overrides Public Function GetMaxCharCount(ByVal byteCount As Integer) As Integer
End Class
```

Hierarchy: System.Object→ Encoding→ UTF7Encoding

UTF8Encoding   Class

System.Text (mscorlib.dll)   *ECMA, serializable*

This class encodes Unicode characters as UTF-8, 8-bit characters. The overloaded constructor allows zero, one, or two boolean parameters. The first argument indicates whether the encoder should both emit the UTF-8 byte order mark code and recognize it. The second boolean argument specifies whether to throw an exception when invalid bytes are encountered.

```
Public Class UTF8Encoding : Inherits Encoding
' Public Constructors
   Public Sub New()
   Public Sub New(ByVal encoderShouldEmitUTF8Identifier As Boolean)
   Public Sub New(ByVal encoderShouldEmitUTF8Identifier As Boolean, ByVal throwOnInvalidBytes As Boolean)
```

' Public Instance Methods

Overrides Public Function **Equals**(ByVal value As Object) As Boolean

Overrides Public Function **GetByteCount**(ByVal chars As Char(), ByVal index As Integer, ByVal count As Integer) _
As Integer

Overrides Public Function **GetByteCount**(ByVal chars As String) As Integer

Overrides Public Function **GetBytes**(ByVal s As String) As Byte()

Overrides Public Function **GetBytes**(ByVal chars As Char(), ByVal charIndex As Integer, ByVal charCount As Integer, _
ByVal bytes As Byte(), ByVal byteIndex As Integer) As Integer

Overrides Public Function **GetBytes**(ByVal s As String, ByVal charIndex As Integer, ByVal charCount As Integer, _
ByVal bytes As Byte(), ByVal byteIndex As Integer) As Integer

Overrides Public Function **GetCharCount**(ByVal bytes As Byte(), ByVal index As Integer, ByVal count As Integer) _
As Integer

Overrides Public Function **GetChars**(ByVal bytes As Byte(), ByVal byteIndex As Integer, ByVal byteCount As Integer, _
ByVal chars As Char(), ByVal charIndex As Integer) As Integer

Overrides Public Function **GetDecoder**() As Decoder

Overrides Public Function **GetEncoder**() As Encoder

Overrides Public Function **GetHashCode**() As Integer

Overrides Public Function **GetMaxByteCount**(ByVal charCount As Integer) As Integer

Overrides Public Function **GetMaxCharCount**(ByVal byteCount As Integer) As Integer

Overrides Public Function **GetPreamble**() As Byte()

End Class

Hierarchy: System.Object→ Encoding→ UTF8Encoding

CHAPTER 19

System.Text.RegularExpressions

System.Text.RegularExpressions implements an object-oriented system for encapsulating regular expressions. The classes allow you to compile expressions and store matches that can be used with any .NET implementation regardless of the programming language. This namespace supports a regular expression syntax similar to Perl 5. Matches to the regular expression from an input string can be retrieved in fine granularity, allowing you to discern substring captures, groups, and multiple matches. Figure 19-1 shows the classes in this namespace.

Capture   Class

System.Text.RegularExpressions (system.dll)   *serializable*

This class represents a single result from a capturing group, which is a segment of a regular expression that is delineated, usually by parentheses. The parentheses signal .NET's regular expression engine to save that segment's result for later use. Capture objects compose the collection returned by Group.Captures. The Value property gets the captured substring. The Index property contains the starting position of the capture in the input string, while Length contains the length of the captured string.

```
Public Class Capture
' Public Instance Properties
   Public ReadOnly Property Index As Integer
   Public ReadOnly Property Length As Integer
   Public ReadOnly Property Value As String
' Public Instance Methods
   Overrides Public Function ToString() As String
End Class
```

Subclasses: Group

Returned By: CaptureCollection.this

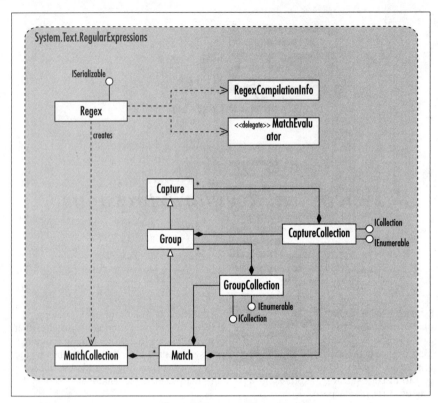

Figure 19–1. The System.Text.RegularExpressions namespace

CaptureCollection   **Class**

System.Text.RegularExpressions (system.dll)   *serializable*

This class contains a set of captures acquired by a single capturing group. A CaptureColl-ection is returned by Group.Captures. An integer indexer returns a single Capture object from this collection. The Count property gets the number of captures in the collection.

Public Class **CaptureCollection** : Implements ICollection, IEnumerable
' *Public Instance Properties*
   Public ReadOnly Property **Count** As Integer Implements ICollection.Count
   Public ReadOnly Property **IsReadOnly** As Boolean
   Public ReadOnly Property **IsSynchronized** As Boolean Implements ICollection.IsSynchronized
   Public Default ReadOnly Property **Item** (ByVal i As Integer) As Capture
   Public ReadOnly Property **SyncRoot** As Object Implements ICollection.SyncRoot
' *Public Instance Methods*
   Public Sub **CopyTo**(ByVal array As Array, ByVal arrayIndex As Integer) Implements ICollection.CopyTo
   Public Function **GetEnumerator**() As IEnumerator Implements IEnumerable.GetEnumerator
End Class

Returned By: Group.Captures

Group
Class

System.Text.RegularExpressions (system.dll)   *serializable*

This class contains a group of results from a capturing group in a regular expression. A capturing group can return zero or more results depending on the use of quantifiers or nested groupings of a subexpression. Captures returns a CaptureCollection composed of individual Capture objects. Captures can use an indexer to return single results from the CaptureCollection.

You can treat a Group as an instance of its parent class (Capture) to get quick access to the last captured substring (an instance of Group is equal to the last item in its Captures property).

```
Public Class Group : Inherits Capture
' Public Instance Properties
    Public ReadOnly Property Captures As CaptureCollection
    Public ReadOnly Property Success As Boolean
' Public Shared Methods
    Public Shared Function Synchronized(ByVal inner As Group) As Group
End Class
```

Hierarchy: System.Object→ Capture→ Group

Subclasses: Match

Returned By: GroupCollection.this

GroupCollection
Class

System.Text.RegularExpressions (system.dll)   *serializable*

This class is a collection of the captured groups in a regular expression. A GroupCollection is indexed by either a string with the name of the capture group, or with an integer number of the capture group as determined in the regular expression (give a name to a capture group by putting ?<name> immediately after the opening parenthesis). So, Match.Groups("name") would retrieve a capture from the subexpression (?<name>expr), and Match.Groups(1) would be the result from the first explicitly grouped subexpression. The entire regular expression is the zero-indexed group (an expression without any groupings is treated as a single group). A GroupCollection is returned by Match.Groups.

```
Public Class GroupCollection : Implements ICollection, IEnumerable
' Public Instance Properties
    Public ReadOnly Property Count As Integer Implements ICollection.Count
    Public ReadOnly Property IsReadOnly As Boolean
    Public ReadOnly Property IsSynchronized As Boolean Implements ICollection.IsSynchronized
    Public Default ReadOnly Property Item (ByVal groupnum As Integer) As Group
    Public Default ReadOnly Property Item (ByVal groupname As String) As Group
    Public ReadOnly Property SyncRoot As Object Implements ICollection.SyncRoot
' Public Instance Methods
    Public Sub CopyTo(ByVal array As Array, ByVal arrayIndex As Integer)  Implements ICollection.CopyTo
    Public Function GetEnumerator() As IEnumerator Implements IEnumerable.GetEnumerator
End Class
```

Returned By: Match.Groups

Match

Class

System.Text.RegularExpressions (system.dll)

serializable

This class is a single match result of a regular expression. As with Capture and Group, Match has no public constructor. It is returned by Regex.Match() or as a member of a MatchCollection returned by Regex.Matches(). A Match instance contains the groups that have been captured in a GroupCollection returned by Groups. A Match inherits from Group and is equivalent to the zero-indexed group in its GroupCollection (the same as Groups(0)).

The NextMatch() method finds the next match result in the search string, starting at the end of the previous match. This method disregards any zero-width assertions on the tail of an expression and begins explicitly after the position of the last character of the previous result (even an empty result).

The Result() method takes a replacement pattern and returns the resulting string based on the current match. A replacement pattern is an expression that uses the group replacement syntax, such as $1 or ${name}. Result() expands the replacement variables corresponding to the captured groups, within its current result, and returns the string.

```
Public Class Match : Inherits Group
' Public Shared Properties
   Public Shared ReadOnly Property Empty As Match
' Public Instance Properties
   Overridable Public ReadOnly Property Groups As GroupCollection
' Public Shared Methods
   Public Shared Function Synchronized(ByVal inner As Match) As Match
' Public Instance Methods
   Public Function NextMatch() As Match
   Overridable Public Function Result(ByVal replacement As String) As String
End Class
```

Hierarchy: System.Object→ Capture→ Group→ Match

Returned By: MatchCollection.this, Regex.Match()

Passed To: MatchEvaluator.{BeginInvoke(), Invoke()}

MatchCollection

Class

System.Text.RegularExpressions (system.dll)

serializable

This class is a collection of Match objects returned by Regex.Matches(). This collection contains each match that an expression finds in the search string. The Count property returns the number of matches found in the string.

```
Public Class MatchCollection : Implements ICollection, IEnumerable
' Public Instance Properties
   Public ReadOnly Property Count As Integer Implements ICollection.Count
   Public ReadOnly Property IsReadOnly As Boolean
   Public ReadOnly Property IsSynchronized As Boolean Implements ICollection.IsSynchronized
   Overridable Public Default ReadOnly Property Item (ByVal i As Integer) As Match
   Public ReadOnly Property SyncRoot As Object Implements ICollection.SyncRoot
' Public Instance Methods
   Public Sub CopyTo(ByVal array As Array, ByVal arrayIndex As Integer)  Implements  ICollection.CopyTo
   Public Function GetEnumerator() As IEnumerator Implements  IEnumerable.GetEnumerator
End Class
```

Returned By: Regex.Matches()

MatchEvaluator   Delegate

System.Text.RegularExpressions (system.dll)   *serializable*

This delegate can be called when a match is found during a replace operation. Several versions of the overloaded Regex.Replace() method take a MatchEvaluator as a parameter. Regex.Replace() walks through a search string looking for matches to a given expression and replaces each match using a specified replacement string. The MatchEvaluator delegate can be called on each match, getting passed the match result as a Match object.

Public Delegate Function **MatchEvaluator**(ByVal match As Match) As String

Passed To: Regex.Replace()

Regex   Class

System.Text.RegularExpressions (system.dll)   *serializable*

This class represents a regular expression. Use it to search for patterns in string data. It provides shared methods that search for a pattern without explicitly creating Regex instances as well as instance methods that allow you to interact with a Regex object.

The various shared methods employed by Regex take the input string to search for as the first argument and the regular expression pattern string as the second. This is equivalent to constructing a Regex instance with a pattern string, using it, and destroying it immediately. Most methods are overloaded as instance methods as well. These do not require a pattern argument, as this is provided with the constructor.

The Match() and Matches() methods search an input string for a single match or all matches. Their overloads are the same. The first argument is the input string. You can specify which position in the string the search should start at using a second integer parameter. Match() also lets you specify the length of substring to search after that position. IsMatch() works the same way as Match(), except that it returns a boolean indicating whether the string contains a match.

The Split() method acts like the System.String.Split() method. It uses the Regex pattern as a delimiter to split the input string into an array of substrings. (The delimiter is not included in the substrings.) You can provide a maximum number of substrings to return, in which case the last substring returned is the remainder of the input string. You can also specify the position to start in the input string and a RegexOptions parameter.

The Replace() method uses a replacement string to replace each pattern match in an input string. The replacement string can include regular characters and backreference variable constructs (e.g., $1 or ${name}). Replace() can iterate through every match found in the input string, or it can specify a maximum number of replacements to perform. Replace() can also take an argument specifying a MatchEvaluator delegate, which is called every time a match is found.

Two additional shared methods can transform strings used with regular expressions. Escape() converts a string containing regular expression metacharacters by replacing them with escaped equivalents (for example, ? would be changed to \?). The set of metacharacters converted is \, *, +, ?, |, {, [, (,), ^, $, ., #, and any whitespace. The Unescape() method replaces escaped characters within a string with their unescaped equivalents. Use Escape() and Unescape() when you need to use one of these metacharacters as a literal in a regular expression.

A set of instance methods for Regex provides information on the capturing groups contained in the expression. GetGroupNames() and GetGroupNumbers() each return an array containing the names of all the capture groups or numbers of all capture groups, respectively. The GroupNameFromNumber() and GroupNumberFromName() methods return the corresponding name or number from the argument given to them.

CompileToAssembly() allows you to create your own type for a regular expression object and save it to disk as an assembly. This is a shared method that takes a RegexCompilation-Info object and assembly information to build the type. The RegexCompilationInfo object contains the regular expression pattern and additional information needed for the compilation.

Public Class **Regex** : Implements System.Runtime.Serialization.ISerializable
' Public Constructors
   Public Sub **New**(ByVal pattern As String)
   Public Sub **New**(ByVal pattern As String, ByVal options As RegexOptions)
' Protected Constructors
   Protected Sub **New**()
' Public Instance Properties
   Public ReadOnly Property **Options** As RegexOptions
   Public ReadOnly Property **RightToLeft** As Boolean
' Public Shared Methods
   Public Shared Sub **CompileToAssembly**(ByVal regexinfos As RegexCompilationInfo(), _
     ByVal assemblyname As System.Reflection.AssemblyName)
   Public Shared Sub **CompileToAssembly**(ByVal regexinfos As RegexCompilationInfo(), _
     ByVal assemblyname As System.Reflection.AssemblyName,   _
     ByVal attributes As System.Reflection.Emit.CustomAttributeBuilder())
   Public Shared Sub **CompileToAssembly**(ByVal regexinfos As RegexCompilationInfo(),   _
     ByVal assemblyname As System.Reflection.AssemblyName,   _
     ByVal attributes As System.Reflection.Emit.CustomAttributeBuilder(), ByVal resourceFile As String)
   Public Shared Function **Escape**(ByVal str As String) As String
   Public Shared Function **IsMatch**(ByVal input As String, ByVal pattern As String) As Boolean
   Public Shared Function **IsMatch**(ByVal input As String, ByVal pattern As String, ByVal options As RegexOptions) _
     As Boolean
   Public Shared Function **Match**(ByVal input As String, ByVal pattern As String) As Match
   Public Shared Function **Match**(ByVal input As String, ByVal pattern As String, ByVal options As RegexOptions) _
     As Match
   Public Shared Function **Matches**(ByVal input As String, ByVal pattern As String) As MatchCollection
   Public Shared Function **Matches**(ByVal input As String, ByVal pattern As String, ByVal options As RegexOptions) _
     As MatchCollection
   Public Shared Function **Replace**(ByVal input As String, ByVal pattern As String, ByVal evaluator As MatchEvaluator) _
     As String
   Public Shared Function **Replace**(ByVal input As String, ByVal pattern As String, ByVal evaluator As MatchEvaluator, _
     ByVal options As RegexOptions) As String
   Public Shared Function **Replace**(ByVal input As String, ByVal pattern As String, ByVal replacement As String) _
     As String
   Public Shared Function **Replace**(ByVal input As String, ByVal pattern As String, ByVal replacement As String, _
     ByVal options As RegexOptions) As String
   Public Shared Function **Split**(ByVal input As String, ByVal pattern As String) As String()
   Public Shared Function **Split**(ByVal input As String, ByVal pattern As String, ByVal options As RegexOptions) _
     As String()
   Public Shared Function **Unescape**(ByVal str As String) As String
' Public Instance Methods
   Public Function **GetGroupNames**() As String()
   Public Function **GetGroupNumbers**() As Integer()
   Public Function **GroupNameFromNumber**(ByVal i As Integer) As String
   Public Function **GroupNumberFromName**(ByVal name As String) As Integer
   Public Function **IsMatch**(ByVal input As String) As Boolean
   Public Function **IsMatch**(ByVal input As String, ByVal startat As Integer) As Boolean

Public Function **Match**(ByVal input As String) As Match
Public Function **Match**(ByVal input As String, ByVal startat As Integer) As Match
Public Function **Match**(ByVal input As String, ByVal beginning As Integer, ByVal length As Integer) As Match
Public Function **Matches**(ByVal input As String) As MatchCollection
Public Function **Matches**(ByVal input As String, ByVal startat As Integer) As MatchCollection
Public Function **Replace**(ByVal input As String, ByVal evaluator As MatchEvaluator) As String
Public Function **Replace**(ByVal input As String, ByVal evaluator As MatchEvaluator, ByVal count As Integer) _
  As String
Public Function **Replace**(ByVal input As String, ByVal evaluator As MatchEvaluator, ByVal count As Integer, _
  ByVal startat As Integer) As String
Public Function **Replace**(ByVal input As String, ByVal replacement As String) As String
Public Function **Replace**(ByVal input As String, ByVal replacement As String, ByVal count As Integer) As String
Public Function **Replace**(ByVal input As String, ByVal replacement As String, ByVal count As Integer, _
  ByVal startat As Integer) As String
Public Function **Split**(ByVal input As String) As String()
Public Function **Split**(ByVal input As String, ByVal count As Integer) As String()
Public Function **Split**(ByVal input As String, ByVal count As Integer, ByVal startat As Integer) As String()
Overrides Public Function **ToString**() As String
' *Protected Instance Methods*
Overrides Protected Sub **Finalize**()
Protected Sub **InitializeReferences**()
Protected Function **UseOptionC**() As Boolean
Protected Function **UseOptionR**() As Boolean
End Class

Passed To: System.Net.WebPermission.{AddPermission(), WebPermission()}

RegexCompilationInfo   Class

System.Text.RegularExpressions (system.dll)   *serializable*

This class holds the information that is needed to compile a regular expression to an
assembly with Regex.CompileToAssembly(). The constructor takes five arguments, which
correspond to its available properties: the pattern string, the RegexOptions option set, the
name of the compiled type, the namespace for the type, and a boolean indicating if the
type is public (true) or private (false).

Public Class **RegexCompilationInfo**
' *Public Constructors*
  Public Sub **New**(ByVal pattern As String, ByVal options As RegexOptions, ByVal name As String, _
    ByVal fullnamespace As String, ByVal ispublic As Boolean)
' *Public Instance Properties*
  Public Property **IsPublic** As Boolean
  Public Property **Name** As String
  Public Property **Namespace** As String
  Public Property **Options** As RegexOptions
  Public Property **Pattern** As String
End Class

Passed To: Regex.CompileToAssembly()

RegexOptions   Enum

System.Text.RegularExpressions (system.dll)   *serializable, flag*

This enumeration contains various options that affect the behavior of pattern matching in various methods from the System.Text.RegularExpressions namespace. The values of this enumeration are passed to these methods as a bitwise-OR combination of the specified options.

```
Public Enum RegexOptions
    None = &H000000000
    IgnoreCase = &H000000001
    Multiline = &H000000002
    ExplicitCapture = &H000000004
    Compiled = &H000000008
    Singleline = &H000000010
    IgnorePatternWhitespace = &H000000020
    RightToLeft = &H000000040
    ECMAScript = &H000000100
End Enum
```

Hierarchy: System.Object→ System.ValueType→ System.Enum(System.IComparable, System.IFormattable, System.IConvertible)→ RegexOptions

Returned By: Regex.Options, RegexCompilationInfo.Options

Passed To: Regex.{IsMatch(), Match(), Matches(), Regex(), Replace(), Split()}, RegexCompilationInfo.{Options, RegexCompilationInfo()}

CHAPTER 20

System.Threading

A "thread" is an abstraction of the platform, providing the impression that the CPU is performing multiple tasks simultaneously; in essence, it offers to the programmer the ability to walk and chew gum at the same time. The .NET framework makes heavy use of threads throughout the system, both visibly and invisibly. The System.Threading namespace contains most of the baseline threading concepts, usable either directly or to help build higher-level constructs (as the .NET Framework Class Library frequently does).

The "thread" itself is sometimes referred to as a "lightweight process" (particularly within the Unix communities). This is because the thread, like the concept of a process, is simply an operating system (or, in the case of .NET, a CLR) abstraction. In the case of Win32 threads, the operating system is responsible for "switching" the necessary execution constructs (the registers and thread stack) on the CPU in order to execute the code on the thread, just as the OS does for multiple programs running simultaneously on the machine. The key difference between a process and a thread, however, is that each process gets its own inviolable memory space—its "process space"—that other processes cannot touch. All threads belong to a single process and share the same process space; therefore, threads can operate cooperatively on a single object. However, this is both an advantage and a disadvantage—if multiple threads can all access a single object, there arises the possibility that the threads will be acting concurrently against the object, leading to some interesting (and unrepeatable) results.

For example, one common problem in VB and MFC code was the inability to process user input while carrying out some other function; this was because the one (and only) thread used to process user input events (button clicks, menu selections, and so on) was also used to carry out the requests to the database, the calculation of results, the generation of pi to the millionth decimal place, and so on. Users could not negate actions ("Oh, shoot, I didn't mean to click that...."), because the user's UI actions—clicking a "Cancel" button, for example—wouldn't be processed until the non-UI action finished first. This would lead the user to believe that the program has "hung."

The first reaction might be to simply fire off every "action" from a UI event in its own thread; this would be a naive reaction at best, as a huge source of bugs and data corruption is more likely. Consider, for a moment, a simple UI that runs off to the database and performs a query when the user clicks a button. It would be tempting to simply spin the database query off in its own thread and update the UI if and when the database query completes.

The problems come up when the query returns—when do we put the results up? If the user has the ability to update the information (before the query results are returned), then does the new data overwrite the user's input? Or should the user's input overwrite the query results? What happens if the user clicks the button again? Should we fire off another query? Worse yet, what happens if the user has moved to a different part of the application? Should the UI "suddenly" flip back to the place from which the query was originated and update the values there? This would make it appear to the user that "some weird bug just took over" the program. But if the query silently updates the data, the user may wonder whether that query ever actually finished.

As is common with such capabilities, however, with power comes responsibility. Callous use of threads within an application can not only create these sorts of conundrums regarding UI design, but also lead to mysterious and inexplicable data corruption. Consider the simple expression x = x + 5. If x is a single object living in the heap, and two threads both simultaneously execute this code, one of several things can occur.

In the first case, the two threads are slightly ahead of or behind one another; the first thread obtains the value of x, adds 5, and stores that value back to x. The second thread, right behind it, does the same. x is incremented by 10. Consider the case, however, when both threads are in exactly the same place in the code. The first thread obtains the value of x (call it 10). The second thread gets switched in and loads the value of x (again, still 10). The first thread switches back in and increments its local value for x (which is 10, now 15). The second thread switches in and increments its local value for x (which is 10, now 15). The first thread stores its new local value for x back into x (15). The second thread switches in and stores its new local value for x (15). Both threads executed, yet the value of x grows by only 5, not 10, as should have happened.

For this reason, threads must often be held up in certain areas of code, in order to wait until another thread is finished. This is called "thread synchronization," sometimes colloquially referred to as "locks." It is the programmer's responsibility to ensure that any thread-sensitive code (such as the previous x=x+5 example) is properly thread-synchronized. Within C++ and VB 6, this could only be done by making use of Win32 synchronization objects such as events and critical sections; however, a simpler mechanism is available in the CLR.

Each object can have a corresponding "monitor" associated with it. This monitor serves as thread-synchronization primitive, since only one thread within the CLR can "own" the monitor. Synchronization is then achieved by forcing threads to wait to acquire the monitor on the object before being allowed to continue; this is very similar to the Win32 critical section. (This monitor is an instance of the Monitor type; see that type for more details.)

Any time locks are introduced into a system, however, two dangers occur: safety and liveness. *Safety* refers to the presence of the kind of data corruption discussed earlier—the lack of enough thread synchronization. *Liveness* is the actual time the threads spend executing, and often represents the opposite danger as safety (the presence of too much thread synchronization, particularly the danger of *deadlock*: two threads frozen forever, each waiting for a lock the other one already holds). An excellent discussion of these two concepts can be found in Doug Lea's book *Concurrent Programming in Java: Design Principles and Pattern, Second Edition* (Addison Wesley, 1999). (Despite Java code samples, 99% of his discussion pertains to threading in .NET as well.)

Frequently programmers wish to perform some sort of asynchronous operation. One approach is to simply create a Thread object and start it off. Unfortunately, this is also somewhat wasteful, since the cost of creating a thread and destroying it (when the thread has finished executing) is quite high. For this reason, it is often more performant to "borrow" an existing and unused thread—this is the purpose of the ThreadPool type, and one such pool already exists for use by the CLR runtime for processes such as the asynchronous execution of delegates (see System.Delegate for more details).

Figure 20-1 shows many of the classes in this namespace. Figure 20-2 shows the delegates, exceptions, and event arguments. Figure 20-3 shows a state diagram for threads.

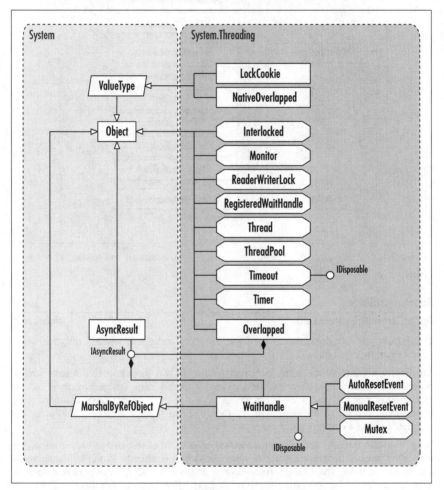

Figure 20–1. The System.Threading namespace

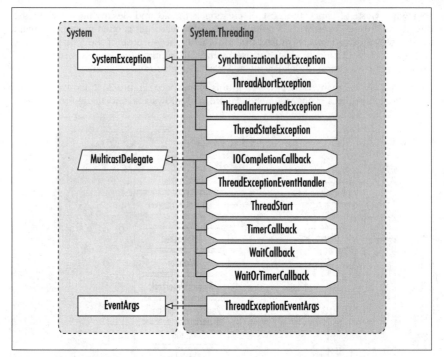

Figure 20-2. Delegates, exceptions, and event arguments in the System.Threading namespace

ApartmentState   Enum

System.Threading (mscorlib.dll)   *serializable*

This type is entirely unnecessary for "normal" .NET code; it is needed only for COM interoperability capability.

Apartments are a COM-threading construct. There are two threading apartments: *single-threaded* (STA) and *multithreaded* (MTA). Once a thread joins an apartment, it cannot join another one. If you want to create or access a COM object from a thread, that thread must belong to an apartment. Further, a given COM component may only be compatible with a certain apartment state.

What if an STA thread needs to call a method on a COM object that is only compatible with MTA threads? In that case, a different thread that is already in the MTA state must service the request. The COM *Service Control Manager* either creates a new thread or uses one allocated for servicing remote procedure calls to accomplish this.

Threads in an MTA apartment cannot directly access STA threads either. Instead, the STA thread contains a message sink, and the method is invoked when the thread in that apartment is free. .NET objects do away with this requirement; however, if some of the threads call COM objects, they must first join an apartment. The Thread class usually handles this automatically, but you can join an apartment directly by assigning a parameter from this enumeration to the Thread.ApartmentState property. Unknown indicates that the thread has not joined an apartment.

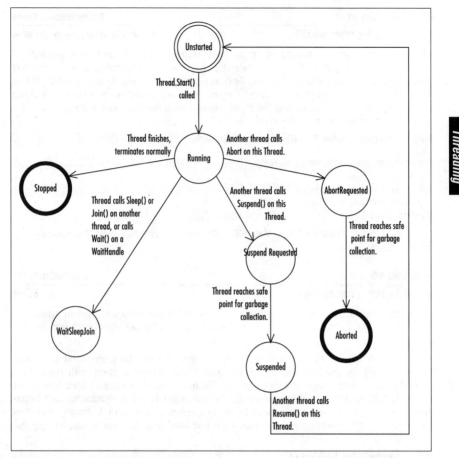

Figure 20–3. Thread state transitions

```
Public Enum ApartmentState
    STA = 0
    MTA = 1
    Unknown = 2
End Enum
```

Hierarchy: System.Object→ System.ValueType→ System.Enum(System.IComparable, System.IFormattable, System.IConvertible)→ ApartmentState

Returned By: Thread.ApartmentState

Passed To: Thread.ApartmentState

AutoResetEvent
NotInheritable Class

System.Threading (mscorlib.dll)
marshal by reference, disposable

This class presents a WaitHandle with two states: signaled and nonsignaled. If nonsignaled, waiting threads block; otherwise they continue executing. It is constructed with an initial signal value and can be Set() to signaled or Reset() to nonsignaled. When signaled, the AutoResetEvent automatically resets to nonsignaled once a single blocking thread has been released. Calling Set() with no blocking threads causes it to remain signaled until another thread waits on it.

```
Public NotInheritable Class AutoResetEvent : Inherits WaitHandle
' Public Constructors
    Public Sub New(ByVal initialState As Boolean)
' Public Instance Methods
    Public Function Reset() As Boolean
    Public Function Set() As Boolean
End Class
```

Hierarchy: System.Object→ System.MarshalByRefObject→ WaitHandle(System.IDisposable)→ AutoResetEvent

Interlocked
NotInheritable Class

System.Threading (mscorlib.dll)
ECMA

The shared members of this class provide thread safety for common built-in arithmetic operations, such as increasing and decreasing a variable by one, and exchanging variables.

If two threads increment the same variable, one thread could be interrupted after both have retrieved the initial value of the variable. If this happens, then both operations store the same value, meaning that the variable has been incremented once instead of twice. The Interlocked methods protect against this kind of error. Increment() and Decrement() increase and decrease a variable by one, respectively, and Exchange() switches two variables. CompareExchange() compares the first two variables and, if true, assigns the third value to the first variable.

```
Public NotInheritable Class Interlocked
' Public Shared Methods
    Public Shared Function CompareExchange(ByRef location1 As Integer, ByVal value As Integer, _
        ByVal comparand As Integer) As Integer
    Public Shared Function CompareExchange(ByRef location1 As Object, ByVal value As Object, _
        ByVal comparand As Object) As Object
    Public Shared Function CompareExchange(ByRef location1 As Single, ByVal value As Single, _
        ByVal comparand As Single) As Single
    Public Shared Function Decrement(ByRef location As Integer) As Integer
    Public Shared Function Decrement(ByRef location As Long) As Long
    Public Shared Function Exchange(ByRef location1 As Integer, ByVal value As Integer) As Integer
    Public Shared Function Exchange(ByRef location1 As Object, ByVal value As Object) As Object
    Public Shared Function Exchange(ByRef location1 As Single, ByVal value As Single) As Single
    Public Shared Function Increment(ByRef location As Integer) As Integer
    Public Shared Function Increment(ByRef location As Long) As Long
End Class
```

IOCompletionCallback Delegate

System.Threading (mscorlib.dll) *serializable*

This delegate is used to communicate with thread pools that are created using the Win32 API. This is a delegate to a method that will be called by an unmanaged process.

```
Public Delegate Sub IOCompletionCallback(ByVal errorCode As UInt32, ByVal numBytes As UInt32, _
    ByVal *pOVERLAP As NativeOverlapped)
```

Passed To: Overlapped.{Pack(), UnsafePack()}

LockCookie Structure

System.Threading (mscorlib.dll) *serializable*

This structure returns a LockCookie representing the type of lock (read or write) released. The same type of lock can be restored by calling ReaderWriterLock.RestoreLock().

```
Public Structure LockCookie
' No public or protected members
End Structure
```

Hierarchy: System.Object→ System.ValueType→ LockCookie

Returned By: ReaderWriterLock.{ReleaseLock(), UpgradeToWriterLock()}

Passed To: ReaderWriterLock.{DowngradeFromWriterLock(), RestoreLock()}

ManualResetEvent NotInheritable Class

System.Threading (mscorlib.dll) *marshal by reference, disposable*

This class is a WaitHandle with two states: signaled and nonsignaled. If nonsignaled, waiting threads block. If signaled, they continue executing. It is constructed with an initial signal value and can be Set() to signaled or Reset() to nonsignaled. Once signaled, you must manually (hence the name of this type) call Reset() to revert it to nonsignaled.

```
Public NotInheritable Class ManualResetEvent : Inherits WaitHandle
' Public Constructors
    Public Sub New(ByVal initialState As Boolean)
' Public Instance Methods
    Public Function Reset() As Boolean
    Public Function Set() As Boolean
End Class
```

Hierarchy: System.Object→ System.MarshalByRefObject→ WaitHandle(System.IDisposable)→ ManualResetEvent

Monitor NotInheritable Class

System.Threading (mscorlib.dll) *ECMA*

This class contains shared methods for thread communication and synchronization. The Enter() and Exit() methods allow you to obtain and release a lock on an object, respectively. If an object lock has already been obtained by another thread, Enter() blocks and resumes executing when the lock is released.

Various languages have the ability to silently emit calls on this type as language built-in primitives. VB.NET's SyncLock ... End SyncLock syntax translates into these two methods: the beginning of the lock block is transformed into a call to Enter(), and the close of the block calls Exit(). (In the presence of exceptions and return calls, the VB.NET compiler must ensure the release of the monitor regardless of how the code exits the SyncLock block.)

TryEnter() attempts to obtain an object lock, but it continues executing and returns false if unsuccessful. Wait() releases an object lock and causes the current thread to wait until another thread calls Pulse() or PulseAll() on the same object. Wait() must be executed from a synchronized block of code.

```
Public NotInheritable Class Monitor
' Public Shared Methods
   Public Shared Sub Enter(ByVal obj As Object)
   Public Shared Sub Exit(ByVal obj As Object)
   Public Shared Sub Pulse(ByVal obj As Object)
   Public Shared Sub PulseAll(ByVal obj As Object)
   Public Shared Function TryEnter(ByVal obj As Object) As Boolean
   Public Shared Function TryEnter(ByVal obj As Object, ByVal millisecondsTimeout As Integer) As Boolean
   Public Shared Function TryEnter(ByVal obj As Object, ByVal timeout As TimeSpan) As Boolean
   Public Shared Function Wait(ByVal obj As Object) As Boolean
   Public Shared Function Wait(ByVal obj As Object, ByVal millisecondsTimeout As Integer) As Boolean
   Public Shared Function Wait(ByVal obj As Object, ByVal millisecondsTimeout As Integer, _
      ByVal exitContext As Boolean) As Boolean
   Public Shared Function Wait(ByVal obj As Object, ByVal timeout As TimeSpan) As Boolean
   Public Shared Function Wait(ByVal obj As Object, ByVal timeout As TimeSpan, ByVal exitContext As Boolean) _
      As Boolean
End Class
```

Mutex   NotInheritable Class

System.Threading (mscorlib.dll)   *marshal by reference, disposable*

A Mutex is an implementation of a WaitHandle. ReleaseMutex() releases a lock on a WaitHandle. A thread that owns a Mutex lock can call any of the Wait() methods (defined in the parent class, WaitHandle) without blocking, but must then release the Mutex the same number of times as the Mutex was obtained.

```
Public NotInheritable Class Mutex : Inherits WaitHandle
' Public Constructors
   Public Sub New()
   Public Sub New(ByVal initiallyOwned As Boolean)
   Public Sub New(ByVal initiallyOwned As Boolean, ByVal name As String)
   Public Sub New(ByVal initiallyOwned As Boolean, ByVal name As String, ByRef createdNew As Boolean)
' Public Instance Methods
   Public Sub ReleaseMutex()
End Class
```

Hierarchy: System.Object→ System.MarshalByRefObject→ WaitHandle(System.IDisposable)→ Mutex

NativeOverlapped   Structure

System.Threading (mscorlib.dll)

This structure has the same layout as the Win32 OVERLAPPED structure, with extra reserved data at the end, which is provided for backward compatibility. Create a NativeOverlapped instance by calling Overlapped.Pack(). Each time an instance is created, it must be freed by calling the shared method Overlapped.Free() to avoid a memory leak.

Public Structure **NativeOverlapped**
' *Public Instance Fields*
   Public **EventHandle** As Integer
   Public **InternalHigh** As Integer
   Public **InternalLow** As Integer
   Public **OffsetHigh** As Integer
   Public **OffsetLow** As Integer
End Structure

Hierarchy: System.Object→ System.ValueType→ NativeOverlapped

Returned By: Overlapped.{Pack(), UnsafePack()}

Passed To: IOCompletionCallback.{BeginInvoke(), Invoke()}, Overlapped.{Free(), Unpack()}

Overlapped   Class

System.Threading (mscorlib.dll)

This class encapsulates the Win32 API OVERLAPPED structure. NativeOverlapped is needed to mimic the structure the API expects, but this class encapsulates the overlapped structure into a .NET class. You can create NativeOverlapped structures by calling Pack(), and create Overlapped objects with the shared Unpack() method. To avoid a memory leak, each NativeOverlapped that you create must also be freed by calling the sharedFree() method. Unpack() does *not* free the memory.

Public Class **Overlapped**
' *Public Constructors*
   Public Sub **New**()
   Public Sub **New**(ByVal offsetLo As Integer, ByVal offsetHi As Integer, ByVal hEvent As Integer, _
      ByVal ar As IAsyncResult)
' *Public Instance Properties*
   Public Property **AsyncResult** As IAsyncResult
   Public Property **EventHandle** As Integer
   Public Property **OffsetHigh** As Integer
   Public Property **OffsetLow** As Integer
End Class

ReaderWriterLock   NotInheritable Class

System.Threading (mscorlib.dll)

This class defines a lock that allows multiple readers, but only one writer. A thread can acquire a lock by calling AcquireReaderLock() or AcquireWriterLock(). ReleaseReaderLock() and ReleaseWriterLock() release the specific locks. Calling ReleaseReaderLock() on a writer lock releases both the writer lock and the reader lock. However, calling ReleaseWriterLock() on a reader lock throws a System.ApplicationException.

ReleaseLock() causes any lock to be released, but it returns a LockCookie, which represents the type of lock that RestoreLock() can use to obtain the same lock. UpgradeToWriterLock() upgrades a reader lock to a writer lock and returns a LockCookie representing the original reader lock. Pass that cookie to DowngradeFromWriterLock() to restore the original reader lock.

Public NotInheritable Class **ReaderWriterLock**
' *Public Constructors*
   Public Sub **New**()
' *Public Instance Properties*
   Public ReadOnly Property **IsReaderLockHeld** As Boolean

Public ReadOnly Property **IsWriterLockHeld** As Boolean
Public ReadOnly Property **WriterSeqNum** As Integer
' *Public Instance Methods*
  Public Sub **AcquireReaderLock**(ByVal millisecondsTimeout As Integer)
  Public Sub **AcquireReaderLock**(ByVal timeout As TimeSpan)
  Public Sub **AcquireWriterLock**(ByVal millisecondsTimeout As Integer)
  Public Sub **AcquireWriterLock**(ByVal timeout As TimeSpan)
  Public Function **AnyWritersSince**(ByVal seqNum As Integer) As Boolean
  Public Sub **DowngradeFromWriterLock**(ByRef lockCookie As LockCookie)
  Public Function **ReleaseLock**() As LockCookie
  Public Sub **ReleaseReaderLock**()
  Public Sub **ReleaseWriterLock**()
  Public Sub **RestoreLock**(ByRef lockCookie As LockCookie)
  Public Function **UpgradeToWriterLock**(ByVal millisecondsTimeout As Integer) As LockCookie
  Public Function **UpgradeToWriterLock**(ByVal timeout As TimeSpan) As LockCookie
End Class

RegisteredWaitHandle

NotInheritable Class

System.Threading (mscorlib.dll)

marshal by reference

ThreadPool.RegisterWaitForSingleObject() returns a RegisteredWaitHandle. To cancel a registered wait (either a new one or one that continuously executes), use Unregister().

Public NotInheritable Class **RegisteredWaitHandle** : Inherits MarshalByRefObject
' *Public Instance Methods*
  Public Function **Unregister**(ByVal waitObject As WaitHandle) As Boolean
' *Protected Instance Methods*
  Overrides Protected Sub **Finalize**()
End Class

Hierarchy: System.Object→ System.MarshalByRefObject→ RegisteredWaitHandle

Returned By: ThreadPool.{RegisterWaitForSingleObject(), UnsafeRegisterWaitForSingleObject()}

SynchronizationLockException

Class

System.Threading (mscorlib.dll)

ECMA, serializable

This exception is thrown when Monitor.Exit(), Monitor.Pulse(), Monitor.PulseAll(), or Monitor.Wait() is called from unsynchronized code.

Public Class **SynchronizationLockException** : Inherits SystemException
' *Public Constructors*
  Public Sub **New**()
  Public Sub **New**(ByVal message As String)
  Public Sub **New**(ByVal message As String, ByVal innerException As Exception)
' *Protected Constructors*
  Protected Sub **New**(ByVal info As System.Runtime.Serialization.SerializationInfo, _
    ByVal context As System.Runtime.Serialization.StreamingContext)
End Class

Hierarchy: System.Object→ System.Exception(System.Runtime.Serialization.ISerializable)→
System.SystemException→ SynchronizationLockException

Thread

System.Threading (mscorlib.dll) **ECMA**

Most interaction with the System.Threading namespace occurs via the Thread type. This type encapsulates most of the logic needed to control the way threads behave.

The most commonly used shared methods, usually referred to as *thread relative statics*, are methods and properties that refer to the currently executing thread. Sleep() causes the calling thread to sleep for a specified amount of time. If for some reason the thread gets woken up, a ThreadInterruptedException is thrown. Because this method can only be called by the current thread and not on a reference to a thread that may also be executing, the thread sleeps immediately and does not need to wait for a safe point for garbage collection as the Suspend() method does (see later in this entry).

GetData() retrieves data from a specified slot in *thread local storage*. To use this method, slots need to be initialized already (see later in this section). SetData() stores data in *thread local storage* to be retrieved using GetData(). AllocateDataSlot() and AllocateNamed-DataSlot() allocate a data slot for use with the previous two methods.

The Thread class also provides the shared property CurrentThread, which returns a reference to the Thread object for the currently running thread. The current thread can then access any of the following instance methods or properties on itself: Abort() causes a thread to abort, throwing a ThreadAbortException and executing any finally blocks. You may catch the ThreadAbortException, but it is automatically re-thrown unless you invoke ResetAbort(), which countermands the Abort() and lets the thread continue to live. Interrupt() interrupts a thread that is in the ThreadState.WaitSleepJoin state. If a thread is not in the ThreadState.WaitSleepJoin state, it is interrupted when it next attempts to enter that state (Join() causes the calling thread to enter that state). The calling thread only starts again once the referenced thread finishes executing and enters the ThreadState.Stopped state. Suspend() suspends a thread. The thread is suspended once it has reached a safe. The current thread can then access any of the following instance methods or properties on itself and point for garbage collection. Resume() resumes a thread that is in the suspended state. Threads in the suspended state are resumed regardless of how many times Suspend() was called. Start() tells a thread to start executing.

```
Public NotInheritable Class Thread
' Public Constructors
   Public Sub New(ByVal start As ThreadStart)
' Public Shared Properties
   Public Shared ReadOnly Property CurrentContext As Context
   Public Shared Property CurrentPrincipal As IPrincipal
   Public Shared ReadOnly Property CurrentThread As Thread
' Public Instance Properties
   Public Property ApartmentState As ApartmentState
   Public Property CurrentCulture As CultureInfo
   Public Property CurrentUICulture As CultureInfo
   Public ReadOnly Property IsAlive As Boolean
   Public Property IsBackground As Boolean
   Public ReadOnly Property IsThreadPoolThread As Boolean
   Public Property Name As String
   Public Property Priority As ThreadPriority
   Public ReadOnly Property ThreadState As ThreadState
' Public Shared Methods
   Public Shared Function AllocateDataSlot() As LocalDataStoreSlot
   Public Shared Function AllocateNamedDataSlot(ByVal name As String) As LocalDataStoreSlot
   Public Shared Sub FreeNamedDataSlot(ByVal name As String)
   Public Shared Function GetData(ByVal slot As LocalDataStoreSlot) As Object
```

```
    Public Shared Function GetDomain() As AppDomain
    Public Shared Function GetDomainID() As Integer
    Public Shared Function GetNamedDataSlot(ByVal name As String) As LocalDataStoreSlot
    Public Shared Sub ResetAbort()
    Public Shared Sub SetData(ByVal slot As LocalDataStoreSlot, ByVal data As Object)
    Public Shared Sub Sleep(ByVal millisecondsTimeout As Integer)
    Public Shared Sub Sleep(ByVal timeout As TimeSpan)
    Public Shared Sub SpinWait(ByVal iterations As Integer)
' Public Instance Methods
    Public Sub Abort()
    Public Sub Abort(ByVal stateInfo As Object)
    Public Sub Interrupt()
    Public Function Join(ByVal millisecondsTimeout As Integer) As Boolean
    Public Function Join(ByVal timeout As TimeSpan) As Boolean
    Public Sub Join()
    Public Sub Resume()
    Public Sub Start()
    Public Sub Suspend()
' Protected Instance Methods
    Overrides Protected Sub Finalize()
End Class
```

Returned By: System.Runtime.InteropServices.Marshal.GetThreadFromFiberCookie()

Passed To: System.Diagnostics.StackTrace.StackTrace()

ThreadAbortException
NotInheritable Class

System.Threading (mscorlib.dll)
ECMA, serializable

This exception is thrown on a running thread when Thread.Abort() is called. This exception is catchable, but it is automatically rethrown (see Thread for more details).

```
Public NotInheritable Class ThreadAbortException : Inherits SystemException
' Public Instance Properties
    Public ReadOnly Property ExceptionState As Object
End Class
```

Hierarchy: System.Object→ System.Exception(System.Runtime.Serialization.ISerializable)→ System.SystemException→ ThreadAbortException

ThreadExceptionEventArgs
Class

System.Threading (system.dll)

This class represents the event arguments passed to a ThreadExceptionEventHandler. Exception contains the exception raised.

```
Public Class ThreadExceptionEventArgs : Inherits EventArgs
' Public Constructors
    Public Sub New(ByVal t As Exception)
' Public Instance Properties
    Public ReadOnly Property Exception As Exception
End Class
```

Hierarchy: System.Object→ System.EventArgs→ ThreadExceptionEventArgs

Passed To: ThreadExceptionEventHandler.{BeginInvoke(), Invoke()}

ThreadExceptionEventHandler   **Delegate**
System.Threading (system.dll)   *serializable*

This event handler allows an event to be raised whenever a thread exception occurs. The System.Windows.Forms.Application.ThreadException property allows you to set one of these handlers, which takes the sender and ThreadExceptionEventArgs as arguments. The ThreadExceptionEventArgs object contains the exception raised.

```
Public Delegate Sub ThreadExceptionEventHandler(ByVal sender As Object, _
    ByVal e As ThreadExceptionEventArgs)
```

ThreadInterruptedException   **Class**
System.Threading (mscorlib.dll)   *serializable*

This exception is thrown on a thread in the ThreadState.WaitSleepJoin state when Thread.Interrupt() is called.

```
Public Class ThreadInterruptedException : Inherits SystemException
' Public Constructors
    Public Sub New()
    Public Sub New(ByVal message As String)
    Public Sub New(ByVal message As String, ByVal innerException As Exception)
' Protected Constructors
    Protected Sub New(ByVal info As System.Runtime.Serialization.SerializationInfo, _
        ByVal context As System.Runtime.Serialization.StreamingContext)
End Class
```

Hierarchy: System.Object→ System.Exception(System.Runtime.Serialization.ISerializable)→ System.SystemException→ ThreadInterruptedException

ThreadPool   **NotInheritable Class**
System.Threading (mscorlib.dll)

Creating or destroying a thread takes a fair amount of work. Therefore, if you pool threads, your program executes more efficiently since you get rid of the overhead associated with creating and destroying threads. There is one thread pool per process. To queue work to execute by this pool of *worker threads*, call any of the ThreadPool shared methods. QueueUserWorkItem() queues a delegate to execute when one of the pool's threads becomes free. RegisterWaitForSingleObject() takes a WaitHandle and executes the specified method either when the WaitHandle is in the signaled state or when a time-out occurs. BindHandle() and UnsafeQueueUserWorkItem() are provided for compatibility with the Win32 API.

```
Public NotInheritable Class ThreadPool
' Public Shared Methods
    Public Shared Function BindHandle(ByVal osHandle As IntPtr) As Boolean
    Public Shared Sub GetAvailableThreads(ByRef workerThreads As Integer, _
        ByRef completionPortThreads As Integer)
    Public Shared Sub GetMaxThreads(ByRef workerThreads As Integer, ByRef completionPortThreads As Integer)
    Public Shared Function QueueUserWorkItem(ByVal callBack As WaitCallback) As Boolean
    Public Shared Function QueueUserWorkItem(ByVal callBack As WaitCallback, ByVal state As Object) As Boolean
    Public Shared Function RegisterWaitForSingleObject(ByVal waitObject As WaitHandle, _
        ByVal callBack As WaitOrTimerCallback, ByVal state As Object, ByVal millisecondsTimeOutInterval As Integer, _
        ByVal executeOnlyOnce As Boolean) As RegisteredWaitHandle
    Public Shared Function RegisterWaitForSingleObject(ByVal waitObject As WaitHandle, _
        ByVal callBack As WaitOrTimerCallback, ByVal state As Object, ByVal millisecondsTimeOutInterval As Long, _
        ByVal executeOnlyOnce As Boolean) As RegisteredWaitHandle
```

Public Shared Function **RegisterWaitForSingleObject**(ByVal waitObject As WaitHandle, _
ByVal callBack As WaitOrTimerCallback, ByVal state As Object, ByVal timeout As TimeSpan, _
ByVal executeOnlyOnce As Boolean) As RegisteredWaitHandle
Public Shared Function **RegisterWaitForSingleObject**(ByVal waitObject As WaitHandle, _
ByVal callBack As WaitOrTimerCallback, ByVal state As Object, ByVal millisecondsTimeOutInterval As UInt32, _
ByVal executeOnlyOnce As Boolean) As RegisteredWaitHandle
Public Shared Function **UnsafeQueueUserWorkItem**(ByVal callBack As WaitCallback, ByVal state As Object) _
As Boolean
Public Shared Function **UnsafeRegisterWaitForSingleObject**(ByVal waitObject As WaitHandle, _
ByVal callBack As WaitOrTimerCallback, ByVal state As Object, ByVal millisecondsTimeOutInterval As Integer, _
ByVal executeOnlyOnce As Boolean) As RegisteredWaitHandle
Public Shared Function **UnsafeRegisterWaitForSingleObject**(ByVal waitObject As WaitHandle, _
ByVal callBack As WaitOrTimerCallback, ByVal state As Object, ByVal millisecondsTimeOutInterval As Long, _
ByVal executeOnlyOnce As Boolean) As RegisteredWaitHandle
Public Shared Function **UnsafeRegisterWaitForSingleObject**(ByVal waitObject As WaitHandle, _
ByVal callBack As WaitOrTimerCallback, ByVal state As Object, ByVal timeout As TimeSpan, _
ByVal executeOnlyOnce As Boolean) As RegisteredWaitHandle
Public Shared Function **UnsafeRegisterWaitForSingleObject**(ByVal waitObject As WaitHandle, _
ByVal callBack As WaitOrTimerCallback, ByVal state As Object, ByVal millisecondsTimeOutInterval As UInt32, _
ByVal executeOnlyOnce As Boolean) As RegisteredWaitHandle
End Class

ThreadPriority   Enum

System.Threading (mscorlib.dll)   *ECMA, serializable*

This enumeration encapsulates the various thread priorities. Threads are scheduled to be executed based on their priority; they default to Normal priority. The runtime can also update thread priorities if a program window is moved between the foreground and background. This is done automatically when you create windowed applications.

Public Enum **ThreadPriority**
    Lowest = 0
    BelowNormal = 1
    Normal = 2
    AboveNormal = 3
    Highest = 4
End Enum

Hierarchy: System.Object→ System.ValueType→ System.Enum(System.IComparable, System.IFormattable, System.IConvertible)→ ThreadPriority

Returned By: Thread.Priority

Passed To: Thread.Priority

ThreadStart   Delegate

System.Threading (mscorlib.dll)   *ECMA, serializable*

This delegate specifies a method for a thread to start executing.

Public Delegate Sub **ThreadStart**()

Passed To: Thread.Thread()

ThreadState   Enum
System.Threading (mscorlib.dll)   *ECMA, serializable, flag*

This enumeration encapsulates the various states a thread may be in. A thread starts in the Unstarted state. Once the Thread.Start() method is called, a thread enters the Running state. If another thread calls Thread.Abort() at any time, the thread shifts into the AbortRequested state, and then into Aborted once the thread reaches a safe point for garbage collection.

If the running thread calls either the shared method Thread.Sleep(), any of the Wait() methods on a WaitHandle, or Thread.Join() on another thread, the executing thread enters the WaitSleepJoin state.

If another thread calls Thread.Interrupt() on a thread in the WaitSleepJoin state, the thread again enters the Running state. When another thread calls Thread.Suspend() on a thread, it enters the SuspendRequested state. Once a thread in the SuspendRequested state reaches a safe point for garbage collection, it enters the Suspended state. A thread then leaves the Suspended state and enters the running state when another thread calls Thread.Resume() on it. When a thread has finished running, it enters the Stopped state.

Once a thread has started, it cannot return to the Unstarted state. Similarly, once a thread has aborted or stopped, it cannot return to the Running state. This enumeration is marked with a <Flags()> attribute, which allows a thread to be in more than one state at a time. For example, if a thread is in the WaitSleepJoin and another thread calls Thread.Abort() on it, it will be in both the WaitSleepJoin and AbortRequested states at the same time.

```
Public Enum ThreadState
    Running = &H000000000
    StopRequested = &H000000001
    SuspendRequested = &H000000002
    Background = &H000000004
    Unstarted = &H000000008
    Stopped = &H000000010
    WaitSleepJoin = &H000000020
    Suspended = &H000000040
    AbortRequested = &H000000080
    Aborted = &H000000100
End Enum
```

Hierarchy: System.Object→ System.ValueType→ System.Enum(System.IComparable, System.IFormattable, System.IConvertible)→ ThreadState

Returned By: Thread.ThreadState

ThreadStateException   Class
System.Threading (mscorlib.dll)   *ECMA, serializable*

This exception is thrown when an invalid method is called on a thread. For example, once a thread has started, it cannot re-enter the ThreadState.Unstarted state. Therefore, an attempt to call Thread.Start() on that thread throws this exception.

```
Public Class ThreadStateException : Inherits SystemException
' Public Constructors
    Public Sub New()
    Public Sub New(ByVal message As String)
    Public Sub New(ByVal message As String, ByVal innerException As Exception)
' Protected Constructors
```

> Protected Sub **New**(ByVal info As System.Runtime.Serialization.SerializationInfo, _
>   ByVal context As System.Runtime.Serialization.StreamingContext)
> End Class

Hierarchy: System.Object→ System.Exception(System.Runtime.Serialization.ISerializable)→
System.SystemException→ ThreadStateException

Timeout
NotInheritable Class

System.Threading (mscorlib.dll)
ECMA

This class provides a sharedInfinite property, which is defined as −1 for use with methods that stop a thread's execution for a specific time period.

> Public NotInheritable Class **Timeout**
> ' *Public Shared Fields*
>   Public const **Infinite** As Integer
> End Class

=-1

Timer
NotInheritable Class

System.Threading (mscorlib.dll)
ECMA, marshal by reference, disposable

This class can execute actions on a periodic basis. Actions can be performed once or multiple times. The constructor takes a TimerCallback delegate, a state object, a due time, and a period. Both due time and period are measured in milliseconds. Use the state argument to hold state information between delegate calls, or pass in null if you don't have any state to maintain. After the timer is created, it begins counting down until due time has expired, and then it invokes the delegate. The period is the amount of time to wait between delegate invocations before resuming the countdown again.

If the period is zero, the timer executes only once. If either due time or period are negative (and not equal to Timeout.Infinite), the constructor fails, throwing an System.ArgumentOutOfRangeException. Change() changes the due time and period after the timer is created. Specify a due time of Timeout.Infinite to halt the timer. An Infinite period prevents the timer from being raised repeatedly.

> Public NotInheritable Class **Timer** : Inherits MarshalByRefObject : Implements IDisposable
> ' *Public Constructors*
>   Public Sub **New**(ByVal callback As TimerCallback, ByVal state As Object, ByVal dueTime As Integer, _
>   ByVal period As Integer)
>   Public Sub **New**(ByVal callback As TimerCallback, ByVal state As Object, ByVal dueTime As Long, _
>   ByVal period As Long)
>   Public Sub **New**(ByVal callback As TimerCallback, ByVal state As Object, ByVal dueTime As TimeSpan, _
>   ByVal period As TimeSpan)
>   Public Sub **New**(ByVal callback As TimerCallback, ByVal state As Object, ByVal dueTime As UInt32, _
>   ByVal period As UInt32)
> ' *Public Instance Methods*
>   Public Function **Change**(ByVal dueTime As Integer, ByVal period As Integer) As Boolean
>   Public Function **Change**(ByVal dueTime As Long, ByVal period As Long) As Boolean
>   Public Function **Change**(ByVal dueTime As TimeSpan, ByVal period As TimeSpan) As Boolean
>   Public Function **Change**(ByVal dueTime As UInt32, ByVal period As UInt32) As Boolean
>   Public Function **Dispose**(ByVal notifyObject As WaitHandle) As Boolean
>   Public Sub **Dispose**() Implements IDisposable.Dispose

```
' Protected Instance Methods
   Overrides Protected Sub Finalize()
End Class
```

Hierarchy: System.Object→ System.MarshalByRefObject→ Timer(System.IDisposable)

TimerCallback   Delegate

System.Threading (mscorlib.dll)   *ECMA, serializable*

Use this delegate with Timer.

```
Public Delegate Sub TimerCallback(ByVal state As Object)
```

Passed To: Timer.Timer()

WaitCallback   Delegate

System.Threading (mscorlib.dll)   *serializable*

This delegate is for a ThreadPool work item.

```
Public Delegate Sub WaitCallback(ByVal state As Object)
```

Passed To: ThreadPool.{QueueUserWorkItem(), UnsafeQueueUserWorkItem()}

WaitHandle   MustInherit Class

System.Threading (mscorlib.dll)   *ECMA, marshal by reference, disposable*

This class encapsulates much of the logic for dealing with synchronization handles, which allow much more fine-grained synchronization control than simple thread locking. Once you have references to one or more WaitHandle subclasses, use the shared WaitOne() or WaitAny() methods to obtain a lock on any single handle or all of the handles, respectively. The WaitOne() instance method acquires the lock for a specific WaitHandle. If a thread blocks and cannot obtain the necessary locks, it enters the ThreadState.WaitSleepJoin state until the locks can be obtained.

```
Public MustInherit Class WaitHandle : Inherits MarshalByRefObject : Implements IDisposable
' Public Constructors
   Public Sub New()
' Public Shared Fields
   Public const WaitTimeout As Integer                                                  =258
' Protected Shared Fields
   protected Shared ReadOnly InvalidHandle As IntPtr                                      =-1
' Public Instance Properties
   Overridable Public Property Handle As IntPtr
' Public Shared Methods
   Public Shared Function WaitAll(ByVal waitHandles As WaitHandle()) As Boolean
   Public Shared Function WaitAll(ByVal waitHandles As WaitHandle(), ByVal millisecondsTimeout As Integer, _
       ByVal exitContext As Boolean) As Boolean
   Public Shared Function WaitAll(ByVal waitHandles As WaitHandle(), ByVal timeout As TimeSpan, _
       ByVal exitContext As Boolean) As Boolean
   Public Shared Function WaitAny(ByVal waitHandles As WaitHandle()) As Integer
   Public Shared Function WaitAny(ByVal waitHandles As WaitHandle(), ByVal millisecondsTimeout As Integer, _
       ByVal exitContext As Boolean) As Integer
   Public Shared Function WaitAny(ByVal waitHandles As WaitHandle(), ByVal timeout As TimeSpan, _
       ByVal exitContext As Boolean) As Integer
' Public Instance Methods
   Overridable Public Sub Close()
```

Overridable Public Function **WaitOne**() As Boolean
Overridable Public Function **WaitOne**(ByVal millisecondsTimeout As Integer, ByVal exitContext As Boolean) _
  As Boolean
Overridable Public Function **WaitOne**(ByVal timeout As TimeSpan, ByVal exitContext As Boolean) As Boolean
' *Protected Instance Methods*
Overridable Protected Sub **Dispose**(ByVal explicitDisposing As Boolean)
Overrides Protected Sub **Finalize**()
End Class

Hierarchy: System.Object→ System.MarshalByRefObject→ WaitHandle(System.IDisposable)

Subclasses: AutoResetEvent, ManualResetEvent, Mutex

Returned By: System.IAsyncResult.AsyncWaitHandle, System.IO.Stream.CreateWaitHandle()

Passed To: RegisteredWaitHandle.Unregister(), ThreadPool.{RegisterWaitForSingleObject(), UnsafeRegisterWaitForSingleObject()}, Timer.Dispose()

WaitOrTimerCallback   Delegate

System.Threading (mscorlib.dll)   *serializable*

This delegate is passed to a ThreadPool. If the wasSignaled parameter is true, then the delegate is invoked in response to a signal; otherwise, it is invoked because the handle timed out.

Public Delegate Sub **WaitOrTimerCallback**(ByVal state As Object, ByVal timedOut As Boolean)

Passed To: ThreadPool.{RegisterWaitForSingleObject(), UnsafeRegisterWaitForSingleObject()}

CHAPTER 21

System.Timers

The **System.Timers** namespace provides the **Timer** class, which periodically raises an **Elapsed** event. It is a server-based component designed to be used in a multithreaded environment and is thus more accurate than many other Windows-based timers. Unlike **System.Windows.Forms.Timer**, a server-based timer is not dependent on a user interface message pump. Figure 21-1 shows the class diagram for this namespace.

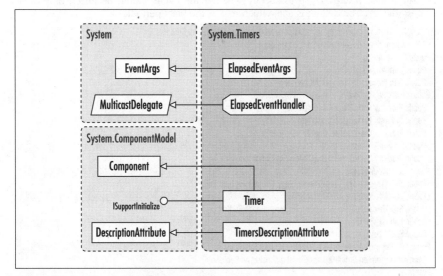

Figure 21-1. The System.Timers namespace

ElapsedEventArgs

Class

System.Timers (system.dll)

This class offers the arguments for an ElapsedEventHandler.

```
Public Class ElapsedEventArgs : Inherits EventArgs
' Public Instance Properties
    Public ReadOnly Property SignalTime As Date
End Class
```

Hierarchy: System.Object→ System.EventArgs→ ElapsedEventArgs

Passed To: ElapsedEventHandler.{BeginInvoke(), Invoke()}

ElapsedEventHandler

Delegate

System.Timers (system.dll)

serializable

This delegate is used for the Timer.Elapsed event.

```
Public Delegate Sub ElapsedEventHandler(ByVal sender As Object, ByVal e As ElapsedEventArgs)
```

Associated Events: Timer.Elapsed()

Timer

Class

System.Timers (system.dll)

marshal by reference, disposable

This class raises an event at regular intervals. It is a server-based timer, which provides much more accuracy than normal Windows timers and ensures that the event is raised at the proper time. To use a Timer, set the Elapsed event, the Interval property, and Enabled to true. Start() and Stop() provide shortcuts, which respectively assign true and false to Enabled. AutoReset allows you to specify whether the event should be raised only once or periodically. The default is true, which makes the Timer periodic.

```
Public Class Timer : Inherits System.ComponentModel.Component : Implements _
    System.ComponentModel.ISupportInitialize
' Public Constructors
    Public Sub New()
    Public Sub New(ByVal interval As Double)
' Public Instance Properties
    Public Property AutoReset As Boolean
    Public Property Enabled As Boolean
    Public Property Interval As Double
    Overrides Public Property Site As ISite
    Public Property SynchronizingObject As ISynchronizeInvoke
' Public Instance Methods
    Public Sub BeginInit() Implements ISupportInitialize.BeginInit
    Public Sub Close()
    Public Sub EndInit() Implements ISupportInitialize.EndInit
    Public Sub Start()
    Public Sub Stop()
' Protected Instance Methods
    Overrides Protected Sub Dispose(ByVal disposing As Boolean)
' Events
    Public Event Elapsed As ElapsedEventHandler
End Class
```

Hierarchy: System.Object→ System.MarshalByRefObject→
System.ComponentModel.Component(System.ComponentModel.IComponent, System.IDisposable)→
Timer(System.ComponentModel.ISupportInitialize)

TimersDescriptionAttribute   Class

System.Timers (system.dll)

This class provides a System.ComponentModel.DescriptionAttribute description for a given timer. It can be used by visual tools to display a helpful description of the component.

Public Class **TimersDescriptionAttribute** : Inherits System.ComponentModel.DescriptionAttribute
' Public Constructors
   Public Sub **New**(ByVal description As String)
' Public Instance Properties
   Overrides Public ReadOnly Property **Description** As String
End Class

Hierarchy: System.Object→ System.Attribute→ System.ComponentModel.DescriptionAttribute→ TimersDescriptionAttribute

Valid On: All

CHAPTER 22

System.Xml

The System.Xml namespace provides support for managing XML documents according to a set of standards defined by the World Wide Web Consortium (W3C). The classes implement objects that comply with the XML 1.0 specification and the Document Object Model (DOM) Core Level 1 and Core Level 2. Additional support is provided for XML Schemas (the System.Xml.Schema namespace), XSLT (System.Xml.Xsl), and XPath (System.Xml.XPath).

Figure 22-1 and Figure 22-2 show the types in this namespace. For more information on these technologies and their use, please consult *XML in a Nutshell*, by Elliote Rusty Harold and W. Scott Means (O'Reilly, 2001) or *Essential XML: Beyond Markup*, by Don Box (Addison Wesley, 2000).

EntityHandling   Enum

System.Xml (system.xml.dll)   *serializable*

This enumeration defines how entities are expanded. ExpandCharEntities expands only character entities, returning the entity text, while general entities are returned as nodes. ExpandEntities expands all entities; this is the default.

```
Public Enum EntityHandling
      ExpandEntities = 1
      ExpandCharEntities = 2
End Enum
```

Hierarchy: System.Object→ System.ValueType→ System.Enum(System.IComparable, System.IFormattable, System.IConvertible)→ EntityHandling

Returned By: XmlValidatingReader.EntityHandling

Passed To: XmlValidatingReader.EntityHandling

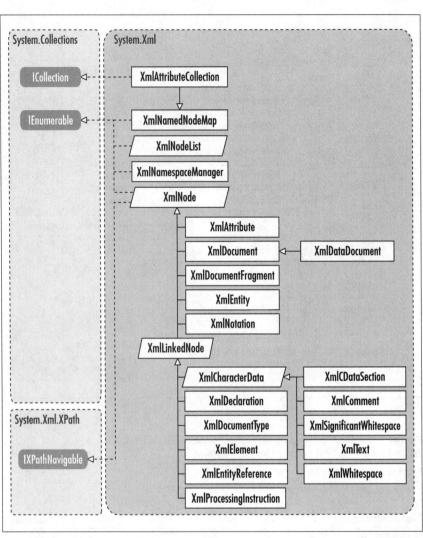

Figure 22–1. XmlNode and related types

Formatting

Enum

System.Xml (system.xml.dll)

ECMA, serializable

This enumeration specifies whether element content that is output from XmlTextWriter is indented. This is only of interest to human consumers of XML; if the destination of the XML document is another machine or software process, the additional whitespace adds only to the file size.

```
Public Enum Formatting
      None = 0
      Indented = 1
End Enum
```

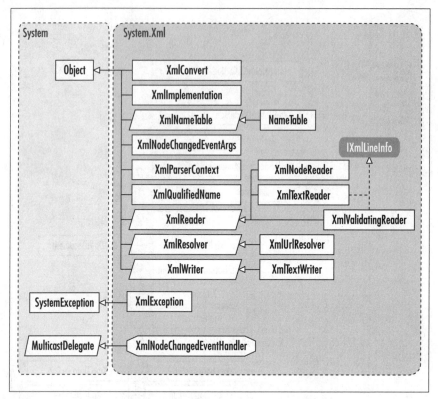

Figure 22–2. More types from System.Xml

Hierarchy: System.Object→ System.ValueType→ System.Enum(System.IComparable, System.IFormattable, System.IConvertible)→ Formatting

Returned By: XmlTextWriter.Formatting

Passed To: XmlTextWriter.Formatting

IHasXmlNode
Interface

System.Xml (system.xml.dll)

This interface is used to get the current or context node from an implementing class, such as XmlDocument or System.Xml.XPath.XPathNavigator. The GetNode() method returns the XmlNode that the navigator is currently positioned on.

```
Public Interface IHasXmlNode
' Public Instance Methods
   Public Function GetNode() As XmlNode
End Interface
```

IXmlLineInfo
Interface

System.Xml (system.xml.dll)

This interface allows XML reader classes (XmlTextReader and XmlValidatingReader) to return line and position information currently being read. If the class is reading data from a stream or other form of input, the HasLineInfo() method returns a boolean indicating if line information is provided.

```
Public Interface IXmlLineInfo
' Public Instance Properties
    Public ReadOnly Property LineNumber As Integer
    Public ReadOnly Property LinePosition As Integer
' Public Instance Methods
    Public Function HasLineInfo() As Boolean
End Interface
```

Implemented By: XmlTextReader, XmlValidatingReader

NameTable
Class

System.Xml (system.xml.dll)
ECMA

This class is a concrete implementation of the XmlNameTable type (described later in this chapter). It is entirely an optimization within the .NET XML stack; it provides a table of string objects for element and attribute names used in an XML document. The XML parser uses these string objects for efficient manipulation of repeated element and attribute names. See XmlNameTable for more discussion of its behavior and usage.

Normally .NET applications have no need to use this class directly. At most, a new instance is passed in blindly when constructing various XML-related types, such as XmlNamespaceManager.

```
Public Class NameTable : Inherits XmlNameTable
' Public Constructors
    Public Sub New()
' Public Instance Methods
    Overrides Public Function Add(ByVal key As Char(), ByVal start As Integer, ByVal len As Integer) As String
    Overrides Public Function Add(ByVal key As String) As String
    Overrides Public Function Get(ByVal key As Char(), ByVal start As Integer, ByVal len As Integer) As String
    Overrides Public Function Get(ByVal value As String) As String
End Class
```

Hierarchy: System.Object→ XmlNameTable→ NameTable

Passed To: System.Xml.Xsl.XsltContext.XsltContext()

ReadState
Enum

System.Xml (system.xml.dll)
ECMA, serializable

This enumeration identifies the current state of an XmlReader instance: closed (Closed); not yet started (Initial); an error is preventing further reading within the document (Error); the read is in process (Interactive); or the end of file (or stream, or wherever the XML is coming from) has been reached (EndOfFile).

```
Public Enum ReadState
    Initial = 0
    Interactive = 1
    Error = 2
    EndOfFile = 3
    Closed = 4
End Enum
```

Hierarchy: System.Object→ System.ValueType→ System.Enum(System.IComparable, System.IFormattable, System.IConvertible)→ ReadState

Returned By: XmlReader.ReadState

ValidationType   Enum

System.Xml (system.xml.dll)   *serializable*

This enumeration is used by XmlValidatingReader to determine the type of validation requested: DTD, schema, XDR, or no validation. If the type is set to Auto, the validation type is determined from the document; if there is a reference to a DTD, then DTD-style validation is performed. This is also true if the document contains references to XML Schema types, and so on. (See XmlValidatingReader for details.)

```
Public Enum ValidationType
    None = 0
    Auto = 1
    DTD = 2
    XDR = 3
    Schema = 4
End Enum
```

Hierarchy: System.Object→ System.ValueType→ System.Enum(System.IComparable, System.IFormattable, System.IConvertible)→ ValidationType

Returned By: XmlValidatingReader.ValidationType

Passed To: XmlValidatingReader.ValidationType

WhitespaceHandling   Enum

System.Xml (system.xml.dll)   *ECMA, serializable*

This enumeration contains settings that determine if whitespace is preserved in text sections of XML documents. This is important if the XML document contains whitespace-sensitive text nodes; for example, HTML is a whitespace-insensitive language.

```
Public Enum WhitespaceHandling
    All = 0
    Significant = 1
    None = 2
End Enum
```

Hierarchy: System.Object→ System.ValueType→ System.Enum(System.IComparable, System.IFormattable, System.IConvertible)→ WhitespaceHandling

Returned By: XmlTextReader.WhitespaceHandling

Passed To: XmlTextReader.WhitespaceHandling

WriteState   Enum

System.Xml (system.xml.dll)   *ECMA, serializable*

As its name implies, this enumeration specifies the state of an XmlWriter instance: closed (Closed), not yet started (Start), or in the process of writing some portion of the XML document (Attribute, Content, Element, or Prolog).

```
Public Enum WriteState
    Start = 0
    Prolog = 1
```

```
        Element = 2
        Attribute = 3
        Content = 4
        Closed = 5
End Enum
```

Hierarchy: System.Object→ System.ValueType→ System.Enum(System.IComparable, System.IFormattable, System.IConvertible)→ WriteState

Returned By: XmlWriter.WriteState

XmlAttribute   Class

System.Xml (system.xml.dll)

This class represents a single attribute of an element. The OwnerElement property returns the element node that contains this attribute. The Specified property indicates if the value was explicitly set or if a default value was used.

```
Public Class XmlAttribute : Inherits XmlNode
' Protected Constructors
   Protected Friend Sub New(ByVal prefix As String, ByVal localName As String, ByVal namespaceURI As String, _
      ByVal doc As XmlDocument)
' Public Instance Properties
   Overrides Public ReadOnly Property BaseURI As String
   Overrides Public Property InnerText As String
   Overrides Public Property InnerXml As String
   Overrides Public ReadOnly Property LocalName As String
   Overrides Public ReadOnly Property Name As String
   Overrides Public ReadOnly Property NamespaceURI As String
   Overrides Public ReadOnly Property NodeType As XmlNodeType
   Overrides Public ReadOnly Property OwnerDocument As XmlDocument
   Overridable Public ReadOnly Property OwnerElement As XmlElement
   Overrides Public ReadOnly Property ParentNode As XmlNode
   Overrides Public Property Prefix As String
   Overridable Public ReadOnly Property Specified As Boolean
   Overrides Public Property Value As String
' Public Instance Methods
   Overrides Public Function CloneNode(ByVal deep As Boolean) As XmlNode
   Overrides Public Sub WriteContentTo(ByVal w As XmlWriter)
   Overrides Public Sub WriteTo(ByVal w As XmlWriter)
End Class
```

Hierarchy: System.Object→ XmlNode(System.ICloneable, System.Collections.IEnumerable, System.Xml.XPath.IXPathNavigable)→ XmlAttribute

Returned By: XmlAttributeCollection.{Append(), InsertAfter(), InsertBefore(), this, Prepend(), Remove(), RemoveAt()}, XmlDocument.CreateAttribute(), XmlElement.{GetAttributeNode(), RemoveAttributeNode(), SetAttributeNode()}

Passed To: XmlAttributeCollection.{Append(), CopyTo(), InsertAfter(), InsertBefore(), Prepend(), Remove()}, XmlElement.{RemoveAttributeNode(), SetAttributeNode()}

XmlAttributeCollection

System.Xml (system.xml.dll)

This class defines a collection of attributes for an XmlElement node. An XmlAttributeCollection is returned by the XmlElement.Attributes property. The collection contains XmlAttribute objects that can be specified by either an object name or a zero-based index. Attribute nodes can be added and removed from the collection with methods, such as InsertBefore(), InsertAfter(), Prepend(), and RemoveAt().

```
Public Class XmlAttributeCollection : Inherits XmlNamedNodeMap : Implements ICollection
' Public Instance Properties
   Overridable Public Default ReadOnly Property ItemOf (ByVal localName As String) (ByVal namespaceURI As String _
      As XmlAttribute
   Overridable Public Default ReadOnly Property ItemOf (ByVal name As String) As XmlAttribute
   Overridable Public Default ReadOnly Property ItemOf (ByVal i As Integer) As XmlAttribute
' Public Instance Methods
   Overridable Public Function Append(ByVal node As XmlAttribute) As XmlAttribute
   Public Sub CopyTo(ByVal array As XmlAttribute(), ByVal index As Integer)
   Overridable Public Function InsertAfter(ByVal newNode As XmlAttribute, ByVal refNode As XmlAttribute) _
      As XmlAttribute
   Overridable Public Function InsertBefore(ByVal newNode As XmlAttribute, ByVal refNode As XmlAttribute) _
      As XmlAttribute
   Overridable Public Function Prepend(ByVal node As XmlAttribute) As XmlAttribute
   Overridable Public Function Remove(ByVal node As XmlAttribute) As XmlAttribute
   Overridable Public Sub RemoveAll()
   Overridable Public Function RemoveAt(ByVal i As Integer) As XmlAttribute
   Overrides Public Function SetNamedItem(ByVal node As XmlNode) As XmlNode
End Class
```

Hierarchy: System.Object→ XmlNamedNodeMap(System.Collections.IEnumerable)→
XmlAttributeCollection(System.Collections.ICollection)

Returned By: XmlNode.Attributes

XmlCDataSection

System.Xml (system.xml.dll)

This class represents a CDATA (character data) section node of a document. A CDATA section is element content that is unparsed, i.e., entities and markup are ignored.

```
Public Class XmlCDataSection : Inherits XmlCharacterData
' Protected Constructors
   Protected Friend Sub New(ByVal data As String, ByVal doc As XmlDocument)
' Public Instance Properties
   Overrides Public ReadOnly Property LocalName As String
   Overrides Public ReadOnly Property Name As String
   Overrides Public ReadOnly Property NodeType As XmlNodeType
' Public Instance Methods
   Overrides Public Function CloneNode(ByVal deep As Boolean) As XmlNode
   Overrides Public Sub WriteContentTo(ByVal w As XmlWriter)
   Overrides Public Sub WriteTo(ByVal w As XmlWriter)
End Class
```

Hierarchy: System.Object→ XmlNode(System.ICloneable, System.Collections.IEnumerable,
System.Xml.XPath.IXPathNavigable)→ XmlLinkedNode→ XmlCharacterData→ XmlCDataSection

Returned By: XmlDocument.CreateCDataSection()

XmlCharacterData

MustInherit Class

System.Xml (system.xml.dll)

This class is a MustInherit parent class for the character data node types: XmlCDataSec-tion, XmlComment, XmlSignificantWhitespace, XmlText, and XmlWhitespace. It defines methods for manipulating the text-based data of these nodes.

Public MustInherit Class **XmlCharacterData** : Inherits XmlLinkedNode
' *Protected Constructors*
  Protected Friend Sub **New**(ByVal data As String, ByVal doc As XmlDocument)
' *Public Instance Properties*
  Overridable Public Property **Data** As String
  Overrides Public Property **InnerText** As String
  Overridable Public ReadOnly Property **Length** As Integer
  Overrides Public Property **Value** As String
' *Public Instance Methods*
  Overridable Public Sub **AppendData**(ByVal strData As String)
  Overridable Public Sub **DeleteData**(ByVal offset As Integer, ByVal count As Integer)
  Overridable Public Sub **InsertData**(ByVal offset As Integer, ByVal strData As String)
  Overridable Public Sub **ReplaceData**(ByVal offset As Integer, ByVal count As Integer, ByVal strData As String)
  Overridable Public Function **Substring**(ByVal offset As Integer, ByVal count As Integer) As String
End Class

Hierarchy: System.Object→ XmlNode(System.ICloneable, System.Collections.IEnumerable, System.Xml.XPath.IXPathNavigable)→ XmlLinkedNode→ XmlCharacterData

Subclasses: XmlCDataSection, XmlComment, XmlSignificantWhitespace, XmlText, XmlWhitespace

XmlComment

Class

System.Xml (system.xml.dll)

This class represents an XmlComment node. An XML comment is contained within <!– and –> markup symbols and is not represented in the resulting XML Infoset tree.

Public Class **XmlComment** : Inherits XmlCharacterData
' *Protected Constructors*
  Protected Friend Sub **New**(ByVal comment As String, ByVal doc As XmlDocument)
' *Public Instance Properties*
  Overrides Public ReadOnly Property **LocalName** As String
  Overrides Public ReadOnly Property **Name** As String
  Overrides Public ReadOnly Property **NodeType** As XmlNodeType
' *Public Instance Methods*
  Overrides Public Function **CloneNode**(ByVal deep As Boolean) As XmlNode
  Overrides Public Sub **WriteContentTo**(ByVal w As XmlWriter)
  Overrides Public Sub **WriteTo**(ByVal w As XmlWriter)
End Class

Hierarchy: System.Object→ XmlNode(System.ICloneable, System.Collections.IEnumerable, System.Xml.XPath.IXPathNavigable)→ XmlLinkedNode→ XmlCharacterData→ XmlComment

Returned By: XmlDocument.CreateComment()

*System.
Xml*

XmlConvert
Class

System.Xml (system.xml.dll)
ECMA

This type is used to convert XML elements into other, non-XML types, such as CLR objects. In particular, it is used to convert XSD types into CLR types, for easy transformation of schema-valid XML documents into .NET objects and back again. It is also used within a variety of other areas, including ADO.NET (for automatic conversion of XML documents into relational tables and rows).

For the most part, .NET programmers use this type indirectly as part of the .NET Web Services stack or else directly in order to convert between XML documents and CLR objects (as part of a home-grown XML-to-RDBMS system, for example).

Note that although a constructor is provided, all methods of any interest are declared shared and therefore require no instance to use. In essence, this type is a collection of C-style functions.

```
Public Class XmlConvert
' Public Constructors
   Public Sub New()
' Public Shared Methods
   Public Shared Function DecodeName(ByVal name As String) As String
   Public Shared Function EncodeLocalName(ByVal name As String) As String
   Public Shared Function EncodeName(ByVal name As String) As String
   Public Shared Function EncodeNmToken(ByVal name As String) As String
   Public Shared Function ToBoolean(ByVal s As String) As Boolean
   Public Shared Function ToByte(ByVal s As String) As Byte
   Public Shared Function ToChar(ByVal s As String) As Char
   Public Shared Function ToDateTime(ByVal s As String) As Date
   Public Shared Function ToDateTime(ByVal s As String, ByVal format As String) As Date
   Public Shared Function ToDateTime(ByVal s As String, ByVal formats As String()) As Date
   Public Shared Function ToDecimal(ByVal s As String) As Decimal
   Public Shared Function ToDouble(ByVal s As String) As Double
   Public Shared Function ToGuid(ByVal s As String) As Guid
   Public Shared Function ToInt16(ByVal s As String) As Short
   Public Shared Function ToInt32(ByVal s As String) As Integer
   Public Shared Function ToInt64(ByVal s As String) As Long
   Public Shared Function ToSByte(ByVal s As String) As SByte
   Public Shared Function ToSingle(ByVal s As String) As Single
   Public Shared Function ToString(ByVal value As Boolean) As String
   Public Shared Function ToString(ByVal value As Byte) As String
   Public Shared Function ToString(ByVal value As Char) As String
   Public Shared Function ToString(ByVal value As Date) As String
   Public Shared Function ToString(ByVal value As Date, ByVal format As String) As String
   Public Shared Function ToString(ByVal value As Decimal) As String
   Public Shared Function ToString(ByVal value As Double) As String
   Public Shared Function ToString(ByVal value As Guid) As String
   Public Shared Function ToString(ByVal value As Short) As String
   Public Shared Function ToString(ByVal value As Integer) As String
   Public Shared Function ToString(ByVal value As Long) As String
   Public Shared Function ToString(ByVal value As SByte) As String
   Public Shared Function ToString(ByVal value As Single) As String
   Public Shared Function ToString(ByVal value As TimeSpan) As String
   Public Shared Function ToString(ByVal value As UInt16) As String
   Public Shared Function ToString(ByVal value As UInt32) As String
   Public Shared Function ToString(ByVal value As UInt64) As String
   Public Shared Function ToTimeSpan(ByVal s As String) As TimeSpan
```

Public Shared Function **ToUInt16**(ByVal s As String) As UInt16
Public Shared Function **ToUInt32**(ByVal s As String) As UInt32
Public Shared Function **ToUInt64**(ByVal s As String) As UInt64
Public Shared Function **VerifyName**(ByVal name As String) As String
Public Shared Function **VerifyNCName**(ByVal name As String) As String
End Class

XmlDataDocument   Class

System.Xml (system.data.dll)

The XmlDataDocument is a marriage of XML and RDBMS technology; it is an XmlDocument-inheriting class that particularly understands ADO.NET DataSet objects. This offers a variety of opportunities to the .NET programmer—for example, a DataSet can be loaded into the XmlDataDocument, and then navigated using traditional DOM-style navigation using the XmlNode API. In fact, because XmlDataDocument also inherits the System.Xml.XPath.IXPathNavigable interface, XPath queries can be issued against the DataSet data, as well.

In order to build this relationship, construct the XmlDataDocument with the DataSet holding the data as its constructor parameter. Alternatively, use the Load() method to read in the data via an XmlReader. The resulting XML can also then be written out to another medium with the WriteTo() method.

Public Class **XmlDataDocument** : Inherits XmlDocument
' Public Constructors
  Public Sub **New**()
  Public Sub **New**(ByVal dataset As System.Data.DataSet)
' Public Instance Properties
  Public ReadOnly Property **DataSet** As DataSet
' Public Instance Methods
  Overrides Public Function **CloneNode**(ByVal deep As Boolean) As XmlNode
  Overrides Public Function **CreateElement**(ByVal prefix As String, ByVal localName As String, _
    ByVal namespaceURI As String) As XmlElement
  Overrides Public Function **CreateEntityReference**(ByVal name As String) As XmlEntityReference
  Overrides Public Function **GetElementById**(ByVal elemId As String) As XmlElement
  Public Function **GetElementFromRow**(ByVal r As System.Data.DataRow) As XmlElement
  Public Function **GetRowFromElement**(ByVal e As XmlElement) As DataRow
  Overrides Public Sub **Load**(ByVal inStream As System.IO.Stream)
  Overrides Public Sub **Load**(ByVal filename As String)
  Overrides Public Sub **Load**(ByVal txtReader As System.IO.TextReader)
  Overrides Public Sub **Load**(ByVal reader As XmlReader)
' Protected Instance Methods
  Overrides Protected Function **CreateNavigator**(ByVal node As XmlNode) As XPathNavigator
End Class

Hierarchy: System.Object→ XmlNode(System.ICloneable, System.Collections.IEnumerable, System.Xml.XPath.IXPathNavigable)→ XmlDocument→ XmlDataDocument

XmlDeclaration   Class

System.Xml (system.xml.dll)

This class contains the XML declaration of a document, which is the first element of an XML document containing the XML version number, encoding, and other optional information about the file.

```
Public Class XmlDeclaration : Inherits XmlLinkedNode
' Protected Constructors
   Protected Friend Sub New(ByVal version As String, ByVal encoding As String, ByVal standalone As String, _
      ByVal doc As XmlDocument)
' Public Instance Properties
   Public Property Encoding As String
   Overrides Public Property InnerText As String
   Overrides Public ReadOnly Property LocalName As String
   Overrides Public ReadOnly Property Name As String
   Overrides Public ReadOnly Property NodeType As XmlNodeType
   Public Property Standalone As String
   Overrides Public Property Value As String
   Public ReadOnly Property Version As String
' Public Instance Methods
   Overrides Public Function CloneNode(ByVal deep As Boolean) As XmlNode
   Overrides Public Sub WriteContentTo(ByVal w As XmlWriter)
   Overrides Public Sub WriteTo(ByVal w As XmlWriter)
End Class
```

Hierarchy: System.Object→ XmlNode(System.ICloneable, System.Collections.IEnumerable, System.Xml.XPath.IXPathNavigable)→ XmlLinkedNode→ XmlDeclaration

Returned By: XmlDocument.CreateXmlDeclaration()

XmlDocument   Class

System.Xml (system.xml.dll)

This class represents an XML document according to the W3C DOM (Document Object Model) specification. The document is represented as a node tree, in which elements and attributes (and their values) are stored as nodes that contain relational information (e.g., parent, child, siblings). XmlDocument derives from the generic XmlNode class and therefore has a node-type of Document.

The set of Create* methods create new objects of any type of node. These objects are created within the context of the XmlDocument; they share the document properties and name table of the parent document. However, they are not inserted into the document. To do this, you need to use the methods for node insertion from XmlNode. A new Xml-Node is created from the root node of the XmlDocument, then methods for walking the node tree and appending or inserting nodes can be used to alter the source document.

Events are noted when any nodes (even created node objects that have not been inserted into the document) from this object change. Register an instance of the Xml-NodeChangedEventHandler delegate with any of the following event types on XmlDocument to receive the corresponding notification: NodeChanged or NodeChanging for notification when a node has or is in the middle of changing (the element name is being modified, an attribute is being modified, added, or removed, and so on); NodeInserted or NodeInserting for notifications of new nodes having been or in the process of being added to the document; and NodeRemoved or NodeRemoving for nodes removed or in the process of being removed. The XmlNodeChangedEventHandler takes two arguments: the object sending the notification (this object), and an XmlNodeChangedEventArgs instance containing information about the change.

```
Public Class XmlDocument : Inherits XmlNode
' Public Constructors
   Public Sub New()
   Public Sub New(ByVal nt As XmlNameTable)
' Protected Constructors
```

Protected Friend Sub **New**(ByVal imp As XmlImplementation)
' *Public Instance Properties*
Overrides Public ReadOnly Property **BaseURI** As String
Public ReadOnly Property **DocumentElement** As XmlElement
Overridable Public ReadOnly Property **DocumentType** As XmlDocumentType
Public ReadOnly Property **Implementation** As XmlImplementation
Overrides Public Property **InnerXml** As String
Overrides Public ReadOnly Property **IsReadOnly** As Boolean
Overrides Public ReadOnly Property **LocalName** As String
Overrides Public ReadOnly Property **Name** As String
Public ReadOnly Property **NameTable** As XmlNameTable
Overrides Public ReadOnly Property **NodeType** As XmlNodeType
Overrides Public ReadOnly Property **OwnerDocument** As XmlDocument
Public Property **PreserveWhitespace** As Boolean
Overridable Public WriteOnly Property **XmlResolver** As XmlResolver
' *Public Instance Methods*
Overrides Public Function **CloneNode**(ByVal deep As Boolean) As XmlNode
Public Function **CreateAttribute**(ByVal name As String) As XmlAttribute
Public Function **CreateAttribute**(ByVal qualifiedName As String, ByVal namespaceURI As String) As XmlAttribute
Overridable Public Function **CreateAttribute**(ByVal prefix As String, ByVal localName As String, _
  ByVal namespaceURI As String) As XmlAttribute
Overridable Public Function **CreateCDataSection**(ByVal data As String) As XmlCDataSection
Overridable Public Function **CreateComment**(ByVal data As String) As XmlComment
Overridable Public Function **CreateDocumentFragment**() As XmlDocumentFragment
Overridable Public Function **CreateDocumentType**(ByVal name As String, ByVal publicId As String, _
  ByVal systemId As String, ByVal internalSubset As String) As XmlDocumentType
Public Function **CreateElement**(ByVal name As String) As XmlElement
Public Function **CreateElement**(ByVal qualifiedName As String, ByVal namespaceURI As String) As XmlElement
Overridable Public Function **CreateElement**(ByVal prefix As String, ByVal localName As String, _
  ByVal namespaceURI As String) As XmlElement
Overridable Public Function **CreateEntityReference**(ByVal name As String) As XmlEntityReference
Overridable Public Function **CreateNode**(ByVal nodeTypeString As String, ByVal name As String, _
  ByVal namespaceURI As String) As XmlNode
Overridable Public Function **CreateNode**(ByVal type As XmlNodeType, ByVal name As String, _
  ByVal namespaceURI As String) As XmlNode
Overridable Public Function **CreateNode**(ByVal type As XmlNodeType, ByVal prefix As String, ByVal name As String, _
  ByVal namespaceURI As String) As XmlNode
Overridable Public Function **CreateProcessingInstruction**(ByVal target As String, ByVal data As String) _
  As XmlProcessingInstruction
Overridable Public Function **CreateSignificantWhitespace**(ByVal text As String) As XmlSignificantWhitespace
Overridable Public Function **CreateTextNode**(ByVal text As String) As XmlText
Overridable Public Function **CreateWhitespace**(ByVal text As String) As XmlWhitespace
Overridable Public Function **CreateXmlDeclaration**(ByVal version As String, ByVal encoding As String, _
  ByVal standalone As String) As XmlDeclaration
Overridable Public Function **GetElementById**(ByVal elementId As String) As XmlElement
Overridable Public Function **GetElementsByTagName**(ByVal name As String) As XmlNodeList
Overridable Public Function **GetElementsByTagName**(ByVal localName As String, _
  ByVal namespaceURI As String) As XmlNodeList
Overridable Public Function **ImportNode**(ByVal node As XmlNode, ByVal deep As Boolean) As XmlNode
Overridable Public Sub **Load**(ByVal inStream As System.IO.Stream)
Overridable Public Sub **Load**(ByVal filename As String)
Overridable Public Sub **Load**(ByVal txtReader As System.IO.TextReader)
Overridable Public Sub **Load**(ByVal reader As XmlReader)
Overridable Public Sub **LoadXml**(ByVal xml As String)
Overridable Public Function **ReadNode**(ByVal reader As XmlReader) As XmlNode

System.
Xml

Overridable Public Sub **Save**(ByVal outStream As System.IO.Stream)
Overridable Public Sub **Save**(ByVal filename As String)
Overridable Public Sub **Save**(ByVal writer As System.IO.TextWriter)
Overridable Public Sub **Save**(ByVal w As XmlWriter)
Overrides Public Sub **WriteContentTo**(ByVal xw As XmlWriter)
Overrides Public Sub **WriteTo**(ByVal w As XmlWriter)
' *Protected Instance Methods*
Overridable Protected Friend Function **CreateDefaultAttribute**(ByVal prefix As String, _
    ByVal localName As String, ByVal namespaceURI As String) As XmlAttribute
Overridable Protected Friend Function **CreateNavigator**(ByVal node As XmlNode) As XPathNavigator
' *Events*
Public Event **NodeChanged** As XmlNodeChangedEventHandler
Public Event **NodeChanging** As XmlNodeChangedEventHandler
Public Event **NodeInserted** As XmlNodeChangedEventHandler
Public Event **NodeInserting** As XmlNodeChangedEventHandler
Public Event **NodeRemoved** As XmlNodeChangedEventHandler
Public Event **NodeRemoving** As XmlNodeChangedEventHandler
End Class

Hierarchy: System.Object→ XmlNode(System.ICloneable, System.Collections.IEnumerable, System.Xml.XPath.IXPathNavigable)→ XmlDocument

Subclasses: XmlDataDocument

Returned By: XmlImplementation.CreateDocument(), XmlNode.OwnerDocument

XmlDocumentFragment
Class

System.Xml (system.xml.dll)

This class represents a lightweight piece or tree section of an XML document. A document fragment has a null parent node. This object is useful for tree insert operations that use the ImportNode() method of the XmlDocument class. To create an XmlDocumentFragment, use the XmlDocument.CreateDocumentFragment() method of an XmlDocument instance.

Public Class **XmlDocumentFragment** : Inherits XmlNode
' *Protected Constructors*
Protected Friend Sub **New**(ByVal ownerDocument As XmlDocument)
' *Public Instance Properties*
Overrides Public Property **InnerXml** As String
Overrides Public ReadOnly Property **LocalName** As String
Overrides Public ReadOnly Property **Name** As String
Overrides Public ReadOnly Property **NodeType** As XmlNodeType
Overrides Public ReadOnly Property **OwnerDocument** As XmlDocument
Overrides Public ReadOnly Property **ParentNode** As XmlNode
' *Public Instance Methods*
Overrides Public Function **CloneNode**(ByVal deep As Boolean) As XmlNode
Overrides Public Sub **WriteContentTo**(ByVal w As XmlWriter)
Overrides Public Sub **WriteTo**(ByVal w As XmlWriter)
End Class

Hierarchy: System.Object→ XmlNode(System.ICloneable, System.Collections.IEnumerable, System.Xml.XPath.IXPathNavigable)→ XmlDocumentFragment

Returned By: XmlDocument.CreateDocumentFragment()

XmlDocumentType   Class

System.Xml (system.xml.dll)

This class represents the DOCTYPE element of an XML document and its contents.

Public Class **XmlDocumentType** : Inherits XmlLinkedNode
' *Protected Constructors*
   Protected Friend Sub **New**(ByVal name As String, ByVal publicId As String, ByVal systemId As String, _
     ByVal internalSubset As String, ByVal doc As XmlDocument)
' *Public Instance Properties*
   Public ReadOnly Property **Entities** As XmlNamedNodeMap
   Public ReadOnly Property **InternalSubset** As String
   Overrides Public ReadOnly Property **IsReadOnly** As Boolean
   Overrides Public ReadOnly Property **LocalName** As String
   Overrides Public ReadOnly Property **Name** As String
   Overrides Public ReadOnly Property **NodeType** As XmlNodeType
   Public ReadOnly Property **Notations** As XmlNamedNodeMap
   Public ReadOnly Property **PublicId** As String
   Public ReadOnly Property **SystemId** As String
' *Public Instance Methods*
   Overrides Public Function **CloneNode**(ByVal deep As Boolean) As XmlNode
   Overrides Public Sub **WriteContentTo**(ByVal w As XmlWriter)
   Overrides Public Sub **WriteTo**(ByVal w As XmlWriter)
End Class

Hierarchy: System.Object→ XmlNode(System.ICloneable, System.Collections.IEnumerable,
System.Xml.XPath.IXPathNavigable)→ XmlLinkedNode→ XmlDocumentType

Returned By: XmlDocument.{CreateDocumentType(), DocumentType}

XmlElement   Class

System.Xml (system.xml.dll)

This class represents an element in an XML document.

Public Class **XmlElement** : Inherits XmlLinkedNode
' *Protected Constructors*
   Protected Friend Sub **New**(ByVal prefix As String, ByVal localName As String, ByVal namespaceURI As String, _
     ByVal doc As XmlDocument)
' *Public Instance Properties*
   Overrides Public ReadOnly Property **Attributes** As XmlAttributeCollection
   Overridable Public ReadOnly Property **HasAttributes** As Boolean
   Overrides Public Property **InnerText** As String
   Overrides Public Property **InnerXml** As String
   Public Property **IsEmpty** As Boolean
   Overrides Public ReadOnly Property **LocalName** As String
   Overrides Public ReadOnly Property **Name** As String
   Overrides Public ReadOnly Property **NamespaceURI** As String
   Overrides Public ReadOnly Property **NextSibling** As XmlNode
   Overrides Public ReadOnly Property **NodeType** As XmlNodeType
   Overrides Public ReadOnly Property **OwnerDocument** As XmlDocument
   Overrides Public Property **Prefix** As String
' *Public Instance Methods*
   Overrides Public Function **CloneNode**(ByVal deep As Boolean) As XmlNode
   Overridable Public Function **GetAttribute**(ByVal name As String) As String
   Overridable Public Function **GetAttribute**(ByVal localName As String, ByVal namespaceURI As String) As String
   Overridable Public Function **GetAttributeNode**(ByVal name As String) As XmlAttribute
   Overridable Public Function **GetAttributeNode**(ByVal localName As String, ByVal namespaceURI As String) _
    As XmlAttribute

System. Xml

Overridable Public Function **GetElementsByTagName**(ByVal name As String) As XmlNodeList
Overridable Public Function **GetElementsByTagName**(ByVal localName As String, _
ByVal namespaceURI As String) As XmlNodeList
Overridable Public Function **HasAttribute**(ByVal name As String) As Boolean
Overridable Public Function **HasAttribute**(ByVal localName As String, ByVal namespaceURI As String) As Boolean
Overrides Public Sub **RemoveAll**()
Overridable Public Sub **RemoveAllAttributes**()
Overridable Public Sub **RemoveAttribute**(ByVal name As String)
Overridable Public Sub **RemoveAttribute**(ByVal localName As String, ByVal namespaceURI As String)
Overridable Public Function **RemoveAttributeAt**(ByVal i As Integer) As XmlNode
Overridable Public Function **RemoveAttributeNode**(ByVal localName As String, ByVal namespaceURI As String) _
As XmlAttribute
Overridable Public Function **RemoveAttributeNode**(ByVal oldAttr As XmlAttribute) As XmlAttribute
Overridable Public Function **SetAttribute**(ByVal localName As String, ByVal namespaceURI As String, _
ByVal value As String) As String
Overridable Public Sub **SetAttribute**(ByVal name As String, ByVal value As String)
Overridable Public Function **SetAttributeNode**(ByVal localName As String, ByVal namespaceURI As String) _
As XmlAttribute
Overridable Public Function **SetAttributeNode**(ByVal newAttr As XmlAttribute) As XmlAttribute
Overrides Public Sub **WriteContentTo**(ByVal w As XmlWriter)
Overrides Public Sub **WriteTo**(ByVal w As XmlWriter)
End Class

Hierarchy: System.Object→ XmlNode(System.ICloneable, System.Collections.IEnumerable,
System.Xml.XPath.IXPathNavigable)→ XmlLinkedNode→ XmlElement

Returned By: XmlAttribute.OwnerElement, XmlDataDocument.GetElementFromRow(),
XmlDocument.{CreateElement(), DocumentElement, GetElementById()}, XmlNode.this

Passed To: XmlDataDocument.GetRowFromElement()

XmlEntity
Class

System.Xml (system.xml.dll)

This class represents an entity in an XML document.

Public Class **XmlEntity** : Inherits XmlNode
' Public Instance Properties
Overrides Public ReadOnly Property **BaseURI** As String
Overrides Public Property **InnerText** As String
Overrides Public Property **InnerXml** As String
Overrides Public ReadOnly Property **IsReadOnly** As Boolean
Overrides Public ReadOnly Property **LocalName** As String
Overrides Public ReadOnly Property **Name** As String
Overrides Public ReadOnly Property **NodeType** As XmlNodeType
Public ReadOnly Property **NotationName** As String
Overrides Public ReadOnly Property **OuterXml** As String
Public ReadOnly Property **PublicId** As String
Public ReadOnly Property **SystemId** As String
' Public Instance Methods
Overrides Public Function **CloneNode**(ByVal deep As Boolean) As XmlNode
Overrides Public Sub **WriteContentTo**(ByVal w As XmlWriter)
Overrides Public Sub **WriteTo**(ByVal w As XmlWriter)
End Class

Hierarchy: System.Object→ XmlNode(System.ICloneable, System.Collections.IEnumerable,
System.Xml.XPath.IXPathNavigable)→ XmlEntity

XmlEntityReference

System.Xml (system.xml.dll)

This class represents an entity reference in an XML document.

```
Public Class XmlEntityReference : Inherits XmlLinkedNode
' Protected Constructors
   Protected Friend Sub New(ByVal name As String, ByVal doc As XmlDocument)
' Public Instance Properties
   Overrides Public ReadOnly Property BaseURI As String
   Overrides Public ReadOnly Property IsReadOnly As Boolean
   Overrides Public ReadOnly Property LocalName As String
   Overrides Public ReadOnly Property Name As String
   Overrides Public ReadOnly Property NodeType As XmlNodeType
   Overrides Public Property Value As String
' Public Instance Methods
   Overrides Public Function CloneNode(ByVal deep As Boolean) As XmlNode
   Overrides Public Sub WriteContentTo(ByVal w As XmlWriter)
   Overrides Public Sub WriteTo(ByVal w As XmlWriter)
End Class
```

Hierarchy: System.Object→ XmlNode(System.ICloneable, System.Collections.IEnumerable, System.Xml.XPath.IXPathNavigable)→ XmlLinkedNode→ XmlEntityReference

Returned By: XmlDocument.CreateEntityReference()

XmlException

System.Xml (system.xml.dll)

ECMA, serializable

This class contains the error thrown by XML-parsing operations. The LineNumber and LinePosition properties store the location of the error in the source document, and Message describes the reason for the error.

```
Public Class XmlException : Inherits SystemException
' Public Constructors
   Public Sub New(ByVal message As String, ByVal innerException As Exception)
' Protected Constructors
   Protected Sub New(ByVal info As System.Runtime.Serialization.SerializationInfo, _
      ByVal context As System.Runtime.Serialization.StreamingContext)
' Public Instance Properties
   Public ReadOnly Property LineNumber As Integer
   Public ReadOnly Property LinePosition As Integer
   Overrides Public ReadOnly Property Message As String
' Public Instance Methods
   Overrides Public Sub GetObjectData(ByVal info As System.Runtime.Serialization.SerializationInfo, _
      ByVal context As System.Runtime.Serialization.StreamingContext)
End Class
```

Hierarchy: System.Object→ System.Exception(System.Runtime.Serialization.ISerializable)→ System.SystemException→ XmlException

XmlImplementation

System.Xml (system.xml.dll)

This class instantiates a new XmlDocument object using the same XmlNameTable of an existing XmlDocument.

```
Public Class XmlImplementation
' Public Constructors
```

```
Public Sub New()
' Public Instance Methods
  Overridable Public Function CreateDocument() As XmlDocument
  Public Function HasFeature(ByVal strFeature As String, ByVal strVersion As String) As Boolean
End Class
```

Returned By: XmlDocument.Implementation

XmlLinkedNode   MustInherit Class

System.Xml (system.xml.dll)

This type of node class is the base class for node types that are not top-level (i.e., nodes that require a parent). For example, XmlCharacterData and XmlElement are derived from XmlLinkedNode.

```
Public MustInherit Class XmlLinkedNode : Inherits XmlNode
' Public Instance Properties
  Overrides Public ReadOnly Property NextSibling As XmlNode
  Overrides Public ReadOnly Property PreviousSibling As XmlNode
End Class
```

Hierarchy: System.Object→ XmlNode(System.ICloneable, System.Collections.IEnumerable, System.Xml.XPath.IXPathNavigable)→ XmlLinkedNode

Subclasses: XmlCharacterData, XmlDeclaration, XmlDocumentType, XmlElement, XmlEntityReference, XmlProcessingInstruction

XmlNamedNodeMap   Class

System.Xml (system.xml.dll)

This class represents a collection of nodes accessed by index or name. This is the MustInherit parent class of XmlAttributeCollection.

```
Public Class XmlNamedNodeMap : Implements IEnumerable
' Public Instance Properties
  Overridable Public ReadOnly Property Count As Integer
' Public Instance Methods
  Overridable Public Function GetEnumerator() As IEnumerator Implements IEnumerable.GetEnumerator
  Overridable Public Function GetNamedItem(ByVal name As String) As XmlNode
  Overridable Public Function GetNamedItem(ByVal localName As String, ByVal namespaceURI As String) _
    As XmlNode
  Overridable Public Function Item(ByVal index As Integer) As XmlNode
  Overridable Public Function RemoveNamedItem(ByVal name As String) As XmlNode
  Overridable Public Function RemoveNamedItem(ByVal localName As String, ByVal namespaceURI As String) _
    As XmlNode
  Overridable Public Function SetNamedItem(ByVal node As XmlNode) As XmlNode
End Class
```

Subclasses: XmlAttributeCollection

Returned By: XmlDocumentType.{Entities, Notations}

XmlNamespaceManager
Class

System.Xml (system.xml.dll)
ECMA

This class represents a collection of namespace prefixes and namespace URIs that are used to manage and resolve namespace information. The namespace manager is constructed using an XmlNameTable. XmlNamespaceManager is used internally by XmlReader to resolve namespace prefixes and track the current scope. XmlNamespaceManager maintains scope in a stack, which can be manipulated with PopScope() and PushScope(). Namespaces must be added explicitly to the namespace manager with AddNamespace(), even if you use an existing XmlNameTable.

```
Public Class XmlNamespaceManager : Implements IEnumerable
' Public Constructors
   Public Sub New(ByVal nameTable As XmlNameTable)
' Public Instance Properties
   Overridable Public ReadOnly Property DefaultNamespace As String
   Public ReadOnly Property NameTable As XmlNameTable
' Public Instance Methods
   Overridable Public Sub AddNamespace(ByVal prefix As String, ByVal uri As String)
   Overridable Public Function GetEnumerator() As IEnumerator Implements IEnumerable.GetEnumerator
   Overridable Public Function HasNamespace(ByVal prefix As String) As Boolean
   Overridable Public Function LookupNamespace(ByVal prefix As String) As String
   Overridable Public Function LookupPrefix(ByVal uri As String) As String
   Overridable Public Function PopScope() As Boolean
   Overridable Public Sub PushScope()
   Overridable Public Sub RemoveNamespace(ByVal prefix As String, ByVal uri As String)
End Class
```

Subclasses: System.Xml.Xsl.XsltContext

Returned By: XmlParserContext.NamespaceManager

Passed To: XmlNode.{SelectNodes(), SelectSingleNode()}, XmlParserContext.{NamespaceManager, XmlParserContext()}, System.Xml.XPath.XPathExpression.SetContext()

XmlNameTable
MustInherit Class

System.Xml (system.xml.dll)
ECMA

This class presents a table of string objects (for element and attribute names) used in an XML document. The XML parser uses these string objects for efficient manipulation of repeated element and attribute names. An XmlNameTable exists for every XmlDocument you create. The XmlImplementation class instantiates a new XmlDocument with the XmlNameTable of another existing XmlDocument.

```
Public MustInherit Class XmlNameTable
' Protected Constructors
   Protected Sub New()
' Public Instance Methods
   MustInherit Public Function Add(ByVal array As Char(), ByVal offset As Integer, ByVal length As Integer) As String
   MustInherit Public Function Add(ByVal array As String) As String
   MustInherit Public Function Get(ByVal array As Char(), ByVal offset As Integer, ByVal length As Integer) As String
   MustInherit Public Function Get(ByVal array As String) As String
End Class
```

Subclasses: NameTable

Returned By: XmlDocument.NameTable, XmlNamespaceManager.NameTable, XmlParserContext.NameTable, XmlReader.NameTable, System.Xml.XPath.XPathNavigator.NameTable

Passed To: XmlDocument.XmlDocument(), XmlNamespaceManager.XmlNamespaceManager(), XmlParserContext.{NameTable, XmlParserContext()}, XmlTextReader.XmlTextReader()

XmlNode   MustInherit Class

System.Xml (system.xml.dll)

This MustInherit class represents a node in a document. A node is the basic object described by the Document Object Model for XML. A node can be an element, an element's attributes, the DOCTYPE declaration, a comment, or the entire document itself. Nodes are ordered in a hierarchical tree in which child, parent, and sibling relationships are "known" by each node.

The XmlNode class is the parent object of the specific node type classes. The properties of this class expose the intrinsic values of the node: NamespaceURI, NodeType, parent, child, sibling nodes, etc. The methods allow a node to add to or removed from a node tree (in the context of an XmlDocument or XmlDocumentFragment), with respect to a reference node.

Public MustInherit Class **XmlNode** : Implements ICloneable, IEnumerable , System.Xml.XPath.IXPathNavigable
' Public Instance Properties
   Overridable Public ReadOnly Property **Attributes** As XmlAttributeCollection
   Overridable Public ReadOnly Property **BaseURI** As String
   Overridable Public ReadOnly Property **ChildNodes** As XmlNodeList
   Overridable Public ReadOnly Property **FirstChild** As XmlNode
   Overridable Public ReadOnly Property **HasChildNodes** As Boolean
   Overridable Public Property **InnerText** As String
   Overridable Public Property **InnerXml** As String
   Overridable Public ReadOnly Property **IsReadOnly** As Boolean
   Overridable Public Default ReadOnly Property **Item** (ByVal name As String) As XmlElement
   Overridable Public Default ReadOnly Property **Item** (ByVal localname As String) (ByVal ns As String As XmlElement
   Overridable Public ReadOnly Property **LastChild** As XmlNode
   MustInherit Public ReadOnly Property **LocalName** As String
   MustInherit Public ReadOnly Property **Name** As String
   Overridable Public ReadOnly Property **NamespaceURI** As String
   Overridable Public ReadOnly Property **NextSibling** As XmlNode
   MustInherit Public ReadOnly Property **NodeType** As XmlNodeType
   Overridable Public ReadOnly Property **OuterXml** As String
   Overridable Public ReadOnly Property **OwnerDocument** As XmlDocument
   Overridable Public ReadOnly Property **ParentNode** As XmlNode
   Overridable Public Property **Prefix** As String
   Overridable Public ReadOnly Property **PreviousSibling** As XmlNode
   Overridable Public Property **Value** As String
' Public Instance Methods
   Overridable Public Function **AppendChild**(ByVal newChild As XmlNode) As XmlNode
   Overridable Public Function **Clone**() As XmlNode
   MustInherit Public Function **CloneNode**(ByVal deep As Boolean) As XmlNode
   Public Function **CreateNavigator**() As XPathNavigator Implements IXPathNavigable.CreateNavigator
   Public Function **GetEnumerator**() As IEnumerator Implements IEnumerable.GetEnumerator
   Overridable Public Function **GetNamespaceOfPrefix**(ByVal prefix As String) As String
   Overridable Public Function **GetPrefixOfNamespace**(ByVal namespaceURI As String) As String
   Overridable Public Function **InsertAfter**(ByVal newChild As XmlNode, ByVal refChild As XmlNode) As XmlNode
   Overridable Public Function **InsertBefore**(ByVal newChild As XmlNode, ByVal refChild As XmlNode) As XmlNode
   Overridable Public Sub **Normalize**()
   Overridable Public Function **PrependChild**(ByVal newChild As XmlNode) As XmlNode
   Overridable Public Sub **RemoveAll**()
   Overridable Public Function **RemoveChild**(ByVal oldChild As XmlNode) As XmlNode
   Overridable Public Function **ReplaceChild**(ByVal newChild As XmlNode, ByVal oldChild As XmlNode) As XmlNode

Public Function **SelectNodes**(ByVal xpath As String) As XmlNodeList
Public Function **SelectNodes**(ByVal xpath As String, ByVal nsmgr As XmlNamespaceManager) As XmlNodeList
Public Function **SelectSingleNode**(ByVal xpath As String) As XmlNode
Public Function **SelectSingleNode**(ByVal xpath As String, ByVal nsmgr As XmlNamespaceManager) As XmlNode
Overridable Public Function **Supports**(ByVal feature As String, ByVal version As String) As Boolean
MustInherit Public Sub **WriteContentTo**(ByVal w As XmlWriter)
MustInherit Public Sub **WriteTo**(ByVal w As XmlWriter)
End Class

Subclasses: XmlAttribute, XmlDocument, XmlDocumentFragment, XmlEntity, XmlLinkedNode, XmlNotation

Returned By: Multiple types

Passed To: XmlDataDocument.CreateNavigator(), XmlDocument.ImportNode(), XmlNamedNodeMap.SetNamedItem(), XmlNodeReader.XmlNodeReader()

XmlNodeChangedAction   Enum

System.Xml (system.xml.dll)   *serializable*

This simple enumeration that describes the change that has occurred within an XmlDocument instance can be one of the following: Change, which indicates that a node within the document has changed in some way; Insert, which indicates that a node has been inserted into the document; or Remove, which indicates that a node has been removed. This is one of the properties specified in the XmlNodeChangedEventArgs parameter to the XmlNodeChangedEventHandler delegate instance registered with the XmlDocument.

Public Enum **XmlNodeChangedAction**
    Insert = 0
    Remove = 1
    Change = 2
End Enum

Hierarchy: System.Object→ System.ValueType→ System.Enum(System.IComparable, System.IFormattable, System.IConvertible)→ XmlNodeChangedAction

Returned By: XmlNodeChangedEventArgs.Action

XmlNodeChangedEventArgs   Class

System.Xml (system.xml.dll)

This type contains information about the changes to a node that are passed when an XmlDocument calls through an XmlNodeChangedEventHandler delegate instance. It contains the changed or changing node, the old and new parents to that node, and an enumeration describing the change (modification, insertion, or removal).

Public Class **XmlNodeChangedEventArgs**
' Public Instance Properties
    Public ReadOnly Property **Action** As XmlNodeChangedAction
    Public ReadOnly Property **NewParent** As XmlNode
    Public ReadOnly Property **Node** As XmlNode
    Public ReadOnly Property **OldParent** As XmlNode
End Class

Passed To: XmlNodeChangedEventHandler.{BeginInvoke(), Invoke()}

XmlNodeChangedEventHandler · Delegate

System.Xml (system.xml.dll) · *serializable*

This declared delegate type must be used to receive event notifications from the XmlDocument instance if code wishes to be notified of changes to the document as they occur.

```
Public Delegate Sub XmlNodeChangedEventHandler(ByVal sender As Object, _
    ByVal e As XmlNodeChangedEventArgs)
```

Associated Events: XmlDataDocument.{NodeChanged(), NodeChanging(), NodeInserted(), NodeInserting(), NodeRemoved(), NodeRemoving()}, XmlDocument.{NodeChanged(), NodeChanging(), NodeInserted(), NodeInserting(), NodeRemoved(), NodeRemoving()}

XmlNodeList · MustInherit Class

System.Xml (system.xml.dll)

This class is an enumerated collection of nodes returned by XmlDocument.GetElementsByTagName(). Nodes contained in the list can be retrieved by index or iterated through via the IEnumerator returned by GetEnumerator(). Changes to the nodes in the list are immediately reflected in the XmlNodeList's properties and methods. For example, if you add a sibling to a node in the list, it appears in the list.

```
Public MustInherit Class XmlNodeList : Implements IEnumerable
' Protected Constructors
    Protected Sub New()
' Public Instance Properties
    MustInherit Public ReadOnly Property Count As Integer
    Overridable Public Default ReadOnly Property ItemOf (ByVal i As Integer) As XmlNode
' Public Instance Methods
    MustInherit Public Function GetEnumerator() As IEnumerator Implements IEnumerable.GetEnumerator
    MustInherit Public Function Item(ByVal index As Integer) As XmlNode
End Class
```

Returned By: XmlDocument.GetElementsByTagName(), XmlElement.GetElementsByTagName(), XmlNode.{ChildNodes, SelectNodes()}

XmlNodeOrder · Enum

System.Xml (system.xml.dll) · *serializable*

These values describe the position of one node relative to another, with respect to document order.

```
Public Enum XmlNodeOrder
    Before = 0
    After = 1
    Same = 2
    Unknown = 3
End Enum
```

Hierarchy: System.Object→ System.ValueType→ System.Enum(System.IComparable, System.IFormattable, System.IConvertible)→ XmlNodeOrder

Returned By: System.Xml.XPath.XPathNavigator.ComparePosition()

XmlNodeReader

System.Xml (system.xml.dll)

This class is a non-cached, forward-only reader that accesses the contents of an Xml-Node. This class can read a DOM subtree, but doesn't provide full-document support such as validation.

```
Public Class XmlNodeReader : Inherits XmlReader
' Public Constructors
   Public Sub New(ByVal node As XmlNode)
' Public Instance Properties
   Overrides Public ReadOnly Property AttributeCount As Integer
   Overrides Public ReadOnly Property BaseURI As String
   Overrides Public ReadOnly Property CanResolveEntity As Boolean
   Overrides Public ReadOnly Property Depth As Integer
   Overrides Public ReadOnly Property EOF As Boolean
   Overrides Public ReadOnly Property HasAttributes As Boolean
   Overrides Public ReadOnly Property HasValue As Boolean
   Overrides Public ReadOnly Property IsDefault As Boolean
   Overrides Public ReadOnly Property IsEmptyElement As Boolean
   Overrides Public Default ReadOnly Property Item (ByVal i As Integer) As String
   Overrides Public Default ReadOnly Property Item (ByVal name As String) (ByVal namespaceURI As String As String
   Overrides Public Default ReadOnly Property Item (ByVal name As String) As String
   Overrides Public ReadOnly Property LocalName As String
   Overrides Public ReadOnly Property Name As String
   Overrides Public ReadOnly Property NamespaceURI As String
   Overrides Public ReadOnly Property NameTable As XmlNameTable
   Overrides Public ReadOnly Property NodeType As XmlNodeType
   Overrides Public ReadOnly Property Prefix As String
   Overrides Public ReadOnly Property QuoteChar As Char
   Overrides Public ReadOnly Property ReadState As ReadState
   Overrides Public ReadOnly Property Value As String
   Overrides Public ReadOnly Property XmlLang As String
   Overrides Public ReadOnly Property XmlSpace As XmlSpace
' Public Instance Methods
   Overrides Public Sub Close()
   Overrides Public Function GetAttribute(ByVal attributeIndex As Integer) As String
   Overrides Public Function GetAttribute(ByVal name As String) As String
   Overrides Public Function GetAttribute(ByVal name As String, ByVal namespaceURI As String) As String
   Overrides Public Function LookupNamespace(ByVal prefix As String) As String
   Overrides Public Function MoveToAttribute(ByVal name As String) As Boolean
   Overrides Public Function MoveToAttribute(ByVal name As String, ByVal namespaceURI As String) As Boolean
   Overrides Public Sub MoveToAttribute(ByVal attributeIndex As Integer)
   Overrides Public Function MoveToElement() As Boolean
   Overrides Public Function MoveToFirstAttribute() As Boolean
   Overrides Public Function MoveToNextAttribute() As Boolean
   Overrides Public Function Read() As Boolean
   Overrides Public Function ReadAttributeValue() As Boolean
   Overrides Public Function ReadInnerXml() As String
   Overrides Public Function ReadOuterXml() As String
   Overrides Public Function ReadString() As String
   Overrides Public Sub ResolveEntity()
   Overrides Public Sub Skip()
End Class
```

Hierarchy: System.Object→ XmlReader→ XmlNodeReader

XmlNodeType

Enum

System.Xml (system.xml.dll)

ECMA, serializable

This enumeration contains identifiers for node types. All DOM Core Level 2 types are included.

```
Public Enum XmlNodeType
        None = 0
        Element = 1
        Attribute = 2
        Text = 3
        CDATA = 4
        EntityReference = 5
        Entity = 6
        ProcessingInstruction = 7
        Comment = 8
        Document = 9
        DocumentType = 10
        DocumentFragment = 11
        Notation = 12
        Whitespace = 13
        SignificantWhitespace = 14
        EndElement = 15
        EndEntity = 16
        XmlDeclaration = 17
End Enum
```

Hierarchy: System.Object→ System.ValueType→ System.Enum(System.IComparable, System.IFormattable, System.IConvertible)→ XmlNodeType

Returned By: XmlNode.NodeType, XmlReader.{MoveToContent(), NodeType}

Passed To: XmlDocument.CreateNode(), XmlTextReader.XmlTextReader(), XmlValidatingReader.XmlValidatingReader()

XmlNotation

Class

System.Xml (system.xml.dll)

This class represents a notation declaration (<!NOTATION . . .>) in an XML document.

```
Public Class XmlNotation : Inherits XmlNode
' Public Instance Properties
    Overrides Public Property InnerXml As String
    Overrides Public ReadOnly Property IsReadOnly As Boolean
    Overrides Public ReadOnly Property LocalName As String
    Overrides Public ReadOnly Property Name As String
    Overrides Public ReadOnly Property NodeType As XmlNodeType
    Overrides Public ReadOnly Property OuterXml As String
    Public ReadOnly Property PublicId As String
    Public ReadOnly Property SystemId As String
' Public Instance Methods
    Overrides Public Function CloneNode(ByVal deep As Boolean) As XmlNode
    Overrides Public Sub WriteContentTo(ByVal w As XmlWriter)
    Overrides Public Sub WriteTo(ByVal w As XmlWriter)
End Class
```

Hierarchy: System.Object→ XmlNode(System.ICloneable, System.Collections.IEnumerable, System.Xml.XPath.IXPathNavigable)→ XmlNotation

XmlParserContext
System.Xml (system.xml.dll)

Class

ECMA

This class contains document context information normally provided by both the XML declaration and DOCTYPE elements for parsing XML fragments. XmlTextReader and XmlValidatingReader use the XmlParserContext for the base URI, internal subset, public and system identifiers, etc.

Public Class **XmlParserContext**
' Public Constructors
   Public Sub **New**(ByVal nt As XmlNameTable, ByVal nsMgr As XmlNamespaceManager, ByVal docTypeName As String _
    , ByVal pubId As String, ByVal sysId As String, ByVal internalSubset As String, ByVal baseURI As String,   _
    ByVal xmlLang As String, ByVal xmlSpace As XmlSpace)
   Public Sub **New**(ByVal nt As XmlNameTable, ByVal nsMgr As XmlNamespaceManager, ByVal xmlLang As String, _
    ByVal xmlSpace As XmlSpace)
   Public Sub **New**(ByVal nt As XmlNameTable, ByVal nsMgr As XmlNamespaceManager, ByVal xmlLang As String, _
    ByVal xmlSpace As XmlSpace, ByVal enc As System.Text.Encoding)
' Public Instance Properties
   Public Property **BaseURI** As String
   Public Property **DocTypeName** As String
   Public Property **Encoding** As Encoding
   Public Property **InternalSubset** As String
   Public Property **NamespaceManager** As XmlNamespaceManager
   Public Property **NameTable** As XmlNameTable
   Public Property **PublicId** As String
   Public Property **SystemId** As String
   Public Property **XmlLang** As String
   Public Property **XmlSpace** As XmlSpace
End Class

Passed To: XmlTextReader.XmlTextReader(), XmlValidatingReader.XmlValidatingReader()

XmlProcessingInstruction
System.Xml (system.xml.dll)

Class

This class represents a processing instruction in an XML document.

Public Class **XmlProcessingInstruction** : Inherits XmlLinkedNode
' Protected Constructors
   Protected Friend Sub **New**(ByVal target As String, ByVal data As String, ByVal doc As XmlDocument)
' Public Instance Properties
   Public Property **Data** As String
   Overrides Public Property **InnerText** As String
   Overrides Public ReadOnly Property **LocalName** As String
   Overrides Public ReadOnly Property **Name** As String
   Overrides Public ReadOnly Property **NodeType** As XmlNodeType
   Public ReadOnly Property **Target** As String
   Overrides Public Property **Value** As String
' Public Instance Methods
   Overrides Public Function **CloneNode**(ByVal deep As Boolean) As XmlNode
   Overrides Public Sub **WriteContentTo**(ByVal w As XmlWriter)
   Overrides Public Sub **WriteTo**(ByVal w As XmlWriter)
End Class

Hierarchy: System.Object→ XmlNode(System.ICloneable, System.Collections.IEnumerable, System.Xml.XPath.IXPathNavigable)→ XmlLinkedNode→ XmlProcessingInstruction

Returned By: XmlDocument.CreateProcessingInstruction()

XmlQualifiedName   Class
System.Xml (system.xml.dll)

This class represents a namespace-qualified local name. This looks like namespace:name within a document. An XmlQualifiedName object is constructed with the element's name and its namespace as string arguments. The namespace field may be empty, in which case the default namespace of the document is assumed.

```
Public Class XmlQualifiedName
' Public Constructors
   Public Sub New()
   Public Sub New(ByVal name As String)
   Public Sub New(ByVal name As String, ByVal ns As String)
' Public Shared Fields
   Public Shared ReadOnly Empty As XmlQualifiedName
' Public Instance Properties
   Public ReadOnly Property IsEmpty As Boolean
   Public ReadOnly Property Name As String
   Public ReadOnly Property Namespace As String
' Public Shared Methods
   Public Shared Function ToString(ByVal name As String, ByVal ns As String) As String
   Public Shared Boolean operator Sub !=(ByVal a As XmlQualifiedName, ByVal b As XmlQualifiedName)
   Public Shared Boolean operator Sub ==(ByVal a As XmlQualifiedName, ByVal b As XmlQualifiedName)
' Public Instance Methods
   Overrides Public Function Equals(ByVal other As Object) As Boolean
   Overrides Public Function GetHashCode() As Integer
   Overrides Public Function ToString() As String
End Class
```

XmlReader   MustInherit Class
System.Xml (system.xml.dll)   ECMA

This class is a simple reader for XML documents. XmlReader provides a non-cached, forward-only navigation through an XML data stream. It does not provide validation, nor does it expand general entities. Two derived classes provide these features: XmlTextReader and XmlValidatingReader.

The XmlReader class parses XML in a streaming-based approach (exemplified by the SAX specification). This means the XML parser presents "interesting pieces" (elements, attributes, namespace declarations, and so forth) in a linear order. Within XmlReader, this ordering of nodes is done using successive calls to the Read() method. An XmlReader is not positioned on a node at first—an initial call to Read() is required to move to the root node of a document. Subsequent calls to Read() move the reader sequentially through the nodes. The NodeType property tells you which type of node the reader is currently positioned on, returning values from the XmlNodeType enumeration. A special node-type value for XmlReader is EndElement. As Read() moves through the stream, it can be positioned on an element's end tag after it has stepped through the element's children. This is not a real node, in the DOM sense, but is required for XmlReader to parse XML data properly. The Skip() method steps through data node by node. A call to Skip() moves the reader to the next real node, disregarding the current node's children.

XML documents can also be parsed in a tree-based approach, using the XmlDocument type.

```
Public MustInherit Class XmlReader
' Protected Constructors
   Protected Sub New()
```

' *Public Instance Properties*

MustInherit Public ReadOnly Property **AttributeCount** As Integer

MustInherit Public ReadOnly Property **BaseURI** As String

Overridable Public ReadOnly Property **CanResolveEntity** As Boolean

MustInherit Public ReadOnly Property **Depth** As Integer

MustInherit Public ReadOnly Property **EOF** As Boolean

Overridable Public ReadOnly Property **HasAttributes** As Boolean

MustInherit Public ReadOnly Property **HasValue** As Boolean

MustInherit Public ReadOnly Property **IsDefault** As Boolean

MustInherit Public ReadOnly Property **IsEmptyElement** As Boolean

MustInherit Public Default ReadOnly Property **Item** (ByVal i As Integer) As String

MustInherit Public Default ReadOnly Property **Item** (ByVal name As String) As String

MustInherit Public Default ReadOnly Property **Item** (ByVal name As String) (ByVal namespaceURI As String _
   As String

MustInherit Public ReadOnly Property **LocalName** As String

MustInherit Public ReadOnly Property **Name** As String

MustInherit Public ReadOnly Property **NamespaceURI** As String

MustInherit Public ReadOnly Property **NameTable** As XmlNameTable

MustInherit Public ReadOnly Property **NodeType** As XmlNodeType

MustInherit Public ReadOnly Property **Prefix** As String

MustInherit Public ReadOnly Property **QuoteChar** As Char

MustInherit Public ReadOnly Property **ReadState** As ReadState

MustInherit Public ReadOnly Property **Value** As String

MustInherit Public ReadOnly Property **XmlLang** As String

MustInherit Public ReadOnly Property **XmlSpace** As XmlSpace

' *Public Shared Methods*

Public Shared Function **IsName**(ByVal str As String) As Boolean

Public Shared Function **IsNameToken**(ByVal str As String) As Boolean

' *Public Instance Methods*

MustInherit Public Sub **Close**()

MustInherit Public Function **GetAttribute**(ByVal i As Integer) As String

MustInherit Public Function **GetAttribute**(ByVal name As String) As String

MustInherit Public Function **GetAttribute**(ByVal name As String, ByVal namespaceURI As String) As String

Overridable Public Function **IsStartElement**() As Boolean

Overridable Public Function **IsStartElement**(ByVal name As String) As Boolean

Overridable Public Function **IsStartElement**(ByVal localname As String, ByVal ns As String) As Boolean

MustInherit Public Function **LookupNamespace**(ByVal prefix As String) As String

MustInherit Public Function **MoveToAttribute**(ByVal name As String) As Boolean

MustInherit Public Function **MoveToAttribute**(ByVal name As String, ByVal ns As String) As Boolean

MustInherit Public Sub **MoveToAttribute**(ByVal i As Integer)

Overridable Public Function **MoveToContent**() As XmlNodeType

MustInherit Public Function **MoveToElement**() As Boolean

MustInherit Public Function **MoveToFirstAttribute**() As Boolean

MustInherit Public Function **MoveToNextAttribute**() As Boolean

MustInherit Public Function **Read**() As Boolean

MustInherit Public Function **ReadAttributeValue**() As Boolean

Overridable Public Function **ReadElementString**() As String

Overridable Public Function **ReadElementString**(ByVal name As String) As String

Overridable Public Function **ReadElementString**(ByVal localname As String, ByVal ns As String) As String

Overridable Public Sub **ReadEndElement**()

MustInherit Public Function **ReadInnerXml**() As String

MustInherit Public Function **ReadOuterXml**() As String

Overridable Public Sub **ReadStartElement**()

Overridable Public Sub **ReadStartElement**(ByVal name As String)

Overridable Public Sub **ReadStartElement**(ByVal localname As String, ByVal ns As String)

```
    MustInherit Public Function ReadString() As String
    MustInherit Public Sub ResolveEntity()
    Overridable Public Sub Skip()
End Class
```

Subclasses: XmlNodeReader, XmlTextReader, XmlValidatingReader

Returned By: XmlValidatingReader.Reader, System.Xml.Xsl.XslTransform.Transform()

Passed To: XmlDocument.{Load(), ReadNode()}, XmlValidatingReader.XmlValidatingReader(), XmlWriter.{WriteAttributes(), WriteNode()}, System.Xml.XPath.XPathDocument.XPathDocument(), System.Xml.Xsl.XslTransform.Load()

XmlResolver   MustInherit Class

System.Xml (system.xml.dll)   *ECMA*

This class resolves external resources according to their URIs. This class is used to retrieve an external DTD or Schema in XML documents and also obtains resources from imported stylesheets (<xsl:import>) and included files (<xml:include>). This MustInherit class is implemented by XmlUrlResolver.

```
Public MustInherit Class XmlResolver
' Protected Constructors
    Protected Sub New()
' Public Instance Properties
    MustInherit Public WriteOnly Property Credentials As ICredentials
' Public Instance Methods
    MustInherit Public Function GetEntity(ByVal absoluteUri As Uri, ByVal role As String, _
        ByVal ofObjectToReturn As Type) As Object
    MustInherit Public Function ResolveUri(ByVal baseUri As Uri, ByVal relativeUri As String) As Uri
End Class
```

Subclasses: XmlUrlResolver

Passed To: XmlDocument.XmlResolver, XmlTextReader.XmlResolver, XmlValidatingReader.XmlResolver, System.Xml.Xsl.XslTransform.{Load(), XmlResolver}

XmlSignificantWhitespace   Class

System.Xml (system.xml.dll)

This class represents a whitespace node in mixed content data, if whitespace is preserved in the XML document (XmlDocument.PreserveWhitespace is True).

```
Public Class XmlSignificantWhitespace : Inherits XmlCharacterData
' Protected Constructors
    Protected Friend Sub New(ByVal strData As String, ByVal doc As XmlDocument)
' Public Instance Properties
    Overrides Public ReadOnly Property LocalName As String
    Overrides Public ReadOnly Property Name As String
    Overrides Public ReadOnly Property NodeType As XmlNodeType
    Overrides Public Property Value As String
' Public Instance Methods
    Overrides Public Function CloneNode(ByVal deep As Boolean) As XmlNode
    Overrides Public Sub WriteContentTo(ByVal w As XmlWriter)
    Overrides Public Sub WriteTo(ByVal w As XmlWriter)
End Class
```

Hierarchy: System.Object→ XmlNode(System.ICloneable, System.Collections.IEnumerable, System.Xml.XPath.IXPathNavigable)→ XmlLinkedNode→ XmlCharacterData→ XmlSignificantWhitespace

Returned By: XmlDocument.CreateSignificantWhitespace()

XmlSpace
Enum

System.Xml (system.xml.dll)
ECMA, serializable

This enumeration provides values for the xml:space scope. Used by XmlParserContext.XmlSpace.

```
Public Enum XmlSpace
    None = 0
    Default = 1
    Preserve = 2
End Enum
```

Hierarchy: System.Object→ System.ValueType→ System.Enum(System.IComparable, System.IFormattable, System.IConvertible)→ XmlSpace

Returned By: XmlParserContext.XmlSpace, XmlReader.XmlSpace, XmlWriter.XmlSpace

Passed To: XmlParserContext.{XmlParserContext(), XmlSpace}, System.Xml.XPath.XPathDocument.XPathDocument()

XmlText
Class

System.Xml (system.xml.dll)

This class represents a text node in an XML document. XmlTest is derived from the XmlCharacterData class and contains the text content of an element.

```
Public Class XmlText : Inherits XmlCharacterData
' Protected Constructors
    Protected Friend Sub New(ByVal strData As String, ByVal doc As XmlDocument)
' Public Instance Properties
    Overrides Public ReadOnly Property LocalName As String
    Overrides Public ReadOnly Property Name As String
    Overrides Public ReadOnly Property NodeType As XmlNodeType
    Overrides Public Property Value As String
' Public Instance Methods
    Overrides Public Function CloneNode(ByVal deep As Boolean) As XmlNode
    Overridable Public Function SplitText(ByVal offset As Integer) As XmlText
    Overrides Public Sub WriteContentTo(ByVal w As XmlWriter)
    Overrides Public Sub WriteTo(ByVal w As XmlWriter)
End Class
```

Hierarchy: System.Object→ XmlNode(System.ICloneable, System.Collections.IEnumerable, System.Xml.XPath.IXPathNavigable)→ XmlLinkedNode→ XmlCharacterData → XmlText

Returned By: XmlDocument.CreateTextNode()

XmlTextReader
Class

System.Xml (system.xml.dll)
ECMA

This class is a text-based reader for XML documents derived from XmlReader. XmlTextReader checks for well-formedness and expands entities, but does not validate data according to a DTD or schema.

Public Class **XmlTextReader** : Inherits XmlReader : Implements IXmlLineInfo
' Public Constructors
Public Sub **New**(ByVal input As System.IO.Stream)
Public Sub **New**(ByVal input As System.IO.Stream, ByVal nt As XmlNameTable)
Public Sub **New**(ByVal xmlFragment As System.IO.Stream, ByVal fragType As XmlNodeType, _
ByVal context As XmlParserContext)
Public Sub **New**(ByVal url As String)
Public Sub **New**(ByVal url As String, ByVal input As System.IO.Stream)
Public Sub **New**(ByVal url As String, ByVal input As System.IO.Stream, ByVal nt As XmlNameTable)
Public Sub **New**(ByVal url As String, ByVal input As System.IO.TextReader)
Public Sub **New**(ByVal url As String, ByVal input As System.IO.TextReader, ByVal nt As XmlNameTable)
Public Sub **New**(ByVal url As String, ByVal nt As XmlNameTable)
Public Sub **New**(ByVal xmlFragment As String, ByVal fragType As XmlNodeType, ByVal context As XmlParserContext)
Public Sub **New**(ByVal input As System.IO.TextReader)
Public Sub **New**(ByVal input As System.IO.TextReader, ByVal nt As XmlNameTable)
' Protected Constructors
Protected Sub **New**()
Protected Sub **New**(ByVal nt As XmlNameTable)
' Public Instance Properties
Overrides Public ReadOnly Property **AttributeCount** As Integer
Overrides Public ReadOnly Property **BaseURI** As String
Overrides Public ReadOnly Property **Depth** As Integer
Public ReadOnly Property **Encoding** As Encoding
Overrides Public ReadOnly Property **EOF** As Boolean
Overrides Public ReadOnly Property **HasValue** As Boolean
Overrides Public ReadOnly Property **IsDefault** As Boolean
Overrides Public ReadOnly Property **IsEmptyElement** As Boolean
Overrides Public Default ReadOnly Property **Item** (ByVal name As String) (ByVal namespaceURI As String As String
Overrides Public Default ReadOnly Property **Item** (ByVal i As Integer) As String
Overrides Public Default ReadOnly Property **Item** (ByVal name As String) As String
Public ReadOnly Property **LineNumber** As Integer Implements IXmlLineInfo.LineNumber
Public ReadOnly Property **LinePosition** As Integer Implements IXmlLineInfo.LinePosition
Overrides Public ReadOnly Property **LocalName** As String
Overrides Public ReadOnly Property **Name** As String
Public Property **Namespaces** As Boolean
Overrides Public ReadOnly Property **NamespaceURI** As String
Overrides Public ReadOnly Property **NameTable** As XmlNameTable
Overrides Public ReadOnly Property **NodeType** As XmlNodeType
Public Property **Normalization** As Boolean
Overrides Public ReadOnly Property **Prefix** As String
Overrides Public ReadOnly Property **QuoteChar** As Char
Overrides Public ReadOnly Property **ReadState** As ReadState
Overrides Public ReadOnly Property **Value** As String
Public Property **WhitespaceHandling** As WhitespaceHandling
Overrides Public ReadOnly Property **XmlLang** As String
Public WriteOnly Property **XmlResolver** As XmlResolver
Overrides Public ReadOnly Property **XmlSpace** As XmlSpace
' Public Instance Methods
Overrides Public Sub **Close**()
Overrides Public Function **GetAttribute**(ByVal i As Integer) As String
Overrides Public Function **GetAttribute**(ByVal name As String) As String
Overrides Public Function **GetAttribute**(ByVal localName As String, ByVal namespaceURI As String) As String
Public Function **GetRemainder**() As TextReader
Overrides Public Function **LookupNamespace**(ByVal prefix As String) As String
Overrides Public Function **MoveToAttribute**(ByVal name As String) As Boolean

Overrides Public Function **MoveToAttribute**(ByVal localName As String, ByVal namespaceURI As String) _
   As Boolean
Overrides Public Sub **MoveToAttribute**(ByVal i As Integer)
Overrides Public Function **MoveToElement**() As Boolean
Overrides Public Function **MoveToFirstAttribute**() As Boolean
Overrides Public Function **MoveToNextAttribute**() As Boolean
Overrides Public Function **Read**() As Boolean
Overrides Public Function **ReadAttributeValue**() As Boolean
Public Function **ReadBase64**(ByVal array As Byte(), ByVal offset As Integer, ByVal len As Integer) As Integer
Public Function **ReadBinHex**(ByVal array As Byte(), ByVal offset As Integer, ByVal len As Integer) As Integer
Public Function **ReadChars**(ByVal buffer As Char(), ByVal index As Integer, ByVal count As Integer) As Integer
Overrides Public Function **ReadInnerXml**() As String
Overrides Public Function **ReadOuterXml**() As String
Overrides Public Function **ReadString**() As String
Public Sub **ResetState**()
Overrides Public Sub **ResolveEntity**()
End Class

Hierarchy: System.Object→ XmlReader→ XmlTextReader(IXmlLineInfo)

XmlTextWriter   Class

System.Xml (system.xml.dll)   *ECMA*

This class adds basic formatting to the text output and is derived from XmlWriter. The Formatting property uses its values to indicate if the output is to be Indented (None is the default). If Formatting is set to Formatting.Indented, the value of the Indentation property is the number of characters to indent each successive level (or child element) in the output. IndentChar sets the character to use for indentation, which must be a valid whitespace character (the default is space). QuoteChar is the character to use to quote attributes and is either a single or double quote.

Public Class **XmlTextWriter** : Inherits XmlWriter
' *Public Constructors*
Public Sub **New**(ByVal w As System.IO.Stream, ByVal encoding As System.Text.Encoding)
Public Sub **New**(ByVal filename As String, ByVal encoding As System.Text.Encoding)
Public Sub **New**(ByVal w As System.IO.TextWriter)
' *Public Instance Properties*
Public ReadOnly Property **BaseStream** As Stream
Public Property **Formatting** As Formatting
Public Property **Indentation** As Integer
Public Property **IndentChar** As Char
Public Property **Namespaces** As Boolean
Public Property **QuoteChar** As Char
Overrides Public ReadOnly Property **WriteState** As WriteState
Overrides Public ReadOnly Property **XmlLang** As String
Overrides Public ReadOnly Property **XmlSpace** As XmlSpace
' *Public Instance Methods*
Overrides Public Sub **Close**()
Overrides Public Sub **Flush**()
Overrides Public Function **LookupPrefix**(ByVal ns As String) As String
Overrides Public Sub **WriteBase64**(ByVal buffer As Byte(), ByVal index As Integer, ByVal count As Integer)
Overrides Public Sub **WriteBinHex**(ByVal buffer As Byte(), ByVal index As Integer, ByVal count As Integer)
Overrides Public Sub **WriteCData**(ByVal text As String)
Overrides Public Sub **WriteCharEntity**(ByVal ch As Char)
Overrides Public Sub **WriteChars**(ByVal buffer As Char(), ByVal index As Integer, ByVal count As Integer)
Overrides Public Sub **WriteComment**(ByVal text As String)

Overrides Public Sub **WriteDocType**(ByVal name As String, ByVal pubid As String, ByVal sysid As String, _
  ByVal subset As String)
Overrides Public Sub **WriteEndAttribute**()
Overrides Public Sub **WriteEndDocument**()
Overrides Public Sub **WriteEndElement**()
Overrides Public Sub **WriteEntityRef**(ByVal name As String)
Overrides Public Sub **WriteFullEndElement**()
Overrides Public Sub **WriteName**(ByVal name As String)
Overrides Public Sub **WriteNmToken**(ByVal name As String)
Overrides Public Sub **WriteProcessingInstruction**(ByVal name As String, ByVal text As String)
Overrides Public Sub **WriteQualifiedName**(ByVal localName As String, ByVal ns As String)
Overrides Public Sub **WriteRaw**(ByVal buffer As Char(), ByVal index As Integer, ByVal count As Integer)
Overrides Public Sub **WriteRaw**(ByVal data As String)
Overrides Public Sub **WriteStartAttribute**(ByVal prefix As String, ByVal localName As String, ByVal ns As String)
Overrides Public Sub **WriteStartDocument**()
Overrides Public Sub **WriteStartDocument**(ByVal standalone As Boolean)
Overrides Public Sub **WriteStartElement**(ByVal prefix As String, ByVal localName As String, ByVal ns As String)
Overrides Public Sub **WriteString**(ByVal text As String)
Overrides Public Sub **WriteSurrogateCharEntity**(ByVal lowChar As Char, ByVal highChar As Char)
Overrides Public Sub **WriteWhitespace**(ByVal ws As String)
End Class

Hierarchy: System.Object→ XmlWriter→ XmlTextWriter

XmlTokenizedType   Enum

System.Xml (system.xml.dll)   *serializable*

This is an enumeration of XML string types based on the XML 1.0 specification.

Public Enum **XmlTokenizedType**
      CDATA = 0
      ID = 1
      IDREF = 2
      IDREFS = 3
      ENTITY = 4
      ENTITIES = 5
      NMTOKEN = 6
      NMTOKENS = 7
      NOTATION = 8
      ENUMERATION = 9
      QName = 10
      NCName = 11
      None = 12
End Enum

Hierarchy: System.Object→ System.ValueType→ System.Enum(System.IComparable,
System.IFormattable, System.IConvertible)→ XmlTokenizedType

XmlUrlResolver   Class

System.Xml (system.xml.dll)   *ECMA*

This class resolves URLs of external resources and retrieves them for parsing. XmlUrlResolver implements XmlResolver and provides methods for retrieving external DTDs,
Schemas, and imported stylesheets via a URL. To retrieve resources on a network, the
Credentials property can be set to provide usernames and passwords, as well as define
authentication schemes. You can set this property by supplying a System.Net.ICredentials
object. By default, this property is set for anonymous access to a URI resource.

```
Public Class XmlUrlResolver : Inherits XmlResolver
' Public Constructors
   Public Sub New()
' Public Instance Properties
   Overrides Public WriteOnly Property Credentials As ICredentials
' Public Instance Methods
   Overrides Public Function GetEntity(ByVal absoluteUri As Uri, ByVal role As String, ByVal ofObjectToReturn As Type) _
      As Object
   Overrides Public Function ResolveUri(ByVal baseUri As Uri, ByVal relativeUri As String) As Uri
End Class
```

Hierarchy: System.Object→ XmlResolver→ XmlUrlResolver

XmlValidatingReader   Class

System.Xml (system.xml.dll)

This class is an XML reader that supports DTD and Schema validation. The type of validation to perform is contained in the ValidationType property, which can be DTD, Schema, XDR, or Auto. Auto is the default and determines which type of validation is required, if any, based on the document. If the DOCTYPE element contains DTD information, that is used. If a schema attribute exists or there is an inline <schema>, that schema is used.

This class implements an event handler that you can set to warn of validation errors during Read() operations. Specifically, a delegate instance of type System.Xml.Schema.ValidationEventHandler can be set for the ValidationEventHandler event in this class. This delegate instance is invoked whenever the XmlValidatingReader finds an schema-invalid construct in the XML document it is reading, giving the delegate a chance to perform whatever error-handling is appropriate. If no event handler is registered, a XmlException is thrown instead on the first error.

```
Public Class XmlValidatingReader : Inherits XmlReader : Implements IXmlLineInfo
' Public Constructors
   Public Sub New(ByVal xmlFragment As System.IO.Stream, ByVal fragType As XmlNodeType, _
      ByVal context As XmlParserContext)
   Public Sub New(ByVal xmlFragment As String, ByVal fragType As XmlNodeType, ByVal context As XmlParserContext)
   Public Sub New(ByVal reader As XmlReader)
' Public Instance Properties
   Overrides Public ReadOnly Property AttributeCount As Integer
   Overrides Public ReadOnly Property BaseURI As String
   Overrides Public ReadOnly Property CanResolveEntity As Boolean
   Overrides Public ReadOnly Property Depth As Integer
   Public ReadOnly Property Encoding As Encoding
   Public Property EntityHandling As EntityHandling
   Overrides Public ReadOnly Property EOF As Boolean
   Overrides Public ReadOnly Property HasValue As Boolean
   Overrides Public ReadOnly Property IsDefault As Boolean
   Overrides Public ReadOnly Property IsEmptyElement As Boolean
   Overrides Public Default ReadOnly Property Item (ByVal name As String) As String
   Overrides Public Default ReadOnly Property Item (ByVal i As Integer) As String
   Overrides Public Default ReadOnly Property Item (ByVal name As String) (ByVal namespaceURI As String As String
   Overrides Public ReadOnly Property LocalName As String
   Overrides Public ReadOnly Property Name As String
   Public Property Namespaces As Boolean
   Overrides Public ReadOnly Property NamespaceURI As String
   Overrides Public ReadOnly Property NameTable As XmlNameTable
   Overrides Public ReadOnly Property NodeType As XmlNodeType
```

Overrides Public ReadOnly Property **Prefix** As String
Overrides Public ReadOnly Property **QuoteChar** As Char
Public ReadOnly Property **Reader** As XmlReader
Overrides Public ReadOnly Property **ReadState** As ReadState
Public ReadOnly Property **Schemas** As XmlSchemaCollection
Public ReadOnly Property **SchemaType** As Object
Public Property **ValidationType** As ValidationType
Overrides Public ReadOnly Property **Value** As String
Overrides Public ReadOnly Property **XmlLang** As String
Public WriteOnly Property **XmlResolver** As XmlResolver
Overrides Public ReadOnly Property **XmlSpace** As XmlSpace
' *Public Instance Methods*
Overrides Public Sub **Close**()
Overrides Public Function **GetAttribute**(ByVal i As Integer) As String
Overrides Public Function **GetAttribute**(ByVal name As String) As String
Overrides Public Function **GetAttribute**(ByVal localName As String, ByVal namespaceURI As String) As String
Overrides Public Function **LookupNamespace**(ByVal prefix As String) As String
Overrides Public Function **MoveToAttribute**(ByVal name As String) As Boolean
Overrides Public Function **MoveToAttribute**(ByVal localName As String, ByVal namespaceURI As String) _
   As Boolean
Overrides Public Sub **MoveToAttribute**(ByVal i As Integer)
Overrides Public Function **MoveToElement**() As Boolean
Overrides Public Function **MoveToFirstAttribute**() As Boolean
Overrides Public Function **MoveToNextAttribute**() As Boolean
Overrides Public Function **Read**() As Boolean
Overrides Public Function **ReadAttributeValue**() As Boolean
Overrides Public Function **ReadInnerXml**() As String
Overrides Public Function **ReadOuterXml**() As String
Overrides Public Function **ReadString**() As String
Public Function **ReadTypedValue**() As Object
Overrides Public Sub **ResolveEntity**()
' *Events*
Public Event **ValidationEventHandler** As ValidationEventHandler
End Class

Hierarchy: System.Object→ XmlReader→ XmlValidatingReader(IXmlLineInfo)

XmlWhitespace   Class

System.Xml (system.xml.dll)

This class represents whitespace in element content. Whitespace is ignored if XmlDocument.PreserveWhitespace is not set to true.

Public Class **XmlWhitespace** : Inherits XmlCharacterData
' *Protected Constructors*
Protected Friend Sub **New**(ByVal strData As String, ByVal doc As XmlDocument)
' *Public Instance Properties*
Overrides Public ReadOnly Property **LocalName** As String
Overrides Public ReadOnly Property **Name** As String
Overrides Public ReadOnly Property **NodeType** As XmlNodeType
Overrides Public Property **Value** As String
' *Public Instance Methods*
Overrides Public Function **CloneNode**(ByVal deep As Boolean) As XmlNode
Overrides Public Sub **WriteContentTo**(ByVal w As XmlWriter)
Overrides Public Sub **WriteTo**(ByVal w As XmlWriter)
End Class

Hierarchy: System.Object→ XmlNode(System.ICloneable, System.Collections.IEnumerable, System.Xml.XPath.IXPathNavigable)→ XmlLinkedNode→ XmlCharacterData→ XmlWhitespace

Returned By: XmlDocument.CreateWhitespace()

XmlWriter   MustInherit Class
System.Xml (system.xml.dll)   *ECMA*

This class is a fast writer used to output XML data to a stream or file. Two methods work with input from an XmlReader object to produce output from the currently positioned node. WriteAttributes() outputs all the node's attributes. WriteNode() dumps the entire current node to the output stream and moves the XmlReader to the next node.

The remaining Write* methods of this class take string arguments that are output as properly formed XML markup. For example, WriteComment() takes a string and outputs it within <!– ... –> markup. WriteStartAttribute() and WriteStartElement() provide some flexibility when writing elements and attributes. These two methods provide the opening contents of each type, given the name, prefix, and namespace. The next call can then provide the value of the element or attribute by other means. For example, you can use WriteString() for a simple string value, or another WriteStartElement() to begin a child element. WriteEndAttribute() and WriteEndElement() close the writing.

The derived XmlTextWriter class provides formatting functionality to the output data.

Public MustInherit Class **XmlWriter**
' Protected Constructors
    Protected Sub **New**()
' Public Instance Properties
    MustInherit Public ReadOnly Property **WriteState** As WriteState
    MustInherit Public ReadOnly Property **XmlLang** As String
    MustInherit Public ReadOnly Property **XmlSpace** As XmlSpace
' Public Instance Methods
    MustInherit Public Sub **Close**()
    MustInherit Public Sub **Flush**()
    MustInherit Public Function **LookupPrefix**(ByVal ns As String) As String
    Overridable Public Sub **WriteAttributes**(ByVal reader As XmlReader, ByVal defattr As Boolean)
    Public Sub **WriteAttributeString**(ByVal localName As String, ByVal value As String)
    Public Sub **WriteAttributeString**(ByVal localName As String, ByVal ns As String, ByVal value As String)
    Public Sub **WriteAttributeString**(ByVal prefix As String, ByVal localName As String, ByVal ns As String, _
        ByVal value As String)
    MustInherit Public Sub **WriteBase64**(ByVal buffer As Byte(), ByVal index As Integer, ByVal count As Integer)
    MustInherit Public Sub **WriteBinHex**(ByVal buffer As Byte(), ByVal index As Integer, ByVal count As Integer)
    MustInherit Public Sub **WriteCData**(ByVal text As String)
    MustInherit Public Sub **WriteCharEntity**(ByVal ch As Char)
    MustInherit Public Sub **WriteChars**(ByVal buffer As Char(), ByVal index As Integer, ByVal count As Integer)
    MustInherit Public Sub **WriteComment**(ByVal text As String)
    MustInherit Public Sub **WriteDocType**(ByVal name As String, ByVal pubid As String, ByVal sysid As String, _
        ByVal subset As String)
    Public Sub **WriteElementString**(ByVal localName As String, ByVal value As String)
    Public Sub **WriteElementString**(ByVal localName As String, ByVal ns As String, ByVal value As String)
    MustInherit Public Sub **WriteEndAttribute**()
    MustInherit Public Sub **WriteEndDocument**()
    MustInherit Public Sub **WriteEndElement**()
    MustInherit Public Sub **WriteEntityRef**(ByVal name As String)
    MustInherit Public Sub **WriteFullEndElement**()
    MustInherit Public Sub **WriteName**(ByVal name As String)
    MustInherit Public Sub **WriteNmToken**(ByVal name As String)
    Overridable Public Sub **WriteNode**(ByVal reader As XmlReader, ByVal defattr As Boolean)

```
    MustInherit Public Sub WriteProcessingInstruction(ByVal name As String, ByVal text As String)
    MustInherit Public Sub WriteQualifiedName(ByVal localName As String, ByVal ns As String)
    MustInherit Public Sub WriteRaw(ByVal buffer As Char(), ByVal index As Integer, ByVal count As Integer)
    MustInherit Public Sub WriteRaw(ByVal data As String)
    Public Sub WriteStartAttribute(ByVal localName As String, ByVal ns As String)
    MustInherit Public Sub WriteStartAttribute(ByVal prefix As String, ByVal localName As String, _
       ByVal ns As String)
    MustInherit Public Sub WriteStartDocument()
    MustInherit Public Sub WriteStartDocument(ByVal standalone As Boolean)
    Public Sub WriteStartElement(ByVal localName As String)
    Public Sub WriteStartElement(ByVal localName As String, ByVal ns As String)
    MustInherit Public Sub WriteStartElement(ByVal prefix As String, ByVal localName As String, ByVal ns As String)
    MustInherit Public Sub WriteString(ByVal text As String)
    MustInherit Public Sub WriteSurrogateCharEntity(ByVal lowChar As Char, ByVal highChar As Char)
    MustInherit Public Sub WriteWhitespace(ByVal ws As String)
End Class
```

Subclasses: XmlTextWriter

Passed To: XmlDocument.Save(), XmlNode.{WriteContentTo(), WriteTo()},
System.Xml.Xsl.XslTransform.Transform()

CHAPTER 23

System.Xml.XPath

XPath is a W3C specification for locating nodes in an XML document. It provides an expression syntax that can determine a node based on its type, location, and relation to other nodes in a document. XPath is generally not useful alone, but works in conjunction with other tools, especially XSLT. Figure 23-1 shows the types in this namespace.

System.Xml.XPath provides types that evaluate expressions and match nodes in XML documents. XPathDocument is a document object designed to provide fast document navigation through XPath and is used by the System.Xml.Xsl classes for XSLT transformations. XPathNavigator is the core entry point for doing XPath expressions; it is MustInherit, allowing for more than just XML documents to be XPath-navigated. For example, an ADO.NET provider could, if it desired, implement the IXPathNavigable interface and return an XPathNavigator that translated XPath queries into a SQL SELECT statement. (See Aaron Skonnard's MSDN Magazine article "Writing XML Providers for Microsoft .NET" for more details about using XML-based technologies over data sources other than XML documents.)

IXPathNavigable   Interface
System.Xml.XPath (system.xml.dll)

This is an interface to XPathNavigator implemented by XPathDocument, System.Xml.XmlNode, and derived classes. It implements one method, CreateNavigator(), which creates an XPath-Navigator instance for the document object.

Public Interface **IXPathNavigable**
' Public Instance Methods
   Public Function **CreateNavigator**() As XPathNavigator
End Interface

Implemented By: XPathDocument, System.Xml.XmlNode

Passed To: System.Xml.Xsl.XslTransform.{Load(), Transform()}

485

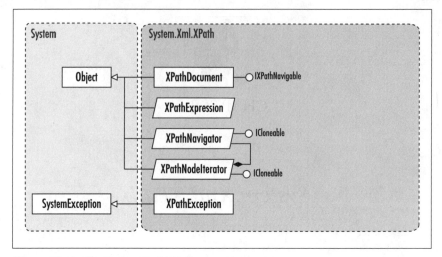

Figure 23-1. The System.Xml.XPath namespace

XmlCaseOrder

Enum

System.Xml.XPath (system.xml.dll)

serializable

This enumeration specifies how nodes are sorted with respect to case. A value of None indicates that case is to be ignored when ordering nodes.

```
Public Enum XmlCaseOrder
    None = 0
    UpperFirst = 1
    LowerFirst = 2
End Enum
```

Hierarchy: System.Object → System.ValueType → System.Enum(System.IComparable, System.IFormattable, System.IConvertible) → XmlCaseOrder

Passed To: XPathExpression.AddSort()

XmlDataType

Enum

System.Xml.XPath (system.xml.dll)

serializable

This enumeration specifies whether to sort node values by type as numeric value (Number) or alphabetically (Text).

```
Public Enum XmlDataType
    Text = 1
    Number = 2
End Enum
```

Hierarchy: System.Object → System.ValueType → System.Enum(System.IComparable, System.IFormattable, System.IConvertible) → XmlDataType

Passed To: XPathExpression.AddSort()

XmlSortOrder **Enum**

System.Xml.XPath (system.xml.dll) *serializable*

This enumeration specifies how nodes are sorted by numerical value, either ascending or descending.

```
Public Enum XmlSortOrder
    Ascending = 1
    Descending = 2
End Enum
```

Hierarchy: System.Object→ System.ValueType→ System.Enum(System.IComparable, System.IFormattable, System.IConvertible)→ XmlSortOrder

Passed To: XPathExpression.AddSort()

XPathDocument **Class**

System.Xml.XPath (system.xml.dll)

This class is a concrete implementation of IXPathNavigable for creating an XPathNavigator that knows how to scan through an XML document. There are overloaded forms of the constructor designed to pull an XML document from various sources—a System.IO.Stream, a string, a System.IO.TextReader (which presumably is pulling from some other valid data source), or a System.Xml.XmlReader. Note that if the XmlReader is currently positioned on top of a particular node within a document, the constructed XPathDocument instance is only valid for that element and its children. This allows partial XPath scans of a given document.

This class serves no other purpose than as a factory for producing XPathNavigator instances.

```
Public Class XPathDocument : Implements IXPathNavigable
' Public Constructors
    Public Sub New(ByVal stream As System.IO.Stream)
    Public Sub New(ByVal uri As String)
    Public Sub New(ByVal uri As String, ByVal space As System.Xml.XmlSpace)
    Public Sub New(ByVal reader As System.IO.TextReader)
    Public Sub New(ByVal reader As System.Xml.XmlReader)
    Public Sub New(ByVal reader As System.Xml.XmlReader, ByVal space As System.Xml.XmlSpace)
' Public Instance Methods
    Public Function CreateNavigator() As XPathNavigator Implements IXPathNavigable.CreateNavigator
End Class
```

*System.
Xml.XPath*

XPathException **Class**

System.Xml.XPath (system.xml.dll) *serializable*

This exception indicates a problem with an XPathExpression, such as an invalid prefix.

```
Public Class XPathException : Inherits SystemException
' Public Constructors
    Public Sub New(ByVal message As String, ByVal innerException As Exception)
' Protected Constructors
    Protected Sub New(ByVal info As System.Runtime.Serialization.SerializationInfo, _
        ByVal context As System.Runtime.Serialization.StreamingContext)
' Public Instance Properties
    Overrides Public ReadOnly Property Message As String
```

' *Public Instance Methods*
  Overrides Public Sub **GetObjectData**(ByVal info As System.Runtime.Serialization.SerializationInfo, _
    ByVal context As System.Runtime.Serialization.StreamingContext)
End Class

Hierarchy: System.Object→ System.Exception(System.Runtime.Serialization.ISerializable)→
System.SystemException→ XPathException

XPathExpression   MustInherit Class

System.Xml.XPath (system.xml.dll)

This class represents a compiled XPath expression. An XPathExpression is returned by the
Compile() method of XPathNavigator from an XPath expression string. The AddSort() method
allows you to specify the order of returned nodes from the expression. SetContext() sets
the namespace to use in the evaluation of the expression.

Public MustInherit Class **XPathExpression**
' *Public Instance Properties*
  MustInherit Public ReadOnly Property **Expression** As String
  MustInherit Public ReadOnly Property **ReturnType** As XPathResultType
' *Public Instance Methods*
  MustInherit Public Sub **AddSort**(ByVal expr As Object, ByVal comparer As System.Collections.IComparer)
  MustInherit Public Sub **AddSort**(ByVal expr As Object, ByVal order As XmlSortOrder,   _
    ByVal caseOrder As XmlCaseOrder, ByVal lang As String, ByVal dataType As XmlDataType)
  MustInherit Public Function **Clone**() As XPathExpression
  MustInherit Public Sub **SetContext**(ByVal nsManager As System.Xml.XmlNamespaceManager)
End Class

Returned By: XPathNavigator.Compile()

Passed To: XPathNavigator.{Evaluate(), Matches(), Select()}

XPathNamespaceScope   Enum

System.Xml.XPath (system.xml.dll)   *serializable*

This enumeration defines the namespace scope for certain XPathNavigator operations. All
includes all namespaces within the scope of the current node (including the xmlns:xml
namespace, whether defined explicitly or not). ExcludeXml includes all namespaces
within the scope of the current node, *except* the xmlns:xml namespace. Local includes all
locally defined namespaces within the scope of the current node.

Public Enum **XPathNamespaceScope**
    All = 0
    ExcludeXml = 1
    Local = 2
End Enum

Hierarchy: System.Object→ System.ValueType→ System.Enum(System.IComparable,
System.IFormattable, System.IConvertible)→ XPathNamespaceScope

Passed To: XPathNavigator.{MoveToFirstNamespace(), MoveToNextNamespace()}

XPathNavigator
MustInherit Class

System.Xml.XPath (system.xml.dll)

This class is a read-only representation of an XPathDocument based on the IXPathNavigable interface. It provides an easy-to-use data object for quick XPath-based navigation, particularly for XSLT transformations.

An XPathNavigator instance maintains its state with the current node position to provide the proper context for any XPath expression evaluation. Initially, the current node is the root node. The current node is changed by using the Select() method or the various MoveTo* methods. If the XPath expression evaluates to a set of nodes, the first node of the set is the current node for the XPathNavigator. All the Select* methods return an XPathNodeIterator object containing the set of nodes returned by the function. Except for plain-old Select(), the Select* functions do not change the current node of the XPathNavigator they are used on. Any actions on the XPathNodeIterator objects that they return also do not affect the originating object.

The Compile() method takes an XPath expression string and encapsulates it into a compiled XPathExpression object. XPathExpression objects are used by Select(), Evaluate(), and Matches() as input to search a node list.

```
Public MustInherit Class XPathNavigator : Implements ICloneable
' Protected Constructors
   Protected Sub New()
' Public Instance Properties
   MustInherit Public ReadOnly Property BaseURI As String
   MustInherit Public ReadOnly Property HasAttributes As Boolean
   MustInherit Public ReadOnly Property HasChildren As Boolean
   MustInherit Public ReadOnly Property IsEmptyElement As Boolean
   MustInherit Public ReadOnly Property LocalName As String
   MustInherit Public ReadOnly Property Name As String
   MustInherit Public ReadOnly Property NamespaceURI As String
   MustInherit Public ReadOnly Property NameTable As XmlNameTable
   MustInherit Public ReadOnly Property NodeType As XPathNodeType
   MustInherit Public ReadOnly Property Prefix As String
   MustInherit Public ReadOnly Property Value As String
   MustInherit Public ReadOnly Property XmlLang As String
' Public Instance Methods
   MustInherit Public Function Clone() As XPathNavigator
   Overridable Public Function ComparePosition(ByVal nav As XPathNavigator) As XmlNodeOrder
   Overridable Public Function Compile(ByVal xpath As String) As XPathExpression
   Overridable Public Function Evaluate(ByVal xpath As String) As Object
   Overridable Public Function Evaluate(ByVal expr As XPathExpression) As Object
   Overridable Public Function Evaluate(ByVal expr As XPathExpression, ByVal context As XPathNodeIterator) _
      As Object
   MustInherit Public Function GetAttribute(ByVal localName As String, ByVal namespaceURI As String) As String
   MustInherit Public Function GetNamespace(ByVal name As String) As String
   Overridable Public Function IsDescendant(ByVal nav As XPathNavigator) As Boolean
   MustInherit Public Function IsSamePosition(ByVal other As XPathNavigator) As Boolean
   Overridable Public Function Matches(ByVal xpath As String) As Boolean
   Overridable Public Function Matches(ByVal expr As XPathExpression) As Boolean
   MustInherit Public Function MoveTo(ByVal other As XPathNavigator) As Boolean
   MustInherit Public Function MoveToAttribute(ByVal localName As String, ByVal namespaceURI As String) _
      As Boolean
   MustInherit Public Function MoveToFirst() As Boolean
   MustInherit Public Function MoveToFirstAttribute() As Boolean
   MustInherit Public Function MoveToFirstChild() As Boolean
```

Public Function **MoveToFirstNamespace**() As Boolean

MustInherit Public Function **MoveToFirstNamespace**(ByVal namespaceScope As XPathNamespaceScope) _
   As Boolean

MustInherit Public Function **MoveToId**(ByVal id As String) As Boolean

MustInherit Public Function **MoveToNamespace**(ByVal name As String) As Boolean

MustInherit Public Function **MoveToNext**() As Boolean

MustInherit Public Function **MoveToNextAttribute**() As Boolean

Public Function **MoveToNextNamespace**() As Boolean

MustInherit Public Function **MoveToNextNamespace**(ByVal namespaceScope As XPathNamespaceScope) _
   As Boolean

MustInherit Public Function **MoveToParent**() As Boolean

MustInherit Public Function **MoveToPrevious**() As Boolean

MustInherit Public Sub **MoveToRoot**()

Overridable Public Function **Select**(ByVal xpath As String) As XPathNodeIterator

Overridable Public Function **Select**(ByVal expr As XPathExpression) As XPathNodeIterator

Overridable Public Function **SelectAncestors**(ByVal name As String, ByVal namespaceURI As String, _
   ByVal matchSelf As Boolean) As XPathNodeIterator

Overridable Public Function **SelectAncestors**(ByVal type As XPathNodeType, ByVal matchSelf As Boolean) _
   As XPathNodeIterator

Overridable Public Function **SelectChildren**(ByVal name As String, ByVal namespaceURI As String) _
   As XPathNodeIterator

Overridable Public Function **SelectChildren**(ByVal type As XPathNodeType) As XPathNodeIterator

Overridable Public Function **SelectDescendants**(ByVal name As String, ByVal namespaceURI As String, _
   ByVal matchSelf As Boolean) As XPathNodeIterator

Overridable Public Function **SelectDescendants**(ByVal type As XPathNodeType, ByVal matchSelf As Boolean) _
   As XPathNodeIterator

Overrides Public Function **ToString**() As String

End Class

Returned By: System.Xml.XmlDataDocument.CreateNavigator(),
System.Xml.XmlNode.CreateNavigator(), IXPathNavigable.CreateNavigator(),
XPathDocument.CreateNavigator(), XPathNodeIterator.Current

Passed To: System.Xml.Xsl.IXsltContextFunction.Invoke(),
System.Xml.Xsl.XsltContext.PreserveWhitespace(), System.Xml.Xsl.XslTransform.{Load(), Transform()}

XPathNodeIterator
MustInherit Class

System.Xml.XPath (system.xml.dll)

This class is a node-set constructed from a compiled XPath expression. This type is
returned by the Select* methods of XPathNavigator. The MoveNext() method moves to the
next node of the node set in document order and does not affect the XPathNavigator on
which the Select() was called.

Public MustInherit Class **XPathNodeIterator** : Implements ICloneable

' *Protected Constructors*

   Protected Sub **New**()

' *Public Instance Properties*

   Overridable Public ReadOnly Property **Count** As Integer

   MustInherit Public ReadOnly Property **Current** As XPathNavigator

   MustInherit Public ReadOnly Property **CurrentPosition** As Integer

' *Public Instance Methods*

   MustInherit Public Function **Clone**() As XPathNodeIterator

   MustInherit Public Function **MoveNext**() As Boolean

End Class

Returned By: XPathNavigator.{Select(), SelectAncestors(), SelectChildren(), SelectDescendants()}

Passed To: XPathNavigator.Evaluate()

XPathNodeType
Enum

System.Xml.XPath (system.xml.dll)
serializable

This enumeration contains the types of nodes that can be listed with the XPathNavigator.NodeType property.

```
Public Enum XPathNodeType
    Root = 0
    Element = 1
    Attribute = 2
    Namespace = 3
    Text = 4
    SignificantWhitespace = 5
    Whitespace = 6
    ProcessingInstruction = 7
    Comment = 8
    All = 9
End Enum
```

Hierarchy: System.Object→ System.ValueType→ System.Enum(System.IComparable, System.IFormattable, System.IConvertible)→ XPathNodeType

Returned By: XPathNavigator.NodeType

Passed To: XPathNavigator.{SelectAncestors(), SelectChildren(), SelectDescendants()}

XPathResultType
Enum

System.Xml.XPath (system.xml.dll)
serializable

This enumeration contains the result types used by the XPathExpression.ReturnType property.

```
Public Enum XPathResultType
    Number = 0
    String = 1
    Navigator = 1
    Boolean = 2
    NodeSet = 3
    Any = 5
    Error = 6
End Enum
```

Hierarchy: System.Object→ System.ValueType→ System.Enum(System.IComparable, System.IFormattable, System.IConvertible)→ XPathResultType

Returned By: XPathExpression.ReturnType, System.Xml.Xsl.IXsltContextFunction.{ArgTypes, ReturnType}, System.Xml.Xsl.IXsltContextVariable.VariableType

Passed To: System.Xml.Xsl.XsltContext.ResolveFunction()

CHAPTER 24

System.Xml.Xsl

The System.Xml.Xsl namespace provides support to Extensible Stylesheet Language Transformations (XSLT). XSLT is a W3C specification that describes how to transform one XML document into another with the use of stylesheet templates. For example, a common use of XSLT is to transform an XML document into standard HTML by transforming the specific elements of the input XML document into comparable HTML elements. XSLT templates use XPath expression syntax to specify which nodes of the input XML are transformed.

The XslTransform class constructs the transform object. It loads a stylesheet and applies its templates to an XML document to output the transformed data. The XsltArgumentList class creates objects for XSLT parameters that can be loaded into the stylesheet at runtime. XsltContext provides the XSLT processor with the current context node information used for XPath expression resolution. Figure 24-1 shows the types in this namespace.

IXsltContextFunction
Interface

System.Xml.Xsl (system.xml.dll)

The Microsoft .NET XSLT engine, like many other XSLT engines, allows custom functions inside of an XSLT stylesheet document. By providing an "extension object" to an XsltArgumentList instance, an XSLT stylesheet can "call out" to methods in the CLR. See the XsltArgumentList description for an example.

```
Public Interface IXsltContextFunction
' Public Instance Properties
    Public ReadOnly Property ArgTypes As XPathResultType()
    Public ReadOnly Property Maxargs As Integer
    Public ReadOnly Property Minargs As Integer
    Public ReadOnly Property ReturnType As XPathResultType
' Public Instance Methods
    Public Function Invoke(ByVal xsltContext As XsltContext, ByVal args As Object(), _
    ByVal docContext As System.Xml.XPath.XPathNavigator) As Object
End Interface
```

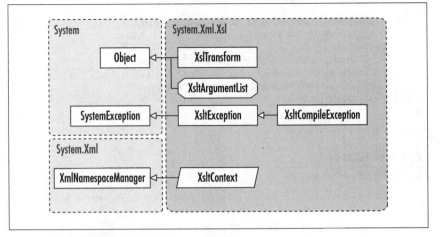

Figure 24–1. The System.Xml.Xsl namespace

Returned By: XsltContext.ResolveFunction()

IXsltContextVariable
Interface

System.Xml.Xsl (system.xml.dll)

As with IXsltContextFunction, this interface is used to help the XSLT engine resolve data objects bound into the XSLT engine's executing context while processing an XML document. See the XsltArgumentList method description for an example of how context functions and variables are used with an XSLT instance.

```
Public Interface IXsltContextVariable
' Public Instance Properties
   Public ReadOnly Property IsLocal As Boolean
   Public ReadOnly Property IsParam As Boolean
   Public ReadOnly Property VariableType As XPathResultType
' Public Instance Methods
   Public Function Evaluate(ByVal xsltContext As XsltContext) As Object
End Interface
```

Returned By: XsltContext.ResolveVariable()

XsltArgumentList
NotInheritable Class

System.Xml.Xsl (system.xml.dll)

The XsltArgumentList class constructs lists of parameters and node fragment objects that can be called from stylesheets. This type is called as the second argument to the Transform() method of XslTransform. Parameters are associated with namespace-qualified names, and objects are associated with their namespace URIs.

The XsltArgumentList can also be used to bind functions and variables into the XSLT engine's execution space—commonly called the XSLT context—for use by the XSLT stylesheet during processing.

```
Public NotInheritable Class XsltArgumentList
' Public Constructors
   Public Sub New()
' Public Instance Methods
```

Public Sub **AddExtensionObject**(ByVal namespaceUri As String, ByVal extension As Object)
Public Sub **AddParam**(ByVal name As String, ByVal namespaceUri As String, ByVal parameter As Object)
Public Sub **Clear**()
Public Function **GetExtensionObject**(ByVal namespaceUri As String) As Object
Public Function **GetParam**(ByVal name As String, ByVal namespaceUri As String) As Object
Public Function **RemoveExtensionObject**(ByVal namespaceUri As String) As Object
Public Function **RemoveParam**(ByVal name As String, ByVal namespaceUri As String) As Object
End Class

Passed To: XslTransform.Transform()

XsltCompileException Class

System.Xml.Xsl (system.xml.dll) *serializable*

The XslTransform.Load() method throws this exception when it encounters an error in an XSLT document.

Public Class **XsltCompileException** : Inherits XsltException
' *Public Constructors*
Public Sub **New**(ByVal inner As Exception, ByVal sourceUri As String, ByVal lineNumber As Integer, _
ByVal linePosition As Integer)
' *Protected Constructors*
Protected Sub **New**(ByVal info As System.Runtime.Serialization.SerializationInfo, _
ByVal context As System.Runtime.Serialization.StreamingContext)
' *Public Instance Properties*
Overrides Public ReadOnly Property **Message** As String
' *Public Instance Methods*
Overrides Public Sub **GetObjectData**(ByVal info As System.Runtime.Serialization.SerializationInfo, _
ByVal context As System.Runtime.Serialization.StreamingContext)
End Class

Hierarchy: System.Object→ System.Exception(System.Runtime.Serialization.ISerializable)→
System.SystemException→ XsltException→ XsltCompileException

XsltContext MustInherit Class

System.Xml.Xsl (system.xml.dll)

This class provides a way to resolve namespaces and determine the current context for XPath variables and expressions. It inherits System.Xml.XmlNamespaceManager and its namespace functions. Additional methods defined for this class resolve variables (ResolveVariable()) as well as references to XPath functions invoked during execution (ResolveFunction()).

Public MustInherit Class **XsltContext** : Inherits System.Xml.XmlNamespaceManager
' *Public Constructors*
Public Sub **New**()
Public Sub **New**(ByVal table As System.Xml.NameTable)
' *Public Instance Properties*
MustInherit Public ReadOnly Property **Whitespace** As Boolean
' *Public Instance Methods*
MustInherit Public Function **CompareDocument**(ByVal baseUri As String, ByVal nextbaseUri As String) As Integer
MustInherit Public Function **PreserveWhitespace**(ByVal node As System.Xml.XPath.XPathNavigator) As Boolean
MustInherit Public Function **ResolveFunction**(ByVal prefix As String, ByVal name As String, _
ByVal ArgTypes As System.Xml.XPath.XPathResultType()) As IXsltContextFunction
MustInherit Public Function **ResolveVariable**(ByVal prefix As String, ByVal name As String) As IXsltContextVariable
End Class

Hierarchy: System.Object→
System.Xml.XmlNamespaceManager(System.Collections.IEnumerable)→ XsltContext

Passed To: IXsltContextFunction.Invoke(), IXsltContextVariable.Evaluate()

XsltException

Class

System.Xml.Xsl (system.xml.dll)

serializable

This class returns XSLT exception errors thrown by XslTransform.Transform().

```
Public Class XsltException : Inherits SystemException
' Public Constructors
    Public Sub New(ByVal message As String, ByVal innerException As Exception)
' Protected Constructors
    Protected Sub New(ByVal info As System.Runtime.Serialization.SerializationInfo, _
        ByVal context As System.Runtime.Serialization.StreamingContext)
' Public Instance Properties
    Public ReadOnly Property LineNumber As Integer
    Public ReadOnly Property LinePosition As Integer
    Overrides Public ReadOnly Property Message As String
    Public ReadOnly Property SourceUri As String
' Public Instance Methods
    Overrides Public Sub GetObjectData(ByVal info As System.Runtime.Serialization.SerializationInfo, _
        ByVal context As System.Runtime.Serialization.StreamingContext)
End Class
```

Hierarchy: System.Object→ System.Exception(System.Runtime.Serialization.ISerializable)→
System.SystemException→ XsltException

Subclasses: XsltCompileException

XslTransform

NotInheritable Class

System.Xml.Xsl (system.xml.dll)

This object uses the Load method to input a stylesheet from either a URL, an XPathNavigator object, an object implementing IXPathNavigable, or an XmlReader object (remember, an XSL stylesheet is an XML document itself). The Transform() method takes a URL, an XPathNavigator object, or an object implementing IXPathNavigable as its first argument, which contains the XML document to transform. The second argument is an XsltArgumentList object; see XsltArgumentList for an example of using bound functions and/or variables.

The transformed result is output to an XmlReader object by default, or you can specify either a System.IO.Stream, XmlWriter, or XmlTextWriter object in the third argument for the output.

```
Public NotInheritable Class XslTransform
' Public Constructors
    Public Sub New()
' Public Instance Properties
    Public WriteOnly Property XmlResolver As XmlResolver
' Public Instance Methods
    Public Sub Load(ByVal stylesheet As System.Xml.XPath.IXPathNavigable)
    Public Sub Load(ByVal stylesheet As System.Xml.XPath.IXPathNavigable, _
        ByVal resolver As System.Xml.XmlResolver)
    Public Sub Load(ByVal url As String)
    Public Sub Load(ByVal url As String, ByVal resolver As System.Xml.XmlResolver)
    Public Sub Load(ByVal stylesheet As System.Xml.XmlReader)
    Public Sub Load(ByVal stylesheet As System.Xml.XmlReader, ByVal resolver As System.Xml.XmlResolver)
```

*System.
Xml.Xsl*

```
Public Sub Load(ByVal stylesheet As System.Xml.XPath.XPathNavigator)
Public Sub Load(ByVal stylesheet As System.Xml.XPath.XPathNavigator, ByVal resolver As System.Xml.XmlResolver)
Public Sub Transform(ByVal input As System.Xml.XPath.IXPathNavigable, ByVal args As XsltArgumentList, _
   ByVal output As System.IO.Stream)
Public Sub Transform(ByVal input As System.Xml.XPath.IXPathNavigable, ByVal args As XsltArgumentList, _
   ByVal output As System.IO.TextWriter)
Public Sub Transform(ByVal input As System.Xml.XPath.IXPathNavigable, ByVal args As XsltArgumentList, _
   ByVal output As System.Xml.XmlWriter)
Public Sub Transform(ByVal inputfile As String, ByVal outputfile As String)
Public Sub Transform(ByVal input As System.Xml.XPath.XPathNavigator, ByVal args As XsltArgumentList, _
   ByVal output As System.IO.Stream)
Public Sub Transform(ByVal input As System.Xml.XPath.XPathNavigator, ByVal args As XsltArgumentList, _
   ByVal output As System.IO.TextWriter)
Public Sub Transform(ByVal input As System.Xml.XPath.XPathNavigator, ByVal args As XsltArgumentList, _
   ByVal output As System.Xml.XmlWriter)
Public Function Transform(ByVal input As System.Xml.XPath.IXPathNavigable, ByVal args As XsltArgumentList) _
   As XmlReader
Public Function Transform(ByVal input As System.Xml.XPath.XPathNavigator, ByVal args As XsltArgumentList) _
   As XmlReader
End Class
```

PART III

Appendixes

The final part of this book contains a number of useful appendixes that supplement information found in Part II. Appendix A, *Regular Expressions*, describes the syntax used in regular expressions, which allow you to define sophisticated patterns to search for in strings. Appendix B, *Format Specifiers*, describes the syntax and presents examples of the format specifiers used with the String.Format method and often with the Console.WriteLine method. Appendix C, *Data Marshaling*, presents a table of .NET data types and their corresponding COM equivalents for COM interop. Appendix D, *Namespaces and Assemblies*, lists the namespaces presented in Part II and the assemblies in which they're located. This information is useful in determining which assemblies you need to reference when compiling your programs. Appendix E, *Type, Method, Property, Event, and Field Index*, provides a list of type members and the types to which they belong.

APPENDIX A

Regular Expressions

The following tables summarize the regular-expression grammar and syntax supported by the regular-expression classes in System.Text.RegularExpression. Each of the modifiers and qualifiers in the tables can substantially change the behavior of the matching and searching patterns. For further information on regular expressions, we recommend the definitive *Mastering Regular Expressions* by Jeffrey E. F. Friedl (O'Reilly).

All the syntax described in the tables should match the Perl5 syntax, with specific exceptions noted.

Table A-1. Character escapes

Escape code sequence	Meaning	Hexadecimal equivalent
\a	Bell	\u0007
\b	Backspace	\u0008
\t	Tab	\u0009
\r	Carriage return	\u000A
\v	Vertical tab	\u000B
\f	Form feed	\u000C
\n	Newline	\u000D
\e	Escape	\u001B
	ASCII character as octal	
\x20	ASCII character as hex	
\cC	ASCII control character	
\u0020	Unicode character as hex	
\non-escape	A nonescape character	

Special case: within a regular expression, \b means word boundary, except in a ( )
set, in which \b means the backspace character.

Table A–2. Substitutions

Expression	Meaning
$group-number	Substitutes last substring matched by group-number
${group-name}	Substitutes last substring matched by (?<group-name>)

Substitutions are specified only within a replacement pattern.

Table A–3. Character sets

Expression	Meaning
.	Matches any character except \n
[characterlist]	Matches a single character in the list
[^characterlist]	Matches a single character not in the list
[char0-char1]	Matches a single character in a range
\w	Matches a word character; same as [a-zA-Z_0-9]
\W	Matches a nonword character
\s	Matches a space character; same as [\n\r\t\f]
\S	Matches a nonspace character
\d	Matches a decimal digit; same as [0-9]
\D	Matches a nondigit

Table A–4. Positioning assertions

Expression	Meaning
^	Beginning of line
$	End of line
\A	Beginning of string
\Z	End of line or string
\z	Exactly the end of string
\G	Where search started
\b	On a word boundary
\B	Not on a word boundary

Table A-5. Quantifiers

Quantifier	Meaning
*	0 or more matches
+	1 or more matches
?	0 or 1 matches
{*n*}	Exactly *n* matches
{*n*,}	At least *n* matches
{*n*,*m*}	At least *n*, but no more than *m* matches
*?	Lazy *, finds first match that has minimum repeats
+?	Lazy +, minimum repeats, but at least 1
??	Lazy ?, zero or minimum repeats
{*n*}?	Lazy {*n*}, exactly *n* matches
{*n*,}?	Lazy {*n*}, minimum repeats, but at least *n*
{*n*,*m*}?	Lazy {*n*,*m*}, minimum repeats, but at least *n*, and no more than *m*

Table A-6. Grouping constructs

Syntax	Meaning
( )	Capture matched substring
(?<*name*>)	Capture matched substring into group *name*[a]
(?<*number*>)	Capture matched substring into group *number*
(?<*name1-name2*>)	Undefine *name2*, and store interval and current group into *name1*; if *name2* is undefined, matching backtracks; *name1* is *optional*
(?:)	Noncapturing group
(?imnsx-imnsx:)	Apply or disable matching options
(?=)	Continue matching only if subexpression matches on right
(?!)	Continue matching only if subexpression doesn't match on right
(?<=)	Continue matching only if subexpression matches on left
(?<!)	Continue matching only if subexpression doesn't match on left
(?>)	Subexpression is matched once, but isn't backtracked

[a] Single quotes may be used instead of angle brackets—for example (?'name').

The named capturing group syntax follows a suggestion made by Friedl in *Mastering Regular Expressions*. All other grouping constructs use the Perl5 syntax.

Table A–7. Back references

Parameter syntax	Meaning
\count	Back reference count occurrences
\k<*name*>	Named back reference

Table A–8. Alternation

Expression syntax	Meaning
|	Logical OR
(?(*expression*)yes|no)	Matches yes if expression matches, else no; the no is optional
(?(*name*)yes|no)	Matches yes if named string has a match, else no; the no is optional

Table A–9. Miscellaneous constructs

Expression Syntax	Meaning
(?imnsx-imnsx)	Set or disable options in midpattern
(?#)	Inline comment
# [to end of line]	X-mode comment

Table A–10. Regular expression options

Option	Meaning
i	Case-insensitive match
m	Multiline mode; changes ^ and $ so they match beginning and ending of any line
n	Capture explicitly named or numbered groups
c	Compile to MSIL
s	Single-line mode; changes meaning of "." so it matches every character
x	Eliminates unescaped whitespace from the pattern
r	Search from right to left; can't be specified in midstream

APPENDIX B

Format Specifiers

Table B-1 lists the numeric format specifiers supported by the String.Format method on the predefined numeric types.

Table B-1. Numeric format specifiers

Specifier	String result	Datatype
C[n]	$XX,XX.XX	Currency
	($XX,XXX.XX)	
D[n]	[-]XXXXXXX	Decimal
E[n] or e[n]	[-]X.XXXXXXE+xxx	Exponent
	[-]X.XXXXXXe+xxx	
	[-]X.XXXXXXE-xxx	
	[-]X.XXXXXXe-xxx	
F[n]	[-]XXXXXXX.XX	Fixed point
G[n]	General or scientific	General
N[n]	[-]XX,XXX.XX	Number
X[n] or x[n]	Hex representation	Hex

This example uses numeric format specifiers without precision specifiers:

```
Imports System

Public Class TestDefaultFormats
    Public Shared Sub Main()
        Dim i As Integer = 654321
        Console.WriteLine("{0:C}", i)       ' $654,321.00
        Console.WriteLine("{0:D}", i)       ' 654321
        Console.WriteLine("{0:E}", i)       ' 6.543210E+005
        Console.WriteLine("{0:F}", i)       ' 654321.00
        Console.WriteLine("{0:G}", i)       ' 654321
```

```
          Console.WriteLine("{0:N}", i)        ' 654,321.00
          Console.WriteLine("{0:X}", i)        ' 9FBF1
          Console.WriteLine("{0:x}", i)        ' 9fbf1
     End Sub
End Class
```

This example uses numeric format specifiers with precision specifiers on a variety of int values:

```
Imports System

Public Class TestIntegerFormats
    Public Shared Sub Main()
        Dim i As Integer = 123
        Console.WriteLine("{0:C6}", i)        '$123.000000
        Console.WriteLine("{0:D6}", i)        '000123
        Console.WriteLine("{0:E6}", i)        '1.230000E+002
        Console.WriteLine("{0:G6}", i)        '123
        Console.WriteLine("{0:N6}", i)        '123.000000
        Console.WriteLine("{0:X6}", i)        '00007B

        i = -123
        Console.WriteLine("{0:C6}", i)        '($123.000000)
        Console.WriteLine("{0:D6}", i)        '-000123
        Console.WriteLine("{0:E6}", i)        '-1.230000E+002
        Console.WriteLine("{0:G6}", i)        '-123
        Console.WriteLine("{0:N6}", i)        '-123.000000
        Console.WriteLine("{0:X6}", i)        'FFFF85

        i = 0
        Console.WriteLine("{0:C6}", i)        '$0.000000
        Console.WriteLine("{0:D6}", i)        '000000
        Console.WriteLine("{0:E6}", i)        '0.000000E+000
        Console.WriteLine("{0:G6}", i)        '0
        Console.WriteLine("{0:N6}", i)        '0.000000
        Console.WriteLine("{0:X6}", i)        '000000
    End Sub
End Class
```

This example uses numeric format specifiers with precision specifiers on a variety of double values:

```
Imports System

Public Class TestDoubleFormats
    Public Shared Sub Main()
        Dim d As Double = 1.23
        Console.WriteLine("{0:C6}", d)        '$1.230000
        Console.WriteLine("{0:E6}", d)        '1.230000E+000
        Console.WriteLine("{0:G6}", d)        '1.23
        Console.WriteLine("{0:N6}", d)        '1.230000

        d = -1.23
        Console.WriteLine("{0:C6}", d)        '($1.230000)
        Console.WriteLine("{0:E6}", d)        '-1.230000E+000
        Console.WriteLine("{0:G6}", d)        '-1.23
        Console.WriteLine("{0:N6}", d)        '-1.230000

        d = 0
        Console.WriteLine("{0:C6}", d)        '$0.000000
```

```
        Console.WriteLine("{0:E6}", d)      '0.000000E+000
        Console.WriteLine("{0:G6}", d)      '0
        Console.WriteLine("{0:N6}", d)      '0.000000
    End Sub
End Class
```

Picture Format Specifiers

Table B-2 lists the valid picture format specifiers supported by the Format method
on the predefined numeric types (see the documentation for System.IFormattable
in the .NET SDK).

Table B-2. Picture format specifiers

Specifier	String result
0	Zero placeholder
#	Digit placeholder
.	Decimal point
,	Group separator or multiplier
%	Percent notation
E+0, E-0 e+0, e-0	Exponent notation
\	Literal character quote
'xx'"xx"	Literal string quote
;	Section separator

This example uses picture format specifiers on some int values:

```
Imports System

    Public Class TestIntegerCustomFormats

        Public Shared Sub Main()
            Dim i As Integer = 123
            Console.WriteLine("{0:#0}", i)                    ' 123
            Console.WriteLine("{0:#0;(#0)}", i)               ' 123
            Console.WriteLine("{0:#0;(#0);<zero>}", i)        ' 123
            Console.WriteLine("{0:#%}", i)                    ' 12300%

            i = -123
            Console.WriteLine("{0:#0}", i)                    ' -123
            Console.WriteLine("{0:#0;(#0)}", i)               ' (123)
            Console.WriteLine("{0:#0;(#0);<zero>}", i)        ' (123)
            Console.WriteLine("{0:#%}", i)                    ' -12300%

            i = 0
            Console.WriteLine("{0:#0}", i)                    ' 0
            Console.WriteLine("{0:#0;(#0)}", i)               ' 0
            Console.WriteLine("{0:#0;(#0);<zero>}", i)        ' <zero>
            Console.WriteLine("{0:#%}", i)                    ' %
        End Sub
    End Class
```

The following example uses these picture format specifiers on a variety of `double` values:

```
Imports System

Class TestDoubleCustomFormats
    Public Shared Sub Main()
        Dim d As Double = 1.23
        Console.WriteLine("{0:#.000E+00}", d)                        ' 1.230E+00
        Console.WriteLine("{0:#.000E+00;(#.000E+00)}", d)  ' 1.230E+00
        Console.WriteLine( _
                "{0:#.000E+00;(#.000E+00);<zero>}", d)       ' 1.230E+00
        Console.WriteLine("{0:#%}", d)                               ' 123%

        d = -1.23
        Console.WriteLine("{0:#.000E+00}", d)                        ' -1.230E+00
        Console.WriteLine("{0:#.000E+00;(#.000E+00)}", d)  ' (1.230E+00)
        Console.WriteLine( _
                "{0:#.000E+00;(#.000E+00);<zero>}", d)       ' (1.230E+00)
        Console.WriteLine("{0:#%}", d)                               ' -123%

        d = 0
        Console.WriteLine("{0:#.000E+00}", d)                        ' 0.000E+01
        Console.WriteLine("{0:#.000E+00;(#.000E+00)}", d)  ' 0.000E+01
        Console.WriteLine( _
                "{0:#.000E+00;(#.000E+00);<zero>}", d)       ' <zero>
        Console.WriteLine("{0:#%}", d)                               ' %
    End Sub
End Class
```

DateTime Format Specifiers

Table B-3 lists the valid format specifiers supported by the `Format` method on the `DateTime` type (see `System.IFormattable`).

Table B-3. DateTime format specifiers

Specifier	String result
D	MM/dd/yyyy
d	dddd, MMMM dd, yyyy
f	dddd, MMMM dd, yyyy HH:mm
F	dddd, MMMM dd, yyyy HH:mm:ss
g	MM/dd/yyyy HH:mm
G	MM/dd/yyyy HH:mm:ss
m, M	MMMM dd
r, R	Ddd, dd MMM yyyy HH':'mm':'ss 'GMT'
s	yyyy-MM-dd HH:mm:ss
S	yyyy-MM-dd HH:mm:ss GMT
t	HH:mm
T	HH:mm:ss
u	yyyy-MM-dd HH:mm:ss

Specifier	String result
U	dddd, MMMM dd, yyyy HH:mm:ss
y, Y	MMMM, yyyy

Here's an example that uses these custom format specifiers on a DateTime value (note that precise output depends on the local computer's settings for the long and short date formats):

```
Imports System

Class TestDateTimeFormats
    Public Shared Sub Main()
        Dim dt As New Date(2000, 10, 11, 15, 32, 14)
        ' Displays "10/11/00 3:32:14 PM"
        Console.WriteLine(dt.ToString())
        ' Displays "10/11/00 3:32:14 PM"
        Console.WriteLine("{0}", dt)
        'Displays "10/11/00"
        Console.WriteLine("{0:d}", dt)
        ' Displays "Wednesday, October 11, 2000"
        Console.WriteLine("{0:D}", dt)
        ' Displays "Wednesday, October 11, 2000 3:32 PM"
        Console.WriteLine("{0:f}", dt)
        ' Displays "Wednesday, October 11, 2000 3:32:14 PM"
        Console.WriteLine("{0:F}", dt)
        ' Displays "10/11/00 3:32 PM"
        Console.WriteLine("{0:g}", dt)
        ' Displays "10/11/00 3:32:14 PM"
        Console.WriteLine("{0:G}", dt)
        ' Displays "October 11"
        Console.WriteLine("{0:m}", dt)
        ' Displays "October 11"
        Console.WriteLine("{0:M}", dt)
        ' Displays "Wed, 11 Oct 2000 15:32:14 GMT"
        Console.WriteLine("{0:r}", dt)
        ' Displays "Wed, 11 Oct 2000 15:32:14 GMT"
        Console.WriteLine("{0:R}", dt)
        ' Displays "3:32 PM"
        Console.WriteLine("{0:t}", dt)
        ' Displays "3:32:14 PM"
        Console.WriteLine("{0:T}", dt)
        ' Displays "2000-10-11 15:32:14Z"
        Console.WriteLine("{0:u}", dt)
        ' Displays "Wednesday, October 11, 2000 10:32:14 PM"
        Console.WriteLine("{0:U}", dt)
        ' Displays "October, 2000"
        Console.WriteLine("{0:y}", dt)
        ' Displays "October, 2000"
        Console.WriteLine("{0:Y}", dt)
        ' Displays "Wednesday the 11 day of Oct in the year 2000"
        Console.WriteLine( _
            "{0:dddd 'the' d 'day of' MMM 'in the year' yyyy}", dt)
    End Sub
End Class
```

APPENDIX C

Data Marshaling

When calling between the runtime environment and existing COM interfaces, the CLR performs automatic data marshaling for CLR types into compatible COM types. Table C-1 describes the Visual Basic to COM default data type mapping.

Table C-1. VB type to COM type mapping

VB type	COM type
Boolean	VARIANT_BOOL
Char	unsigned short
System.Sbyte	Char
Byte	Unsigned char
Short	Short
System.UInt16	Unsigned short
Integer	Int
System.UInt32	Unsigned int
Long	Hyper
System.UInt64	Unsigned hyper
Single	Single
Double	Double
Decimal	DECIMAL
Object	VARIANT
String	BSTR
Date	DATE[a]
System.Guid	GUID
1-dimensional arrays	SAFEARRAY
Value types	Equivalently named struct

Table C-1. VB type to COM type mapping (continued)

VB type	COM type
Enum	Equivalently named enum
Interface	Equivalently named interface
Class	Equivalently named CoClass

a COM dates are less precise, causing comparison problems.

APPENDIX D

Namespaces and Assemblies

This appendix allows you to look up a namespace and determine which assemblies export that namespace. This information is helpful when constructing the appropriate /reference:<file list> command-line option for the VB compiler. Note that the Visual Basic compiler references *mscorlib.dll* and *Microsoft.VisualBasic.dll* by default.

For a complete list of default assemblies, see the global C# response file, *csc.rsp*, in *%SystemRoot%\Microsoft.NET\Framework\VERSION*, where *VERSION* is the version number of the framework (the first release of .NET is v1.0.3705). You can modify *csc.rsp* to affect all compilations run on your machine, or you can create a local *csc.rsp* in your current directory. The local response file is processed after the global one. You can use the /noconfig switch with *csc.exe* to disable the local and global *csc.rsp* files entirely.

Namespace	DLLs
Accessibility	*Accessibility.dll*
EnvDTE	*envdte.dll*
IEHost.Execute	*IEExecRemote.dll*
Microsoft.CLRAdmin	*mscorcfg.dll*
Microsoft.CSharp	*cscompmgd.dll*
	System.dll
Microsoft.IE	*IEHost.dll*
	IIEHost.dll
Microsoft.JScript	*Microsoft.JScript.dll*
Microsoft.JScript.Vsa	*Microsoft.JScript.dll*
Microsoft.Office.Core	*office.dll*
Microsoft.VisualBasic	*Microsoft.VisualBasic.dll*
	System.dll

Namespace	DLLs
Microsoft.VisualBasic. Compatibility.VB6	*Microsoft.VisualBasic.Compatibility. Data.dll*
	Microsoft.VisualBasic.Compatibility.dll
Microsoft.VisualBasic. CompilerServices	*Microsoft.VisualBasic.dll*
Microsoft.VisualBasic.Vsa	*Microsoft.VisualBasic.Vsa.dll*
Microsoft.VisualC	*Microsoft.VisualC.Dll*
Microsoft.Vsa	*Microsoft.JScript.dll*
	Microsoft.Vsa.dll
Microsoft.Vsa.Vb.CodeDOM	*Microsoft.Vsa.Vb.CodeDOMProcessor. dll*
Microsoft.Win32	*mscorlib.dll*
	System.dll
Microsoft_VsaVb	*Microsoft_VsaVb.dll*
RegCode	*RegCode.dll*
System	*mscorlib.dll*
	System.dll
System.CodeDom	*System.dll*
System.CodeDom.Compiler	*System.dll*
System.Collections	*mscorlib.dll*
System.Collections. Specialized	*System.dll*
System.ComponentModel	*System.dll*
System.ComponentModel.Design	*System.Design.dll*
	System.dll
System.ComponentModel.Design. Serialization	*System.Design.dll*
	System.dll
System.Configuration	*System.dll*
System.Configuration. Assemblies	*mscorlib.dll*
System.Configuration.Install	*System.Configuration.Install.dll*
System.Data	*System.Data.dll*
System.Data.Common	*System.Data.dll*
System.Data.OleDb	*System.Data.dll*
System.Data.SqlClient	*System.Data.dll*
System.Data.SqlTypes	*System.Data.dll*
System.Diagnostics	*mscorlib.dll*
	System.Configuration.Install.dll
System.Diagnostics.Design	*System.Design.dll*
System.Diagnostics. SymbolStore	*ISymWrapper.dll*
	mscorlib.dll
System.DirectoryServices	*System.DirectoryServices.dll*
System.Drawing	*System.Drawing.dll*
System.Drawing.Design	*System.Drawing.Design.dll*
	System.Drawing.dll

Namespace	DLLs
System.Drawing.Drawing2D	*System.Drawing.dll*
System.Drawing.Imaging	*System.Drawing.dll*
System.Drawing.Printing	*System.Drawing.dll*
System.Drawing.Text	*System.Drawing.dll*
System.EnterpriseServices	*System.EnterpriseServices.dll*
System.EnterpriseServices. Compen-satingResourceManager	*System.EnterpriseServices.dll*
System.EnterpriseServices.Internal	*System.EnterpriseServices.dll*
System.Globalization	*mscorlib.dll*
System.IO	*mscorlib.dll* *System.dll*
System.IO.IsolatedStorage	*mscorlib.dll*
System.Management	*System.Management.dll*
System.Management. Instrumentation	*System.Management.dll*
System.Messaging	*System.Messaging.dll*
System.Messaging.Design	*System.Design.dll* *System.Messaging.dll*
System.Net	*System.dll*
System.Net.Sockets	*System.dll*
System.Reflection	*mscorlib.dll*
System.Reflection.Emit	*mscorlib.dll*
System.Resources	*mscorlib.dll* *System.Windows.Forms.dll*
System.Runtime.CompilerServices	*mscorlib.dll*
System.Runtime. InteropServices	*mscorlib.dll*
System.Runtime.InteropServices. CustomMarshalers	*CustomMarshalers.dll*
System.Runtime.InteropSer-vices.Expando	*mscorlib.dll*
System.Runtime.Remoting	*mscorlib.dll*
System.Runtime.Remoting.Activation	*mscorlib.dll*
System.Runtime.Remoting.Channels	*mscorlib.dll* *System.Runtime.Remoting.dll*
System.Runtime.Remoting.Chan-nels.Http	*System.Runtime.Remoting.dll*
System.Runtime.Remoting.Chan-nels.Tcp	*System.Runtime.Remoting.dll*
System.Runtime.Remoting.Contexts	*mscorlib.dll*
System.Runtime.Remoting.Lifetime	*mscorlib.dll*
System.Runtime.Remoting.Messaging	*mscorlib.dll*
System.Runtime.Remoting.Metadata	*mscorlib.dll*
System.Runtime.Remoting.Metadata. W3cXsd2001	*mscorlib.dll*

Namespace	DLLs
System.Runtime.Remoting.Meta-dataServices	*System.Runtime.Remoting.dll*
System.Runtime.Remoting.Proxies	*mscorlib.dll*
System.Runtime.Remoting.Services	*mscorlib.dll*
	System.Runtime.Remoting.dll
System.Runtime.Serialization	*mscorlib.dll*
System.Runtime.Serialization.For-matters	*mscorlib.dll*
System.Runtime.Serialization.For-matters. Binary	*mscorlib.dll*
System.Runtime.Serialization.For-matters. Soap	*System.Runtime.Serialization. Formatters.Soap.dll*
System.Security	*mscorlib.dll*
System.Security. Cryptography	*mscorlib.dll*
System.Security.Cryptography.X509Certificates	*mscorlib.dll*
	System.dll
System.Security.Cryptography.Xml	*System.Security.dll*
System.Security.Permissions	*mscorlib.dll*
	System.dll
System.Security.Policy	*mscorlib.dll*
System.Security.Principal	*mscorlib.dll*
System.ServiceProcess	*System.ServiceProcess.dll*
System.ServiceProcess.Design	*System.Design.dll*
	System.ServiceProcess.dll
System.Text	*mscorlib.dll*
System.Text.RegularExpressions	*System.dll*
System.Threading	*mscorlib.dll*
	System.dll
System.Timers	*System.dll*
System.Web	*System.Web.dll*
System.Web.Caching	*System.Web.dll*
System.Web.Configuration	*System.Web.dll*
System.Web.Handlers	*System.Web.dll*
System.Web.Hosting	*System.Web.dll*
System.Web.Mail	*System.Web.dll*
System.Web.RegularExpressions	*System.Web.RegularExpressions.dll*
System.Web.Security	*System.Web.dll*
System.Web.Services	*System.Web.Services.dll*
System.Web.Services. Configuration	*System.Web.Services.dll*
System.Web.Services.Description	*System.Web.Services.dll*
System.Web.Services.Discovery	*System.Web.Services.dll*
System.Web.Services.Protocols	*System.Web.Services.dll*
System.Web.SessionState	*System.Web.dll*
System.Web.UI	*System.Web.dll*

Namespace	DLLs
System.Web.UI.Design	System.Design.dll
System.Web.UI.Design.WebControls	System.Design.dll
System.Web.UI.HtmlControls	System.Web.dll
System.Web.UI.WebControls	System.Web.dll
System.Web.Util	System.Web.dll
System.Windows.Forms	System.Windows.Forms.dll
System.Windows.Forms. Component-Model.Com2Interop	System.Windows.Forms.dll
System.Windows.Forms.Design	System.Design.dll
	System.Windows.Forms.dll
System.Windows.Forms. Property-GridInternal	System.Windows.Forms.dll
System.Xml	System.Data.dll
	System.XML.dll
System.Xml.Schema	System.XML.dll
System.Xml.Serialization	System.XML.dll
System.Xml.XPath	System.XML.dll
System.Xml.Xsl	System.XML.dll

APPENDIX E

Type, Method, Property, Event, and Field Index

Use this index to look up a type or member and see where it is defined. For a type (a class or interface), you can find the enclosing namespace. If you know the name of a member (a method, property, event, or field), you can find all the types that define it.

AddHours(): Calendar, DateTime
AddInterfaceImplementation(): TypeBuilder
AddMembership: SocketOptionName
AddMethod(): IExpando
AddMilliseconds(): Calendar, DateTime
AddMinutes(): Calendar, DateTime
AddMonths(): Calendar, DateTime, GregorianCalendar, HebrewCalendar, HijriCalendar, JapaneseCalendar, JulianCalendar, KoreanCalendar, TaiwanCalendar, ThaiBuddhistCalendar
AddNamespace(): XmlNamespaceManager
AddOtherMethod(): EventBuilder, PropertyBuilder
AddParam(): XsltArgumentList
AddPermission(): SocketPermission, WebPermission
AddProperty(): IExpando
AddRange(): ArrayList, CounterCreationDataCollection, EventLogPermissionEntryCollection, HttpWebRequest, PerformanceCounterPermissionEntryCollection, String-Collection, TraceListenerCollection
AddRef(): Marshal
AddResourceFile(): AssemblyBuilder
Address: HttpWebRequest, IPAddress, IPEndPoint, ServicePoint, WebProxy
AddressFamily: EndPoint, IPAddress, IPEndPoint, Socket, System.Net.Sockets
AddressList: IPHostEntry
AddrOfPinnedObject(): GCHandle
AddSeconds(): Calendar, DateTime
AddSentinel(): SignatureHelper
AddSort(): XPathExpression
AddSourceMembership: SocketOptionName
AddSurrogate(): SurrogateSelector
AddTicks(): DateTime
AddValue(): SerializationInfo
AddWeeks(): Calendar, GregorianCalendar
AddWithoutValidate(): WebHeaderCollection
AddYears(): Calendar, DateTime, GregorianCalendar, HebrewCalendar, HijriCalendar, JapaneseCalendar, JulianCalendar, KoreanCalendar, TaiwanCalendar, ThaiBuddhistCalendar
ADEra: GregorianCalendar
AdjustToUniversal: DateTimeStyles
Administer: PerformanceCounterPermissionAccess
After: XmlNodeOrder
AlgorithmId: AssemblyAlgorithmIdAttribute
Aliases: IPHostEntry
All: AttributeTargets, MemberTypes, StreamingContextStates, TransportType, WatcherChangeTypes, WhitespaceHandling, XPathNamespaceScope, XPathNodeType
AllCultures: CultureTypes
AllKeys: NameValueCollection
Alloc(): GCHandle
AllocateDataSlot(): Thread

AllocateNamedDataSlot(): Thread
AllocCoTaskMem(): Marshal
AllocHGlobal(): Marshal
AllowAutoRedirect: HttpWebRequest
AllowCurrencySymbol: NumberStyles
AllowDecimalPoint: NumberStyles
AllowExponent: NumberStyles
AllowHexSpecifier: NumberStyles
AllowInnerWhite: DateTimeStyles
AllowLeadingSign: NumberStyles
AllowLeadingWhite: DateTimeStyles, NumberStyles
AllowMultiple: AttributeUsageAttribute
AllowParentheses: NumberStyles
AllowThousands: NumberStyles
AllowTrailingSign: NumberStyles
AllowTrailingWhite: DateTimeStyles, NumberStyles
AllowWhiteSpaces: DateTimeStyles
AllowWriteStreamBuffering: HttpWebRequest
AllPorts: SocketPermission
AltDirectorySeparatorChar: Path
Ambiguous: HttpStatusCode
AmbiguousMatchException: System.Reflection
AMDesignator: DateTimeFormatInfo
And: OpCodes
And(): BitArray
Annotation: OpCodeType
Ansi: CharSet
AnsiBStr: UnmanagedType
AnsiClass: TypeAttributes
ANSICodePage: TextInfo
Any: CallingConventions, IPAddress, NumberStyles, XPathResultType
AnyWritersSince(): ReaderWriterLock
ApartmentState: System.Threading, Thread
AppDomain: System
AppDomainSetup: System
AppDomainUnloadedException: System
Append: FileMode
Append(): StringBuilder, XmlAttributeCollection
AppendChild(): XmlNode
AppendData(): XmlCharacterData
AppendFormat(): StringBuilder
AppendPrivatePath(): AppDomain
AppendText(): File, FileInfo
AppleTalk: AddressFamily, ProtocolFamily
ApplicationBase: AppDomainSetup
ApplicationData: SpecialFolder
ApplicationException: System
ApplicationName: AppDomainSetup
Arabic: GregorianCalendarTypes
Archive: FileAttributes
ArgIterator: System
Arglist: OpCodes
ArgTypes: IXsltContextFunction

ArgumentException: System
ArgumentNullException: System
ArgumentOutOfRangeException: System
Arguments: ProcessStartInfo
ArithmeticException: System
Array: System
ArrayList: System.Collections
ArraySubType: MarshalAsAttribute
ArrayTypeMismatchException: System
ArrayWithOffset: System.Runtime.InteropServices
AsAny: UnmanagedType
Ascending: XmlSortOrder
ASCII: Encoding
ASCIIEncoding: System.Text
Asin(): Math
Assembly: AttributeTargets, EnumBuilder, FieldAttributes,
    IsolatedStorageScope, MethodAttributes, Module,
    System.Reflection, Type, TypeBuilder, TypeDelegator
AssemblyAlgorithmIdAttribute: System.Reflection
AssemblyBuilder: System.Reflection.Emit
AssemblyBuilderAccess: System.Reflection.Emit
AssemblyCompanyAttribute: System.Reflection
AssemblyConfigurationAttribute: System.Reflection
AssemblyCopyrightAttribute: System.Reflection
AssemblyCultureAttribute: System.Reflection
AssemblyDefaultAliasAttribute: System.Reflection
AssemblyDelaySignAttribute: System.Reflection
AssemblyDescriptionAttribute: System.Reflection
AssemblyFileVersionAttribute: System.Reflection
AssemblyFlagsAttribute: System.Reflection
AssemblyFormat: BinaryFormatter, SoapFormatter
AssemblyIdentity: IsolatedStorage
AssemblyInformationalVersionAttribute: System.Reflec-
    tion
AssemblyKeyFileAttribute: System.Reflection
AssemblyKeyNameAttribute: System.Reflection
AssemblyLoad: AppDomain
AssemblyLoadEventArgs: System
AssemblyLoadEventHandler: System
AssemblyName: SerializationInfo, System.Reflection
AssemblyNameFlags: System.Reflection
AssemblyNameProxy: System.Reflection
AssemblyProductAttribute: System.Reflection
AssemblyQualifiedName: EnumBuilder, Type, TypeBuilder,
    TypeDelegator
AssemblyRegistrationFlags: System.Runtime.InteropSer-
    vices
AssemblyResolve: AppDomain
AssemblyTitleAttribute: System.Reflection
AssemblyTrademarkAttribute: System.Reflection
AssemblyVersionAttribute: System.Reflection
Assert(): Debug, Trace
AssertUIEnabled: DefaultTraceListener
AsyncCallback: System

AsyncResult: Overlapped
AsyncState: IAsyncResult
AsyncWaitHandle: IAsyncResult
Atan(): Math
Atan2(): Math
Atm: AddressFamily, ProtocolFamily
Attribute: System, WriteState, XmlNodeType, XPathNode-
    Type
AttributeCount: XmlNodeReader, XmlReader, XmlText-
    Reader, XmlValidatingReader
Attributes: ConstructorBuilder, EventInfo, FieldBuilder,
    FieldInfo, FileSystemInfo, MethodBase, Method-
    Builder, NotifyFilters, ParameterBuilder, Parameter-
    Info, PropertyBuilder, PropertyInfo, Type, XmlElement,
    XmlNode
AttributeTargets: System
AttributeUsageAttribute: System
AttrsImpl: ParameterInfo
Audit: EventLogPermissionAccess
Authenticate(): AuthenticationManager, IAuthentication-
    Module
AuthenticationManager: System.Net
AuthenticationType: IAuthenticationModule
Authority: Uri, UriPartial
Authorization: System.Net
Auto: CharSet, LayoutKind, ValidationType
AutoClass: TypeAttributes
AutoDispatch: ClassInterfaceType
AutoDual: ClassInterfaceType
AutoFlush: Debug, StreamWriter, Trace
AutoLayout: TypeAttributes
AutoReset: Timer
AutoResetEvent: System.Threading
Available: Socket
AverageBase: PerformanceCounterType
AverageCount64: PerformanceCounterType
AverageTimer32: PerformanceCounterType

B

Background: ThreadState
BadGateway: HttpStatusCode
BadImageFormatException: System
BadRequest: HttpStatusCode
Banyan: AddressFamily, ProtocolFamily
BaseAdd(): NameObjectCollectionBase
BaseAddress: ProcessModule, WebClient
BaseClear(): NameObjectCollectionBase
BaseDirectory: AppDomain
BaseGet(): NameObjectCollectionBase
BaseGetAllKeys(): NameObjectCollectionBase
BaseGetAllValues(): NameObjectCollectionBase
BaseGetKey(): NameObjectCollectionBase
BaseHasKeys(): NameObjectCollectionBase

BasePriority: Process, ProcessThread

BaseRemove(): NameObjectCollectionBase

BaseRemoveAt(): NameObjectCollectionBase

BaseSet(): NameObjectCollectionBase

BaseStream: BinaryReader, BinaryWriter, StreamReader, StreamWriter, XmlTextWriter

BaseType: EnumBuilder, Type, TypeBuilder, TypeDelegator, UnmanagedMarshal

BaseURI: XmlAttribute, XmlDocument, XmlEntity, XmlEntityReference, XmlNode, XmlNodeReader, XmlParserContext, XmlReader, XmlTextReader, XmlValidatingReader, XPathNavigator

BaseValue: CounterSample

Basic: UriHostNameType

Before: XmlNodeOrder

BeforeFieldInit: TypeAttributes

Begin: SeekOrigin

BeginAccept(): Socket

BeginCatchBlock(): ILGenerator

BeginConnect(): Socket

BeginExceptFilterBlock(): ILGenerator

BeginExceptionBlock(): ILGenerator

BeginFaultBlock(): ILGenerator

BeginFinallyBlock(): ILGenerator

BeginGetHostByName(): Dns

BeginGetRequestStream(): FileWebRequest, HttpWebRequest, WebRequest

BeginGetResponse(): FileWebRequest, HttpWebRequest, WebRequest

BeginInit(): EventLog, FileSystemWatcher, PerformanceCounter, Timer

BeginInvoke(): AssemblyLoadEventHandler, AsyncCallback, CrossAppDomainDelegate, ElapsedEventHandler, EntryWrittenEventHandler, ErrorEventHandler, EventHandler, FileSystemEventHandler, HttpContinueDelegate, IOCompletionCallback, MatchEvaluator, MemberFilter, ModuleResolveEventHandler, ObjectCreationDelegate, PowerModeChangedEventHandler, RenamedEventHandler, ResolveEventHandler, SessionEndedEventHandler, SessionEndingEventHandler, ThreadExceptionEventHandler, ThreadStart, TimerCallback, TimerElapsedEventHandler, TypeFilter, UnhandledExceptionEventHandler, UserPreferenceChangedEventHandler, UserPreferenceChangingEventHandler, WaitCallback, WaitOrTimerCallback, XmlNodeChangedEventHandler

BeginRead(): FileStream, IsolatedStorageFileStream, NetworkStream, Stream

BeginReceive(): Socket

BeginReceiveFrom(): Socket

BeginResolve(): Dns

BeginScope(): ILGenerator

BeginSend(): Socket

BeginSendTo(): Socket

BeginWrite(): FileStream, IsolatedStorageFileStream, NetworkStream, Stream

BelowNormal: ProcessPriorityClass, ThreadPriority, ThreadPriorityLevel

Beq: OpCodes

Beq_S: OpCodes

Bge: OpCodes

Bge_S: OpCodes

Bge_Un: OpCodes

Bge_Un_S: OpCodes

Bgt: OpCodes

Bgt_S: OpCodes

Bgt_Un: OpCodes

Bgt_Un_S: OpCodes

BigEndianUnicode: Encoding

BinaryFormatter: System.Runtime.Serialization.Formatters.Binary

BinaryReader: System.IO

BinarySearch(): Array, ArrayList

BinaryWriter: System.IO

Bind(): Socket

Binder: BinaryFormatter, Formatter, IFormatter, SoapFormatter, System.Reflection

BindHandle(): ThreadPool

BindingFlags: System.Reflection

BindToField(): Binder

BindToMethod(): Binder

BindToMoniker(): Marshal

BindToType(): SerializationBinder

BitArray: System.Collections

BitConverter: System

BitVector32: System.Collections.Specialized

Ble: OpCodes

Ble_S: OpCodes

Ble_Un: OpCodes

Ble_Un_S: OpCodes

BlockCopy(): Buffer

Blocking: Socket

BlockSource: SocketOptionName

Blt: OpCodes

Blt_S: OpCodes

Blt_Un: OpCodes

Blt_Un_S: OpCodes

Bne_Un: OpCodes

Bne_Un_S: OpCodes

BodyName: Encoding

Bool: UnmanagedType

Boolean: System, TypeCode, XPathResultType

BooleanSwitch: System.Diagnostics

Both: SocketShutdown

Box: OpCodes

Box(): Pointer

Br: OpCodes

ClassName: MissingMemberException
ClassSemanticsMask: TypeAttributes
Clear(): Array, ArrayList, CollectionBase, DictionaryBase, EventLog, Hashtable, HybridDictionary, IDictionary, IList, ListDictionary, NameValueCollection, Queue, SortedList, Stack, StringCollection, StringDictionary, TraceListenerCollection, XsltArgumentList
ClearCache: GC
ClearCachedData(): CultureInfo
ClearPrivatePath(): AppDomain
ClearShadowCopyPath(): AppDomain
ClientCertificate: ServicePoint
ClientCertificates: HttpWebRequest
Clone: StreamingContextStates
Clone(): Array, ArrayList, AssemblyName, BitArray, CharEnumerator, CultureInfo, DateTimeFormatInfo, Delegate, Hashtable, ICloneable, NumberFormatInfo, OperatingSystem, Queue, SortedList, Stack, String, Version, XmlNode, XPathExpression, XPathNavigator, XPathNodeIterator
CloneNode(): XmlAttribute, XmlCDataSection, XmlComment, XmlDataDocument, XmlDeclaration, XmlDocument, XmlDocumentFragment, XmlDocumentType, XmlElement, XmlEntity, XmlEntityReference, XmlNode, XmlNotation, XmlProcessingInstruction, XmlSignificantWhitespace, XmlText, XmlWhitespace
Close(): BinaryReader, BinaryWriter, BufferedStream, Debug, EventLog, EventLogTraceListener, FileStream, FileWebResponse, HttpWebResponse, IsolatedStorageFile, IsolatedStorageFileStream, MemoryStream, NetworkStream, PerformanceCounter, Process, RegistryKey, Socket, Stream, StreamReader, StreamWriter, StringReader, StringWriter, TcpClient, TextReader, TextWriter, TextWriterTraceListener, Timer, Trace, TraceListener, UdpClient, WaitHandle, WebResponse, XmlNodeReader, XmlReader, XmlTextReader, XmlTextWriter, XmlValidatingReader, XmlWriter
Closed: ReadState, WriteState
CloseMainWindow(): Process
ClosePunctuation: UnicodeCategory
CloseSharedResources(): PerformanceCounter
CLSCompliantAttribute: System
Clt: OpCodes
Clt_Un: OpCodes
Cluster: AddressFamily, ProtocolFamily
CoClass: CoClassAttribute
CoClassAttribute: System.Runtime.InteropServices
CodeBase: Assembly, AssemblyBuilder, AssemblyName
CodePage: Encoding
CodeTypeMask: MethodImplAttributes
Collect(): GC
CollectionBase: System.Collections
CollectionsUtil: System.Collections.Specialized
Color: UserPreferenceCategory

ComAliasNameAttribute: System.Runtime.InteropServices
Combine(): Delegate, Path
CombineImpl(): Delegate, MulticastDelegate
ComConversionLossAttribute: System.Runtime.InteropServices
COMException: System.Runtime.InteropServices
ComImportAttribute: System.Runtime.InteropServices
ComInterfaceType: System.Runtime.InteropServices
CommandLine: Environment
ComMemberType: System.Runtime.InteropServices
Comment: Cookie, XmlNodeType, XPathNodeType
Comments: FileVersionInfo
CommentUri: Cookie
CommonApplicationData: SpecialFolder
CommonProgramFiles: SpecialFolder
Company: AssemblyCompanyAttribute
CompanyName: FileVersionInfo
Compare(): CaseInsensitiveComparer, CompareInfo, Comparer, DateTime, Decimal, IComparer, SortKey, String, TimeSpan
CompareDocument(): XsltContext
CompareExchange(): Interlocked
CompareInfo: CultureInfo, System.Globalization
CompareOptions: System.Globalization
CompareOrdinal(): String
ComparePosition(): XPathNavigator
Comparer: System.Collections
CompareTo(): Boolean, Byte, Char, DateTime, Decimal, Double, Enum, Guid, IComparable, Int16, Int32, Int64, SByte, Single, String, TimeSpan, UInt16, UInt32, UInt64, Version
CompatibleImpl: IDispatchImplType
Compile(): XPathNavigator
Compiled: RegexOptions
CompileToAssembly(): Regex
Complete: Authorization
CompletedSynchronously: IAsyncResult
Compressed: FileAttributes
CompressedStack: System.Threading
ComputeCounterValue(): CounterSampleCalculator
ComRegisterFunctionAttribute: System.Runtime.InteropServices
ComSourceInterfacesAttribute: System.Runtime.InteropServices
ComUnregisterFunctionAttribute: System.Runtime.InteropServices
ComVisibleAttribute: System.Runtime.InteropServices
Concat(): String
Cond_Branch: FlowControl
ConditionalAttribute: System.Diagnostics
ConditionString: ConditionalAttribute
Configuration: AssemblyConfigurationAttribute
ConfigurationFile: AppDomainSetup

StringDictionary, TraceListenerCollection, XmlAttributeCollection

CoreNewLine: TextWriter

Cos(): Math

Cosh(): Math

Count: ArrayList, BitArray, CaptureCollection, CollectionBase, CookieCollection, CookieContainer, DictionaryBase, EventLogEntryCollection, GroupCollection, Hashtable, HybridDictionary, ICollection, KeysCollection, ListDictionary, MatchCollection, NameObjectCollectionBase, Queue, ReadOnlyCollectionBase, SortedList, Stack, StringCollection, StringDictionary, TraceListenerCollection, XmlNamedNodeMap, XmlNodeList, XPathNodeIterator

CounterCreationData: System.Diagnostics

CounterCreationDataCollection: System.Diagnostics

CounterDelta32: PerformanceCounterType

CounterDelta64: PerformanceCounterType

CounterExists(): PerformanceCounterCategory

CounterFrequency: CounterSample

CounterHelp: CounterCreationData, PerformanceCounter

CounterMultiBase: PerformanceCounterType

CounterMultiTimer: PerformanceCounterType

CounterMultiTimer100Ns: PerformanceCounterType

CounterMultiTimer100NsInverse: PerformanceCounterType

CounterMultiTimerInverse: PerformanceCounterType

CounterName: CounterCreationData, InstanceDataCollection, PerformanceCounter

Counters: PerformanceCounterInstaller

CounterSample: System.Diagnostics

CounterSampleCalculator: System.Diagnostics

CounterTimer: PerformanceCounterType

CounterTimerInverse: PerformanceCounterType

CounterTimeStamp: CounterSample

CounterType: CounterCreationData, CounterSample, PerformanceCounter

CountPerTimeInterval32: PerformanceCounterType

CountPerTimeInterval64: PerformanceCounterType

Cpblk: OpCodes

Cpobj: OpCodes

Create: FileMode

Create(): DirectoryInfo, EndPoint, File, FileInfo, IPEndPoint, IWebRequestCreate, PerformanceCounterCategory, WebRequest

CreateAttribute(): XmlDocument

CreateCaseInsensitiveHashtable(): CollectionsUtil

CreateCaseInsensitiveSortedList(): CollectionsUtil

CreateCDataSection(): XmlDocument

CreateComInstanceFrom(): Activator, AppDomain

CreateComment(): XmlDocument

Created: FileSystemWatcher, HttpStatusCode, WatcherChangeTypes

CreateDefault(): WebRequest

CreateDelegate(): Delegate

CreateDirectory(): Directory, IsolatedStorageFile

CreateDocument(): XmlImplementation

CreateDocumentFragment(): XmlDocument

CreateDocumentType(): XmlDocument

CreateDomain(): AppDomain

CreateElement(): XmlDataDocument, XmlDocument

CreateEntityReference(): XmlDataDocument, XmlDocument

CreateEventSource(): EventLog

CreateGlobalFunctions(): ModuleBuilder

CreateInstance: BindingFlags

CreateInstance(): Activator, AppDomain, Array, Assembly

CreateInstanceAndUnwrap(): AppDomain

CreateInstanceFrom(): Activator, AppDomain

CreateInstanceFromAndUnwrap(): AppDomain

CreateMask(): BitVector32

CreateMethodBody(): MethodBuilder

CreateNavigator(): IXPathNavigable, XmlDataDocument, XmlNode, XPathDocument

CreateNew: FileMode

CreateNode(): XmlDocument

CreateNoWindow: ProcessStartInfo

CreateObjRef(): MarshalByRefObject

CreatePermission(): DnsPermissionAttribute, EventLogPermissionAttribute, PerformanceCounterPermissionAttribute, SocketPermissionAttribute, WebPermissionAttribute

CreateProcessingInstruction(): XmlDocument

CreateQualifiedName(): Assembly

CreateSection(): BitVector32

CreateSignificantWhitespace(): XmlDocument

CreateSpecificCulture(): CultureInfo

CreateSubdirectory(): DirectoryInfo

CreateSubKey(): RegistryKey

CreateText(): File, FileInfo

CreateTextNode(): XmlDocument

CreateTimer(): SystemEvents

CreateType(): EnumBuilder, TypeBuilder

CreateWaitHandle(): Stream

CreateWhitespace(): XmlDocument

CreateWrapperOfType(): Marshal

CreateXmlDeclaration(): XmlDocument

CreationTime: FileSystemInfo, NotifyFilters

CredentialCache: System.Net

Credentials: FileWebRequest, HttpWebRequest, IWebProxy, WebClient, WebProxy, WebRequest, XmlResolver, XmlUrlResolver

CrossAppDomain: StreamingContextStates

CrossAppDomainDelegate: System

CrossMachine: StreamingContextStates

CrossProcess: StreamingContextStates

Culture: AssemblyCultureAttribute

CultureInfo: AssemblyName, System.Globalization

DefineInitializedData(): ModuleBuilder, TypeBuilder

DefineLabel(): ILGenerator

DefineLiteral(): EnumBuilder

DefineLPArray(): UnmanagedMarshal

DefineMethod(): TypeBuilder

DefineMethodOverride(): TypeBuilder

DefineNestedType(): TypeBuilder

DefineParameter(): ConstructorBuilder, MethodBuilder

DefinePInvokeMethod(): ModuleBuilder, TypeBuilder

DefineProperty(): TypeBuilder

DefineResource(): AssemblyBuilder, ModuleBuilder

DefineSafeArray(): UnmanagedMarshal

DefineType(): ModuleBuilder

DefineTypeInitializer(): TypeBuilder

DefineUninitializedData(): ModuleBuilder, TypeBuilder

DefineUnmanagedMarshal(): UnmanagedMarshal

DefineUnmanagedResource(): AssemblyBuilder, Module-
Builder

DefineVersionInfoResource(): AssemblyBuilder

DelaySign: AssemblyDelaySignAttribute

Delegate: AttributeTargets, System

Delete(): Directory, DirectoryInfo, EventLog, File, FileInfo,
FileSystemInfo, PerformanceCounterCategory

Deleted: FileSystemWatcher, WatcherChangeTypes

DeleteData(): XmlCharacterData

DeleteDirectory(): IsolatedStorageFile

DeleteEventSource(): EventLog

DeleteFile(): IsolatedStorageFile

DeleteSubKey(): RegistryKey

DeleteSubKeyTree(): RegistryKey

DeleteValue(): RegistryKey

Delimiter: Type

Delta: DaylightTime

Depth: XmlNodeReader, XmlReader, XmlTextReader, Xml-
ValidatingReader

Dequeue(): Queue

Descending: XmlSortOrder

Description: AssemblyDescriptionAttribute, IODescriptionAttribute, MonitoringDescriptionAttribute, Switch,
TimersDescriptionAttribute

Deserialize(): BinaryFormatter, Formatter, IFormatter,
SoapFormatter

DeserializeMethodResponse(): BinaryFormatter

Desktop: UserPreferenceCategory

DesktopDirectory: SpecialFolder

DestroyStructure(): Marshal

Detail: SoapFault

Device: FileAttributes

Dgram: SocketType

DictionaryBase: System.Collections

DictionaryEntry: System.Collections

Directory: FileAttributes, FileInfo, System.IO

DirectoryInfo: System.IO

DirectoryName: FileInfo, NotifyFilters

DirectoryNotFoundException: System.IO

DirectorySeparatorChar: Path

DisallowPublisherPolicy: AppDomainSetup

Discard: Cookie

DiscardBufferedData(): StreamReader

DispatchWrapper: System.Runtime.InteropServices

DispIdAttribute: System.Runtime.InteropServices

DisplayName: CultureInfo, RegionInfo, Switch

DisplaySettingsChanged: SystemEvents

Dispose(): BinaryReader, BinaryWriter, EventLog, Event-
LogTraceListener, FileStream, FileSystemWatcher,
FileWebResponse, HttpWebResponse, IDisposable,
IsolatedStorageFile, IsolatedStorageFileStream, Net-
workStream, PerformanceCounter, Process, Socket,
StreamReader, StreamWriter, StringReader, String-
Writer, TcpClient, TextReader, TextWriter, TextWriter-
TraceListener, Timer, TraceListener, WaitHandle

Div: OpCodes

Div_Un: OpCodes

Divide(): Decimal

DivideByZeroException: System

Dll: PEFileKinds

DllImportAttribute: System.Runtime.InteropServices

DllNotFoundException: System

Dns: System.Net, UriHostNameType

DnsPermission: System.Net

DnsPermissionAttribute: System.Net

DoCallBack(): AppDomain

DocTypeName: XmlParserContext

Document: XmlNodeType

DocumentElement: XmlDocument

DocumentFragment: XmlNodeType

DocumentType: XmlDocument, XmlNodeType

DoFixups(): ObjectManager

Domain: Cookie, IsolatedStorageScope, NetworkCredential

DomainIdentity: IsolatedStorage

DomainUnload: AppDomain

DontFragment: SocketOptionName

DontLinger: SocketOptionName

DontRoute: SocketFlags, SocketOptionName

Double: System, TypeCode

DoubleToInt64Bits(): BitConverter

DowngradeFromWriterLock(): ReaderWriterLock

DownloadData(): WebClient

DownloadFile(): WebClient

DropMembership: SocketOptionName

DropMulticastGroup(): UdpClient

DropSourceMembership: SocketOptionName

DTD: ValidationType

Dup: OpCodes

DuplicateWaitObjectException: System

Duration(): TimeSpan

DynamicBase: AppDomainSetup

F

Fail(): Debug, DefaultTraceListener, Trace, TraceListener
FailureAudit: EventLogEntryType
FalseString: Boolean
FamANDAssem: FieldAttributes, MethodAttributes
Family: FieldAttributes, MethodAttributes, SocketAddress
FamORAssem: FieldAttributes, MethodAttributes
FastCall: CallingConvention
FaultActor: SoapFault
FaultCode: SoapFault
FaultString: SoapFault
Favorites: SpecialFolder
Field: AttributeTargets, MemberTypes
FieldAccessException: System
FieldAccessMask: FieldAttributes
FieldAttributes: System.Reflection
FieldBuilder: System.Reflection.Emit
FieldHandle: FieldBuilder, FieldInfo
FieldInfo: System.Reflection
FieldNames: IFieldInfo
FieldOffsetAttribute: System.Runtime.InteropServices
FieldToken: System.Reflection.Emit
FieldType: FieldBuilder, FieldInfo
FieldTypes: IFieldInfo
File: StreamingContextStates, System.IO
FileAccess: System.IO
FileAttributes: System.IO
FileBuildPart: FileVersionInfo
FileDescription: FileVersionInfo
FileInfo: System.IO
FileLoadException: System.IO
FileMajorPart: FileVersionInfo
FileMinorPart: FileVersionInfo
FileMode: System.IO
FileName: BadImageFormatException, FileLoadException, FileNotFoundException, FileVersionInfo, ManifestResourceInfo, NotifyFilters, ProcessModule, ProcessStartInfo
FileNotFoundException: System.IO
FilePrivatePart: FileVersionInfo
FileShare: System.IO
FileStream: System.IO
FileSystemEventArgs: System.IO
FileSystemEventHandler: System.IO
FileSystemInfo: System.IO
FileSystemWatcher: System.IO
FileVersion: FileVersionInfo
FileVersionInfo: ProcessModule, System.Diagnostics
FileWebRequest: System.Net
FileWebResponse: System.Net
FillBuffer(): BinaryReader
Filter: FileSystemWatcher
FilterAttribute: Type
FilterName: Type

FilterNameIgnoreCase: Type
FilterTypeName: Module
FilterTypeNameIgnoreCase: Module
Final: MethodAttributes
Finalize(): CompressedStack, FileStream, IsolatedStorageFile, LocalDataStoreSlot, NetworkStream, Object, Regex, RegisteredWaitHandle, RegistryKey, Socket, StreamWriter, TcpClient, TcpListener, Thread, Timer, WaitHandle, WeakReference
FinalQuotePunctuation: UnicodeCategory
FindInterfaces(): Type
FindMembers(): Type
FindServicePoint(): ServicePointManager
FindTypes(): Module
FireFox: AddressFamily, ProtocolFamily
FirstChild: XmlNode
FirstDay: CalendarWeekRule
FirstDayOfWeek: DateTimeFormatInfo
FirstFourDayWeek: CalendarWeekRule
FirstFullWeek: CalendarWeekRule
FixedSize(): ArrayList
Flags: AssemblyFlagsAttribute, AssemblyName
FlagsAttribute: System
FlattenHierarchy: BindingFlags
Float: NumberStyles
Floor(): Decimal, Math
FlowControl: OpCode, System.Reflection.Emit
Flush(): BinaryWriter, BufferedStream, Debug, FileStream, IsolatedStorageFileStream, MemoryStream, NetworkStream, RegistryKey, Stream, StreamWriter, TextWriter, TextWriterTraceListener, Trace, TraceListener, XmlTextWriter, XmlWriter
Forbidden: HttpStatusCode
Format: UnicodeCategory
Format(): Enum, ICustomFormatter, String
FormatException: System
FormatProvider: TextWriter
Formatter: System.Runtime.Serialization
FormatterAssemblyStyle: System.Runtime.Serialization.Formatters
FormatterConverter: System.Runtime.Serialization
FormatterServices: System.Runtime.Serialization
FormatterTypeStyle: System.Runtime.Serialization.Formatters
Formatting: System.Xml, XmlTextWriter
ForwardRef: MethodImplAttributes
Found: HttpStatusCode
Fragment: Uri, UriBuilder
FrameCount: StackTrace
Free(): GCHandle, Overlapped
FreeBSTR(): Marshal
FreeCoTaskMem(): Marshal
FreeHGlobal(): Marshal
FreeNamedDataSlot(): Thread

FreePage: ThreadWaitReason

Friday: DayOfWeek

FriendlyName: AppDomain

FromBase64CharArray(): Convert

FromBase64String(): Convert

FromDays(): TimeSpan

FromFileTime(): DateTime

FromGlobalAccessCache(): RuntimeEnvironment

FromHex(): Uri

FromHours(): TimeSpan

FromMilliseconds(): TimeSpan

FromMinutes(): TimeSpan

FromOACurrency(): Decimal

FromOADate(): DateTime

FromSeconds(): TimeSpan

FromTicks(): TimeSpan

FromXml(): DnsPermission, SocketPermission, WebPermission

Full: FormatterAssemblyStyle

FullDateTimePattern: DateTimeFormatInfo

FullName: Assembly, AssemblyName, EnumBuilder, FileSystemInfo, Type, TypeBuilder, TypeDelegator

FullPath: FileSystemEventArgs, FileSystemInfo

FullTypeName: SerializationInfo

FullyQualifiedName: Module, ModuleBuilder

FunctionPtr: UnmanagedType

FusionLog: BadImageFormatException, FileLoadException, FileNotFoundException

G

GatewayTimeout: HttpStatusCode

GC: System

GCHandle: System.Runtime.InteropServices

GCHandleType: System.Runtime.InteropServices

General: UserPreferenceCategory

GenerateGuidForType(): Marshal

GenerateProgIdForType(): Marshal

Get(): BitArray, KeysCollection, NameTable, NameValueCollection, XmlNameTable

GetAbbreviatedDayName(): DateTimeFormatInfo

GetAbbreviatedEraName(): DateTimeFormatInfo

GetAbbreviatedMonthName(): DateTimeFormatInfo

GetAccessors(): PropertyBuilder, PropertyInfo

GetActiveObject(): Marshal

GetAddMethod(): EventInfo

GetAllDateTimePatterns(): DateTimeFormatInfo

GetArray(): ArrayWithOffset

GetArrayMethod(): ModuleBuilder

GetArrayMethodToken(): ModuleBuilder

GetArrayRank(): Type

GetAssemblies(): AppDomain

GetAssembly(): Assembly

GetAssemblyName(): AssemblyName,

AssemblyNameProxy

GetAttribute(): XmlElement, XmlNodeReader, XmlReader, XmlTextReader, XmlValidatingReader, XPathNavigator

GetAttributeFlagsImpl(): EnumBuilder, Type, TypeBuilder, TypeDelegator

GetAttributeNode(): XmlElement

GetAttributes(): File

GetAvailableThreads(): ThreadPool

GetBaseDefinition(): MethodBuilder, MethodInfo

GetBaseException(): Exception

GetBits(): Decimal

GetBoolean(): SerializationInfo

GetBuffer(): MemoryStream

GetByIndex(): SortedList

GetByte(): Buffer, SerializationInfo

GetByteCount(): ASCIIEncoding, Encoder, Encoding, UnicodeEncoding, UTF7Encoding, UTF8Encoding

GetBytes(): ASCIIEncoding, BitConverter, Encoder, Encoding, UnicodeEncoding, UTF7Encoding, UTF8Encoding

GetCallingAssembly(): Assembly

GetCategories(): PerformanceCounterCategory

GetChar(): SerializationInfo

GetCharCount(): ASCIIEncoding, Decoder, Encoding, UnicodeEncoding, UTF7Encoding, UTF8Encoding

GetChars(): ASCIIEncoding, Decoder, Encoding, UnicodeEncoding, UTF7Encoding, UTF8Encoding

GetComInterfaceForObject(): Marshal

GetCommandLineArgs(): Environment

GetComObjectData(): Marshal

GetCompareInfo(): CompareInfo

GetComSlotForMethodInfo(): Marshal

GetConstructor(): Type

GetConstructorImpl(): EnumBuilder, Type, TypeBuilder, TypeDelegator

GetConstructors(): EnumBuilder, Type, TypeBuilder, TypeDelegator

GetConstructorToken(): ModuleBuilder

GetCookieHeader(): CookieContainer

GetCookies(): CookieContainer

GetCounters(): PerformanceCounterCategory

GetCreationTime(): Directory, File

GetCredential(): CredentialCache, ICredentials, NetworkCredential

GetCultures(): CultureInfo

GetCurrentDirectory(): Directory

GetCurrentMethod(): MethodBase

GetCurrentProcess(): Process

GetCurrentThreadId(): AppDomain

GetCustomAttribute(): Attribute

GetCustomAttributes(): Assembly, Attribute, ConstructorBuilder, EnumBuilder, FieldBuilder, ICustomAttributeProvider, MemberInfo, MethodBuilder, Module, ParameterInfo, PropertyBuilder, TypeBuilder, TypeDelegator

GetData(): AppDomain, Thread
GetDateTime(): SerializationInfo
GetDateTimeFormats(): DateTime
GetDaylightChanges(): TimeZone
GetDayName(): DateTimeFormatInfo
GetDayOfMonth(): Calendar, GregorianCalendar, HebrewCalendar, HijriCalendar, JapaneseCalendar, JulianCalendar, KoreanCalendar, TaiwanCalendar, ThaiBuddhistCalendar
GetDayOfWeek(): Calendar, GregorianCalendar, HebrewCalendar, HijriCalendar, JapaneseCalendar, JulianCalendar, KoreanCalendar, TaiwanCalendar, ThaiBuddhistCalendar
GetDayOfYear(): Calendar, GregorianCalendar, HebrewCalendar, HijriCalendar, JapaneseCalendar, JulianCalendar, KoreanCalendar, TaiwanCalendar, ThaiBuddhistCalendar
GetDaysInMonth(): Calendar, GregorianCalendar, HebrewCalendar, HijriCalendar, JapaneseCalendar, JulianCalendar, KoreanCalendar, TaiwanCalendar, ThaiBuddhistCalendar
GetDaysInYear(): Calendar, GregorianCalendar, HebrewCalendar, HijriCalendar, JapaneseCalendar, JulianCalendar, KoreanCalendar, TaiwanCalendar, ThaiBuddhistCalendar
GetDecimal(): SerializationInfo
GetDecoder(): Encoding, UnicodeEncoding, UTF7Encoding, UTF8Encoding
GetDefaultMembers(): Type
GetDefaultProxy(): WebProxy
GetDirectories(): Directory, DirectoryInfo
GetDirectoryName(): Path
GetDirectoryNames(): IsolatedStorageFile
GetDirectoryRoot(): Directory
GetDomain(): Thread
GetDomainID(): Thread
GetDouble(): SerializationInfo
GetDynamicModule(): AssemblyBuilder
GetElementById(): XmlDataDocument, XmlDocument
GetElementFromRow(): XmlDataDocument
GetElementsByTagName(): XmlDocument, XmlElement
GetElementType(): EnumBuilder, Type, TypeBuilder, TypeDelegator
GetEmptyWebProxy(): GlobalProxySelection
GetEncoder(): Encoding, UTF7Encoding, UTF8Encoding
GetEncoding(): Encoding
GetEndComSlot(): Marshal
GetEntity(): XmlResolver, XmlUrlResolver
GetEntryAssembly(): Assembly
GetEnumerator(): Array, ArrayList, BitArray, CaptureCollection, CollectionBase, CookieCollection, CredentialCache, DictionaryBase, EventLogEntryCollection, GroupCollection, Hashtable, HybridDictionary, IDictionary, IEnumerable, IsolatedStorageFile,

KeysCollection, ListDictionary, MatchCollection, NameObjectCollectionBase, Queue, ReadOnlyCollectionBase, SerializationInfo, SortedList, Stack, String, StringCollection, StringDictionary, TraceListenerCollection, XmlNamedNodeMap, XmlNamespaceManager, XmlNode, XmlNodeList
GetEnvironmentVariable(): Environment
GetEnvironmentVariables(): Environment
GetEra(): Calendar, DateTimeFormatInfo, GregorianCalendar, HebrewCalendar, HijriCalendar, JapaneseCalendar, JulianCalendar, KoreanCalendar, TaiwanCalendar, ThaiBuddhistCalendar
GetEraName(): DateTimeFormatInfo
GetEvent(): EnumBuilder, Type, TypeBuilder, TypeDelegator
GetEventLogs(): EventLog
GetEvents(): EnumBuilder, Type, TypeBuilder, TypeDelegator
GetEventToken(): EventBuilder
GetException(): ErrorEventArgs
GetExceptionCode(): Marshal
GetExceptionPointers(): Marshal
GetExecutingAssembly(): Assembly
GetExportedTypes(): Assembly, AssemblyBuilder
GetExtension(): Path
GetExtensionObject(): XsltArgumentList
GetField: BindingFlags
GetField(): EnumBuilder, IReflect, Module, Type, TypeBuilder, TypeDelegator
GetFieldFromHandle(): FieldInfo
GetFields(): EnumBuilder, IReflect, Module, Type, TypeBuilder, TypeDelegator
GetFieldSigHelper(): SignatureHelper
GetFieldToken(): ModuleBuilder
GetFile(): Assembly, AssemblyBuilder
GetFileColumnNumber(): StackFrame
GetFileLineNumber(): StackFrame
GetFileName(): Path, StackFrame
GetFileNames(): IsolatedStorageFile
GetFileNameWithoutExtension(): Path
GetFiles(): Assembly, AssemblyBuilder, Directory, DirectoryInfo
GetFileSystemEntries(): Directory
GetFileSystemInfos(): DirectoryInfo
GetFolderPath(): Environment
GetFormat(): CultureInfo, DateTimeFormatInfo, IFormatProvider, NumberFormatInfo
GetFrame(): StackTrace
GetFullPath(): Path
GetGeneration(): GC
GetGetMethod(): PropertyBuilder, PropertyInfo
GetGroupNames(): Regex
GetGroupNumbers(): Regex
GetHash(): Hashtable

GetHashCode(): ArgIterator, ArrayWithOffset, Attribute, BitVector32, Boolean, Byte, CaseInsensitiveHash-CodeProvider, Char, CompareInfo, Cookie, CultureInfo, DateTime, Decimal, Delegate, Double, Encoding, EndpointPermission, Enum, EventToken, FieldToken, Guid, HttpWebRequest, HttpWebResponse, IHash-CodeProvider, Int16, Int32, Int64, IntPtr, IPAddress, IPEndPoint, Label, MethodBuilder, MethodToken, MulticastDelegate, Object, OpCode, ParameterToken, PropertyToken, RegionInfo, SByte, Section, ServicePoint, SignatureHelper, SignatureToken, Single, Socket, SocketAddress, SortKey, StreamingContext, String, StringToken, TextInfo, TimeSpan, Type, TypeToken, UInt16, UInt32, UInt64, UIntPtr, UnicodeEncoding, Uri, UriBuilder, UTF8Encoding, ValueType, Version, XmlQualifiedName

GetHINSTANCE(): Marshal

GetHostByAddress(): Dns

GetHostByName(): Dns

GetHostName(): Dns

GetHour(): Calendar

GetHRForException(): Marshal

GetHRForLastWin32Error(): Marshal

GetId(): ObjectIDGenerator

GetIDispatchForObject(): Marshal

GetILGenerator(): ConstructorBuilder, MethodBuilder

GetILOffset(): StackFrame

GetIndexParameters(): PropertyBuilder, PropertyInfo

GetInstance(): DateTimeFormatInfo, NumberFormatInfo

GetInstanceNames(): PerformanceCounterCategory

GetInt16(): SerializationInfo

GetInt32(): SerializationInfo

GetInt64(): SerializationInfo

GetInterface(): EnumBuilder, Type, TypeBuilder, TypeDelegator

GetInterfaceMap(): EnumBuilder, Type, TypeBuilder, TypeDelegator

GetInterfaces(): EnumBuilder, Type, TypeBuilder, TypeDelegator

GetInvocationList(): Delegate, MulticastDelegate

GetITypeInfoForType(): Marshal

GetIUnknownForObject(): Marshal

GetKey(): NameValueCollection, SortedList

GetKeyList(): SortedList

GetLastAccessTime(): Directory, File

GetLastWin32Error(): Marshal

GetLastWriteTime(): Directory, File

GetLeftPart(): Uri

GetLength(): Array

GetLifetimeService(): MarshalByRefObject

GetLoadedModules(): Assembly

GetLocalVarSigHelper(): SignatureHelper

GetLogicalDrives(): Directory, Environment

GetLowerBound(): Array

GetManagedCategoryGuid(): IRegistrationServices, RegistrationServices

GetManagedThunkForUnmanagedMethodPtr(): Marshal

GetManifestResourceInfo(): Assembly, AssemblyBuilder

GetManifestResourceNames(): Assembly, AssemblyBuilder

GetManifestResourceStream(): Assembly, AssemblyBuilder

GetMaxByteCount(): ASCIIEncoding, Encoding, UnicodeEncoding, UTF7Encoding, UTF8Encoding

GetMaxCharCount(): ASCIIEncoding, Encoding, UnicodeEncoding, UTF7Encoding, UTF8Encoding

GetMaxThreads(): ThreadPool

GetMember(): EnumBuilder, IReflect, Type, TypeBuilder, TypeDelegator

GetMembers(): EnumBuilder, IReflect, Type, TypeBuilder, TypeDelegator

GetMethod(): IReflect, Module, StackFrame, Type

GetMethodFromHandle(): MethodBase

GetMethodImpl(): Delegate, EnumBuilder, Module, Type, TypeBuilder, TypeDelegator

GetMethodImplementationFlags(): ConstructorBuilder, MethodBase, MethodBuilder

GetMethodInfoForComSlot(): Marshal

GetMethods(): EnumBuilder, IReflect, Module, Type, TypeBuilder, TypeDelegator

GetMethodSigHelper(): SignatureHelper

GetMethodToken(): ModuleBuilder

GetMilliseconds(): Calendar

GetMinute(): Calendar

GetModule(): Assembly, ConstructorBuilder, MethodBuilder

GetModules(): Assembly

GetMonth(): Calendar, GregorianCalendar, HebrewCalendar, HijriCalendar, JapaneseCalendar, JulianCalendar, KoreanCalendar, TaiwanCalendar, ThaiBuddhistCalendar

GetMonthName(): DateTimeFormatInfo

GetMonthsInYear(): Calendar, GregorianCalendar, HebrewCalendar, HijriCalendar, JapaneseCalendar, JulianCalendar, KoreanCalendar, TaiwanCalendar, ThaiBuddhistCalendar

GetName(): Assembly, Enum

GetNamedDataSlot(): Thread

GetNamedItem(): XmlNamedNodeMap

GetNames(): Enum

GetNamespace(): XPathNavigator

GetNamespaceOfPrefix(): XmlNode

GetNativeOffset(): StackFrame

GetNativeVariantForObject(): Marshal

GetNestedType(): EnumBuilder, Type, TypeBuilder, TypeDelegator

GetNestedTypes(): EnumBuilder, Type, TypeBuilder, TypeDelegator

GetNext(): Formatter
GetNextArg(): ArgIterator
GetNextArgType(): ArgIterator
GetNextSelector(): ISurrogateSelector, SurrogateSelector
GetNextTextElement(): StringInfo
GetNode(): IHasXmlNode
GetNumericValue(): Char
GetObject(): Activator, ObjectManager
GetObjectData(): ArgumentException, ArgumentOut-
OfRangeException, Assembly, AssemblyName, BadIm-
ageFormatException, DBNull, Delegate, Exception,
FileLoadException, FileNotFoundException, Format-
terServices, Hashtable, ISerializable, ISerialization-
Surrogate, MissingMemberException, Module,
MulticastDelegate, NameObjectCollectionBase,
NotFiniteNumberException, ObjectDisposedExcep-
tion, ReflectionTypeLoadException, RuntimeTypeHan-
dle, SoapFault, TypeInitializationException,
TypeLoadException, WeakReference, XmlException,
XPathException, XsltCompileException, XsltException
GetObjectForIUnknown(): Marshal
GetObjectForNativeVariant(): Marshal
GetObjectsForNativeVariants(): Marshal
GetOffset(): ArrayWithOffset
GetParam(): XsltArgumentList
GetParameters(): ConstructorBuilder, MethodBase,
MethodBuilder
GetParent(): Directory
GetPathRoot(): Path
GetPermission(): IsolatedStorage, IsolatedStorageFile
GetPreamble(): Encoding, UnicodeEncoding, UTF8Encod-
ing
GetPrefixOfNamespace(): XmlNode
GetProcessById(): Process
GetProcesses(): Process
GetProcessesByName(): Process
GetProgIdForType(): IRegistrationServices, Registra-
tionServices
GetProperties(): EnumBuilder, IReflect, Type, TypeBuilder,
TypeDelegator
GetProperty: BindingFlags
GetProperty(): IReflect, Type
GetPropertyImpl(): EnumBuilder, Type, TypeBuilder, Type-
Delegator
GetPropertySigHelper(): SignatureHelper
GetProxy(): IWebProxy, WebProxy
GetPublicKey(): AssemblyName
GetPublicKeyToken(): AssemblyName
GetRaiseMethod(): EventInfo
GetRange(): ArrayList
GetRealObject(): IObjectReference
GetReferencedAssemblies(): Assembly
GetRegistrableTypesInAssembly(): IRegistrationServices,
RegistrationServices

GetRemainder(): XmlTextReader
GetRemainingCount(): ArgIterator
GetRemoveMethod(): EventInfo
GetRequestStream(): FileWebRequest, HttpWebRequest,
WebRequest
GetResponse(): FileWebRequest, HttpWebRequest,
WebRequest
GetResponseHeader(): HttpWebResponse
GetResponseStream(): FileWebResponse, HttpWebRe-
sponse, WebResponse
GetRowFromElement(): XmlDataDocument
GetRuntimeDirectory(): RuntimeEnvironment
GetSatelliteAssembly(): Assembly
GetSByte(): SerializationInfo
GetSecond(): Calendar
GetSerializableMembers(): FormatterServices
GetService(): IServiceProvider
GetSetMethod(): PropertyBuilder, PropertyInfo
GetSignature(): SignatureHelper
GetSignatureToken(): ModuleBuilder
GetSignerCertificate(): Module
GetSingle(): SerializationInfo
GetSocketOption(): Socket
GetSortKey(): CompareInfo
GetStartComSlot(): Marshal
GetStore(): IsolatedStorageFile
GetStream(): TcpClient
GetString(): ASCIIEncoding, Encoding, SerializationInfo
GetStringBuilder(): StringWriter
GetStringConstant(): ModuleBuilder
GetSubKeyNames(): RegistryKey
GetSurrogate(): ISurrogateSelector, SurrogateSelector
GetSymWriter(): ModuleBuilder
GetSystemVersion(): RuntimeEnvironment
GetTempFileName(): Path
GetTempPath(): Path
GetTextElement(): TextElementEnumerator
GetTextElementEnumerator(): StringInfo
GetThreadFromFiberCookie(): Marshal
GetToken(): ConstructorBuilder, FieldBuilder, Method-
Builder, ParameterBuilder
GetTotalMemory(): GC
GetType(): AppDomain, Assembly, Module, Module-
Builder, Object, Type
GetTypeArray(): Type
GetTypeCode(): Boolean, Byte, Char, Convert, DateTime,
DBNull, Decimal, Double, Enum, IConvertible, Int16,
Int32, Int64, SByte, Single, String, Type, UInt16,
UInt32, UInt64
GetTypedObjectForIUnknown(): Marshal
GetTypeForITypeInfo(): Marshal
GetTypeFromAssembly(): FormatterServices
GetTypeFromCLSID(): Type
GetTypeFromHandle(): Type

GetTypeFromProgID(): Type
GetTypeHandle(): Type
GetTypeInfoName(): Marshal
GetTypeLibGuid(): Marshal
GetTypeLibGuidForAssembly(): Marshal
GetTypeLibLcid(): Marshal
GetTypeLibName(): Marshal
GetTypes(): Assembly, Module, ModuleBuilder
GetTypeToken(): ModuleBuilder
GetUInt16(): SerializationInfo
GetUInt32(): SerializationInfo
GetUInt64(): SerializationInfo
GetUnderlyingType(): Enum
GetUnicodeCategory(): Char
GetUninitializedObject(): FormatterServices
GetUnmanagedThunkForManagedMethodPtr(): Marshal
GetUnmanagedType: UnmanagedMarshal
GetUpperBound(): Array
GetUserStoreForAssembly(): IsolatedStorageFile
GetUserStoreForDomain(): IsolatedStorageFile
GetUtcOffset(): TimeZone
GetValue(): Array, FieldBuilder, FieldInfo, PropertyBuilder, PropertyInfo, RegistryKey, SerializationInfo
GetValueDirect(): FieldInfo
GetValueList(): SortedList
GetValueNames(): RegistryKey
GetValues(): Enum, NameValueCollection, WebHeaderCollection
GetVersionInfo(): FileVersionInfo
GetWeekOfYear(): Calendar
GetYear(): Calendar, GregorianCalendar, HebrewCalendar, HijriCalendar, JapaneseCalendar, JulianCalendar, KoreanCalendar, TaiwanCalendar, ThaiBuddhistCalendar
Ggp: ProtocolType
GlobalAssemblyCache: Assembly
GlobalProxySelection: System.Net
Gone: HttpStatusCode
GregorianCalendar: System.Globalization
GregorianCalendarTypes: System.Globalization
Group: MulticastOption, System.Text.RegularExpressions
GroupCollection: System.Text.RegularExpressions
GroupNameFromNumber(): Regex
GroupNumberFromName(): Regex
Groups: Match
Guid: System
GUID: EnumBuilder, Type, TypeBuilder, TypeDelegator
GuidAttribute: System.Runtime.InteropServices

H

Handle: FileStream, HandleRef, IsolatedStorageFileStream, Process, Socket, WaitHandle
HandleCount: Process
HandleRef: System.Runtime.InteropServices
HasAttribute(): XmlElement
HasAttributes: XmlElement, XmlNodeReader, XmlReader, XPathNavigator
HasChildNodes: XmlNode
HasChildren: XPathNavigator
HasDefault: FieldAttributes, ParameterAttributes, PropertyAttributes
HasElementType: Type
HasElementTypeImpl(): EnumBuilder, Type, TypeBuilder, TypeDelegator
HasExited: Process
HasExtension(): Path
HasFeature(): XmlImplementation
HasFieldMarshal: FieldAttributes, ParameterAttributes
HasFieldRVA: FieldAttributes
HashAlgorithm: AssemblyName
Hashtable: System.Collections
HasId(): ObjectIDGenerator
HasKeys(): NameValueCollection
HasLineInfo(): IXmlLineInfo
HasNamespace(): XmlNamespaceManager
HasSecurity: MethodAttributes, TypeAttributes
HasShutdownStarted: Environment
HasThis: CallingConventions
HasValue: XmlNodeReader, XmlReader, XmlTextReader, XmlValidatingReader
HaveResponse: HttpWebRequest
HeaderIncluded: SocketOptionName
HeaderName: Encoding
Headers: FileWebRequest, FileWebResponse, HttpWebRequest, HttpWebResponse, ISoapMessage, SoapMessage, WebClient, WebRequest, WebResponse
HebrewCalendar: System.Globalization
HebrewEra: HebrewCalendar
HelpLink: Exception
HexEscape(): Uri
HexNumber: NumberStyles
HexUnescape(): Uri
Hidden: FileAttributes, ProcessWindowStyle
HideBySig: MethodAttributes
High: ProcessPriorityClass
Highest: ThreadPriority, ThreadPriorityLevel
HijriCalendar: System.Globalization
HijriEra: HijriCalendar
History: SpecialFolder
Host: SocketPermissionAttribute, Uri, UriBuilder
Hostname: EndpointPermission
HostName: IPHostEntry
HostNameType: Uri

InitializeLifetimeService(): AppDomain, MarshalByRef-Object

InitializeReferences(): Regex

InitialQuotePunctuation: UnicodeCategory

InitLocals: ConstructorBuilder, MethodBuilder

Initobj: OpCodes

InitOnly: FieldAttributes

InitStore(): IsolatedStorage

InlineBrTarget: OperandType

InlineField: OperandType

InlineI: OperandType

InlineI8: OperandType

InlineMethod: OperandType

InlineNone: OperandType

InlinePhi: OperandType

InlineR: OperandType

InlineSig: OperandType

InlineString: OperandType

InlineSwitch: OperandType

InlineTok: OperandType

InlineType: OperandType

InlineVar: OperandType

InnerException: Exception

InnerText: XmlAttribute, XmlCharacterData, XmlDeclaration, XmlElement, XmlEntity, XmlNode, XmlProcessingInstruction

InnerXml: XmlAttribute, XmlDocument, XmlDocumentFragment, XmlElement, XmlEntity, XmlNode, XmlNotation

INormalizeForIsolatedStorage: System.IO.IsolatedStorage

Insert: XmlNodeChangedAction

Insert(): ArrayList, CounterCreationDataCollection, EventLogPermissionEntryCollection, IList, PerformanceCounterPermissionEntryCollection, ProcessThreadCollection, String, StringBuilder, StringCollection, TraceListenerCollection

InsertAfter(): XmlAttributeCollection, XmlNode

InsertBefore(): XmlAttributeCollection, XmlNode

InsertData(): XmlCharacterData

InsertRange(): ArrayList

Install(): EventLogInstaller, PerformanceCounterInstaller

InstalledFontsChanged: SystemEvents

InstalledUICulture: CultureInfo

InstalledWin32Cultures: CultureTypes

Instance: BindingFlags

InstanceData: System.Diagnostics

InstanceDataCollection: System.Diagnostics

InstanceDataCollectionCollection: System.Diagnostics

InstanceExists(): PerformanceCounterCategory

InstanceName: InstanceData, PerformanceCounter

Instrument: EventLogPermissionAccess, PerformanceCounterPermissionAccess

Int16: System, TypeCode

Int32: System, TypeCode

Int64: System, TypeCode

Int64BitsToDouble(): BitConverter

Integer: NumberStyles

Interactive: ReadState

Interface: AttributeTargets, TypeAttributes, UnmanagedType

InterfaceIsDual: ComInterfaceType

InterfaceIsIDispatch: ComInterfaceType

InterfaceIsIUnknown: ComInterfaceType

InterfaceMapping: System.Reflection

InterfaceMethods: InterfaceMapping

InterfaceType: InterfaceMapping

InterfaceTypeAttribute: System.Runtime.InteropServices

Interlocked: System.Threading

Intern(): String

InternalBufferOverflowException: System.IO

InternalBufferSize: FileSystemWatcher

InternalCall: MethodImplAttributes

InternalHigh: NativeOverlapped

InternalImpl: IDispatchImplType

InternalLow: NativeOverlapped

InternalName: FileVersionInfo

InternalServerError: HttpStatusCode

InternalSubset: XmlDocumentType, XmlParserContext

InternalValidationEventHandler: XmlValidatingReader

InternetCache: SpecialFolder

InterNetwork: AddressFamily, ProtocolFamily

InterNetworkV6: AddressFamily, ProtocolFamily

Interrupt(): Thread

Intersect(): DnsPermission, SocketPermission, WebPermission

Interval: Timer

IntPtr: System

InvalidateCachedArrays(): NameValueCollection

InvalidCastException: System

InvalidComObjectException: System.Runtime.InteropServices

InvalidFilterCriteriaException: System.Reflection

InvalidHandle: WaitHandle

InvalidOleVariantTypeException: System.Runtime.InteropServices

InvalidOperationException: System

InvalidPathChars: Path

InvalidProgramException: System

InvariantCulture: CultureInfo

InvariantInfo: DateTimeFormatInfo, NumberFormatInfo

Invoke(): AssemblyLoadEventHandler, AsyncCallback, ConstructorBuilder, ConstructorInfo, CrossAppDomainDelegate, ElapsedEventHandler, EntryWrittenEventHandler, ErrorEventHandler, EventHandler, FileSystemEventHandler, HttpContinueDelegate, IOCompletionCallback, IXsltContextFunction, MatchEvaluator, MemberFilter, MethodBase,

MethodBuilder, ModuleResolveEventHandler,
ObjectCreationDelegate, PowerModeChangedEvent-
Handler, RenamedEventHandler, ResolveEvent-
Handler, SessionEndedEventHandler,
SessionEndingEventHandler, ThreadExceptionEvent-
Handler, ThreadStart, TimerCallback, TimerElapsed-
EventHandler, TypeFilter,
UnhandledExceptionEventHandler, UserPreference-
ChangedEventHandler, UserPreferenceChangingEven-
tHandler, WaitCallback, WaitOrTimerCallback,
XmlNodeChangedEventHandler

InvokeMember(): EnumBuilder, IReflect, Type, Type-
Builder, TypeDelegator

InvokeMethod: BindingFlags

InvokeOnEventsThread(): SystemEvents

IObjectReference: System.Runtime.Serialization

IOCompletionCallback: System.Threading

IOControl(): Socket

IODescriptionAttribute: System.IO

IOException: System.IO

IP: ProtocolType, SocketOptionLevel

IPAddress: System.Net

IPEndPoint: System.Net

IPHostEntry: System.Net

IPOptions: SocketOptionName

IpTimeToLive: SocketOptionName

IPv4: UriHostNameType

IPv6: UriHostNameType

Ipx: AddressFamily, ProtocolFamily, ProtocolType

Irda: AddressFamily, ProtocolFamily

IReflect: System.Reflection

IRegistrationServices: System.Runtime.InteropServices

IsAbstract: MethodBase, Type

IsAlive: Thread, WeakReference

IsAllocated: GCHandle

IsAnsiClass: Type

IsArray: Type

IsArrayImpl(): EnumBuilder, Type, TypeBuilder, TypeDelegator

IsAssembly: FieldInfo, MethodBase

IsAssignableFrom(): Type, TypeBuilder

IsAsync: FileStream, IsolatedStorageFileStream

IsAttached: Debugger

IsAutoClass: Type

IsAutoLayout: Type

IsBackground: Thread

IsBadFileSystemCharacter(): Uri

IsBrowserDisplay: Encoding

IsBrowserSave: Encoding

IsBypassed(): IWebProxy, WebProxy

IsByRef: Type

IsByRefImpl(): EnumBuilder, Type, TypeBuilder, TypeDelegator

IsClass: Type

IsCOMObject: Type

IsComObject(): Marshal

IsCOMObjectImpl(): EnumBuilder, Type, TypeBuilder,
TypeDelegator

IsCompleted: IAsyncResult

IsCompliant: CLSCompliantAttribute

IsConstructor: MethodBase

IsContextful: Type

IsContextfulImpl(): Type

IsControl(): Char

IsDaylightSavingTime(): TimeZone

IsDBNull(): Convert

IsDebug: FileVersionInfo

IsDefault: XmlNodeReader, XmlReader, XmlTextReader,
XmlValidatingReader

IsDefaultAttribute(): Attribute

IsDefaultPort: Uri

IsDefined(): Assembly, Attribute, ConstructorBuilder,
Enum, EnumBuilder, FieldBuilder, ICustomAttributeProvider, MemberInfo, MethodBuilder, Module,
ParameterInfo, PropertyBuilder, TypeBuilder, TypeDelegator

IsDescendant(): XPathNavigator

IsDigit(): Char

IsEmpty: XmlElement, XmlQualifiedName

IsEmptyElement: XmlNodeReader, XmlReader, XmlText-
Reader, XmlValidatingReader, XPathNavigator

IsEnum: Type

IsEquivalentInstaller(): EventLogInstaller

ISerializable: System.Runtime.Serialization

ISerializationSurrogate: System.Runtime.Serialization

IsError: ObsoleteAttribute

IServiceProvider: System

IsExcludedCharacter(): Uri

IsExplicitLayout: Type

IsFamily: FieldInfo, MethodBase

IsFamilyAndAssembly: FieldInfo, MethodBase

IsFamilyOrAssembly: FieldInfo, MethodBase

IsFile: Uri

IsFinal: MethodBase

IsFinalizingForUnload(): AppDomain

IsFixedSize: Array, ArrayList, Hashtable, HybridDictionary,
IDictionary, IList, ListDictionary, SortedList

IsHexDigit(): Uri

IsHexEncoding(): Uri

IsHideBySig: MethodBase

IsImport: Type

IsIn: ParameterBuilder, ParameterInfo

IsInfinity(): Double, Single

IsInitOnly: FieldInfo

IsInst: OpCodes

IsInstanceOfType(): Type

IsInterface: Type

IsInterned(): String

IsJITOptimizerDisabled: DebuggableAttribute
IsJITTrackingEnabled: DebuggableAttribute
IsLayoutSequential: Type
IsLcid: ParameterInfo
IsLeapDay(): Calendar, GregorianCalendar, HebrewCalendar, HijriCalendar, JapaneseCalendar, JulianCalendar, KoreanCalendar, TaiwanCalendar, ThaiBuddhistCalendar
IsLeapMonth(): Calendar, GregorianCalendar, HebrewCalendar, HijriCalendar, JapaneseCalendar, JulianCalendar, KoreanCalendar, TaiwanCalendar, ThaiBuddhistCalendar
IsLeapYear(): Calendar, DateTime, GregorianCalendar, HebrewCalendar, HijriCalendar, JapaneseCalendar, JulianCalendar, KoreanCalendar, TaiwanCalendar, ThaiBuddhistCalendar
IsLetter(): Char
IsLetterOrDigit(): Char
IsLiteral: FieldInfo
IsLittleEndian: BitConverter
IsLocal: IXsltContextVariable
IsLogging(): Debugger
IsLoopback: Uri
IsLoopback(): IPAddress
IsLower(): Char
IsMailNewsDisplay: Encoding
IsMailNewsSave: Encoding
IsMarshalByRef: Type
IsMarshalByRefImpl(): Type
IsMatch(): Regex
IsMetric: RegionInfo
IsMulticast: EventInfo
IsName(): XmlReader
IsNameToken(): XmlReader
IsNaN(): Double, Single
IsNegativeInfinity(): Double, Single
IsNestedAssembly: Type
IsNestedFamANDAssem: Type
IsNestedFamily: Type
IsNestedFamORAssem: Type
IsNestedPrivate: Type
IsNestedPublic: Type
IsNeutralCulture: CultureInfo
IsNotPublic: Type
IsNotSerialized: FieldInfo
IsNumber(): Char
Iso: AddressFamily, ProtocolFamily
ISoapMessage: System.Runtime.Serialization.Formatters
ISOCurrencySymbol: RegionInfo
IsolatedStorage: System.IO.IsolatedStorage
IsolatedStorageException: System.IO.IsolatedStorage
IsolatedStorageFile: System.IO.IsolatedStorage
IsolatedStorageFileStream: System.IO.IsolatedStorage
IsolatedStorageScope: System.IO.IsolatedStorage

IsOptional: ParameterBuilder, ParameterInfo
IsOut: ParameterBuilder, ParameterInfo
IsParam: IXsltContextVariable
IsPatched: FileVersionInfo
IsPathRooted(): Path
IsPInvokeImpl: FieldInfo
IsPointer: Type
IsPointerImpl(): EnumBuilder, Type, TypeBuilder, TypeDelegator
IsPositiveInfinity(): Double, Single
IsPrefix(): CompareInfo
IsPreRelease: FileVersionInfo
IsPrimitive: Type
IsPrimitiveImpl(): EnumBuilder, Type, TypeBuilder, TypeDelegator
IsPrivate: FieldInfo, MethodBase
IsPrivateBuild: FileVersionInfo
IsPublic: FieldInfo, MethodBase, RegexCompilationInfo, Type
IsPunctuation(): Char
IsReaderLockHeld: ReaderWriterLock
IsReadOnly: Array, ArrayList, BitArray, CaptureCollection, CookieCollection, CultureInfo, DateTimeFormatInfo, GroupCollection, Hashtable, HybridDictionary, IDictionary, IList, ListDictionary, MatchCollection, NumberFormatInfo, SortedList, StringCollection, XmlDocument, XmlDocumentType, XmlEntity, XmlEntityReference, XmlNode, XmlNotation
IsReservedCharacter(): Uri
IsResource(): Module
IsRestricted(): WebHeaderCollection
IsRetval: ParameterInfo
IsSamePosition(): XPathNavigator
IsSealed: Type
IsSeparator(): Char
IsSerializable: Type
IsSpecialBuild: FileVersionInfo
IsSpecialName: EventInfo, FieldInfo, MethodBase, PropertyInfo, Type
IsStartElement(): XmlReader
IsStatic: FieldInfo, MethodBase
IsSubclassOf(): Type, TypeBuilder
IsSubsetOf(): DnsPermission, SocketPermission, WebPermission
IsSuffix(): CompareInfo
IsSurrogate(): Char
IsSymbol(): Char
IsSynchronized: Array, ArrayList, BitArray, CaptureCollection, CookieCollection, GroupCollection, Hashtable, HybridDictionary, ICollection, ListDictionary, MatchCollection, Queue, SortedList, Stack, StringCollection, StringDictionary
IsTerminating: UnhandledExceptionEventArgs
IsThreadPoolThread: Thread

Ldc_I4_S: OpCodes
Ldc_I8: OpCodes
Ldc_R4: OpCodes
Ldc_R8: OpCodes
Ldelem_I: OpCodes
Ldelem_I1: OpCodes
Ldelem_I2: OpCodes
Ldelem_I4: OpCodes
Ldelem_I8: OpCodes
Ldelem_R4: OpCodes
Ldelem_R8: OpCodes
Ldelem_Ref: OpCodes
Ldelem_U1: OpCodes
Ldelem_U2: OpCodes
Ldelem_U4: OpCodes
Ldelema: OpCodes
Ldfld: OpCodes
Ldflda: OpCodes
Ldftn: OpCodes
Ldind_I: OpCodes
Ldind_I1: OpCodes
Ldind_I2: OpCodes
Ldind_I4: OpCodes
Ldind_I8: OpCodes
Ldind_R4: OpCodes
Ldind_R8: OpCodes
Ldind_Ref: OpCodes
Ldind_U1: OpCodes
Ldind_U2: OpCodes
Ldind_U4: OpCodes
Ldlen: OpCodes
Ldloc: OpCodes
Ldloc_0: OpCodes
Ldloc_1: OpCodes
Ldloc_2: OpCodes
Ldloc_3: OpCodes
Ldloc_S: OpCodes
Ldloca: OpCodes
Ldloca_S: OpCodes
Ldnull: OpCodes
Ldobj: OpCodes
Ldsfld: OpCodes
Ldsflda: OpCodes
Ldstr: OpCodes
Ldtoken: OpCodes
Ldvirtftn: OpCodes
Leave: OpCodes
Leave_S: OpCodes
LeaveDebugMode(): Process
LegalCopyright: FileVersionInfo
LegalTrademarks: FileVersionInfo
Length: Array, BitArray, BufferedStream, Capture, FileInfo, FileStream, IsolatedStorageFileStream, Memory-Stream, NetworkStream, Stream, String,

StringBuilder, XmlCharacterData
LengthRequired: HttpStatusCode
LetterNumber: UnicodeCategory
Level: TraceSwitch
LicenseFile: AppDomainSetup
LineNumber: IXmlLineInfo, XmlException, XmlTextReader, XsltException
LinePosition: IXmlLineInfo, XmlException, XmlTextReader, XsltException
LineSeparator: UnicodeCategory
Linger: SocketOptionName
LingerOption: System.Net.Sockets
LingerState: TcpClient
LingerTime: LingerOption
ListDictionary: System.Collections.Specialized
Listen(): Socket
Listeners: Debug, Trace
ListSeparator: TextInfo
Literal: FieldAttributes
Load(): AppDomain, Assembly, XmlDataDocument, Xml-Document, XslTransform
LoadedAssembly: AssemblyLoadEventArgs
LoaderExceptions: ReflectionTypeLoadException
LoaderOptimization: AppDomainSetup, System
LoaderOptimizationAttribute: System
LoadFrom(): Assembly
LoadModule(): Assembly
LoadWithPartialName(): Assembly
LoadXml(): XmlDocument
Local: XPathNamespaceScope
LocalAddress: MulticastOption
LocalApplicationData: SpecialFolder
LocalBuilder: System.Reflection.Emit
LocalDataStoreSlot: System
Locale: UserPreferenceCategory
LocalEndpoint: TcpListener
LocalEndPoint: Socket
Localized: GregorianCalendarTypes
Localloc: OpCodes
LocalMachine: Registry, RegistryHive
LocalName: XmlAttribute, XmlCDataSection, XmlCom-ment, XmlDeclaration, XmlDocument, XmlDocument-Fragment, XmlDocumentType, XmlElement, XmlEntity, XmlEntityReference, XmlNode, XmlNodeReader, Xml-Notation, XmlProcessingInstruction, XmlReader, Xml-SignificantWhitespace, XmlText, XmlTextReader, XmlValidatingReader, XmlWhitespace, XPathNavigator
LocalPath: Uri
LocalType: LocalBuilder
Location: Assembly, AssemblyBuilder
Lock(): FileStream
LockCookie: System.Threading
Log: EventLog, EventLogInstaller
Log(): Debugger, Math

Method: AttributeTargets, ComMemberType, Delegate, FileWebRequest, HttpWebRequest, HttpWebResponse, MemberTypes, WebRequest
MethodAccessException: System
MethodAttributes: System.Reflection
MethodBase: System.Reflection
MethodBuilder: System.Reflection.Emit
MethodHandle: ConstructorBuilder, MethodBase, MethodBuilder
MethodImplAttributes: System.Reflection
MethodInfo: System.Reflection
MethodName: ISoapMessage, SoapMessage
MethodNotAllowed: HttpStatusCode
MethodRental: System.Reflection.Emit
METHODS_TO_SKIP: StackTrace
MethodToken: System.Reflection.Emit
MiddleEastFrench: GregorianCalendarTypes
Millisecond: DateTime
Milliseconds: TimeSpan
Min(): Math
Minargs: IXsltContextFunction
Minimized: ProcessWindowStyle
Minor: Version
MinPort: IPEndPoint
MinusOne: Decimal
Minute: DateTime
Minutes: TimeSpan
MinValue: Byte, Char, DateTime, Decimal, Double, Int16, Int32, Int64, SByte, Single, TimeSpan, UInt16, UInt32, UInt64
MinWorkingSet: Process
Missing: System.Reflection, Type
MissingFieldException: System
MissingMemberException: System
MissingMethodException: System
Mkrefany: OpCodes
Mode: PowerModeChangedEventArgs
ModifierLetter: UnicodeCategory
ModifierSymbol: UnicodeCategory
Module: AttributeTargets, EnumBuilder, System.Reflection, Type, TypeBuilder, TypeDelegator
ModuleBuilder: System.Reflection.Emit
ModuleMemorySize: ProcessModule
ModuleName: ProcessModule
ModuleResolve: Assembly
ModuleResolveEventHandler: System.Reflection
Modules: Process
Monday: DayOfWeek
Monitor: System.Threading
MonitoringDescriptionAttribute: System.Diagnostics
Month: DateTime
MonthDayPattern: DateTimeFormatInfo
MonthNames: DateTimeFormatInfo
Mouse: UserPreferenceCategory

Move(): Directory, File
Moved: HttpStatusCode
MovedPermanently: HttpStatusCode
MoveNext(): CharEnumerator, IEnumerator, SerializationInfoEnumerator, StringEnumerator, TextElementEnumerator, XPathNodeIterator
MoveTo(): DirectoryInfo, FileInfo, XPathNavigator
MoveToAttribute(): XmlNodeReader, XmlReader, XmlTextReader, XmlValidatingReader, XPathNavigator
MoveToContent(): XmlReader
MoveToElement(): XmlNodeReader, XmlReader, XmlTextReader, XmlValidatingReader
MoveToFirst(): XPathNavigator
MoveToFirstAttribute(): XmlNodeReader, XmlReader, XmlTextReader, XmlValidatingReader, XPathNavigator
MoveToFirstChild(): XPathNavigator
MoveToFirstNamespace(): XPathNavigator
MoveToId(): XPathNavigator
MoveToNamespace(): XPathNavigator
MoveToNext(): XPathNavigator
MoveToNextAttribute(): XmlNodeReader, XmlReader, XmlTextReader, XmlValidatingReader, XPathNavigator
MoveToNextNamespace(): XPathNavigator
MoveToParent(): XPathNavigator
MoveToPrevious(): XPathNavigator
MoveToRoot(): XPathNavigator
MTA: ApartmentState
MTAThreadAttribute: System
Mul: OpCodes
Mul_Ovf: OpCodes
Mul_Ovf_Un: OpCodes
MulticastDelegate: System
MulticastInterface: SocketOptionName
MulticastLoopback: SocketOptionName
MulticastNotSupportedException: System
MulticastOption: System.Net.Sockets
MulticastTimeToLive: SocketOptionName
MultiDomain: LoaderOptimization
MultiDomainHost: LoaderOptimization
Multiline: RegexOptions
MultipleChoices: HttpStatusCode
Multiply(): Decimal
Mutex: System.Threading

N

Name: AssemblyName, ConstructorBuilder, Cookie, CultureInfo, DirectoryInfo, EnumBuilder, EventLogTraceListener, FieldBuilder, FileInfo, FileStream, FileSystemEventArgs, FileSystemInfo, MemberInfo, MethodBuilder, Module, OpCode, ParameterBuilder, ParameterInfo, PropertyBuilder, RegexCompilationInfo, RegionInfo, RegistryKey, ResolveEventArgs, SerializationEntry, SerializationInfoEnumerator,

Thread, TraceListener, TypeBuilder, TypeDelegator, WaitForChangedResult, XmlAttribute, XmlCDataSection, XmlComment, XmlDeclaration, XmlDocument, XmlDocumentFragment, XmlDocumentType, XmlElement, XmlEntity, XmlEntityReference, XmlNode, XmlNodeReader, XmlNotation, XmlProcessingInstruction, XmlQualifiedName, XmlReader, XmlSignificantWhitespace, XmlText, XmlTextReader, XmlValidatingReader, XmlWhitespace, XPathNavigator

NameImpl: ParameterInfo

NameObjectCollectionBase: System.Collections.Specialized

NameResolutionFailure: WebExceptionStatus

Namespace: EnumBuilder, RegexCompilationInfo, Type, TypeBuilder, TypeDelegator, XmlQualifiedName, XPathNodeType

NamespaceManager: XmlParserContext

Namespaces: XmlTextReader, XmlTextWriter, XmlValidatingReader

NamespaceURI: XmlAttribute, XmlElement, XmlNode, XmlNodeReader, XmlReader, XmlTextReader, XmlValidatingReader, XPathNavigator

NameTable: System.Xml, XmlDocument, XmlNamespaceManager, XmlNodeReader, XmlParserContext, XmlReader, XmlTextReader, XmlValidatingReader, XPathNavigator

NameValueCollection: System.Collections.Specialized

NaN: Double, Single

NaNSymbol: NumberFormatInfo

Native: MethodImplAttributes

NativeName: CultureInfo

NativeOverlapped: System.Threading

Navigator: XPathResultType

NCName: XmlTokenizedType

ND: ProtocolType

Neg: OpCodes

Negate(): Decimal, TimeSpan

NegativeInfinity: Double, Single

NegativeInfinitySymbol: NumberFormatInfo

NegativeSign: NumberFormatInfo

NestedAssembly: TypeAttributes

NestedFamANDAssem: TypeAttributes

NestedFamily: TypeAttributes

NestedFamORAssem: TypeAttributes

NestedPrivate: TypeAttributes

NestedPublic: TypeAttributes

NestedType: MemberTypes

NetBios: AddressFamily, ProtocolFamily

NetworkAccess: System.Net

NetworkCredential: System.Net

NetworkDesigners: AddressFamily, ProtocolFamily

NetworkStream: System.Net.Sockets

NetworkToHostOrder(): IPAddress

NeutralCultures: CultureTypes

Newarr: OpCodes

NewGuid(): Guid

NewLine: Environment, TextWriter

Newobj: OpCodes

NewParent: XmlNodeChangedEventArgs

NewSlot: MethodAttributes

Next: FlowControl

Next(): Random

NextBytes(): Random

NextDouble(): Random

NextMatch(): Match

NextSample(): PerformanceCounter

NextSibling: XmlElement, XmlLinkedNode, XmlNode

NextValue(): PerformanceCounter

NMTOKEN: XmlTokenizedType

NMTOKENS: XmlTokenizedType

NoChecksum: SocketOptionName

NoContent: HttpStatusCode

NoCurrentDateDefault: DateTimeStyles

Node: XmlNodeChangedEventArgs

NodeChanged: XmlDocument

NodeChanging: XmlDocument

NodeInserted: XmlDocument

NodeInserting: XmlDocument

NoDelay: SocketOptionName, TcpClient

NodeRemoved: XmlDocument

NodeRemoving: XmlDocument

NodeSet: XPathResultType

NodeType: XmlAttribute, XmlCDataSection, XmlComment, XmlDeclaration, XmlDocument, XmlDocumentFragment, XmlDocumentType, XmlElement, XmlEntity, XmlEntityReference, XmlNode, XmlNodeReader, XmlNotation, XmlProcessingInstruction, XmlReader, XmlSignificantWhitespace, XmlText, XmlTextReader, XmlValidatingReader, XmlWhitespace, XPathNavigator

NoInlining: MethodImplAttributes

NonAuthoritativeInformation: HttpStatusCode

None: AssemblyNameFlags, AssemblyRegistrationFlags, CharSet, ClassInterfaceType, CompareOptions, DateTimeStyles, EventAttributes, EventLogPermissionAccess, FileShare, Formatting, IPAddress, IsolatedStorageScope, NumberStyles, ParameterAttributes, PerformanceCounterPermissionAccess, PropertyAttributes, RegexOptions, SocketFlags, ValidationType, WhitespaceHandling, XmlCaseOrder, XmlNodeType, XmlSpace, XmlTokenizedType

NonpagedSystemMemorySize: Process

NonPublic: BindingFlags

NonSerializedAttribute: System

NonSpacingMark: UnicodeCategory

Nop: OpCodes

Normal: FileAttributes, GCHandleType, ProcessPriorityClass, ProcessWindowStyle, ThreadPriority, ThreadPriorityLevel

Normalization: XmlTextReader
Normalize(): INormalizeForIsolatedStorage, XmlNode
Not: OpCodes
Not(): BitArray
NotAcceptable: HttpStatusCode
Notation: XmlNodeType
NOTATION: XmlTokenizedType
NotationName: XmlEntity
Notations: XmlDocumentType
NotContentIndexed: FileAttributes
NotFiniteNumberException: System
NotFound: HttpStatusCode
NotifyFilter: FileSystemWatcher
NotifyFilters: System.IO
NotImplemented: HttpStatusCode
NotImplementedException: System
NotModified: HttpStatusCode
NotPublic: TypeAttributes
NotSerialized: FieldAttributes
NotSpecified: LoaderOptimization
NotSupportedException: System
Now: DateTime
NS: AddressFamily, ProtocolFamily
Nternal: OpCodeType
Null: BinaryWriter, Stream, StreamReader, StreamWriter, TextReader, TextWriter
NullReferenceException: System
Number: NumberStyles, XmlDataType, XPathResultType
NumberDecimalDigits: NumberFormatInfo
NumberDecimalSeparator: NumberFormatInfo
NumberFormat: CultureInfo
NumberFormatInfo: System.Globalization
NumberGroupSeparator: NumberFormatInfo
NumberGroupSizes: NumberFormatInfo
NumberNegativePattern: NumberFormatInfo
NumberOfItems32: PerformanceCounterType
NumberOfItems64: PerformanceCounterType
NumberOfItemsHEX32: PerformanceCounterType
NumberOfItemsHEX64: PerformanceCounterType
NumberStyles: System.Globalization
NumParamBytes(): Marshal

O

Object: System, TypeCode
ObjectCreationDelegate: System.Runtime.InteropServices
ObjectDisposedException: System
ObjectIDGenerator: System.Runtime.Serialization
ObjectManager: System.Runtime.Serialization
ObjectName: ObjectDisposedException
ObjectType: SerializationEntry, SerializationInfoEnumerator
Objmodel: OpCodeType

ObsoleteAttribute: System
OEMCodePage: TextInfo
Off: TraceLevel
OffendingNumber: NotFiniteNumberException
Offline: FileAttributes
Offset: Section
OFFSET_UNKNOWN: StackFrame
OffsetHigh: NativeOverlapped, Overlapped
OffsetLow: NativeOverlapped, Overlapped
OffsetOf(): Marshal
OK: HttpStatusCode
OldFullPath: RenamedEventArgs
OldName: RenamedEventArgs, WaitForChangedResult
OldParent: XmlNodeChangedEventArgs
OnChanged(): FileSystemWatcher
OnClear(): CollectionBase, DictionaryBase, EventLogPermissionEntryCollection, PerformanceCounterPermissionEntryCollection
OnClearComplete(): CollectionBase, DictionaryBase
OnCreated(): FileSystemWatcher
OnDeleted(): FileSystemWatcher
OnDeserialization(): AssemblyName, Hashtable, IDeserializationCallback, NameObjectCollectionBase, WebHeaderCollection
One: Decimal
OnError(): FileSystemWatcher
OnExited(): Process
OnGet(): DictionaryBase
OnInsert(): CollectionBase, CounterCreationDataCollection, DictionaryBase, EventLogPermissionEntryCollection, PerformanceCounterPermissionEntryCollection
OnInsertComplete(): CollectionBase, DictionaryBase
OnRemove(): CollectionBase, DictionaryBase, EventLogPermissionEntryCollection, PerformanceCounterPermissionEntryCollection
OnRemoveComplete(): CollectionBase, DictionaryBase
OnRenamed(): FileSystemWatcher
OnSet(): CollectionBase, DictionaryBase, EventLogPermissionEntryCollection, PerformanceCounterPermissionEntryCollection
OnSetComplete(): CollectionBase, DictionaryBase
OnSwitchSettingChanged(): Switch, TraceSwitch
OnValidate(): CollectionBase, DictionaryBase
OpCode: System.Reflection.Emit
OpCodes: System.Reflection.Emit
OpCodeType: OpCode, System.Reflection.Emit
Open: FileMode
Open(): File, FileInfo
OpenOrCreate: FileMode
OpenPunctuation: UnicodeCategory
OpenRead(): File, FileInfo, WebClient
OpenRemoteBaseKey(): RegistryKey
OpenStandardError(): Console
OpenStandardInput(): Console

OpenStandardOutput(): Console
OpenSubKey(): RegistryKey
OpenText(): File, FileInfo
OpenWrite(): File, FileInfo, WebClient
OperandType: OpCode, System.Reflection.Emit
OperatingSystem: System
OPTIL: MethodImplAttributes
Optional: ParameterAttributes
OptionalAttribute: System.Runtime.InteropServices
OptionalCalendars: CultureInfo
OptionalParamBinding: BindingFlags
Options: Regex, RegexCompilationInfo
Or: OpCodes
Or(): BitArray
Ordinal: CompareOptions
OriginalFilename: FileVersionInfo
OriginalPath: FileSystemInfo
OriginalString: SortKey
Osi: AddressFamily, ProtocolFamily
OSVersion: Environment
Other: StreamingContextStates
OtherLetter: UnicodeCategory
OtherNotAssigned: UnicodeCategory
OtherNumber: UnicodeCategory
OtherPunctuation: UnicodeCategory
OtherSymbol: UnicodeCategory
Out: Console, ParameterAttributes
OutAttribute: System.Runtime.InteropServices
OuterXml: XmlEntity, XmlNode, XmlNotation
OutOfBand: SocketFlags
OutOfBandInline: SocketOptionName
OutOfMemoryException: System
OutStream: BinaryWriter
OverflowException: System
Overlapped: System.Threading
OwnerDocument: XmlAttribute, XmlDocument, XmlDocumentFragment, XmlElement, XmlNode
OwnerElement: XmlAttribute

P

Pack: StructLayoutAttribute
Pack(): Overlapped
PacketInformation: SocketOptionName
PackingSize: System.Reflection.Emit, TypeBuilder
PadLeft(): String
PadRight(): String
PagedMemorySize: Process
PagedSystemMemorySize: Process
PageIn: ThreadWaitReason
PageOut: ThreadWaitReason
PaletteChanged: SystemEvents
ParagraphSeparator: UnicodeCategory
ParamArrayAttribute: System

Parameter: AttributeTargets
ParameterAttributes: System.Reflection
ParameterBuilder: System.Reflection.Emit
ParameterInfo: System.Reflection
ParameterModifier: System.Reflection
ParameterToken: System.Reflection.Emit
ParameterType: ParameterInfo
ParamName: ArgumentException
ParamNames: ISoapMessage, SoapMessage
ParamTypes: ISoapMessage, SoapMessage
ParamValues: ISoapMessage, SoapMessage
Parent: CultureInfo, DirectoryInfo
ParentNode: XmlAttribute, XmlDocumentFragment, XmlNode
Parse(): Boolean, Byte, Char, DateTime, Decimal, Double, Enum, Int16, Int32, Int64, IPAddress, SByte, Single, TimeSpan, UInt16, UInt32, UInt64, Uri
ParseCombiningCharacters(): StringInfo
ParseExact(): DateTime
Partial: SocketFlags
PartialContent: HttpStatusCode
Password: NetworkCredential, UriBuilder
Path: Cookie, FileSystemWatcher, System.IO, UriBuilder, UriPartial
PathAndQuery: Uri
PathSeparator: Path
PathTooLongException: System.IO
Pattern: RegexCompilationInfo
PaymentRequired: HttpStatusCode
PeakPagedMemorySize: Process
PeakVirtualMemorySize: Process
PeakWorkingSet: Process
Peek: SocketFlags
Peek(): Queue, Stack, StreamReader, StringReader, TextReader
PeekChar(): BinaryReader
PEFileKinds: System.Reflection.Emit
Pending: WebExceptionStatus
Pending(): TcpListener
PercentDecimalDigits: NumberFormatInfo
PercentDecimalSeparator: NumberFormatInfo
PercentGroupSeparator: NumberFormatInfo
PercentGroupSizes: NumberFormatInfo
PercentNegativePattern: NumberFormatInfo
PercentPositivePattern: NumberFormatInfo
PercentSymbol: NumberFormatInfo
PerDomainCapacity: CookieContainer
PerformanceCounter: System.Diagnostics
PerformanceCounterCategory: System.Diagnostics
PerformanceCounterInstaller: System.Diagnostics
PerformanceCounterPermission: System.Diagnostics
PerformanceCounterPermissionAccess: System.Diagnostics
PerformanceCounterPermissionAttribute:

System.Diagnostics

PerformanceCounterPermissionEntry: System.Diagnostics

PerformanceCounterPermissionEntryCollection: System.Diagnostics

PerformanceCounterType: System.Diagnostics

PerformanceData: Registry, RegistryHive

PerMilleSymbol: NumberFormatInfo

PermissionAccess: EventLogPermissionAttribute, EventLogPermissionEntry, PerformanceCounterPermissionAttribute, PerformanceCounterPermissionEntry

PermissionEntries: EventLogPermission, PerformanceCounterPermission

Persistence: StreamingContextStates

Personal: SpecialFolder

Phi: FlowControl

PI: Math

Pinned: GCHandleType

PinvokeImpl: FieldAttributes, MethodAttributes

Pipelined: HttpWebRequest

PipelineFailure: WebExceptionStatus

Platform: OperatingSystem

PlatformID: System

PlatformNotSupportedException: System

PMDesignator: DateTimeFormatInfo

Pointer: System.Reflection

Policy: UserPreferenceCategory

Poll(): Socket

Pop: OpCodes

Pop(): Stack

Pop0: StackBehaviour

Pop1: StackBehaviour

Pop1_pop1: StackBehaviour

Popi: StackBehaviour

Popi_pop1: StackBehaviour

Popi_popi: StackBehaviour

Popi_popi_popi: StackBehaviour

Popi_popi8: StackBehaviour

Popi_popr4: StackBehaviour

Popi_popr8: StackBehaviour

Popref: StackBehaviour

Popref_pop1: StackBehaviour

Popref_popi: StackBehaviour

Popref_popi_popi: StackBehaviour

Popref_popi_popi8: StackBehaviour

Popref_popi_popr4: StackBehaviour

Popref_popi_popr8: StackBehaviour

Popref_popi_popref: StackBehaviour

PopScope(): XmlNamespaceManager

PopulateObjectMembers(): FormatterServices

Port: Cookie, EndpointPermission, IPEndPoint, SocketPermissionAttribute, Uri, UriBuilder

Position: BufferedStream, FileStream, IsolatedStorageFileStream, MemoryStream, NetworkStream,

ParameterBuilder, ParameterInfo, Stream

PositionImpl: ParameterInfo

PositiveInfinity: Double, Single

PositiveInfinitySymbol: NumberFormatInfo

PositiveSign: NumberFormatInfo

Pow(): Math

Power: UserPreferenceCategory

PowerModeChanged: SystemEvents

PowerModeChangedEventArgs: Microsoft.Win32

PowerModeChangedEventHandler: Microsoft.Win32

PowerModes: Microsoft.Win32

PreAuthenticate: FileWebRequest, HttpWebRequest, WebRequest

PreAuthenticate(): AuthenticationManager, IAuthenticationModule

PreconditionFailed: HttpStatusCode

Prefix: OpCodeType, XmlAttribute, XmlElement, XmlNode, XmlNodeReader, XmlReader, XmlTextReader, XmlValidatingReader, XPathNavigator

Prefix1: OpCodes

Prefix2: OpCodes

Prefix3: OpCodes

Prefix4: OpCodes

Prefix5: OpCodes

Prefix6: OpCodes

Prefix7: OpCodes

Prefixref: OpCodes

Prelink(): Marshal

PrelinkAll(): Marshal

Prepend(): XmlAttributeCollection

PrependChild(): XmlNode

Preserve: XmlSpace

PreserveSig: DllImportAttribute, MethodImplAttributes

PreserveSigAttribute: System.Runtime.InteropServices

PreserveWhitespace: XmlDocument

PreserveWhitespace(): XsltContext

PreviousSibling: XmlLinkedNode, XmlNode

Primitive: OpCodeType

Priority: Thread

PriorityBoostEnabled: Process, ProcessThread

PriorityClass: Process

PriorityLevel: ProcessThread

Private: FieldAttributes, MethodAttributes, ResourceAttributes

PrivateBinPath: AppDomainSetup

PrivateBinPathProbe: AppDomainSetup

PrivateBuild: FileVersionInfo

PrivateMemorySize: Process

PrivateScope: FieldAttributes, MethodAttributes

PrivateUse: UnicodeCategory

PrivilegedProcessorTime: Process, ProcessThread

Process: System.Diagnostics

ProcessExit: AppDomain

ProcessingInstruction: XmlNodeType, XPathNodeType

ProcessModule: System.Diagnostics
ProcessModuleCollection: System.Diagnostics
ProcessName: Process
ProcessorAffinity: Process, ProcessThread
ProcessPriorityClass: System.Diagnostics
ProcessStartInfo: System.Diagnostics
ProcessThread: System.Diagnostics
ProcessThreadCollection: System.Diagnostics
ProcessWindowStyle: System.Diagnostics
Product: AssemblyProductAttribute
ProductBuildPart: FileVersionInfo
ProductMajorPart: FileVersionInfo
ProductMinorPart: FileVersionInfo
ProductName: FileVersionInfo
ProductPrivatePart: FileVersionInfo
ProductVersion: FileVersionInfo
ProgIdAttribute: System.Runtime.InteropServices
ProgramFiles: SpecialFolder
Programs: SpecialFolder
Prolog: WriteState
Property: AttributeTargets, MemberTypes
PropertyAttributes: System.Reflection
PropertyBuilder: System.Reflection.Emit
PropertyInfo: System.Reflection
PropertyToken: PropertyBuilder, System.Reflection.Emit
PropertyType: PropertyBuilder, PropertyInfo
PropGet: ComMemberType
PropSet: ComMemberType
ProtectionRealm: Authorization
ProtocolError: WebExceptionStatus
ProtocolFamily: System.Net.Sockets
ProtocolType: Socket, System.Net.Sockets
ProtocolVersion: HttpWebRequest, HttpWebResponse,
  ServicePoint
ProtocolViolationException: System.Net
Proxy: FileWebRequest, HttpWebRequest, WebRequest
ProxyAuthenticationRequired: HttpStatusCode
ProxyNameResolutionFailure: WebExceptionStatus
PtrToStringAnsi(): Marshal
PtrToStringAuto(): Marshal
PtrToStringBSTR(): Marshal
PtrToStringUni(): Marshal
PtrToStructure(): Marshal
Public: BindingFlags, FieldAttributes, MethodAttributes,
  ResourceAttributes, TypeAttributes
PublicId: XmlDocumentType, XmlEntity, XmlNotation,
  XmlParserContext
PublicKey: AssemblyNameFlags, StrongNameKeyPair
Pulse(): Monitor
PulseAll(): Monitor
Pup: AddressFamily, ProtocolFamily, ProtocolType
Push(): Stack
Push0: StackBehaviour
Push1: StackBehaviour

Push1_push1: StackBehaviour
Pushi: StackBehaviour
Pushi8: StackBehaviour
Pushr4: StackBehaviour
Pushr8: StackBehaviour
Pushref: StackBehaviour
PushScope(): XmlNamespaceManager
PutDispProperty: BindingFlags
PutRefDispProperty: BindingFlags

Q

QName: XmlTokenizedType
Query: Uri, UriBuilder
QueryInterface(): Marshal
QueryString: WebClient
Queue: System.Collections
QueueUserWorkItem(): ThreadPool
QuoteChar: XmlNodeReader, XmlReader, XmlTextReader,
  XmlTextWriter, XmlValidatingReader

R

R4: UnmanagedType
R8: UnmanagedType
RaiseDeserializationEvent(): ObjectManager
Random: System
Rank: Array
RankException: System
RateOfCountsPerSecond32: PerformanceCounterType
RateOfCountsPerSecond64: PerformanceCounterType
Raw: ProtocolType, SocketType
RawBase: PerformanceCounterType
RawFraction: PerformanceCounterType
RawValue: CounterSample, InstanceData, Performance-
  Counter
Rdm: SocketType
Read: FileAccess, FileShare
Read(): BinaryReader, BufferedStream, Console,
  FileStream, IsolatedStorageFileStream, Memory-
  Stream, NetworkStream, Stream, StreamReader,
  StringReader, TextReader, XmlNodeReader, Xml-
  Reader, XmlTextReader, XmlValidatingReader
Read7BitEncodedInt(): BinaryReader
ReadAttributeValue(): XmlNodeReader, XmlReader, Xml-
  TextReader, XmlValidatingReader
ReadBase64(): XmlTextReader
ReadBinHex(): XmlTextReader
ReadBlock(): TextReader
ReadBoolean(): BinaryReader
ReadByte(): BinaryReader, BufferedStream, FileStream,
  IsolatedStorageFileStream, Marshal, MemoryStream,
  Stream
ReadBytes(): BinaryReader

ReadCategory(): PerformanceCounterCategory
ReadChar(): BinaryReader
ReadChars(): BinaryReader, XmlTextReader
ReadDecimal(): BinaryReader
ReadDouble(): BinaryReader
ReadElementString(): XmlReader
ReadEndElement(): XmlReader
Reader: XmlValidatingReader
ReaderWriterLock: System.Threading
ReadInnerXml(): XmlNodeReader, XmlReader, XmlText-
   Reader, XmlValidatingReader
ReadInt16(): BinaryReader, Marshal
ReadInt32(): BinaryReader, Marshal
ReadInt64(): BinaryReader, Marshal
ReadIntPtr(): Marshal
ReadLine(): Console, StreamReader, StringReader, Text-
   Reader
ReadNode(): XmlDocument
ReadOnly: FileAttributes, PerformanceCounter
ReadOnly(): ArrayList, CultureInfo, DateTimeFormatInfo,
   NumberFormatInfo
ReadOnlyCollectionBase: System.Collections
ReadOuterXml(): XmlNodeReader, XmlReader, XmlText-
   Reader, XmlValidatingReader
ReadSByte(): BinaryReader
ReadSingle(): BinaryReader
ReadStartElement(): XmlReader
ReadState: System.Xml, XmlNodeReader, XmlReader,
   XmlTextReader, XmlValidatingReader
ReadString(): BinaryReader, XmlNodeReader, XmlReader,
   XmlTextReader, XmlValidatingReader
ReadToEnd(): StreamReader, StringReader, TextReader
ReadTypedValue(): XmlValidatingReader
ReadUInt16(): BinaryReader
ReadUInt32(): BinaryReader
ReadUInt64(): BinaryReader
ReadWrite: FileAccess, FileShare
Ready: ThreadState
ReAllocCoTaskMem(): Marshal
ReAllocHGlobal(): Marshal
RealTime: ProcessPriorityClass
Reason: SessionEndedEventArgs, SessionEndingEventArgs
Receive: SocketShutdown
Receive(): Socket, UdpClient
ReceiveBuffer: SocketOptionName
ReceiveBufferSize: TcpClient
ReceiveFailure: WebExceptionStatus
ReceiveFrom(): Socket
ReceiveLowWater: SocketOptionName
ReceiveTimeout: SocketOptionName, TcpClient
Recent: SpecialFolder
RecordArrayElementFixup(): ObjectManager
RecordDelayedFixup(): ObjectManager
RecordFixup(): ObjectManager

Redirect: HttpStatusCode
RedirectKeepVerb: HttpStatusCode
RedirectMethod: HttpStatusCode
RedirectStandardError: ProcessStartInfo
RedirectStandardInput: ProcessStartInfo
RedirectStandardOutput: ProcessStartInfo
Refanytype: OpCodes
Refanyval: OpCodes
ReferencedAssembly: ManifestResourceInfo
ReferenceEquals(): Object
Referer: HttpWebRequest
ReflectedType: ConstructorBuilder, EnumBuilder, Field-
   Builder, MemberInfo, MethodBuilder, PropertyBuilder,
   Type, TypeBuilder
ReflectionTypeLoadException: System.Reflection
Refresh(): FileSystemInfo, Process
Regex: System.Text.RegularExpressions
RegexCompilationInfo: System.Text.RegularExpressions
RegexOptions: System.Text.RegularExpressions
RegionInfo: System.Globalization
Register(): AuthenticationManager
RegisterAssembly(): IRegistrationServices, Registra-
   tionServices
RegisteredModules: AuthenticationManager
RegisteredWaitHandle: System.Threading
RegisterObject(): ObjectManager
RegisterObjectCreationCallback(): ExtensibleClassFac-
   tory
RegisterPrefix(): WebRequest
RegisterTypeForComClients(): IRegistrationServices,
   RegistrationServices
RegisterWaitForSingleObject(): ThreadPool
RegistrationServices: System.Runtime.InteropServices
Registry: Microsoft.Win32
RegistryHive: Microsoft.Win32
RegistryKey: Microsoft.Win32
RelativeSearchPath: AppDomain
Release(): Marshal
ReleaseComObject(): Marshal
ReleaseLock(): ReaderWriterLock
ReleaseMutex(): Mutex
ReleaseReaderLock(): ReaderWriterLock
ReleaseThreadCache(): Marshal
ReleaseWriterLock(): ReaderWriterLock
Rem: OpCodes
Rem_Un: OpCodes
Remainder(): Decimal
RemoteEndPoint: Socket
Remoting: StreamingContextStates
Remove: XmlNodeChangedAction
Remove(): ArrayList, CounterCreationDataCollection, Cre-
   dentialCache, Delegate, EventLogPermissionEntryCol-
   lection, Hashtable, HybridDictionary, IDictionary,
   IList, IsolatedStorage, IsolatedStorageFile,

ListDictionary, NameValueCollection, Performance-
CounterPermissionEntryCollection, ProcessThreadCol-
lection, SortedList, String, StringBuilder,
StringCollection, StringDictionary, TraceListenerCol-
lection, WebHeaderCollection, XmlAttributeCollection
RemoveAll(): XmlAttributeCollection, XmlElement, Xml-
Node
RemoveAllAttributes(): XmlElement
RemoveAt(): ArrayList, CollectionBase, IList, SortedList,
StringCollection, TraceListenerCollection, XmlAt-
tributeCollection
RemoveAttribute(): XmlElement
RemoveAttributeAt(): XmlElement
RemoveAttributeNode(): XmlElement
RemoveChild(): XmlNode
RemoveEventHandler(): EventInfo
RemoveExtensionObject(): XsltArgumentList
RemoveImpl(): Delegate, MulticastDelegate
RemoveInstance(): PerformanceCounter
RemoveMember(): IExpando
RemoveNamedItem(): XmlNamedNodeMap
RemoveNamespace(): XmlNamespaceManager
RemoveParam(): XsltArgumentList
RemoveRange(): ArrayList
RemoveSurrogate(): SurrogateSelector
Renamed: FileSystemWatcher, WatcherChangeTypes
RenamedEventArgs: System.IO
RenamedEventHandler: System.IO
ReorderArgumentArray(): Binder
ReparsePoint: FileAttributes
Repeat(): ArrayList
Replace(): Regex, String, StringBuilder
ReplaceChild(): XmlNode
ReplaceData(): XmlCharacterData
ReplacementStrings: EventLogEntry
RequestCanceled: WebExceptionStatus
RequestedRangeNotSatisfiable: HttpStatusCode
RequestEntityTooLarge: HttpStatusCode
RequestTimeout: HttpStatusCode
RequestUri: FileWebRequest, HttpWebRequest, WebRe-
quest
RequestUriTooLong: HttpStatusCode
RequireSecObject: MethodAttributes
ReRegisterForFinalize(): GC
Reserved2: PropertyAttributes
Reserved3: ParameterAttributes, PropertyAttributes
Reserved4: ParameterAttributes, PropertyAttributes
ReservedMask: EventAttributes, FieldAttributes, Method-
Attributes, ParameterAttributes, PropertyAttributes,
TypeAttributes
Reset(): AutoResetEvent, CharEnumerator, IEnumerator,
ManualResetEvent, SerializationInfoEnumerator,
StringEnumerator, TextElementEnumerator
ResetAbort(): Thread

ResetContent: HttpStatusCode
ResetIdealProcessor(): ProcessThread
ResetState(): XmlTextReader
Resolve(): Dns
ResolveEntity(): XmlNodeReader, XmlReader, XmlText-
Reader, XmlValidatingReader
ResolveEventArgs: System
ResolveEventHandler: System
ResolveFunction(): XsltContext
ResolveUri(): XmlResolver, XmlUrlResolver
ResolveVariable(): XsltContext
ResourceAttributes: System.Reflection
ResourceLocation: ManifestResourceInfo, System.Reflec-
tion
ResourceResolve: AppDomain
Responding: Process
Response: WebException
ResponseHeaders: WebClient
ResponseUri: FileWebResponse, HttpWebResponse,
WebResponse
RestoreLock(): ReaderWriterLock
Result(): Match
Resume: PowerModes
Resume(): Thread
Ret: OpCodes
Rethrow: OpCodes
Return: FlowControl
ReturnType: ConstructorBuilder, IXsltContextFunction,
MethodBuilder, MethodInfo, XPathExpression
ReturnTypeCustomAttributes: MethodBuilder, Method-
Info
ReturnValue: AttributeTargets
Retval: ParameterAttributes
ReuseAddress: SocketOptionName
ReuseSlot: MethodAttributes
Reverse(): Array, ArrayList
Revision: Version
RFC1123Pattern: DateTimeFormatInfo
RightToLeft: Regex, RegexOptions
Roaming: IsolatedStorageScope
Rollback(): EventLogInstaller, PerformanceCounterIn-
staller
Root: DirectoryInfo, XPathNodeType
Round(): Decimal, Math
RTSpecialName: EventAttributes, FieldAttributes, Method-
Attributes, PropertyAttributes, TypeAttributes
Run: AssemblyBuilderAccess
RunAndSave: AssemblyBuilderAccess
Running: ThreadState
Runtime: MethodImplAttributes
RuntimeEnvironment: System.Runtime.InteropServices
RuntimeTypeHandle: System

S

SafeArray: UnmanagedType
SafeArrayRankMismatchException: System.Runtime.InteropServices
SafeArraySubType: MarshalAsAttribute
SafeArrayTypeMismatchException: System.Runtime.InteropServices
SafeArrayUserDefinedSubType: MarshalAsAttribute
Same: XmlNodeOrder
Sample: InstanceData
Sample(): Random
SampleBase: PerformanceCounterType
SampleCounter: PerformanceCounterType
SampleFraction: PerformanceCounterType
Saturday: DayOfWeek
Save: AssemblyBuilderAccess
Save(): AssemblyBuilder, XmlDocument
SByte: System, TypeCode
Schedule(): Formatter
Schema: ValidationType
Schemas: XmlValidatingReader
SchemaType: XmlValidatingReader
Scheme: Uri, UriBuilder, UriPartial
SchemeDelimiter: Uri
Scope: IsolatedStorage
ScopeName: Module
Screensaver: UserPreferenceCategory
Sealed: TypeAttributes
Second: DateTime
Seconds: TimeSpan
Section: System.Collections.Specialized
Secure: Cookie
SecureChannelFailure: WebExceptionStatus
Security: NotifyFilters
Seek(): BinaryWriter, BufferedStream, FileStream, IsolatedStorageFileStream, MemoryStream, NetworkStream, Stream
SeekOrigin: System.IO
SeeOther: HttpStatusCode
Segments: Uri
SEHException: System.Runtime.InteropServices
Select: GlobalProxySelection
Select(): Socket, XPathNavigator
SelectAncestors(): XPathNavigator
SelectChildren(): XPathNavigator
SelectDescendants(): XPathNavigator
SelectError: SelectMode
SelectMethod(): Binder
SelectMode: System.Net.Sockets
SelectNodes(): XmlNode
SelectProperty(): Binder
SelectRead: SelectMode
SelectSingleNode(): XmlNode
SelectWrite: SelectMode

Send: SocketShutdown
Send(): Socket, UdpClient
SendBuffer: SocketOptionName
SendBufferSize: TcpClient
SendChunked: HttpWebRequest
SendFailure: WebExceptionStatus
SendLowWater: SocketOptionName
SendTimeout: SocketOptionName, TcpClient
SendTo: SpecialFolder
SendTo(): Socket
Seqpacket: SocketType
Sequential: LayoutKind
SequentialLayout: TypeAttributes
Serializable: TypeAttributes
SerializableAttribute: System
SerializationBinder: System.Runtime.Serialization
SerializationEntry: System.Runtime.Serialization
SerializationException: System.Runtime.Serialization
SerializationInfo: System.Runtime.Serialization
SerializationInfoEnumerator: System.Runtime.Serialization
Serialize(): BinaryFormatter, EndPoint, Formatter, IFormatter, IPEndPoint, SoapFormatter
Server: HttpWebResponse
ServerFault: System.Runtime.Serialization.Formatters
ServerProtocolViolation: WebExceptionStatus
ServicePoint: HttpWebRequest, System.Net
ServicePointManager: System.Net
ServiceUnavailable: HttpStatusCode
SessionEnded: SystemEvents
SessionEndedEventArgs: Microsoft.Win32
SessionEndedEventHandler: Microsoft.Win32
SessionEnding: SystemEvents
SessionEndingEventArgs: Microsoft.Win32
SessionEndingEventHandler: Microsoft.Win32
SessionEndReasons: Microsoft.Win32
Set(): AutoResetEvent, BitArray, ManualResetEvent, NameValueCollection, WebHeaderCollection
SetAddOnMethod(): EventBuilder
SetAll(): BitArray
SetAppDomainPolicy(): AppDomain
SetAttribute(): XmlElement
SetAttributeNode(): XmlElement
SetAttributes(): File
SetByIndex(): SortedList
SetByte(): Buffer
SetCachePath(): AppDomain
SetCodeBase: AssemblyRegistrationFlags
SetComObjectData(): Marshal
SetConstant(): FieldBuilder, ParameterBuilder, PropertyBuilder
SetContext(): XPathExpression
SetCookies(): CookieContainer
SetCreationTime(): Directory, File

SetCurrentDirectory(): Directory
SetCustomAttribute(): AssemblyBuilder, Constructor-
   Builder, EnumBuilder, EventBuilder, FieldBuilder,
   MethodBuilder, ModuleBuilder, ParameterBuilder,
   PropertyBuilder, TypeBuilder
SetData(): AppDomain, Thread
SetDynamicBase(): AppDomain
SetEntryPoint(): AssemblyBuilder
SetError(): Console
SetField: BindingFlags
SetGetMethod(): PropertyBuilder
SetImplementationFlags(): ConstructorBuilder, Method-
   Builder
SetIn(): Console
SetLastAccessTime(): Directory, File
SetLastError: DllImportAttribute
SetLastWriteTime(): Directory, File
SetLength(): BufferedStream, FileStream, IsolatedStor-
   ageFileStream, MemoryStream, NetworkStream,
   Stream
SetLocalSymInfo(): LocalBuilder
SetMarshal(): FieldBuilder, MethodBuilder, Parameter-
   Builder
SetNamedItem(): XmlAttributeCollection, Xml-
   NamedNodeMap
SetObjectData(): ISerializationSurrogate
SetOffset(): FieldBuilder
SetOut(): Console
SetParent(): TypeBuilder
SetPrincipalPolicy(): AppDomain
SetProperty: BindingFlags
SetPublicKey(): AssemblyName
SetPublicKeyToken(): AssemblyName
SetRaiseMethod(): EventBuilder
SetRange(): ArrayList
SetRemoveOnMethod(): EventBuilder
SetSetMethod(): PropertyBuilder
SetShadowCopyFiles(): AppDomain
SetShadowCopyPath(): AppDomain
SetSocketOption(): Socket
SetSymCustomAttribute(): ConstructorBuilder, Method-
   Builder, ModuleBuilder
SetThreadPrincipal(): AppDomain
SetType(): SerializationInfo
SetupInformation: AppDomain
SetUserEntryPoint(): ModuleBuilder
SetValue(): Array, FieldBuilder, FieldInfo, PropertyBuilder,
   PropertyInfo, RegistryKey
SetValueDirect(): FieldInfo
ShadowCopyDirectories: AppDomainSetup
ShadowCopyFiles: AppDomain, AppDomainSetup
Shl: OpCodes
ShortDatePattern: DateTimeFormatInfo
ShortInlineBrTarget: OperandType

ShortInlineI: OperandType
ShortInlineR: OperandType
ShortInlineVar: OperandType
ShortTimePattern: DateTimeFormatInfo
Shr: OpCodes
Shr_Un: OpCodes
Shutdown(): Socket
Sign(): Math
SignalTime: ElapsedEventArgs
Signature: ConstructorBuilder, MethodBuilder, Missing-
   MemberException
SignatureHelper: System.Reflection.Emit
SignatureToken: System.Reflection.Emit
Significant: WhitespaceHandling
SignificantWhitespace: XmlNodeType, XPathNodeType
Simple: FormatterAssemblyStyle
Sin(): Math
Single: System, TypeCode
SingleDomain: LoaderOptimization
Singleline: RegexOptions
Sinh(): Math
Site: FileSystemWatcher, Timer
Size: IntPtr, NotifyFilters, OpCode, SocketAddress, Struct-
   LayoutAttribute, TypeBuilder, UIntPtr
Size1: PackingSize
Size16: PackingSize
Size2: PackingSize
Size4: PackingSize
Size8: PackingSize
SizeConst: MarshalAsAttribute
Sizeof: OpCodes
SizeOf(): Marshal
SizeParamIndex: MarshalAsAttribute
Skip(): XmlNodeReader, XmlReader
Sleep(): Thread
Sna: AddressFamily, ProtocolFamily
SoapFault: System.Runtime.Serialization.Formatters
SoapFormatter: System.Runtime.Serialization.Format-
   ters.Soap
SoapMessage: System.Runtime.Serialization.Formatters
Socket: SocketOptionLevel, System.Net.Sockets
SocketAddress: System.Net
SocketException: System.Net.Sockets
SocketFlags: System.Net.Sockets
SocketOptionLevel: System.Net.Sockets
SocketOptionName: System.Net.Sockets
SocketPermission: System.Net
SocketPermissionAttribute: System.Net
SocketShutdown: System.Net.Sockets
SocketType: Socket, System.Net.Sockets
Sort(): Array, ArrayList
SortableDateTimePattern: DateTimeFormatInfo
SortedList: System.Collections
SortKey: System.Globalization

Sub: OpCodes
Sub_Ovf: OpCodes
Sub_Ovf_Un: OpCodes
SubKeyCount: RegistryKey
Substring(): String, XmlCharacterData
Subtract(): DateTime, Decimal, TimeSpan
Success: Group, WebExceptionStatus
SuccessAudit: EventLogEntryType
Sunday: DayOfWeek
Supports(): XmlNode
SupportsPipelining: ServicePoint
SuppressChangeType: BindingFlags
SuppressFinalize(): GC
Surrogate: UnicodeCategory
SurrogateSelector: BinaryFormatter, Formatter, IFormatter, SoapFormatter, System.Runtime.Serialization
Suspend: PowerModes
Suspend(): Thread
Suspended: ThreadState, ThreadWaitReason
SuspendRequested: ThreadState
SwapMethodBody(): MethodRental
Switch: OpCodes, System.Diagnostics
SwitchingProtocols: HttpStatusCode
SynchronizationLockException: System.Threading
Synchronized: MethodImplAttributes
Synchronized(): ArrayList, Group, Hashtable, Match, Queue, SortedList, Stack, TextReader, TextWriter
SynchronizingObject: EventLog, FileSystemWatcher, Process, Timer
SyncRoot: Array, ArrayList, BitArray, CaptureCollection, CookieCollection, GroupCollection, Hashtable, HybridDictionary, ICollection, ListDictionary, MatchCollection, Queue, SortedList, Stack, StringCollection, StringDictionary
SysInt: UnmanagedType
System: FileAttributes, SpecialFolder
SystemAllocation: ThreadWaitReason
SystemConfigurationFile: RuntimeEnvironment
SystemDefaultCharSize: Marshal
SystemDefinedImpl: IDispatchImplType
SystemDirectory: Environment
SystemEvents: Microsoft.Win32
SystemException: System
SystemFrequency: CounterSample
SystemId: XmlDocumentType, XmlEntity, XmlNotation, XmlParserContext
SystemMaxDBCSCharSize: Marshal
SystemShutdown: SessionEndReasons
SysUInt: UnmanagedType

T

Tailcall: OpCodes
TaiwanCalendar: System.Globalization
TakesSingleByteArgument(): OpCodes
Tan(): Math
Tanh(): Math
Target: Delegate, GCHandle, WeakReference, XmlProcessingInstruction
TargetException: System.Reflection
TargetInvocationException: System.Reflection
TargetMethods: InterfaceMapping
TargetParameterCountException: System.Reflection
TargetSite: Exception
TargetType: InterfaceMapping
TBStr: UnmanagedType
Tcp: ProtocolType, SocketOptionLevel, TransportType
TcpClient: System.Net.Sockets
TcpListener: System.Net.Sockets
Templates: SpecialFolder
Temporary: FileAttributes
TemporaryRedirect: HttpStatusCode
Terminated: ThreadState
Text: XmlDataType, XmlNodeType, XPathNodeType
TextElementEnumerator: System.Globalization
TextInfo: CultureInfo, System.Globalization
TextReader: System.IO
TextWriter: System.IO
TextWriterTraceListener: System.Diagnostics
ThaiBuddhistCalendar: System.Globalization
ThaiBuddhistEra: ThaiBuddhistCalendar
ThisCall: CallingConvention
Thread: System.Threading
ThreadAbortException: System.Threading
ThreadExceptionEventArgs: System.Threading
ThreadExceptionEventHandler: System.Threading
ThreadInterruptedException: System.Threading
ThreadPool: System.Threading
ThreadPriority: System.Threading
ThreadPriorityLevel: System.Diagnostics
Threads: Process
ThreadStart: System.Threading
ThreadState: ProcessThread, System.Diagnostics, System.Threading, Thread
ThreadStateException: System.Threading
ThreadStaticAttribute: System
ThreadWaitReason: System.Diagnostics
ThreeLetterISOLanguageName: CultureInfo
ThreeLetterISORegionName: RegionInfo
ThreeLetterWindowsLanguageName: CultureInfo
ThreeLetterWindowsRegionName: RegionInfo
Throw: FlowControl, OpCodes
ThrowException(): ILGenerator
ThrowExceptionForHR(): Marshal
Thursday: DayOfWeek

TickCount: Environment
Ticks: DateTime, TimeSpan
TicksPerDay: TimeSpan
TicksPerHour: TimeSpan
TicksPerMillisecond: TimeSpan
TicksPerMinute: TimeSpan
TicksPerSecond: TimeSpan
TimeChanged: SystemEvents
TimeCritical: ThreadPriorityLevel
TimedOut: WaitForChangedResult
TimeGenerated: EventLogEntry
TimeOfDay: DateTime
Timeout: FileWebRequest, HttpWebRequest, System.Threading, WebExceptionStatus, WebRequest
Timer: System.Threading, System.Timers
Timer100Ns: PerformanceCounterType
Timer100NsInverse: PerformanceCounterType
TimerCallback: System.Threading
TimerElapsed: SystemEvents
TimerElapsedEventArgs: Microsoft.Win32
TimerElapsedEventHandler: Microsoft.Win32
TimerId: TimerElapsedEventArgs
TimersDescriptionAttribute: System.Timers
TimeSeparator: DateTimeFormatInfo
TimeSpan: System
TimeStamp: Cookie, CounterSample
TimeStamp100nSec: CounterSample
TimeWritten: EventLogEntry
TimeZone: System
Title: AssemblyTitleAttribute
TitlecaseLetter: UnicodeCategory
ToArray(): ArrayList, MemoryStream, Queue, Stack
ToBase64CharArray(): Convert
ToBase64String(): Convert
ToBoolean(): BitConverter, Convert, FormatterConverter, IConvertible, IFormatterConverter, XmlConvert
ToByte(): Convert, Decimal, FormatterConverter, IConvertible, IFormatterConverter, XmlConvert
ToByteArray(): Guid, WebHeaderCollection
ToChar(): BitConverter, Convert, FormatterConverter, IConvertible, IFormatterConverter, XmlConvert
ToCharArray(): String
ToDateTime(): Calendar, Convert, FormatterConverter, GregorianCalendar, HebrewCalendar, HijriCalendar, IConvertible, IFormatterConverter, JapaneseCalendar, JulianCalendar, KoreanCalendar, TaiwanCalendar, ThaiBuddhistCalendar, XmlConvert
Today: DateTime
ToDecimal(): Convert, FormatterConverter, IConvertible, IFormatterConverter, XmlConvert
ToDouble(): BitConverter, Convert, Decimal, FormatterConverter, IConvertible, IFormatterConverter, XmlConvert
ToFileTime(): DateTime

ToFourDigitYear(): Calendar, GregorianCalendar, HebrewCalendar, HijriCalendar, JapaneseCalendar, JulianCalendar, KoreanCalendar, TaiwanCalendar, ThaiBuddhistCalendar
ToGuid(): XmlConvert
ToInt16(): BitConverter, Convert, Decimal, FormatterConverter, IConvertible, IFormatterConverter, XmlConvert
ToInt32(): BitConverter, Convert, Decimal, FormatterConverter, IConvertible, IFormatterConverter, IntPtr, XmlConvert
ToInt64(): BitConverter, Convert, Decimal, FormatterConverter, IConvertible, IFormatterConverter, IntPtr, XmlConvert
Token: EventToken, FieldToken, MethodToken, ParameterToken, PropertyToken, SignatureToken, StringToken, TypeToken
ToLocalTime(): DateTime, TimeZone
ToLongDateString(): DateTime
ToLongTimeString(): DateTime
ToLower(): Char, String, TextInfo
ToOACurrency(): Decimal
ToOADate(): DateTime
ToObject(): Enum
TopObject: SoapFormatter
ToPointer(): IntPtr, UIntPtr
ToSByte(): Convert, Decimal, FormatterConverter, IConvertible, IFormatterConverter, XmlConvert
ToShortDateString(): DateTime
ToShortTimeString(): DateTime
ToSingle(): BitConverter, Convert, Decimal, FormatterConverter, IConvertible, IFormatterConverter, XmlConvert
ToString(): AppDomain, Assembly, AssemblyName, BadImageFormatException, BitConverter, BitVector32, Boolean, Byte, Capture, Char, COMException, CompareInfo, ConstructorBuilder, Convert, Cookie, CultureInfo, DateTime, DBNull, Decimal, DirectoryInfo, Double, EndpointPermission, Enum, Exception, FileInfo, FileLoadException, FileNotFoundException, FileVersionInfo, FormatterConverter, Guid, IConvertible, IFormattable, IFormatterConverter, Int16, Int32, Int64, IntPtr, IPAddress, IPEndPoint, MethodBuilder, Module, Object, OpCode, OperatingSystem, Process, ProcessModule, Regex, RegionInfo, RegistryKey, SByte, Section, SignatureHelper, Single, SocketAddress, SortKey, StackFrame, StackTrace, String, StringBuilder, StringWriter, TextInfo, TimeSpan, Type, TypeBuilder, UInt16, UInt32, UInt64, UIntPtr, Uri, UriBuilder, ValueType, Version, WebHeaderCollection, XmlConvert, XmlQualifiedName, XPathNavigator
TotalDays: TimeSpan
TotalHours: TimeSpan
TotalMilliseconds: TimeSpan
TotalMinutes: TimeSpan
TotalProcessorTime: Process, ProcessThread

TotalSeconds: TimeSpan
ToTimeSpan(): XmlConvert
ToTitleCase(): TextInfo
ToType(): IConvertible
ToUInt16(): BitConverter, Convert, Decimal, Formatter-Converter, IConvertible, IFormatterConverter, XmlConvert
ToUInt32(): BitConverter, Convert, Decimal, Formatter-Converter, IConvertible, IFormatterConverter, UIntPtr, XmlConvert
ToUInt64(): BitConverter, Convert, Decimal, Formatter-Converter, IConvertible, IFormatterConverter, UIntPtr, XmlConvert
ToUniversalTime(): DateTime, TimeZone
ToUpper(): Char, String, TextInfo
ToXml(): DnsPermission, SocketPermission, WebPermission
Trace: System.Diagnostics
TraceError: TraceSwitch
TraceInfo: TraceSwitch
TraceLevel: System.Diagnostics
TraceListener: System.Diagnostics
TraceListenerCollection: System.Diagnostics
TraceSwitch: System.Diagnostics
TraceVerbose: TraceSwitch
TraceWarning: TraceSwitch
TrackResurrection: WeakReference
Trademark: AssemblyTrademarkAttribute
TransferEncoding: HttpWebRequest
Transform(): XslTransform
Transition: ThreadState
TransliteratedEnglish: GregorianCalendarTypes
TransliteratedFrench: GregorianCalendarTypes
Transport: EndpointPermission, SocketPermissionAttribute
TransportType: System.Net
Trim(): String
TrimEnd(): String
TrimStart(): String
TrimToSize(): ArrayList, Queue, SortedList
TrueString: Boolean
Truncate: FileMode
Truncate(): Decimal
TrustFailure: WebExceptionStatus
TryEnter(): Monitor
TryParse(): Double
Tuesday: DayOfWeek
TwoDigitYearMax: Calendar, GregorianCalendar, Hebrew-Calendar, HijriCalendar, JapaneseCalendar, JulianCalendar, KoreanCalendar, TaiwanCalendar, ThaiBuddhistCalendar
TwoLetterISOLanguageName: CultureInfo
TwoLetterISORegionName: RegionInfo
Type: SocketOptionName, System

TypeAttributes: System.Reflection
TypeBuilder: System.Reflection.Emit
TypeCode: System
TypeConstructorName: ConstructorInfo
TypeDelegator: System.Reflection
TypeFilter: System.Reflection
TypeFormat: BinaryFormatter, SoapFormatter
TypeHandle: EnumBuilder, Type, TypeBuilder, TypeDelegator
TypeId: Attribute
typeImpl: TypeDelegator
TypeInfo: MemberTypes
TypeInitializationException: System
TypeInitializer: Type
TypeLoadException: System
TypeName: TypeInitializationException, TypeLoadException
TypeOfService: SocketOptionName
TypeRepresentsComType(): IRegistrationServices, RegistrationServices
TypeRequiresRegistration(): IRegistrationServices, RegistrationServices
TypeResolve: AppDomain
Types: ReflectionTypeLoadException
TypesAlways: FormatterTypeStyle
TypesWhenNeeded: FormatterTypeStyle
TypeToken: EnumBuilder, System.Reflection.Emit, TypeBuilder
TypeUnloadedException: System

U

U1: UnmanagedType
U2: UnmanagedType
U4: UnmanagedType
U8: UnmanagedType
Udp: ProtocolType, SocketOptionLevel, TransportType
UdpClient: System.Net.Sockets
UInt16: System, TypeCode
UInt32: System, TypeCode
UInt64: System, TypeCode
UIntPtr: System
Unaligned: OpCodes
Unauthorized: HttpStatusCode
UnauthorizedAccessException: System
UnblockSource: SocketOptionName
Unbox: OpCodes
Unbox(): Pointer
UnderlyingField: EnumBuilder
UnderlyingSystemType: EnumBuilder, IReflect, Type, TypeBuilder, TypeDelegator
Unescape(): Regex, Uri
UnhandledException: AppDomain
UnhandledExceptionEventArgs: System

UnhandledExceptionEventHandler: System
Unicode: CharSet, Encoding
UnicodeCategory: System.Globalization
UnicodeClass: TypeAttributes
UnicodeEncoding: System.Text
Unindent(): Debug, Trace
Uninstall(): EventLogInstaller, PerformanceCounterInstaller
UninstallAction: EventLogInstaller, PerformanceCounterInstaller
Union(): DnsPermission, SocketPermission, WebPermission
UniversalSortableDateTimePattern: DateTimeFormatInfo
Unix: AddressFamily, ProtocolFamily
Unknown: AddressFamily, ApartmentState, ProtocolFamily, ProtocolType, SocketType, ThreadState, ThreadWaitReason, UriHostNameType, XmlNodeOrder
UnknownWrapper: System.Runtime.InteropServices
Unload(): AppDomain
Unlock(): FileStream
Unmanaged: MethodImplAttributes
UnmanagedExport: MethodAttributes
UnmanagedMarshal: System.Reflection.Emit
UnmanagedType: System.Runtime.InteropServices
Unpack(): Overlapped
Unregister(): AuthenticationManager, RegisteredWaitHandle
UnregisterAssembly(): IRegistrationServices, RegistrationServices
UnsafeAddrOfPinnedArrayElement(): Marshal
UnsafePack(): Overlapped
UnsafeQueueUserWorkItem(): ThreadPool
UnsafeRegisterWaitForSingleObject(): ThreadPool
Unspecified: AddressFamily, PackingSize, ProtocolFamily, ProtocolType
UnspecifiedTypeSize: TypeBuilder
Unstarted: ThreadState
UnsupportedMediaType: HttpStatusCode
Unused: HttpStatusCode
UpgradeToWriterLock(): ReaderWriterLock
UploadData(): WebClient
UploadFile(): WebClient
UploadValues(): WebClient
UppercaseLetter: UnicodeCategory
UpperFirst: XmlCaseOrder
Uri: System, UriBuilder
UriBuilder: System
UriFormatException: System
UriHostNameType: System
UriPartial: System
UriSchemeFile: Uri
UriSchemeFtp: Uri
UriSchemeGopher: Uri
UriSchemeHttp: Uri

UriSchemeHttps: Uri
UriSchemeMailto: Uri
UriSchemeNews: Uri
UriSchemeNntp: Uri
UseLoopback: SocketOptionName
USEnglish: GregorianCalendarTypes
UseOptionC(): Regex
UseOptionR(): Regex
UseProxy: HttpStatusCode
User: IsolatedStorageScope
UserAgent: HttpWebRequest
UserDomainName: Environment
UserEscaped: Uri
UserInfo: Uri
UserInteractive: Environment
UserName: Environment, EventLogEntry, NetworkCredential, UriBuilder
UserPreferenceCategory: Microsoft.Win32
UserPreferenceChanged: SystemEvents
UserPreferenceChangedEventArgs: Microsoft.Win32
UserPreferenceChangedEventHandler: Microsoft.Win32
UserPreferenceChanging: SystemEvents
UserPreferenceChangingEventArgs: Microsoft.Win32
UserPreferenceChangingEventHandler: Microsoft.Win32
UserProcessorTime: Process, ProcessThread
UserRequest: ThreadWaitReason
Users: Registry, RegistryHive
UseShellExecute: ProcessStartInfo
UseUserOverride: CultureInfo
UsingNamespace(): ILGenerator
UtcNow: DateTime
UTF7: Encoding
UTF7Encoding: System.Text
UTF8: Encoding
UTF8Encoding: System.Text

V

ValidationEventHandler: XmlTextReader, XmlValidatingReader
ValidationType: System.Xml, XmlValidatingReader
ValidOn: AttributeUsageAttribute
Value: Capture, ClassInterfaceAttribute, ComAliasNameAttribute, ComSourceInterfacesAttribute, ComVisibleAttribute, Cookie, DBNull, DictionaryEntry, DispIdAttribute, DllImportAttribute, FieldOffsetAttribute, GuidAttribute, IDictionaryEnumerator, IDispatchImplAttribute, InterfaceTypeAttribute, LCIDConversionAttribute, LoaderOptimizationAttribute, MarshalAsAttribute, Missing, OpCode, ProgIdAttribute, RuntimeTypeHandle, SerializationEntry, SerializationInfoEnumerator, StructLayoutAttribute, XmlAttribute, XmlCharacterData, XmlDeclaration, XmlEntityReference, XmlNode,

VT_UI8: VarEnum
VT_UINT: VarEnum
VT_UNKNOWN: VarEnum
VT_USERDEFINED: VarEnum
VT_VARIANT: VarEnum
VT_VECTOR: VarEnum
VT_VOID: VarEnum
VtableLayoutMask: MethodAttributes

W

Wait: ThreadState
Wait(): Monitor
WaitAll(): WaitHandle
WaitAny(): WaitHandle
WaitCallback: System.Threading
WaitForChanged(): FileSystemWatcher
WaitForChangedResult: System.IO
WaitForExit(): Process
WaitForInputIdle(): Process
WaitForPendingFinalizers(): GC
WaitHandle: System.Threading
WaitOne(): WaitHandle
WaitOrTimerCallback: System.Threading
WaitReason: ProcessThread
WaitSleepJoin: ThreadState
WaitTimeout: WaitHandle
Warning: EventLogEntryType, TraceLevel
WatcherChangeTypes: System.IO
Weak: GCHandleType
WeakReference: System
WeakTrackResurrection: GCHandleType
WebClient: System.Net
WebException: System.Net
WebExceptionStatus: System.Net
WebHeaderCollection: System.Net
WebName: Encoding
WebPermission: System.Net
WebPermissionAttribute: System.Net
WebProxy: System.Net
WebRequest: System.Net
WebResponse: System.Net
Wednesday: DayOfWeek
Whitespace: XmlNodeType, XPathNodeType, XsltContext
WhitespaceHandling: System.Xml, XmlTextReader
Win32NT: PlatformID
Win32S: PlatformID
Win32Windows: PlatformID
Winapi: CallingConvention
Window: UserPreferenceCategory
WindowApplication: PEFileKinds
WindowsCodePage: Encoding
WindowStyle: ProcessStartInfo
WorkingDirectory: ProcessStartInfo

WorkingSet: Environment, Process
WrappedObject: CurrencyWrapper, DispatchWrapper, UnknownWrapper
Wrapper: HandleRef
Write: FileAccess, FileShare
Write(): BinaryWriter, BufferedStream, Console, Debug, DefaultTraceListener, EventLogTraceListener, FileStream, IsolatedStorageFileStream, MemoryStream, NetworkStream, Stream, StreamWriter, StringWriter, TextWriter, TextWriterTraceListener, Trace, TraceListener
Write7BitEncodedInt(): BinaryWriter
WriteArray(): Formatter
WriteAttributes(): XmlWriter
WriteAttributeString(): XmlWriter
WriteBase64(): XmlTextWriter, XmlWriter
WriteBinHex(): XmlTextWriter, XmlWriter
WriteBoolean(): Formatter
WriteByte(): BufferedStream, FileStream, Formatter, IsolatedStorageFileStream, Marshal, MemoryStream, Stream
WriteCData(): XmlTextWriter, XmlWriter
WriteChar(): Formatter
WriteCharEntity(): XmlTextWriter, XmlWriter
WriteChars(): XmlTextWriter, XmlWriter
WriteComment(): XmlTextWriter, XmlWriter
WriteContentTo(): XmlAttribute, XmlCDataSection, XmlComment, XmlDeclaration, XmlDocument, XmlDocumentFragment, XmlDocumentType, XmlElement, XmlEntity, XmlEntityReference, XmlNode, XmlNotation, XmlProcessingInstruction, XmlSignificantWhitespace, XmlText, XmlWhitespace
WriteDateTime(): Formatter
WriteDecimal(): Formatter
WriteDocType(): XmlTextWriter, XmlWriter
WriteDouble(): Formatter
WriteElementString(): XmlWriter
WriteEndAttribute(): XmlTextWriter, XmlWriter
WriteEndDocument(): XmlTextWriter, XmlWriter
WriteEndElement(): XmlTextWriter, XmlWriter
WriteEntityRef(): XmlTextWriter, XmlWriter
WriteEntry(): EventLog
WriteFullEndElement(): XmlTextWriter, XmlWriter
WriteIf(): Debug, Trace
WriteIndent(): TraceListener
WriteInt16(): Formatter, Marshal
WriteInt32(): Formatter, Marshal
WriteInt64(): Formatter, Marshal
WriteIntPtr(): Marshal
WriteLine(): Console, Debug, DefaultTraceListener, EventLogTraceListener, TextWriter, TextWriterTraceListener, Trace, TraceListener
WriteLineIf(): Debug, Trace
WriteMember(): Formatter

WriteName(): XmlTextWriter, XmlWriter
WriteNmToken(): XmlTextWriter, XmlWriter
WriteNode(): XmlWriter
WriteObjectRef(): Formatter
WriteProcessingInstruction(): XmlTextWriter, XmlWriter
WriteQualifiedName(): XmlTextWriter, XmlWriter
Writer: TextWriterTraceListener
WriteRaw(): XmlTextWriter, XmlWriter
WriterSeqNum: ReaderWriterLock
WriteSByte(): Formatter
WriteSingle(): Formatter
WriteStartAttribute(): XmlTextWriter, XmlWriter
WriteStartDocument(): XmlTextWriter, XmlWriter
WriteStartElement(): XmlTextWriter, XmlWriter
WriteState: System.Xml, XmlTextWriter, XmlWriter
WriteString(): XmlTextWriter, XmlWriter
WriteSurrogateCharEntity(): XmlTextWriter, XmlWriter
WriteTimeSpan(): Formatter
WriteTo(): MemoryStream, XmlAttribute, XmlCDataSection, XmlComment, XmlDeclaration, XmlDocument, XmlDocumentFragment, XmlDocumentType, XmlElement, XmlEntity, XmlEntityReference, XmlNode, XmlNotation, XmlProcessingInstruction, XmlSignificantWhitespace, XmlText, XmlWhitespace
WriteUInt16(): Formatter
WriteUInt32(): Formatter
WriteUInt64(): Formatter
WriteValueType(): Formatter
WriteWhitespace(): XmlTextWriter, XmlWriter

X

XDR: ValidationType
XmlAttribute: System.Xml
XmlAttributeCollection: System.Xml
XmlCaseOrder: System.Xml.XPath
XmlCDataSection: System.Xml
XmlCharacterData: System.Xml
XmlComment: System.Xml
XmlConvert: System.Xml
XmlDataDocument: System.Xml
XmlDataType: System.Xml.XPath
XmlDeclaration: System.Xml, XmlNodeType
XmlDocument: System.Xml
XmlDocumentFragment: System.Xml
XmlDocumentType: System.Xml
XmlElement: System.Xml
XmlEntity: System.Xml
XmlEntityReference: System.Xml
XmlException: System.Xml
XmlImplementation: System.Xml
XmlLang: XmlNodeReader, XmlParserContext, XmlReader, XmlTextReader, XmlValidatingReader, XmlWriter, XPathNavigator

XmlLinkedNode: System.Xml
XmlNamedNodeMap: System.Xml
XmlNameSpace: ISoapMessage, SoapMessage
XmlNamespaceManager: System.Xml
XmlNameTable: System.Xml
XmlNode: System.Xml
XmlNodeChangedAction: System.Xml
XmlNodeChangedEventArgs: System.Xml
XmlNodeChangedEventHandler: System.Xml
XmlNodeList: System.Xml
XmlNodeOrder: System.Xml
XmlNodeReader: System.Xml
XmlNodeType: System.Xml
XmlNotation: System.Xml
XmlParserContext: System.Xml
XmlProcessingInstruction: System.Xml
XmlQualifiedName: System.Xml
XmlReader: System.Xml
XmlResolver: System.Xml, XmlDocument, XmlTextReader, XmlValidatingReader, XslTransform
XmlSignificantWhitespace: System.Xml
XmlSortOrder: System.Xml.XPath
XmlSpace: System.Xml, XmlNodeReader, XmlParserContext, XmlReader, XmlTextReader, XmlTextWriter, XmlValidatingReader, XmlWriter
XmlText: System.Xml
XmlTextReader: System.Xml

About the Authors

Ted Neward is an independent consultant, working with firms ranging in size from Fortune 50 to early-phase startups to define and build back-end enterprise systems. He is the author of numerous technical white papers (*http://www.javageeks.com*), as well as the book *Server-Based Java Programming*, and the older books *Core OWL 5.0* and *Advanced OWL 5.0*. Ted is also an instructor for DevelopMentor, where he teaches liberally from both the Java and .NET curriculum. Originally from Long Island, New York, Ted now lives in the Sacramento area with his wife, Charlotte, and his two sons, Michael and Matthew. When not teaching or writing on .NET or Java, Ted spends most of his time researching the .NET and Java environments. He can be reached at *tneward@javageeks.com*.

Budi Kurniawan is an IT consultant specializing in Internet and object-oriented programming and has taught both Microsoft and Java technologies. Budi is among the first people to develop commercial .NET applications and components and is currently writing the *.NET Real-World Projects* book to be published by APress this year, which includes the world's first .NET Pacman game. He is also the author of *Java for the Web with Servlets, JSP, and EJB* (New Riders) and the developer of the most popular Java Upload Bean from BrainySoftware.com.

Budi has a Masters by Research degree in Electrical Engineering from Sydney University, Australia, after completing a thesis project on image processing. Budi has also published articles for more than 10 publications. He can be contacted at *budi@brainysoftware.com*.

Colophon

Our look is the result of reader comments, our own experimentation, and feedback from distribution channels. Distinctive covers complement our distinctive approach to technical topics, breathing personality and life into potentially dry subjects.

The animal on the cover of *VB.NET Core Classes in a Nutshell* is a crawfish. Crawfish, or crayfish, are freshwater crustaceans. They can be found all over the world, but more than half of the approximately 500 species is found in North America.

Crawfish are similar in structure to lobsters, though much smaller (3-4 inches long). A crawfish's head and thorax are joined, followed by a segmented body. The head has a sharp snout, eyes on moveable stalks, and sensory antennae. It has four pairs of walking legs, which it also uses to probe for food, and two claws that extend from the front of its body, used for pinching. Crawfish are brown or greenish, except for some cave-dwelling types that are colorless and eyeless.

Females lay anywhere from 10 to 800 eggs, which attach to the females' swimming legs until they hatch. Newly hatched crawfish look like miniature adults. They molt 6-10 times in the first year during rapid growth, then less in the second year. Crawfish usually live only two years.

Linley Dolby and Catherine Morris were the production editors for *VB.NET Core Classes in a Nutshell*. Catherine Morris was the proofreader. Emily Quill, Linley Dolby, Ann Schirmer, and Claire Cloutier provided quality control.

Pam Spremulli designed the cover of this book, based on a series design by Edie Freedman. The cover image is a 19th-century engraving from the Dover Pictorial Archive. Emma Colby produced the cover layout with QuarkXPress 4.1 using Adobe's ITC Garamond font. David Futato produced the CD label with QuarkXPress 4.1 using Adobe's ITC Garamond font

David Futato designed the interior layout based on a series design by Nancy Priest. The print version of this book was created by translating the DocBook XML markup of its source files into a set of gtroff macros using a filter developed at O'Reilly & Associates by Norman Walsh. Steve Talbott designed and wrote the underlying macro set on the basis of the GNU *troff–gs* macros; Lenny Muellner adapted them to XML and implemented the book design. The GNU groff text formatter version 1.11.1 was used to generate PostScript output. The text and heading fonts are ITC Garamond Light and Garamond Book. The illustrations that appear in the book were produced by Robert Romano and Jessamyn Read using Macromedia FreeHand 9 and Adobe Photoshop 6. This colophon was written by Linley Dolby.